The History of Mathematical Proof in Aı

This radical, profoundly scholarly book explores the purposes and nature of proof in a range of historical settings. It overturns the view that the first mathematical proofs were in Greek geometry and rested on the logical insights of Aristotle by showing how much of that view is an artefact of nineteenth-century historical scholarship. It documents the existence of proofs in ancient mathematical writings about numbers, and shows that practitioners of mathematics in Mesopotamian, Chinese and Indian cultures knew how to prove the correctness of algorithms, which are much more prominent outside the limited range of surviving classical Greek texts that historians have taken as the paradigm of ancient mathematics. It opens the way to providing the first comprehensive, textually based history of proof.

Jeremy Gray, Professor of the History of Mathematics, Open University

'Each of the papers in this volume, starting with the amazing "Prologue" by the editor, Karine Chemla, contributes to nothing less than a revolution in the way we need to think about both the substance and the historiography of ancient non-Western mathematics, as well as a reconception of the problems that need to be addressed if we are to get beyond myth-eaten ideas of "unique Western rationality" and "the Greek miracle". I found reading this volume a thrilling intellectual adventure. It deserves a very wide audience.'

Hilary Putnam, Cogan University Professor Emeritus, Harvard University

KARINE CHEMLA is Senior Researcher at the CNRS (Research Unit SPHERE, University Paris Diderot, France), and a Senior Fellow at the Institute for the Study of the Ancient World at New York University. She is also Professor on a Guest Chair at Northwestern University, Xi'an, as well as at Shanghai Jiaotong University and Hebei Normal University, China. She was awarded a Chinese Academy of Sciences Visiting Professorship for Senior Foreign Scientists in 2009.

The History of Mathematical
Proof In Ancient Traditions

—

Edited by KARINE CHEMLA 林力娜

CAMBRIDGE
UNIVERSITY PRESS

CAMBRIDGE
UNIVERSITY PRESS

University Printing House, Cambridge CB2 8BS, United Kingdom

Cambridge University Press is part of the University of Cambridge.

It furthers the University's mission by disseminating knowledge in the pursuit of education, learning and research at the highest international levels of excellence.

www.cambridge.org
Information on this title: www.cambridge.org/9781107527539

© Cambridge University Press 2012

First published 2012
First paperback edition 2015

A catalogue record for this publication is available from the British Library

ISBN 978-1-107-52753-9 Paperback

Contents

Figures

Contributors

FRANÇOIS CHARETTE Independent scholar (retired), Gärtringen, Germany

KARINE CHEMLA Directrice de recherche, REHSEIS, UMR SPHERE, CNRS and University Paris Diderot, PRES Sorbonne Paris Cité, France

ORNA HARARI Department of Philosophy and Department of Classics, Tel Aviv University, Israel

JENS HØYRUP Emeritus Professor, Section for Philosophy and Science Studies, Roskilde University, Roskilde, Denmark

AGATHE KELLER Chargée de recherche, REHSEIS, UMR SPHERE, CNRS and University Paris Diderot, PRES Sorbonne Paris Cité, France

G. E. R. LLOYD Professor, Needham Research Institute, Cambridge, UK

IAN MUELLER Emeritus Professor, Philosophy and Conceptual Foundations of Science, University of Chicago, USA (deceased 2010)

REVIEL NETZ Professor, Department of Classics, Stanford University, Palo Alto, USA

CHRISTINE PROUST Directrice de recherche, REHSEIS, UMR SPHERE, CNRS and University Paris Diderot, PRES Sorbonne Paris Cité, Paris, France

DHRUV RAINA Professor, School of Social Sciences, Jawaharlal Nehru University, New Delhi, India

KEN SAITO Professor, Department of Human Sciences, Osaka Prefecture University, Japan

NATHAN SIDOLI Assistant Professor, School of International Liberal Studies, Waseda University, Tokyo, Japan

TIAN MIAO Senior Researcher, IHNS, Chinese Academy of Science, Beijing, China

BERNARD VITRAC Directeur de recherche, ANHIMA, CNRS UMR 8210, Paris, France

ALEXEI VOLKOV Assistant Professor, Center for General Education and Institute of History, National Tsing-Hua University, Hsinchu, R.O.C., Taiwan

Note on references

The following books are frequently referred to in the notes. We use the following abbreviations to refer to them.

CG2004   Chemla, K. and Guo Shuchun (2004) *Les Neuf Chapitres: le classique mathématique de la Chine ancienne et ses commentaires.* Paris.

C1817   Colebrooke, H. T. (1817) *Algebra with Arithmetic and Mensuration from the Sanscrit of Brahmagupta and Bhāscara.* Translated by H. T. Colebrooke. London.

H1995   Hayashi, T. (1995) *The Bakhshali Manuscript: An Ancient Indian Mathematical Treatise.* Groningen.

H2002   Høyrup, J. (2002) *Lengths, Widths, Surfaces: A Portrait of Old Babylonian Algebra and Its Kin.* New York.

LD1987   Li Yan, Du Shiran ([1963] 1987) *Mathematics in Ancient China: A Concise History* (Zhongguo gudai shuxue jianshi). Beijing. Updated and translated in English by J. N. Crossley and A. W. C. Lun, *Chinese Mathematics: A Concise History.* Oxford.

N1999   Netz, R. (1999) *The Shaping of Deduction in Greek Mathematics.* Cambridge.

T1893/5   Tannery, P. (1893–5) *Diophanti Alexandrini opera omnia cum graecis commentariis, edidit et latine interpretatus,* vol. i: 1893; vol. ii: 1895. Leipzig.

Acknowledgements

The book that the reader has in his or her hands is based on the research carried out within the context of a working group that convened in Paris for three months during the spring of 2002. The core members of the group were: Geoffrey Lloyd, Ian Mueller, Dhruv Raina, Reviel Netz and myself. Other colleagues took part in some or all of the weekly discussions: Alain Bernard, Armelle Debru, Marie-José Durand-Richard, Pierre-Sylvain Filliozat, Catherine Jami, Agathe Keller, François Patte, Christine Proust, Tian Miao, Bernard Vitrac and Alexei Volkov. As a complement to its work, this group organized a workshop to tackle questions for which no specialist could be found within the original set of participants (www.piea-ipas.msh-paris.fr/IMG/pdf/RAPPORT_groupe_Chemla.pdf). The whole endeavour has been made possible thanks to the International Advanced Study Program set up by the Maison des sciences de l'homme, Paris, in collaboration with Reid Hall, Columbia University at Paris. It is my pleasure to express to these institutions my deepest gratitude. I completed the writing of the introduction at the Dibner Institute, MIT, to which I am pleased to address my heartfelt thanks. Stays at the Max Planck Institute, Berlin, in 2007, and at Le Mas Pascal, Cavillargues, in 2008 and 2009, have provided the quietness needed to complete the project. Thanks for that to Hans-Jörg Rheinberger, Jean-Pascal Jullien and Gilles Vandenbroeck. For the preparation of this volume, the core members of the group acted as an editorial board. I express my deepest gratitude to those who accepted the anonymous work of being referees. Micah Ross, Guo Yuanyuan, Wang Xiaofei, Leonid Zhmud and Zhu Yiwen have played a key role in the elaboration of this book. I have pleasure here in expressing my deepest thanks to them as well as to those who read versions of this introduction: Bruno Belhoste, Evelyn Fox Keller, Ramon Guardans and Jacques Virbel.

Prologue | Historiography and history of mathematical proof: a research programme

KARINE CHEMLA

Pour Oriane, ces raisonnements sur les raisonnements

I Introduction: a standard view

The standard history of mathematical proof in ancient traditions at the present day is disturbingly simple.

This perspective can be represented by the following assertions. (1) Mathematical proof emerged in ancient Greece and achieved a mature form in the geometrical works of Euclid, Archimedes and Apollonius. (2) The full-fledged theory underpinning mathematical proof was formulated in Aristotle's *Posterior Analytics*, which describes the model of demonstration from which any piece of knowledge adequately known should derive. (3) Before these developments took place in classical Greece, there was no evidence of proof worth mentioning, a fact which has contributed to the promotion of the concept of 'Greek miracle'. This account also implies that mathematical proof is distinctive of Europe, for it would appear that no other mathematical tradition has ever shown interest in establishing the truth of statements.[1] Finally, it is assumed that mathematical proof, as it is practised today, is inherited exclusively from these Greek ancestors.

Are things so simple? This book argues that they are not. But we shall see that some preliminary analysis is required to avoid falling into the old, familiar pitfalls. Powerful rhetorical devices have been constructed which perpetuate this simple view, and they need to be identified before any meaningful discussion can take place. This should not surprise us. As Geoffrey Lloyd has repeatedly stressed, some of these devices were shaped in the context of fierce debates among competing 'masters of truth' in ancient Greece, and these devices continue to have effective force.[2]

---

[1] See, for example, M. Kline's crude evaluation of what a procedure was in Mesopotamia and how it was derived, quoted in J. Høyrup's chapter, p. 363. The first lay sinologist to work on ancient Chinese texts related to mathematics, Edouard Biot, does not formulate a higher assessment – see the statement quoted in A. Volkov's chapter, p. 512. On Biot's special emphasis on the lack of proofs in Chinese mathematical texts, compare Martija-Ochoa 2001–2: 61.

[2] See chapter 3 in Lloyd 1990: 73–97, Lloyd 1996a. Lloyd has also regularly emphasized how 'The concentration on the model of demonstration in the *Organon* and in Euclid, the one that

Studies of mathematical proof as an aspect of the intellectual history of the ancient world have echoed the beliefs summarized above – in part, by concentrating mainly on Euclid's *Elements* and Archimedes' writings, the subtleties of which seem to be infinite. The practice of proof to which these writings bear witness has impressed many minds, well beyond the strict domain of mathematics. Since antiquity, versions of Euclid's *Elements*, in Greek, in Arabic, in Latin, in Hebrew and later in the various vernacular languages of Europe, have regularly constituted a central piece of mathematical education, even though they were by no means the only element of mathematical education. The proofs in these editions were widely emulated by those interested in the value of incontrovertibility attached to them and they inspired the discussions of many philosophers. However, some versions of Euclid's *Elements* have also been used since early modern times – in Europe and elsewhere – in ways that show how mathematical proof has been enrolled for unexpected purposes.

One stunning example will suffice to illustrate this point. At the end of the sixteenth century, European missionaries arrived at the southern door of China. As a result of the difficulties encountered in entering China and capturing the interest of Chinese literati, the Jesuit Matteo Ricci devised a strategy of evangelism in which the science and technology available in Europe would play a key part. One of the first steps taken in this programme was the publication of a Chinese version of Euclid's *Elements* in 1607. Prepared by Ricci himself in collaboration with the Chinese convert and high official Xu Guangqi, this translation was based on Clavius' edition of the *Elements*, which Ricci had studied in Rome, while he was a student at the Collegio Romano. The purpose of the translation was manifold. Two aspects are important for us here. First, the purportedly superior value of the type of geometrical knowledge introduced, when compared to the mathematical knowledge available to Chinese literati at that time, was expected to plead in favour of those who possessed that knowledge, namely, European missionaries. Additionally, the kind of certainty such a type of proof was prized for securing in mathematics could also be claimed for the theological teachings which the missionaries introduced simultaneously and which made use of reasoning similar to the proof of Euclidean geometry.[3] Thus, in the first large-scale intellectual contact between Europe

proceeds via valid deductive argument from premises that are themselves indemonstrable but necessary and self-evident, that concentration is liable to distort the *Greek* materials already – let alone the interpretation of Chinese texts.' (Lloyd 1992: 196.)

[3] On Ricci's background and evangelization strategy, see Martzloff 1984. Martzloff 1995 is devoted more generally to the translations of Clavius's textbooks on the mathematical sciences

and China mediated by the missionaries, mathematical proof played a role having little to do with mathematics *stricto sensu*. It is difficult to imagine that such a use and such a context had no impact on its reception in China.[4] This topic will be revisited later.

The example outlined is far from unique in showing the role of mathematical proof outside mathematics. In an article significantly titled 'What mathematics has done to some and only some philosophers', Ian Hacking (2000) stresses the strange uses that mathematical proof inspired in philosophy as well as in theological arguments. In it, he diagnoses how mathematics, that is, in fact, the experience of mathematical proof, has 'infected'

into Chinese at the time. Engelfriet 1993 discusses the relationship between Euclid's *Elements* and teachings on Christianity in Ricci's European context. More generally, this article outlines the role which Clavius allotted to mathematical sciences in Jesuit schools and in the wider Jesuit strategy for Europe. For a general and excellent introduction to the circumstances of the translation of Euclid's *Elements* into Chinese, an analysis and a complete bibliography, see Engelfriet 1998. Xu Guangqi's biography and main scholarly works were the object of a collective endeavour: Jami, Engelfriet and Blue 2001. Martzloff 1981, Martzloff 1993 are devoted to the reception of this type of geometry in China, showing the variety of reactions that the translation of the *Elements* aroused among Chinese literati. On the other hand, the process of introduction of Clavius' textbook for arithmetic was strikingly different. See Chemla 1996, Chemla 1997a.

[4] Leibniz appears to have been the first scholar in Europe who, one century after the Jesuits had arrived in China, became interested in the question of knowing whether 'the Chinese' ever developed mathematical proofs in their past. In his letter to Joachim Bouvet sent from Braunschweig on 15 February 1701, Leibniz asked whether the Jesuit, who was in evangelistic mission in China, could give him any information about geometrical proofs in China: 'J'ay souhaité aussi de sçavoir si ce que les Chinois ont eu anciennement de Geometrie, *a esté accompagné de quelques demonstrations*, et particulièrement s'ils ont sçu il y a long temps l'égalité du quarré de l'hypotenuse aux deux quarrés des costés, ou quelque autre telle proposition de la Geometrie non populaire.' (Widmaier 2006: 320; my emphasis.) In fact, Leibniz had already expressed this interest few years earlier, in a letter written in Hanover on 2 December 1697, to the same correspondent: 'Outre l'Histoire des dynasties chinoises . . ., il faudroit avoir soin de l'Histoire des inventions [,] des arts, des loix, des religions, et d'autres établissements[.] Je voudrois bien sçavoir par exemple s'il[s] n'ont eu il y a long temps quelque chose d'approchant de nostre Geometrie, et si l'égalité du quarré de l'Hypotenuse à ceux des costés du triangle rectangle leur a esté connue, et *s'ils ont eu cette proposition par tradition ou commerce des autres peuples, ou par l'experience, ou enfin par demonstration, soit trouvée chez eux ou apportée d'ailleurs.*' (Widmaier 2006: 142–4, my emphasis.) To this, Bouvet replied on 28 February 1698: 'Le point au quel on pretend s'appliquer davantage comme le plus important est leur chronologie . . . Apres quoy on travaillera sur leur histoire naturelle et civile[,] sur leur physique, leur morale, leurs loix, leur politique, leurs Arts, leurs mathematiques et leur medecine, qui est une des matieres sur quoy je suis persuadé que la Chine peut nous fournir de[s] plus belles connaissances.' (Widmaier 2006: 168.) In his letter from 1697 (Widmaier 2006: 144–6), Leibniz expressed the conviction that, even though 'their speculative mathematics' could not hold the comparison with what he called 'our mathematics', one could still learn from them. To this, in a sequel to the preceding letter, Bouvet expressed a strong agreement (Widmaier 2006: 232). Mathematics, especially proof, was already a 'measure' used for comparative purposes.

'some central parts of [the] philosophy [of some philosophers], parts that have nothing intrinsically to do with mathematics' (p. 98).

What is important for us to note for the moment is that through such non-mathematical uses of mathematical proof the actors' perception of proof has been colored by implications that were foreign to mathematics itself. This observation may help to account for the astonishing emotion that often permeates debates on mathematical proof – ordinary ones as well as more academic ones – while other mathematical issues meet with indifference.[5] On the other hand, these historical uses of proof in non-mathematical domains, as well as uses still often found in contemporary societies, led to overvaluation of some values attached to proof (most importantly the incontrovertibility of its conclusion and hence the rigour of its conduct) and the undervaluing and overshadowing of other values that persist to the present. In this sense, these uses contributed to biases in the historical and philosophical discussion about mathematical proof, in that the values on which the discussion mainly focused were brought to the fore by agendas most meaningful outside the field of mathematics. The resulting distortion is, in my view and as I shall argue in greater detail below, one of the main reasons why the historical analysis of mathematical proof has become mired down and has failed to accommodate new evidence discovered in the last decades.[6] Moreover, it also imposed restrictions on the philosophical inquiry into proof. Accordingly, the challenge confronting us is to reinstate some autonomy in our thinking about mathematical proof. To meet this challenge effectively, a critical awareness derived from a historical outlook is essential.

II Remarks on the historiography of mathematical proof

The historical episode just invoked illustrates how the type of mathematical proof epitomized by Euclid's *Elements* (notwithstanding the differences between the various forms the book has taken) has been used by some (European) practitioners to claim superiority of their learning over that of other practitioners. In the practice of mathematics as such, proof became a means of distinction among practices and consequently among social groups. In the nineteenth century, the same divide was projected back into history. In parallel with the professionalization of science and the shaping of

---

[5] The same argument holds with respect to 'science'. For example, the social and political uses of the discourses on 'methodology' within the milieus of practitioners, as well as vis-à-vis wider circles, were at the focus of Schuster and Yeo 1986. However, previous attempts paid little attention to the uses of these discourses outside Europe.

[6] I was led to the same diagnosis through a different approach in Chemla 1997b.

a scientific community, history and philosophy of science emerged during that century as domains of inquiry in their own right.[7] Euclid's *Elements* thus became an object of the past, to be studied as such, along with other Greek, Arabic, Indian, Chinese and soon Babylonian and Egyptian sources that were progressively discovered.[8] By the end of the nineteenth century, as François Charette shows in his contribution, mathematical proof had again become the weapon with which some Greek sources were evaluated and found superior to all the others: a pattern similar to the one outlined above was in place, but had now been projected back in history. The standard history of mathematical proof, the outline of which was recalled at the beginning of this introduction, had taken shape. In this respect, the dismissive assertion formulated in 1841 by Jean-Baptiste Biot – Edouard Biot's father – was characteristic and premonitory, when he exposed

this peculiar habit of mind, following which the Arabs, as the Chinese and Hindus, limited their scientific writings to the statement of a series of rules, which, once given, ought only to be verified by their applications, without requiring any logical demonstration or connections between them: this gives those Oriental nations a remarkable character of dissimilarity, I would even add of intellectual inferiority, comparatively to the Greeks, with whom any proposition is established by reasoning, and generates logically deduced consequences.[9]

This book challenges the historical validity of this thesis. The issue at hand is not merely to determine whether this representation of a worldwide history of mathematical proof holds true or not. We shall also question whether the idea that this quotation conveys is relevant with respect to

---

[7] See for example Laudan 1968, Yeo 1981, Yeo 1993, especially chapter 6.

[8] Between 1814 and 1818, Peyrard, who had been librarian at the Ecole Polytechnique, translated Euclid's *Elements* as well as his other writings on the basis of a manuscript in Greek that Napoleon had brought back from the Vatican. He had also published a translation of Archimedes' books (Langins 1989.) Many of those active in developing history and philosophy of science in France (Carnot, Brianchon, Poncelet, Comte, Chasles), especially mathematics, had connections to the Ecole Polytechnique. More generally, on the history of the historiography of mathematics, including the account of Greek texts, compare Dauben and Scriba 2002.

[9] This is a quotation with which F. Charette begins his chapter (p. 274). See the original formulation on p. 274. At roughly the same time, we find under William Whewell's pen the following assessment: 'The Arabs are in the habit of giving conclusions without demonstrations, precepts without the investigations by which they are obtained; as if their main object were practical rather than speculative, – the calculation of results rather than the exposition of theory. Delambre [here, Whewell adds a footnote with the reference] has been obliged to exercise great ingenuity, in order to discover the method in which Ibn Iounis proved his solution of certain difficult problems.' (Whewell 1837: 249.) Compare Yeo 1993: 157. The distinction which 'science' enables Whewell to draw between Europe and the rest of the world in his *History of the Inductive Sciences* would be worth analysing further but falls outside the scope of this book.

proof. As we shall see, comparable debates on the practice of proof have developed within the field of mathematics at the present day too.

First lessons from historiography, or: how sources have disappeared from the historical account of proof

Several reasons suggest that we should be wary regarding the standard narrative.

To begin with, some historiographical reflection is helpful here. As some of the contributions in this volume indicate, the end of the eighteenth century and the first three-quarters of the nineteenth century by no means witnessed a consensus in the historical discourse about proof comparable to the one that was to become so pervasive later. In the chapter devoted to the development of British interest in the Indian mathematical tradition, Dhruv Raina shows how in the first half of the nineteenth century, Colebrooke, the first translator of Sanskrit mathematical writings into a European language, interpreted these texts as containing a kind of algebraic analysis forming a well arranged science with a method aided by devices, among which symbols and literal signs are conspicuous. Two facts are worth stressing here.

On the one hand, Colebrooke compared what he translated to D'Alembert's conception of analysis. This comparison indicates that he positioned the Indian algebra he discovered with respect to the mathematics developed slightly before him and, let me emphasize, specifically with respect to 'analysis'. When Colebrooke wrote, analysis was a field in which rigour had not yet become a central concern. Half a century later in his biography of his father, Colebrooke's son would assess the same facts in an entirely different way, stressing the practical character of the mathematics written in Sanskrit and its lack of rigour. As Raina emphasizes, a general evolution can be perceived here. We shall come back to this evolution shortly.

On the other hand, Colebrooke read in the Sanskrit texts the use of 'algebraic methods', the rules of which were proved in turn by geometric means. In fact, Colebrooke discussed 'geometrical and algebraic demonstrations' of algebraic rules, using these expressions to translate Sanskrit terms. He showed how the geometrical demonstrations 'illustrated' the rules with diagrams having particular dimensions. We shall also come back later to this detail. Later in the century, as Charette indicates, the visual character of these demonstrations was opposed to Greek proofs and assessed positively or negatively according to the historian. As for 'algebraic proofs', Colebrooke compared some of the proofs developed by Indian authors to those of Wallis, for example, thereby leaving little doubt as to Colebrooke's estimation of these sources: namely, that Indian scholars had carried out genuine algebraic proofs. If we recapitulate the previous argument, we see that Colebrooke read in the Sanskrit texts a rather elaborate system of proof in which the algebraic rules used in the application of algebra were themselves proved. Moreover, he pointed resolutely to the use in these writings of 'algebraic proofs'. It is striking that these remarks were not taken up in later historiography. Why did this evidence disappear from subsequent accounts?[10] This first observation raises doubts about the completeness of the record on which the standard narrative examined is based. But there is more.

Reading Colebrooke's account leads us to a much more general observation: algebraic proof as a *kind* of proof essential to mathematical practice today is, in fact, absent from the standard account of the early history of mathematical proof. The early processes by which algebraic proof was constituted are still *terra incognita* today. In fact, there appears to be a correlation between the evidence that vanished from the standard historical narrative and segments missing in the early history of proof. We can interpret this state of the historiography as a symptom of the bias in the historical approach to proof that I described above. Various chapters in this book will have a contribution to make to this page in the early history of mathematical proof.

Let us for now return to our critical examination of the standard view from a historiographical perspective. Charette's chapter, which sketches the evolution of the appreciation of Indian, Chinese, Egyptian and Arabic source material during the nineteenth century with respect to mathematical proof, also provides ample evidence that many historians of that time discussed what they considered proofs in writings which they qualified as 'Oriental'. For some, these proofs were inferior to those found in Euclid's *Elements*. For others, these proofs represented alternatives to Greek ones, the rigour characteristic of the latter being regularly assessed as a burden or even verging on rigidity. The deficit in rigour of Indian proofs was thus not systematically deemed an impediment to their consideration as proofs, even interesting ones. It is true that historians had not yet lost their awareness that this distinctive feature made them comparable to early modern proofs.

One characteristic of these early historical works is even more telling when we contrast it with attitudes towards 'non-Western' texts today: when confronted with Indian writings in which assertions were not

---

[10] The same question is raised in Srinivas 2005: 213–14. The author also emphasizes that Colebrooke and his contemporary C. M. Whish both noted that there were proofs in ancient mathematical writings in Sanskrit.

accompanied by proofs, we find more than one historian in the nineteenth century expressing his conviction that the assertion had once been derived on the basis of a proof. As late as the 1870s, this characteristic held true of, for instance, G. F. W. Thibaut in his approach to the geometry of the *Sulbasutras*, described below by Agathe Keller. It is true that Thibaut criticized the dogmatic attitude he attributed to Sanskrit writings dealing with science, in which he saw opinions different from those expounded by the author treated with contempt – a fact that he related to how proofs were presented. It is also true that the practical religious motivations driving the Indian developments in geometry he studied diminished their value to him. In his view, these motivations betrayed the lack of free inquiry that should characterize scientific endeavour. Note here how these judgements projected the values attached to science in Thibaut's scholarly circles back into history.[11] Yet he never doubted that proofs were at the basis of the statements contained in the ancient texts. For example, for the general case of 'Pythagorean theorem', he was convinced that the authors used some means to 'satisfy themselves of the general truth' of the proposition. And he judged it a necessary task for the historian to restore these reasonings. This is how, for the specific case when the two sides of the right-angled triangle have equal length, Thibaut unhesitatingly attributed the reasoning recorded in Plato's *Meno* to the authors of the *Sulbasutras*. As the reader will find out in the historiographical chapters of this book, he was not the only one to hold such views. On the other hand, it is revealing that while he was looking for geometrical proofs from which the statements of the *Sulbasutras* were derived, Thibaut discarded evidence of arithmetical reasoning contained in ancient commentaries on these texts. He preferred to attribute to the authors from antiquity a geometrical proof that he would freely restore. In other words, he did not consider commentators of the past worth attending to and, in particular, did not describe how they proceeded in their proofs.

To sum up the preceding remarks, even if, in the nineteenth century, 'the Greeks' were thought to have carried out proofs that were quite specific, there were historians who recognized that other types of proofs could be found in other kinds of sources. Even when proofs were not recorded, historians might grant that the achievements recorded in the writings had been obtained by proofs that they thus strove to restore. However, as Charette concludes with respect to the once-known 'non-Western' source material, 'much of the twentieth-century historiography simply disre-

---

[11] The moral, political and religious dimensions of the discourse on methodology have begun to be explored. See, for example, the introduction and various chapters in Schuster and Yeo 1986. More remains to be done.

garded the evidence already available'. One could add that the assumption that outside the few Greek geometrical texts listed above, there were no proofs at all in ancient mathematical sources has become predominant today. It is clearly a central issue for our project to understand the processes which marginalized some of the known sources to such an extent that they were eventually erased from the early history of mathematical proof. In any event, the elements just recalled again suggest caution regarding the standard narrative.

Other lessons from historiography, or: nineteenth-century ideas on computing

Raina and Charette highlight another process that gained momentum in the nineteenth century and that will prove quite meaningful for our purpose. They show how mathematics provided a venue for progressive development of an opposition between styles soon understood to characterize distinct 'civilizations'. In fact, as a result of this development, by the end of the century 'the Greeks' were more generally contrasted with all the other 'Orientals', because they privileged geometry over any other branch of mathematics, while 'the others' were thought of as having stressed computations and rules, that is, algorithms, arithmetic and algebra, instead.[12] Charette discusses the various means by which historians accommodated the somewhat abundant evidence that challenged this division.

This remark simultaneously reveals and explains a wide lacuna in the standard account of the early history of proof: this account is mute with respect to proofs relating to arithmetical statements or addressing the correctness of algorithms. From this perspective, Colebrooke's remarks on 'algebraic analysis' take on a new significance, since they pertain precisely to proofs of that kind. In addition, the absence of algebraic proof from the standard early history, noted above, appears to be one aspect of a systematic gap. If we exclude the quite peculiar kind of number theory to be found in the 'arithmetic books' of Euclid's *Elements*, or in Diophantus' *Arithmetics*, the standard history has little to say about how practitioners developed proofs for statements related to numbers and computations. Yet there is no doubt that all societies had number systems and developed means of

[12] From the statement by J. B. Biot in 1841 (quoted by F. Charette) to the statement by M. Kline in 1972 (quoted by Høyrup) – both cited above – there is a remarkable stability in the arguments by which algorithms are trivialized: they are interpreted as verbal instructions to be followed without any concern for justification. An analysis of the historiography of computation would certainly be quite helpful in situating such approaches within a broader context. This point will be taken up later.

computing with them. Can we believe that proving the correctness of these algorithms was not a key issue for Athenian public accounts or for the Chinese bureaucracy?[13] Could these rely on checks left to trial and error? Clearly, there is a whole section missing in the early history of proof as it took shape in the last centuries.[14]

In fact, there appear two correlated absences in the narrative we are analysing: on the one hand, most traditions are missing,[15] while on the other hand, proofs of a certain type are lacking. Is it because we have no evidence for this kind of proof? Such is not the case, and it will come as no surprise to discover that most of the chapters on proof that follow address precisely those theorems dealing with numbers or algorithms. From a historiographic perspective, again, it would be quite interesting to understand better the historical circumstances that account for this lacuna.

Creating the standard history

As Charette recalls in the conclusion of his chapter, the standard early history of mathematical proof took shape and became dominant in relation to the political context of the European imperialist enterprise. As was the case with the European missionaries in China a few centuries earlier, mathematical proof played a key role in the process of shaping 'European civilization' as superior to the others – a process to which not only science, but also history of science, more generally contributed at that time. The analysis developed above still holds, and I shall not repeat it. The role that was allotted to proof in this framework tied it to issues that extended far beyond the domain of mathematics. These ties explain, in my view, why mathematical proof has meant so much to so many people – a point that still holds true today. These uses of proof have also badly constrained its historical and philosophical analysis, placing emphasis on some values rather than others for reasons that lay outside mathematics.

---

[13] What is at stake today in the trustworthiness of computing is discussed in MacKenzie 2001.

[14] The failure that results from not having yet systematically developed the portion of the history of mathematical proof has unfortunate consequences in how some philosophers of mathematics deal with 'calculations', as opposed to 'proofs'. To take an example among those to whom I refer in this introduction, however insightful Hacking 2000 may be, the paragraph entitled 'The unpuzzling character of calculation' (pp. 101–3) records some common misconceptions about computing that call for rethinking. See fn. 45.

[15] As is often the case, when 'non-Western traditions' – as they are sometimes called – are missing, other traditions in the West have been marginalized in, or even left out from, the historiography. Lloyd directly addresses this fact in his own contribution to this volume.

Understanding what other elements played a part in the shaping of our narrative is another way of developing our critical awareness of the narrative.

As R. Yeo has argued regarding the case of early Victorian Britain in the publications mentioned above, the professionalization of science and the development of the sense of a 'scientific community', as well as the need of the practitioners to reinforce the unity of 'science' for themselves and its value in the eyes of the public, can be correlated with an increase in the size and number of publications devoted to the 'scientific method'. The distinctive features of the method enabled it to maintain the cohesion of the community and enhance the value of the social group in the eyes of the public. It shaped the social and professional status of those who were soon to be called 'scientists'. Philosophy of science and history of science emerged and developed as disciplines through this historical process and were instrumental in the pursuit of the question of method. How were the understanding and discussion of mathematical proof influenced by this global trend? In my view, this is a key issue for our topic, to which we shall come back below but which awaits further research.[16]

A consideration of the mainstream development of academic mathematics during the nineteenth century casts more light on our narrative from yet another perspective. It also allows the perception of other elements that may have played a part in constructing the narrative. Indeed, the approach to proofs of the past at different time periods correlates with more general trends in the mathematics of the time. On the one hand, as we saw, in the first decades of the nineteenth century, Colebrooke was reading his Indian

---

[16] Clearly, proof was a topic of explicit discussion within disciplinary writings, as the first edition of George Peacock's *Treatise of Algebra* (1830) shows. The pages starting from paragraph 142, on p. 109, were devoted to the question: 'What constitutes a demonstration?' Further, John Stuart Mill's discussion of methodology, in his *A System of Logic, Ratiocinative and Inductive*, first published in 1843, encompassed an analysis of mathematical proof and led him to offer an interpretation of Euclidean proofs as reliant on an inductive foundation and their certainty as an illusion (p. 296). This example shows how reflections of mathematical proofs were influenced by wider discussion of methodology. By comparison, Auguste Comte's considerations on demonstrations were less systematic. Conversely, another question is worth exploring: what role did ideas about and practices of mathematical proofs play in shaping the various discourses about methodology? Even though considerations about demonstration are pervasive in the methodological books of that period, it seems to me that this feature has received little attention. An exception is the discussion of Whewell's ideas regarding the various practices of proof in the context of his wider concern for the teaching of mathematics and physics in Yeo 1993: 218–22. In this case, questions of method relate to pedagogic efficiency and tie mathematics to natural science. Hacking 1980 (reprinted as chapter 13 in Hacking 2002: 200–13) sheds interesting light on the question of the emergence of methodology in the seventeenth century. On the issue of mathematical proof as such, this article is updated in Hacking 2000.

sources with mathematical analysis in mind. His comparisons were with Wallis or D'Alembert. On the other hand, at the end of the nineteenth century, when Greek geometry overshadowed all other evidence for the early history of proof, the value of rigour had been growing in significance for some decades, and academic mathematics was witnessing the beginning of a new practice of axiomatic systems which would soon become the dominant trend in the twentieth century.[17]

These arguments suggest that different factors brought about the shift in historiography outlined above and could account for the outline of the now-standard narrative of the early history of proof. Some of these factors clearly relate to the state of mathematics at a given time, both institutionally and intellectually, but others are not directly related to it. The influence of some of these factors may be felt at the present day and could explain the lingering belief in this narrative as well as the significance widely attached to it. However, the same arguments invite us to look at this narrative with critical eyes: the narrative belongs to its time and the time may have come that we need to replace it.

Dissatisfactions: overemphasizing certainty

For more than three decades now, some historians of mathematics have published articles and books arguing that the Chinese, Babylonian and Indian sources on which they were working contained mathematical proofs.[18]

---

[17] It would be interesting to document these correlations in greater detail. See e.g. I. Toth's work on the history of axiomatization. Other changes in the mathematics of the nineteenth century also probably had an impact on the historiography in exactly the same way such as the increasing marginalization of computing and the division between pure and applied mathematics, which were soon perceived as two distinct pursuits and to be carried out in separate institutions. Thibaut's critical remarks, mentioned above, on the practical orientation of the mathematics in the *Sulbasutras* are probably an echo of the latter trend and illustrate a typical motif of nineteenth- and twentieth-century historical publications. Regarding the marginalization of computing and its impact on historiography, I refer to the forthcoming joint publication by Marie-José Durand-Richard, Agathe Keller and Dhruv Raina.

[18] For the Chinese case, let us mention the first research works on the topic published in English: Wagner 1975, Wagner 1978, Wagner 1979. One must also mention the first works in Chinese systematically addressing the issue: the 8th issue of the journal *Kejishi wenji* (Collection of papers on the history of science and technology), in 1982; the 11th issue of the journal *Kexueshi jikan* (Collected papers in history of science); Wu Wenjun 1982. Since then, the publications are too numerous to be listed here. The reader can find a more complete bibliography in CG2004. The first publication on the topic of proofs that could be read in the Mesopotamian sources is Høyrup 1990. Since then, Høyrup has continued exploring this issue, and other specialists of the field have joined him to support and develop this thesis. A synthesis of the outcomes of this research programme, the results of which were widely adopted by the narrow circle of specialists of Mesopotamian mathematics, was published: H2002. As for the Indian case, we can refer the reader to H1995: 75–7, Jain 1995. These were followed more recently by Patte 2004, Srinivas 2005, Keller 2006, among others.

They worked independently of each other and the proofs they discussed were quite different in nature. Moreover, their interpretation of the facts confronting them was not uniform. However, they brought forward extensive evidence, partly new, partly old, which challenged the received view of the early history of mathematical proof. It is interesting to note that, in a way, they were partly returning to a past historiography.

A puzzling fact is that, beyond the strict circle of specialists in the same domain, these results were at best ignored, but, more frequently, were rejected outright. Clearly, these publications have so far not managed to bring about any change in the view of the early history of mathematical proof held by historians and philosophers of science at large, or the wider population.

This sustained failed reception needed to be analysed. Thus, this book is not only devoted to the history but also contains a section on the historiography of mathematical proof. Needless to say, much more remains to be done in this domain. These circumstances also explain why I chose to begin this introduction with historiographical remarks. Some further factors are at play in how mathematical proof is approached in our societies at large, and we need to recognize these factors in order to restore some freedom to the discussion and come to grips with the new evidence.

On the basis of the analysis outlined above, we see two types of obstacles which could hinder the development of the discussion. Firstly, the whole question of mathematical proof is entangled with extrascholarly uses in which it plays an important part – among these uses are those of the issues addressed earlier which are related to claims of identity.[19] Additionally, and in relation to this point, an image of what a mathematical proof endeavours has crystallized and blurs the analysis. My claim is that this image is biased and that dealing with the new evidence mentioned above presents an opportunity for us to locate this distortion and to think about mathematical proof anew.

We have reached the crux of the argument. Let me explain in greater detail. The essential value usually attached to mathematical proof – topmost for its wide cultivation and esteem outside the sphere of mathematics – is that, as the word 'proof' itself indicates, it yields certainty: the conclusion which has been proved can (hopefully) be accepted as true.[20] Securing the

---

[19] How social groups construct identity through science or history of science is more generally a key issue, on which much more research ought to be done.

[20] Grabiner 1988 argues that certainty and applicability were the two features through which mathematics was most influential to 'Western thought'. Certainly, these two features occupy a prominent position in Xu Guangqi's preface to the Chinese translation of Euclid's *Elements* (Engelfriet 1998: 291–7). Grabiner's analysis of how the certainty yielded by proof was influential, especially in theology, reveals dimensions of the importance regularly attached

truth of a piece of knowledge and convincing an opponent of the incontrovertibility of an assertion seem to be what mathematical proof offers and the ideal it embodies.

Clearly, if we adopt this view of proof, we are immediately forced to admit that starting points (definitions, axioms) are mandatory for the activity of proof, if we are to achieve these goals. Moreover, the validity of these starting points must be agreed upon, regardless of how this agreement is reached. In his chapter, Geoffrey Lloyd treats at length the variety of terms used to designate these starting points in ancient Greece and the intensity of interest in, and debate about, them that this variety reflects. On this basis, and this is where requirements such as rigour appear to come in, valid arguments are required to derive assertions from the starting points in a trustworthy way, and new assertions depend on the first ones or the starting points, and so on.

In other words, as soon as one has granted the premise that the goal of mathematical proof is to prove in an indisputable way, then the conclusion follows unavoidably that this aim can be only achieved within the framework of an axiomatic–deductive system of one sort or another. In the context of this assumption, Euclid's *Elements* is the first known mathematical writing that contains proofs, and any claim that a given source contains proofs has to be judged accordingly. And such claims have actually been judged by that very standard.

This is, in my view, the simple device by which Greek geometrical writings have become so central to the discussion of proof that they cannot possibly be challenged, and this position lies at the core of the recent rejection of the claim that Babylonian, Chinese or Indian sources contained proofs by some part of the community of history and philosophy of science (among others). The reasoning will look simplistic to many. However, I claim that this is precisely the core of the matter.[21] If I am right, this is the point on which critical analysis must be exercised for us to open our historical inquiry into proof wider. The feature of mathematical proof just examined is certainly quite meaningful, and was indeed deemed so outside mathematics. However, on what basis do we grant 'incontrovertibility' as *the* essential value and goal of mathematical proof within mathematics itself?

---

to this value. Hacking 2000 is a bright analysis of what certainty and its cognate values have meant for some philosophers.

[21] I formulated the reasoning relying on present-day perception of what yields certainty. Although certainty, starting points and modes of reasonings based on the latter to secure the former remained a stable constellation of elements in the history of discussions about mathematical proof, the meanings and contents attached to them displayed variation in history. As Orna Harari shows in her chapter in this book, earlier views were quite different from present-day ones. Compare Mancosu 1996, especially chapter 1.

To examine this question, let us restrict the discussion to mathematical proof as such, as carried out within the context of mathematics. The recollection of a simple fact will prove useful here: many mathematical proofs produced throughout history by duly acknowledged scholars were not presented within axiomatic–deductive systems.[22] In fact, the periods during which advanced mathematical writings were predominantly composed in such a way are much shorter than the periods when they were not. In tandem with the lack of interest in an axiomatic–deductive organization of mathematical knowledge, the authors often did not place much emphasis on rigour. Yet they referred to what they wrote as proofs.[23] One may argue that these practitioners of mathematics overlooked some difficulties and made errors. But these objections cannot possibly obliterate the innumerable theories proposed and results obtained with precisely such types of proof. These remarks have an inescapable consequence: it reveals that for a fair number of practitioners of mathematics the goals of proof cannot have been *only* ascertaining incontrovertibility and assuring certainty through achieving conviction, if such was ever their goal at all. Nevertheless, they considered it worthwhile to look for proofs, and their practice of proof was no less productive from a mathematical point of view.

In my view, this perception of proof still holds true today. Even though, in their discourse on the contemporary practices of proof, mathematicians may stress the axiomatic–deductive framework within which they work and emphasize the certainty yielded by proofs as well as the rigour necessary in their production,[24] the functions they ascribe to proof in their

[22] Ironically enough, the proof that lies at the core of Plato's *Meno* and that has exerted a huge influence in the history of philosophy (Hacking 2000) is not formulated within an axiomatic–deductive system. Philosophers of the present day such as Lakatos 1970 held 'a no-foundation view of mathematics' (Hacking 2000: 124). Unfortunately such views have not yet shown any clear impact on the history of ancient mathematics. Rav 1999: 15–19 lists several examples of major domains of mathematics of the present day, for which axioms have not been proposed and that are nevertheless felt to be rigorous. He further emphasizes the various meanings of 'axioms' as used in modern practice.

[23] I am not aware of any historical publication which denies that Leibniz, Euler, Poncelet, Poincaré or others of their ilk wrote down actual proofs and suggests that these men should be erased from the history of mathematical proof: whatever the evaluation may be, it is without contest that they contributed to shaping practices of proof. More revealing examples are discussed in Jaffe and Quinn 1993: 7–8. The fact that Jaffe and Quinn refer to cases of 'weak standards of proof' and suggest that, in some cases, 'expressions such as "motivation" or "supporting argument" should replace "proof"' in actors' language indicates that in the contemporary mathematical literature the label 'proof' refers to a great variety of types of arguments (Jaffe and Quinn 1993: 7, 10). This topic recurs below.

[24] See the very different and lucid account in Thurston 1994: 10–11. Among other refreshing insights into the activity of proof, Thurston rejects the 'hidden assumption that there is

actual work seem quite different and multifaceted, in fact. Some insight on this point can be gained from the contributions to a debate that broke out in the pages of the *Bulletin of the American Mathematical Society* about a decade ago.[25] The paper by Jaffe and Quinn that launched the discussion recognized the importance of 'speculating' – which they called 'theoretical mathematics' – for the development of mathematics, in addition to proofs which secure certainty. However, the authors expressed concerns regarding the confusion that could arise from confounding rigorous proofs (ones that bring certainty), insights, arguments and so on. As a consequence, they suggested norms of publication that would distinguish explicitly between, on the one hand, 'theorem', 'show', 'construct', 'proof' and, on the other hand, 'conjecture', 'predict', 'motivation', and 'supporting argument'.[26] One may venture to recognize in this opposition a divide of the type we are examining with respect to history.

It is impossible to review the debate in detail here. However, for our purposes, it is interesting to observe the intensity of reaction that this suggestion elicited in the mathematical community. From the responses published in the *Bulletin*, a much more complex image of the activity of proof emerges, in which rigorous proofs appear to arouse mixed feelings and cohabit with all kinds of other modalities of proof.[27] Moreover, the relation of proof to other aspects of mathematical activity appears to be quite intricate and calls for further analysis. In relation to our topic, I interpret the fact that, ironically, many mathematicians do not find it difficult to recognize as proofs arguments from Chinese or Indian texts although other scholars deny them this quality as an additional sign of this coexistence of motley practices of proof in the mathematical community. Were further evidence still necessary, these facts indicate that there are conflicting ideas among mathematicians about what a proof is or should be. Why, in such circumstances, should historians or philosophers opt for one idea as the correct one and civilize the past, let alone the present, on this basis?

uniform, objective and firmly established theory and practice of proof' (p. 1.) A comparable, yet different, account of proof, which is quite critical of standard views, is provided by Rav 1999.

[25] Some of the pieces written for this debate were already mentioned above. Here are the references to the entire core exchange: Jaffe and Quinn 1993, Atiyah, Borel, Chaitin, Friedan, Glimm, Gray, Hirsch, Lane, Mandelbrot, Ruelle, Schwarz, Uhlenbeck, Thom, Witten and Zeeman 1994, Jaffe and Quinn 1994, Thurston 1994.

[26] Jaffe and Quinn 1993: 10.

[27] The relationship between the written text of the proof and the collective oral activity related to proof that emerges from these testimonies presents a potentially worrying complexity to the historian, whose only sources are written vestiges with a faint relation to real processes of proof production.

In connection with this issue, and to return to the question whether certainty is the main motivation for looking for proofs today, it is interesting to note that many responses to the original paper by Jaffe and Quinn manifest a concern that too strict a control in order to assure certainty could entail losses for the discipline. By contrast, the debate also allows one to observe how many different functions and expectations mathematicians attach to proof: bringing 'clarity and reliability'; providing 'feedback and corrections', 'new insights and unexpected new data' (Jaffe *et al.* 1993), 'clues to new and unexpected phenomena' (Jaffe *et al.* 1994), 'ideas and techniques' (Atiyah *et al.* 1994), 'understanding',[28] 'mathematical concepts which are quite interesting in themselves, and lead to further mathematics'; 'helping support of certain vision for the structure of' a mathematical object (Thurston 1994).[29] Only with this variety of objectives in mind can we account for some otherwise mysterious practices. For instance, how else could we explain why rewriting a proof for already well-established statements can be fruitful?[30] Restricting ourselves to consideration of proof in the more limited domain of mathematics brought to light a wealth of reasons which motivated the writing of proofs for mathematicians.[31] Moreover, it suggests the great loss for the historical inquiry on mathematical proof if these proofs, the values attached to them, and the motivations to formulate them and write them down were not considered.

[28] A comment by Martin Davis on the four-colour theorem nicely illustrates this point: the problem with the computer proof, in his view, is not so much the lack of certainty it entails, but the fact that it does not put us in a position to understand where the '4' comes from, and whether it is accidental or not (Martin Davis, 2 October 2007, personal communication).

[29] As I alluded to it above, rigour is a contested value in these pages (see the contributions by Mandelbrot, Thom). What is more, it must be stressed that in contemporary mathematics, as it may have been the case for the Aristotle of the *Posterior Analytics*, the value attached to rigour is perhaps linked more to the understanding and additional insights it provides than to the increased certainty it yields. Hilbert 1900, for example, testifies to the idea that rigour yields fruitfulness and provides a guide to determine the importance of a problem (in the English translation: Hilbert 1902: 441). However, as Rav 1999 stresses, even when proofs are wrong or inadequate, they remain the main source from which new concepts emerge and new theories are developed. He further suggests that it is in proofs, rather than in theorems, that mathematicians look for mathematical knowledge and understanding: 'Conceptual and methodological innovations are inextricably bound to the search for and the discovery of proofs, thereby establishing links between theories, systematizing knowledge and spurring further developments.' (Rav 1999: 6).

[30] This point was stressed in Chemla 1992, which relies on how Rota 1990 had discussed the issue.

[31] Some historians have attempted to widen the history of proof by suggesting that the actors of the past used various means to convince their peers of the truth of a statement. In this vein attention has been paid to the rhetorical means that the actors employed. The preceding remarks show why this does not help frame a wide enough perspective on the activity of proof.

New perspectives, or: the project of the book

From this vantage point, two conclusions can be discerned.

Firstly, we see how a history of proof limited to inquiry into how practitioners devised the means of establishing a statement in an incontrovertible way runs the risk of being truncated. This, in my view, is what happens when the Babylonian, Chinese and Indian evidence is left out.

Secondly, and conversely, the outline sketched above suggests another kind of programme for a history of mathematical proof, one likely to be more open and allow us to derive benefits from the multiplicity of our sources. We may be interested in understanding the aims pursued by different collectives of practitioners in the past when they manifested an interest in the reasons why a statement was true or an algorithm was correct. We may also wonder how they shaped the practices of proof in relation to the aims they pursued and how they left written evidence of these practices.[32]

In fact, some of these other functions associated with proof were explicitly identified in the past and they were at times perceived as more important than assuring certainty. In relation to this, epistemological values distinct from that of incontrovertibility have been used to assess proofs. In this respect, one can recall the seventeenth-century debates about how to secure increased clarity through mathematical proofs, thereby achieving conviction and understanding. Seen in this light, the versions of Euclid's *Elements* of the past were not much prized, and new kinds of *Elements* were composed to fulfil more adequately the new requirements demanded from mathematical proof.[33] This example illustrates how different types of proof were created in relation to different agendas for proving.

How would such a programme translate with respect to ancient traditions? This is the inquiry of the present book, as one step towards opening a wider space for a historical and epistemological investigation into mathematical proof.

The book is mainly – we shall see why 'mainly' shortly – devoted to the earliest known proofs in mathematics. By the term 'proof', it should be now clear why we simply mean texts in which the ambition of accounting for the truth of an assertion or the correctness of an algorithm can be identified as one of the actors' intentions. In other words, we do not restrict our corpus

---

[32] This analysis and this programme develop the suggestion I formulated in Chemla 1997b: 229–31.

[33] On this question, see chapter 4, 'L'interprétation d'Euclide chez Pascal et Arnauld', in Gardies 1984: 85–108.

a priori by reference to norms and values that would appear to us as characterizing proofs in an essential way.

From this basis, the various chapters aim at identifying the variety of goals and functions that were assigned to proof in different times and places as well as the variety of practices that were constructed accordingly. In brief, the authors seek to analyse *why* and *how* practitioners of the past chose to execute proofs. Moreover, they attempt to understand how the activity of proving was tied to other dimensions of mathematical activity and, when possible, to determine the social or professional environments within which these developments took place.

Beyond such an agenda, several more general questions remain on our horizon.

From a historical point of view, we need to question whether the history of mathematical proof presents the linear pattern which today seems to be implicitly assumed. How did the various practices of proof clearly distinguished in present day mathematical practice inherit from and draw on earlier equally distinct practices? In more concrete terms, we seek to understand how the various practices of proof identified in ancient traditions or their components (like ways of proceeding or motivations), developed, circulated and interacted with one another. These are some of the questions that arise when attempting to account for the construction of proof as a central but multifaceted mathematical endeavour that unfolded in history in a less straightforward way than it was once believed.

From an epistemological point of view, on the other hand, we are interested in the understanding about mathematical proof in general that can be derived from studying these early sources from this perspective.

Further lessons from historiography, or: the historical analysis of critical editions

The analysis developed so far was needed to raise an awareness of the various meanings that have overloaded – and still overload – the term 'proof' in the historiography of mathematics. We brought to light how agendas involved in this issue fettered the development of a broader programme which would consider proof as a practice and analyse it in all its dimensions. Before we outline how the present book contributes to this larger programme, further preliminary remarks of another type are still needed.

Our approach to proofs from the past is mediated by written texts. In his contribution to the debate evoked above, wherein he described the collective work involved in the making of a proof eventually produced and written down by an individual, W. Thurston makes us fully aware of the bias that such an approach represents. In fact, there are further difficulties linked to the nature of the sources with which the historian works.

Some of these sources, like Babylonian tablets, were discovered in archaeological excavations, on a spot where they were used by actors. Others came down to us through the written tradition. In most cases, the physical medium has travelled.[34] In the end of the best-case scenario, those that can be read are available to us through critical editions. Through the various processes of transmission and reshaping of the primary sources, the agendas related to proof described earlier may have left an imprint. In such cases, our analysis of the source material would be biased at its root.

We shall illustrate this problem with a fundamental example, which will bring us back to nineteenth-century historiography of proof and a dimension of its formation that we have not yet contemplated. Above, we outlined the contribution that this book makes to analysing the evolution of European historiography of science with respect to 'non-Western' proofs. As a complementary account, the first section of Part I in the book focuses on the approach to Greek geometrical texts that developed in the late nineteenth century and the beginning of the twentieth century. Three chapters examine how the critical editions of Euclid's *Elements* and Archimedes' writings produced by the philologist Johann Heiberg, on which we still depend for our access to these texts, reflect, and hence convey, his own vision of the mathematics of ancient Greece. These chapters illustrate a new element involved in the historiographic turn described above: the production of critical editions. Let us sketch why they invite us to maintain a critical distance from the way sources have come down to us, lest we unconsciously absorb the agendas that shaped these editions.

The problem affecting these critical editions was first exposed by Wilbur Knorr, in an article published in 1996, the title of which was quite explicit: 'The wrong text of Euclid: on Heiberg's text and its alternatives'.[35] In it, Knorr explained why in his view, Heiberg shaped Euclid's text on the basis of his own assumptions regarding the practice of axiomatic–deductive systems in ancient Greece. Knorr's article began with a critical examination of a debate which at the end of the nineteenth century opposed Heiberg to

---

[34] The research programme entitled 'Looking at it from Asia and Africa: a critical analysis of the processes that shaped the sources of history of science', led by Florence Bretelle-Establet and to which A. Bréard, C. Jami, A. Keller, C. Proust and myself contributed helped me clarify my views on these questions.

[35] Knorr 1996. A paper that appeared posthumously took up this issue once again: Knorr 2001.

Klamroth, a historian who specialized in Arabic mathematics. The debate concerned the role ascribed to the editions and translations into Arabic and Latin carried out between the eighth and the thirteenth centuries – the so-called 'indirect tradition' – in the making of the critical edition of the *Elements*. Heiberg's position was that the Greek manuscripts dating from the ninth century onwards – the 'direct tradition' – were closer to Euclid's original text. In contrast, Klamroth argued that the Arabic and Latin witnesses, less complete from a logical point of view, bore testimony to earlier states of the text, whereas the Greek documents had already been contaminated by the various uses to which the text had been put in the centuries between its composition by Euclid and the transliteration into minuscule that took place in Byzantium. In brief, Heiberg was committed to the view that Euclid's *Elements* contained a minimum of logical gaps in the mathematical composition which it delineated. This supposition dictated the choice of sources on which he based his edition and motivated his rejection of other documents as derivative. This is how his selective treatment of the written evidence contributed to reshaping Euclid closer to his own vision. Taking up Klamroth's thesis, Knorr held the opposite view: for him, the Arabic and Latin witnesses were closer to the original Euclid, and the additions of logical steps were carried out by later editors of the *Elements*. The consequence of the resurgence of the debate was clear: some textual doubts were thereby raised regarding Euclid's original formulation of his proofs.

In articulating a critical analysis of this kind regarding the nineteenth-century edition of the *Elements* still widely used today for the first time since the publication of Heiberg's volumes, Knorr launched a research programme of tremendous importance to our topic. How much does our perception of the practice of proof in the *Elements* depend on the choices carried out by Heiberg? In other words, how far is his vision of Euclidean proof, formed at the end of the nineteenth century, conveyed through the text of his critical edition? Such are the fundamental questions raised. The example illustrates clearly, I believe, a much more general problem, which can be formulated as follows: how do critical editions affect the theses held by historians of science and the transmission of this inheritance to the next generations of scholars?

This general issue is to be kept in mind with respect to all the sources mentioned in this volume. However, beyond providing the illustration of a general difficulty, the example of the *Elements* is in itself of specific importance for our topic. In fact, the problem it raises extends beyond the case of the *Elements*, since soon after the publication of Knorr's first paper, a difficulty of the same kind became manifest with respect to Heiberg's critical edition of Archimedes' writings.[36] What can we learn about the issue of proof by examining the philologist's impact on our present-day vision of Euclid and Archimedes?

The three chapters of this book that are devoted to the analysis of the nineteenth-century editions of Greek geometrical texts from antiquity – the first one dealing with the *Elements*, the second one with the general issue of the critical edition of diagrams and the third one with Archimedes' texts – represent three critical approaches to Heiberg's philological choices and their impact on the editing of the proofs. Their argumentation benefits from the wealth of twentieth-century publications on the Arabic and Latin translations and editions of the Greek geometrical texts. Let us outline here briefly the distinct textual problems on which these chapters focus. Each chapter represents one way in which our understanding of the proofs preserved in the geometrical writings of ancient Greece is affected by their representation developed in the editions commonly employed.

In his contribution to the volume, Bernard Vitrac examines different *types* of divergences between proofs, to which the various manuscripts that bear witness to Euclid's *Elements* testify. More specifically, Vitrac focuses on a corpus of differences that were caused by deliberate intervention. Since these transformations were most certainly carried out by an author in the past who wanted to manipulate the logical or mathematical nature of the text, they indicate clearly the points at which we are in danger of attributing to Euclid reworking of the *Elements* undertaken after him.

Three types of divergences are examined. The first one, about which the debate described above broke out, relates to the terseness of the text of proofs: some proofs are found to be more complete from a logical point of view in some manuscripts than in others. Vitrac brings to light that the interpretation made by the two opponents in the debate relied on divergent views of the possible evolution of such a book as the *Elements*. Klamroth's thesis presupposed that the evolution of the text could only be a progressive expansion, motivated by the desire to make the deductive system more and more complete from a logical or a mathematical point of view. In contrast, Heiberg suggested that the Arabic and Latin versions were based on an epitome of the Euclidean text, on which account he could marginalize their use in restoring the *Elements*. Vitrac provides an analysis of the various logical gaps and concludes that the later additions to the Greek text that the indirect tradition allows us to perceive in the Greek manuscripts are linked to a logical concern regarding the mathematical content of the text.

---

[36] Chemla 1999.

This also holds true for most of the material added (propositions, lemmas, porisms). These remarks seem to support Klamroth's view. In this respect, Vitrac considers the indirect tradition as more authentic, a fact which calls for a re-examination of proofs in the various versions of Euclid's *Elements*. Vitrac suggests, however, that the enlargement and 'improvement' of the *Elements* could have started in Greek and continued in Arabic and Latin. The extant versions all seem to bear signs of corruption by such activity.

The second type of divergence between the sources Vitrac examines relates to the order in which propositions are arranged. This order constitutes a key ingredient in an axiomatic–deductive structure. In fact, the order does vary according to the version of the text. The decisions implemented by any critical edition hence represent an interpretation of Euclid's original deductive structure. However, on this count, Vitrac suggests the provisional conclusion that the indirect tradition more frequently bears witness to modifications of this type.

The third kind of divergence which he analyses has perhaps the greatest impact on our perception of Euclid's proofs, since it relates to major differences between the sources: substitution of proofs, integration of these substitutions in a set of related proofs, addition or subtraction of cases, and double proofs, of which Heiberg kept only one according to criteria that need to be examined. Such cases indicate that proofs and their modification were the subject of a continuous effort, part of which was integrated into the editions of the *Elements* available to us today.

In conclusion, before we consult the critical editions of Arabic, Arabo-Hebrew or Arabo-Latin versions of Euclid's *Elements*, it may be difficult to go substantially further in the analysis of the proofs or the deductive system attributed to Euclid. Most probably, this goal may remain forever out of reach. However, we can already appreciate the extent to which the textual decisions made by the philologist affect the discourse on the practice of proof in ancient Greece. This remark shows that the discourse on the practice of proof in ancient Greece may not be as solidly founded as was previously thought. As Vitrac suggests in his conclusion, rather than holding to the romantic ideal of some day retrieving the original *Elements*, it may be far more reasonable and interesting to consider the various versions of Euclid's *Elements* for which we have evidence. This new perspective would provide us with a better grasp of the various forms that the text took in history – namely, the forms through which different generations of scholars read and used the *Elements*.

Ken Saito and Nathan Sidoli critically examine the work of the philologist from an entirely different perspective. The purpose of their chapter is to draw attention to the fact that the diagrams inserted by Heiberg in his edition of Euclid's *Elements*, among others, are quite different from those actually and stably contained in the manuscripts. The sources indicate that the diagrams were more often than not quite particular, representing the general case not by means of a generic figure, but rather by means of a remarkable and singular configuration. By contrast, Saito and Sidoli show how Heiberg tacitly altered the diagrams, modernizing them and thereby conspicuously making them look more faithful to the situation under study and more generic than they actually were. These operations inserted diagrams in the nineteenth-century edition of the *Elements* which displayed an artificial continuity between past practices and mathematical practices at the time, not only with respect to their appearance, but also with respect to their way of expressing the general. Furthermore, the Greek diagrams were thereby shown as being demonstrably more different from the diagrams having specific dimensions contained in the Sanskrit or Chinese sources than the manuscripts actually indicated. Such issues may look minor, but they are not. In fact, Saito (2006) discusses a case in which the option chosen by the philologist in the restoration of the figure has had a crucial impact on the restored text. His conclusion is that, on both counts, Heiberg's choice seems to admit the results of a later intervention as genuine.[37] It is important to notice that, in modernizing the diagrams in this way, Heiberg removed any hint of the actors' ways of drawing and using figures, thereby impeding through his edition any study of the ancient practices with geometrical figures.

Saito's and Sidoli's critical analysis of the figures that Heiberg included in his editions such as the *Elements* is in full agreement with what Reviel Netz shows in the following chapter about Heiberg's edition of Archimedes' writings. In this chapter, Netz analyses more generally by which kinds of operation Heiberg's philological interventions left a lingering imprint on Greek mathematical texts of antiquity as we read them today. However, concentrating on the Danish philologist's critical edition of Archimedes' writings, particularly the second edition published between 1910 and 1915, Netz demonstrates further the specifics of Heiberg's editorial operations with respect to the Syracusan's *Opera Omnia*. Netz's analysis distinguishes three types of intervention that, in his words 'produce[d] an Archimedes who was textually explicit, consistent, rigorous and yet opaque'. In particular, Netz's overall broader argument reveals how Heiberg shaped Archimedes'

---

[37] Saito 2006: 97–144 compares Heiberg's diagrams in Book i of the *Elements* with those of the Greek manuscripts which formed the basis of his critical edition.

proofs according to his vision. In conclusion, we understand better *how* we were mistaken, when we took Heiberg's words for Archimedes' writings as the manuscripts bear witness to them.

To start with, Netz examines the diagrams of the critical edition. Clearly, like cases analysed by Saito and Sidoli, the diagrams used by Heiberg differ markedly from the evidence contained in the manuscripts, and Heiberg drew the diagrams according to his own understanding of what the original diagrams might have looked like. Yet Netz argues that the manuscripts represent a coherent and perfectly valid practice with diagrams. Further, three criteria allow him to discern how the ancient diagrams, drawn within the context of this practice, systematically differ from those which Heiberg substituted. Note that one of Netz's criteria relates to a feature already discussed by Saito and Sidoli: Heiberg tended to picture elements of the diagram as unequal that the manuscripts, in contrast to the discourse, drew as equal. Interestingly, the two chapters suggest slightly different interpretations of this ancient element of practice. The broader analysis developed by Netz further leads him to restore an ancient and consistent regime of conceiving and using diagrams which Heiberg's critical edition concealed and replaced with another more modern usage, for which there exists no ancient evidence. In addition, Netz argues that, in relation to this transformation, the role of the diagrams in the text underwent a dramatic shift: although the ancient evidence preserves diagrams that were an integral component of the argumentative text, Heiberg turned the diagrams into mere 'aids', dispensable elements for reading a discursive text that was 'logically self enclosed'. This first conclusion thus identifies one way in which the critical edition distorted the texts of Archimedes' proofs with respect to the extant manuscripts.

The second systematic intervention by Heiberg which Netz analyses is the bracketing of words, sentences and passages in Archimedes' writings, despite the fact that the manuscripts all agree on the wording of these passages. In other words, by rejecting portions as belonging to the original text, Heiberg modified the received text of Archimedes' writings in conformity with the representation that he had formed for Archimedes as a sharp contrast to Euclid. While, for Heiberg, Euclid was characterized by the careful expression of the full-fledged argument, Archimedes' style was, in his view, to focus on the main line of the proof, leaving aside 'obvious' details. Accordingly, Heiberg designated many passages of the received text as possible interpolations. Heiberg thus made Archimedes' style more coherent than what the manuscript evidence shows. Netz brings to light Heiberg's uneven pattern of bracketing and suggests factors which account for it. What is important for us here are the conclusions that Netz's analysis allows him to derive with respect to the text of proofs: Heiberg's bracketing occurs mainly in the texts for proofs, at precisely those points which suggest that Heiberg felt that overly simple arguments in the course of a proof could not be due to Archimedes. The more elementary the treatises, the more bracketing Heiberg carried out. In conclusion, Heiberg imposed on the text of the proof his expectation regarding Archimedes' way of proof.

Lastly, Netz brings to light the subtle ways at the global level of the corpus of texts in which Heiberg established Archimedes as a mathematician who adopted a uniform style and wrote down his treatises according to the same systematic pattern. By contrast, Netz suggests that Archimedes' writings manifested variety in several ways and at different levels. What matters most for us, again, is how the philologist's operations have a bearing on our perception of proofs and the sequence of them in 'axiomatic–deductive organizations'. And, here, the description of the editorial situation that Netz offers us is quite striking. He reveals how Heiberg forced divisions between propositions, types of propositions and components of propositions onto texts that did not lend themselves equally well to the operations and thus artificially created the sense of a standardized mathematical text, in conformity to modern expectations. In addition, Netz reveals Heiberg himself decided to give some propositions the status of postulate and others that of definition, with the manuscripts containing nothing of the sort. In that way, beyond the Archimedean corpus, the whole corpus of Greek geometrical texts acquired more coherence than what the written evidence records.

Together, these three chapters bring to light various respects by which the critical editions tacitly convey nineteenth-century or early-twentieth-century representations in place of Greek mathematical proofs to inattentive readers. Still more will be developed on this point in relation to Diophantus below. These conclusions provide impetus for developing further research on these topics, in order to understand how representations of ancient mathematics were formed in the nineteenth century and how they adhered to other representations and uses of Greek antiquity. Another chapter of the book inquires further in this direction of research. It complements our critical analysis of the historical formation of our understanding of Greek ideas of proof and shows how fruitful further research of that kind could be for sharpening our critical awareness.

In this chapter, Orna Harari draws on the hindsight of history and questions the conviction widely shared today that Aristotle's theory of demonstration in the *Posterior Analytics* can be interpreted in reference to its presumptive illustration, that is, Euclid's *Elements*. In fact, she establishes that this use of these two pieces of evidence in relation to each other became commonplace only in modern times. This brings us back to the issue of the part played in our story by the philosophy of science as it took shape as a discipline in the nineteenth century.

To make this point, Harari digs into the history of the discussions that bore on the question of the conformity of mathematical proofs – particularly, those contained in Euclid's *Elements* – to Aristotle's theory of demonstration. Her historical inquiry highlights that the present-day discussions of the issue are at odds with how the question was understood and tackled from late antiquity until the Renaissance. In contrast to the discussions by John Philoponus and Proclus which took Aristotle's theory as their foundation and inquired into whether and how mathematical proofs, and which mathematical proofs conformed to the Aristotelian theory, the contemporary view reversed the perspective. It took Euclid's *Elements* as a basis on which Aristotle's theory of demonstration had to be interpreted and understood. This repositioning reveals a fundamental shift in the interpretation of Aristotle's *Posterior Analytics*. By analysing how Philoponus and Proclus discussed the issue, she emphasizes that, despite essential differences between their approaches, they both understood the key problems to be whether proofs established mathematical attributes that belong to their subjects essentially and whether the middle term of a syllogism could serve as the cause of the conclusion. Thus, for these authors, the problem of the applicability of Aristotle's theory of demonstration related to the *non-formal* requirements of the theory. The same criterion holds true for the discussion until the Renaissance. By contrast, whatever conclusions they reach, contemporary interpretations of the question only consider the *formal* requirements. The main point of the discussion has hence become whether an interpretation of the syllogism could be offered that could accommodate what is to be found in, say, Euclid's *Elements*. Harari's contribution thereby exposes the anachronism underpinning the common, present-day reading of the relationship of Euclid and Aristotle to each other and highlights how much stranger they might become – both to us and to each other – if we attempted to restore them back to the context of the discussions and problems from which they emerged, so far as this is possible. Can we establish a correlation between the modern readings of Euclid and Aristotle and the way in which the critical editions discussed above were carried out? Such questions are interesting to keep in mind generally when analysing the various editions of Euclid's *Elements* produced throughout history.

These remarks conclude our analysis of past historiographies of proof and our identification of the factors at play in shaping and maintaining them. Among these factors, we identified elements of the contexts in which historiographic ideas were formed, the values which past historians had deemed central, the agendas they adopted and the critical editions they produced. We are now brought back to the new agenda we suggested above: what can be gained by widening our perspective on the practices of proof while considering a richer collection of sources?

III Broader perspectives on the history of proof

Widening our perspective on Greek texts: epistemological values and goals attached to proof

The biases in the history of proof on which the foregoing analysis shed light first coloured the treatment of the source material written in Greek. Historical approaches to proof in ancient Greece have so far concentrated mainly on a restricted corpus of texts and have limited the issues addressed. The ensuing account was accordingly confined in its scope and left wide ranges of evidence overlooked. Some of the chapters in this book deal precisely with part of this evidence. To begin with, Geoffrey Lloyd's chapter indicates some of the benefits that could be derived from a radical broadening of the corpus of Greek proofs under consideration. In particular, he discusses some of the new questions that emerge from this extended context, with regard to the practices of proof in ancient Greece.

Lloyd first reminds us of the fact that, despite the importance histo-riography granted to Euclid's *Elements* and cognate geometrical texts, mathematical arguments in ancient Greece were by no means restricted to proofs of the type that this corpus embodies. As Lloyd illustrates by means of examples, Greek sources on mathematical sciences provide ample evidence of other forms of argument as well as discussions on the relative value of proofs.[38] Enlarging the set of sources under consideration thus opens a space in which the various practices of proof and the values attached to them become an object of historical inquiry. Some of these sources bear witness to the fact that some authors found it important to use various modes of reasoning. Lloyd recalls the case of Archimedes, who expounds in *The Method* why it is fruitful to consider a figure as composed of indivisibles and to interpret it in a mechanical way in order to yield the result sought for. However, as Lloyd insists, although Archimedes deemed such reasoning essential to the discovery of the result to be proved, in

---

[38] Lloyd has made this point on other domains of inquiry; compare for instance Lloyd 1996b.

Archimedes' view, this type of argument could not be conclusive and had to be followed by another purely geometrical proof. Our explorations into matters of proof will allow us to come back to this example below, from a new perspective. Let us stress for now that different kinds of reasoning have different kinds of value.

Furthermore, Lloyd stresses that in numerous domains of inquiry in ancient Greece, there were debates about the value of their starting points or the proper methods to follow, and securing conviction was a key issue. Keeping too narrow a focus on mathematics in this respect conceals important phenomena. Here two points are worth emphasizing.

Firstly, within this extended framework, it appears that proofs carried out according to an axiomatic–deductive pattern were developed in several areas and were by no means confined to mathematics, although even in antiquity, geometry came to be perceived as a singular field in this respect. The recurring use of such a practice of proof echoes the variety of terms used throughout the sources to demand 'irrefutable' arguments. One is hence led to wonder how far, as regards ancient Greece, the history of an axiomatic–deductive practice can be conducted while remaining within the history of mathematics, or to what extent the interpretation of this practice can be based only on mathematical sources. Here too, we encounter the impact of a form of anachronism. Since this kind of proof is at the present day deemed to be essential to, and even characteristic of, mathematics, historiography has approached the question of axiomatic–deductive proof mainly from within the field of mathematics, disregarding the fact that it was employed much more widely in antiquity. What greater understanding of such a practice of proof would a broad historical inquiry of proof *more geometrico* yield? This is the issue at stake here.

Secondly, such an importance granted to one type of method and organization of knowledge cannot hide a much wider phenomenon which Lloyd wants to emphasize: the numerous debates on the correct way of conducting an inquiry. We seem to have here an idiosyncrasy of ancient Greek writings, or at least among the writings that have been handed down to us. The unique multiplicity of 'second-order disputes' evidenced in 'most areas of inquiry' leads Lloyd to suggest a third expansion.

Lloyd grants that disputes between practitioners of mathematics or other domains of inquiry are a widespread phenomenon worldwide in the ancient world. However, his comparison of such debates, in ancient Greece and elsewhere, leads him to an important observation, namely, that the modes of settling debates in various collectives appear to differ. Lloyd thus invites us to consider engaging in a discussion on the standards of proof in order to conclusively resolve debates as a *social* phenomenon. The new and important research programme which he proposes intends to account for the development of such attempts to adjudicate debates in social terms. In other words, Lloyd calls for developing a social account of the emergence of second-order discussions on proof.

These suggestions show how, by concentrating on a set of texts wider than the usual geometrical writings, one can define new horizons for research on proof in Greek sources. In recent years, though, new approaches to proofs in the writings that provided the standard historiography with its basis have taken shape. These approaches are interesting for us, since they have brought to the fore epistemological values other than being conducive to truth which, as far as our sources can tell, may have been attached to proof, thereby side-lining the issue of certainty that has dominated the discussion on ancient proofs. To mention but one example, I shall show how, in my view, Ken Saito has advocated a new way of interpreting proofs in the core corpus.

Saito takes as his starting point the thesis that, when one considers this collection of texts *as a whole*, there emerges from the corpus a set of 'elementary techniques' that form a 'tool-box' on which Greek geometers relied.[39] Moreover, he argues that the practitioners developed knowledge of how to combine the elements in the tool-box in *standard* and *locally valid* methods – combinations which he also calls 'techniques', or 'patterns of argument'. In Saito's view, the 'method of exhaustion', which was named and discussed as such only in the seventeenth century, constitutes an example of such a method. His approach not only yields an analysis of the method as a specific sequence of elements taken from the tool-box, but it also embeds a technique that has been long recognized into a larger set of similar techniques which recur in proofs. What is worth stressing is his remark that, for reasons yet unknown, these methods do not seem to have been described at a meta-mathematical level or even named at the time. Nevertheless, the sources bear witness to patterns of proof which circulate between proofs and to the stabilization of a form of knowledge about them.

An initial hypothesis can be formulated with respect to these methods: it is by reading the text of a proof *per se* and *not* merely as establishing the

---

[39] The insight about the 'tool-box' was introduced and worked out by Saito from 1994 on (see Saito and Tassora 1998 and www.greekmath.org/diagram/). It was further developed in N1999: 216–35. The latter book figures prominently among the publications that opened new perspectives in the approach to deduction in the Greek mathematical texts of what I called the 'core corpus'. I develop here reflections on a tiny part of the new ideas that were introduced in this wider context. Saito's project on the Greek mathematical tool-box has not yet come to completion. To present his ideas here, I rely on personal communication and on drafts that he sent me in 2005 and which contain abstracts of part of his project.

truth of a proposition that such techniques could be grasped. The hypothesis accounts for how the techniques brought to light took shape. It may also account for one of the motivations at play in making proofs explicit and writing them down. One can go one step further and speculate about why, as far as we know, in ancient Greece the methods in question were neither named, nor analysed in any second-order discussion. This point leads me to a second hypothesis with respect to the text of a proof: were not some of the proofs written down with the purpose of displaying a given technique which they put into play? In that case, general techniques would have been expressed through the proofs of *particular* propositions and thereby also motivated the expression of these proofs in writing. In other words, some proofs were to be read as a kind of *paradigm*, making a statement of more general validity than a first reading would indicate. The interpretation of the texts of these proofs would be comparable in that respect to how a problem and the procedure for solving it made sense in the Babylonian or Chinese writings.[40] Whatever the case, the essential point here is that the text of a proof was not read only as establishing a proposition, but also as a possible source for working techniques. Moreover, the generality and importance of a textual unit in these books would not lie only in the proposition itself, but also in the technique brought into play in its proof.

Let us consider these various points one by one to grasp what is more generally at stake here.

To begin with, the first hypothesis formulated above suggests that readers were likely to read a proof *for itself* and not merely for its capacity to establish the statement proved. There is nothing surprising about this assumption. The recent debate on which we commented in Section II bore witness to such uses of the text of proofs: some of these mathematicians testified to the fact that they read proofs, seeking, among other things, techniques and also concepts. This constitutes a challenge for us: how are we, as historians, to gather evidence in order to take this dimension of the interest in proof into account more generally and rigorously? Interestingly enough, the hypothesis on the practice of proof prompted by Saito's suggestion echoes with how, as we shall see, proofs of the correctness of algorithms were conducted in the earliest extant Chinese sources attesting to practices of proof.[41] In all these contexts, the proofs appear not to have been only means

---

[40] On the latter, a discussion and bibliography can be found in Chemla 2009. Note that I use paradigm in the sense that grammarians use this word. Also note that the text of a proof could either state a general technique or document its existence by the fact of bringing it into play.

[41] See below and Chemla 1992, Chemla 1997b.

for an end, but their texts were also read as conveying other meanings. The 'techniques' read in the proofs do not have the same nature in different contexts. However, what is important to note here is that in all these cases the epistemological value of the proof cannot be exhausted by the question of determining whether it duly establishes the statement to be proved.

According to the first hypothesis too, the reader looked for something *general* in a proof – a method, the use of which could extend beyond the limits of a proposition. The fact that, as Saito showed, some techniques of somewhat general validity were actually composed indicates the possible outcome of such a search. A straightforward interpretation of the text of each proof taken separately would miss this feature of the practice of proof. The virtue of the techniques thereby identified was their potential usefulness in other contexts: if we follow this interpretation, a certain *fruitfulness* was recognized in it. These concerns indicate epistemological values that actors may have attached to proofs and that too narrow a focus on certainty could hide from our view.

The preceding remarks illustrate what kind of benefits could be derived from re-examining standard texts with wider expectations in mind. They also bring to light an issue that will prove essential in what follows. The way in which actors have read proofs or have written them down, the *motivation* driving the composition of explicit proofs, cannot be taken for granted. As I have indicated, reading meanings into proofs is apparently a widely shared practice. However, this does not mean that practitioners belonging to different scholarly cultures read the meanings in texts in the same way or that the texts intended the meanings to be read in the same way. Whether one accepts only the first hypothesis or both hypotheses as formulated, the perception of the various dimensions of the Greek texts to which I have just alluded requires an unusual and specific reading of the text. If one admits the second hypothesis, texts of proofs were to be read as paradigms. Interestingly enough, as we saw in Section II of this introduction, the diagrams in Greek texts seem to have required the same kind of reading, at least if we agree on the fact that the original figures resembled those in the manuscripts and not those which Heiberg drew. Interpretation of the sources appears more generally to be a delicate procedure, on which our ability to perceive the various dimensions of the proofs examined will depend. As I shall argue below, this problem is intrinsic to our endeavour: it is, in my view, tied to the fact that shaping a practice of proof has always involved designing a kind of text to work out and deliver the proofs. The task of interpreting the texts thus cannot be separated from the job of describing the practice of proof to which they adhere.

The lines of inquiry just outlined illustrate some of the issues that more generally have imposed themselves as central issues in the following chapters of the book. To begin with, these issues are taken up from different perspectives in the next two chapters of the book, both also devoted to Greek sources.

The issue of generality in relation to proof directs Ian Mueller's analysis of marginalized Greek writings dealing with numbers, albeit from a different perspective. Because they have been overshadowed by the treatment of arithmetic in Books VII to IX of Euclid's *Elements*, the techniques of proof used by Nicomachus in his *Introduction to Arithmetic* and by Diophantus in *On Polygonal Numbers* have not yet been the object of detailed analysis. Ian Mueller chooses to focus on them because they deal with numbers – polygonal numbers – in a singular way, approaching them through the prism of configuration and procedure of generation. These features raise the problem of defining the polygonal numbers as general objects, making general statements about them, and proving such statements in a general way. The challenge is to reach generality not only with respect to all polygonal numbers of a specific type, such as triangular or square numbers, but also to define and work with n-agonal numbers.

Both Nicomachus and Diophantus attempted to meet with this challenge, by composing treatments of these numbers in general, stating propositions about them, and accounting for the validity of these statements. In particular, both authors set themselves the task of establishing the value of the nth j-agonal number. The conclusion of Mueller's analysis is that both attempts equally fail to establish the conclusion aimed at with full generality. Nonetheless, the differences between the ways the two authors shape textual elements to approach polygonal numbers, formulate statements about them and design modes of proving to deal with the topic raise considerable interest. This is what emerges from Mueller's detailed description of the different techniques of reasoning by which both authors address these numbers and try to establish their properties.

Nicomachus makes use of specific diagrams that iconically represent the numbers as configurations of units. In addition, Nicomachus introduces a key tool – sequences of numbers – in a way that will be characteristic of his approach. To begin with, he constructs arithmetical ways of generating these sequences. He then strives to establish relationships between these sequences and the first sequences of polygonal numbers (triangular, square, pentagonal and so on). It is for this task that Nicomachus' diagrams are brought into play. Because of their features, these diagrams can be used to indicate the reason of the correctness of the relationship only for the first terms of the sequences. However, this is how Nicomachus argues in favour of the general statement, whereby his establishment of this general statement differs from modern standards. In the second step, Nicomachus further brings to light patterns in the modes of generation of the first sequences, thereby indicating the general structure of the set of sequences of polygonal numbers and pointing to further relationships between these sequences. Again, Nicomachus indicates the general pattern and argues for it by highlighting the pattern for the first sequences. And again this is where his approach falls short of modern standards. The most general statement by which Nicomachus summarizes his procedure of proof consists of a *table* of numbers. It collects in its rows the sequences introduced and more. Since it displays the pattern of relationship between the lines, the table allows Nicomachus to generate subsequent lines by deploying the same pattern further and thereby determining the value of any polygonal number.

The textual elements brought into play (diagrams, sequences and table of numbers) and the ways of using and articulating them by modes of reasoning contrast sharply with how Diophantus approaches the same topic. The core of Diophantus' treatise *On Polygonal Numbers* consists of purely arithmetical and general propositions. These propositions state arithmetical properties in the form of relationships holding between numbers. Diophantus proves these relationships through representations of numbers as lines, using the representations in a way that is specific to this branch of inquiry. Diophantus attempts to formulate the value of the nth j-agonal number as a *proposition* of this kind. The diagrams used and the propositions stated thus exhibit a style completely different from Nicomachus'. However, their kind of generality is precisely what constitutes the problem for concluding the proof. It is in Diophantus' attempt to connect these general statements to polygonal numbers with full generality that Mueller identifies the gap in Diophantus' proof. The tools Diophantus uses here are too general to allow him to recapture the details of the general objects that polygonal numbers represent. He manages to establish the link only for the first n-agonal numbers.

These two texts devoted to the same topic illustrate quite vividly the plurality of practices in Greek mathematics, the study of which Lloyd advocated. Mueller highlights differences in the ways of making diagrams and relating them to the mathematical objects being studied. He shows the distinct ways in which diagrams are employed in the arguments being developed, thereby bringing to light two distinct kinds of arithmetical methods. Additional interest in this case study derives from what is revealed when the proofs are considered from the viewpoint of generality. Clearly, both texts betray an ambition to reach a high level of generality. Mueller's contrastive analysis discloses how distinct means are constructed and combined for the proofs to fulfil this ambition. Despite their failure in modern eyes to achieve their goal, the two sets of proofs in the texts appear to form two strikingly different, but carefully designed, architectures of arguments inspired by the task that the authors had set for themselves. Taking the value of generality into account in his interpretation allows Mueller to use finer tools and describe with greater accuracy the argumentative structures and the differences between them. Mueller thus highlights *how* the conduct of proofs can bear the hallmark of epistemological values prized by the actors.

More generally, Mueller's analysis indicates how much more there can be to the study of a practice of proof than simply assessing whether proofs adequately establish their conclusions or not. The kinds of elements the practitioners design for their proofs, the ways in which they use them, and other questions, all essential for a historical inquiry into the activity of proof, will appear quite fruitful in the following chapters. In particular, the question of how a kind of text has been designed for a certain practice of proof – a question that the multiplicity of the proofs examined brings to the fore – appears relevant again for the further analysis of the sources. Its fundamental character will soon become even clearer.

Further widening: the text of a proof

In his *Arithmetics*, Diophantus opts for a completely different style of composition and presents solutions for hundreds of problems relating to integers. Each problem is followed by the reasoning that leads to the determination of a solution. To formulate the problems and the kind of proof following them, both of which involve statements relating to numbers and unknowns, Diophantus regularly makes use of symbols. In his chapter, Reviel Netz focuses on the question of determining the role played by this symbolism in the development of the reasonings Diophantus proposed to establish the solutions to the problems.

The fact that the symbols introduced are essential to Diophantus' project is made clear by the fact that they are the main topic of the introduction to his book. On the other hand, Diophantus stands in contrast to his known predecessors in that he makes explicit the reasoning by which he establishes the solutions to problems. Therefore, the question of how the former are linked to the latter is not only natural, but also essential to an analysis of Diophantus' activity of proving. Such is the main question of the chapter. It pertains, as one can see, to the text with which an argument is conducted.

Aware that the symbols of Diophantus must be distinguished from those of Vieta, Netz first studies the specific historical context in which they were designed and describes them in detail, on which basis he examines how the editors of the nineteenth century transcribed them in their critical editions and translations. His conclusions are twofold. On the one hand, Netz shows that the symbols are located at the level of noun-phrases, but are not used for either the relations or the structural terms specific to a problem. Moreover, he establishes their nature of being 'allographs' of the words they stand for, that is, they write these words in another way. On the other hand, Netz reveals that the use of these symbols is nowhere as systematic in the manuscripts as Paul Tannery presented them in his 1893–5 edition.[42] Tannery designed the proofs, rather than the statement of problems, as the locus for the use of symbols, a fact which does not correspond to what is found in the manuscripts. Moreover, Tannery introduced a distinction between some terms which he systematically rendered as symbols and other terms which he always wrote down in full, thereby establishing two different kinds of terms, in contrast to the manuscripts which use abbreviations for both kinds in comparable ways. We meet again with the necessity of a critical awareness regarding the critical editions carried out in the nineteenth century.

This preliminary analysis provides a sound basis on which Netz can address the main question raised by his chapter: what is the correlation between Diophantus' use of such symbols and the specific kind of proof he systematically presented? In Netz's view, Diophantus undertook to gather problems he had received and complete their collection in a systematic way. Moreover, his ambition was to present them for a literate, elite readership. In relation to this goal, Diophantus opted for a solution of each problem in the form of 'analysis'. Hence Netz also addresses a part of the history of proof that falls outside the scope of Euclid's *Elements*. This holds true not only because these proofs proceed through analysis. In addition, the point in Diophantus' *Arithmetics* is not to establish the truth of a statement, but rather to fulfil a task correctly. In a context in which the procedure of the solution provided for problems was also a topic for debate, Netz argues, writing down the reasoning which establishes how the task was correctly fulfilled contributed to showing the suitability of the mode of solution adopted. In other words, for Netz, the proof here intended to highlight the natural and rational character of the method chosen to solve a given

---

[42] Compare T1893/5. The 1974 reprint of the book is freely available on Gallica: http://gallica.bnf.fr/.

problem. To this end, Diophantus shaped, primarily thanks to his symbols, a kind of text that would enable the reader to survey in the best way possible the method followed. This is how Netz argues in support of his thesis that the expressions formed with the specific symbols introduced are consubstantial with the project and the kind of proof specific to Diophantus' *Arithmetics*.

Note that here again, as in Mueller's chapter, the examined proofs proceed through operating with statements of equality between numbers. However, in the *Arithmetics*, the symbols developed helped carry out such operations in a specific way, linked to the peculiar features of Diophantus' reasonings. Since they were allographs, they allowed the reader to keep the meaning of the computations in mind. On that count, these symbols differ from modern symbolism. This difference in nature possibly echoes a difference in use: Diophantus' symbols do not seem to have been used for proving through blind computations, as is the case with modern symbolism. Instead, they helped form a kind of writing transparent with respect to the meaning of the statement. Since the symbols were abbreviations, they enhanced the *surveyability* of the expressions, in the same way as the technical writing of a number helps understand the structure of the number.[43] This conclusion raises a general question. The surveyability of a procedure or a proof depends on the kind of text constructed to write down and work with the proof or procedure. Which resources did various groups of practitioners create, or borrow, to this end? Netz's contribution can be viewed as a step towards a systematic inquiry in that direction. We shall soon meet with further evidence that can be fruitfully analysed from the same perspective.

To create this form of writing, Diophantus made use of possibilities available in the written culture of his time, but used them in a way specific to his project. As Netz stresses, Euclid's *Elements* also exhibits evidence of creating a specific language, characterized by distinctive formulaic expressions. Thus we meet with the same phenomenon already emphasized on several occasions above from yet another perspective: the kind of text used is correlated to the type of proof developed. Given the fact that the kinds of proof and the project embodied by the *Elements* differ from the objectives of Diophantus, the kind of writing employed in the *Elements* differs from those used by Diophantus.

---

[43] Neugebauer also interpreted some features of Mesopotamian ways of writing mathematics as making statements surveyable. Høyrup 2006 quotes at length the passages by Neugebauer on this point and discusses them, with respect to Mesopotamian, Greek, Latin, Arabic and Indian sources as well as sources written in vernacular European languages.

From another viewpoint, Diophantus' text can be contrasted with other types of problem texts, which also attest to mathematical work on and with operations or computations. Several of the following chapters consider types of writing of the latter kind. Both the use of operations on statements of equality and the introduction of symbols to carry out these operations found in the *Arithmetics* contrast with what other traditions formatted as algorithmic solutions to problems, for which the correctness needed to be, and was, established. Even if these other writings bear witness to other means of proof, via other techniques and in pursuit of other goals, many parallels can be drawn between the *Arithmetics* and these other texts. These texts all deal with operations and operations on operations, illustrating how different modes of manipulating mathematical operations were devised in history. Most of these texts reveal an ideal of writing sequences and combinations of operations in such a way that the meaning becomes transparent. However, despite the fact that they shared a common feature, in what follows we shall see that how this ideal was achieved depended on the context and the type of text constructed. Lastly, these writings all raise the question of what was meant by a problem and the procedure attached to it. Was a particular problem representative only of itself, or was it read more generally as a paradigm for all problems in the same class? Netz develops an interpretation of the way in which Diophantus conceived of generality. Whether or not this interpretation is accepted, it stresses an essential point: the symbols used by Diophantus were not abstract. This feature sheds an additional light on how these symbols differed from modern ones. Moreover, it implies that if they had a general meaning, it was conveyed in a specific way, requiring again a specific reading.

This chapter thus leads to two general conclusions, essential for our purposes. Firstly, Netz's article analyses how different groups of mathematicians created different kinds of text in relation to the practice of proof they adopted. Note that this approach offers one of the ways in which one could systematically develop the programme suggested by Lloyd and account for the variety of practices of proof in ancient Greece. More generally, Netz foregrounds the fact that proofs have been conducted in history with various kinds of texts, each being shaped in relation to the operations specific to a given kind of proof. The text of the proof is correlated to the act of proving. The general question raised by Netz in his approach to Greek sources may be phrased as 'What types of text were shaped for the conduct of which kind of proofs?' and has already proved relevant above. Clearly, this question opens a field of inquiry into proof that could be – and will prove so below – extremely fruitful. In particular, we can expect that the development of this inquiry provides means for interpreting these texts more accurately.

In conjunction with the first point, Netz's treatment yields insight into how different the purposes for developing proofs may have been. This brings us back to the programme suggested above for our historical inquiry into proof, namely, the restoration of the motivations behind the development of proofs and the description of the diversity in their conduct accordingly. However, before we go further in widening the set of sources to be considered with these issues in mind, a last point must be emphasized.

Netz's discussion illustrates how the resources Diophantus introduced for a given type of proof were adopted to design the text of another kind of proof, i.e. algebraic proofs, in modern times. More precisely, Netz's analysis highlights why Diophantus' proofs are not algebraic in nature. Nonetheless, the shaping of the modern algebraic proof made use, for the conduct of a reasoning, of symbolic resources similar to those designed within the framework of the *Arithmetics*. This conclusion offers our first insight into the history of algebraic proofs. What are its other components and how did they take shape? These are some of the questions to which we shall come back below.

Proving the correctness of algorithms

The ideal of transparency, which Netz interprets as informing the symbolism used by Diophantus, is also the main force driving the way Babylonian practitioners of mathematics composed the text of algorithms, according to the interpretation of Jens Høyrup. Before explaining this point further, let us first recall some basic features of the writings to which we now turn. These documents are, for the most part, composed of problems followed by algorithms which solve them. The fact that the algorithm correctly solves the problem is the statement to be proved, in contrast to what we find in Euclid's *Elements*, where proofs mainly deal with the truth of theorems.[44] In such contexts, proving means establishing that the procedure carries

---

[44] The claim here takes into account the fact that the statement of a problem in the *Elements* does not include the statement of how to carry out a task. Interestingly enough, except for some specific cases, the scholarship devoted to Euclid's *Elements* has paid much less attention to problems than to theorems. There are exceptions like Harari 2003. However, the problems still await further study *qua* problems. How was the solution written down as text and how did the proof relate to the formulation of the solution as such? These are questions that seem to me to be promising for future research. It may well be that after these problems have been studied more in depth, the statement contrasting proofs in Euclid's *Elements* with those of algorithms may have to be made more precise.

out correctly the task for which it is given, that is, that the algorithm yields the desired result. In this framework, the ideal of transparency that the Mesopotamian tablets embody consists of the fact established by Høyrup that the texts for procedures were *simultaneously* prescribing computations and indicating the reasons underlying their correctness.[45] Since we have no second-order comments by Babylonians explaining how these texts should be interpreted, it took some time before this property was recognized.

Once again, like the previous examples, this case shows how given collectives of practitioners shaped specific kinds of text to work with operations and establish their correctness. It also highlights how this formation and standardization of texts invited problems of interpretation. The technical character of the texts hindered their interpretation by historians, who failed to identify how proofs were expressed and hence drew derogatory conclusions, such as M. Kline's.

In this case, however, recognizing the proof in the text required understanding something with respect to proof as well, that is, that the rationale of a procedure can, at times, be given in the description of the procedure itself and not as a separate text – this is precisely the manifestation of the ideal of transparency in this context, which demonstrates that the same ideal can appear in various ways. More accurately, when we examine Mesopotamian texts such as those with which Høyrup establishes his point from this perspective, we observe that the texts of algorithms do not only contain specific prescriptions for operations that achieve transparency, but also contain elements of the reasoning that develops along the statement of the algorithm. Again, widening the corpus of proofs under consideration leads us to deeper insights into how a proof can be formulated.

This expansion of the corpus also broadens our understanding of the motivations for writing down proofs in the ancient traditions. In Høyrup's

---

[45] One speaks of the 'correctness' of the algorithm. On this theme, it may be helpful to clarify two points about which I often read misleading comments. Firstly, the text of an algorithm is the statement to be proved and *not* its proof. It is on the basis of this distinction that one can make the point that in Mesopotamian tablets, the two texts (the statement of the algorithm and the formulation of its proof) merged with each other. Moreover, to perceive this requires a specific reading, whereby two layers of meaning are discerned in the statement of the algorithm. Secondly, the aim in proving the correctness of an algorithm is *not only* to show that the algorithm yields an exact *value* – or to establish how accurate or inaccurate the value is – but *also* to establish that the sequence of operations prescribed yields the desired *magnitude*. So the depiction of algorithms only in association to approximations is doubly misleading. These basic misconceptions lie at the root of what most commentators who have been discounting computation have claimed. The section entitled 'The unpuzzling character of calculation' in Hacking 2000: 101–3 comments on the text of an algorithm, overlooking the fact that this is the statement to be proved and not the proof. The same pages make other claims that are contradicted by the conclusions reached here.

view, the proofs he reads in the formulation of the procedure intend to guarantee an *understanding* of the reasons why the operations should be carried out. He even suggests they are proofs precisely because they have this goal. We see how the exclusive focus on the function of proof as yielding certainty would leave out these sources as irrelevant for a history of proof. However, these texts demonstrate that one motivating interest in proofs and their transcription in one way or another may have been not only – or perhaps not at all – to *convince* someone of the truth of a statement but to make one *understand* the statement. This is still a strong motivation for mathematicians today, as is evidenced, for example, by the debate analysed in Section II and it has been so all through the history of mathematics.

Let us pause for a while to consider the goal of 'understanding' within the context of a practice of proof intended to establish the correctness of algorithms. Far from being the final point of the analysis, it is in fact only its beginning. The possibility that some proofs aim at providing an 'understanding' raises an essential question, for which the Babylonian case allows further inquiry: what techniques or *dispositifs* were devised to provide an 'understanding' of the algorithms in the milieus of scribes? By Høyrup's restoration, geometrical diagrams seem to have supported the procedure. Moreover, these diagrams were made in a way which allowed material transformations of their shape. The specific terms which prescribed the operations designated such material transformations which helped make sense of the computations. The arguments supporting this hypothesis come from a close analysis of the terms used to write down the algorithm. However, this conclusion would have remained only speculation, had not Høyrup discovered some texts from Susa that make explicit the kind of training required by such a mode of understanding.

These texts are revealing for several reasons. The explanations in them that produce the 'understanding' are developed very specifically within the framework of paradigmatic situations similar to those described in the outline of some geometrical problems. We hold that these explanations reveal how the context of geometrical problems may have provided situations as well as numerical values with which the understanding of the effect of operations could be grasped. The texts from Susa also reveal how diagrams with highly particular dimensions were used in the same way. This parallel between geometrical figures and problems, as well as this way of using geometrical problems, compellingly evokes the case of some Chinese mathematical sources, about which two points can be established. Firstly, the problems were not only a question to be addressed, but, as the paradigms that they were, they also provided a semantic field for interpreting the operations of the algorithm or the operations required for the proof of correctness. Secondly, just as problems provided particular numerical data, geometrical figures displayed simple dimensions, and they were used in the same way to make explicit the meaning of operations.[46] In a moment, we shall come back to this comparison, but note that exactly the same situation holds true for Sanskrit sources analysed by Colebrooke.[47]

In addition, the Susa texts that Høyrup analyses formulate the explanations by describing the result of each operation in two ways: on the one hand, a numerical value is provided and, on the other hand, an interpretation of the magnitude which is determined is made explicit in the geometrical terms of the field of interpretation. Such a kind of 'meaning' for the effect of operations recalls what is found in Chinese texts. In the latter sources, a specific concept (*yi*) is reserved to designate that 'meaning', and the meaning is made explicit by reference to the situations introduced in the statements of problem. In my own chapter on early China, I discuss the interpretation of this concept and provide cases where it is used in Chinese sources. In correlation with this parallel, in early Chinese mathematical writings we also find algorithms that are transparent regarding the reasons of their correctness: the successive operations are prescribed in such a way as to *simultaneously* indicate their 'meaning', which can be exhibited directly in the context of the situation described by the problem.[48]

This parallel shows that the early mathematical cultures which worked with algorithms developed partially similar techniques for 'understanding', even though they did so in different ways, as we shall make clearer below. More broadly, these remarks raise a general issue. They invite us to study systematically the devices, or *dispositifs*, that various human collectives constructed for 'understanding' and interpreting the 'meaning' of operations, or conversely, the kind of 'interpretation' that was rejected. Interestingly enough, this question enables a perspective from which we may cast a new light on the 'Method' described by Archimedes in the text devoted to this topic, which Lloyd discusses in his chapter. Indeed, what Archimedes offers with his 'mechanical method' is a way of 'interpreting a figure' in terms of weight – specifically, an interpretation from which he can

---

[46] See chapter A, in CG2004: 28–38 and Chemla 2009, which presents a fully developed analysis of these issues.

[47] See p. 6.

[48] Chemla 1991. Chemla 2010 analyses more generally the two fundamental ways in which the text of an algorithm can refer to the reasons for its correctness. Both can be recognized in the way in which texts for algorithms were recorded in the tablets discussed by Høyrup.

derive a result. Even though he discards this method as inappropriate for a proof, as did a tradition of scholars who developed comparable proofs, the question remains open for us to understand *what this kind of interpretation actually achieved for him.*[49]

Getting back to our Mesopotamian documents, I am aware that some historians may question whether such modes of establishing the correctness of algorithms ought to be considered proofs. The Babylonian source material allows us to shed light on the difficulty that this division would entail in the history of mathematics. In fact, the techniques that the scribes used to provide an 'understanding' of the type discussed above could be, and appear to have been later on, taken up in other practices of proof – where the qualification as 'proof' is less disputed. As Høyrup has suggested in previous publications, there is a strong historical continuity between the modes of argumentation alluded to above, which appear to have been developed in Babylonian scribal milieus on the one hand and what are explicitly recorded as proofs in Arabic algebraic texts from the ninth century onwards on the other hand.[50] If only for this reason, these techniques of 'understanding' do belong, in my view, to the history of mathematical proof. The continuity evoked is of the same kind as that mentioned above with respect to the textual techniques devised by Diophantus to develop his arguments.

As a provisional conclusion, one may suggest that the text of a proof is a technical text, the shaping of which may have benefited from all kinds of resources available. Conversely, in some cases, the formation of a technical text for working out a kind of proof led to developing techniques that could be brought to bear in other mathematical activities. In the case of Babylonian tablets, not only the operations used in a procedure, but – as is clearly shown by the Susa texts – also the transformations of algorithms,

---

[49] In the same way, Krob 1991 has developed a proof of a combinatorial theorem based on an interpretation involving a plate, beads and pebbles. Such features are unusual in mathematical publications. They occur more frequently in some fields, like combinatorics, than in others. The reasons why it is so are worth exploring, since they shed light on social aspects of proving. It is clear that precisely because of these features, not all mathematicians of the present day will accept the proof Krob 1991 gives as a proof. This approach to the question, however, leaves unanswered the questions which I find quite fascinating: what does the interpretation do for the reasoning? And why do practitioners find it appealing to make use of such devices or *dispositifs* of interpretation within proofs? Approaching the problem through the controversies among mathematicians would yield interesting results.

[50] See, for instance, Høyrup 1986. In his recent edition and translation into French of al-Khwarizmi's book on algebra, Rashed 2007 puts forward a different hypothesis for the history of these proofs, interpreting them rather as composed within the framework of Euclidean geometry.

such as embedding them into other algorithms or modifying their lists of operations, could be established on the basis of problems and/or figures. In the case of Diophantus, equalities were transformed *qua* equalities. Both techniques were adopted in Arabic algebraic texts.

In addition to providing insights into how actors carried out interpretation for the algorithms recorded on Babylonian tablets, Høyrup suggests that the need for understanding perhaps developed in relation to teaching. In other words, he links the professional context of training scribes in Mesopotamia to the development of certain kinds of proof. Interestingly enough, as we shall see below, such a hypothesis nicely fits with A. Volkov's thesis regarding the use of proofs for a teaching context in East Asia.

Christine Proust's chapter suggests capturing an interest in the correctness of algorithms in another kind of Mesopotamian tablet, which contain texts consisting of only numbers. Note that, here, the work of the exegete is particularly challenging, since she has to argue for an interpretation of texts that contain no words, only numbers. The method Proust uses to read these traces is deeply subtle but of particular interest for us.

At first sight, the tablets at the focus of Proust's attention appear merely to betray an interest in 'checking' the numerical results yielded by an algorithm. Seen in that light, they recall some of the texts discussed by Høyrup, in which a similar concern can be identified. However, as we shall see, the two types of text call for different modes of interpretation.

The tablet VAT 8390, discussed by Høyrup, contains a 'verification' part, comparable in some sense to the 'synthesis' following the 'analysis' in Diophantus' *Arithmetics*. This part of the text relies on the values produced by the algorithm as well as on the procedure described by the statement of the problem to show that the values obtained satisfy the relationships stated in the problem. However, the actual function of this section in the text should not be interpreted too hastily: as Høyrup emphasizes, it does not merely yield a 'numerical control' of the solution, since the way in which the 'verification' procedure is written down requires the same kind of 'understanding' from the reader as that attached to the text of the direct algorithm. The nature and practice of the 'verification' must thus be considered somewhat further, without being taken for granted *a priori*.

Textual structures of this type are characteristic of other tablets, in which, once an algorithm has yielded a result, this result is then subjected to another procedure, immediately appended to the original one and which has often been interpreted as a verification of it. The tablets on which Proust focuses in her chapter display such a structure. The main algorithm she examines is the one used to compute reciprocals of regular numbers.[51] Once the computation of a reciprocal has been recorded on the tablet, the same algorithm is applied to the result and shows that one thereby returns to the starting point of the original algorithm. In fact, more accurately, this structure is typical of only one type of tablet devoted to the algorithm computing reciprocals, precisely those tablets that contain only numbers. These tablets record successive numbers produced through the flow of computations according to a determined and highly specific layout until the result is yielded, and then record numbers obtained through applying the algorithm to the result. However, as Proust emphasizes, another type of text also refers to the same algorithm. In these other tablets, the algorithm is expressed in words and the text prescribes the operations to be carried out in succession. Among all the tablets containing either formulation (the two never occur on the same tablet), Proust chooses to concentrate on two tablets (Tablet A and Tablet B), one for each kind of expression. In fact, she selects the two texts that repeat the same pattern in a significant number of sections.

The verbal expression of the algorithm had been essential for Sachs to interpret the purely numerical expression for it. However, once he had established that the two tablets relate to the same algorithm, a key question remained, which Proust addresses: why do we have two expressions of the same algorithm? What are the specific meanings conveyed by each of them? And, especially in her case, what does the numerical tablet say?

To answer these questions, Proust combines several methods. She restores the practices of computation to which both tablets adhere, bringing to light that they relate to the flow of computations in different ways. She also compares the tablets to other parallel specimens. Lastly, she examines every detail of the numerical tablet (Tablet A): the layout, the numbers chosen, the way of conducting the algorithm in the direct and the reverse computations. Through sophisticated reasoning, Proust can establish that the second part of each section – the one containing the computations in the reverse direction – did most probably *not* play the part of checking the results of the direct algorithm. She further demonstrates that the layout designed to record the numbers, as evidenced in Tablet A, was created for such kind of texts and introduces a way of managing the space of the tablet that was *artificial*. This conclusion leads her to suggest that the spatial elements of the layout, like columns, are precisely those which convey the meanings expressed by Tablet A. We see here at its closest how the composition of a kind of text relates to the work carried out with a text. In her view, the columns may be

---

[51] For greater technical detail, I refer the reader to Proust's chapter.

interpreted as related to the statement of rules which ground the correctness of the algorithm. Proust thereby accounts for the meaning behind the numerical display as found in Tablet A, suggesting that it made sense for its readers in a way comparable to how an algebraic formula makes sense for us today. For her, the numerical text enjoys a kind of transparency in regard to the algorithm treated, making the operation of the procedure explicit. The reader could thereby see why and how the algorithm worked. This is how Proust argues that the numerical text bears witness to an interest in the correctness of the algorithm for computing reciprocals. Note that Proust's argument is in agreement with what Høyrup has shown. Although they operate in different ways, they both highlight that a specific kind of inscription has been designed to note down an algorithm while pointing out the reasons for its correctness. In some sense, Proust's thesis with respect to these tablets concurs with Netz's conclusions on the *Arithmetics*. In her view, Tablet A bears witness to the development of an artificial kind of text designed to make the algorithm surveyable. Yet, in both cases, different aspects of the working of the computations are made surveyable. Note further that, once more, the fact that actors constructed a specific kind of text to make specific statements with respect to algorithms means that historians have to design sophisticated methods to argue how such texts should be interpreted and what they mean. Here an interest in the correctness of the procedure can only be perceived through lengthy consideration of the text itself.

Let us pause here for a while and consider what we have accomplished in this subsection so far. We have entered the world of proving the correctness of algorithms. As was stressed in Section II of this Introduction, this was precisely a part missing from the standard account of the history of proof in the ancient world. By enlarging the set of sources and the issues about proofs considered, we began to see the emergence of a new continent. But there is more.

We saw above that an operation – take multiplication, for example – computes two things: a number and a meaning. A multiplication can produce the value which is claimed to be the product of two numbers. Or it can be interpreted as computing the area of a rectangle. On this basis, we see that Proust analyses texts addressing the former feature of the operation, whereas Høyrup considers texts that deal with the latter feature. In what follows, we shall proceed in the development of this segment of the history of proof, showing how various groups of actors have established the correctness of algorithms.

Proust's final point about Tablet A relates to its specific structure, namely, the display of an application of the algorithm followed by the display of its application to the result. On that count, her conclusion is that the overall structure of the text makes a statement regarding the fact that the algorithm for computing reciprocals is its own reverse algorithm. Similar tablets can be found for square-root extractions, displaying that squaring and square-root extraction are in the same way the reverse of one another. A similar interest in algorithms that are the reverse of one another – where one algorithm cancels the effect of the other – emerges as central to a type of proof to which Chinese early mathematical sources bear witness.[52] It is to this type of proof that my own chapter is devoted.

Algebraic proofs in an algorithmic context

Like some of the Babylonian tablets analysed above, the earliest Chinese writings attesting to mathematical activity *stricto sensu* are composed of problems and algorithms solving them. The practice of proof to which they bear witness also aims at establishing the correctness of algorithms.

Among these writings, those that were handed down through the written tradition are of a type quite different from that of the Babylonian tablets just examined.[53] The most important one for our purpose, *The Nine Chapters on Mathematical Procedures (Jiuzhang suanshu)*, was probably completed in the first century CE and considered a 'classic' soon thereafter. In correlation with this adoption, commentaries on it were composed, some of which were felt to be so essential to the reading of *The Nine Chapters* that they were handed down with it. These are the commentary composed by Liu Hui and completed in 263 as well as the one written under the supervision of Li Chunfeng and presented to the throne in 656. Two key facts regarding the commentaries prove essential for us in relation to mathematical proof.

First of all, the commentaries attest to how ancient readers approached the classic as such. This highlights why, as historians, when we interpret *The Nine Chapters*, we are in quite a different situation from that confronting historians who deal with sources for which no ancient commentary

---

[52] Chemla 1997–8.

[53] In addition to the source material handed down through the written tradition, we now have recourse to writings that archaeologists excavated from tombs. The most important of them, the *Book of Mathematical Procedures (Suanshushu)*, found in a tomb sealed in *c.* 186 BCE, is useful for, but not central to, our purpose. Such sources can be compared to the Babylonian tablets with respect to the way in which they were found and the conditions in which we can interpret them. However, it is not yet clear within which milieus and how they were used.

exists.[54] As alluded to above, *The Nine Chapters*, like Babylonian tablets, describes some of the algorithms in such a way that they are transparent in regard to the reasons accounting for the correctness of the computations they prescribe. At this stage in the reasoning, 'transparency' is an observer's category. However, it is crucial that, with respect to this Chinese document, the commentators did read the text of the algorithm as transparent and made precisely these reasons explicit in their exegesis. 'Transparency' can thus also be shown to correspond to an actor's category.

It is in this context that the commentators bring to light exactly the same type of 'meaning' that Høyrup suggests reading in the transparent algorithms found in Babylonian tablets. In the Chinese case, we can thus demonstrate that this is the way in which the earliest observable readers actually did 'interpret' the texts. Such evidence supports the hypothesis that the practitioners of mathematics in ancient China designed a kind of text to formulate algorithms, similar to that shaped in Mesopotamia to express algorithms transparent about the reasons of their correctness. The proof expressed in this way was read as such by ancient readers.[55] From the point of view of the reception, after all, the historical continuity between Babylonian and Arabic sources also indicates that Babylonian proofs were read in this way by subsequent practitioners. On the other hand, from the point of view of the text itself, it is remarkable that in different contexts, the mode of expression chosen for indicating the reasons of the correctness was the same. In my view, this remark indirectly reinforces Høyrup's argument, in that it shows the usefulness of this property of the statements for practitioners. The important point here is that for the Chinese commentators, in my interpretation, such a reading was a way of making the 'meaning' of the classic explicit. It is in order to designate that 'meaning' that they used the concept of *yi*, which I introduced above.[56]

This brings us back to the question, for which we now have plenty of evidence, of how the commentators made use of the context of a problem, or the geometrical analysis of a body, to formulate the 'meaning' they read

[54] Using ancient commentaries to interpret an ancient text does not mean that we attribute anything found in the commentaries to the text commented upon without caution. Chemla 1997–8 constitutes an example of how the two kinds of sources are treated separately and only thereafter articulated with each other.

[55] The commentators read the expression of the reasons for the correctness in various elements of the classic. The structure of the text is one of them; compare Chemla 1991. The terms used in *The Nine Chapters* to prescribe an operation is another one – see, for instance, Chemla 1997–8. Chemla 2010 attempts to give a systematic treatment of this question and to highlight elements of a history of these kinds of text.

[56] On the fact that commentators assumed that the classic indicated the 'meaning' or 'reasoning', see Chemla 2003, Chemla 2008a, Chemla 2008b.

in the classic. Further analysis reveals that, beyond the similarity which we suggested above with the Babylonian case as interpreted by Høyrup, the understanding made explicit in the Chinese commentaries was not only provided by 'geometrical' interpretations, but could also be achieved, more generally, by recourse to the situation described in the statement of any kind of problem.[57] In this sense, the way of generating a semantic analysis of operations differed. A landscape of similarities and differences starts emerging in our world history of mathematical proof in ancient traditions.

Secondly, the fact that the commentators made explicit the reasons underlying the correctness of the algorithms in such cases is one aspect of a much more general phenomenon. In effect, the commentaries *systematically* established the correctness of the algorithms contained in *The Nine Chapters*, thereby bearing witness to a considered practice of proof for such kinds of statements.

My own chapter focuses on one dimension of this practice, which, as far as I know, appears to be specific to ancient China. This dimension, which reveals another fundamental operation used to establish the correctness of procedures, sheds light on why the texts of algorithms are not all transparent about the reasons for their correctness.

As I show, in some cases, to establish that an algorithm correctly fulfilled the task for which it was given, the commentators, on the one hand, established another algorithm fulfilling the same task and, on the other hand, carried out operations on the text of this algorithm to transform it into the proper algorithm, the correctness of which was to be established. Moreover, in such cases the commentary usually made explicit the reasons they adduced for explaining why, although the former algorithm was transparent, the classic substituted the latter algorithm for it.

My chapter mainly focuses on the section of such a proof in which the algorithm is reworked by means of transformations carried out on the list of operations directly. My claim is that, within a context in which mathematics was worked out on the basis of algorithms, this section of the proof represents a practice of algebraic proof.

By algebraic proof, I mean, in this context, a proof that starts from a statement of equality, first established in a given way that is not of interest here and then transforms this original equality *as such and in a valid way* into other equalities, until the desired equality is obtained. The first part of my claim is thus that the commentaries record proofs of precisely this kind, with the only difference being that algorithms, and not equalities, are

---

[57] Compare chapter A in CG2004, Chemla 2009.

transformed. We would then have a form of algebraic proof in an algorithmic format.

The second part of my claim relates to the concern for the validity of such a method of proof. In fact, an analysis of the commentaries reveals that the exegetes considered the question of the validity of the operations applied to an algorithm as such.

A close inspection shows that the exegetes linked the validity of their operations to the set of numbers introduced in *The Nine Chapters*, which includes not only integers but also fractions and quadratic irrationals. The key point, in their eyes, was that these quantities allowed the expression of the results of divisions and root extraction exactly, thereby allowing the inverse operation of multiplication to cancel the effect of these operations and restore the original number. This point recalls the Mesopotamian tablets described by Proust, which demonstrate the same concern. Why was this fact important for practitioners of mathematics in Mesopotamia? Further inquiry into that question could prove interesting for our topic.

At the same time, I argue that it is when the commentators establish the correctness of algorithms for carrying out the arithmetic with fractions that they address the validity of applying some of the operations to lists of operations. Several points must be stressed here.

Firstly, the analysis of this dimension of the practice of proof preserved from ancient China brings to light an essential point, which allows us to capture a key feature of algebraic proof: the validity of such kinds of proof is essentially linked to the set of numbers with which one operates and how one operates with them. This point, I argue, was understood in ancient China, but it is a point of general validity regarding algebraic proof.

Secondly, the question arises whether dimensions of algebraic proofs as we practise them today may have historically taken shape within practices of proving the correctness of algorithms.

This brings me back to a point raised at the beginning of this introduction. I insisted on the fact that the standard account of the history of mathematical proof had nothing to say about the history of how the correctness of algorithms was established in the past. At this point, I am in a position to summarize our findings on this question. We now see even more clearly that this was a lacuna which contributed to the marginalization of sources that were 'non-Western' and sources that bore witness to practices of proof related to computations. In addition, we also see that this lacuna may also prevent us from providing a historical account of the emergence of algebraic proof.

Last, but not least, if the answer to the previous question proves positive, a new historical question presents itself quite naturally: one may further wonder whether the algebraic proof in an algorithmic context as demonstrated in ancient China could not have played a part in the actual emergence of the algebraic proof as we practise it today.

This set of issues demonstrates the ways in which the broadening of our corpus leads to the formulation of new directions of research in the early history of mathematical proof.

Proving as an element of the interpretation of a classic

The Chinese case just examined is not the only historical instance in which the formulation of mathematical proofs took place within the framework of commentaries on a classic. Agathe Keller's chapter is devoted to the earliest known Indian source in which an interest for mathematical proof can be identified: it turns out to be the seventh-century commentary by Bhaskara I on the mathematical chapter of the fifth-century astronomical treatise *Aryabhatiya*. As in the Chinese case, Keller shows how the development of arguments to establish the correctness of procedures is part of the activity of an exegete who comments on a classic.[58]

The proof is part of Bhaskara's way of justifying the classic, unless it justifies his own interpretation of the classic. A Sanskrit classic is composed of *sutras*, the interpretation of which requires skills. It is within this context that, when the classic deals with mathematics, proof – together with grammar – seems to be a means for a commentator to inquire into the meaning of the classic and to advance his interpretation. Despite the fact that commenting on a classic provided the impetus for making proofs explicit in both Sanskrit and Chinese, the way in which proofs relate to the interpretation seems to present differences between the two contexts.

In the case discussed by Keller, the classic, i.e. the *Aryabhatiya*, indicates algorithms. The commentator Bhaskara states them fully, showing by means of Paninian grammar *how* the *sutras* mean the suggested algorithms and then accounting for why the suggested algorithms are correct. Bhaskara manifests his expectation that the classic does not provide explanations. By contrast, he introduces a set of terms (explaining, verifying, proving) that indicate how he understands the epistemological status of parts of his commentary.

Keller provides evidence to support an interpretation of what 'explaining', 'verifying' and 'proving' meant for him, in terms of actual intellectual

---

[58] Srinivas 2005 insists more generally on the fact that in Indian writings proofs occur in commentaries, and in Appendix A he provides a list of these commentaries.

acts. Moreover, she delineates the techniques used by the commentator to account for an algorithm.

Here, similarities with the Chinese sources appear. One of the key techniques Bhaskara uses is to highlight how a given procedure is in fact supported by a fundamental, general procedure, in the terms of which the original procedure can be rewritten. Such a technique also appears in Chinese commentaries, where a technical term 'meaning (yi')' is used exclusively to refer to the kind of meaning of the procedure that a proof brings to light in this way.[59] This similarity between the two contexts possibly derives from the fact that the activity of interpreting a classic inspired similar conceptions of the 'higher meaning' of an algorithm.

Showing that different procedures can in fact be explained in the terms of the same fundamental, general procedure is one way in which proofs highlight relationships between algorithms which at first glance might appear unrelated. In such cases, something circulates among the proofs, and thanks to the proofs, in a way that can be compared to the techniques brought to light by Saito in the core corpus of Greek geometrical texts. This circulation again requires a reading of the proof in and of itself, and not merely as a means to prove the correctness of a procedure. Moreover, what circulates between the proofs differs depending on the context. In Sanskrit and Chinese sources, a procedure circulates, that is, a statement of the same kind as the proposition to be proved. In other terms, the technique of proof is at the same time a new statement. Again, this echoes present-day mathematicians' claim that proofs are a source of knowledge for them. However, the procedure in question is not ordinary, since the mere fact that it can be put to such uses indicates that it is more fundamental and more general than others. One may hypothesize that the identification of procedures of this kind formed one of the goals that motivated the interest in proving in these contexts.[60] In this case, the historian would miss one of the epistemological expectations with respect to proving, were he to analyse it only from the viewpoint of its ability to establish the statement to be proved.

It is also interesting that, in the context of Bhaskara's commentary as well as in the Chinese commentaries, figures were introduced for types of

[59] On this 'meaning' yi', see the glossary I compiled, CG2004: 1022–3.

[60] For Chinese sources, there is evidence supporting the claim. Compare Chemla 1992, Chemla 1997b. We reach a conclusion that was already an outcome of Lakatos' analysis of the activity of proving in Lakatos 1970. This convergence is not surprising: we share with Lakatos' enterprise a starting point, that is, that there is more to proof than mere deduction. However, the nature of the statements produced in the contexts Lakatos studied and those we studied differs, showing that one could go deeper in the analysis of how proofs yield mathematical knowledge (concepts, statements and techniques).

'explanation' which are referenced with specific terms. Once the 'explanation' is given in the form of such a diagram, it comes to a close. Is it that the argument is left for the reader to develop or is it that it was developed orally? It is difficult to tell. However, we recognize a feature of proofs that was frequently mentioned in nineteenth-century accounts of 'Indian' mathematical reasoning but was subject to divergent assessments, as Charette's chapter shows. Seen from another angle, we may note that the written formulation of a proof carried out in relation to a diagram took quite different forms in history. Further development of a comparative analysis of such texts arises as a possible venue for future research.

On the other hand, the commentator used the term 'explanation' (*pratipadita*) to refer specifically to another component that he introduced: problems solved by means of the algorithm described. In which ways did the problems contribute to providing an explanation of the algorithms? Here too, the source material calls for a comparative analysis of the part allotted by different traditions to problems for establishing an algorithm.

The evidence discussed so far illustrates the variety of contexts that may have prompted an interest in writing down proofs. The sources analysed by Keller and myself show how commenting upon a canonical text has been an activity by which proofs were made explicit. In addition Høyrup suggests the hypothesis that teaching could have motivated an interest in formulating proofs. In fact, the two explanations are not mutually exclusive, if we embrace Volkov's hypothesis that Chinese commentaries were composed within the context of mathematical education. We come back to this hypothesis below. In addition, the evidence discussed so far also shows the variety of motivations that led to the formulation of proofs in the ancient traditions. What they contribute to our historical approach and understanding of mathematical proof is an issue to be taken up in the conclusion. Before we can address our conclusions, however, one more dimension of our world history is worth considering.

The persistence of traditions of proof in Asia

One may be tempted to believe that it is relevant to adopt the perspective of a world history to deal with mathematical proof in ancient traditions, but that after the seventeenth century, the story to be told is that of the 'Western' practices and their adoption worldwide. The final two chapters of the book illustrate two ways in which such a view must be qualified. They constitute the only incursions of this book into later traditions of proof. The main reason for including them in the book is that they reveal historically interesting modes of continuity with what was analysed above.

Alexei Volkov devotes his chapter to an apparently discrete topic: mathematical examinations in China and the sphere of Chinese influence in East Asia. However, the link to our questions appears immediately. The issue at hand for him is that of the relation between the practices of examination in mathematics and mathematical proof as evidenced by the commentaries on Chinese classics. This question leads him to focus on the extant evidence regarding the teaching of mathematics in this part of the world.

Among all the channels through which mathematical knowledge was taught throughout Chinese history, the channel of state institutions is the least poorly documented. Relying on the extant Chinese administrative sources, Volkov describes the textbooks used for mathematics in the state educational system from the seventh century onwards and the way in which they were used. It is important for us that among these textbooks, one finds precisely *The Nine Chapters on Mathematical Procedures* along with the commentaries by Liu Hui and Li Chunfeng introduced above.[61] Moreover, Volkov discusses in great detail how the terse description of the kind of examinations the students had to take by the administrative sources can be interpreted concretely.

The interpretation of the extant administrative sources would have remained a matter of speculation, had not Volkov discovered a piece of evidence in nineteenth-century Vietnamese sources. Some elements of context are needed to understand this point better. As in Japan and Korea, Vietnamese state institutions had a history closely linked to that of their parallel institutions in China. In particular, from the Tang dynasty onwards, Chinese state institutions for teaching were imitated in East Asia and the textbooks used by these institutions were transmitted in this process. Moreover, state examinations in mathematics were held in all other contexts, including in Vietnam, as Volkov shows. This explains how Vietnamese sources clarify practices carried out in China: the margins often keep alive traditions that are modified in the centre.

In Vietnam, an additional factor played a decisive role: at the beginning of the nineteenth century, Western books had not yet become influential there. The extant mathematical writings composed in Vietnam until that time consequently appear to belong mainly to a tradition on which Chinese

---

[61] Please note that Volkov opts for another interpretation of the title of the Chinese book, translating it in a different way. Appendix 2 in his chapter presents various transcriptions and translations for the title of Chinese mathematical texts.

books exerted a strong influence. It is in such a Vietnamese source that Volkov found a model for mathematical examination which he translates and analyses in his chapter.

This piece of evidence leads him to put forward the hypothesis that the shape taken in China by the mathematical classics and the seventh-century commentaries may reflect precisely the requirements of the teaching institution. On this basis, one can shed light on the connection between these texts and the examination system from another angle. It is quite striking, indeed, that the administrative texts analysed by Volkov describe the tasks to be carried out by students in the seventh-century Chinese state institutions with technical terms that can be found *inter alia* in *The Nine Chapters* and the commentaries on the mathematical classics that were mentioned above. This holds true, as Volkov stresses, for words like *wen* 'problem', or *da* 'answer', which refer to components of texts like *The Nine Chapters*. However, most importantly, this also holds true for terms like *yi'* 'meaning', which is the second type of meaning given above for a procedure, a meaning that is intimately connected to the activity of proving. Such a link between the two types of sources supports Volkov's thesis that commentaries played a key part in the training of students, since terms like *yi'* are not to be found in the texts of the mathematical classics themselves, but only in commentaries.[62] In conclusion, Volkov suggests a social context for the interest in the proofs of the correctness of algorithms in ancient China.

Two points are worth emphasizing for our main argument here. Firstly, let me stress again what was said above: if Volkov's hypothesis holds true, we would have at least two cases – East Asia and Babylon – in which the professional context of teaching was instrumental for composing proofs, even though the proofs actually written down differed in the two contexts. Secondly, it is worth noting that this piece of evidence confirms the longevity of practices of proof in East Asia. This is but one example which shows

[62] One may even go a step further. We mentioned above two commentaries on *The Nine Chapters*: the one completed by Liu Hui in 263, and the one presented to the throne by Li Chunfeng in 656. In fact, several scholars have produced clues which indicate that the text of the two commentaries may have been commingled during the process of transmission (in CG2004: 472–3, I have summarized the current contributions treating this difficult issue which awaits further research). For the question discussed here, it may be relevant to note that many clues suggest that the concept of *yi'*, when used in relation to procedures, may belong to the layer of commentary from the seventh century. If this is confirmed, the connection between the administrative sources and the seventh-century commentary would be even more striking. The correlation between the terms used in both types of documents should invite us, in my view, to take the occurrence of the terms in the commentaries on the classics into account when interpreting the administrative prescriptions.

that the late history of practices of proof bears witness to circulations and preservations that challenge the standard account sketched above.[63]

At the beginning of his chapter, Volkov recalls how the sinologist Edouard Biot, in his 1847 *Essai sur l'histoire de l'instruction publique en Chine*, dismissively belittled the format of problems in Chinese mathematical texts, their absence of proof and the elementary level of state education. With respect to what was discussed above, the additional denigration of everything classed as educational in the historiography of mathematics may be partly responsible for the lack of discernment regarding sources that could have modified Biot's assessment at least to a certain extent.

In China, the approach to mathematics of the past was strikingly different, if we judge it on the basis of Li Rui's *Detailed Outline of Mathematical Procedures for the Right-Angled Triangle* completed in 1806, which Tian Miao analyses in her chapter. This text illustrates a second form of prolonged relevance of ancient practices of proof, which reveals several interesting features.

To be more precise, Li Rui's practice of proof exemplifies a revival of past Chinese practices of proof and shows how they were at that time transformed mathematically while simultaneously reshaped under the influence of – or rather as an alternative to – practices of proof identified as 'Western'.

The topic on which Li Rui chose to write his book, the right-angled triangle, was one in which, as he knew, an interest was documented in both Chinese and Greek antiquity. The ninth of *The Nine Chapters* is devoted to the right-angled triangle and it is the subject of theorems in the part of Clavius' edition of Euclid's *Elements* that Ricci and Xu Guangqi translated into Chinese in 1607.

Li Rui approached the right-angled triangle as was done in the tradition which descends from *The Nine Chapters*. Among the various identifiable traces of this approach, one notes that his book takes the form of problems for which solutions are provided in the form of algorithms. In addition, Li Rui makes use of the traditional terminology developed throughout Chinese history and completed in the Song dynasty to designate the quantities attached to a triangle.

On the other hand, Tian argues, the influence of the *Elements* can be perceived in the fact that Li Rui provided a systematic set of solutions to all the problems that can be encountered. Moreover, he organized this set according to the dependencies of its elements. In the system produced, the

---

[63] A similar kind of continuity in the practice of proof is described by François Patte, in his work on sixteenth-century Sanskrit commentaries; see Patte 2004.

solution to any problem depended only on those before it. The proofs of the correctness of the algorithms were thus a key element for deciding over the structure of the system.

Tian highlights several mathematical innovations in the book. To begin with, Li Rui invoked combinatorial methods to state and solve any problem that could be asked about a right-angled triangle. Moreover, Li Rui innovatively employed the ancient 'heavenly unknown (*tianyuan*)'[64] method to establish the correctness of the algorithms which solve each of the problems in the most uniform way possible. The earliest surviving evidence for this method, which is equivalent to the modern practice of using polynomial algebra to set up an equation which solves a problem, dates to 1248, the year that Li Ye completed his *Sea-Mirror of the Circle Measurements (Ceyuan haijing)*. After having been forgotten in China, the method had been recovered by Mei Juecheng in the first half of the eighteenth century, thanks to the understanding Mei gained through his acquaintance with European books of algebra.[65] In particular, Mei deciphered the meaning of the algebraic symbolisms for writing down polynomials and equations that had been developed in China a few centuries earlier and had since been lost.

Li Rui could thus rely on the method and its related symbolisms that had been rescued from oblivion only a few decades before he wrote his book. When using the symbolism to establish algebraically the correctness of the algorithms he stated, Li Rui was using symbols that differed in form from those of Diophantus, but which had played a similar part in the past. Like Li Ye, Li Rui used these symbolic notations to account for the correctness of the equation – the 'procedure' – yielded to solve a general problem. However, the way in which Li Rui was now using them modified the status of the proofs carried out with them. The main point that Tian highlights in this respect is that, when considering given quantities attached to a triangle as data, Li Rui discriminated among the different categories of triangles according to the relative size of the data in them. More precisely, in contrast to Li Ye before him, Li Rui formulated as many problems as there were distinguishable cases so that he could prove the correctness of the general equation in a way that would be valid for each case and that would establish

---

[64] The literal interpretation of the expression *tianyuan* is 'celestial origin'. This interpretation permits the identification of occurrences of the concept before the thirteenth century in the set of mathematical classics gathered in the seventh century; see above. I shall come back to this point in a future publication.

[65] On this episode, compare Needham and Wang Ling 1959: 53, Horng Wann-sheng 1993: 175–6, Yabuuti Kiyosi 2000: 141–3.

the equation with full generality. This distinction between cases relates to a concern about the validity of the operations in the proof and the generality of the proven statement. Li Rui distinguished cases in such a way that the proof carried out through polynomial computations would be valid for all triangles of the same case. This step ensured the correctness of the kind of algebraic proof which he conducted in a way that Li Ye's proofs before him did not.

As a consequence, Li Rui established *general* equations through polynomial computations – the proof of their correctness – that were valid for the particular category of triangles delineated and he probably developed this structure of proof intentionally. Otherwise, there would be no reason for him to differentiate different cases of a given type. Yet, even though this feature reveals that Li Rui was interested in the generality of procedures, like the ancient Chinese mathematical texts, he expressed this property for each case within the context of a particular problem, which he thus used as a paradigm. We see here again that the search for generality and the ways in which generality is expressed both account for specific features of the practice of proof that was constructed.

Several other elements manifest how, through his mathematical practice, Li Rui simultaneously presented himself as continuing the tradition of his Chinese predecessors of the past and yet changed it. His deployment of geometrical diagrams to provide yet another (geometric) proof of the correctness of the equation is one of these elements. However, although the diagrams clearly call to mind Li Ye's own diagrams in his *Yigu yanduan*, completed in 1259, or Yang Hui's 1261 commentary on *The Nine Chapters*, they betray differences, due not least of all to an influence of Western practices with geometrical figures. Further, like Xu Guangqi before him, Li Rui seems to be using the concept of 'meaning (*yi'*)' in a way that displays affinity with how the commentators on *The Nine Chapters* used the same term. This reveals a continuity of mathematical theory that has not yet been addressed adequately.

In addition, Tian surmises that Li Rui was also interested in showing the power of the 'procedure of the right-angled triangle (*gougushu*)' – the ancient name and formulation for Pythagoras' theorem – to solve any problem in a uniform way. Li's book can be interpreted as having explicitly developed the system covered by this older procedure, even if it had been presented in the past in relation to a particular problem.

In conclusion, the *Detailed Outline of Mathematical Procedures for the Right-Angled Triangle* demonstrates a synthesis of goals for and techniques of proof, which take their origins from both East and West. The book composes a new type of text with which to carry out proofs, one that integrates different agendas. Most importantly, however, if we follow Tian's interpretation of it, we can read Li Rui's discourse and practice as illustrating the politics of the proof, in that they attempt to embody the ideal of proving in the 'Chinese way', and *not* in the 'Western' way. Some decades later, the politics of the historiography of mathematical proof would become by far more visible.

IV Conclusion: a research programme on mathematical proofs

It is time to gather the various threads that we have followed and conclude, by considering our findings with respect to ancient mathematics and the research programme that they open for us.

Let us begin with facts. What we have seen emerging in Section III is the outline of a history of proving the correctness of algorithms in the ancient world. Mesopotamian, Chinese and Indian sources bear witness to the fact that practitioners have attended to the correctness of the algorithms with which they have practised mathematics. An analysis of their attempts helps us identify some of the fundamental operations involved in such proofs. We have seen that these practitioners have striven to establish how an algorithm correctly yields the desired magnitude and the value that can be attached to it. To do so, they have designed devices or *dispositifs* that have allowed them to formulate the 'meaning' of operations. The proofs they constructed share common features. They also demonstrate specificities in the way in which proof was practised.

Among the specificities noted in the way of approaching the correctness of algorithms, one fact proved of special relevance for a history of proving. Chinese sources demonstrate the fact that operations – meta-operations, if one wishes – were sometimes applied to the sequence of operations that an algorithm constitutes. These meta-operations were used to transform an algorithm known to be true, *qua* algorithm, into another algorithm, the correctness of which was to be established. Moreover, these sources bear witness to the fact that a connection was established between the validity of these meta-operations and the numbers with which one worked. I suggested the conclusion that we have here a kind of 'algebraic proof within an algorithmic context'.

This remark leads to several questions. What kind of understanding can practices developed specifically to prove the correctness of algorithms yield into the nature of algebraic proofs, on the one hand, and the process of their emergence, on the other? If a historical link can be established between the two, what evidence can we find regarding the historical process by which both kinds of proof were connected? This question opens onto another one, much more general: through what concrete historical processes did algebraic proof take shape and develop?

The analyses developed in this introduction have brought to light several elements inherent to that kind of proof as we experience it: textual techniques, reflections on numbers and problems of generality. What other elements constitute algebraic proof and how did this cluster crystallize? What type of historicity is attached to it? This book offers a contribution to this agenda by identifying elements essential to algebraic proof and hypothesizing a historical scenario regarding the kinds of practice in which these elements took shape. Clearly, much more remains to be done.

These first results show the benefits that broadening of the scope of sources taken into consideration can produce through the change of perspective we advocated in the approach to proofs and their history. A scarcely considered branch of the history of proof thus emerges: namely, the history of proving the correctness of algorithms. And as it takes shape, it elucidates parts of the history of proof that still await better understanding. In correlation with opening new pages in the history of proof, we have been naturally led to approach the topic of proof more comprehensively. From this global perspective, we understand more clearly the link between the devaluation of computation as a mathematical activity, which was and still is quite widespread, and the exclusive focus on only some proofs, written in ancient Greece, that has dominated the history of mathematics. Now, what changes will this outline of the history of proving the correctness of algorithms bring in the history of proof? How far will these tools of analysis allow historians to examine anew other proofs, for instance proofs written in Greek? These remain open questions.

Our exploration of ancient practices of proof has met with another important issue, which is worth pondering further. As suggested by Lloyd, Høyrup, Keller and Volkov among others, the interest in proof and, more specifically, in writing proofs down has been stimulated by distinct activities and social contexts. Among those activities and contexts we have seen, let us mention the rivalry between competing schools of thought or the development and promotion of one tradition as opposed to another, teaching mathematics or interpreting a classic, all activities that need not have been exclusive of each other. The list is by no means exhaustive. Still, this remark brings to the fore two points that are important much more generally. On the one hand, proving is an activity that takes place in specific social and professional groups which have specific agendas. On the other hand, as we saw, the practices of proof betray a variety of modalities which one can attempt to correlate to the social groups which sustain them. This leaves us with two tasks: finding the means to describe the practices in their variety and identifying the social and professional contexts that are relevant to account for their formation and relative stability.

Such a research programme is quite meaningful to inquire into the history of proof in the ancient world. Indeed, only along these lines can we hope to bring to light and accommodate the variety of practices in a way more satisfactory than the old model of competing civilizations which has been pre-eminent from the nineteenth century onwards. However, the research programme is laden with difficulties. The evidence available with respect to ancient time periods is in general so scanty that rigorously reconstructing the social environment in which proofs were actually com-posed is an ideal for the most part out of reach. One can only put forward hypotheses. In that context, concentrating on the description of the varying practices appears to be an initial means of overcoming the difficulties and perhaps discerning from mathematical sources different social groups that carried out the practice of proof.

This is the project on which we focus in the book and what our explo-rations into matters of proof open to reflections of wider relevance. The conclusions which we propose bring forth some suggestions for the task of describing practices of proof whose value appears to me to exceed the scope of the ancient world to which we have restricted ourselves. Let me comment on some of these suggestions by way of conclusion.

Among the various sets of sources which they treat, the chapters in this book identify different goals ascribed to proof, different values attached to proving and different qualities required from a proof. In this Introduction, I have outlined some of them. We have seen that some proofs seem to be con-ducted in order to understand the statement proved or the text which states it. In other cases, proofs have appeared to have had as one of their goals the identification of fundamental operations or the display of a technique. We have also seen that in some contexts, proofs were expected to be general or to comply with an ideal of generality. In others, they should bring clarity, yield fruitfulness or manifest simplicity. Much more remains to be done in identifying goals and values practitioners have attached – and still attach today – to proof and the constraints they imposed on themselves.

What is important is that in each of these cases the identification of these elements, far from being the end of the inquiry, constitutes only its beginning. Indeed, the main question then raised is to identify *how* the way in which the proof is conducted or written down helps practitioners to reach the goals, achieve the values or implement the qualities they value. This is where the issue of the practices of proof is inextricably linked to the issue of the expectations actors have with respect to proofs. In relation to this issue, I introduced the notion of devices or *dispositifs* that actors have created in various contexts to carry out key operations with respect to the proof. We have seen that the *dispositifs* constructed by Mesopotamian scribes or Chinese scholars to make explicit the 'meaning' of operations in an algorithm had commonalities as well as specific differences. The differences between the two Greek texts dealing with polygonal numbers that Mueller described can also be approached in these terms: the *dispositifs* used by the authors to treat their topic show two distinct attempts at achieving generality. Seen in this light, axiomatic–deductive systems appear to be a *dispositif* designed to yield certainty. Describing these *dispositifs* appears to me as a method to attend more closely to differences between the various practices of proof, thereby breaking down what is all too often presented collectively as 'the mathematical practice'.

Can we spot transformations in the modalities of proof that demonstrate a change of values or a combination of a larger set of values? Which of these goals, of these values, of these qualities were held together? Which combinations can we identify and how have these various constraints been held together? Which of them seem to have been in tension with each other, because they were difficult to fulfil simultaneously? Archimedes' practices of proof offer a case study that can be approached from this perspective. All the questions that arise in this context now explain, I hope, how an overly strict focus on the value of certainty would yield an essentially truncated account of mathematical proof. Clearly, such an approach does not do justice to the variety of agendas that were ascribed to proof and to the variety of practices that were developed accordingly.

When describing the diverse practices of proof exhibited in ancient sources, the various chapters of the book collectively bring to the fore another fact that is, in my view, both important and of general relevance. They converge on the conclusion that various types of technical texts have been designed for the conduct of proofs, depending on the context in which these proofs have been written down and the constraints bearing on them. Let me gather various hints that support this conclusion.

The texts of proofs we have mentioned consist of distinct basic components. Among them, one can list equalities, proportions or lists of operations. Moreover, within the context of distinct practices of proof, these basic components appear to have been composed in various ways and to have been combined in distinct kinds of technical texts. Among the kinds of texts and inscriptions we encountered, let me recall a few: texts for algorithms transparent with respect to the reasons of their correctness; the material *dispositifs* by means of which their meaning was made explicit; symbolic inscriptions of different sorts (including those of Diophantus, those which Colebrooke first described in the Sanskrit texts, and those of the Chinese past revivified by Li Rui); and texts composed with formulaic languages. In addition, it regularly appeared that paradigms in the form of particular figures or mathematical problems were used to formulate general proofs.

This variety of texts developed for proofs merely reflects the variety of contexts within which proofs were carried out. This means that the design of texts is, in an important sense, an indicator of the context in which they were composed. Moreover, the shaping of kinds of texts to carry out proofs is an aspect of the practice of proof as such which has been little studied so far. This shaping demands study, even if only as a limited component of the practice of proof. However, there is another equally fundamental reason to study this range of phenomena.

The examples just summarized remind us of the fact that the interpretation of the text of a proof is a thorny issue, and it is so *in relation* to the effort involved in the construction of a kind of text adequate for the execution of proofs of a certain type. In other words, it is *because* each human collective which carried out mathematical proofs deliberately designed texts for this activity that these texts cannot be interpreted straightforwardly.[66] This claim can be illustrated easily with the example of the recently mentioned transparent algorithms. In order to read a proof in the statement of the algorithm itself, the historian has to establish the way in which the texts made sense. The interpretation of paradigms as paradigms would constitute another example.

These remarks explain why the relation between the type of text used and the kind of proof developed is an essential topic for future research. It is essential not only because the shaping of texts to carry out proofs is an aspect of the practice of proof in itself, but also because inquiring into this issue yields better tools to interpret the texts in question.

---

[66] In this respect, we return to the conclusions that emerged from the collective effort published in Chemla 2004.

Such are some of the general issues that emerged from our historical analysis of ancient practices of proofs. As such, they appear to me to provide useful directions of research if we are to develop more generally a genuinely historical approach to the activity of proving and understand the motley practices of mathematical proofs as such. What results can these issues yield for the study of modern proofs? Let this task constitute our future endeavour.

Bibliography

Atiyah, M., Borel, A., Chaitin, G. J., *et al.* (1994) 'Responses to "Theoretical mathematics: toward a cultural synthesis of mathematics and theoretical physics", by A. Jaffe and F. Quinn', *Bulletin of the American Mathematical Society* **30**: 178–207.

Chemla, K. (1991) 'Theoretical aspects of the Chinese algorithmic tradition (first to third century)', *Historia Scientiarum* **42**: 75–98 (+errata in the following issue).

(1992) 'Résonances entre démonstration et procédure: remarques sur le commentaire de Liu Hui (IIIe siècle) aux *Neuf chapitres sur les procédures mathématiques* (1er siècle)', in *Regards Obliques sur l'Argumentation en Chine*, ed. K. Chemla, *Extrême-Orient, Extrême-Occident* **14**: 91–129.

(1996) 'Que signifie l'expression "mathématiques européennes" vue de Chine?', in *L'Europe mathématique: Histoires, mythes, identités (Mathematical Europe: History, Myth, Identity)*, ed. C. Goldstein, J. Gray and J. Ritter. Paris: 219–45.

(1997a) 'Reflections on the worldwide history of the rule of false double position, or: how a loop was closed', *Centaurus, an International Journal of the History of Mathematics, Science and Technology* **39**: 97–120.

(1997b) 'What is at stake in mathematical proofs from third-century China?', *Science in Context* **10**: 227–51.

(1997–8) 'Fractions and irrationals between algorithm and proof in ancient China', *Studies in History of Medicine and Science*, N.S. **15**: 31–54.

(1999) 'Commentaires, éditions et autres textes seconds: quel enjeu pour l'histoire des mathématiques? Réflexions inspirées par la note de Reviel Netz', *Revue d'histoire des mathématiques* **5**: 127–48.

(2003) 'Les catégories textuelles de "Classique" et de "Commentaire" dans leur mise en oeuvre mathématique en Chine ancienne', in *Figures du texte scientifique*, ed. J.-M. Berthelot. Paris: 55–79.

(ed.) (2004) *History of Science, History of Text*. Dordrecht.

(2008a) 'Antiquity in the shape of a canon: views on antiquity from the outlook of mathematics', in *Perceptions of Antiquity in Chinese Civilization*, ed. D. Kuhn and H. Stahl. Heidelberg: 191–208.

(2008b) *Classic and Commentary: An Outlook Based on Mathematical Sources.* Preprint MPING, vol. **344**. Berlin.

(2009) 'On mathematical problems as historically determined artifacts: reflections inspired by sources from ancient China', *Historia Mathematica* **36**: 213–46.

(2010) 'Proof in the wording: two modalities from ancient Chinese algorithms', in *Explanation and Proof in Mathematics: Philosophical and Educational Perspectives*, ed. G. Hanna, H. N. Jahnke and H. Pulte. Dordrecht: 253–85.

Dauben, J., and Scriba, C. J. (eds.) (2002) *Writing the History of Mathematics: Its Historical Development.* Basel.

Engelfriet, P. (1993) 'The Chinese Euclid and its European context', in *L'Europe en Chine: Interactions scientifiques, religieuses et culturelles aux XVIIe et XVIIIe siècles*, ed. C. Jami and H. Delahaye. Paris: 111–35.

(1998) *Euclid in China: The Genesis of the First Translation of Euclid's* Elements *in 1607 and Its Reception up to 1723.* Leiden.

Gardies, J.-L. (1984) *Pascal entre Eudoxe et Cantor.* Paris.

Grabiner, J. (1988) 'The centrality of mathematics in the history of Western thought', *Mathematics Magazine* **61**: 220–30.

Hacking, I. (1980) 'Proof and eternal truths: Descartes and Leibniz', in *Descartes: Philosophy, Mathematics and Physics*, ed. S. Gaukroger. Brighton: 169–80.

(2000) 'What mathematics has done to some and only some philosophers', in *Mathematics and Necessity: Essays in the History of Philosophy*, ed. T. Smiley. Oxford: 83–138.

(2002) *Historical Ontology.* Cambridge, Mass.

Harari, O. (2003) 'Existence and constructions in Euclid's *Elements*', *Archive for History of Exact Sciences* **57**: 1–23.

Hilbert, D. (1900) 'Mathematische Probleme', *Nachrichten von der Königlichen Gesellschaft der Wissenschaften zu Göttingen, Mathematisch–Physikalische Klasse* : 253–97.

(1902) 'Mathematical Problems', *Bulletin of the American Mathematical Society* **8**: 437–79.

Horng Wann-sheng (1993) 'Chinese mathematics at the turn of the nineteenth century: Jiao Xun, Wang Lai and Li Rui', in *Philosophy and Conceptual History of Science in Taiwan*, ed. C. H. Lin and D. Fu. Dordrecht: 167–208.

Høyrup, J. (1986) 'Al-Khwarizmi, Ibn Turk, and the "Liber mensurationum": on the origins of Islamic algebra', *Erdem* **2**: 445–84.

(1990) 'Algebra and naive geometry: an investigation of some basic aspects of Old Babylonian mathematical thought', *Altorientalische Forschungen* **17**: 27–69, 262–324.

(2006) 'Artificial languages in Ancient Mesopotamia: a dubious and a less dubious case', *Journal of Indian Philosophy* **34**: 57–88.

Jaffe, A., and Quinn, F. (1993) '"Theoretical mathematics": toward a cultural synthesis of mathematics and theoretical physics', *Bulletin of the American Mathematical Society* **29**: 1–13.

(1994) 'Responses to comments on "Theoretical mathematics"', *Bulletin of the American Mathematical Society* **30**: 208–11.

Jain, P. K. (1995) 'A critical edition, English translation and commentary of the upodghata, savidhaprakarana and kuttakadhikara of the *Suryaprakasa* of Suryadasa (A commentary on Bhaskaracarya's *Bijaganita*)', PhD thesis, Simon Fraser University, Canada.

Jami, C., Engelfriet, P., and Blue, G. (eds.) (2001) *Statecraft and Intellectual Renewal in Late Ming China: The Cross-Cultural Synthesis of Xu Guangqi (1562–1633)*. Leiden.

Keller, A. (2006) *Expounding the Mathematical Seed: A Translation of Bhaskara I on the Mathematical Chapter of the Aryabhatiya*, 2 vols. Basel.

Knorr, W. R. (1996) 'The wrong text of Euclid: on Heiberg's text and its alternatives', *Centaurus* **38**: 208–76.

(2001) 'On Heiberg's Euclid', *Science in Context* **14**: 133–43.

Krob, D. (1991) 'Algèbres de Lie partiellement commutatives libres', in *Séminaire de Mathématique, Rouen, 1989/90*. Rouen: 81–90.

Lakatos, I. (1970) *Conjectures and Refutations*. Cambridge.

Langins, J. (1989) 'Histoire de la vie et des fureurs de François Peyrard, bibliothécaire de l'Ecole polytechnique de 1795 à 1804 et traducteur renommé d'Euclide et d'Archimède', *Bulletin de la SABIX* **3**: 2–12.

Laudan, L. (1968) 'Theories of scientific method from Plato to Mach: a bibliographical review', *History of Science* **7**: 1–63.

Lloyd, G. E. R. (1990) *Demystifying Mentalities*. Cambridge.

(1992) 'The Agora perspective', in *Regards obliques sur l'argumentation en Chine*, ed. K. Chemla, *Extrême-Orient, Extrême-Occident* **14**: 185–98.

(1996a) *Adversaries and Authorities: Investigations into Ancient Greek and Chinese Science*. Cambridge.

(1996b) 'The theories and practices of demonstration', in *Aristotelian Explorations*, ed. G. E. R. Lloyd. Cambridge: 7–37.

MacKenzie, D. A. (2001) *Mechanizing Proof: Computing, Risk, and Trust*. Cambridge, Mass.

Mancosu, P. (1996) *Philosophy of Mathematics and Mathematical Practice in the Seventeenth Century*. Oxford.

Martija-Ochoa, I. (2001–2) 'Edouard et Jean-Baptiste Biot: L'astronomie chinoise en France au xixe siècle', Diplôme d'études approfondies, University Paris Diderot, Département d'histoire et de philosophie des sciences.

Martzloff, J.-C. (1981) 'La géométrie euclidienne selon Mei Wending', *Historia Scientiarum* **21**: 27–42.

(1984) 'Sciences et techniques dans l'œuvre de Ricci', *Recherches de science religieuse* **72**: 37–49.

(1993) 'Eléments de réflexion sur les réactions chinoises à la géométrie euclidienne à la fin du XVIIe siècle: Le *Jihe lunyue* de Du Zhigeng vu principalement à partir de la préface de l'auteur et deux notices bibliographiques rédigées par des lettrés illustres', *Historia Mathematica* **20**: 160–79.

(1995) 'Clavius traduit en chinois', in *Les jésuites à la Renaissance: Système éducatif et production du savoir*, ed. L. Giard. Paris: 309–22.

Needham, J., and Wang Ling (1959) 'Section 19: Mathematics', in *Science and Civilisation in China*, vol. III, ed. J. Needham. Cambridge: 1–168.

Patte, F. (2004) *BHĀSKARĀCĀRYA, Le Siddhāntaśiromaṇi, I–II : L'oeuvre mathématique et astronomique de Bhāskarācārya*, 2 vols. Geneva.

Rashed, R. (2007) *Al-Khwarizmi: Le commencement de l'algèbre*. Paris.

Rav, Y. (1999) 'Why do we prove theorems?', *Philosophia Mathematica* **7**: 5–41.

Rota, G.-C. (1990) 'Les ambiguïtés de la pensée mathématique', *Gazette des mathématiciens* **45**: 54–64.

Saito, K. (2006) 'A preliminary study in the critical assessment of diagrams in Greek mathematical works', *SCIAMVS* **7**: 81–144.

Saito, K., and Tassora, R. (1998) *Restoration of the Tool-Box of Greek Mathematics: Summary of Research Project, Grant-in-Aid for Scientific Researches (C2) in 1995–98*. Osaka.

Schuster, J. A., and Yeo, R. R. (eds.) (1986) *The Politics and Rhetoric of Scientific Method: Historical Studies*. Dordrecht.

Srinivas, M. D. (2005) 'Proofs in Indian mathematics', in *Contributions to the History of Indian Mathematics*, ed. G. G. Emch, R. Sridharan and M. D. Srinivas. New Delhi: 209–48.

Thurston, W. P. (1994) 'On proof and progress in mathematics', *Bulletin of the American Mathematical Society* **30**: 161–77.

Wagner, D. B. (1975) 'Proof in ancient Chinese mathematics: Liu Hui on the volumes of rectilinear solids', Candidatus magisterii thesis, University of Copenhagen.

(1978) 'Liu Hui and Tsu Keng-Chih on the volume of a sphere', *Chinese Science* **3**: 59–79.

(1979) 'An early Chinese derivation of the volume of a pyramid: Liu Hui, 3rd century AD', *Historia Mathematica* **6**: 164–88.

Whewell, W. (1837) *History of the Inductive Sciences from the Earliest to the Present Times*, vol. 1. Cambridge.

Widmaier, R. (2006) *Gottfried Wilhelm Leibniz: Der Briefwechsel mit den Jesuiten in China (1689–1714)*. Hamburg.

Wu Wenjun (ed.) (1982) *Jiuzhang suanshu yu Liu Hui* (The Nine Chapters on Mathematical Procedures *and Liu Hui*). Beijing.

Yabuuti Kiyosi (K. Baba and C. Jami, trans.) (2000) *Une Histoire des mathématiques chinoises*. Paris.

Yeo, R. (1981) 'Scientific method and the image of science: 1831–1890', in *The Parliament of Science*, ed. R. MacLeod and P. Collins. London: 65–88.

(1993) *Defining Science: William Whewell, Natural Knowledge, and Public Debate in Early Victorian Britain*. Cambridge.

1 | The Euclidean ideal of proof in *The Elements* and philological uncertainties of Heiberg's edition of the text

BERNARD VITRAC, TRANSLATION MICAH ROSS

Introduction

One of the last literary successors of Euclid, Nicolas Bourbaki, wrote at the beginning of his *Éléments d'histoire des mathématiques*:

> L'originalité essentielle des Grecs consiste précisément en un effort conscient pour ranger les démonstrations mathématiques en une succession telle que le passage d'un chaînon au suivant ne laisse aucune place au doute et contraigne l'assentiment universel ... Mais, dès les premiers textes détaillés qui nous soient connus (et qui datent du milieu du ve siècle), le « canon » idéal d'un texte mathématique est bien fixé. Il trouvera sa réalisation la plus achevée chez les grands classiques, Euclide, Archimède, Apollonius; la notion de démonstration, chez ces auteurs, ne diffère en rien de la nôtre.[1]

I am unsure what was intended by the last possessive, whether it acts as the royal or editorial *we* designating the 'author', or if it ought to be understood in a more general way: 'la nôtre' could mean that of the Modernists, of the twentieth-century mathematicians, of the French, or formalists. All jokes aside, the affirmation supposes a well-defined and universally accepted conception of what constitutes a mathematical proof. The aforementioned conception, the citation for which is found in a chapter titled 'Fondements des mathématiques, Logique, Théorie des ensembles', is at once logical, psychological (through a rejection of doubt), and 'sociological' (based on universal consensus). Perhaps this assertion ought to be considered nothing more than a distant echo of the Aristotelian affirmation that all scientific assertions (not just mathematical statements) are necessary and universal.

The following list of Greek geometers is also interesting. It contains the classics, and the triumvirate was probably intended to follow chronological order. Here, then, *Euclid* is not simply a convenient label, sometimes used to designate one or several of the many adaptations of Euclid's famous work, as when one speaks about the Euclid of Campanus (*c.* 1260–70), the Arab

---

[1] Bourbaki 1974: 10.

Euclid or the Euclid of the sixteenth century. Rather, this *Euclid* indicates the third-century Hellenistic geometer and author of the *Elements*. To speak about the Hellenistic Euclid, to describe the contents of his composition with precision – which certainly implies the fact that it qualifies as a 'classic' – and to adopt or reject its approach towards proof presumes a reasonably certain knowledge of the text of the *Elements*. Precisely this knowledge, however, is in doubt.

To examine these assumptions, in the first part I revisit some information (or hypotheses) concerning the transmission of ancient Greek texts, particularly the text of the *Elements*. I emphasize there the indirect character of our knowledge about this subject, and I review the history of the text proposed by the Danish philologist J. L. Heiberg, at the time when he produced, in the 1880s, the critical edition of the Greek text to which the majority of modern studies on Euclid still refer.[2] I raise some uncertainties and mention the recent criticism of W. Knorr.[3] In the second part, I give examples of differences between preserved versions of the text, illustrating the uncertainties which dismantle our knowledge about the Euclidean text, notably the texts of certain proofs.

Reflections on the History of the Text of the *Elements*

A brief history of the ancient Greek texts

Lest the present study become too complicated,[4] let us admit that there existed in thirteen books a Hellenistic edition (ἔκδοσις) of the *Elements* (τὰ Στοιχεῖα), corresponding, at least in rough outline, to that which has come down to us and *produced* by Euclid or one of his closest students.[5] In

---

[2] Heiberg and Menge, 1883–1916. It has been partially re-edited and (seemingly) revised by E. S. Stamatis: Heiberg and Stamatis, 1969–77. In the following, I will designate these editions by the *EHM* and *EHS* respectively.

[3] Knorr 1996.

[4] The literature on this subject is immense. I have consulted Pasquali 1952, Dain 1975, Reynolds and Wilson 1988, Dorandi 2000 (which contains extensive information about papyri) and Irigoin 2003 (a collection of articles published between 1954 and 2001, plus several unpublished studies).

[5] At least two other possibilities are conceivable, by analogy with some known cases of ancient scholarly editions:

- Euclid had produced two versions of his text: the first, a provisional copy, for a restricted circle of students, correspondents or friends; the other, revised and authorized. This corresponds with the composition of the *Conics* of Apollonius, as described by the author himself in the introduction of Book I (of his revised version). Consequently, this hypothesis

Greek antiquity, when there existed neither printing press nor any form of copyright, *edition* signified 'the introduction of a text into circulation among a circle of readers larger than the school, friends and students of the author' – in other words, a 'publication' in the minimal sense of having been 'rendered public' and of having been reproduced from a manuscript revised and corrected by the author (or a collaborator).[6] The books of the Hellenistic era (third to first century before our era) were written in majuscule and, in theory, on only one side of papyrus scrolls of a modest and relatively standardized size. Thus, they were rather limited in contents.[7] In the case of the *Elements*, this tradition implies a likely division into fifteen rolls, each containing one book, with the exception of the lengthy Book x.[8]

Of course, like practically any other text from Greek antiquity, the 'original' (which was not necessarily an autograph copy)[9] has not come down to us. The rather limited lifespan of such papyrus scrolls required that they be periodically recopied, with each copy capable of introducing new faults and, even more importantly, alterations. Certainly chance played a role in the preservation of particular papyri, but, in the long run, because of the fragility of the writing material, a text could come to us only if certain communities found enough interest in it to reproduce it frequently.

In the course of these recopyings, two particularly important technical operations occurred in the history of the ancient Greek book:

- the change from papyrus scrolls (*volumina*) first to papyrus codices but later to parchment codices, and
- the Byzantine transliteration.

> allows the possibility of variations by the author from the beginning of the textual tradition. Nonetheless, there is no evidence of this process for the *Elements*.
> - Euclid had not gone to the trouble of producing an ἔκδοσις in the technical sense of the term. His writings had been circulated in his 'school' (in a form that we evidently do not know), and the edition was made some time later, such as at the beginning of the Roman era in the circle of Heron of Alexandria. This scenario is traced in the history of the body of 'scholarly' works of Aristotle, officially edited only after the first century before our era, by Andronicos of Rhodes, among others.
>
> In order to be able to dismiss such a (completely speculative) hypothesis, fully detailed testaments about the role of the *Elements* in the course of the three centuries before our era must be in evidence, and this is not the case. On the contrary, we are nearly certain that Heron had made an important contribution to the *Elements* – in particular from a textual point of view – but the epoch in which he lived (traditionally, after the work of Neugebauer, the second half of the first century is named) is not free from dispute. This second hypothesis has been suggested to me by A. Jones. I thank him for it.
>
> [6] The most famous case is that of the edition of the works of Plotinus by Porphyry.
> [7] See Reynolds and Wilson 1988: 2–3.
> [8] Dorandi 1986.
> [9] See Dorandi 2000: 51–75.

The first operation, apparently begun in Rome at the beginning of our era, is nothing more than the adoption of the book with pages, written on both sides and with contents definitely more important than the *volumen*. This shift allows the composition of textual collections and the development of marginal commentaries which previously appeared in a separate scroll. Writings that were not converted into this format had a relatively small chance of being transmitted down to us. The texts known only through papyrus scrolls are small in number and frequently nothing more than fragments. In other words, in the case of the *Elements*, the creation of (at least one) archetypal codex must be postulated. We know nothing of when this fabrication occurred or who (whether a mathematician or an institution similar to a library with a centre for copying) undertook this labour. However, the adoption of the codex was a rather slow operation which spanned from the first through to the fourth centuries of our era, and beyond. The fact that this adoption was applied in wholesale to the texts from previous eras probably ought to be attributed to the revival of the study of classical texts under the Antonines (second century).[10]

The other operation, the Byzantine transliteration, was more limited than the change from scrolls to codices. It was done in the Byzantine empire from the end of the eighth century. The Byzantine transliteration consisted of using a form of cursive minuscule for the edition of texts in place of the majuscule writing termed *uncial*. Previously, cursive minuscule had been limited to the drafting of administrative documents, but uncial had proven too large and thus 'costly' for use with parchment. Here, too, the success and systematization of the process were certainly linked with a renewed interest in ancient texts during the course of the 'Byzantine Renaissance', which began in the 850s and was associated with individuals like Leo the Wise (or the Philosopher), the patriarch Photius and Arethas of Cesarea. Such transliteration was a rather delicate technical operation composed of two phases – the first (and the largest) of which fell in the ninth and tenth centuries, the second in the years 1150–1300.[11] Here, again, translation acted as a filter. Non-transliterated texts progressively ceased to be read. Save for some fortunate circumstances, they disappeared.

For the ancient writings which survived these two transformations, we may, if we are reasonably optimistic, emphasize on the one hand the fact that on occasions in these two situations, the editors intervened in important ways, and the specimens were produced according to particularly

[10] On the change from scroll to codex, see the accessible summary by Reynolds and Wilson 1988: 23–6. Cf. also Blanchard 1989.

[11] Cf. Irigoin 2003: 6–7.

'authorized' manners which played a decisive role in the transmission. These two circumstances produced the archetypal codex (or codices) of the Roman era and the transliterated example or examples in minuscule beginning in the ninth century. On the other hand, on these occasions there was the risk and opportunity that the substance or presentation of these texts would be radically modified.

The oldest preserved complete examples of the *Elements* in thirteen books were produced immediately after the transliteration into minuscule which has just been called into question.

They are:

- one manuscript from the Vatican Library, *Vaticanus gr*. 190, assigned to the years 830–50 according to palaeographic and codicological considerations;[12]
- one manuscript from the Bodleian Library at Oxford, *D'Orville 301*, which, other than its exceptional state of conservation, has the advantage of having been explicitly dated, since its copying, ordered from the cleric Stephanos by Arethas, who was then deacon, was completed in September 888.

Two remarks are in order:

(1) These pieces of evidence are from more than a thousand years after the hypothetical original of Euclid.
(2) The case of the *Elements* is, however, one of the most favourable (or, perhaps, least unfavourable?) in the collection of profane Greek texts.

Other than these two precious copies, about eighty manuscripts containing the text (either complete or in part) are known; of these roughly thirty predate the fifteenth century. Likewise, a palimpsest, dated to the end of the seventh or the beginning of the eighth century and written in uncial, contains extracts from Books x and xIII.[13] It thus seems assured that the study of the *Elements* had not completely ceased during the so-called Dark Ages of Byzantine history (650–850). Also known are several papyrus fragments,[14] the oldest of which are ascribed to the first century and the most

---

[12] Cf. Irigoin 2003: 215 (original publication, 1962). Cf. Follieri 1977, particularly 144; Mogenet and Tihon 1985, 23–4 (Vatican fr. 190 = ms probably from the first half of the ninth century) and 80–1. At the time of Heiberg, this copy was assigned to the tenth century, and the manuscript in the Bodleian was considered the oldest. One sometimes still finds this debatable assertion.

[13] See Heiberg 1885.

[14] Cf. *EHS*: I: 187–9 and Fowler 1987: 204–14 and Plates 1–3.

recent to the third century. In contrast to the manuscripts, the papyri have the privileged position of being documents from Antiquity. An author represented among the papyri is likely to have been used in teaching. In the mathematical realm, the bulk of papyri preserved for us represent two categories: (1) very elementary school documents, and (2) astronomical texts. It is therefore significant that Euclid is the only geometer of the 'scholarly' tradition who appears in this type of text.

Direct and indirect traditions

Nicolas Bourbaki probably did not consult the manuscripts of the *Elements* to determine his opinion about the subject of the Euclidean ideal of proof, and it is the same for the majority of Euclid's modern readers. Generally, they rely on a translation, or if they know ancient Greek, on a critical edition produced by a modern philologist. In the case of the Greek texts of the *Elements*, the critical edition was produced by J. L. Heiberg. If he reads the work in Greek, the reader labours under the illusion that he has read what Euclid has written. In this respect, the philological terminology and its label 'direct tradition' can be misleading. The 'direct' tradition designates the set of Greek manuscripts and papyri which contain the text either in its totality or in part. Despite this label, we must not forget the considerable number of intermediaries that came between us and the author, even in the direct tradition. These intermediaries include not only the copyists, who we would like to believe did nothing more than passively reproduce the text, but also, more importantly, those who took an active part in the transmission of the text – in particular ancient and medieval re-editors and, last of all, the philologists who, beginning with the collection of the available information, have constructed the critical edition that we read today. I have thus reported, too briefly, the several elements of the history of the preceding ancient Greek texts to make the point that our knowledge about the text of the *Elements*, like that of the majority of other ancient Greek texts, is essentially indirect.

Classical philology is not without resources. It has developed methods to 'reverse' the course of time. These methods make it possible to trace the relationships between manuscripts, to detect the mistakes of the copyists, and in the 'good' cases to reconstitute an ancestor of the tradition, often immediately before the transliteration, sometimes an ancient prototype from late antiquity or from the Roman era. In the case of a Hellenistic author, this result is still rather removed from the 'original' and thus necessitates appeals to other sources. These sources constitute the so-called indirect tradition

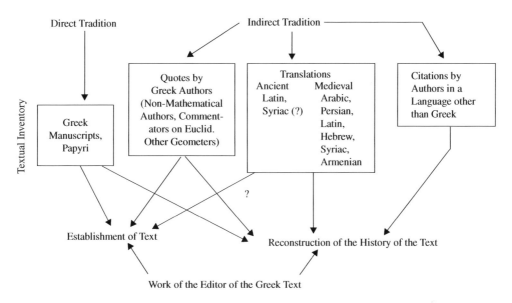

Figure 1.1 Textual history: the philological approach.

(see Figure 1.1). Generally, it is used to decide between variant manuscripts or as confirmation in the testing of conjectures about the state of the text before the production of the oldest preserved manuscripts.

In brief, the work of the editor comprises two dimensions: (1) the establishment of the text, and (2) the reconstruction of what philologists call the 'textual history', that is to follow the avatars of the manuscripts, but also the commentaries and translations through which we have access to the text, to review the evidence about the use of the work in education, in controversies, or its presence in libraries. Although the one dimension is certainly articulated with respect to the other, it is nonetheless convenient to distinguish between them.

For the reconstruction of the textual history, all information ought to be taken into account. Because the collected sources will probably be contradictory (variants among manuscripts, incompatible quotations, etc.), it is necessary to classify the information and search for plausible explanations (accidents in copying, editorial action by a re-editor, influence of a commentary through marginal notations, decisions of the translator, influence of pedagogical, philosophical or mathematical context) in order to provide an account of the development of the manuscript. Since the history of the text serves to justify the choices made in its establishment (see the flow-chart, in Figure 1.1 above), it must be understood how the two aspects of the philological work are articulated.

In the case of the *Elements*, the group of sources which constitutes the indirect tradition is rich. First of all, in the case of citations by ancient authors, the *Elements* received commentaries on several occasions (namely, by Heron of Alexandria, Pappus of Alexandria, Proclus of Lycia, Simplicius (?)).[15] The *Elements* were also used abundantly by the authors of late antiquity. Some extracts of several of these commentaries are found in the thousands of marginal annotations contained in the manuscripts of the text. Moreover, tracing the indirect tradition of the translations, quotations and commentaries in languages other than Greek is practically unmanageable, even when the task is limited to ancient and medieval periods. Consequently, it is impossible to imagine an exhaustive textual history undertaken by a single individual.

The first task for whoever wants to edit the text will be to limit the pertinent information, in a way that is not only selective enough to be operational, but also wide-ranging enough that no essential elements are left behind. In the matter of editing a Greek text, in Greek, it is reasonable that the philologists privilege the direct tradition of manuscripts and papyri for the establishment of the text. They also emphasize the obvious limits of the different elements of the indirect tradition. Whether the quotations are in Greek or not, philologists note that the citations were sometimes made from memory. As for the translations, they introduce into the process of transmission not only the passage from one language to another in which the linguistic structures may be somewhat different, but also the preliminary operation of the comprehension of the text, which is not necessarily implied for a professional copy. Indeed, there is even something about which to be happy when the Greek text no longer exists. Hellenists are generally grateful to the Latin, Syriac, Arabic, Persian, Armenian and Hebrew translators for having preserved whole fields of ancient literature. In the case of mathematics, the medieval Arabic translations have had great importance for our knowledge of Apollonius, Diocles, Heron, Menelaus, Ptolemy and Diophantus, to mention only the best-known cases. These examples suggest not only that the savants of the Arab world had assiduously sought out Greek manuscripts – indeed, they have borne frequent witness to this subject – but also that they had some skill in finding them in formerly Hellenized areas. The decline of Greek as a scientific language and the ascendancy of Syriac and then Arabic made translation necessary.

The possibility is thus foreseen that, in so doing, these translations had preserved an earlier state of the text than that transmitted by the

---

[15] The first and last are accessible indirectly, thanks to the Persian commentator an-Nayrîzî. Heron is also cited several times by Proclus.

manuscripts elaborated in the Byzantine world. Consequently, important decisions must be made about instances in which the medieval translations show important textual divergences from the version of the same work preserved in Greek. As we will see, it is exactly this situation which occurs in the case of the *Elements* of Euclid.

In the case of such divergences, at least two explanations may be imagined:

(1) The medieval translators took great liberties with the text, and they did not hesitate to adapt it to their own ends.
(2) Their versions were based on Greek models appreciably different from those which we know. Thus, we can imagine that these models were (i) more authentic, or, (ii) on the contrary, more corrupt, than our manuscripts.

In either case, it will be necessary to make an account of the history of the text, to establish the innovative informality or rigorous fidelity of the translators, to account for the methods and the context of the transmission. It is clear that, within the framework of hypotheses 1 or 2(ii), translations will not be taken into account in the establishment of the text. But if we prove that the translators scrupulously respected their models (non 1), which were less corrupted (2(i)) – let us remain realistic, though – what then?

The textual inventory in the case of the *Elements*

In order to produce his critical edition (1883–8), Heiberg had (partially) collated about twenty manuscripts. He continued this task for fifteen years after the publication of the aforementioned edition, extending the scope to nearly thirty other manuscripts. He compared his edition with papyrus fragments, as they were discovered.[16] In order to establish his text, he used seven of the eight manuscripts from before the thirteenth century. He systematically explored the indirect tradition of quotations by Greek authors and the tradition of fragments of ancient Latin translation. As for the medieval versions, they were not particularly well known. Heiberg used several previous works and, as far as the phase of Arabic translations of the ninth century was concerned, he accepted the description published by M. Klamroth in 1881,[17] at which time he inventoried the materials useful

---

[16] See Heiberg 1885 and Heiberg 1903.
[17] At the time when he edited the chapter devoted to the medieval Arabic history of the text of the *Elements* in Heiberg 1882, he seems not to know Klamroth 1881, which he later criticized in his 1884 article.

for the establishment of his edition. A debate – but not to say a polemic[18] – between the two scholars followed on the subject of the obligation of recognizing the value of the indirect tradition from the medieval era.

At any rate, Heiberg knew that there had been at least two Arabic translations, that of al-Hajjâj (produced before 805 and modified by the author for the Kalif al-Ma'mun between 813 and 833), then that of Ishâq ibn Hunayn (†910–11) revised by Thâbit ibn Qurra (†901). Klamroth believed himself to have the al-Hajjâj version for Books I–VI and XI–XIII and that of Ishâq for Books I–X. The Hebrew and Arabo-Latin translations likewise began to be studied. Heiberg also knew (especially) about several recensions (falsely) attributed to Nâsir ad-Dîn at-Tûsî (1201–73) and that of Campanus (†1296).[19]

From the comparison of Greek manuscripts produced by Heiberg and from the statement that Klamroth had furnished concerning the Arabic Euclid emerges an assessment of the situation which I will describe roughly in the following way:

- For the 'direct' Greek tradition, it is necessary to distinguish two versions of the text in the collection of the thirteen Books of the *Elements*, and even three for XI.36–XII.17. A simple structural comparison of the manuscripts is sufficient to establish this point. The two divergent versions of the complete text[20] are represented on the one hand by the manuscript *Vaticanus gr.* 190 (*P*) – the oldest complete manuscript – and, on the other, by the strongly connected *BFVpqS* manuscripts,[21] as well as the Bologna manuscript (denoted as *b*),[22] for the whole of the text, save the section XI.36–XII.17. In these twenty-one Propositions, the Bologna manuscript presents a structure completely different from that of *P* and *BFVpqS*, which on the whole are less divergent from each other than they are with respect to *b*.
- For the indirect tradition of the Arabic translations, the report of Klamroth was that there was a considerable difference between the Greek and Arabic traditions. This difference went beyond the scope of the

---

[18] I allow myself to recall the first part of Rommevaux, Djebbar and Vitrac 2001: 227–33 and 235–44, in which I analyse the arguments of the two parties.

[19] For a synthesized presentation of the Arabic, Arabo-Latin and Arabo-Hebrew traditions as they are known today, see Brentjes 2001a: 39–51 and De Young 2004: 313–23.

[20] This is what I have termed 'dichotomy 3' (see Appendix, Table 3).

[21] Codex Bodleianus, D'Orville, 301 (*B*), Codex Florentinus, Bibl. Laurentienne, xxviii, 3 (*F*), Codex Vindobonensis, philos. Gr. 103 (*V*); Codex Parisinus gr. 2466 (*p*); Codex Parisinus gr. 2344 (*q*); Codex *Scolariensis gr.* 221, F, iii, 5 (*S*). The sigla used here are the same as those used by Heiberg.

[22] Codex Bononiensis, Bibl. communale, n°. 18–19.

unavoidable variations between manuscripts. Klamroth further declared that the Arabic tradition was characterized by a particular 'thinness' and several structural alterations in presentation (specifically, in modification of order, division or regrouping).[23]

The history of the text of the *Elements* in antiquity

Let us consider now the history of the text of the *Elements*. Starting with these inventories, let us examine the interpretation of the different pieces of evidence which our two scholars proposed. The interpretation of Klamroth is simple: the 'thinness' of the Arabic (and Arabo-Latin) tradition is an indication of its greater purity. The textual destiny of the *Elements* has been the amplification of its contents, particularly for pedagogical reasons. The medieval evidence about the translators' methods and the context in which they worked shows that the medieval translators had a real concern about the completeness of translated texts. The gaps (with respect to the Greek text) cannot be ascribed to negligence on the part of these translators. The additions are interpolations in the Greek tradition. Consequently, for Klamroth, it is necessary to take the indirect tradition into account, not only for the history of the text, but also in the establishment of the text.[24]

The history of the text proposed by Heiberg is completely different. This history is clearly dependent on the way in which the transmission of the *Elements* was conceptualized by Hellenists since the Renaissance, particularly since the Latin translation produced by Zamberti, taken directly from the Greek and published at Venice in 1505.[25] The presentation of this last work raised two essential questions:

(1) For Zamberti, the 'return' to the Greek text was a remedy for the abuses to which the text had been subjected in medieval editions. The focus of his concern was the then highly renowned Latin recension of Campanus. This edition had just been printed at Venice in 1482 and was itself composed from an Arabo-Latin translation. A debate arose about the (linguistic and mathematical) competence of the translators and the quality of the models which would establish for quite some time the idea that the indirect medieval tradition could be discarded.

(2) Zamberti presented his *Elements* as if the definitions and the statements of the propositions were due to Euclid, while the proofs were

---

[23] He thus identified a well-established line of demarcation between the direct tradition and the indirect tradition. I have named this distinction 'dichotomy 1' (see Appendix, Table 1).

[24] Generally, this position has been taken up by Knorr in his powerful 1996 study.

[25] See Weissenborn 1882.

attributable to Theon of Alexandria. In fact, we have a (single) example of this authorial division. Theon indicates explicitly, in his *Commentary to the Almagest*, that he had been given an edition of the *Elements* and that he had modified the last Proposition of Book VI (VI.33 Heib.) in order to append an assertion concerning proportionality of sectors and arcs upon which they stand in equal circles. Zamberti's attribution of proofs to Theon was undoubtedly inferred from the glosses 'of the edition of Theon (ἐκ τῆς Θέωνος ἐκδόσεως)' marked on the Greek manuscripts used by him. Consequently, since it was understood that Theon had re-edited the *Elements* in the second half of the fourth century of our era, the question arose of what ought to be ascribed to Euclid and what ought to ascribed to the editorial actions of Theon. For someone like R. Simson (1756), the answers were particularly clear. All that was worthy of admiration originated with Euclid; all the deficiencies were due to the incompetence of the re-editor.

Thus, the debate on the subject was open. When F. Peyrard, around 1808, undertook to check the Greek text for his new French translation of *Elements* which was based on the Oxford edition of 1703, he discovered among the manuscripts which had been brought back from Italy by Gaspard Monge (after the Napoleonic campaigns) a copy belonging to the Vatican Library (*Vaticanus gr.* 190), which contained neither mention 'of the edition of Theon' nor the additional portion at VI.33 and which differed considerably from the twenty-two other manuscripts known to him. From this divergence, he deduced that this manuscript, unlike the others, preceded the re-edition of Theon and that it moreover contained the text of Euclid![26] He at once decided to make a new edition of the Greek text.

Heiberg accepted (with some reworking) the interpretations of Peyrard, particularly the idea that all the manuscripts with the exception of *Vaticanus gr.* 190 were derived from Theon's edition. He called these the 'Theonine'.[27] As for the Vatican copy, he was more careful. Heiberg noted that the copyist admits in the margins of Proposition XI.38 *vulgo*[28] and Proposition XIII.6 to have consulted two editions, one 'ancient' and the other 'new'. Proposition XIII.6 existed in the first but was missing in the other. Exactly the oppo-

---

[26] Peyrard 1814: xiii, xxv.

[27] Consequently, in the following, I will use the abbreviation **Th** to designate the aforementioned family of manuscripts.

[28] Several Propositions appearing in the *editio princeps* (and reproduced in the following editions) were discarded by Heiberg who designated them in this way lest there be some confusion in numbering. XI.38 *vulgo* was No. 38 in the preceding editions. It was rejected by Heiberg in the Appendix. His Proposition 38 was thus No. 39 in the previous editions.

site was the case for Proposition XI.38 *vulgo*. Heiberg considered that the manuscript – which he would call *P* in homage to Peyrard – had been produced beginning with at least two models, one of which was pre-Theonian, and the other was Theonian. His edition was thus founded on the comparison of *P* with *Th* and on an examination of the total or partial agreement or disagreement between the two families.[29] From there, he claimed he had determined the editorial actions of Theon of Alexandria, and passed severe judgement on the changes. Theon's re-edition of the *Elements* did not compare favourably with the editions of the great poetical texts produced by the Alexandrian philologists of the second and third centuries before the modern era.[30]

If we return to the terms of our previous line of reasoning and if we accept this history of the text, we ought to distinguish two textual archetypal manuscripts: the first representing the re-edition of Theon and realized in the 370s, and the second corresponding to the pre-Theonine model called *P*. However, the alterations which Theon is supposed to have effected on the text, as deduced by a comparison with the manuscript *P*, are so limited that with a few exceptions (which are listed in the Appendices), Heiberg believed he could combine the two versions in one text with a single *apparatus criticus*.

For the divergent Greek text (*b* XI.36–XII.17), his solution was somewhat different. It seems that the discovery of this manuscript must be attributed to Heiberg in the context of the previously mentioned debate. In an 1884 article, he presented this new Greek evidence, taking the opportunity to respond to the arguments presented by Klamroth. The reason for his approach was that this 'dissenting' Greek text and the Arabic translations are incontestably related in this portion of the text. Precisely this incomplete but incontestable structural agreement in opposition to the tradition in *P* + *Th* constitutes the principal argument in the article by W. Knorr. However, noting that the text of *b*, copied in the eleventh century and also Theonine, is particularly deficient in section XI.36–XII.17, Heiberg introduced into the history of the text a Byzantine redactor, the author of an abridged version of the *Elements*, in order to explain the difference. From this abbreviated work was derived *b* XI.36–XII.17 and the models used by the Arabic translators. The consequences for the edition of the text were clear. Aside from some specific references to the Latin recension of Campanus, the indirect medieval tradition which had been connected from

---

[29] See *EHS*: v, 1, xxv–xxxvi.
[30] lviii. The comparison is irrelevant: see Rommevaux, Djebbar and Vitrac 2001: 246–7.

the beginning to a lower-quality model was not taken into account by the Danish editor. The portion *b* xi.36–xii.17 was relegated to Appendix II of Volume 4 of the edition, together with portions of the text which Heiberg deemed inauthentic.

In other words, his decisions (or rather his non-decisions) resulted in a critical edition that can be described as 'conservative'. In order to clarify the meaning of this term, let us recall that the Greek text had undergone five editions in recent times: the *editio princeps* by S. Grynée (Bâle, 1533), the edition by D. Gregory (Oxford, 1703), the edition by F. Peyrard (Paris, 1814–18), that of E. F. August (Berlin, 1826–29) and finally Heiberg's own edition. I do not intend to examine in detail their respective merits, but two or three facts are clear. The first two editions were produced from manuscripts belonging to the family later characterized as 'Theonine'. Despite the many discussions of the sixteenth century, 170 years had passed before the appearance of a new edition, which Peyrard judged to be no better than the preceding!

At any rate, Peyrard's edition scarcely agrees with his history of the text. After he affirmed that the Vatican manuscript contained the text of Euclid, he continued to follow the text of the *editio princeps* of 1533 (and thus the Theonine family of texts) in several passages where the divergences are especially well-marked. The quest for authenticity was not of primary importance. It was more important to present a mathematically correct Euclid. We may suppose that it is for this reason that Peyrard continued to follow the Theonine family which is more correct in the case of ix.19 and more general in the case of xi.38, but privileged *P* which is (apparently) less faulty in the case of iii.24 and more complete in the case of xiii.6. Peyrard also wanted his edition to be easy to use. Quite bluntly, Peyrard admits to having retained what is now designated as Proposition x.13 *vulgo* lest he introduce a shift in the enumeration of the Propositions of the book with respect to the previous editions – even though this proposition is omitted in *P* and is clearly an interpolation! More generally, he preserves most of the additional material (various additions, lemmas, alternate proofs) which *P* would have been able to dismiss as inauthentic had it been taken into account.

It was not until the edition of Heiberg that the primacy of manuscript *P* was truly assumed. A large part (but not all!) of the material thereafter considered additional was added to the Appendices inserted at the end of each of the four volumes. Whenever the textual divergence is marked and the result (in *Th*) is identified as the product of a voluntary modification, the reading of *P* is retained, even if this destroys the mathematical coherence, as in the previously mentioned example of ix.19.[31] Contrary to Peyrard, Heiberg does not admit that Euclid could have provided several proofs for the same result, which would constitute what I have called above an 'authorial variation'. We will return to this important topic later. For now, let us say simply that the criteria of Heiberg are simple. In the case of double proofs, he retains as the sole, authentic proof that which occurs first in **P**, whether it is better than the other or not.

The limitations of this edition thus result from the adopted history of the text and the resulting principles of selection, while the merits of the edition derive from a more coherent observation of these choices than Peyrard managed. Another (and not the least) of its merits is that the text as published corresponds rather well with something which had existed, namely manuscript **P** of the Vatican,[32] whereas the archetypal texts reconstituted by the modern editors of ancient texts are sometimes nothing more than fictions or philological monsters. What it represents with respect to the ancient text is more uncertain. The incidental remarks of the copyist of **P** already suggest a certain contamination between (at least) two branches of the tradition.

Until the 1970s it was believed that the manuscripts resulting from the transliteration were faithful copies of ancient models, with the only change being the replacement of one type of writing with another. Nowadays belief in this practice is not so sure, and there are even a number of cases in which it may be frankly doubted.[33] We will see an argument (see below, p. 111) which casts doubts on the two oldest witnesses of the *Elements* (**P** and **B**). Let us assume that the copyist of **P** followed what was termed the 'ancient edition', and that he compared the 'ancient edition' with the 'new edition' only after the copying. (Indeed, there is a good probability that this was the case.) Even so, our faith in the antiquity of the text produced in this way depends entirely on the confidence accorded to the history of the text proposed by Heiberg. In particular, the strength of the argument rests on the validity of the interpretation he proposes for the distinction between **P** and **Th** in connection with the re-edition by Theon of Alexandria, around 370.

This history was accepted by T. L. Heath and J. Murdoch – who have significantly contributed to its diffusion – and thus by the majority of specialists. Disconnectedly and periodically challenged, this history was

---

[31] See Vitrac 2004: 10–12.

[32] In a certain number of passages, and more generally for minor variants, Heiberg preserved the text of the Theonian family. Cf. the list that he gives in *EHS*: v, 1, xxxiv–xxxv.

[33] See Irigoin 2003: 37–53. The (very illuminating) example from the Hippocratic corpus is the object of the article reproduced on pp. 251–69 (original publication 1975).

thoroughly called into question by W. Knorr in his article of 1996. In particular, our late colleague there affirms that all the preserved Greek manuscripts depend on the edition of Theon, that the differences between the Vatican manuscript and the *Th* family are microscopic, and that these differences are not characteristic of a re-edition. Stated differently, if the opinion of Knorr is adopted, the Euclid edited by Heiberg ought to correspond, at best, to the text in circulation at Alexandria in the second half of the fourth century of our era.

The arguments of Knorr are not all of the same value – far from it.[34] The difference between *P* and *Th* is real. It is not a question only of divergences attributable to errors by the copyist which philologists try to dismiss. The reader can convince himself of the extent of differences between *P* and *Th* by consulting the list which I give in Table 3 of the Appendix. However, it should also be emphasized that there is not, in this internal dichotomy in the Greek, any substitution of proofs (!), any change in the order of the Propositions, or any Lemma which exists in one of the two versions but not in the other. When there are double proofs, the order is always the same as in *P* and in *Th*.

At the present stage of my work, I see only two solutions: (i) to adopt Knorr's opinion, or (ii) to conclude that the goal of Theon's re-edition was not a large-scale alteration. About Theon's motivations, we know next to nothing. He presents us with a single indication relating to the contents (the addition at vi.33). It is possible, for example, to conceive of the hypothesis that Theon's re-edition was in fact the transcription of the edition(s) written on scrolls into a version in the form of a codex or codices. If the text of the previous *vulgata* appeared satisfactory to him, the goal would not have been to propose a different mathematical composition, but to revitalize the treatise by adopting a new format for the old book. The second half of the fourth century represents a relatively late date, but it is known that the pagan circles sometimes resisted innovations which seemed to meet with their first successes in Christian quarters.[35] And, what is known, if not about Theon himself, then at least about his daughter Hypatia, suggests that he was connected with pagan, neo-Platonic intellectual circles. Moreover, even if this explanation is adopted, nothing guarantees that he was the first to unfold this way, nor that he was the only one. On the other hand, it is certain that this version played an important role in the transmission of the *Elements*, as is proven by the statements contained in the family of manuscripts titled *Th*.

---

[34] See Rommevaux, Djebbar and Vitrac 2001: 233–5 and 244–50.
[35] See van Haelst 1989: 14, 26–35.

The second scenario which might account for the limited but real variation shown between *P* and *Th* satisfies me more than Knorr's reconstruction.
We have only two criteria external to the text by which we can understand
the aforementioned re-edition: the glosses 'of the edition of Theon (ἐκ τῆς
Θέωνος ἐκδόσεως)' and the presence or absence of the addition at vi.33. We
have so little information about the history of the text[36] that it is a little too
daring to throw out some part of our information without external support
for the decision. As for the problem discussed here, I do not believe that my
hypotheses change anything regarding the state of the texts that the Greek
manuscripts enable us to establish. It is probably approximately the text as
it circulated around the turn of the third and fourth centuries of our era. Is
it possible to advance from here? With regard to the edition of a minimally
coherent Greek text, I am not sure. However, other sources clarifying the
history of the text are provided to us, thanks to the indirect tradition and,
in this arena, our situation is a little more favourable than the time-frame of
the Klamroth–Heiberg debate.

New contributions to the textual inventory

With regard to the indirect tradition of the quotations by Greek authors, we
have two more valuable sources:

- The Persian commentator an-Nayrîzî has transmitted to us a certain
  number of testimonies about the commentaries of Heron and Simplicius,
  whose original Greek texts are now lost. Some of them provide interesting
  information about the history of the text.[37] Heiberg had taken note of this
  evidence. He had even taken part in the edition of *Codex Leidensis* 399
  through which the commentary was first known, although this edition
  was produced after Heiberg's edition of the *Elements*. He gives an analysis
  of these new materials, among other things, in an important 1903 article.
- In the same vein, he had nothing except a very fragmentary knowledge
  about the commentary on Book x, attributed to Pappus and preserved
  in an Arabic translation by al-Dimashqî, from which Woepcke, around

---

[36] In this regard, the indirect medieval tradition, so rich in new textual variants, teaches us
nothing about the history of the text during antiquity, particularly about the existence or not
of several editions of the *Elements*.

[37] In the case of Heron, see Brentjes 1997–8: 71–7; in this article Brentjes suggests that other
Arabic authors knew about the commentary by Heron independently of an-Nayrîzî, in
particular Ibn al-Haytham. In Brentjes 2000: 44–7, she shows that it is probably true for
al-Karâbîsî, also. Heron proposed a number of textual emendations, among other things. See
Vitrac 2004: 30–4.

1855, published only extracts. Thenceforth, the text was edited and translated into multiple languages.[38]

In the course of the two decades during which Heiberg worked on the
tradition of the text of Euclid, new information, accessible thanks to the
indirect tradition,[39] could have led him to alter certain editorial decisions
made in the years 1883–6 at the time when he argued with Klamroth.
These alterations might have stemmed notably from taking into account
manuscript *b* (in the portion where it diverges) and the indirect medieval tradition. The works which he published in the years 1888–1903 are
indispensable to those who use his critical edition. Regrettably, Heiberg
did not produce a second revised edition, as he did for Archimedes, after
the discovery of the so-called Archimedes Palimpsest.[40] This text gave
access to the previously unavailable Greek texts of *On Floating Bodies* and
The Method of Mechanical Theorems. To his eyes, the necessity of a revised
edition was probably much smaller in the case of the *Elements* of Euclid,
but the resumption of such a work would perhaps have led him to revise his
position concerning the indirect medieval tradition.

We know this tradition somewhat better than Klamroth or Heiberg,
thanks to a more developed textual inventory. At least a score of manuscripts of the version called Ishâq–Thâbit have been identified today,[41]
whereas Klamroth knew only two! Multiple works on the methods and
contexts of medieval translations from Greek into Syriac or Arabic, or from
Arabic into Latin or Hebrew, either in general or more directed toward
mathematical texts, including the *Elements*, have been undertaken. Busard
has published seven Arabo-Latin versions from the twelfth and thirteenth
centuries[42] as well as a Greco-Latin version from the twelfth century discovered by J. Murdoch.[43] We even have partial editions of the Books v and

---

[38] See notably Thomson and Junge 1930. It might be argued that this partial knowledge led
Heiberg to some debatable conclusions concerning the collection of the 'Vatican' scholia (see
Vitrac 2003: 288–92) and the pre-Theonine state of the text of Book x (see Euclid/Vitrac, 1998:
III 381–99). Let us add that the integrity of the text attributed to Pappus and the uniqueness of
the author (*pace* Thomson and Junge 1930) are not at all certain (see Euclid/Vitrac, 1998:III:
418–19).

[39] It ought to include the new information contained by the scholia found in the margins of the
Greek manuscripts and we once again know about these sources thanks to the monumental
work of Heiberg. See *EHS*, v, 1–2 and Heiberg 1888, to which should be added Heiberg 1903.

[40] Regrettably, in his 'revision' (*EHS*), Stamatis did not supplement 'Heiberg with Heiberg'.

[41] See Folkerts 1989 (with the corrections of Brentjes 2001: 52, n. 13). Some of these manuscripts
contain fragments attributed to the translation by al-Hajjâj.

[42] Respectively Busard 1967–1972–1977 (*HC*), 1983 (*Ad. I*), 1984 (*GC*); Busard and Folkerts
1992 (*RC*); Busard 1996, 2001 (*JT*), 2005 (Campanus). Complete references are provided in the
bibliography.

[43] Busard 1987.

VII–IX from the so-called Ishâq–Thâbit version.[44] A second manuscript of the commentary by an-Nayrîzî made it possible to complete the evidence from the (mutilated) *Codex Leidensis* regarding the principles in Book I.[45] Several other commentaries (al-Mahânî,[46] al-Farâbî,[47] Ibn al-Haytham,[48] al-Jayyâni,[49] 'Umar al-Khayyâm[50]) have also been edited, translated and analysed. The wealth of materials since made available is exceptional. It is obvious that the history of the text of the *Elements* during the Middle Ages and perhaps even from the beginning of the Renaissance ought to be entirely rewritten.

This is clearly not what I propose to do in the remainder of this chapter, as this task surpasses my competence. I will adopt a more limited perspective and focus on more modest aims. What does this renewed knowledge about the indirect tradition teach us about the history of the text in antiquity, more particularly about the redaction of mathematical proofs? What are the limits?

In so doing, I attempt to explore the consequences of the hypotheses put forth by Knorr. In his striking 1996 study, knowing that I was in the process of carrying out an annotated French translation (which was then partially published), he suggested that I compare the Greek text established by Heiberg with that of two Arabo-Latin translations, the first attributed to Adelard of Bath and the second ascribed to Gerard of Cremona, the former composed around 1140, and the latter about 1180.

Knorr was convinced that these versions transmitted to us a text less altered than the one contained in the Greek manuscripts. He believed that it was possible to reconstitute a Greek archetype from the group of medieval

---

[44] Engroff 1980; De Young 1981.

[45] See Arnzen 2002. See also the new partial edition of the Latin translation by Gerard of Cremona, initially published as vol. IX of *EHM*: Tummers 1994. The preserved Arab and Latin versions of the text of an-Nayrîzî may be described as passably divergent. See Brentjes 2001b: 17–55.

[46] *Risâla li-al-Mâhânî fî al-mushkil min amr al-nisba* (*Épitre d'al-Mâhânî sur la difficulté relative à la question du rapport*). Edition and French translation in Vahabzadeh 1997. Reprinted, with English translation, in Vahabzadeh 2002: 31–52; *Tafsîr al-maqâla al-'âshira min kitâb Uqlîdis* (*Explication du Dixième Livre de l'ouvrage d'Euclide*). Edition and French translation in Ben Miled 2005: 286–92.

[47] *Sharh al-mustaglaq min musâdarât al-maqâla al-ûlâ wa-l-hâmisa min Uqlîdis*. The text was translated into Hebrew by Moses ibn Tibbon. See Freudenthal 1988: 104–219.

[48] *Sharh musâdarât Uqlîdis*. Partial edition, English translation and commentaries in Sude 1974.

[49] *Maqâla fî sharh al-nisba* (*Commentaire sur le rapport*). Facsimile of manuscript Algier 1466/3, fos. 74r–82r and English translation in Plooij 1950. Edition and French translation in Vahabzadeh 1997.

[50] *Risâla fî sharh mâ ashkala min musâdarât Kitâb Uqlîdis* (*Épitre sur les problèmes posés par certaines prémisses problématiques du Livre d'Euclide*). French translation in Djebbar 1997 and 2002: 79–136. Edition of Arabic text with French translation in Rashed and Vahabzadeh 1999: 271–390.

translations. This hypothetical archetype represented the state of the text prior to the re-edition of Theon, a re-edition from which he believed any of the preserved Greek manuscripts stemmed. The adoption of this point, one suspects, would overturn the entire ancient history of the text and have grave consequences for the establishment of the text, not only at the structural level, but also for the redaction of each proof as is shown in the example of xii.17 analysed in detail by Knorr.

In order to present my results (and my doubts), I must first give the reader some idea of the size and nature of the collection of textual divergences found by the comparison of the direct Greek tradition with the indirect medieval tradition.

Extent and nature of the textual divergences between versions of the *Elements*

Typology of deliberate structural alterations

It is obviously not possible either to give an exhaustive list of deliberate alterations which the text of the *Elements* has undergone or to detail the relatively complex methods of detection and identification of specific divergences. I am not interested in the variants that the philologists use: variant spellings, small additions and/or microlacunae, *saut du même au même*, and dittographies (that is, reduplications of lines of text). The errors shared between copies of the same text make it possible to establish the genealogy of manuscripts. They constitute textual markers, all the more interesting because they are reproduced by generations of copyists who did not notice them because they could not understand the text or did not try to understand it.

I have tried to determine the variants which are connected with the deliberate modifications made by those responsible for the re-edition of the Greek text or the possible revisers of the Arabic translations, such as Thâbit ibn Qurra, not those related to the 'mechanical' errors directly associated with the process of copying. This concern goes particularly for the global modifications of proofs.[51] When such variations existed among the Greek manuscripts, they had a good chance of surviving the process of translation. Even the structure of the text of the *Elements*, composed

---

[51] For the local variants of the Greek text, another phenomenon must be taken into account: the multiple uses of the margins of manuscripts after the adoption of the codex. See Euclid/Vitrac 2001: IV 44–5.

of rather easily identifiable textual units, facilitates this work. In the same way, the formulaic character of Greek geometrical language has been maintained in the translations and permits the identification of local variants which would probably be more difficult in a philosophical or medical text.

My sample size is sufficiently large to propose a typology, although the qualitative considerations are provisional and clearly depend on the given range of the analysed corpus.[52] In the absence of critical editions of the Arabic versions and in accounting for the multitude of recensions, epitomes and annotated versions inspired by Euclid's work, we cannot pretend to determine with any degree of certainty the extent of the corpus to be taken into consideration. For the present purposes, I use the various components of the direct tradition, the so-called Greco-Latin version[53] and the available information concerning the Arabic translation attributed to Ishâq ibn Hunayn and revised by Thâbit ibn Qurra, as well as the fragments attributed to al-Hajjâj in the manuscripts of the Ishâq–Thâbit version, the Arabo-Latin translations attributed respectively to Adelard of Bath and Gerard of Cremona. This group corresponds to what the specialists of the Arabic Euclid call the 'primary transmission', in order to distinguish it from the secondary elaborations (recensions, epitomes, …).[54]

I currently work with a list of about 220 structural alterations of which the principal genres and species appear in Figure 1.2. They relate to well-defined textual units: Definition, Postulate, Common Notion, Proposition, Case, Lemma, Porism, even a collection of such units, particularly when there is a change in the order of presentation. The debate which divided Klamroth and Heiberg in the 1880s concerned a corpus of this genre, itself strongly determined by the indications provided in the medieval recensions such as those of Nasîr at-Din at-Tûsî and of the author known as pseudo-Tûsî.[55]

The 'global/local' distinction is necessary because of the question of the proofs. It is easy to identify the phenomenon of double proofs. Generally the second proofs are introduced by an indicator 'ἄλλως' ('in another way')

---

[52] I add that the information which I have gleaned about the medieval Arabic (and Hebrew) tradition is second-hand and depends on the accessibility of the publication or the goodwill with which my friends and colleagues have responded to my requests. Particular thanks are due to S. Brentjes, T. Lévy and A. Djebbar.

[53] A very literal version, directly translated from Greek into Latin in southern Italy during the thirteenth century, discovered and studied by J. Murdoch in 1966 and edited by H. L. L. Busard in 1987.

[54] See Brentjes 2001: 39–41 and De Young 2004: 313–19. Other information is likewise accessible, thanks to the Greek or Arabic commentators, as well as through the scholia in Greek and Arabic manuscripts.

[55] See Rommevaux, Djebbar and Vitrac 2001: 235–8 and 284–5.

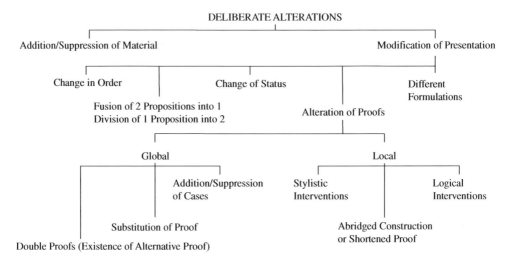

Figure 1.2 Euclid's *Elements*. Typology of deliberate structural alterations.

or 'ἢ καὶ οὕτως …' ('Or, also thus …').[56] In the same way, in the Arabo-Latin translation of Gerard of Cremona, the great majority of the second proofs are explicitly presented as such, thanks to indications of the type '*in alio libro … invenitur*' ('in another book is found …'). On the other hand the identification of proofs as distinct is much more delicate when it is a question of comparing two solitary proofs appearing in different versions – for example, when one compares a proof from a Greek manuscript and its corresponding proof in the Arabic translation, or one from Adelard of Bath and the other from Gerard of Cremona. The intricacies of the manuscript transmission prevent two proofs which have only minimal variations from being considered as *truly different*. If this were not so, there would be as many proofs of a Proposition as there are versions or, even, manuscripts!

This is why it has proven necessary to introduce the division between local and global. Ideally, it ought to be possible to identify the 'core argument' which characterizes a proof and to distinguish it from the type of 'packaging' which is stylistically or didactically relevant but which is neither mathematically nor logically essential. The expression 'substitution of proof' (global modification) will be reserved for those cases where there is a replacement of one core argument by another. The distinction between 'core' and 'packaging' is not always easy to establish, but it may be thought that the distinction will be better understood if the different methods of 'packaging' have been previously delineated. In other words, in order that

---

[56] Nonetheless, there are confusions. Thus, the addition at vi.27 is introduced as if it were an alternative proof (ἄλλως). See *EHS*: ii 231.2.

the category of *global* differences – that is, substitution of proof – be well defined, it is necessary also to propose a typology[57] of changes for which I will reserve the qualifier *local* (see the figure 1.1 above).

Let us also give a few explanations or examples for the variations for which the designation is perhaps not immediately apparent:

- There is a doubling when a Proposition concerning two Cases is replaced by two distinct, consecutive Propositions. This expansion is observed in the indirect medieval tradition for x.31 and 32, xi.31 and 34. The inverse operation is fusion. Of course, these alterations are not the same as the substitution of a proof. Thus, the *doubling* might correspond to a logical or (in the case of very long proofs) pedagogical concern. Even stylistic concerns might be represented, but they would not alter the mathematical content of the proofs.
- The change of status may, for example, affect a Porism (corollary). This is the case of the Porism to Heib. x.72, transformed into an independent Proposition in the indirect medieval tradition. According to another example, the (apocryphal) principle that 'two lines do not contain an area' is presented as Postulate No. 6 in some of the Greek manuscripts (*PF*), in the translation by al-Hajjâj[58] and in the work of Adelard, but as Common Notion No. 9 in another part (*BVb*) of the direct tradition, in the translation of Ishâq–Thâbit, and in the work by Gerard of Cremona.
- There is, for example, a different formulation in Proposition ii.14. The translations of al-Hajjâj and the Adelardian tradition propose to present the quadrature of a triangle, while the Greek manuscripts, the Ishâq–Thâbit and Gerard of Cremona translations undertake the quadrature of an unspecified rectilinear figure. This is related to another category of variations represented by the absence of Proposition i.45 in the first group of witnesses just mentioned. In the same way, the Porism to vi.19 is formulated differently in the manuscript *P* (for a figure) and in the manuscript *Th* (for a triangle). Here, too, the variant is connected with the existence of the Porism to vi.20, No. 2 (for a figure), found in only the so-called Theonine manuscripts. The divergences may thus be correlated at long range.
- As for the local variants with some possible logical and pedagogical purpose, we will see some examples in what follows. Let us specify only those which approach the category 'abridged demonstrations'. This category concerns the use of proofs described as analogical proofs (AP) and

---

[57] See this point introduced in Euclid/Vitrac 2001: iv 41–69, in particular the chart on p. 55.
[58] See De Young 2002–3: 134.

potential proofs (PP) introduced by the formulae: 'So also for the same reasons …' (= 'διὰ τὰ αὐτὰ δὴ καὶ …') (AP), 'Similarly we will prove (alternatively, it will be shown) that …' (= 'ὁμοίως δὴ δείξομεν (alternatively, δειχθήσεται) ὅτι…') (PP). These phrases refer to the desire to shorten the text. The first is the equivalent of our *mutatis mutandis*; it allows the omission of a completely similar argument with a particular figure or elements from a different figure. The second is a false 'prophecy'. It is invoked precisely not to have to prove in detail what it introduces.

The 'abbreviated' proofs are not uncommon in the *Elements* (they number about 250), but in certain cases, it is easy to imagine that a later editor has used this Euclidean stylistic convention to abridge his text. It is rather striking that the Arabo-Latin versions are on the whole much more concise than the Greek text and sometimes have complete proofs, where the latter uses one of the formulae just cited. In Proposition xii.6, the version carried by manuscript *P* uses a potential proof ('δειχθήσεται'), whereas that of the so-called Theonine manuscripts advances an analogical proof ('διὰ τὰ αὐτὰ δή'). The appearance of these formulae is therefore not independent of the transmission of the text.[59]

Quantitative aspect

The 220 structural modifications in my database include: more than 60 Definitions of about 130, 8 of 11 Common Notions, 29 of 35 Porisms, 41 of 42 Lemmas and additions, 173 Propositions of 474 (actually, 465 in the Greek tradition) which is a little more than a third of the total.[60] These modifications are very unequally distributed through the Books, depending on the type of textual units. Taking a cue from medieval scholars, I have grouped together the principal global variations according to three (not completely, but almost) independent criteria:

(a) The presence or absence of certain portions of the text (35 Definitions, 8 Common Notions, 27 Porisms, 41 Lemmas and additions, 25 Propositions).
(b) A change in the order of presentation. There are roughly 30 which relate to about 30 Definitions and more than 60 Propositions.
(c) The (structural) alteration of proofs. For now, I have listed about 80 which concern a little fewer than 100 Propositions.[61]

---

[59] For other examples, see the references given in Euclid/Vitrac 2001: iv 46–7, n. 51, 53.
[60] Some relate to a group of Propositions, for a total greater than 220.
[61] See Vitrac 2004: 40–2.

In comparing Heiberg's text with the text of the Arabo-Latin translations by Adelard of Bath and by Gerard of Cremona, I have noted (at least) three textual dichotomies (in decreasing order of importance):[62]

> Dichotomy 1: Edition Heiberg ($\cup P$) *versus* medieval tradition
> (existence of 18 Definitions, 12 Propositions, 19 Porisms, all the additional material (!), numerous changes in order, the majority of substitutions of proofs)
>
> Dichotomy 2 (in Books I–x): Adelardian tradition *versus* Gerard of Cremona translation (al-Hajjâj / Ishâq–Thâbit?)[63]
> (existence of 16 Definitions, 10 Propositions, 2 Porisms, some changes in order, double proofs in GC)
>
> Dichotomy 3: *P versus* **Th**
> (existence of 3 Propositions, 2 Porisms, 3 additions, 2 inversions of Definitions, several modifications)

To return to certain elements from our first part, the Heiberg edition is founded on Dichotomy 3. The Danish editor refused to account for Dichotomy 1 demonstrated by Klamroth. Knorr finally proposed an interpretation somewhat similar to that of Heiberg. His interpretation was linear and consisted of two terms (pre-Theonine/Theonine), simply replacing *P* with the hypothetical Greek archetype which he believed possible to reconstruct for the medieval tradition. Taking into account the information at his disposal, Heiberg was not able to identify Dichotomy 2. Knorr appears to have ignored it, which is at the very least surprising, as he declared that the Arabo-Latin versions which he used (Adelard and Gerard) were neither divergent, nor contaminated. This break in the indirect tradition in Books I–x dashes hopes of reconstructing a common archetype for the indirect medieval tradition.[64] As for the local variants, they number in the hundreds, probably amounting to 1000–1500 and concerning about 80 per cent of the Propositions in the Greek text. It might be thought that a single instance of an analogical proof or a simple stylistic intervention in a Proposition is hardly significant. If examples of this type are disregarded, 70 per cent of the Propositions from the Euclidean treatise nonetheless

---

[62] For details, see the three tables given in the Appendix.

[63] Accounting for the Arabo-Latin versions adds a supplementary difficulty from my point of view (to return to the Greek) since it is a doubly indirect tradition. But the structural divergences which we observe between Adelard of Bath and Gerard of Cremona nearly always find an explanation in their Arabic precursors, in particular in the differences between al-Hajjâj and Thâbit, as they are described – for right or wrong – by the copyists, commentators and authors of the recension (for example at-Tûsî).

[64] It is particularly clear in Book x; see Rommevaux, Djebbar and Vitrac 2001: 252–70.

remain, the difference being especially apparent in the arithmetical Books VII–VIII, as a matter of fact more 'salvaged' by these variants than the geometric portions, in particular Book X and the stereometric Books.

An example of a local variant

The rather simple example which I propose is that of Proposition XI.1. It shows how accounting for the indirect medieval tradition allows us to go beyond the confrontation between *P* and *Th* to which Heiberg was confined. The codicological primacy which he accords to the Vatican manuscript is not inevitable because all Greek manuscripts, including *P*, have been subjected to various late enrichments. It also probably indicates the intention of these specific additions.

As with several other initial proofs in the stereometric books, in XI.1 Euclid tries to demonstrate a property he probably would have been better off accepting (i.e. as a postulate) – namely, the fact that a line which has some part in a plane is contained in the plane.[65] Here, the philological aspect interests me, even though the changes in the text were probably the result of the perception of an insufficiency in the proof. The text is as follows:

(a)

Εὐθείας γραμμῆς μέρος μέν τι οὐκ ἔστιν ἐν τῷ ὑποκειμένῳ ἐπιπέδῳ, μέρος δέ ἐν μετεωροτέρῳ.	Some part of a straight line is not in a subjacent plane and another part is in a higher plane.

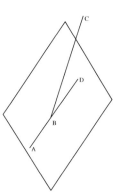

Εἰ γὰρ δυνατόν, εὐθείας γραμμῆς τῆς ΑΒΓ μέρος μέν τι τὸ ΑΒ ἔστω ἐν τῷ ὑποκειμένῳ ἐπιπέδῳ, μέρος δέ τι τὸ ΒΓ ἐν μετεωροτέρῳ.	For, if possible, let some part AB of the straight line ABC be in the subjacent plane, another part, BC, in a higher plane.
Ἔσται δέ τις τῇ ΑΒ συνεχὴς εὐθεῖα ἐπ' εὐθείας ἐν τῶν ὑποκειμένῳ ἐπιπέδῳ.	There will then exist in the subjacent plane some straight line continuous with AB in a straight line.
ἔστω ἡ ΒΔ· δύο ἄρα εὐθειῶν τῶν ΑΒΓ, ΑΒΔ κοινὸν τμῆμά ἐστιν ἡ ΑΒ· ὅπερ ἐστὶν ἀδύνατόν,	Let it be BD; therefore, of the two straight lines ABC and ABD, the common part is AB; which is impossible,

---

[65] On the weaknesses of the foundations of the Euclidean stereometry, see Euclid/Vitrac, 4, 2001: 31 and my commentary to Prop. XI.1, 2, 3, 7.

(b) Then the two textual families distinguished by Heiberg diverge:

P	ἐπειδήπερ ἐὰν κέντρῳ τῷ Β καὶ διαστήματι τῷ ΑΒ κύκλον γράψωμεν, αἱ διάμετροι ἀνίσους ἀπολήψονται τοῦ κύκλου περιφερείας.	Because, if we describe a circle with the centre B and distance AB, the diameters will cut unequal arcs of the circle
BFVb	εὐθεῖα γαρ εὐθεῖα οὐ συμβάλλει κατὰ πλείομα σημεῖα ἢ καθ' ἕν· εἰ δὲ μή, ἐφαρμόσουσιν ἀλλήλαις αἱ εὐθεῖαι.	for a straight line does not meet a straight line in more points than one; otherwise the lines will coincide.

(c) The general conclusion follows, then the closing of the theorem:

Εὐθείας ἄρα γραμμῆς μέρος μέν τι οὐκ ἔστιν ἐν τῷ ὑποκειμένῳ ἐπιπέδῳ, μέρος δέ ἐν μετεωροτέρῳ·	Therefore, it is not the case that some part of a straight line is in a subjacent plane and another part is in a higher plane.
ὅπερ ἔδει δεῖξαι.[66]	Which is what was to be proved.

Conforming to the general rule which he follows, Heiberg has retained the reading of *P* in his text, and he consigns the reading of the Theonine manuscripts in his *apparatus criticus*.[67] From the stylistic point of view, one can see that:

- The two variants are what I call *post-factum* explanations because they have the form '*q*, because *p*', rather than 'if *p*, then *q*'. The 'cause' (*p*) is stated after the fact (*q*) of which it is supposed to be the cause.[68]
- The variant *P* is introduced by the conjunction 'ἐπειδήπερ', which is sufficient to arouse suspicions about its authenticity.[69] Moreover, I call what appears here an 'active, personal, conjugated form' ('γράψωμεν') since the normal Euclidean form of conjugation in the portion of the deductive argument is the middle voice,[70] which reinforces the suspicion of inauthenticity.

---

[66] See *EHS*: IV: 4.8–5.3.

[67] This same variant appears in the margin of *P*, but by a later hand, followed by the addition: 'οὕτως ἐν ἄλλοις εὕρηται, ἔπειτα τὸ· εὐθείας ἄρα γραμμῆς' (alternatively, this is found in other [copies]: 'Of a straight line …').

[68] See Euclid/Vitrac 2001: IV 50, 56, 67–9.

[69] There exist, in the text of Book XII as edited by Heiberg, about fifteen passages introduced by the conjunction 'ἐπειδήπερ', all of which contain elementary explanations found neither in manuscript *b*, nor in the Arabo-Latin translations by Adelard of Bath and by Gerard of Cremona. In the whole of the *Elements*, 38 instances occur. As already indicated by Knorr 1996: 241–2, we know that there are relatively late interpolations in manuscripts used by Heiberg. *A posteriori*, we can see that Heiberg considered seven of these passages interpolations on the basis of criteria other than their absence in manuscript *b* and the indirect tradition.

[70] See Euclid/Vitrac, 2001: IV 47.

Let us now consult the indirect medieval tradition, for example the Arabo-Latin translation by Gerard of Cremona,[71] compared to parts (a) and (c) of the text edited by Heiberg:

Parts (a) and (c) of Heiberg's text	Gerard of Cremona's version
Εὐθείας γραμμῆς μέρος μέν τι οὐκ ἔστιν ἐν τῷ ὑποκειμένῳ ἐπιπέδῳ, μέρος δέ τι ἐν μετεωροτέρῳ.	Recte linee pars non est una in superficie et pars alia in alto.

	Quoniam non est possibile ut ita sit, quod in exemplo declarabo.
Εἰ γὰρ δυνατόν, εὐθείας γραμμῆς τῆς ΑΒΓ μέρος μέν τι τὸ ΑΒ ἔστω ἐν τῷ ὑποκειμένῳ ἐπιπέδῳ, μέρος δέ τι τὸ ΒΓ ἐν μετεωροτέρῳ.	Si ergo possibile fuerit, sit pars linee ABG que est AB in superficie posita et sit alia pars que est BG in alto.
Ἔσται δέ τις τῇ ΑΒ συνεχὴς εὐθεῖα ἐπ' εὐθείας ἐν τῷ ὑποκειμένῳ ἐπιπέδῳ.	Protaham ergo a linea AB in data superficie lineam coniunctam linee AB
ἔστω ἡ ΒΔ· δύο ἄρα εὐθειῶν τῶν ΑΒΓ, ΑΒΔ κοινὸν τμῆμά ἐστιν ἡ ΑΒ·	que sit BD. Linea ergo ABG est linea recta et linea ABD est linea recta, ergo linea AB duabus lineis BG et BD secundum rectitudinem coniungitur.
ὅπερ ἐστὶν ἀδύνατόν.	Quod est omnino contrarium.
Εὐθείας ἄρα γραμμῆς μέρος μέν τι οὐκ ἔστιν ἐν τῷ ὑποκειμένῳ ἐπιπέδῳ, μέρος δέ ἐν μετεωροτέρῳ·	Non est ergo linee recte pars in superficie et pars in alto.
ὅπερ ἔδει δεῖξαι.	Et illus est quod demonstrare voluimus.

Despite the Arabic intermediary, the reader will easily recognize the faithfulness of this Latin translation to the Greek, with two exceptions:

- the Latin adds a clause intended to introduce an indirect reasoning (a systematic characteristic shared with several manuscripts of the Ishâq–Thâbit translation)
- it has neither of the *post-factum* explanations of the Greek (part b).

[71] Busard 1984: 338–9.

It is possible to imagine (at least) two scenarios: either these post-factum explanations are inauthentic, or the translator (or the editor Thâbit), noting the divergence among the Greek manuscripts and the deficiency of the proposed explanations, refrained from retaining one or the other. In other words, he has 'cleaned up' the text.

The mathematical deficiency of the explanation in *P* is obvious. It allows the points ABCD to be co-planar. In order to prove the co-planarity of lines ABC and ABD starting from the fact that they are secant (they even have a segment in common), one would have to use XI.2 – which in turn invokes XI.1! Thus, and this is Heiberg's reading, an argument akin to *lectio difficilior* may be implemented and the text of the Theonine manuscripts may be declared an improvement. Hence, his editorial decision. This scenario is hardly likely.

In fact, in certain manuscripts of the *Th* family, particularly *V*, there exists a scholium proposing a proof of the impossibility of two straight lines having a common segment, that is the concluding point of our indirect proof: [72]

For two straight lines, there is no common segment. Thus, for the two straight lines ABC and ABD, let AB be a common segment, and on the straight line ABC, let B be taken as the centre and let BA be the radius and let circle AEZ be drawn. Then, since B is the centre of the circle AEZ and since a straight line ABC has been drawn through the point B, line ABC is thus a diameter of the circle AEZ. Now, the diameter cuts the circle in two. Thus AEC is a semi-circle. Then, since point B is the centre of circle AEZ and since straight line ABD passes through point B, line ABD is thus a diameter of circle AEZ. However, ABC has also been demonstrated to be a diameter of the same AEZ. Now semi-circles of the same circle are equal to each other. Therefore, the semi-circle AEC is equal to semi-circle AED, the smallest to the largest. This is impossible. Thus, for the two straight lines, there is no common segment. Therefore, [they are completely] distinct. From that starting point, it is no longer possible to continuously prolong the lines by any given line, but [only] a [given] line and, that because, as has been shown, [namely] that for two straight lines, there is no common segment.

This scholium does not exist in *P*, but its absence may be explained if it is the origin of the *post-factum* explanation, albeit in severely abbreviated form, inserted in the text of the manuscript. Thus, there was no longer need to recopy the aforementioned scholium. It is likely that the explanations appearing in the Theonine manuscripts come from the insertion of an abridgment of some (another) scholium into the text. There is even a chance that we know the source of these marginal annotations. In his commentary to Proposition I.1, Proclus reports an objection by the Epicurean Zenon of

---

[72] Cf. *EHS*: v, 2, 243.27–244.22.

Sidon. The Euclidean proof of i.1 presupposes that there is not a common segment for two distinct straight lines,[73] precisely what is here declared to be impossible. The commentator denies the objection, using three arguments, the first and last of which are close to the contents of the two *post-factum* explanations (in **Th** and **P** respectively), as well as to the scholia.[74]

In this example, there is every reason to believe that the first scenario was the better one, that the 'Euclidean' proof of xi.1 was similar to that of the indirect tradition. Heiberg could not have known the Gerard of Cremona translation (discovered by A. A. Björnbo at the beginning of the twentieth century), but he could have consulted Campanus's edition, which has neither of the *post-factum* explanations.

It goes without saying that the difference, from a mathematical point of view, is minuscule. However, from the point of view of the history and use of the text, it is the number of alterations of this type – in the hundreds[75] – which is significant. Additions like those which we have just seen regarding xi.1 have been introduced on different occasions, undoubtedly independently of each other, since each version – including the Arabo-Latin translations which escape nearly uncorrupted by this phenomenon – has some which are proper to it.[76] This work of improvement undoubtedly owes much to the marginal annotations eventually integrated into the text itself. Yet it partially blurs the distinction between 'text' and 'commentary'.

For the majority of them, these additions ensure the 'saturation' of the text. The interpretation of the *Elements* which the annotators presuppose is more logical than mathematical. Indeed, for them, Euclid's text represents the very apprenticeship of deduction more than a means for the acquisition of the fundamental results of geometry. Even if the role of the marginal annotations has probably been less effective in the case of structural divergences, we will see that the purpose which they pursue – when it can be determined – is frequently the same.

From the point of view of the history of the text, the abundance of these sometimes independent improvements implies that for the *Elements* and for certain other mathematical texts the methods of transmission were much more flexible than those postulated by philologists whose model rests on the tradition of poetic texts. It is not possible either to put the different examples of a text in a linearly ordered schema (*stemma*) or even to admit the simple primacy accorded to a manuscript, such as Heiberg accorded to **P**. Clearly,

---

[73] See Friedlein 1873: 215.11–13, 215.15–16.

[74] See Friedlein 1873: 215. 17–216. 9.

[75] For example, about 600 sentences are intended to point out a hypothesis or what was the object of a previous proof. About twenty terminological explanations, mostly in Book x, may be added.

[76] See Euclid/Vitrac 2001: iv 63.

in the discussion of problematic places, variant readings of the indirect medieval tradition ought to be accounted for. This was exactly what Knorr recommended. He even thought that it was possible to reconstruct a Greek archetype for the whole of the medieval tradition.

In other words, by comparing the different states of the text for each attested divergence, we ought to be able to identify the least inauthentic version (or versions). Taking into account the three principal types of structural variants that we have recognized, this amounts to:

- solving the question of authenticity for each contested textual unit (the determination of the 'materiel' contained there)
- selecting a method of presentation (in particular, an order) when several are known; and
- knowing, for the cases of substitution or double proofs, which of the two is older.

To pronounce such judgements supposes criteria. There are essentially two of them:

(i) the first concerns the 'quantity' of material transmitted by various versions, and
(ii) the second bears on the form of this material (order of presentation, modification of proofs).

These criteria rest on the presuppositions that the historians accept regarding the nature of the text of the *Elements* and on the hypotheses that they imagine regarding its transmission. According to Klamroth (and Knorr), the textual history has essentially been an amplification. Thus, for example, except by accident, a Proposition missing from a 'thin' version (containing less material than another or even several others) will be judged inauthentic.

As for the transformations of form, if it is not an accident of transmission but a deliberate alteration of the structure of the text (supposing that it is possible to discriminate between the two), the criterion, as stated explicitly by W. Knorr, will be improvement – that is, whether it met with success or failure, whether it was really justified or invalid, the deliberate modification of the form (order, proof) of the text sought to better the composition. Obviously, this is an optimistic vision of the history of mathematics.

To see how to apply these principles and to understand the nature of the structural modifications that we have called up, it is easiest to produce some examples. The limitations of the aforementioned criteria will appear more clearly when we examine their application to the proofs (see below, pp. 111–13).

Questions of authenticity and the logical architecture of the *Elements*

If the different versions are considered from the point of view of the 'material contents', the question of authenticity is perhaps the least complex of the three, at least as far as the first dichotomy is concerned. There exists in the Greek manuscripts material which I describe as 'additional'. This additional material includes cases, some portions identified as additions, the double proofs, and the Lemmas.[77] The critical edition of Heiberg, completed in 1888, four years after the debate with Klamroth, condemns the lot of this material as inauthentic. In this regard, the (rather relative) thinness of **P** compared with the other Greek manuscripts is one of the criteria which justifies its greater antiquity.[78] Now this additional material, to nearly a single exception,[79] is absent from the medieval Arabic and Arabo-Latin tradition. However, Heiberg did not alter his position and did not accept this conclusion about the 'thinness' of the indirect tradition as a gauge of its purity. According to Heiberg – and this too is a hypothesis about the nature of the treatise – the *Elements* could not be so thin that it suffered from deductive lacunae, but such thinness is the case with the medieval versions.

I do not believe that anyone (and certainly not Klamroth or Knorr) contested the global deductive structure of the *Elements*. If the *Elements* is compared with the geometric treatises of Archimedes or Apollonius, the local 'texture' may not be so different, but the principal variation resides in the fact that the *Elements* was edited as if it supposed no previous geometric knowledge. The identification of what would be a deductive lacuna in Euclid is thus a crucial point, but not always a simple one. Indeed, all the exegetical history of the Euclidean treatise, from antiquity until David Hilbert, has shown that the logical progression of the *Elements*, probably like any geometric text composed in natural language, rests on implicit presuppositions.[80] The identification of the deductive lacunae supposes that consciously permitted 'previous knowledge' is always capable of clearly being distinguished from 'implicit presumption'.

Let us take the example of Proposition xii.15. Here it is established that:

The bases of equal cones and cylinders are inversely [proportional] to the heights; and among the cones and cylinders, those in which the bases are inversely [proportional] to the heights are equal,

---

[77] For details, see Table 1 of the Appendix.
[78] See Table 3 of the Appendix.
[79] The addition of special cases in Prop. iii.35, 36 and 37.
[80] See the beautiful study by Mueller 1981.

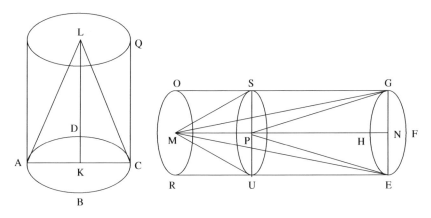

Figure 1.3   Euclid's *Elements*, **Proposition xii.15.**

a property likewise shown for the parallelepipeds (xi.34) and pyramids
(xii.9).

In the first part of the proof, let us suppose the cones or cylinders on
bases ABCD and EFGH, with heights KL and MN, are equal. If KL is not
equal to MN, NP equal to KL is introduced and the cone (or cylinder) on
base EFGH with height NP is considered (see Figure 1.3).

Schematically, in abbreviated notation, we have (by v.7) a trivial
proportion:

cylinder AQ = cylinder EO ⇒ cylinder AQ: cylinder ES:: cylinder EO:
cylinder ES

in which a substitution is made for each of the two ratios:

cylinder AQ: cylinder ES:: base ABCD: base EFGH   (which is justified
by xii.11)

cylinder EO: cylinder ES:: height MN: height PN (**S**).
From which: base ABCD: base EFGH:: height MN: height PN (CQFD)

However, the proportion (**S**) is an 'implicit presumption' in the Arabo-
Latin versions. Admittedly, it may be easily deduced by those who understand Propositions vi.1 and 33, as well as xi.25, that is the way one employs
the celebrated Definition v.5. In the Greek manuscripts, though, the
situation is different. Proportion (**S**) is justified on the basis of previous
knowledge: xii.13 in **P** and *Th*, xii.14 in **b**.[81] These Propositions xii.13–14
do not exist in the indirect medieval tradition and thus it may be inferred

---

[81] Here, the indirect medieval tradition is not in accord with ms **b** which presents the most
satisfying textual state from the deductive point of view! For details, see Euclid/Vitrac 2001: iv
334–44.

from their absence, as Heiberg has done, that there is a deductive 'lacuna' in the proof of xii.15. However, from the point of view of the history of the text, the question immediately arises about whether or not the insertion of Propositions xii.13–14 represents an addition aimed at filling a lacuna perceived in the original proof of xii.15. Let us add that the assertions of Heiberg on this subject are often a little hasty because the status of authenticity cannot be judged independently of the status of the proofs.

For example, the indirect tradition does not contain Proposition x.13 ('If two magnitudes be commensurable and one of them be incommensurable with any magnitude, the remaining one will also be incommensurable with the same'). Heiberg suggests that the absence of this Proposition introduces deductive lacunae in several Propositions which exist in the Arabic translations. In these Propositions, the Greek text explicitly uses x.13. However, in fact, when the proofs in the aforementioned translations are examined, they are formulated a little differently than in Greek and x.12 ('Magnitudes commensurable with the same magnitude are commensurable with one another too') is employed in place of x.13. Consequently, there is not a deductive lacuna![82] By consulting the indirect tradition of Greek citations in Pappus, the idea may be supported that x.13 did not exist in his version of the *Elements*.[83] Thus, the most natural conclusion is that x.13 is effectively an inauthentic addition and its addition has allowed reconsideration of the proofs of the other Propositions.

Through a simple comparison of the different versions, I have examined each of the Propositions whose authenticity has been called into question. My conclusion regarding this point – the details would exceed the scope of this essay – is that the real deductive lacunae, proper to the indirect tradition, are, so far as can be judged, far from numerous:

• Two in Book xii,[84] with the provision that in any event the stereometric Books constitute a particular case in the transmission of the *Elements* (see below).

---

[82] See Vitrac 2004: 25–6.

[83] See Euclid/Vitrac 1998: iii 384–5.

[84] The second is due to the absence, this time in *b* as well as in the indirect medieval tradition, of Proposition xii.6 and the Porisms to xii.7–8 which generalize the results established for pyramids on a triangular base to pyramids on an unspecified polygonal base, respectively in Propositions xii.5, 7 and 8. There also, Euclid may have considered this generalization as intuitively obvious given the decomposition of all polygons into triangles and the rule concerning proportions established in (Heib.) v.12: 'If any number of magnitudes be proportional, as one of the antecedents is to one of the consequents, so will all the antecedents be to all the consequents.' The non-thematization of pyramids on an unspecified polygonal base is comparable to what we have seen above regarding ii.14 (triangle unspecified rectilinear figure) in only the Adelardo-Hajjajian tradition. The difference is that it introduces a deductive

- One in Proposition iv.10 of the Adelardo-Hajjajian tradition, connected to the absence of iii.37, probably due to an accident in transmission, namely, the mutilation of the end of a Greek (or possibly Syriac?) scroll containing Book iii.

Books i–x, perhaps the only ones to have been both translated by Ishâq and reworked by Thâbit,[85] contain no supplementary deductive lacunae. In other words, the deductive lacunae which appear there already existed in the Greek text which served as their model. The most striking case is that of the Lemmas designed to fill what can be regarded as a 'deductive leap', especially in Book x.[86] In fact, there are in (some manuscripts of) the Ishâq–Thâbit and Gerard of Cremona translations a number of additions that fulfil the same role of completion.[87] When compared with the direct tradition, they are presented as additions, mathematically useful, but well distinguished from the Euclidean text. Those who composed our Greek manuscripts had no such scruples.

The addition of the so-called missing propositions and part of the additional material (Lemmas of deductive completion, some of the Porisms) serve with a certain fluidity the obvious intention of improving the proofs and reinforcing the deductive structure. The second part of the Porism to x.6 allows the resolution of the same problem as the lemma {x.29/30}. The Proposition xi.38 *vulgo* is clearly a lemma to xii.17. The Proposition was probably inspired by a marginal scholium and then moved to the end of Book xi.[88] The textual variants of xii.6 suggest that perhaps it was initially introduced as a Porism to xii.5 and eventually transformed into a Proposition. For the other additional Porisms, it would certainly be excessive to speak about a deductive lacuna to be filled. However, v.7 Por. and v.19 Por explicitly justify the use of inversion and conversion of ratios. The Porisms to vi.20, ix.11, xi.35 serve to *make explicit* a deductive dependence on the Propositions x.6 Por., ix.12 and xi.36, respectively. Our examples, found in Books x–xii, show that this work of enrichment began in the Greek tradition, but the Arabic and Arabo-Latin versions tell us that the

---

lacuna in the proofs of Propositions xii.10–11. Here the properties established previously for pyramids and prisms are shown for cones and cylinders, by using the method of exhaustion. To do this, the pyramids are considered as having polygonal bases with an arbitrary number of sides, inscribed in the circular bases of the cones and cylinders.

[85] See below, pp. 116–19.

[86] I have called them the 'lemmas of deductive completion' in order to distinguish them from lemmas with only a pedagogical use. See the list given in Euclid/Vitrac 1998:iii 391. To these might be added Lemma xii.4/5.

[87] See Euclid/Vitrac 1998: iii 392–4.

[88] See Euclid/Vitrac 2001: iv 229–30.

enrichment was not confined to the final, more complicated portion of the text in question.

It is even probable that the entire treatise has been subjected to such treatment. For example, the arithmetic books of the Ishâq–Thâbit and Gerard of Cremona versions possess four supplementary Propositions with respect to the Greek. Ishâq–Thâbit ix.30–31 are added to improve (Heib.) ix.30–31, and Ishâq–Thâbit viii.24–25 are the converses of (Heib.) viii.26–27. In fact, the proof of (Ishâq–Thâbit) viii.24 (plane numbers) is nothing more than the second part of (Heib.) ix.2! Hence the idea, again suggested by Heron, to remove this portion in order to introduce it as a Proposition in its own right and to do the same for the converse of viii.27 (solid numbers) to simplify the proof of ix.2.[89]

Insofar as the Euclidean approach is deductive, the work just described represents a real improvement of the text as much from a logical perspective as from a mathematical point of view. A number of implicit presumptions which might be described as harmless but real deductive lacunae have been identified and eliminated. However, the logical concerns have been sometimes pushed beyond what is reasonable. For example, in the desire to make the contrapositives appear in the text, Propositions viii.24–27 in the Ishâq–Thâbit version expect the reader to know that two numbers are similar plane numbers if and only if they have the ratio that a square number has to a square number to one another. The Lemma x.9/10 – an addition probably connected to Ishâq–Thâbit viii.24–25 – thence deduces that non-similar plane numbers do not have the ratio that a square number has to a square number to one another.

Likewise, the (important) Propositions x.5–6 establish that the 'commensurable magnitudes have to one another the ratio which a number has to a number' (5) and the inverse (6). In the Greek manuscripts, but not in the primary indirect tradition, two other Propositions (Heib.) x.7–8 have been inserted: 'Incommensurable magnitudes have not to one another the ratio which a number has to a number' (7, contrapositive of 6) and its inverse (8, contrapositive of 5)!

Propositions viii.14–15 show that 'if a square (resp. cube) [number] measures a square (resp. cube) [number], the side will also measure the side; and, if the side measures the side, the square (resp. cube) will also measure the square (resp. cube)'. In the Greek manuscripts these Propositions are followed by their contrapositives (Heib. viii.16–17, for example): 'If a square number does not measure a square number, neither

[89] See Vitrac 2004: 25.

will the side measure the side; and, if the side does not measure the side, neither will the square measure the square.' If the indirect tradition is consulted, an interesting division is observed:

- In the translation of Ishâq–Thâbit the contrapositives do not exist, but each of the Propositions VIII.14–15 is followed by a Porism which expresses the same thing.[90]
- In the translation of al-Hajjâj[91] and in the Adelardian tradition[92] is found a single Proposition combining the equivalent of Heib. VIII.16–17. The assertion about cube numbers is simply left as a potential proof.
- Gerard of Cremona transmits the two version successively.[93]

I think there is hardly any doubt in this case. The Propositions VIII.16–17 of the Greek manuscripts are inauthentic and all the versions, including those of the indirect tradition, contain augmentations or additions which proceed along different modalities and which are probably of Greek origin. Logical concerns have certainly played a role in the transmission of the text.[94]

The change in the order of VI.9–13

The examples that we have examined until now are rather simple in the sense that their motivations appear rather clearly to be the improvement of a defective proof (cf. XI.1), or filling a gap or explaining a deductive connection (supplementary material and Propositions). In a significant number of cases we have seen the advantages of taking into account the Arabic and Arabo-Latin indirect tradition. However, it ought not to be believed that this simplicity is always the case or that the indirect tradition systematically presents us with the state of the text least removed from the original. As we have already seen regarding the supplementary Propositions, the alteration of Books X–XIII is especially clear in the Greek, although among the

---

[90] See De Young 1981: 151, 154–5, 431, 435.

[91] This we know thanks to Nâsir ad-Dîn at-Tûsî. See Lévy 1997: 233.

[92] See Busard 1983 (Prop. VIII. 15 *Ad. I*): 239.359–240.371.

[93] See Busard 1984, respectively, 201.11–16 (= VIII. 14 Por. GC), 202. 11–16 (= VIII.15 Por GC) and 202.19–40 (= VIII.16 GC).

[94] One might add here the supplementary Porism to Prop. IX.5 found in the Ishâq–Thâbit and Gerard of Cremona translations. IX.4 establishes that a cube, multiplied by a cube, yields a cube, and IX.5 states that if a cube, multiplied by a number, yields a cube, the multiplier was a cube. The Porism to IX.5 affirms that a cube, multiplied by a non-cube, yields a non-cube and that if a cube, multiplied by a number, yields a non-cube, the multiplier was a non-cube. In a subfamily of Ishâq–Thâbit manuscripts, this Porism has been moved after IX.4. In Gerard of Cremona, there is a Porism after IX.4 and one after IX.5! See De Young 1981: 201, n. 7, 202–3, 480–1 and Busard 1984 213.29–31 and 213.51–6.

Greek order	Medieval order
9: From a given straight line to cut off a prescribed part.	13: To two given straight lines to find a mean proportional.
10: To cut a given uncut straight line similarly to a given cut straight line.	11: To two given straight lines to find a third proportional.
11: To two given straight lines to find a third proportional.	12: To three given straight lines to find a fourth proportional.
12: To three given straight lines to find a fourth proportional.	9: From a given straight line to cut off a prescribed part.
13: To two given straight lines to find a mean proportional.	10: To cut a given uncut straight line similarly to a given cut straight line.

arithmetical books, the Ishâq–Thâbit version (itself inspired by Heron) is the best evidence of this 'betterment'. The consideration of changes in order confirms the complexity of the phenomenon. In Book vi, Propositions vi.9–13 (according to the numbers of the Heiberg edition), resolve the five problems listed in the table above.

In the indirect tradition, the order of presentation runs 13–11–12–9–10. The solutions of the problems are independent of each other. Thus the inversion has no influence on the deductive structure, but vi.13 uses (part of) vi.8 Por.:

From this it is clear that, if in a right-angled triangle a perpendicular be drawn from the right angle to the base, the straight line so drawn is a mean proportional between segments of the base.[95]

The Proposition has thus been moved in order to place it in contact with the used result. Since there are clearly two groups – one concerning proportionality, the other about sections – the coherence of the two themes has been maintained by also moving vi.11–12 (or, in the case of Adelard's translation, only vi.11 because it lacks vi.12 as a result of a 'Hajjajian' lacuna).[96] This order of the indirect tradition appears to be an improvement over the Greek.

[95] In the majority of Greek manuscripts, a second assertion declares that each side of a right angle is also the mean proportional between the entire base and one of the segments of it (which has a common extremity with the aforementioned side). It is absent in *V*, for example. Heiberg considered it inauthentic and bracketed it (see *EHS* ii: 57.1–3). Both parts exist in the Ishâq–Thâbit version and Adelard of Bath and Gerard of Cremona, but the complete Porism does not figure in the Leiden Codex (the an-Nayrîzî version). Moreover a scholium, attributed to Thâbit, explains that the Porism had not been found among the Greek manuscripts. Without a doubt, this is in error. In (at least) two mss of the Ishâq–Thâbit version, a gloss indicates that Thâbit had not found what corresponds to only the second part of the Porism (excised by Heiberg). See Engroff 1980: 28–9.

[96] This we know thanks to the recension of pseudo-Tûsî. See Lévy 1997: 222–3.

When the various versions are considered,[97] the inversions are not the result of happenstance in binding or in later inexpert replacement of lost pages. As in our example, they leave practically all the deductive structure intact and they even improve it. Of course, not all the examples are equally simple, and the same principle clearly cannot be applied to the inversions in the Definitions, for which it seems that a criterion, which I call 'aesthetic' for lack of anything better, has prevailed. The evidence is divided but at this stage in my work, it seems to me that the preliminary conclusions about the orders conflict with what can be determined about the content.[98] Namely, for problems regarding order, notably in Books v–x, the indirect tradition received the greatest number of improvements!

Although changes in order may be limited, they are interesting because they have an advantage with respect to the authenticity or alteration of proofs. Such changes are hardly conducive to contamination. Admittedly, we have several remarks by Thâbit ibn Qurra affirming that he had found a different order of presentation in another manuscript,[99] but no one saw fit to reproduce the Propositions twice in each of the orders. In contrast, for the problems of authenticity, the contamination between textual families concerns the whole text, beginning particularly with the margins of the manuscripts. As for the substitutions of proofs, we will see that they are the cause, at least in part, of the phenomenon of double proofs.

From the substitution of proof to the phenomenon of double proofs: the example of x.105

The Propositions (Heib.) x.66–70 and 103–107 establish that the twelve types of irrational lines obtained through addition and subtraction distinguished by Euclid are stable with respect to commensurability. In the Greek version,

---

[97] Things are a little different at the level of individual manuscripts which have not been preserved though the accidents of transmission.

[98] For example, in the Greek, the order of the Propositions (Heib.) vii.21–22 (each the converse of the other) runs opposite to the order in medieval indirect tradition. The inversion has no influence on the deductive structure, but the proof of (Heib.) vii.21 uses vii. 20. It is probable this time that the inversion was made in the direct tradition, in order to make the two connected deductive theorems consecutive.

[99] For example, in Book vi which was just discussed. In (at least) three mss of the Ishâq–Thâbit version, the following gloss appears after (Ishâq–Thâbit) vi.9 = (Heib.) vi.13. 'Thâbit says: we have found, in certain Greek manuscripts, in the place of this Proposition, that which we have made the thirteenth.' Undoubtedly, the existence of *two* distinct orders ought to be understood as having been observed by the Editor among the Greek manuscripts which he consulted. (Thus, the change is Greek in origin.) The editor retained the better order (which was that already in al-Hajjâj). See Engroff 1980: 29, who mentions two mss. The gloss also exists in ms Tehran Malik 3586 (the oldest preserved copy of the Ishâq–Thâbit version), fo.75a. I thank A. Djebbar for this information.

two alternative proofs for Propositions x.105–106 are inserted at different places in the manuscripts.[100] Called here 'superficial' as opposed to the original 'linear' Greek proofs, they apply to and argue about rectangular areas. Let us explain this difference by an example, Proposition (Heib.) x.105:

A [straight line] commensurable with a minor straight line is a minor.

First proof in Greek[101]	*Aliter* in Greek = first proof in medieval tradition
Let AB be a minor straight line and CD commensurable with AB; I say that CD is also minor.	Let A be a minor straight line and B [be] commensurable with A; I say that B is minor.

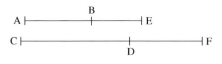

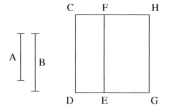

We will consider the two components (AE, EB) of AB and let DF be constructed so that (AB, BE, CD, DF) are in proportion. By vi.22, their squares will also be in proportion and, thence by x.11, x.23 Por. it will be shown (CD, DF) have the same properties as (AB, BE). Thus, by definition, CD will be a minor.	Let CD be a commensurate straight line. Let the rectangles be constructed: CE = square on A, width: CF, FG = square on B, width: FH. CE is the square on minor A so CE is the fourth apotome (x.100). We have Comm. (A, B). Thus: Comm. (CE, FG) and Comm. (CF, FH). FH is the fourth apotome (x.103). The square on B = Rect. (EF, FH), thus B is a minor (x.94)

- In each of the linear proofs, the argument concerns the two parts of an irrational straight line. The same type of argument is repeated ten times. Though repetitive, the approach has the advantage of not employing anything other than the Definitions of different types and the theory of

---

[100] In the Greek manuscripts the proof *aliter* to x.105–106 is inserted at the end of Book x, after the alternative proof to x.115, which without a doubt implies that they had been compiled in this place, after the transcription of Book x, in a limited space. Thus, they are in the margins of manuscripts **B** and **b**. In one of the prototypes of the tradition, x.107 *aliter* has been lost or omitted, probably for reasons of length, or because it was confused with x.117 *vulgo* which follows immediately (but which is mathematically unrelated).

[101] My diagrams are derived from those found in the edition of Heiberg (*EHS*: III 191 and 229, respectively). Those of the manuscripts are less general. The segments AE, CF are very nearly equal (the same goes for A, B in *aliter*) and divided similarly.

proportions. Deductively, the linear proofs may be characterized as minimalist.

• The superficial proofs introduce areas, which, from the point of view of the linguistic style used, might seem more geometric than the proofs using the theory of proportions, which is a second-order language. But, in fact, they strengthen the deductive structure because they establish new connections by using Propositions (Heib.) x.57–59 + 63–65 + 66 (resp. 94–96 + 100–102 + 103). In addition, these superficial proofs – like the linear ones – present results expressed for commensurability in length but the former proofs may be immediately generalized to commensurability in power.

The first anomaly occurs in x.107. No alternative proof exists, although this Proposition, along with two others, constitutes a triad of quite similar Propositions. Alternative proofs are no longer known for the parallel triad of x.68–70, which concerns the irrationals produced by addition, whereas the other triad x.105–107 treats the corresponding irrationals produced by subtraction.[102] However, in the indirect Arabic and Arabo-Latin tradition, there is a textual family in which these two triads of Propositions have (only) superficial proofs. This is the case in Arabic, with the recension of Avicenna, and in Latin, with the translation of Adelard I. Evidence from the copyist of the manuscript Esc. 907 establishes a link between the superficial proofs and the translation of al-Hajjâj.[103] The Ishâq–Thâbit version is less coherent. It contains the linear proofs of the Greek tradition in the triad x.68–70 and the superficial proofs for the triad x.105–107. In the manuscript from the Escorial and the translation of Gerard of Cremona, which agree on this point, the situation is nearly the inverse to the Greek translation. There are only the superficial proofs for x.105–107 (like the indirect tradition), but they present proofs of this type as *aliter* for the first triad, whereas the Greek texts includes them only for (two Propositions of) the second triad!

Let us add that the same type of substitution (and thus, generalization) is possible in Propositions (Heib.) x.67 + 104 which concern the two corresponding types of bimedials and apotomes of a bimedial.[104] Such substitution is precisely what is found in the recensions of at-Tûsî and pseudo-Tûsî, but not in the Arabic or Arabo-Latin translations.

---

[102] On the plan of Book x, see Euclid/Vitrac 1998: III 63–8.

[103] See De Young 1991: 659.

[104] However, this is not possible for Prop. Heib. x.66 (binomials) and 103 (apotomes) because, in this case, it is required to show that the order (from one to six) of the straight lines commensurable in length is the same. This crucial point is required for the superficial proofs concerning the other ten types of irrationals.

If the principle of improvement advanced by Knorr is applied, we are led to think that the linear proofs of the Greek are authentic, with the superficial proofs clearly being ameliorations from a mathematical point of view. This attempt at strengthening the deductive structure and generalizing was begun in Greek, as demonstrated by the proofs *aliter* to x.105–106. It is likely that there was also a proof *aliter* to x.107 which has disappeared. The opposite hardly makes any sense. Its disappearance is probably due to codicological reasons.

However, the question of knowing who produced the alternative proofs for the Propositions of the first triad remains unanswered. A likely hypothesis is that the same editor is responsible for the parallel modification of the two triads and he happened to be a Greek. But it could also be imagined that it was a contribution from the indirect tradition, occurring as the result of an initiative by al-Hajjâj. This latter explanation is the interpretation of Gregg De Young.[105] The examples of at-Tûsî and pseudo-Tûsî show that improvements continued into the medieval tradition, but it should not be forgotten that these were authors of recensions, not translators. As for the structure for the Ishâq–Thâbit version, it may be explained in different ways – either by the existence of a Greek model combining the two approaches or by an attempt at compromise on the part of the editor Thâbit. In the first case, there would have been at least three different states of the text. In the second case, Thâbit would have combined the first (linear) triad from the translation of Ishâq (considered closer to the Greek) and the second (superficial) triad presented in the earlier translation! In neither of these scenarios does recourse to the indirect tradition simplify the identification of the oldest proofs.

Whatever scenario is chosen, it must be admitted that there was a substitution of proofs in one branch of the tradition. The substitution occurred in the model(s) of al-Hajjâj, if the superficial proofs are considered later improvements, but in the Greek, if the opposite explanation is adopted. This fact is not surprising.[106] In the situations in which the Greek tradition contains double proofs, the medieval versions contain only one of them. (This is confirmed by the remarks of Thâbit and Gerard when they make such comments as 'in another copy, we have found …' and thus, probably, in Greek models of which we have no evidence.)

It is possible to take a lesson from this example. The existence of double proofs in the Byzantine manuscripts could be explained, for the majority of

---

[105] See De Young 1991: 660–1.

[106] It is noted for i.44p; ii.14; iii.7p, 8p, 25, 31, 33p, 35, 36; iv.5; v.5, 18; vi.9p, 20p, 31; viii.11p-12p; 22–23; x.1, 6, 14, 26p, 27–28, 29–30, 68–70, 105–107, 115; xi.30, xiii.5. The note 'p' signifies that the variant pertains only to a portion of the proof.

cases, by the fact that the aforementioned manuscripts have compiled the proofs from different versions which contained these proofs in isolation. If what we have seen about Propositions x.107 and x.68–70 is recalled, the process of transliteration and the desire to safeguard a flourishing tradition seems to us to constitute a propitious occasion for compiling proofs, however incomplete.

Returning to discussions concerning the history of the text, we ought to first note that the double proofs do not fall within what is called authorial variants. Euclid did not propose several proofs with the same results. Thus the Greek manuscripts closest to the operation of transliteration (**P** and **B**) are most likely the results of a compilation of the tradition, rather than of simple reproduction – changing only the writing – of a venerably aged model.[107]

The limits of Knorr's criteria

It is often possible to perceive one or more reasons for the other types of structural changes that I described earlier (additions, modifications of the order). Thus Knorr thought it possible to order the different states of the text, if not according to authenticity, then at least relative to the degree of alteration. We have already noted that this criterion of improvement applies locally, and the example of changes in the order suggested to us that it does not seem always to have been exercised for the benefit of the one and the same version. The phenomenon of the substitution of proofs evidences another difficulty.

The criterion of improvement works well enough as long as there is only a single parameter (or even more,[108] but all acting in the same direction) which governs the replacement of a proof or the modification of a presentation. But, when there are at least two acting in opposite directions, the change which is more *sophisticated* from a certain point of view may be less desirable from another point of view. Let us reconsider our example of Proposition x.105. Admittedly, from a mathematical point of view, there is an improvement (generalization), but from the logical, or metamathematical, point of view – and it is no doubt one of the points of view adopted by

---

[107] See n. 33.

[108] The most frequent parameters governing the replacement of proofs are the reinforcement of the deductive structure, the substitution of a direct proof with an indirect proof (a criterion notably explained by Heron – see Vitrac 2004: 17–18 (regarding iii.9 *aliter*) – and Menelaus), the addition of the case of a figure and the level of discourse used (geometric objects *versus* proportions; a criterion clearly noted by Pappus).

those who deliberately changed the text of the *Elements* – different criteria could be used. From the logical, or metamathematical, point of view, the criteria are:

- Render the deductive structure more dense, as the superficial proofs have done, or conversely minimize the structure in order not to introduce what would eventually become accidental 'causalities', that is, links of dependence, as found among the linear proofs.
- Prefer either a type of object language over a second-order language – that is, a relational terminology, like the theory of proportions – or, on the contrary, privilege a concise but more general second-order language. A choice of this kind explains the *aliter* family of proofs conceived for Propositions VI.20, 22, 31, X.9, XI.37.[109] The same choice exists also in our families of proofs, but in these instances it acts in the opposite direction with respect to reinforcing the deductive structure.

It would then be welcome to be able to organize these criteria hierarchically. The deductively minimalist attitude seems well represented in the *Elements*. For example, deductive minimalism may safely be assumed to underpin the decision to postpone as long as possible the intervention of the parallel postulate in Book I. It appears again in the decision to establish a number of results from plane geometry before the theory of proportions is introduced at the beginning of Book V, even though this theory would have allowed considerable abbreviation. The idea that geometry ought to restrict itself to a minimal number of principles had already been explained by Aristotle.[110] Deduction is not neglected, but emphasis is placed on the 'fertility' of the initial principles, rather than on the possible interaction of the resultants which are deduced from them.

There are thus different ways to put emphasis on the deductive structure. The case of our proofs from Book X is not unique. The ten Propositions from Book II and the first five from Book XIII are successively set out in a quasi-independent manner based on the least number of principles, even if this means reproducing several times certain portions of the arguments.[111] Remarkably, we know that for the sequences II.2–10 and XIII.1–5 alternative proofs had been elaborated, annulling this deductive mutual independence in order to construct a chain in the case of II.2–10 or to deduce XIII.1–5 from certain results from Books II and V. Even better, thanks to the testimony of

---

[109] See Vitrac 2004: 18–20.

[110] *De cælo*, III, 4, 302 b26–30.

[111] Similarly in the group *El.* III.1, 3, 9, 10 (considering the first proofs of III.9–10).

the Persian commentator an-Nayrîzî, we know that the author of the first suggestion was Heron of Alexandria. It is thus tempting, as Heiberg did in his *Paralipomena* of 1903, to attribute to him the other alteration (in XIII) that shares the same spirit.[112] If, in order to strengthen the deductive structure, it is appropriate to argue about segments rather than the surfaces described thereon as in the case of Books II and XIII,[113] it will be noted that the opposite is the case in the example from Book X which has just been discussed. Reinforcement of the aforementioned structure is realized through the introduction of surfaces. For us to attribute it to Heron, it is necessary to be sure that the parameter most important to him was indeed the densification of the deductive structure. Without any external confirmation or other historical information, as in the case of Books II and III, this scenario remains a stimulating hypothesis, but only a hypothesis![114]

Conclusions: contributions and limitations of the indirect tradition

From the study of a better-known indirect tradition, several lessons may be drawn. Newly available information confirms certain results of the Klamroth–Heiberg debate. Consideration of a greater number of versions of the *Elements* than Heiberg or Klamroth could have used reinforces the existence of a dichotomy between the direct and indirect traditions.

(1) Although they agree (albeit with opposite interpretations of the fact), the 'thinness' of the indirect tradition is not so marked as Klamroth and Heiberg would have us believe, especially in Books I–X. The most complete inventory of variants, probably Greek in origin, which we have now (by induction or thanks to information transmitted by Arab scholars or copyists), has several consequences:

   • It puts into perspective the different textual dichotomies. For example, No. 3 (*P* / *Th*), within the Greek direct tradition, is quite modest with

---

[112] See Heiberg 1903: 59. I have espoused the same hypothesis in Euclid/Vitrac 2001: IV 399–400.

[113] The insertion of III.10 *aliter*, explicitly attributed to Heron by an-Nayrîzî, has the same effect of strengthening the deductive structure.

[114] A single thing seems likely. The version of Euclid which Pappus had – if he is indeed the author of the second table of contents of Book X contained in the first Book of Commentary to the aforementioned book transmitted under his name – contained the linear proofs. In effect, Propositions X.60–65 and X.66–70 were inverted (similarly for X.97–102/103–107) and this fact precludes the existence of superficial proofs for X.68–70.

respect to No. 1 (direct tradition/indirect medieval tradition) or even to No. 2, within the Arabic and Arabo-Latin translations.[115]

- It convinces us that some part of what exists in Greek, and preserved by Heiberg in his edition, is very probably inauthentic.
- It gives a possible interpretation to some 'isolated' variants in Greek by integrating them into a broader picture which makes sense. For example, it makes sense of families of alternative proofs created by the same editorial principles.[116]

(2) However, because of the number of variants, the homogeneity of the entire indirect tradition, which Klamroth believed existed, no longer exists in Books I–X. I have called this dichotomy 2, within the Arabic, Arabo-Latin and, it seems, the Hebraic traditions. For certain portions, notably Books III, VIII and X, it seems that (at least) two rather structurally different editions existed and they contaminated each other significantly. Consequently, it will be impossible to reconstitute a unique Greek prototype for this portion of the whole of the medieval tradition as Knorr had wanted.[117]

If the study of the material contents, order, presentation, and proofs of the preserved versions of the thirteen books is resumed, it is not to be expected to find that among the preserved versions, one of them, for instance Adelard I or Ishâq–Thâbit, may be declared closer to the original in all its dimensions than all the other versions. The 'local' criteria used by Klamroth, Heiberg and Knorr, either focusing on the material contents (according to the principle of expansion) or on the improvement of the form, do not converge upon a global criterion which applies to the entirety of the collection of the thirteen books. The result is thus that the indirect tradition appears more authentic in regard to the material contents but not for the order of presentation. For the problems of order and of presentation, conversely, the indirect

---

[115] See Tables 1–3 of the Appendix.

[116] We have seen an example of this with the superficial proofs of x.105–106. Another family of double proofs may be reconstituted for Propositions VI. 20p, 22, 31, x.9, xi.37. See Vitrac 2004: 18–20.

[117] It should be emphasized that Knorr had not considered the problem at its full scale:

- He considered at most a group of 21 Propositions and proceeded by induction.
- He did not take into account more than one single criterion of structural divergence – that of material contents – with one exception: the proof of xii.17, poorly handled in the indirect tradition and interpreted not as an accident of transmission but in terms of development.
- He took into account neither changes in order nor the rich collection of double proofs.
- He did not ask himself the question of whether the two Arabo-Latin translations that he used, Adelard and Gerard, were representative of the whole of the indirect tradition. Whether these translations are representative is not at all certain in the stereometric books (cf. below, pp. 118–19).

tradition has the benefit of many more improvements, and the Greek tradition seems to have been very conservative in this area.

(3) Furthermore, the conclusions drawn from the results of the comparison of versions change according to the book or group of books being studied. For example, interaction between Euclid and the Nicomachean tradition has had an impact on the text of the arithmetical Books. If x.68–70 and 105–107 and xiii.1–5 are judged by the criteria of improvement, the medieval versions (particular Adelard's) are more sophisticated than the Greek text, at least as far as the contents are concerned. At the end of Book iii (and perhaps also in response to an initiative by Heron), the medieval versions are also more sophisticated with regard to the material contents,[118] although the opposite is much more frequent.

Along the same lines, the mathematically insufficient proofs (according to the criteria of the ancients) in the *Elements* are four in number if the direct and indirect traditions are combined: viii.22–23, ix.19 and xii.17. If, as Knorr argues, we assume the errors are from Euclid and not textual corruptions, we arrive then, by applying his criteria, at the following conclusions:

- For viii.22–23, the original proofs are those common to both the Greek and to the Hajjajian tradition; the proofs presented by the Ishâq–Thâbit version are improvements.[119]
- For ix.19, the original proof is that of manuscript *P*; those of *Th* and of the indirect tradition are improvements.
- For xii.17, the original proof is that of the indirect tradition; those of *b* as well as of *P* and *Th* are improvements.[120]

The type of statements must also be taken into account. The Definitions occupy a privileged place in philosophical exegesis. The Porisms are particularly prone to the vagaries of transmission because they may easily be confused with additions. [121]

[118] There is the addition of the case of figures in the Propositions (Heib.) iii.25, 33, 35, 36; iv.5. The copyists ascribe them to the version of al-Hajjâj, and even to his *second* version if al-Karâbîsî is to be believed. See Brentjes 2000: 48, 50. Other cases are also added in iii.37 without al-Hajjâj being mentioned.

[119] See De Young 1991: 657–9.

[120] For my part, contrary to Knorr, I believe that the criterion of improvement does not apply for ix.19 or xii.17. I also believe that the proofs of *P* in one case and the proofs of the indirect tradition in the other are corrupt. For ix.19, see Vitrac 2004: 10–12. For xii.17, see Euclid/ Vitrac 2001: iv 369–71.

[121] Heiberg 1884: 20 observed that with the Definitions and Corollaries (Porisms) 'die Araber ... sehr frei verfahren haben'. In fact, it is not even simple to say exactly how many Porisms there are in the Greek text. Heiberg identifies 30 of them as such but makes a second Porism

(4) To explain this state of affairs, I see at least two explanations, that perhaps work in tandem:

- Either our different witnesses of the text reflect a general contamination[122] and a global criterion – at the scale of the complete treatise – cannot be reached.
- Or the principles that underpin the local criteria are inadequate. If certain branches of the tradition have epitomized the *Elements*, then the principle used by Klamroth and Knorr that the text of the *Elements* grew increasingly amplified proves inadequate. These principles may also miss their goals if it is not possible to identify the motivations of the ancient re-editors when they sought to improve the form of a mathematical text. We have seen that the criterion of mathematical refinement is sometimes difficult to use.

(5) Certain characteristics of the preserved versions and different external confirmations have convinced us that there has been both contamination and epitomization. Thus, not only is the text of the version by Ishâq, as revised by Thâbit, without any additional deductive lacuna in Books I–X, but the medieval evidence teaches us that the revision of Thâbit implied the consultation of other manuscripts and, consequently, the collation of alternative proofs.[123] In so doing, various versions of the Greek or Arabic texts, if not contaminated by, were at

from what, in the manuscripts, is nothing more than an addition to the Porism to VI.20 and an insertion of a heading [Porism] before the large recapitulation following X.111, although he did not do this for the summary following X.72! For fifteen Porisms, there is one or more Greek manuscripts in which the heading <Porism> is missing. Fifteen Porisms are placed before the standard clause ('what ought to be proved'), particularly true for ***P***. Eleven are inserted after the clause. Normally, a Porism begins with the expression, 'From this, it is clear that' ('ἐκ δὴ τούτου φανερὸν ὅτι ...'), but in seven cases (IV.5, VI.20, IX.11, X.9, X.111, X.114 and XII.17), the formulation is not canonical. The possibility of confusion appears in the fact that ten Porisms retained by Heiberg were amplified by inauthentic additions. If the indirect tradition is consulted, it ought not to be forgotten that two Porisms from the Greek are related to substitutions of proof (III.31, IV.5) and to an addition (X.114) which do not exist in this tradition. Thus, it is not at all surprising that these Porisms did not exist in it. By holding to comparable cases, the indirect tradition counts eleven Porisms from the Greek, but two exist in a different form. The Porism to X.111 exists as a Proposition and the one to XII.17 appears as part of a proof (as is also the case in certain Greek manuscripts). This 'πόρισμα' exists only in the margin of ***P*** and not in the other manuscripts! It may be remarked that neither has the standard formulation and that the indirect tradition has none of the other five Porisms 'heterodox' to the Greek text. For the others, their number decreases (to seven from nine in I–IX to which could be added three supplementary Porisms from the Ishâq–Thâbit version (to VIII.14, 15; IX.5), to one from four in X, to nil from six in XI–XIII).

[122] This is the opinion of Brentjes, at least as concerns the Arabic and Arabo-Latin traditions. See Brentjes 1996: 205.

[123] See Engroff 1980: 20–39.

least compared with each other in order to produce Thâbit's revision of Ishâq's translation. There is no reason for astonishment: these scholars were not working to provide guidance to modern philologists who want to establish the history of the text of the *Elements*. They sought to procure a complete and stimulating mathematical text. Knowing the hazards of manuscript transmission, they compared different copies, and I believe that Thâbit ibn Qurra used other Arabic translations, probably that of al-Hajjâj, and even some Greek commentaries, in particular that of Heron of Alexandria, which has some consequences for the structure of the revised text. At some points, it is more sophisticated than the Greek text of Heiberg.[124] In the Arabo-Latin domain, the Gerard of Cremona version also proceeds by juxtaposition of different texts, some of which Thâbit had already combined, but also the alternate proofs that the tradition attributes to al-Hajjâj and which often appears in the Latin of Adelard of Bath.

(6) The case of the translation (or translations) of al-Hajjâj is much more difficult to judge because we know it only very incompletely and indirectly through several citations by copyists of manuscripts of the Ishâq–Thâbit versions and through the evidence of Tûsî and pseudo-Tûsî.[125] Virtually all the characteristics that distinguish it – primarily its thinness and the structure of several families of proofs – appear in the Arabo-Latin version of Adelard of Bath.[126] Its antiquity and its thinness make it tempting to ascribe to it a privileged role. Nonetheless, the evidence from the preface of the Leiden Codex introducing the commentary of an-Nayrîzî is troubling.[127] The principle of amplification, to which Klamroth (and Knorr) subscribe concerning the textual development, suppose that no deliberately abridged version has played a role in the transmission of the text. It is to precisely this phenomenon of abbreviation that the preface to the second translation (or revision) of al-Hajjâj makes reference. Thus, I am not sure that this principle,

---

[124] This is particularly clear in Books VIII–IX, first of all for the alternative proofs proposed for VIII.22–23, then the insertion of the converses to Prop. (Heib.) VIII.24–25 and the simplification of the proof of IX.2, finally the addition of the Propositions (Ishâq–Thâbit) IX.30–31 to simplify the proofs of IX.32–33 (= Heib. IX.30–31), without forgetting the addition of Porisms (cf. n. 121).

[125] See Engroff 1980: 20–39. Recently Gregg de Young has discovered an anonymous commentary relatively rich in references to divergences between the versions of Ishâq–Thâbit and al-Hajjâj. See de Young, 2002/2003.

[126] Twenty structural divergences are supposed to characterize the version of al-Hajjâj. Of these, sixteen appear in Adelard. The other four from Book IX and the first part of Book X – the lost portion in Adelard's translation – appear in the related Latin versions by Herman of Carinthia and Robert of Chester.

[127] See the text and French translation in Djebbar 1996: 97, 113, partially cited below as n. 142.

which functions rather well in the case of dichotomy 1, also applies to dichotomy 2.[128]

(7) Moreover, the case of the stereometric books, on which Knorr founded his argument, seems problematic to me. The Arabo-Latin translations are particularly close to each other in these books. Knorr relied on this point to deduce that the same thing would happen to their Arabic models and thus also the versions of al-Hajjâj and Ishâq–Thâbit.[129] What I have called dichotomy 2 hardly occurs there at all.[130] However, there are, in two manuscripts of this last version (Copenhagen, Mehrens 81; Istanbul, Fâtih 3439), glosses indicating that Book x is the last which Ishâq has translated and that what follows is 'Hajjajian'. The author of the gloss to the manuscript in Copenhagen specifies exactly that it 'comes from the second translation of al-Hajjâj', i.e., the abridgement.[131] From this reference, Klamroth deduced that Ishâq had translated only Books i–x and that Thâbit had taken xi–xiii from the translation of al-Hajjâj. This thesis has been challenged by Engroff and I obviously have no expertise on this point, but it seems to me that the stereometric books undeniably constitute a particular case.[132] Even then, at-Tûsî had remarked that there is no structural divergence between what he believed to be the two versions of the stereometric books.[133] I would add that there is not, to my knowledge, any mention of the sort 'Thâbit says …' beyond Book x.[134]

A final element must be taken into account. In Proposition XIII.11 it is established that the side of a pentagon inscribed in a circle with a rational diameter is irrational, of the 'minor' type. Thus, in Book x, 'ἄλογος' is translated as 'asamm' ('deaf') by al-Hajjâj and 'ghayr muntaq' ('un-expressible') by Ishâq–Thâbit. The divergence appears, for example, between Avicenna and the manuscript Petersburg 2145 on the one hand and the other Ishâq–Thâbit manuscripts on the other

---

[128] It seems to me that Brentjes equally admits the idea that the so-called al-Hajjâj version No. 2 represents an improved and abridged re-edition. See Brentjes 1996: 221–2.

[129] See Knorr 1996: 259–60.

[130] See Table 2 of the Appendix.

[131] See Engroff 1980: 9.

[132] See Engroff 1980: 9–10, 12–13. Let us add that at the end of Book xi in the manuscript Tehran Malik 3586, a gloss indicates that Thâbit ibn Qurra had revised only Books i–x and that Books xi, xii and xiii are Hajjajian! See Brentjes 2000: 53.

[133] See Rommevaux, Djebbar and Vitrac 2001: 275, n. 184.

[134] In the anonymous commentary cited above at n. 125, the references relative to the divergences between the versions of Ishâq–Thâbit and al-Hajjâj stop after the first third of Book x. This observation is well explained in the line of the gloss inserted in the manuscript Tehran Malik 3586 (cf. above, n. 132).

hand.[135] It is interesting to note that in Proposition (Heib.) XIII.11 (= IsTh 14), the manuscript Petersb. 2145, as well as Tehran Malik 3586 and Rabat 1101, record 'asamm!'[136] This does not necessarily mean that Ishâq did not translate Books XI–XIII,[137] but it at least suggests that at some moment of transmission, the stereometric books existed only in a single version.[138] This homogeneity, recorded by Tûsî, might even be the cause of the glosses inserted in the three manuscripts of the Ishâq–Thâbit version that I just mentioned.[139]

(8) Two consequences may be drawn from the preceding considerations. First, Knorr's hypothesis that the indirect tradition derived from a single Greek archetype, based only on the stereometric books – in fact only on the portion XI.36–XII.17 – is challenged. Second, I have said that there are, in the versions of al-Hajjâj and Ishâq–Thâbit, three and two deductive lacunae respectively. Those of Ishâq–Thâbit occur in Book XII. But, if the hypothesis of Klamroth or one of his variations is adopted, we know the translation of Ishâq–Thâbit only for Books I–X. The translation here is without deductive lacunae, which, considering the work of the Reviser, is to be expected. As for the translation of al-Hajjâj, the evidence of the preface in the Leiden manuscript suggests that it could scarcely be other than an epitome!

(9) These consequences being noted, it ought not to be forgotten that it is thanks to the indirect tradition itself that we have been able to determine some of its limitations. The medieval versions, notably those of Ishâq–Thâbit and Gerard of Cremona, are more attentive to problems of textual origin than the Greek manuscripts and thereby more informative about the divergences between versions observed by their authors. The contamination is clearly not the doing of medieval scholars only. The subject of double proofs demonstrates this. The abundance of additional material and local alterations of the

---

[135] See Rommevaux, Djebbar and Vitrac 2001: 259, 288–9.

[136] I thank A. Djebbar for this information.

[137] It is possible to doubt such an abstention by Ishâq given that there are two series of definitions for Book XI in Tehran Malik 3586, the latter being attributed to Hunayn ibn Ishâq and, probably, there was some confusion here between the father and the son (see Brentjes 2000: 54). However, Ishâq may well have brought his translation to an end with the Definitions for Book XI, which have been (piously) conserved, though he did not translate what followed. Thus, one again arrives at the thesis of Klamroth.

[138] Although she disagrees with the thesis of Klamroth, Brentjes pointed out that in regard to Definition XI, the first version of Tehran Malik 3586 (the Ishâq–Thâbit version) and the version given by al-Karâbîsî, who, (according to Brentjes), follows Hajjajian version, have minuscule differences. See Brentjes 2000: 53. This seems to me to concur with the preceding remark.

[139] See above, nn. 131–132.

sort of *post-factum* explanations in Byzantine Greek manuscripts (cf. above the example of XI.1) shows that the Greek text is itself enriched through recourse to the relevant elements of the commentary, probably through the intermediacy of marginal annotations by simple readers or by scholars.

(10) The intervention of the epitomes in the indirect tradition is quite probable. There are, however, different ways of abridging a text like that of the *Elements*. An editor could eliminate portions considered inauthentic or some theorems dealing with a theme judged too particular. Regroupings could be made. Abbreviated proofs could be substituted, using in particular the previously discussed formulae for potential and analogical proofs or by removing the uninstantiated general statements, which are often less comprehensible than the example (set out in *ecthesis* and *diorism*) accompanied by a diagram and labelled with letters. More radically, all the proofs could be removed, and only what Bourbaki called a 'fascicule de résultats' might be retained, or some number of books no longer considered indispensable might be cut out. In this case, the very structure of the treatise and its plan, which have often been criticized, would be changed. Such recensions are not at all rare beginning from the sixteenth century, but in the majority of ancient and medieval versions, even in a recension like that of Campanus which introduces numerous local changes, the Euclidean progression through thirteen books is maintained, even if at some stage supplementary books (XIV, XV, XVI, ...) were added.

Alternatively, the other operations of abbreviations listed above are all mentioned in the medieval prefaces, such as those of al-Maghribî,[140] the recension now called pseudo-Tûsî[141] or the Leiden Codex, wherein the authors described recensions or epitomes. Moreover, as we have noted above, according to the preface of the Leiden Codex, al-Hajjâj, in order to win the favour of the new Khalif al-Ma'mûn, improved his first translation 'by rendering it more concise and shortening it. He did not find an addition without removing it, nor a lacuna without filling it, nor a fault without repairing and correcting it, until he had purged, improved, summarized and shortened it all.'[142] It is possible

---

[140] One can read a Latin translation in Heiberg 1884: 16–17, with several errors of identification about the cited Arabic authors (and even about the author of the preface! See Rommevaux, Djebbar and Vitrac 2001: 230, 239). It allows us however to have some idea of the liberties taken by the authors of recensions. Completed by Sabra 1969: 14–5 who corrects the identifications and Murdoch 1971: 440 (col. b).

[141] It is taken up again by Murdoch in the article cited in the preceding note.

[142] Translation in Djebbar 1996: 97.

that this passage contains some rhetorical exaggerations or stock phrases about the improvement of a text. If the quest for conciseness seems hardly debatable, the preface indicates neither the motivations for the suppressions nor the criteria used to identify the 'additions'. It is conceivable that al-Hajjâj knew of other Greek versions, more concise than the text or texts initially translated, to which the phenomenon of the epitomization had itself already been applied.

(11) We know that at least one abridged version of the *Elements* had been produced in antiquity by Aigeias of Hierapolis. Mentioned by Proclus, he wrote therefore no later than the fifth century of the modern era. The difference with the second version of al-Hajjâj is that there is no evidence that it played a role in the transmission of the text. However, besides the obvious textual enrichment, it is not possible to completely exclude the intervention of one or several abridged Greek versions.

The relative 'thinness' of the al-Hajjâj version, as far as can be known, can indeed be explained in different ways depending on the portion of text considered. Proposition II.14, which treats the quadrature of the triangle (with the associated absence of I.45), and Propositions XII.5, 7 and 8, which treat pyramids on a triangular base, proceed from the same attitude, and, in these cases, there are good reasons to think that the origin of this minimalist treatment has a Greek origin.[143] For the absence of Proposition III.37 I have noted that it was probably an accident of transmission. The absence of the bulk of the additional material, of several Definitions in Books V, VI, VII and XI and of the Porisms in the stereometric books may perhaps be explained because al-Hajjâj had identified them as additions. Similarly, several other Propositions missing from his version (VI.12, VIII.11a–12a, X.16, X.27–28), but present in the Ishâq–Thâbit translation, might be the result of additions lacking from the Greek or Syriac manuscripts consulted by al-Hajjâj, or they might have possessed these assertions, but he judged them to be useless, as they very nearly are.

(12) The existence of abridged versions in Greek also made up part of the hypothesis of Heiberg, and he described the model of manuscript *b* in this way for its divergent part (XI.36–XII.17).[144] Manuscript *b* is, however, very flawed. It contains problems in the lettering of the

---

[143] Let us recall that Proposition XII.6 and the Porisms to XII.7 and 8 are missing in manuscript *b*. For II.14, Simplicius seemingly knew two versions of the theorem: the 'rectangular' version in his commentary to the *Physics* of Aristotle (*CAG*, 62. 8 Diels) and the 'triangular' version in his commentary to *De cælo*: (*CAG*, ed. 414.1 Heiberg).

[144] See above, pp. 81–2.

diagrams, *saut du même au même*, and even, as it seems to me, faults in reading the uncial script. Manuscript *b* could thus be the result of a new transliteration, being more faulty since it was further removed from the ninth century, and produced (for reasons which elude us) at the same time as the copy, in the eleventh century, of the Bologna manuscript from a model which was either truly ancient (the hypothesis of Knorr) or proceeding from another archetype, such as an abridged version of the 'Aigeias' type. Here, I call upon the possibility of an ancient model, whereas Heiberg imagined a Byzantine recension.

Whatever the case may have been, I do not believe that this really changes the attitude that the editor of the Greek text may have adopted toward it. The appeal to *b* XI.36–XII.17 may prove useful for removing some cases of textual divergences between *P* and *Th*, in the aforementioned portion. However, adopting these readings would probably create a philological monster which never existed. Perhaps it can yet be used to improve the edition of a similar Arabic version. Knorr wanted to adopt the text of *b*, rather than what he called 'the wrong text' of Heiberg, because he hoped that a comparison of the primary Arabic translations would permit the reconstitution of a Greek archetype of comparable antiquity for the remainder of the treatise. This reconstitution is impossible, at least for the present state of our knowledge.

Therefore, the conception of a new critical edition of the Greek text seems useless to me for the moment. The critical editions of the various identified Arabic, Arabo-Latin and Arabo-Hebrew versions would be preferable. It would be necessary to produce an 'instruction manual' for the reader to navigate these versions according to the problem, the time period, the language of culture, even the Euclid available to (another) interested author. Such a manual would be especially necessary in the cases of double proofs or substitutions of proofs, cases which the indirect tradition has considerably enriched.

This necessity has long been perceived by the historians of the medieval and modern periods. Undoubtedly, the Hellenist would also admit the same necessity. The movement to 'return' to the original which inspired the work of the philologists of the nineteenth century seems to need a break. A less partial knowledge of the indirect tradition provides us not only with much richer information at a local level, but also with more uncertainty about its ancient components. Thus stripped of our (false) certainties, we may feel a little frustrated, but the hope remains that new discoveries of ancient papyri, manuscripts of medieval translations of Euclid or of its commentators will allow us to move forward.

Appendix

The appendix contains three tables (each describing one of the breaks observed in the textual tradition of Euclid's *Elements*). I have used the following abbreviations:

Df., Definition; Post., Postulates; CN, Common Notion; Prop. proposition; Por. Porism (= corollary); The notation $N/N+1$ designates the lemma between Propositions N and $N+1$. Brackets indicate portions considered inauthentic by Heiberg, but which exist in Greek manuscripts.

(+) or (−) signify the presence or absence of a textual element, respectively;
(÷2): fusion of two elements into one;
(×2): subdivision of an element into two.
aliter marks the existence of a second proof, possibly partial (indicated by 'p') or the existence of a second definition.

Ad., version called Adelard I (Busard 1983); GC, version attributed to Gerard of Cremona (Busard 1984); gr.-lat., Greco-Latin version (Busard 1987); Heib., Heiberg's edition; IsTh, Ishâq–Thâbit version; *P*, manuscript Vatic. Gr. 190; *Th*, Greek manuscripts called Theonians (on *P* / *Th*, see above, pp. 82–5); mg., marginalia.

Dichotomy 1 (Heiberg's edition *versus* medieval Arabic and Arabo-Latin tradition[a])

Type of divergence	Textual elements	
	Definitions	Df. III. additional (+); Df. IV.3–7 (−); Df. IV.5–7 (−); Df. XI.15, 17 (−); Df. XI.23 (−); Df. XI.25–28 (−)
	Propositions	III.12 (−); {VII.20 *vulgo*^b} (−); {VII.22 *vulgo*} (−); Ishâq-Thâbit IX.30–31 (+); x.7–8 (−); x.9 (iii) (−); x.13 (−); {x.13 *vulgo*} (−); x.16 (−); x.24 (−); x.112–114 (−); {x.117 *vulgo*} (−); {XI.38 *vulgo*} (−); XII.6 (−); XII.13 (−); XII.14 (−)
	Porisms	{II.4Por} (+); {III.31Por,}, IV.5 Por. (−); v.4 (or 7) Por. (−); v.19 Por., VI.20 Por.1 (−); IX.2 Por (+); IX.5 Por (+); IX.11 Por. (−); x.4 Por. (−); x.6 Por. (−); x.9 Por. (−); x.23 Por. (−); x.114 Por. (−); XI.33 Por. (−); XI.35 Por. (−); XII.7 Por (−); XII.8 Por (−); XIII.16 Por. (−); XIII.17 Por. (−)
(+ / −)	Additional material	
	Special Cases	{Pseudo-special case in III.11} (−); Special case in III.20, 24, 27 (−); Special case in III.35, 36, 37 (+); Special case in v.8 (−); {Special case in VI.27} (−); {Special case in XI.23} (−)
	Additions	{Addition to III.16 Por.} (−); {Addition to VI.33} (−); Addition to x.1 (−); 12 {Additions} {to x.10, 18, to x.23 Por, to x.32/33; to x.36, 37, 38, 39, 40, 41, to Df. x (series ii); to x.85–90}; Addition (?) to XIII.18 (−)
	Double Proofs	{III.7p, 8p; VI.20p, 30; VII.31 *aliter*} (−); {x.1 *aliter*} (+); {XI.22; XII.17p *aliter*} (−); {XIII.1–3 *aliter* (+); {XIII.5 *aliter*} (−); {XIII.1–5 *aliter* by analysis/synthesis} (−); {XIII.18p *aliter*} (−)

Lemmas[c]		vi.22/23; x.9/10; x.13/14; x.16/17; x.18/19; {x.20/21}; x.21/22; {x.27/28}; x.28/29 {1}, {2}; {x.29/30}; {x.31/32}; {x.32/33}; {x.33/34}; {x.34/35}; x.41/42; x.53/54; x.59/60; xi.23/24; xii.2/3; xii.4/5; xiii.2/3; xiii.13/14; Lemma after xiii.18
Changes in order	In Df.	Df. v.12–13; Df. vi.3–4; Df. vii.13–14; Df. vii.17–20; Df. xi.9–22
	In Prop.	v.12–13; vi.9–13; vi.18–20; vi.31–32; vii.21–22; vii.29–32; x.10–11; x.14–15; x.25–26; x.111–111Por; xi.33–34; xii.8–9; xii.11–12; xiii.4–5; xiii.8–12; xiii.14–15
Modifications	Substitution of proof	iii.14p, 31p, 37; iii.33 (Construction); x.105–107; xi.37
		Df. xi.1–2 (÷2)
		iii.1 Por; x.72 Por. (transformed into a Proposition)
	Formulations ≠	iii.25; v.23
		viii.16–17 = Ad.15 = GC viii.14 Por. + 15 Por.
		Inversion x.111, 111 Por. and transformation (in Prop.); xi.31 (×2); xi.34 (×2)
Total		139

Notes:

[a] In this table, the medieval tradition (as defined above, p. 89) serves as a reference: (+), (–), (÷2), (×2) signify presence, absence, fusion, subdivision respectively in this tradition.

[b] On the meaning of *vulgo*, see n. 28.

[c] The case of the Lemmas is slightly different. Heiberg explicitly dismisses some ({}), keeps others, all the while maintaining that they are all certainly interpolated (with the sole possible exception of x.28/29 {1}, {2}).

Dichotomy 2 (Adelardian traditions *versus* Ishâq–Thâbit tradition received by Gerard of Cremona)[a]

Type of divergence	Textual elements	In Books I to x	In Books XI to XIII
(+ / −)	Definitions	Df. III.6, 9; Df. IV.2; Df. V.10, 11, 18 (−) in Ad.	Df. XI.9 (−) in GC
		Df. IsT V.17bis additional; Df. V.17ter (−) in Ad.	Df. XI.22 (−) in Ad.
		Df. IsT VI.2, 4 *aliter*, VI.6 additional (+) in (GC)	2 Df. XI. *aliter* in GC
		Df. VI.3, 4, {5}; Df. VII.3–5 (−) in Ad.	
		Df. IsT VII.9bis additional in GC	
		Substitution of Df. IsTh VII.15–16 additional in Ad.	
	Common notion	{CN4/5} (−) in Ad.	
	Propositions	I.45; III.37; VI.12; VIII.11–12(a) (−) in Ad.	
		IsTh VIII.24–25 additional (+) in GC	
		x.27–28, 32 (−) in Ad.	
	Porisms	VI.20Por. (n°2) in GC	
		Additional Porisms to VIII.14–15 (+) in GC	
	Additional material Additions	I.35P *aliter* = addition to I.35 in GC	
		Additions to Df. V.5, 7, 9–10 in GC	
		Addition at x.54 in GC	
	Double proofs in GC	I.44P *aliter*; II.4 *aliter*; III.9, 10, 25, 31P, 33 *aliter*; III.35, 36 *aliter*; IV.5, 8, 15 *aliter*; V.5 *aliter*; V.18 *aliter*; VI.9, 22, 31 *aliter*; VIII.22–23 *aliter*; x.6, 30, 33, 68–70, 91, 111, 115 *aliter*; XI.30 *aliter*	
	Lemmas	x.32/33 (+) in GC	
		GC x.40/41 (Cf. Heiberg 41/42)	

Changes in order	In Df.	Df. vii.21–23
	In Prop.	vi.23–26; vii.7–13; viii.19–20; ix.11–12; ix.14–19–20; ix.25–26–27; x.10–12–14–15
Modifications	Substitutions of proof	Substitution of proof in v.6, 18; vi.20, viii.22–23 in GC
		Substitution of Proof at x.68–70 in Ad.
	Formulations ≠	Variations of formulation in Df. iii.11
		Replacement of Df. v.4 in Ad. (continuous proportion)
		Ad., Post.6 = GC CN 10 = grec CN 9
		i.15 Por.; iv.15 Por.
		Statements ≠ for ii.1–9
		'Triangle' variation for ii.14 in Ad.
		Variation in lettering for vii (simple in Ad. / double in GC)
		Ad. viii.15 = GC viii.16 (= Heib. viii.16–17) = GC viii.14 Por. + viii.15 Por.
		Fusion of x.29–30 into a single Proposition and removal (in the Adelardian tradition)
		Subdivision of x.31–32 into four Propositions in GC or into three in the Adelardian tradition
Total		83 3

Note:

a Adelardian tradition: Ad. + RC (Busard and Folkerts, 1992) + JT (Busard 2001). From a structural point of view, the versions of Hermann of Carinthia (Busard 1967–1972–1977) and Campanus (Busard 2005) belong to the tradition. It is necessary to take these versions into consideration because Ad. is mutilated (through the loss of Book ix and the first third of Book x). The specialists ascribe the structural particularities of the Adelardian tradition to its dependence on a model something like al-Ḥajjāj. The version of Gerard of Cremona juxtaposes two textual families (without mixing them too much). The first is similar to the Adelardian tradition, the other approaches the Isḥāq–Thābit version.

Dichotomy 3 _P versus Th_

Type of divergence[a]	Textual element	In Books I to IX	In Books X to XIII
(+ / −)	Propositions	VII.20 _vulgo_ exists in **Th** & gr. lat. In mg. by a late hand in **P** VII.22 _vulgo_ exists in **Th** & gr. lat. In mg. by a late hand in **P**	x.13 _vulgo_ exists in **Th** & gr. lat. In mg. by hand **2** in **P**
	Porisms	II.4 Por. exists in **Th** & gr. lat. by a late hand in **P** Does not exist in Pap. Oxyrh.29 v.4 Por. exists in **Th** & in gr.-lat. v.4 Por. in mg. by a late hand in **P** v.7 Por. exists in **P** but not in **Th** v.19 Por. exists in **Th** & in gr.-lat. v.19 Por. in mg. by hand 1 in **P** IX.11 Por. exists in only **P**	
	Additional material		
	Special case	Case+ in VI.27 in **Th** & gr. lat. In mg. by a late hand in **P**	
	Additions	In III.16 Por. N°2 exists in **Th** & gr. lat. In mg. by a late hand in **P** In v.4 exists in **Th** & in gr. lat., but not in **P** In VI.33 for 'sector' with modifications of the statement and of the discussion in **Th** and gr. lat. In mg. by a late hand in **P**	

Double proofs		II.4 *aliter.* exists in *Th* & gr. lat. In mg. by a late hand in *P* VII.31 *aliter.* exists in *Th* & gr. lat. Does not exist in *P*	X.1 *aliter.* exists in *Th* & gr. lat. In mg. by hand **1** in *P* X.6 *aliter.* exists in *Th* & gr. lat. In mg. by hand **1** in *P* X.9 *aliter.* exists in *Th* & gr. lat. In mg. by hand **1** in *P*
Changes in order	in Df.	Inversion of Df. V.6–7 in *P*	Inversion Df. XI 27–28 (icos.; dodec.) in *P* (dodec.; icos.) in *Th* & gr. lat.
Modifications	Formulations ≠	Proof of IX.19 corrupted in *P* correct in *Th*	Proof in XI.1 with addition of explanations ≠ in *P* and in *Th* 'solid parallelepiped' in place of 'cube' for XI.38 in *Th* Modification of lettering in XII.17
		IV.5 Por., IV.15 Por. VI.19 Por: 'trigonon' (= triangle) in *Th* & gr. lat. & addition *supralin.* in *P*, by a late hand; 'eidos' in text in *P* by hand 1 XII.7 Por.	
Total		17	8

Note:

[a] No substitution of proof (!), no change in order for the Propositions; no Lemma which exists in one of the two versions and not in the other. When there is a double proof, the order is always the same in *P* as in *Th*. The difference occurs mostly in the marginal additions of *P* (by the copyist = hand 1 or by a late hand) after consultation with a copy of the family *Th*.

Bibliography

Editions and translations of versions of Euclid's *Elements*

Besthorn, R. O., J. L. Heiberg, then G. Junge, J. Raeder and W. Thomson (eds.) (1893–1932) *Codex Leidensis 399/1: Euclidis* Elementa *ex interpretatione al'Hadschdschaschii cum Commentariis al' Narizii*. Arabic text and Latin trans., Hauniae, Lib. Gyldendaliana: I, 1 and 2 (= L. I), 1893–7; II, 1 and 2 (= L. II and III), 1900–5; III, 1, 2 and 3 (= L. IV–VI), 1910–32.

Busard, H. L. L. and M. Folkerts (eds.) (1992, *RC*) *Robert of Chester's (?) Redaction of Euclid's* Elements, *the so-called Adelard* II *Version*. Basel.

Busard, H. L. L. (ed.) (1967–1972–1977, *HC*) *The Translation of the* Elements *of Euclid from the Arabic into Latin by Hermann of Carinthia (?)*. L. I–VI in *Janus* 54, 1967, 1–140; L. VII–IX, *Janus* 59, 1972, 125–187; L. VII–XII, Mathematical Centre Tracts **84**, Amsterdam, Mathematisch Centrum, 1977.

Busard, H. L. L. (ed.) (1983, *Ad. I*) *The First Latin Translation of Euclid's* Elements *Commonly Ascribed to Adelard of Bath*. Toronto.

Busard, H. L. L. (ed.) (1984, *GC*) *The Latin Translation of the Arabic Version of Euclid's* Elements *Commonly Ascribed to Gerard of Cremona*. Leiden.

Busard, H. L. L. (ed.) (1996) *A Thirteenth-Century Adaptation of Robert of Chester's Version of Euclid's* Elements. Munich.

Busard, H. L. L. (ed.) (2001, *JT*) *Johannes de Tinemue's Redaction of Euclid's* Elements, *The so-called Adelard* III *Version*. Stuttgart.

Busard, H. L. L. (ed.) (1987, *gr.-lat.*) *The Mediaeval Latin Translation of Euclid's* Elements *Made Directly from the Greek*. Stuttgart.

Busard, H. L. L. (ed.) (2005) *Campanus of Novara and Euclid's* Elements. Stuttgart.

De Young, G. (1981) 'The arithmetic books of Euclid's *Elements*'. Ph.D. thesis, Harvard University.

Engroff, J. W. (1980) 'The Arabic tradition of Euclid's *Elements*: Book V'. Ph.D. thesis, Harvard University.

Euclide d'Alexandrie, *Les Eléments* (Euclid/Vitrac). Translation and commentary by Bernard Vitrac. 4 volumes: I (general introduction by M. Caveing. L. I–IV): 1990; II (L. V–IX): 1994; III (L. X): 1998; IV (L. XI–XIII): 2001. Paris.

Heiberg, J. L. and H. Menge (eds.) (1883–1916, *EHM*) *Euclidis opera omnia*. I *Elementa* i–iv (1883); II *El.* v–ix (1884); III *El.* x (1886); IV *El.* xi–xiii (1885); V *El.* xiv–xv, *Scholia, Prolegomena critica* (1888); VI *Data, Marini Commentarius in Eucl. Data* (1896); VII *Optica, Opticorum recensio Theonis, Catoptrica* (1895); VIII *Phaenomena, Scripta musica, Fragmenta* (1916); IX *Supplementum*. Leipzig.

Heiberg, J. L. and E. S. Stamatis (eds.) (1969–77, *EHS*) *Euclidis* Elementa, post Heiberg ed. E. S. Stamatis. I, *El.* i–iv (1969); II, *El.* v–ix (1970); III, *El.* x (1972); IV, *El.* xi–xiii (1973); V, 1. *El.* xiv–xv, *Scholia in lib.* i–v (1977); V, 2. *Scholia in lib.* vi–xiii (1977). Leipzig.

Peyrard, F. (1814–18) *Les œuvres d'Euclide en grec, en latin et en français*. Paris.

Editions and translations of commentators

Pappus of Alexandria

Thomson, W. and G. Junge (eds.) (1930) *The Commentary of Pappus on Book X of Euclid's* Elements, Edited and translated W. Thomson, comm. G. Junge and W. Thomson. Cambridge, Mass. (Reprinted. New York 1968.)

Theon of Alexandria

Mogenet, J. and Tihon, A. (eds.) (1985) *Le 'grand commentaire' de Théon d'Alexandrie aux* Tables faciles *de Ptolémée*, Livre I, Studi e Testi 315. Vatican City.

Proclus Lycaeus

Friedlein, G. (ed.) (1873) *Procli Diadochi in primum Euclidis Elementorum librum Commentarii*. Leipzig. (Reprinted: Hildesheim 1967.)

al-Mâhânî

Abû 'Abdallâh Muhammad ibn 'Isâ al-Mâhânî, *Risâla li-al-Mâhânî fî al-mushkil min amr al-nisba* (Épitre d'al-Mâhânî sur la difficulté relative à la question du rapport). Edition and French translation in Vahabzadeh 1997. (Reprinted, with English translation, in Vahabzadeh 2002: 31–52.)

Abû 'Abdallâh Muhammad ibn 'Isâ al-Mâhânî, *Tafsîr al-maqâla al-'âshira min kitâb Uqlîdis*. Edition and French translation (*Explication du Dixième Livre de l'ouvrage d'Euclide*) in Ben Miled, M. (2005) *Opérer sur le continu: Traditions arabes du Livre X des Éléments d'Euclide*. Carthage: 286–92 [completed with an anonymous commentary, *ibid.*: 296–333].

al-Fârâbî

Abû Nasr Muhammad ibn Muhammad ibn Tarhân al-Fârâbî, *Sharh al-mustaglaq min musâdarât al-maqâla al-ûlâ wa-l-hâmisa min Uqlîdis*. Hebrew translation by Moses ibn Tibbon in Freudenthal 1988.

an-Nayrîzî

Arnzen, R. (ed.) (2002) *Abû l-'Abbâs an-Nayrîzî, Exzerpte aus (Ps.-?)Simplicius' Kommentar zu den Definitionen, Postulaten und Axiomen in Euclids Elementa I, eingeleitet, ediert und mit arabischen und lateinischen Glossaren versehen von R. Arnzen*. Cologne.

Tummers, P. M. J. E. (ed.) (1994), *Anaritius' Commentary on Euclid: The Latin Translation* I–IV. Artistarium Supplementa IX. Nijmegen.

al-Jayyânî

Abû 'Abdallâh Muhammad ibnMu'âd al-Jayyânî al-Qâsî, *Maqâla fi sharh al-nisba* (Commentary on Proportion). Facsimile of the Algier manuscript 1466/3, fo. 74r–82r and English in Plooij 1950; edition and French translation in Vahabzadeh 1997.

Ibn al-Haytham

Abû 'Alî al-Hasan ibn al-Hasan Ibn al-Haytham, *Sharh musâdarât Uqlîdis*. Partial edition, English translation and commentary in Sude, B. H. (1974) 'Ibn al-Haytham's Commentary on the Premises of Euclid's *Elements*: Books I–VI', Ph.D. thesis, Princeton University.

al-Khayyâm

'Umar al-Khayyâm, *Risâla fi sharh mâ ashkala min musâdarât Kitâb Uqlîdis* (Epître sur les problèmes posés par certaines prémisses problématiques du Livre d'Euclide). French translation (based on the Arabic edition of the text by A. I. Sabra) in Djebbar, A. (1997) *'L'émergence du concept de nombre réel positif dans l'Épître d'al-Khayyâm (1048–1131). Sur l'explication des prémisses problématiques du Livre d'Euclide'* Orsay, Université de Paris-Sud. Mathématiques. Prépublications 97–39. Re-edited, with corrections, in Fahrang, *Quarterly Journal of Humanities and Cultural Studies* **14**: 79–136 (2002). Arabic edition of the text with French translation by B. Vahabzadeh in Rashed, R. and Vahabzadeh, B. (1999) *Al-Khayyâm mathématicien*. Paris: 271–390.

Studies

Blanchard, A. (ed.) (1989) *Les débuts du codex*. Turnhout.
Bourbaki, N. (1974) *Éléments d'histoire des mathématiques*, 2nd edn. Paris.
Brentjes, S. (1996) 'The relevance of non-primary sources for the recovery of the primary transmission of Euclid's *Elements* into Arabic', in *Tradition, Transmission, Transformation*, Proceedings of Two Conferences on Pre-Modern Science held at the University of Oklahoma, ed. F. J. Ragep, S. P. Ragep and S. Livesey. Leiden: 201–25.
   (1997–98) 'Additions to Book I in the Arabic Traditions of Euclid's *Elements*', *Studies in History of Medicine and Science* XV: 55–117.

(2000) 'Ahmad al-Karâbîsî's Commentary on Euclid's "Elements"', in *Sic Itur ad Astra: Studien zur Geschichte der Mathematik und Naturwissenschaften*, Festschrift für den Arabisten Paul Kunitzsch zum 70. Geburtstag, ed. M. Folkerts and R. Lorch. Wiesbaden: 31–75.

(2001a) 'Observations on Hermann of Carinthia's version of the *Elements* and its relation to the Arabic Transmission', *Science in Context* 14(1/2): 39–84.

(2001b) 'Two comments on Euclid's *Elements?* On the relation between the Arabic text attributed to al-Nayrîzî and the Latin text ascribed to Anaritius', *Centaurus* 43: 17–55.

Dain, A. (1975) *Les manuscrits*, 3rd edn. Paris.

De Young, G. (1991) 'New traces of the lost al-Hajjâj Arabic Translations of Euclid's *Elements*', *Physis* 38: 647–66.

(2002–3) 'The Arabic version of Euclid's *Elements* by al-Hajjâj ibn Yûsuf ibn Matar', *Zeitschrift für Geschichte der arabisch-islamischen Wissenchaften* 15: 125–64.

(2004) 'The Latin translation of Euclid's *Elements* attributed to Gerard of Cremona in relation to the Arabic transmission', *Suhayl* 4: 311–83.

Djebbar, A. (1996) 'Quelques commentaires sur les versions arabes des *Eléments* d'Euclide et sur leur transmission à l'Occident musulman', in *Mathematische Probleme im Mittelalter: Der lateinische und arabische Sprachbereich*, ed. M. Folkerts. Wiesbaden: 91–114.

Dorandi, T. (1986) 'Il Libro x degli *Elementi* di Euclide', *Prometheus* 12: 225.

(2000) *Le stylet et la tablette: Dans le secret des auteurs antiques*. Paris.

Folkerts, M. (1989) *Euclid in Medieval Europe*. Winnipeg.

Follieri, E. (1977) 'La minuscola libraria dei secoli ix e x', in *La paléographie grecque et byzantine*, ed. J. Glénisson, J. Bompaire and J. Irigoin. Paris: 139–65.

Fowler, D. H. (1987) *The Mathematics of Plato's Academy*. Oxford.

Freudenthal, G. (1988) 'La philosophie de la géométrie d'al-Fârâbî: son commentaire sur le début du 1er livre et le début du ve livre des *Eléments* d'Euclide', *Jerusalem Studies in Arabic and Islam* 11: 104–219.

Heiberg, J. L. (1882) *Litterargeschichtliche Studien über Euklid*. Leipzig.

(1884) 'Die arabische Tradition der Elemente Euklids', *Zeitschrift für Mathematik und Physik, hist.-litt. Abt.* 29: 1–22.

(1885) 'Ein Palimpsest der Elemente Euklidis', *Philologus* 44: 353–66.

(1888) *Om Scholierne til Euklids Elementer* (with a French summary). Copenhagen.

(1903) 'Paralipomena zu Euklid', *Hermes, Zeitschrift für classische Philologie* xxxviii: 46–74, 161–201, 321–56.

Irigoin, J. (2003) *La tradition des textes grecs: Pour une critique historique*. Paris.

Klamroth, M. (1881) 'Über den arabischen Euklid', *Zeitschrift der Deutschen Morgenländischen Gesellschaft* 35: 270–326, 788.

Knorr, W. R. (1996) 'The wrong text of Euclid: on Heiberg's text and its alternatives', *Centaurus* **36**: 208–76.

Lévy, T. (1997) 'Une version hébraïque inédite des *Eléments* d'Euclide', in *Les voies de la science grecque: Études sur la transmission des textes de l'Antiquité au dix-neuvième siècle*, ed. D. Jacquart. Geneva: 181–239.

Murdoch, J. (1971) 'Euclid: transmission of the *Elements*', in *Dictionary of Scientific Biography*, ed. C. C. Gillispie, vol. IV. New York: 437–59.

Pasquali, G. (1952) *Storia della tradizione e critica del testo*, 2nd edn. Florence.

Plooij, E. B. (1950) *Euclid's Conception of Ratio and his Definition of Proportional Magnitudes as Criticised by Arabian Commentators*, Rotterdam.

Reynolds, L. G. and N. G. Wilson (1988) *D'Homère à Érasme: La transmission des classiques grecs et latins*. Paris.

Rommevaux, S., A. Djebbar and B. Vitrac (2001) 'Remarques sur l'histoire du texte des *Éléments* d'Euclide', *Archive for History of Exact Sciences* **55**: 221–95.

Sabra, A. I. (1969) 'Simplicius's proof of Euclid's parallels postulate', *Journal of the Warburg and Courtauld Institutes* **32**: 1–24.

Vahabzadeh, B. (1997) 'Trois commentaires arabes sur les concepts de rapport et de proportionnalité'. Ph.D. thesis. Université de Paris VII.

(2002) 'Al-Mâhânî's Commentary on the concept of ratio', *Arabic Sciences and Philosophy* **12**: 9–52.

Van Haelst, J. (1989) 'Les origines du codex', in *Les débuts du codex*, ed. A. Blanchard. Turnhout: 13–35.

Vitrac, B. (2003) 'Les scholies grecques aux *Éléments* d'Euclide', *Revue d'Histoire des Sciences* **56**: 275–92.

(2004) 'A propos des démonstrations alternatives et autres substitutions de preuve dans les *Éléments* d'Euclide', *Archive for History of Exact Sciences* **59**: 1–44.

Weissenborn, H. (1882) *Die Übersetzungen des Euklid durch Campano und Zamberti*. Halle.

2 | Diagrams and arguments in ancient Greek mathematics: lessons drawn from comparisons of the manuscript diagrams with those in modern critical editions

KEN SAITO AND NATHAN SIDOLI

Introduction

In some ways, the works of ancient Greek geometry can be regarded as arguments about diagrams. Anyone who has ever looked at a medieval manuscript containing a copy of an ancient geometrical text knows that the most conspicuous characteristic of these works is the constant presence of diagrams.[1] Anyone who has ever read a Greek mathematical text, in any language, knows that the most prevalent feature of Greek mathematical prose is the constant use of letter names, which refer the reader's attention to the accompanying diagrams.

In recent years, particularly due to a chapter in Netz's *The Shaping of Deduction in Greek Mathematics* entitled 'The lettered diagram', historians of Greek mathematics have had a renewed interest in the relationship between the argument in the text and the figure that accompanies it.[2] Research projects that were motivated by this interest, however, quickly had to come to grips with the fact that the edited texts of canonical works of Greek geometry, although they contained a wealth of information about the manuscript evidence for the text itself, often said nothing at all about the diagrams. For years, the classical works of Apollonius, Archimedes and, most importantly, the *Elements* of Euclid have been read in edited Greek texts and modern translations that contain diagrams having little or no relation to the diagrams in the manuscript sources. Because they are essentially mathematical reconstructions, the diagrams in modern editions are often mathematically more intelligible than those in the manuscripts, but they are often historically misleading and occasionally even mathematically misleading.[3]

---

[1] In some cases, the diagrams were never actually drawn, but even their absence is immediately evident from the rectangular boxes that were left for them.

[2] N1999: 12–67.

[3] In this chapter, we will see a number of examples of modern diagrams that are more mathematically consistent with our understanding of the argument and a few that may have

In fact, a few scholars of the ancient mathematical sciences have for many years made critical studies of the manuscript figures, and Neugebauer often called for the critical and conceptual study of ancient and medieval diagrams.[4] These scholars, however, were mostly working on the exact sciences, particularly astronomy and, perhaps due to the tendency of historians of science to divide their research along contemporary disciplinary lines that would have made little sense to ancient mathematicians, these works have generally formed a minority interest for historians of ancient mathematics. Indeed, in his later editions, Heiberg paid more attention to the manuscript figures than he did in his earlier work, but by this time his editions of the canonical works were already complete. In fact, for his edition of Euclid's *Elements*, it appears that the diagrams were adopted from the tradition of printed texts without consulting the manuscript sources.

In this chapter, after briefly sketching the rise of scholarly interest in producing critical diagrams, we investigate the characteristics of manuscript diagrams in contrast to modern reconstructions. To the extent that the evidence will allow, we distinguish between those features of the manuscript diagrams that can be attributed to ancient practice and those that are probably the result of the medieval manuscript tradition, through which we have received the ancient texts. We close with some speculations about what this implies for the conceptual relationship between the figure and the text in ancient Greek mathematical works.

Heiberg's edition of Euclid's *Elements*

Heiberg (1883–8), on the basis of a study of manuscripts held in European libraries, prepared his edition of the *Elements* from seven manuscripts and the critical apparatus accompanying his text makes constant reference to these sources.[5] Nevertheless, there is usually no apparatus for the diagrams and hence no mention of their source.[6] An examination of the previous

led to historical misunderstandings for this reason. Mathematically misleading modern diagrams, on the other hand, are relatively rare; Neugebauer discusses one example from the edition of Theodosius' *On Days and Nights* prepared by Fecht. Neugebauer 1975: 752; Fecht 1927.

[4] For example see the section IV D, 2, 'Figures in Texts' in his *A History of Ancient Mathematical Astronomy*. Neugebauer 1975: 751–5.

[5] Heiberg 1903 later published a more detailed account of the manuscript sources and the reasons for his editorial choices. For a more extended discussion of Heiberg's work on the *Elements* and a discussion of the overall history of the text see Vitrac's contribution in this volume.

[6] While this is largely the case there are some exceptions. For example, the diagrams for *Elem.* XI.39 and XIII.15 are accompanied with apparatus. Heiberg and Stamatis 1969–77: IV, 73 and 166.

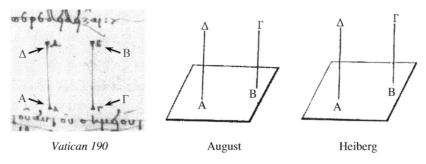

Figure 2.1 Diagrams for Euclid's *Elements*, Book XI, Proposition 12.

printed editions of the text, however, makes it clear that the diagrams accompanying Heiberg's edition were drawn entirely, or for the most part, by copying those in the edition of August (1826–9).[7] The August edition would have been particularly convenient for copying the diagrams, since, as was typical for a German technical publication of its time, the diagrams were printed together in fold-out pages at the end of the volumes.

Although nearly all the diagrams appear to have been so copied, a single example may be used to demonstrate this point. For *Elem.* XI.12, concerning the construction of a perpendicular to a given plane, the diagrams in all the manuscripts consist simply of two equal lines, ΔA and BΓ, placed side by side and labelled such that points Δ and B mark the top of the two lines. In Figure 2.1, we compare the diagram for *Elem.* XI.12 in *Vatican 190*, as representative of all the manuscripts, with that in both the August and Heiberg editions.[8] While *Vatican 190* is typical of the manuscript diagrams, that in Heiberg's text is clearly copied from the August diagram. Although the given plane is not shown in the manuscript figures, it appears in both the printed editions and it is used with the techniques of linear perspective to make the two lines appear to be in different planes from the plane of the drawing. Most significantly, however, there is a labelling error in the line BΓ. Point Γ is supposed to be in the given plane, and hence must be at the bottom of line BΓ, as in *Vatican 190*. This error was transmitted when the diagram was

---

[7] The diagrams to the arithmetical books are a clear exception. The August diagrams are dotted lines, whereas Heiberg's edition returns to the lines we find in the manuscripts. There also other, individual cases where the diagrams were redrawn, presumably because those in the August edition were considered to be mathematically unsatisfactory. For example, the diagram to *Elem.* XI.38 has been redrawn for Heiberg's edition, whereas all the surrounding diagrams are clearly copied. See also the diagram for *Elem.* XII.17. Compare Heiberg and Stamatis 1969–77: IV 75 and 128 with August 1826–9: Tab. IX and Tab. X.

[8] In this chapter, we refer to manuscripts by an abbreviated name in *italics*. Full library shelf marks are given in the references. For the Euclidian manuscripts see also Vitrac's chapter in this volume.

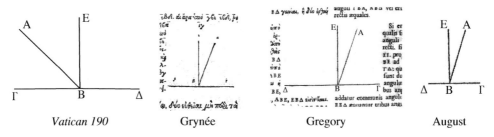

Figure 2.2 Diagrams for Euclid's *Elements*, Book I, Proposition 13.

copied, despite the fact that it could have been easily corrected from considerations of the orientation required by the text.

Indeed, whereas through the course of the modern period, following the general trends of classical scholarship, the editors of successive publications of the *Elements* tended to consult a wider and wider range of manuscripts and give their readers more and more information about these manuscripts, the diagrams that accompanied these editions were generally made on the basis of the diagrams in the previous editions.

As an example of this practice, we may take *Elem.* I.13, which concerns the sum of the angles on either side of a straight line that falls on another straight line. The manuscripts all agree in depicting angle ABΓ as opening to the left, as shown in Figure 2.2 by the example of *Vatican 190*.[9] Nevertheless, all printed editions, following the *editio princeps* of Grynée (1533), print angle ABΓ opening to the right.

In some sense, this may have been a result of the division of labour of the publishers themselves. Whereas the editions were prepared by classical scholars and typeset by printers who were knowledgeable in the classical languages and generally had some sensitivity to the historical issues involved in producing a printed text from manuscript sources, the diagrams were almost certainly drafted by professional illustrators, who would have been skilled in the techniques of visual reproduction but perhaps uninterested in the historical issues at hand. Nevertheless, the fact that the scholars who prepared these editions and the editors who printed them were content to use the diagrams of the previous editions as their primary sources says a great deal about their views of the relative importance of the historical sanctity of the text and of the diagrams in Greek mathematical works.

Already, during the course of Heiberg's career, the attitudes of scholars towards the importance of the manuscript diagrams began to change. In the late 1890s, in the edition he prepared with Besthorn of al-Nayrīzī's

---

[9] See Saito 2006: 110 for further images of the manuscript figures.

commentaries to the *Elements*, the diagrams were taken directly from *Leiden 399*, and hence often quite different from those printed in his edition of the Greek.[10] By the time he edited Theodosius' *Spherics*, he must have become convinced of the importance of giving the diagrams critical attention, because the finished work includes diagrams based on the manuscripts, generally accompanied with a critical note beginning 'In fig.'[11]

Editions of manuscript diagrams

Because the manuscript diagrams for spherical geometry are so strikingly different from what we have grown to expect since the advent of the consistent application of techniques of linear perspective in the early modern period, the editions of ancient Greek works in spherical astronomy were some of the first in which the editors began to apply critical techniques to the figures. For example in the eighth, and last, volume of the complete works of Euclid, for his edition of the *Phenomena*, Menge (1916) provided diagrams based on the manuscript sources and in some cases included critical notes.

One of the most influential editions with regard to the critical treatment of diagrams was that made by Rome (1931–43) of the commentaries by Pappus and Theon to Ptolemy's *Almagest*. The diagrams in this long work were taken from the manuscript sources and their variants are discussed in critical notes placed directly below the figures themselves.[12] Rome's practices influenced other scholars working in French and the editions by Mogenet (1950), of Autolycus' works in spherical astronomy, and Lejeune (1956), of the Latin translation of Ptolemy's *Optics*, both contain manuscript figures with critical notes.

More recently, the majority tendency has been to provide manuscript diagrams with critical assessment. For example, the editions by Jones (1986) and Czinczenheim (2000) of Book VII of Pappus' *Collection* and

---

[10] Besthorn *et al.* 1897–1932.

[11] Heiberg 1927. In fact, these critical notes are difficult to notice, since they are found among the notes for the Greek text. The notes for the Greek text, however, are prefaced by numbers referring to the lines of the text, whereas the diagrams are always located in the Latin translation, which has no line numbers. Neugebauer 1975: 751–5 seems to have missed them, since he makes no mention of them in his criticism of the failure of classical scholars to pay sufficient attention to the manuscript diagrams of the works of spherical astronomy.

[12] In connection with the early interest that Rome and Neugebauer showed in manuscript figures, we should mention the papers they wrote on Heron's *Dioptra*, the interpretation of which depends in vital ways on understanding the diagram. Rome 1923; Neugebauer 1938–9; Sidoli 2005.

Theodosius' *Spherics*, respectively, both contain critical diagrams, and a recent translation of Archimedes' *Sphere and Cylinder* also includes a critical assessment of the manuscript figures.[13]

Nevertheless, although there are critically edited diagrams for many works, especially those of the exact sciences, the most canonical works – the works of Archimedes and Apollonius, the *Elements* of Euclid and the *Almagest* of Ptolemy – because they were edited by Heiberg early in his career, are accompanied by modern, redrawn diagrams. Hence, because a study of Greek mathematics almost always begins with the *Elements*, and because the manuscript diagrams of this work contain many distinctive and unexpected features, it is essential that we reassess the manuscript evidence.

Characteristics of manuscript diagrams

In this section, focusing largely on the *Elements*, we examine some of the characteristic features of the manuscript diagrams as material objects that distinguish them from their modern counterparts. Manuscript diagrams are historically contingent objects which were read and copied and redrawn many times over the centuries. In some cases, they may tell us about ancient practice, in other cases, about medieval interpretations of ancient practice, and in some few cases, they simply tell us about the idiosyncratic reading of a single scribe. In the following sections, we begin with broad general tendencies that can almost certainly be ascribed to the whole history of the transmission, and then move into more individual cases where the tradition shows modification and interpretation. In this chapter, we present summary overviews, not systematic studies.

Overspecification

One of the most pervasive features of the manuscript figures is the tendency to represent more regularity among the geometric objects than is demanded by the argument. For example, we find rectangles representing parallelograms, isosceles triangles representing arbitrary triangles,

---

[13] Netz 2004. In fact, however, the figures printed by Czinczenheim contain some peculiar features. Although she claims to have based her diagrams on those of *Vatican 204*, they often contain curved lines of a sort almost never seen in Greek mathematical manuscripts and certainly not in *Vatican 204*. Thus, although her critical notes are useful, the visual representation of the figures is often misleading.

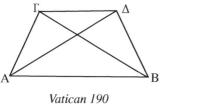
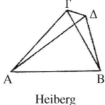

Vatican 190   Heiberg

Figure 2.3 Diagrams for Euclid's *Elements*, Book I, Proposition 7.

squares representing rectangles, and symmetry in the figure where none is required by the text.[14] This tendency towards greater regularity, which we call 'overspecification', is so prevalent in the Greek, Arabic and Latin transmissions of the *Elements* that it almost certainly reflects ancient practice.

We begin with an example of a manuscript diagram portraying more symmetry than is required by the text. *Elem.* I.7 demonstrates that two given straight lines constructed from the extremities of a given line, on the same side of it, will meet in one and only one point. In Figure 2.3, where the given lines are AΓ and BΓ, the proof proceeds indirectly by assuming some lines equal to these, say AΔ and BΔ, meet at some other point, Δ, and then showing this to be impossible. As long as they are on the same side of line AB, points Γ and Δ may be assumed to be anywhere and the proof is still valid. Heiberg, following the modern tradition, depicts this as shown in Figure 2.3. All of the manuscripts used by Heiberg agree, however, in placing points Γ and Δ on a line parallel to line AB and arranged such that triangle ABΔ and triangle ABΓ appear to be equal.[15] In this way, the figure becomes perfectly symmetrical and, to our modern taste, fails to convey the arbitrariness that the text allows in the relative positions of points Γ and Δ.

We turn now to a case of the tendency of arbitrary angles to be represented as orthogonal. *Elem.* I.35 shows that parallelograms that stand on the same base between the same parallels are equal to each other. In Figure 2.4, the proof that parallelogram ABΓΔ equals parallelogram EBΓZ follows from the addition and subtraction of areas represented in the figure and would make no sense without an appeal to the figure in order to understand these operations. In the modern figures that culminate in Heiberg's edition, the parallelograms are both depicted with oblique angles, whereas

---

[14] In this chapter, we give only a few select examples. Many more examples, however, can be seen by consulting the manuscript diagrams themselves. For Book I of the *Elements*, see Saito 2006. For Books II–VI of the *Elements*, as well as Euclid's *Phenomena* and *Optics*, see the report of a three-year research project on manuscript diagrams, carried out by Saito, available online at www.hs.osakafu-u.ac.jp/~ken.saito/.

[15] See Saito 2006: 103 for further images of the manuscript figures.

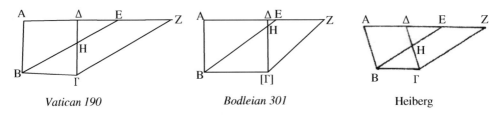

Figure 2.4 Diagrams for Euclid's *Elements*, Book I, Proposition 35.

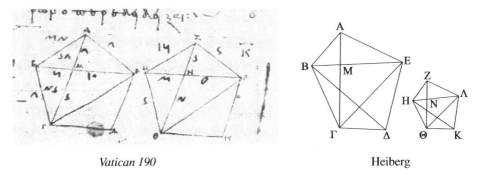

Figure 2.5 Diagrams for Euclid's *Elements*, Book VI, Proposition 20.

in the manuscripts the base parallelogram ΑΒΓΔ is always depicted as a rectangle, as seen in *Bodleian 301*, and often even as a square, as seen in *Vatican 190*.[16] Once again, to our modern sensibility, the diagrams appear to convey more regularity than is required by the proof. That is, the angles need not be right and the sides need not be the same size, and yet they are so depicted in the manuscripts.

We close with one rather extreme example of overspecification. *Elem.* VI.20 shows that similar polygons are divided into an equal number of triangles, of which corresponding triangles in each polygon are similar, and that the ratio of the polygons to one another is equal to the ratio of corresponding triangles to one another, and that the ratio of the polygons to one another is the duplicate of the ratio of a pair of corresponding sides. Although the enunciation is given in such general terms, following the usual practice of Greek geometers, the enunciation and proof is made for a particular instantiation of these objects; in this case, a pair of pentagons. In Figure 2.5, the modern diagram printed by Heiberg depicts two similar, but unequal, irregular pentagons. In *Bodleian 301*, on the other hand, we find two pentagons that are both regular and equal. This diagram strikes the modern eye as inappropriate for this situation because the proposition is not about equal, regular pentagons, but rather similar polygons of

---

[16] See Saito 2006: 131 for further images of the manuscript figures.

any shape.[17] In the modern figure, because the pentagons are irregular, we somehow imagine that they could represent any pair of polygons, although, in fact a certain specific pair of irregular pentagons are depicted.

The presence of overspecification is so prevalent in the diagrams of the medieval transmission of geometric texts that we believe it must be representative of ancient practice. Moreover, there is no mathematical reason why the use of overspecified diagrams should not have been part of the ancient tradition. For us, the lack of regularity in the modern figures is suggestive of greater generality. The ancient and medieval scholars, however, apparently did not have this association between irregularity and greater generality, and, except perhaps from a statistical standpoint, there is no reason why these concepts should be so linked. The drawing printed by Heiberg is not a drawing of 'any' pair of polygons, it is a drawing of two particular irregular pentagons. Since the text states that the two polygons are similar, they could be represented by any two similar polygons, as say those in *Bodleian 301* which also happen to be equal and regular. Of course statistically, an arbitrarily chosen pair of similar polygons is more likely to be irregular and unequal, but statistical considerations, aside from being anachronistic, are hardly relevant. The diagram is simply a representation of the objects under discussion. For us, an irregular triangle is somehow a more satisfying representation of 'any' triangle, whereas for the ancient and medieval mathematical scholars an arbitrary triangle might be just as well, if not better, depicted by a regular triangle.

Indifference to visual accuracy

Another widespread tendency that we find in the manuscripts is the use of diagrams that are not graphically accurate depictions of the mathematical objects discussed in the text. For example, unequal lines may be depicted as equal, equal angles may be depicted as unequal, the bisection of a line may look more like a quadrature, an arc of a parabola may be represented with the arc of a circle, or straight lines may be depicted as curved. These tendencies show a certain indifference to graphical accuracy and can be divided into two types, which we call 'indifference to metrical accuracy' and 'indifference to geometric shape'.

We begin with an example that exhibits both overspecification and indifference to metrical accuracy. *Elem.* 1.44 is a problem that shows how to

---

[17] In fact, the proof given in the proposition is also about a more specific polygon in that it has five sides and is divided into three similar triangles, but it achieves generality by being generally applicable for any given pair of rectilinear figures. This proof is an example of the type of proof that Freudenthal 1953 called *quasi-general*.

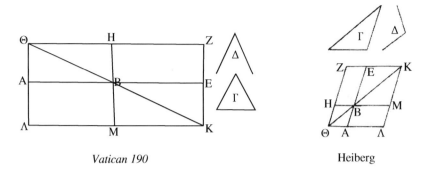

Vatican 190   Heiberg

Figure 2.6 Diagrams for Euclid's *Elements*, Book i, Proposition 44.

construct, on a given line, a parallelogram that contains a given angle and is equal to a given triangle. As exemplified by *Vatican 190* in Figure 2.6, in all the manuscripts, the parallelogram is represented by a rectangle, and in the majority of the manuscripts that Heiberg used for his edition there is no correlation between the magnitudes of the given angle and triangle and those of the constructed angle and parallelogram.[18] In the modern figure, printed by Heiberg and seen in Figure 2.6, however, not only is the constructed figure depicted as an oblique parallelogram, but the magnitudes of the given and constructed objects have been set out as equal.

We turn now to an occurrence of metrical indifference that is, in a sense, the opposite of overspecification. In *Elem.* ii.7, Euclid demonstrates a proposition asserting the metrical relationship obtaining between squares and rectangles constructed on a given line cut at random. The overall geometric object is stated to be a square and it contains two internal squares. Nevertheless, as seen in the examples of *Vatican 190* and *Bodleian 301* in Figure 2.7, the majority of Heiberg's manuscripts show these squares as rectangles.[19] We should note also the extreme overspecification of *Bodleian 301*, in which all of the internal rectangles appear to be equal. In general, there seems to be a basic indifference as to whether or not the diagram should visually represent the most essential metrical properties of the geometric objects it depicts.

[18] In this chapter, when we speak of the majority of the manuscripts, we mean the majority of the manuscripts selected by the text editor as independent witnesses for the establishment of the text. We should be wary of assuming, however, that the majority reading is the best, or most pristine. See Saito 2006: 140, for further images of the manuscript figures. In *Vienna 31*, as is often the case with this manuscript, we find the magnitudes have been drawn so as to accurately represent the stipulations of the text (see the discussion of this manuscript in 'Correcting the diagram', below).

[19] See Saito 2008 for further images of the manuscript diagrams. In *Vienna 31* and *Bologna 18–19*, the squares, indeed, look like squares.

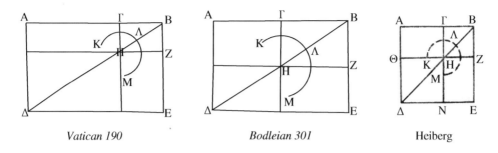

Figure 2.7 Diagrams for Euclid's *Elements*, Book II, Proposition 7.

As well as metrical indifference, the manuscript diagrams often seem to reveal an indifference toward the geometric shape of the objects as specified by the text. The most prevalent example of this is the use of circular arcs to portray all curved lines. As an example, we may take the diagram for Apollonius *Con.* 1.16. As seen in Figure 2.8, the diagram in *Vatican 206* shows the two branches of an hyperbola as two semicircles. Indeed, all the diagrams in this manuscript portray conic sections with circular arcs. Heiberg's diagram, on the other hand, depicts the hyperbolas with hyperbolas.

This diagram, however, is also interesting because it includes a case of overspecification, despite the fact that Eutocius, already in the sixth century, noticed this overspecification and suggested that it be avoided.[20] In Figure 2.8, the line AB appears to be drawn as the axis of the hyperbola, such that HK and ΘΛ are shown as orthogonal ordinates, whereas the theorem treats the properties of any diameter, such that HK and ΘΛ could also be oblique ordinates. Eutocius suggested that they be so drawn in order to make it clear that the proposition is about diameters, not the axis. Nevertheless, despite Eutocius' remarks, the overspecification of this figure was preserved into the medieval period, and indeed was maintained by Heiberg in his edition of the text.[21] This episode indicates that overspecification was indeed in effect in the ancient period and that although Eutocius objected to this particular instance of it, he was not generally opposed, and even here his objection was ignored.

As well as being used to represent the more complicated curves of the conics sections, circular arcs are also used to represent straight lines. As Netz has shown,[22] this practice was consistently applied in the diagrams for

[20] Heiberg 1891–3: 224; Decorps-Foulquier 1999: 74–5.
[21] A more general figure, which would no doubt have pleased Eutocius, is given in Taliaferro, Densmore and Donahue 1998: 34.
[22] Netz 2004.

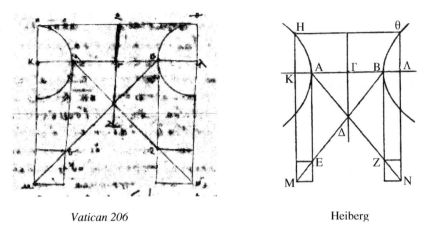

Vatican 206   Heiberg

Figure 2.8 Diagrams for Apollonius' *Conica*, Book I, Proposition 16.

Archimedes' *Sphere and Cylinder* for a polygon with short sides that might be visually confused with the arcs of the circumscribed circle.[23]

In the manuscript diagrams of *Elem.* IV.16, however, we have good evidence that the curved lines are the result of later intervention by the scribes. *Elem.* IV.16 is a problem that shows how to construct a regular 15-gon in a circle (Figure 2.9). The manuscript evidence for this figure is rather involved and, in fact, none of the manuscripts that Heiberg used contain the same diagram in the place of the primary diagram, although there is some obvious cross-contamination in the secondary, marginal diagrams.[24] Nevertheless, it is most likely that the archetype was a metrically inexact representation of the sides of the auxiliary equilateral triangle and regular pentagon depicted with straight lines, as found in *Bologna 18–19*

---

[23] In the present state of the evidence, it is difficult to determine with certainty whether or not the curved lines in the Archimedes tradition go back to antiquity, but there is no good reason to assert that they do not. All of our extant Greek manuscripts for the complete treatise of *Sphere and Cylinder* are based on a single Byzantine manuscript, which is now lost. This is supported by the fragmentary evidence of the oldest manuscript, the so-called Archimedes Palimpsest, whose figures also contain curved lines. The diagrams in an autograph of William of Moerbeke's Latin translation, *Vatican Ottob. 1850*, however, made on the basis of a different Greek codex, also now lost, have straight lines, but this does not prove anything. The source manuscript may have had straight lines or Moerbeke may have changed them. Whatever the case, we now have three witnesses, two of which agree on curved lines and one of which contains straight lines.

[24] See Saito 2008: 171–3 for a full discussion. This previous report, however, was written before the manuscripts could be consulted in person. Since Saito has now examined most of the relevant manuscripts, it is clear from the colour of the lines, the pattern of erasures and so on, that the curved lines are part of the later tradition. See www.hs.osakafu-u.ac.jp/~ken.saito/ diagram/ for further updates.

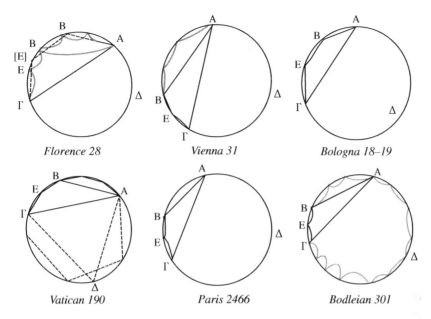

| Florence 28 | Vienna 31 | Bologna 18–19 |

| Vatican 190 | Paris 2466 | Bodleian 301 |

Figure 2.9 Diagrams for Euclid's *Elements*, Book IV, Proposition 16. Dashed lines were drawn in and later erased. Grey lines were drawn in a different ink or with a different instrument.

and in the erased part of *Florence 28*.[25] In *Bodleian 301* and *Paris 2466* we see examples in which the scribe has made an effort to draw lines AB and AΓ so as to portray more accurately the sides of a regular pentagon and an equilateral triangle, respectively. In *Bodleian 301*, the external sides of the figures are clearly curved, while in *Paris 2466* this curvature is slight. In *Vienna 31*, the original four lines were straight and metrically accurate, as is usual for this manuscript, and a later hand added further curved lines. In *Vatican 190*, it appears that all the sides of the auxiliary triangle and pentagon were drawn in at some point and then later erased, presumably so as to bring the figure into conformity with the evidence of some other source.

Not only were circles used for straight lines, but we also have at least one example of straight lines being used to represent a curved line. This rather interesting example of indifference to visual accuracy comes from one of the most fascinating manuscripts of Greek mathematics, the so-called Archimedes Palimpsest, a tenth-century manuscript containing various Hellenistic treatises including technical works by Archimedes that was

[25] In *Florence 28*, the metrically inaccurate figure with straight lines was erased and drawn over with a metrically accurate figure with curved lines. The colour of the ink makes it clear that the rectilinear lines that remain from the original are AΓ and the short part of AB that coincides with the new curved line AB.

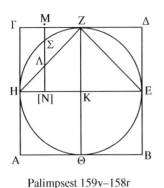

Palimpsest 159v–158r

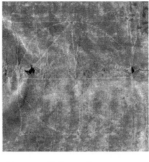

Reversed X-ray fluorescence
calcium image

Optical multispectral image

Figure 2.10 Diagrams for Archimedes' *Method*, Proposition 12.

palimpsested as a prayer book some centuries later.[26] In the section of the treatise that Heiberg called *Method* 14, Archimedes discusses the metrical relationships that obtain between a prism, a cylinder and a parabolic solid that are constructed within the same square base.[27] In Figure 2.10, the base of the prism is rectangle EΔΓH, that of the cylinder is semicircle EZH, while that of the parabolic solid is triangle EZH. Thus, in this diagram, a parabola is represented by an isosceles triangle. Since the parabola is defined in the text by the relationship between the ordinates and abscissa, and since the triangle intersects and meets the same lines as the parabola, this was apparently seen as a perfectly acceptable representation. In this way, the triangle functions as a purely schematic representation of the parabola. Indeed, without the text we would have no way to know that the diagram represents a parabola.

Diagrams in solid geometry

The schematic nature of ancient and medieval diagrams becomes most obvious when we consider the figures of solid geometry. Although there are some diagrams in the manuscripts of solid geometry that attempt to give a pictorial representation of the geometric objects, for the most part, they forego linear perspective in favour of schematic representation. This means that they do not serve to convey a sense of the overall spacial relationships

---

[26] The circuitous story of this manuscript is told by Netz and Noel 2007.

[27] This section of the *Method* is discussed by Netz, Saito and Tchernetska 2001–2. The diagram found in the palimpsest is difficult to see in the original. Here, we include two images developed by researchers in the Archimedes Palimpsest Project. The diagram is in the left-hand column of the text spanning pages 159v–158r. These images, licensed under the Creative Commons Attribution 3.0 Unported Access Rights, are available online at www.archimedespalimpsest.org.

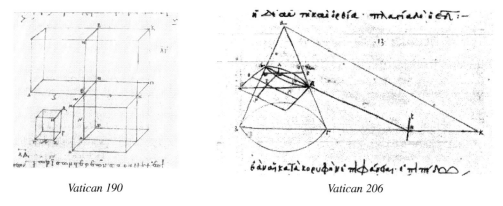

Vatican 190   *Vatican 206*

Figure 2.11 Diagrams for Euclid's *Elements*, Book xi, Proposition 33 and Apollonius' *Conica*, Book i, Proposition 13.

obtaining among the objects, but rather to convey specific mathematical relationships that are essential to the argument.

Some conspicuous exceptions to this general tendency should be mentioned. For example, the diagrams for the rectilinear solids treated in *Elem.* xi and xii and the early derivations of the conic sections in the cone, in *Con.* i, appear to use techniques of linear perspective to convey a sense of the three-dimensionality of the objects. In Figure 2.11, we reproduce the diagram for *Elem.* xi.33 from *Vatican 190* and that for *Con.* i.13 from *Vatican 206.*

In all of these cases, however, it is possible to represent the three-dimensionality of the objects simply and without introducing any object not explicitly named in the proof merely for the sake of the diagram. For example, in Figure 2.1 above, the plane upon which the perpendicular is to be constructed does not appear in the manuscript figure. Hence, even in these three-dimensional diagrams, techniques of linear perspective are used only to the extent that they do not conflict with the schematic nature of the diagram. Auxiliary, purely graphical elements are not used, nor is there any attempt to convey the visual impression of the mathematical objects through graphical techniques. An example of this is the case of circles seen at an angle. Although it is not clear that there was a consistent theory of linear perspective in antiquity, ancient artists regularly drew circles as ovals and Ptolemy, in his *Geography*, describes the depiction of circles seen from an angle as represented by ovals,[28] nevertheless, in the medieval manuscripts such oblique circles are always drawn with two

---

[28] Knorr 1992: 280–91; Berggren and Jones 2000: 116.

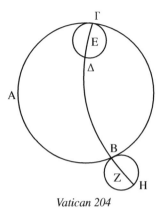

Vatican 204

Figure 2.12 Diagrams for Theodosius' *Spherics*, Book II, Proposition 6.

circular arcs that meet at cusps, as seen in Figure 2.11.[29] This confirms that the diagrams were not meant to be a visual depiction of the objects, but rather a representation of certain essential mathematical properties.

Likewise, in the figures of spherical geometry, if the sphere itself is not named or required by the proof, we will often see the objects themselves simply drawn free-floating in the plane, to all appearances as though they were actually located in the plane of the figure. Theodosius' *Spher.* II.6 shows that if, in a sphere, a great circle is tangent to a lesser circle, then it is also tangent to another lesser circle that is equal and parallel to the first. In Figure 2.12, we find the great circle in the sphere, ABΓ, and the two equal and parallel lesser circles that are tangent to it, ΓΔ and BH, all lying flat in the same plane, with no attempt to portray their spacial relationships to each other or the sphere in which they are located.

The diagram for *Spher.* II.6 thus highlights the schematic nature of diagrams in the works of spherical geometry. The theorem is about the type of tangency that obtains between a great circle and two equal lesser circles and this tangency is essentially the only thing conveyed by the figure. The actual spacial arrangement of the circles on the sphere must either be imagined by the reader or drawn out on some real globe.[30]

---

[29] With respect to linear perspective, there is still a debate as to whether or not the concept of the vanishing point was consistently applied in antiquity. See Andersen 1987 and Knorr 1991. As Jones 2000: 55–6 has pointed out, Pappus' commentary to Euclid's *Optics* 35 includes a vanishing point, but it is not located in accordance with the modern principles of linear perspective.

[30] We argue elsewhere that Theodosius was, indeed, concerned with the practical aspects of drawing figures on solid globes, but that this practice was not explicitly discussed in the *Spherics*; Sidoli and Saito 2009.

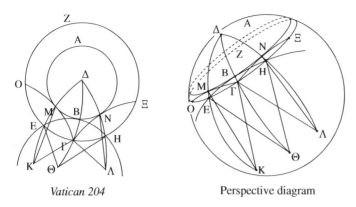

Vatican 204	Perspective diagram

Figure 2.13 Diagrams for Theodosius' *Spherics*, Book II, Proposition 15.

The schematic role of diagrams in spherical geometry becomes unmistakable when we compare the diagram of one of the more involved propositions as found in the manuscripts with one intended to portray the same objects using principles of linear perspective. *Spher.* II.15 is a problem that demonstrates the construction of a great circle passing through a given point and tangent to a given lesser circle. As can be seen in Figure 2.13, merely by looking at the manuscript diagram, without any discussion of the objects and their arrangement, it is rather difficult to get an overall sense of what the diagram is meant to represent. Nevertheless, certain essential features are conveyed, such as the conpolarity of parallel circles, the tangency and intersection of key circles, and so on. It is clear that the manuscript diagram is meant to be read in conjunction with the text as referring to some other object, either an imagined sphere or more likely a real sphere on which the lines and circles were actually drawn. It tells the reader how to understand the labelling and arrangement of the objects under discussion, so that the text can then be read as referring to these objects. The modern figure, on the other hand, by selecting a particular vantage point as most opportune and then allowing the reader to see the objects from this point, does a better job of conveying the overall spacial relationships that obtain among the objects.[31]

---

[31] We should point out, however, that the modern diagram in Figure 2.13, as well as being in linear perspective, employes a number of graphical techniques that we do not find in the manuscript sources, such as the use of non-circular curves, dotted lines, highlighted points, and so on.

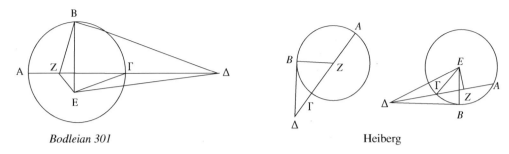

Bodleian 301   Heiberg

Figure 2.14 Diagrams for Euclid's *Elements*, Book III, Proposition 36.

One diagram for multiple cases

In the foregoing three sections, we have discussed characteristics of the medieval diagrams that are so prevalent that they almost certainly reflect ancient practice. We turn now to characteristics that are more individual but which, nevertheless, form an essential part of the material transmission through which we must understand the ancient texts.

For a few propositions that are divided into multiple cases, we find, nevertheless, the use of a single diagram to represent the cases. There is some question about the originality of most of these, and in fact it appears that, in general, Euclid did not include multiple cases and that those propositions that do have cases were altered in late antiquity.[32] Nevertheless, even if the cases are all due to late ancient authors, they are historically interesting and the manuscript tradition shows considerable variety in the diagrams. This indicates that single diagrams for multiple cases were probably in the text at least by late antiquity and that the medieval scribes had difficulty understanding them and hence introduced the variety that we now find.

As an example, we consider *Elem.* III.36. The proposition shows that if, from a point outside a circle, a line is drawn cutting the circle, it will be cut by the circle such that the rectangle contained by its parts will be equal to the square drawn on the tangent from the point to the circle. That is, in Figure 2.14, the rectangle contained by AΔ and ΔΓ is equal to the square on ΔB. In the text, as we now have it, this is proved in two cases, first where line AΔ passes through the centre of the circle and second where it

---

[32] See Saito 2006: 85–90 for the case of a single figure containing two cases in *Elem.* III.25, in which the division into cases was almost certainly not due to Euclid. The Arabic transmission of the *Elements* gives further evidence for the elaboration of a single figure into multiple figures. In the eastern Arabic tradition, we find a single figure for both *Elem.* III.31 and IV.5 (see for example, *Uppsala 20*: 42v and 38v), while in the Andalusian Arabic tradition, which was also transmitted into Latin, we find multiple figures for these propositions (compare *Rabāṭ 53*: 126–8 and 145–6 with Busard 1984: 83–5 and 102–5).

does not. In Heiberg's edition, and *Vienna 31* (which often has corrected diagrams), there is an individual figure for each case. In the majority of Heiberg's manuscripts, however, there is only a single figure and it contains two different points that represent the centre, one for each case. In Figure 2.14, we reproduce the two diagrams from Heiberg's edition, which are mathematically the same as those in *Vienna 31*, and an example of the single figure taken from *Bodleian 301*. In the single diagram, as found in *Bodleian 301*, there are two centres, points E and Z, and neither of them lies at the centre of the circle. Nevertheless, if we suppose that they are indeed centres, the proof can be read and understood on the basis of this figure.

Despite these peculiarities, there are a number of reasons for thinking that this figure is close to the original on which the others were based. It appears in the majority of Heiberg's manuscripts, and the other diagrams contain minor problems, such as missing or misplaced lines, or are obviously corrected.[33] Moreover, the single figure appears to have caused widespread confusion in the manuscript tradition. In most of the manuscripts, there are also marginal figures which either correct the primary figure or provide a figure that is clearly meant for a single case.

Hence, although we cannot, at present, be certain of the history of this theorem and its figure, the characteristics and variety of the figures should be used in any analysis of the text that seeks to establish its authenticity or authorship. This holds true for nearly all of the propositions that were clearly subject to modification in the tradition.

Correcting the diagrams

Medieval scribes also made what they, no doubt, considered to be corrections to the diagrams both by redrawing the figures according to their own interpretation of the mathematics involved and by checking the diagrams against those in other versions of the same treatise and, if they were different, correcting on this basis. We will call the first practice 'redrawing' and the latter 'cross-contamination'. We have already seen the example of *Elem.* iv.16, on the construction of the regular 15-gon (see Figure 2.9), in which the scribes corrected for metrical indifference and drew the lines of the polygon as curved lines to distinguish them better from the arcs of the circumscribing circle.

---

[33] See Saito 2008: 78–9 for a discussion of variants of this diagram in the manuscripts of the *Elements*.

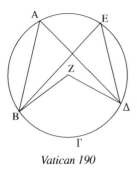   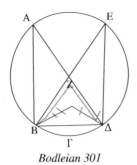   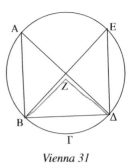

   Vatican 190   Bodleian 301   Vienna 31

Figure 2.15 Diagrams for Euclid's *Elements*, Book III, Proposition 21.

In a number of cases, the tendencies toward overspecification and graphical indifference resulted in a figure that was difficult to interpret as a graphical object. For example, we may refer again to Figure 2.14 in which two different centres of the circle are depicted, neither of which appears to lie at the centre of the circle. In such cases, the scribes often tried to correct the figure so that it could be more readily interpreted without ambiguity.

As an example of a redrawn diagram, we take *Elem.* III.21, which proves that, in a circle, angles that subtend the same arc are equal to one another. As seen in Figure 2.15, *Vatican 190* portrays the situation by showing the two angles BAΔ and BEΔ as clearly separated from the angle at the centre, angle BZΔ, which is twice both of them. In the majority of Heiberg's manuscripts, however, as seen in *Bodleian 301* and *Vienna 31*, through overspecification the lines BA and EΔ have been drawn parallel to each other and at right angles to BΔ, so that the lines AΔ and BE appear to intersect at the centre of the circle. In the course of the proposition, however, centre Z is found and lines BZ and ZΔ are joined. In order to depict centre Z as distinct from the intersection of lines AΔ and BE, centre Z has been placed off centre, often by later hands, as seen in the examples of *Bodleian 301* and *Vienna 31*.[34] Because of the variety of the manuscript figures, it does not seem possible to be certain of the archetype, but it probably either had point Z as the intersection of AΔ and BE, as in the example of *Vienna 31*, or it had a second centre called Z but not located at the centre of the circle, as in the example of *Bodleian 301*.[35] Later readers, then, found this situation confusing and corrected the diagrams accordingly. In this case, the redrawing was done directly on top of the original figure.

---

[34] See Saito 2008: 67 for further discussion of this diagram.
[35] In *Bodleian 301*, a later hand appears to have crossed out this original second centre, Z, and moved it closer to the centre of the circle.

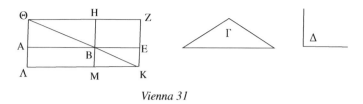

Vienna 31

Figure 2.16 Diagrams for Euclid's *Elements*, Book I, Proposition 44.

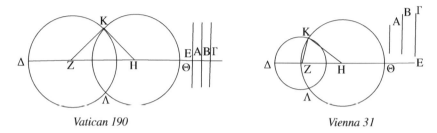

Vatican 190   *Vienna 31*

Figure 2.17 Diagrams for Euclid's *Elements*, Book I, Proposition 22.

The redrawing, however, might also be done at the time when the text was copied and the figures drafted. In this case, the source diagram is lost in this part of the tradition. Of the manuscripts used by Heiberg, the diagrams in *Vienna 31* are often redrawn for metrical accuracy, but less often for overspecification.[36] For the diagram accompanying *Elem.* I.44, the figure in *Vienna 31* (see Figure 2.16) should be compared with that in *Vatican 190* (see Figure 2.6). As can be seen, the given area Γ is indeed the size of the parallelogram constructed on line AB, but the parallelogram is depicted as a rectangle and this is reflected in the fact that the given angle, Δ, is depicted as right. In this case, the diagram is metrically accurate but it still represents any parallelogram with a rectangle.

For an example in which the diagram in *Vienna 31* has been corrected both for metrical accuracy and overspecification, we consider *Elem.* I.22, which demonstrates the construction of a triangle with three given sides. As seen in Figure 2.17, the older tradition, here exemplified by *Vatican 190*, represents the constructed triangle with the isosceles triangle ZKH, and the given lines with the equal lines A, B and Γ. In some of the manuscripts, however, the constructed triangle ZKH is drawn as an irregular acute triangle.[37] In Figure 2.17 we see the example of *Vienna 31*, in which the

---

[36] As we saw in the foregoing example, in the case of *Elem.* III.21, however, the original scribe of *Vienna 31* did not correct the diagram, but a correction was added by a later hand.

[37] See Saito 2006: 118 for a larger selection of the manuscript figures. The fact that *Vatican 190* belongs to the older tradition is confirmed by the Arabic transmission.

constructed triangle is depicted as an irregular, acute triangle and all of its sides are depicted as the same length as the sides that have been given for the construction. Indeed, here we have a figure that is fully in accord with modern tastes.

For *Elem.* I.22, of the manuscripts used by Heiberg in his edition, *Bodleian 301* also depicts the constructed triangle as an irregular, acute triangle, similar to that in *Vienna 31*. The fact that *Vienna 31* and *Bodleian 301* have a similar irregular, acute triangle could either indicate that scribes in both traditions independently had the idea to draw an irregular, acute triangle and randomly drew one of the same shape or, more likely, a scribe in one tradition saw the figure in the other and copied it. There is considerable evidence that this kind of cross-contamination took place. As another example that we have already seen, we may mention *Elem.* III.21 in which both *Vienna 31* and *Bodleian 301* show a second centre drawn in freehand at some time after the original drawing was complete. Moreover, in the case of *Elem.* III.21, in *Florence 28*, which has the same primary diagram as *Bodleian 301*, we find a marginal diagram like that in *Vatican 190*, while in *Bologna 18–19*, which has the same primary diagram as *Vatican 190*, we find a marginal diagram like that in *Florence 28*.

Hence, as well as being used as a cross-reference for the primary diagram, the figures of a second or third manuscript were often drawn into the margin as a secondary diagram. Although we are now only at the beginning stages of such studies, this process of cross-contamination suggests the possibility of analysing the transmission dependencies of the diagrams themselves without necessarily relying on those of the text. Indeed, there is now increasing evidence that the figures, like the scholia, were sometimes transmitted independently of the text.[38] The process of cross-contamination has left important clues in the manuscript sources that should be exploited to help us understand how the manuscript diagrams were used and read.

Ancient and medieval manuscript diagrams

Since the ancient and medieval diagrams are material objects that were transmitted along with the text, we should consider the ways they were copied, read and understood with respect to the transmission of the text.

---

[38] For examples of the independent transmission of the scholia of Aristarchus' *On the Sizes and Distances of the Sun and Moon* and Theodosius' *Spherics* see Noack 1992 and Czinczenheim 2000. The independent transmission of the manuscript figures for Calcidius' Latin translation of Plato's *Timaeus* has been shown by Tak 1972.

Although, for the most part, the text and diagrams appear to have been copied as faithfully as possible, at various times in the Greek transmission, and perhaps more often in the Arabic tradition, mathematically minded individuals re-edited the texts and redrew the diagrams.

For the most part, in Greek manuscripts the diagrams are drawn into boxes that were left blank when the text was copied, whereas in the Arabic and Latin manuscripts the diagrams were often drawn by the same scribe as copied the text, as is evident from the fact that the text wraps around the diagram. Nevertheless, except during periods of cultural transmission and appropriation, the diagrams appear to have been generally transmitted by scribes who based their drawings on those in their source manuscripts, despite the fact that the diagrams can largely be redrawn on the basis of a knowledge of the mathematics contained in the text. Hence, the diagrams in the medieval manuscripts give evidence for two, in some sense conflicting, tendencies: (1) the scribal transmission of ancient treatises based on a concept of the sanctity of the text and (2) the use of the ancient works in the mathematical sciences for teaching and developing those sciences and the consequent criticism of the received text from the perspective of a mathematical reading.

For these reasons, when we use the medieval diagrams as evidence for ancient practices, when we base our understanding of the intended uses of the diagrams on these sources, we should look for general tendencies and not become overly distracted by the evidence of idiosyncratic sources.

Diagrams and generality

The two most prevalent characteristics of the manuscript diagrams are what we have called overspecification and indifference to visual accuracy. The consistent use of overspecification implies that the diagram was not meant to convey an idea of the level of generality discussed in the text. The diagram simply depicts some representative example of the objects under discussion and the fact that this example is more regular than is required was apparently not considered to be a problem. In the case of research, discussion or presentation, a speaker could of course refer to the level of generality addressed by the text, or, in fact, could simply redraw the diagram. The indifference to visual accuracy implies that the diagram was not meant to be a visual depiction of the objects under discussion but rather to use visual cues to communicate the important mathematical relationships. In this sense, the diagrams are schematic representations. They help the reader navigate the thicket of letter names in the text, they relate the letter names to specific objects and they convey the most relevant mathematical characteristics of those objects. Again, in the course of research, discussion or presentation, a speaker could draw attention to other aspects of the objects that are not depicted, or again could simply redraw the diagrams.

We have referred to the fact that the diagrams could have been redrawn in the regular course of mathematical work, and, in fact, the evidence of the medieval transmission of scientific works shows that mathematically minded readers had a tendency to redraw the diagrams in the manuscripts they were transmitting.[39] This brings us to another essential fact of the manuscript diagrams. They were conceived, and hence designed, to be objects of transmission, that is, as a component of the literary transmission of the text. Nevertheless, the extent to which mathematics was a literary activity was changing throughout the ancient and medieval periods and indeed the extent to which individual practitioners would have used books in the course of their study or research is an open question. This much, however, is virtually certain: the total number of people studying the mathematical sciences at any time was much greater than the number of them who owned copies of the canonical texts. Hence, in the process of learning about and discussing mathematics the most usual practice would have been to draw some temporary figure and then to reason about it.

In fact, there is evidence that, contrary to the impression of the diagrams in the manuscript tradition, ancient mathematicians were indeed interested in making drawings that were accurate graphic images of the objects under discussion. We argue elsewhere that the diagrams in spherical geometry, as represented by Theodosius' *Spherics*, were meant to be drawn on real globes and that the problems in the *Spherics* were structured so as to facilitate this process.[40] As is clear from Eutocius' commentary to Archimedes' *Sphere and Cylinder*, Greek mathematicians sometimes designed mechanical devices in order to solve geometric problems and to draw diagrams accurately.[41] In contrast to the triangular parabola we saw in *Method* 14, Diocles, in *On Burning Mirrors*, discusses the use of a horn ruler to draw a graphically accurate parabola through a set of points.[42] Hence, we must distinguish between the diagram as an object of transmission and the diagram as an instrument of mathematical learning and investigation.

---

[39] See Sidoli 2007 for some examples of mathematically minded readers who redrew the figures in the treatises they were transmitting.

[40] Sidoli and Saito 2009.

[41] Netz 2004: 275–6 and 294–306.

[42] Toomer 1976: 63–7.

In fact, we will probably never know much with certainty about the parabolas that were drawn by mathematicians investigating conic theory or the circles that were drawn on globes by teachers discussing spherical geometry. Nevertheless, insofar as mathematical teaching and research are human activities, we should not doubt that the real learning and research was done by drawing diagrams and reasoning about them, not simply by reading books or copying them out. Hence, the diagrams in the manuscripts were meant to serve as signposts indicating how to draw these figures and mediating the reader's understanding of the propositions about them.

We may think of the manuscript diagrams as schematic guides for drawing figures and for navigating their geometric properties. In some cases, and for individuals with a highly developed geometric imagination, these secondary diagrams might simply be imagined, but for the most part they would actually have been drawn out. The diagrams achieve their generality in a similar way as the text, by presenting a particular instantiation of the geometric objects, which shows the readers how they are laid out and labelled so that the readers can themselves draw other figures in such a way that the proposition still holds. Hence, just as the words of the text refer to any geometric objects which have the same conditions, so the diagrams of the text refer to any diagrams that have the same configurations.

We may think of the way we use the diagram of a difficult proposition, such as that of the manuscript diagram for *Spher.* II.15 in Figure 2.13, in the same way that we think of the way we use the subway map of the Tokyo Metro.[43] We may look at the manuscript diagram in Figure 2.13 before we have worked through the proposition to get a sense of how things are laid out, just as we may look at the Tokyo subway map before we set out for a new place, to see where we will transfer and so forth. Although this may help orientate our thinking, in neither case does it fully prepare us for the actual experience. The schematic representation of the sphere in Figure 2.13 tells us nothing of its orientation in space, an intuition of which we will need to develop in order to actually understand the proposition. The Tokyo subway map tells us nothing about trains, platforms and tickets, all of which we will need to negotiate to actually go anywhere in Tokyo. In both cases, the image is a schematic that conveys only information essential to an activity that the reader is assumed to be undertaking.

There is, however, also an important distinction. The Tokyo subway map points towards a very specific object – or rather a system of objects that are

---

[43] The Tokyo subway map, in a number of different languages, can be downloaded from www.tokyometro.jp/e/.

always in flux, and probably not nearly as determinate as we would like to believe – nevertheless, a system of objects with a very specific locality and temporality. A Tokyo subway map is useless for Paris. If it was drawn this year, it will contain stations and lines that did not exist ten years ago and ten years from now it will again be out of date. The manuscript diagram in Figure 2.13, however, has no such specificity. It can refer to any sphere and does. Anyone who wants to draw a great circle on a sphere tangent to a given line and through a given point can use this diagram in conjunction with its proposition to do so. In the centuries since this proposition was written, a great many readers must have drawn figures of this construction – on the plane, on the sphere, in their mind's eye – and this diagram, strange and awkward as it is, somehow referred to all of them. It is in such a way that the overspecified, graphically inaccurate diagrams that we find in the manuscript tradition achieve the generality for which they were intended.

Bibliography

Manuscripts

Bodleian 301: Bodleian Library, D'Orville 301. Ninth century.
Bologna 18–19: Bologna, Biblioteca comunale, 18–19. Eleventh century.
Florence 28: Florence Laurenziana 28.3 Tenth century.
Leiden 399: Bibliotheek van de Universiteit Leiden, Or. 399.1. 1144–1145 (539 AH).
Paris 2466: Bibliothèque nationale de France, Gr. 2466. Twelfth century.
Rabāṭ 53: Rabāṭ, al-Maktaba al-Malikiyya, al-Khyzāna al-H. assaniyya, 53. 1607–1608 (1016 AH).
Uppsala 20: Uppsala Universitetsbibliotek, O. Vet. 20. 1042–1043 (434 AH).
Vatican 190: Bibliotheca Apostolica Vaticana, Gr. 190. Ninth century.
Vatican 206: Bibliotheca Apostolica Vaticana, Gr. 206. Twelfth–thirteenth century.
Vatican 204: Bibliotheca Apostolica Vaticana, Gr. 204. Ninth–tenth century.
Vatican Ottob. 1850: Bibliotheca Apostolica Vaticana, Lat. Ottob. 1850. Thirteenth century.
Vienna 31: Vienna Gr. 31. Eleventh–twelfth century.

Modern scholarship

Andersen, K. (1987) 'The central projection in one of Ptolemy's map constructions', *Centaurus* **30**: 106–13.
August, E. F. (1826–9) *ΕΥΚΛΕΙΔΟΥ ΣΤΟΙΧΕΙΑ, Euclidis Elementa.* Berlin.

Berggren, J. L., and Jones, A. (2000) *Ptolemy's* Geography: *An Annotated Translation of the Theoretical Chapters*. Princeton, N.J.

Besthorn, R. O., Heiberg, J. L., Junge, G., Raeder, J. and Thomson, W. (1897–1932) *Codex Leidensis 399, vol.* i, *Euclidis* Elementa *ex interpretatione al-Hadschdschadschii cum commentariis al-Narizii*. Copenhagen. (Reprinted in 1997 by F. Sezgin (ed.), Frankfurt.)

Busard, H. L. L. (ed.) (1984) *The Latin Translation of the Arabic Version of Euclid's* Elements, *Commonly Ascribed to Gerard of Cremona*. Leiden.

Czinczenheim, C. (2000) 'Edition, traduction et commentaire des *Sphériques* de Théodose', PhD thesis, Université Paris iv.

Decorps-Foulquier, M. (1999) 'Sur les figures du traité des *Coniques* d'Apollonius de Pergé édité par Eutocius d'Ascalon', *Revue d'histoire des mathématiques* **5**: 61–82.

Fecht, R. (ed., and trans.) (1927) Theodosii, *De habitationibus liber, De diebus et noctibus libri duo. Abhandlungen der Gesellschaft der Wissenschaften zu Göttingen, Philosophisch–Historische Klasse*, n.s. **19**(4). Berlin.

Freudenthal, H. (1953) 'Zur Geschichte der vollständigen Induktion', *Archives Internationales d'Histoire des Sciences* **6**: 17–37.

Gregory (Gregorius), D. (1703) *ΕΥΚΛΕΙΔΟΥ ΤΑ ΣΩΖΟΜΕΝΑ, Euclidis quae supersunt omnia*. Oxford.

Grynée (Grynaeus), S. (1533) *ΕΥΚΛΕΙΔΟΥ ΣΤΟΙΧΕΙΩΝ ΒΙΒΛ► ΙΕ► ΕΚ ΤΩΝ ΘΕΩΝΟΣ ΣΥΝΟΥΣΙΩΝ*. Basel.

Heiberg, J. L. (ed. and trans.) (1883–1888) *Euclidis* Elementa, 4 vols. Leipzig. (Reprinted with minor changes in Heiberg and Stamatis 1969–77.)

(1891–3) *Apollonii Pergaei quae graece extant cum commentariis antiquis*. Leipzig.

(1903) 'Paralipomena zu Euklid', *Hermes* **38**: 46–74, 161–201, 321–56.

(1927) *Theodosius Tripolites* Sphaerica. *Abhandlungen der Gesellschaft der Wissenschaften zu Göttingen, Philosophisch–Historische Klasse*, n.s. **19**(3). Berlin.

Heiberg, J. L., and Stamatis, E. (eds.) (1969–77) *Euclidis* Elementa, 5 vols. Leipzig.

Jones, A. (ed., and trans.) (1986) *Pappus of Alexandria: Book 7 of the* Collection, 2 vols. New York.

(2000) 'Pappus' notes to Euclid's *Optics*', in *Ancient and Medieval Traditions in the Exact Sciences: Essays in Memory of Wilbur Knorr*, ed. P. Suppes, J. M. Moravcsik and H. Mendell. Stanford, Calif.: 49–58.

Knorr, W. (1991) 'On the principle of linear perspective in Euclid's *Optics*', *Centaurus* **34**: 193–210.

(1992) 'When circles don't look like circles: an optical theorem in Euclid and Pappus', *Archive for History of Exact Sciences* **44**: 287–329.

Lejeune, A. (ed., and trans.) (1956) L'Optique *de Claude Ptolémée dans la version latine d'après l'arabe de l'émir Eugène de Sicile*. Louvain.

(1989) *L'Optique de Claude Ptolémée dans la version latine d'après l'arabe de l'émir Eugène de Sicile*. Leiden. (Reprint, with new French translation, of Lejeune 1956.)

Menge, H. (1916) *Euclidis phaenomena et scripta musica, Opera omnia vol.* VIII. Leipzig.

Mogenet, J. (1950) *Autolycus de Pitane, histoire du texte suivie de l'édition critique des traités de la Sphère en mouvement et des levers et couchers*. Louvain.

Netz, R. (2004), *The Works of Archimedes, vol.* I, *The Two Books* On the Sphere and the Cylinder. Cambridge.

Netz, R. and Noel, W. (2007) *The Archimedes Codex*. New York.

Netz, R., Saito, K. and Tchernetska, N. (2001–2) 'A new reading of *Method* proposition 14: preliminary evidence from the Archimedes Palimpsest (Parts 1 and 2)', *SCIAMVS* **2**: 9–29 and **3**: 109–25.

Neugebauer, O. (1938–9) 'Über eine Methode zur Distanzbestimmung Alexandria-Rom bei Heron I and II', *Det Kongelige Danske Videnskabernes Selskab* **26** (2 and 7): 3–26 and 3–11.

(1975) *A History of Ancient Mathematical Astronomy*. New York.

Noack, B. (1992) *Aristarch von Samos: Untersuchungen zur Überlieferungsgeschichte der Schrift* περὶ μεγεθῶν καὶ ἀποστρημάτων ἡλίου καὶ σελήνης. Wiesbaden.

Rome, A. (1923) 'Le problème de la distance entre deux villes dans la *Dioptra* de Héron', *Annales de la Société scientifique de Bruxelles* **43**: 234–58.

(1931–43) *Commentaires de Pappus et Théon d'Alexandrie sur l'Almageste*, 3 vols. Rome.

Saito, K. (2006) 'A preliminary study in the critical assessment of diagrams in Greek mathematical works', *SCIAMVS* **7**: 81–144.

(2008) *Diagrams in Greek Mathematical Texts*, Report of research grant 17300287 of the Japan Society for the Promotion of Science. Sakai. (See www. hs.osakafu-u.ac.jp/~ken.saito/diagram/ for further updates.)

Sidoli, N. (2005) 'Heron's *Dioptra* 35 and analemma methods: an astronomical determination of the distance between two cities', *Centaurus* **47**: 236–58.

(2007) 'What we can learn from a diagram: the case of Aristarchus's *On the Sizes and Distances of the Sun and the Moon*', *Annals of Science* **64**: 525–47.

Sidoli, N. and Saito, K. (2009) 'The role of geometrical construction in Theodosius's *Spherics*', *Archive for History of Exact Sciences* **63**: 581–609.

Tak, J. G. van der (1972) 'Calcidius' illustration of the astronomy of Heraclides of Pontus', *Mnemosyne* **25** Ser. 4: 148–56.

Taliaferro, R. C. (with D. Densmore and W. H. Donahue) (1998) *Apollonius of Perga: Conics Books* I–III. Santa Fe, N.M.

Toomer, G. J. (1976) *Diocles* On Burning Mirrors. New York.

3 | The texture of Archimedes' writings: through Heiberg's veil

REVIEL NETZ

The reading of Archimedes will always be inextricably intertwined with the reading of Heiberg. The great Danish philologer, involved with so many other projects in Greek science and elsewhere,[1] had Archimedes become his life project: the subject of his original dissertation, *Quaestiones Archimedeae* (1879), which formed the basis for his first Teubner edition of Archimedes' *Opera Omnia* (1880) and then, following upon the discovery of codices B and C, the second Teubner edition of the *Opera Omnia* (1910–15). The second edition appears to have settled the main questions of the relationship between the manuscripts, and has established the readings with great authority and clarity (it is this second and definitive edition which I study here). This is especially impressive, given how few technical resources Heiberg had for the reading of codex C – the famous Palimpsest. Even if today we can go further than Heiberg did, this is to a large extent thanks to the framework produced by Heiberg himself: so that, even if his edition is superseded, his legacy shall remain. Let this article not be read as a criticism of Heiberg – the most acute reader Archimedes has ever had.

The historical significance of Heiberg's publication is due not only to his scholarly stature, but also to his precise position in the modern reception of Archimedes. Classical scholarship is a tightly defined network of texts and readers, organized by a strict topology. The 'standard edition' has a special position. Its very pagination comes to define how quotations are to be made. Indeed, even more can be said for Archimedes specifically. First, the rise of modern editions inspired by German philological methods, in the late nineteenth century, coincided with an early phase of an interest in the history of science. Thus Heath's work of translating and popularizing Greek mathematics in the English-speaking world took place in the same decades that Heiberg was producing his edition of Archimedes. The version of Archimedes still in use by most English readers – Heath 1897 – depends, paradoxically, on Heiberg's first (and deficient) edition. Czwalina's German translation (1922–5) was based on the second edition, as was Ver Eecke's French translation (1921). Perhaps the most useful version among those widely available today,

---

[1] For Heiberg's somewhat incredible bibliography, see Spang-Hanssen 1929.

Mugler's Budé's text (1970–2) goes further: it not merely translates the text of the second edition of Archimedes, but also provides a facing Greek text – which directly reproduces the original edition by Heiberg! Mugler's decision to avoid any attempt to revise Heiberg may well have been due to another curious twist of fate: by the 1970s, the Palimpsest had gone missing so that a new edition appeared impossible. Stamatis' version (1970–4) repeats the same procedure, with modern Greek instead of French.

An edition is ontologically distinct from its sources. It is a synthesis of various manuscripts into a single printed text. The editor, aiming to preserve a past legacy, inevitably transforms it. It is a truism that Heiberg's version of Archimedes is not the same as the manuscript tradition – let alone the same as Archimedes' original 'publication' (whatever this term may mean). Once again: the point is not to criticize Heiberg. The point is to try to understand the distinguishing features of his edition, which may even form part of the image of Archimedes in the twenty-first century. In this chapter I survey a number of transformations introduced by Heiberg into his text. These fall into three parts, very different in character. First, Heiberg ignored the manuscript evidence for the diagrams, producing instead his own diagrams (this, indeed, may be the only point for which his philology may be faulted; I return to discuss Heiberg's possible justifications below). Second, at the local textual level, Heiberg marked passages he considered to be late glosses and thus not coming from the pen of Archimedes. Third, at the global textual level, through various choices of modern format as well as textual extrapolation, Heiberg introduced a certain homogeneity of presentation to the Archimedean text. The net result of all those transformations was to produce an Archimedes who was textually explicit, consistent, rigorous and yet opaque. I move on to show this in detail.

The texture of Archimedes' diagrams

This is not the place to discuss the complex philological question of the origins of the diagrams as extant in our manuscripts. I sum up, instead, the main facts. Of the three known early Byzantine manuscripts, one – the Palimpsest or codex C – is extant. The two others are represented by copies: a plethora of independent copies of codex A, allowing a very confident reconstruction of the original; and Moerbeke's Latin translation based in part on codex B (and in part based also on codex A). For most works we can reconstruct two early Byzantine traditions (codices A and C for SC I, SC II, SL, DC; codices A and B for PE I; codices B and C for FB I, FB II. For PE II alone we have some evidence from all three traditions).[2] The agreement between A and C is striking. We can also see that Moerbeke's Latin translation involved a considerable transformation of the diagrams he had available to him from codex A. This may serve to explain why, when we don't have the separate evidence of A and just compare codices B and C, the two appear different: this is likely to be the influence of Moerbeke's transformation. In short, the evidence suggests that the various early Byzantine manuscripts were *probably* identical in their diagrams. This is *certainly* the case for the two independent early Byzantine manuscripts A and C, for the works SC I, SC II, SL and DC – representing the bulk of Archimedes' extant work in pure geometry.

In all likelihood, such resemblance stems from a close dependence on a Late Ancient archetype. Whether or not this archetype can be pushed back to the original publication by Archimedes – whatever *that* could mean – is an open question. To the extent that the manuscript evidence displays striking, original practices, a kind of *lectio difficilior* makes it more likely that it is an original practice. The argument could never be very strong and it is probably for this cogent reason that Heiberg avoided offering an edition of the manuscripts' diagrams. However, even if the following need not represent the original form of Archimedes' works, it certainly represents one important way in which Archimedes was read for at least some part of antiquity. In understanding Archimedes' modern reception, it is helpful to compare this with the ancient reception to which the manuscripts testify. In what follows, then, I compare Heiberg's diagrams with the Late Ancient archetype reconstructed for the two books on *Sphere and Cylinder* (concentrating on these two books for the reason that I have already completed their edition). I arrange my comments as three comparisons – three ways in which Heiberg transformed the original found in the manuscripts.

Heiberg goes metrical

I put side by side the two diagrams for SC I.16 (see Figure 3.1). The differences as regards the triangle – in fact, a 'flat' view of a cone – are immaterial. Neither do I emphasize at the moment the differences in overall layout (it is clear that Heiberg saves more on space, aiming at a more economic production; this may have been imposed by the press). The major difference has to do with the nature of the circles Λ, Θ and K. Heiberg has them concentric,

---

[2] Here and in what follows I use a system of abbreviation of the titles of works by Archimedes, as follows: SC (*Sphere and Cylinder*), DC (*Measurement of the Circle*), CS (*Conoids and Spheroids*), SL (*Spiral Lines*), PE (*Planes in Equilibrium*), Aren. (*Arenarius*), QP (*Quadrature of Parabola*), FB (*Floating Bodies*), Meth. (*Method*), Stom. (*Stomachion*), Bov. (*Cattle Problem*).

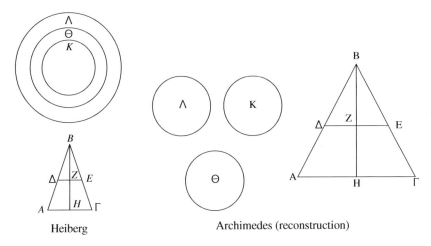

Figure 3.1 Heiberg's diagrams for *Sphere and Cylinder* I.16 and the reconstruction of Archimedes' diagrams.

in a descending order of size. The manuscripts have them arranged side by side, all of equal size.

The proposition constructs the circles in a complex way which is then shown to determine that the circle Λ equals the surface of the cone ΒΑΓ, circle K equals the surface of the cone ΒΔΕ, and Θ the difference between the surfaces, that is the surface of the truncated cone at the lines ΑΔΕΓ. It is therefore geometrically required that Λ>K, Λ>Θ (the relationship between K, Θ, though, is not determined by the proposition).

It is clear that Heiberg's diagram provides more metrical information than the manuscript diagrams do. In this particular case, indeed, Heiberg provides *more* metrical information than is determined by the proposition; while the manuscripts provide *less* than is determined by the proposition. This immediately suggests why the manuscripts' practice is in fact rational. Let us suppose that the manuscripts would set out to diagram the precise metrical relations determined by the proposition. It would make sense, then, to have both Θ and K smaller than Λ. However, how to represent the relationship between Θ and K? Once Λ appears bigger than both Θ and K, this is already taken to suggest that diagrams are metrically informative; and so the reader would look for the diagram relationship between Θ and K so as to provide him or her with the intended metrical relation. Thus, a diagram where, say, Λ is greater than both Θ and K, the two, say, equal to each other, falsely suggests that the intended metrical properties are: Λ>Θ=K. The difficulty of representing indeterminate metrical relations inside a metrical diagram is obvious.

The manuscripts' diagram avoids this difficulty altogether. The three equal circles – in flagrant violation of the textual requirement that $\Lambda > \Theta$, $\Lambda > K$ – imply that the diagram carries no metrical consequences (at least so far as these three circles are concerned) and therefore the diagram itself leaves the metrical relationship between K and Θ indeterminate.

This is a systematic feature of the manuscripts' diagrams. There are twenty-four cases where a system of homogeneous, unequal magnitudes (typically all circles, or all lines) is represented by equal magnitudes set side by side, as well as five cases where a system of homogeneous unequal magnitudes is represented by magnitudes some of which (in contradiction to the text) are represented equally. There are only four cases where a system of unequal magnitudes is allowed to be represented by a diagram where all traces are appropriately unequal.

The consequence of this convention is clear: the ancient diagrams are not read off as metrical. As a corollary, they are read more for their configurational information. This is obvious from the comparison with Heiberg: in the latter's diagram of I.16, the readers' expectation clearly is not that the three circles should indeed all be concentric. Indeed, the reader must understand that such figures are pure magnitudes and do not stand to each other in any spatial, configurational sense. While the conical surface $AB\Gamma$ does indeed envelope the smaller surfaces ΔBE, $A\Delta E\Gamma$, no such envelopment is understood between the three circles K, Λ and Θ that merely represent three magnitudes manipulated in the course of the proposition. Now, this does not make Heiberg's diagram *false*. It simply highlights what Heiberg's reader – in direct opposition to the reader of the ancient diagrams – is supposed to edit away in his reading of the diagram. Heiberg's reader is supposed to edit away a certain piece of configurational information (the circles *merely appear* to envelop each other), whereas the ancient reader was supposed to edit away a certain piece of metrical information (the circles *merely appear* equal). One can say that both representational systems foreground one dimension of information, overruling the other dimension: The metrical dimension of information is foregrounded in Heiberg and overrules the configurational dimension; the configurational dimension of information is foregrounded in the ancient diagram and overrules the metrical dimension.

This may serve to elucidate the following. Interestingly, the five cases where the ancient diagrams represent unequals by unequals – propositions SC I.15, 33, 34, 44 – all involve *lines*. Consider the typical case of I.15 (see Figure 3.2). B is the radius of the circle A, Γ – the side of a cone set up on that circle, E – a mean proportional between the two. The metrical relationship $B < E < \Gamma$ is indeed determined. Further, the circle Δ is drawn

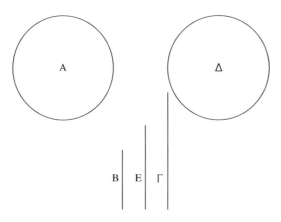

Figure 3.2 A reconstruction of Archimedes' diagram for *Sphere and Cylinder* I.15.

around the radius E. It thus follows also that $A < \Delta$. The diagram displays the inequality between the lines $B < E < \Gamma$ but not the equally determined inequality between the circles $A < \Delta$. There are six other cases, however, where unequal lines are represented by equal diagram traces. The rule then appears to be that the manuscripts' diagrams have a very strong preference to mark unequal plane figures as equal, but only a tendency to mark unequal line segments as unequal. Why should that be the case? Clearly, lines are less configurationally charged than plane figures are. The representation of a system of line traces does not suggest so powerfully a configuration made of those lines in spatial arrangement, and it is easier to read as a purely quantitative representation (indeed, such lines form the principle of representation used by Greek mathematicians when dealing with numbers or with general magnitudes, whose significance is purely quantitative, as in Euclid's *Elements* V, VII–IX). The principle is clear, then: the more the diagrams are taken to convey configurational meaning, the less metrical they are made. Lines – whose non-configurational character is easy to establish – may sometimes take metrical characteristics; but with plane figures, metrical characteristics are altogether avoided.

The upshot of this is obvious: diagrams which mostly carry configurational information, to the exclusion of the metrical, can also be rigorous. As Poincaré pointed out long ago, diagrams may be geometrically correct, to the extent that they are taken to be purely topological.[3] Of course, Poincaré

---

[3] Poincaré 1913: 60. Needless to say, topology or 'analysis situs' (as Poincaré would say) meant something different a century ago: in particular, this to Poincaré had absolutely nothing to do with Set Theory and instead had everything to do with a study of spatial relations abstracted away from any metrical conditions – which of course makes 'topology' even more obviously relevant to the study of schematic diagrams.

himself knew Greek mathematics only via editions such as Heiberg's. Little could he guess that the ancient manuscripts for Archimedes had just the kind of diagrams he considered logically viable!

Heiberg goes three-dimensional

A group of propositions early in *Sphere and Cylinder* I involves the comparison of cones or cylinders with the pyramids or prisms they enclose: propositions 7–12. Proposition 12 selects a diagram focused on the base alone, but the diagrams of propositions 7–11 require that we look at the entire solid construction. The manuscripts' diagrams (with a single exception, on which more below) produce a representation with a markedly 'flat' effect, whereas Heiberg produces several times a partly perspectival image with a three-dimensional effect.

The figure for I.9 (see Figure 3.3) may be taken as an example. What is the view selected by the manuscripts' diagram? Perhaps we may think of it as a view from above, slightly slanted so as to make the vertex Δ appear to fall not on the centre of the circle but somewhat below. The view selected by Heiberg's diagram is much 'lower', so that the point Δ appears higher above the plane of the base circle, allowing the pyramid to emerge out and produce an illusionistic three-dimensional effect. The net result is that Heiberg's figure impresses the eye with the picture of an external object; the manuscripts' diagram is reduced to a mere schema of interconnected lines.

This definitely should not be understood as a mark of poor draughtsmanship on the part of the manuscripts. Indeed, the one exception is telling: I.11 has a clear three-dimensional representation of a cylinder, and here the motivation is clear: since the proposition refers in detail to both the top and bottom bases of the cylinder, a view from 'above', where the bases coincide or nearly coincide, would have been useless. It turns out, therefore, that once the view from above was excluded, the manuscripts were capable of producing a lower view, with its consequent three-dimensional illusionistic effect. Strikingly and decisively, we note that the manuscripts' diagrams for I.11 represent the bases by almond-shapes (standardly used elsewhere for the representation of conic sections).[4] This is a deliberate foreshortening effect – which Heiberg himself eschews in his own diagram. Clearly, Heiberg has established a certain compromise between three-dimensional representation and geometric fidelity, to

---

[4] This practice is commented upon, for the Arabic tradition, in Toomer 1990: lxxxv, and it is indeed widespread in the various manuscript traditions of Greek mathematics.

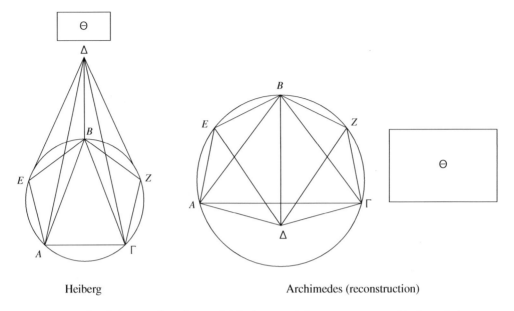

Heiberg   Archimedes (reconstruction)

Figure 3.3 Heiberg's diagram for *Sphere and Cylinder* 1.9 and the reconstruction of Archimedes' diagram.

which he is consistent. The manuscripts, on the other hand, insist on the preference, where possible, of a more schematic representation, even while they mark their ability to produce a full three-dimensional representation.

The manuscripts' decision clearly is not motivated by simple considerations of space. As we have seen in the preceding section, the manuscripts tend to have much bigger figures. No one invests in an Archimedes' manuscript for considerations of practical utility, so that these manuscripts should all be seen as luxury items,[5] so that one is allowed more space. A printed book, of course, is not typically based on a patronage economy and its calculations are different. I do think that a certain consideration of layout is relevant, however: what we do see in the manuscripts' diagrams is a certain preference for the horizontal arrangement, perhaps reflecting the origins of such diagrams within the spaces of papyrus columns.[6] This would in itself make a three-dimensional representation less preferable. But note that this is a mere tendency in the manuscripts' diagrams: as we will see with 1.12 below,

---

[5] The main proof for the lack of practical purpose in Byzantine Archimedes manuscripts is in their plethora of uncorrected, trivial errors. The extant Palimpsest shows not a single correction by a later hand (indeed, it was consigned to become a palimpsest!). We have a credible report from one of the scribes copying codex A that this, too, was replete with uncorrected errors (a reported supported by the pattern of errors in the extant copies of A): see Heiberg 1915: x.

[6] On the tendency of papyrus illustrations to orient horizontally, see Weitzmann 1947.

some diagrams in the manuscripts take a vertical arrangement (even though this arrangement is not determined by the geometrical situation). I do think the manuscripts avoid the three-dimensional representation, among other things, because of their preference for the horizontal over the vertical; what I wish to stress is that this shows how little weight they allow the pictorial quality of the diagram – so that the minor consideration of a preferred orientation trumps over that of the three-dimensional representation.

Note now that our discussion touches on a small stretch of text, but this is in fact in itself meaningful. The Archimedean corpus is sometimes dedicated to purely plane figures (*Spiral Lines, Planes in Equilibrium, Measurement of Circle, Stomachion, Quadrature of Parabola*) but, even in the several cases where Archimedes studies solid objects, these are studied essentially via some plane section passing through them (*Floating Bodies* II, *Method, Conoids and Spheroids, Sphere and Cylinder* II). *Sphere and Cylinder* I forms an exception because of its mathematical theme of the comparison of curved, concave surfaces – one which calls for a direct three-dimensional treatment.[7] Now consider I.12, where Archimedes' treatment of the three-dimensional cone is mediated via the plane base (where two lines form tangents to the circle of the base). Such is the standard Archimedean diagram. In the manuscripts, the diagrams of I.12 and of I.9 are closely aligned together, displaying a similar configuration of criss-crossing lines; whereas Heiberg's diagrams open up a chasm between the two situations, the solid picture of I.9 marked against the planar view of I.12 (see Figure 3.4). I would venture to say as much: that by making I.9 appear more *solid*, Heiberg simultaneously makes I.12 appear more *planar*. If I.9 is designed to bring to mind a picture of what a pyramid looks like, then I.12 should be seen to be designed so as to bring to mind a picture of what a circle looks like. But if I.9 is a mere schematic representation of lines in configuration, then the same must be said of I.12 as well: it is not a *picture* of a two-dimensional figure. It is, instead, a geometrically valid way of providing information, visually, about such a figure.

This, of course, is an interpretation that goes beyond the evidence. The facts on three-dimensional representation are simple: such representation is avoided as far as possible by the manuscripts, but is produced, wherever

---

[7] Among the lost works by Archimedes, the *Centres of Weights of Solids* may well have been based on planar sectional treatment – which Archimedes invariably pursues in the closely related *Method* (where various spheres, conoids and prisms are represented by planar cuts). One wonders how Archimedes' treatment of semi-regular solids was handled: the account in Pappus (Hultsch 1876: 350–8) carries no diagrams and is based on a purely numerical characterization of the figures.

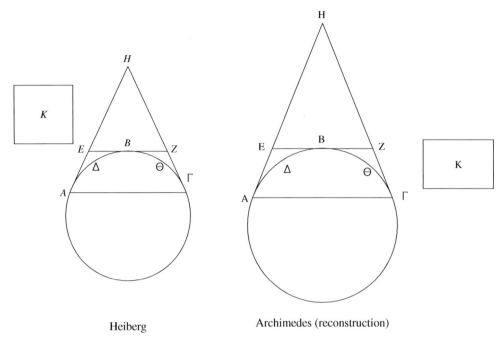

Heiberg   Archimedes (reconstruction)

Figure 3.4 Heiberg's diagram for *Sphere and Cylinder* I.12 and the reconstruction of Archimedes' diagram.

applicable (which is rare), by Heiberg. My interpretation of this evidence is based on the facts shown above – the non-metrical character of the manuscripts' diagrams – as well as those to which I now turn: their non-iconic character.

Heiberg goes iconic

I have suggested that Heiberg goes beyond the manuscripts, in making the two-dimensional figures more of a 'picture' of the object they are designed to represent. So far, my argument has been based purely on the contrast of such two-dimensional diagrams to their three-dimensional counterparts. What we require, then, is to see whether there are cases where Heiberg's representation of two-dimensional figures inserts into them a visual 'correctness' absent in the manuscripts. We have to a certain extent seen this already with the quantitative, metrical character of Heiberg's diagrams. Even more striking, however, is a certain systematic way by which Heiberg's two-dimensional diagrams are qualitatively more 'correct' than those of the manuscripts.

I turn now to SC I.33 (see Figure 3.5). I note quickly the metrical facts. The figure by Heiberg has A much bigger than the main circle, which is

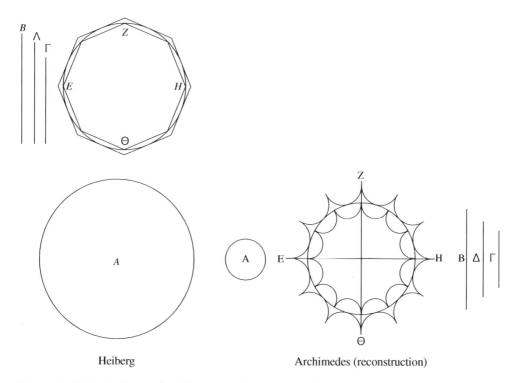

Heiberg   Archimedes (reconstruction)

Figure 3.5 Heiberg's diagram for *Sphere and Cylinder* I.33 and the reconstruction of Archimedes' diagram.

indeed 'correct'; the manuscripts' smaller A is in a sense 'false'.[8] The manuscripts agree with Heiberg, however, in the arrangement of the line segments, all in keeping with the practice described above (pp. 167–8).

Qualitatively, Heiberg represents the propositions' requirement – of a 4*n*-sided regular polygon circumscribed and inscribed about a circle – by two octagons. The manuscripts, instead, have a system made of two nested sequences of curved lines, 12 outside and 12 inside. The visual effect could not have been more different and here we see the manuscripts' diagrams becoming markedly non-iconic. A sequence of 12 curved lines, each nearly a semicircle, does not make the visual impression of a polygon.

The manuscripts, in this case, have a very good reason to choose their non-iconic system of representation. As we can see from Heiberg's diagram, it is difficult to make the visual resolution between such a polygon and a

---

[8] Incidentally, note that I did not count such false planar inequalities in my treatment of the non-metrical character of the manuscripts' diagrams. My survey focused on the (very common) case where *homogeneous* objects are put side by side – typically unmarked circles or lines. I did not look into the case of heterogeneous objects, such as the simple circle A alongside the more complex main circle in I.33.

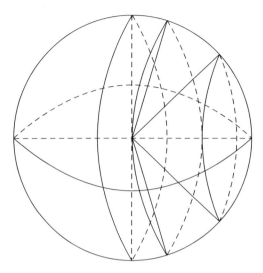

Figure 3.6 The general case of a division of the sphere.

circle. A square perhaps could still do, but this offers a very special case of the $4n$-sided regular polygon: considered as a division of the sphere, it reduces to a system of two cones, without any truncated cones. The octagon already brings in a truncated cone, but this is the limiting truncated cone lying directly on the diameter of the sphere. Only with the dodecagon do we begin to see the general case of a division of the sphere based on $4n$-sided regular polygons, with a limiting truncated cone lying directly on the diameter, another truncated cone next to it, and finally a non-truncated cone away from the diameter (Figure 3.6). Of course, a regular dodecagon is nearly impossible to distinguish, visually, from a circle, but the entire point of avoiding a limiting case for the diagram is the desire to limit the extent to which the visual impression of the diagram creates false expectations. The same desire, then, accounts for the radical, non-iconic representation itself: no one is going to base an argument concerning polygons on the visual impression made by the curved arcs. Indeed, the visual impression as such does not play into the argument. What matters, for the argument, is the similarity of the polygons and the purely topological structure they determine – a circle nested precisely between two polygons, triggering Archimedes' results on concave surfaces.

This diagrammatic practice is not isolated: it defines the character of Archimedes' SC I. As soon as the structure of a polygon inscribed inside the circle is introduced, in proposition 21, and right through the ensuing argument, the manuscripts systematically deploy such representations based on curved lines – in fifteen propositions altogether (I.21, 23–6, 28, 30,

32–3, 37–42). I find it hard to see how a scribe, asked to copy a manuscript where polygons are represented by polygons, would produce a manuscript where polygons are represented by a system of curved lines. This *lectio difficilior* argument is the best I have for showing that, if not introduced by a scribe, such diagrammatic practice is likely authorial. Perhaps our simplest hypothesis is that the diagrams as a whole derive, largely speaking, from Archimedes himself.

The texture of Archimedes' diagrams: summary

Whether by Archimedes or not, the non-iconic character of the representation of polygons in SC I is a striking example of how schematic the manuscripts' diagrams are – and how Heiberg has turned such schematic representations into *pictures*. This is of course consistent with the manuscripts' preference for a 'flat' representation as against Heiberg's pictorial pyramids, as well as with the much wider manuscript practice of metrical simplification, typically that of representing unequal magnitudes by equal figures.

Heiberg has clearly transformed the manuscripts' schematic diagrams into pictorially 'correct' ones. By so doing, however, he has also constructed diagrams of a different logical character. If diagrams are expected to be pictorially correct, then one is expected to read them for some metrical information; and if so, the information one gathers from the diagrams is potentially false (since no metrical drawing can answer the infinite precision demanded by mathematics) as well as potentially overdetermined (since a particular metrical configuration may introduce constraints that are less general than the case required by the proposition). The schematic and more 'topological' character of the manuscripts' diagrams, on the other hand, makes them logically useful. One can rely on the manuscripts' diagrams as part of the argument, without thereby compromising the logical validity of the proof.

A major claim of my book (N1999) was that diagrams play a role in Greek mathematical reasoning.[9] I have suggested there – following Poincaré – that the diagrams may have been used *as if* they were merely topological. My consequent study of the palaeography of Greek diagrams has revealed a striking and more powerful result: the diagrams, at least as preserved by early Byzantine manuscripts, simply *were* topological. Heiberg's choice to obscure this character of the diagrams was not only philologically but also philosophically motivated. Clearly, he did not perceive diagrams to form

---

[9] N1999, especially chapters 1, 2, 5.

part of the logic of the text and for that reason, on the one hand, did not value them enough to care for their proper edition and, on the other hand, preferred to produce them as mere 'illustrations' – as visual aids revealing to the mind a *picture* of the object under discussion. The implication – false for Archimedes as for Greek mathematics more generally – would be that the text is logically self-enclosed, that all claims are textually explicit. This, then, was the first transformation introduced by Heiberg into the texture of Archimedes' reasoning.

The texture of Archimedes' text: the local level

An overview of Heiberg's practice of excision

A characteristic feature of Heiberg's edition is his use of square brackets in the sense of text present in the manuscripts, which however is to be excluded as non-authorial. This, incidentally, is not the current practice among classical philologers, where the '{}' are used for the same purpose, whereas square brackets are used to signal text restored by the editor – for which Heiberg himself used the '<>' brackets.[10] This practice should be compared with two other options Heiberg had available to him.

(1) One was to omit excluded text from his printed text altogether, relegating it into the critical apparatus alone. Such, indeed, is Heiberg's practice whenever *already any of the manuscripts exclude the passage*. For instance, SL 68.15–16 has the printed text συμπεσεῖται δε αυτα τα TZ, 'This will meet TZ', which Heiberg has on the authority of codices BG. Heiberg's apparatus has the comment: 'αυτα] G, τα αυτα A(C), ipsi B' (G is the siglum used for one of the Renaissance copies of codex A), that is: the reconstructed manuscript A certainly read *ta auta ta* (as this is the text read in all copies save the relatively mathematically sophisticated G), and so probably (Heiberg was unsure, but he was right) codex C; in codex B, Moerbeke translated the relevant words as if they were *auta ta* alone – though once again, Moerbeke is relatively mathematically sophisticated.

Heiberg could in principle have printed '[τα] αυτα τα', commenting in the apparatus 'τα] del. prae. BG'. This he did not do: his practice was to relegate such excluded words to the apparatus alone. On the other hand, in such cases where there was unanimous textual authority for a particular passage which Heiberg preferred to omit, his practice was to print that passage in the main text, surrounded by square brackets.

---

[10] See e.g. http://odur.let.rug.nl/~vannijf/epigraphy1.htm.

(2) Another option was to avoid the square brackets altogether, leaving his doubts to footnotes. He does so occasionally – particularly, it seems, when the exclusion involves both an excision as well as an addition to the text. So, for instance, footnote 2 in PE I, II.149, where the text is printed simply as πεποιησθω:

'πεποιησθω lin. 19 fortasse vestigium recensionis posterioris est. u. Quaest. Arch. p. 70. γεγονετω scripsit *Torellius* cum *Basil.*', that is '*let it be made* in line 19 may be due to a late re-edition; see Quaest. Arch. p. 70 [Heiberg's PhD]. Torelli [The Oxford 1792 edition] as well as Basil [the first edition from 1544] have *let it come to be*'.

Heiberg could have instead printed [πεποιησθω] γεγονετω, with a note in the apparatus 'γεγονετω] πεποιησθω ABC, scripsi prae. Tor., Basil.' By printing, simply, πεποιησθω, Heiberg shows in this case more respect to the manuscripts' authority and allows a smoother reading of the main printed text.

Heiberg's strategy is well balanced. It is designed to help the reader navigate the main text as readable prose, without encumbering the apparatus (a necessary consequence of (1) above) or the footnotes (a necessary consequence of (2) above). The square brackets are a helpful feature of the text. They allow the reader to consider two possible ways of reading the text – with or without the excluded passage – and to see for herself which she likes best.

We should contrast Heiberg's treatment of the text with his treatment of the diagrams. He made sure as much of the manuscript evidence as possible remained visible as regards the text, even taking pains to print text in whose inauthenticity he was certain – all of this, while removing the evidence for the manuscripts' diagrams nearly in its entirety!

However respectful Heiberg's practice may have been towards the manuscripts' textual evidence, its outcome was to define a certain set of expectations concerning the local texture of Archimedes' writing. Heiberg effectively shares with us his view: 'Archimedes could not write like this', and readers would take notice of views with such authority. Let us consider, then, Heiberg's judgements.

I move on to describe the pattern of Heiberg's square brackets. The first point to note is their unequal distribution among the treatises. I have gone through the corpus, counting all square brackets and classifying them as 'single words' (with the possible addition of the definite article), 'phrases' (i.e. no more than a single claim or construction), 'passages' (consisting of several phrases) and 'long passages' (the border between these and 'passages' is difficult to define, but I mean an entire train of thought, going

Table 3.1 Heiberg's use of square brackets

Treatise	Length (Teubner pages of Greek)	Bracketed by Heiberg (~BEPP)	Notes (discussed below)
Floating Bodies I	13	1 word (~0.05)	Doric, Palimpsest
Arenarius	22	3 words (~0.15)	Doric, discursive
Method	41	4 words, 2 phrases (~0.25)	Koine, Palimpsest
Spiral Lines	60	5 words, 2 phrases, 1 passage (~0.35)	Doric
Floating Bodies II	~26	8 words (~0.35)	Doric, Palimpsest
Quadrature of Parabola	27	6 words, 3 phrases (~0.55)	Doric
Conoids and Spheroids	100	10 words, 10 phrases, 2 long passages (~0.95)	Doric
Planes in Equilibrium II	25	3 words, 5 phrases, 2 passages (~1.4)	Doric, Eutocius extant
Planes in Equilibrium I	20	7 words, 12 phrases, 2 passages (~2.6)	Doric, Eutocius extant
Measurement of the Circle	6	7 words, 1 phrase, 1 passage (~3.1)	Koine, Eutocius extant
Sphere and Cylinder II	31	12 words, 20 phrases, 12 passages, 3 long passages (~8.7)	Koine, Eutocius extant
Sphere and Cylinder I	83	11 words, 48 phrases, 29 passages, 12 long passages (~9)	Koine, Eutocius extant

Note: The table is arranged by ascending BEPP (Stom. and Bov. are not included in this survey).

beyond a single argument or so). In Table 3.1, I list for each treatise its length in Teubner Greek pages, as well as its square-bracketed passages. I believe that a good way of quantifying the impact of such square brackets is not by mere word-count – excising five times a single-word passage is more significant than excising a single five-word passage – and instead I develop an ad-hoc 'logarithmic' count, with each 'single word' counting for one unit, each 'phrase' counting for three units, each 'passage' for nine and each 'long passage' for twenty-seven. I then sum up this logarithmic value as the 'Bracketing Equivalent'. I then calculate the 'Bracketing Equivalent per Page' or BEPP, which is the Bracketing Equivalent divided by the number of Teubner pages. This entire exercise is of course somewhat absurd, but it does arrange the data in a useful way.

Several factors emerge. Heiberg's tendency was to introduce brackets much more into those texts for which we have an extant commentary by Eutocius (PE, DC, SC). Second, he introduced brackets into Koine treatises (DC, SC i–ii, Meth.) more than to Doric treatises (thus, of the treatises for which we have a commentary by Eutocius, PE in Doric has far fewer brackets than DC, let alone SC). On the other hand, he was reluctant to introduce brackets into texts for which he had textual authority from the Palimpsest (thus, he introduced few brackets into the text of the *Method*, even though it is extant in Koine). Finally, he practically did not intervene in the more discursive text of the *Arenarius*. I move on to comment on those factors.

Eutocius

A common source of square brackets (especially at the level of words) is the comparison of the manuscripts' text to that of Eutocius' quotation. Heiberg's judgement here may be faulted on philological grounds: it is now widely understood that many ancient quotations did not aim at precision,[11] and the transformations introduced by Eutocius (e.g. a different particle) can be explained by the new grammatical context into which the quotation is inset by Eutocius. Furthermore, the texts for which there is a commentary by Eutocius are the more elementary, and it appears that Heiberg suspected that such texts were more heavily retouched by their readers: a reasonable assumption, seeing that the more advanced works by necessity had much fewer readers. The net result is to make the advanced works the benchmark against which all the treatises are judged.

Dialect

Archimedes the Syracusan may have written at least some of his works in Doric – even when addressing Koine readers in Alexandria. The manuscripts present a variety of positions, between stretches of text written in what appears like pure Doric, through more mixed passages and all the way to texts in normal Hellenistic Koine. Heiberg's edition turns this variety into just two options: treatises that Heiberg considered to have been transmitted in the Doric throughout antiquity (which we may call 'Doric treatises'), and those he considered to have been turned into Koine at some point in antiquity (which we may call 'Koine treatises'). Thus, the presence

---

[11] A case studied in great detail is the quotations of Plato by his epitomizer Alcinous: Whittaker 1990: xvii–xxx.

of Koine anywhere in the manuscript tradition of 'Doric treatises' – a presence which is often considerable, even preponderant – is taken by Heiberg to represent no more than the failure of scribes whose Doric may not have not have been up to Archimedes' text. I shall return to discuss all of this in considering the global texture of Archimedes. What is clear, however, is that Heiberg's initial decision – whether or not to treat a treatise as 'Doric' – had consequences at the local level. Understandably enough, Heiberg felt less compelled to preserve the text of the 'Koine treatises', considering them the product of some late re-edition, as opposed to Archimedes' pristine words preserved in the Doric. Thus the 'Doric works' come to serve as the benchmark against which the verbal texture of Archimedes as a whole is to be judged. This is comparable to the 'Eutocius' effect and indeed may be related to it. (Was the transition to Koine related to the presence of Eutocius' commentaries?)

Palimpsest

Since the text of the *Method* is printed by Heiberg in its original Koine, we would expect him to bracket its text more extensively. As I will point out in the next section, the *Method* provides enough textual difficulties to allow for such editorial intervention. In fact, Heiberg leaves the text of the *Method* almost as it is. The reason must be, I believe, what we may call a purely sociological or even psychological factor. The text of the *Method* is recovered from the Palimpsest, through Heiberg's major palaeographic tour de force. In sociological terms, Heiberg has already displayed his professional skill by his very recovery of the text and is therefore less under pressure to scrutinize it so as to display his professionalism. In psychological terms, I suspect Heiberg must have become attached to the words he did manage to read – it would be a pity to go through all the trouble just so as to discover some late gloss! (A reader of the Palimpsest myself, I am all too familiar with this urge.) For whatever reason, the fact is that the texts recovered from the Palimpsest are among those Heiberg trusts the most. Since these also happen to be among the more advanced works by Archimedes (in particular FB II as well as the *Method*) this has the tendency of confirming the role of the advanced works as paradigmatic.

Arenarius

The *Arenarius* is an outsider in the Archimedean corpus: written mostly in discursive prose rather than in the style of proofs and diagrams, it presents many verbal and stylistic variations on the norm elsewhere.[12] The same goes for Heiberg's interventions in this text. In II.236.24, Heiberg brackets the particle *men* which is unanswered by the obligatory *de*; in II.258.11 he brackets the particle *eti* which seems to be a mere scribal error anticipating the following preposition *epi*. The case of 222.31, with the words *tou kulindrou* bracketed, is more complex. The text as it stands in the manuscript does not make any sense, as Greek grammar or as mathematics. Heiberg not only brackets *tou kulindrou* but also adds in a particle *oun* and changes the gender of a relative pronoun. In short, Heiberg's interventions are philological rather than mathematical in character; that they are so few is a mark of Heiberg's tact as an editor. Of course, Heiberg's apparatus records many more variations that Heiberg introduced into the main text and indeed all three brackets could equally have been relegated to the apparatus alone. Needless to say, the *Arenarius* does not thereby obtain a canonical position for Heiberg's reading of Archimedes: here, the lack of intervention signals, paradoxically, a marginal status. What the *Arenarius* reminds us is that Heiberg's exclusions are so closely focused on the proofs-and-diagrams style. Indeed, there are, I believe, no words bracketed inside the *introductions* to Archimedes' works.

To sum up: Heiberg intervened in Archimedes' text mostly to exclude words and passages that, in his view, do not square with what should have been Archimedes' style of proof, as judged mostly by the advanced works extant in Doric.

Heiberg's practice of excision: close-up on *Sphere and Cylinder*

The mathematics of Archimedes, especially in the more advanced works, is very difficult. Generally speaking, Heiberg's brackets tend to keep it that way. Many of the excluded passages take the form of brief explanations to relatively simple arguments. The excluded passages make the text of Archimedes locally *transparent*, and this is what Heiberg avoids – in this way also introducing a certain consistency which is absent from the manuscripts' evidence.

Consider SC 1.4. Archimedes constructs a triangle ΘΚΛ, with ΚΘ given and the angle at Θ right. It is also required that ΚΛ be equal to a certain line H. At this point the text comments (1 16.25): 'For this is possible, since H is greater than ΘΚ.' This comment is bracketed by Heiberg. There seem to be three reasons for Heiberg's bracketing.

---

[12] N1999: 199.

First, this is an argument headed by the particle *gar*, usually translated 'for': having established a claim, the text moves on to offer further grounds for it. Heiberg's tendency, especially in the books on *Sphere and Cylinder*, was to excise a great proportion of *gar* statements. There are altogether 155 occurrences of the particle in the text of SC I, II outside of the introductions, but of these 58 occur not in the context of a backwards-looking argument but in the context of some meta-mathematical formulaic expression using a *gar*, such as the heading of the *reductio* mode of reasoning: 'for if possible', *ei gar dunaton*. Remaining are 95 occurrences. Of these 54 are inside Heiberg's brackets; only 41 are considered genuine. The 54 excised *gars* represent fewer than 50 excisions (a few long passages excised by Heiberg include more than a single *gar*), all of them constituting at least a phrase (Heiberg never excises a *gar* alone – which of course would have produced an asyndeton). Heiberg excised altogether 124 phrases and passages from the text of SC I, II, and so we see that about 40 per cent of these excisions are claimed by *gars*. Note however that many of the remaining excisions have a similar logical character, even while using a connector other than *gar*: e.g. a *dēlon*, 'clearly' phrase in SC I.34 130.20–1, or even an *ara*, 'therefore' phrase in SC I.32 120.8. In most cases, the excision is motivated by the elementary character of the claim made.

This can be seen from the distribution of excisions of *gar* between the two treatises. Of the 68 *gars* in SC I, Heiberg excises 45 or about two-thirds; of the 27 *gars* in SC II, Heiberg excises 9, that is a third. The major difference between the two treatises is that SC II is usually much more complex than most of SC I.[13] The rule then begins to emerge: Heiberg excises *gars* in the context of relatively simple mathematics.

Going back finally to our example from SC I.4, we can now see one reason why Heiberg chose to bracket it: in this example, the text looks back to explain why a certain construction is possible. This condition, however, is relatively simple: in constructing a right-angled triangle, the hypotenuse must be greater than the side. Heiberg's view was that Archimedes could well have just taken such a condition for granted.

For this, Heiberg had something of a corroboration. Here I pass to the second ground for Heiberg's excision: his search for *consistency*. In the preceding proposition 3, Archimedes requires an analogous construction, and there the text does not provide an explicit backwards-looking argument, merely stating (I 14.8) 'for this is possible' (this is bracketed by

---

[13] As a comparison: in the advanced treatise *Spiral Lines*, Heiberg brackets 2 out of 33 *gars* – which forms, however, a large part of his overall editorial intervention in that treatise.

Heiberg, for reasons that will be made clear immediately). Why should the text be fuller here than in the preceding proposition? Consistency, therefore, requires an excision.

I now move to the third reason for Heiberg's bracketing. To understand it, let us note the following: the received text for Archimedes' propositions 3 and 4 seems to open a strange gap between propositions 3 and 4. Why would Archimedes offer no more than a brief 'this is possible' claim in proposition 3, expanding it in proposition 4? If anything, the opposite – going from a more spelled-out expression to a briefer one – would be more natural. On the other hand, the entire picture makes perfect sense if we pursue the following hypothesis. Now, the text of Eutocius contains a commentary to proposition 3, starting with the following words: 'And let [the construction be made]. For this is possible, with KL being produced *etc.*' (III 18.24–5). Let us assume that Archimedes' text had none of the backwards-looking argument, and that some late reader has taken Eutocius' commentary, first inserting the words 'for this is possible' from Eutocius' commentary into the text of proposition 3, then using Eutocius as a kind of crib from which to insert a very brief backwards-looking argument into proposition 4 (for which there is no commentary by Eutocius).

We see how the various factors – the presence of Eutocius' commentary, the elementary nature of the claims made, the use of a backwards-looking argument, textual inconsistency – all come together to inform Heiberg's considerations.

Was Heiberg right? I tend to believe he was, at least in part. This, for the following reason. Either we take the words 'for this is possible' in proposition 3 to represent Eutocius' original words, inserted into the text of Archimedes; or we take them as Archimedes' original words, quoted by Eutocius as part of his commentary. Now, the word order of those words is *dunaton gar touto*. This word order is natural as an anticipation of the genitive absolute used by Eutocius in his commentary; inside Archimedes' full phrase, the word order expected would more likely be *touto gar dunaton*. The excision in proposition 3 therefore seems likely. And if so, it becomes somewhat more likely that the words in proposition 4, too, are due to some late reader. But then again, perhaps Archimedes' text was strangely inconsistent, offering no argument in proposition 3 but some minimal argument in proposition 4? Obviously, such questions can be answered only based on some overarching argument concerning Archimedes' style, an argument which would have to be derived – circularly – from the established text of Archimedes.

In some cases, and in particular in the longer passages, Heiberg's excisions seem very reasonable. One of the clearest cases is SC I.13 (I 56.10–24).

This should be read in full to get a sense of the manuscript evidence Heiberg had to contend with (I quote together with my numbering of claims in the argument. It should be clear that this is something of an extreme case, though not at all a unique one):

(16) But that ratio which TΔ has to H in square – TΔ has this ratio to PZ in length [(17) for H is a mean proportional between TΔ, PZ (18) through <its being a mean proportional> between ΓΔ, EZ, too; how is this? (19) For since ΔT is equal to TΓ, (20) while PE <is equal> to EZ, (21) therefore ΓΓ is twice TΔ, (22) and PZ <is twice> PE; (23) therefore it is: as ΔΓ to ΔT, so PZ to ZE. (24) Therefore the <rectangle contained> by ΓΔ, EZ is equal to the <rectangle contained> by TΔ PZ. (25) But the <rectangle contained> by ΓΔ, EZ is equal to the <square> on H; (26) therefore the <rectangle contained> by TΔ, PZ, too, is equal to the <square> on H; (27) therefore it is: as TΔ to H, so H to PZ; (28) therefore it is: as TΔ to PZ, the <square> on TΔ to the <square> on H; (29) for if three lines are proportional, it is: as the first to the third, the figure on the first to the figure on the second which is similar and similarly set up]

The expression 'how is this?' inside claim 18 is without parallel in the corpus, and seems like a didactic order to a pupil (or, perhaps, an autodidact's *cri de coeur*?). The passage from 19 to 21 is indeed extraordinarily simple (from A = B to A + B being twice A). The final explicit quotation from Euclid's *Elements* is natural coming from a didactic context. And overall the argument is very simple, strikingly so given its length. It is therefore quite likely that the entire passage from 'how is this?' in the end of claim 18 down to the end of claim 29 is a scholion inserted into the manuscript tradition. Heiberg's choice, however, was to bracket starting from step 17 itself – this, apparently, merely because step 17 begins with a *gar*.

It would be easy for us to condemn Heiberg's use of square brackets as disrespectful to the manuscripts' evidence, or as involving massive circular reasoning. But Heiberg's practice is not unreasonable and is likely to be correct at least in part. I doubt any editor could have come up with a single system better than Heiberg – short, that is, of the confession of editorial ignorance which might have been best of all (and which Heiberg, in a sense, did finally follow – by allowing the bracketed words to be printed inside the main text). I stand by my judgement of Heiberg as a superb, and superbly tactful, philologer. Having said that, however, the fact remains that we cannot really say how correct he was. There are three texts at play here:

(A) Heiberg's text with the bracketed segments inserted, i.e. the manuscripts' reading.
(B) Heiberg's text with the bracketed segments removed.
(C) Archimedes' original text.

Heiberg's intention was of course to take A and, by transforming it into B, to make it come as close to C as possible. It is indeed certain that A and C are not identical. However, it is impossible to judge how close B is in fact to C. The only judgement we can make with confidence has to do with the relationship between A and B. The transformation introduced by Heiberg into the manuscripts' text is motivated by two main considerations: the avoidance of explicit argument in the context of relatively simple mathematics; and the avoidance of textual inconsistencies. This determines the image of Archimedes as projected by Heiberg's method of excision: neither transparent nor inconsistent. I do not address right now the question whether this image is, or is not, correct. I merely point out the presence of this image, before moving on to consider the influence of this image in Heiberg's treatment of the texture of Archimedes at the global level.

The texture of Archimedes' text: the global level

As usual, my point is not to criticize Heiberg. In some ways, any edition involves a transformation at the global level. The 'feel' of an *Opera Omnia* in its Teubner print is very distinct from that of codices A or C which, in turn, would have felt, possibly, even more different from their antecedent of a basket of rolls in ancient Alexandria. Some of Heiberg's decisions were of this inevitable character: so, for instance, an *Opera Omnia* must proceed in some order, and the fact that this calls for editorial decision does not thereby make the editor unfaithful to his author. On the other hand, in some other forms Heiberg made choices for presentation that went beyond the manuscripts' evidence, mostly informed by a sense of overall mathematical consistency.

The order of Archimedes' works

Knorr was upset over that issue:[14]

Following the start made by Torelli in 1792, Heiberg had in 1879 attempted to determine the relative chronology of the treatises then known to him. But in setting them out in his ensuing editions of Archimedes he chose to retain the traditional order in the principal manuscripts, based on the prototype A, and then tacked on the few remaining works and fragments preserved in other sources.

---

[14] Knorr 1978: 212–13.

Heiberg's ordering has been adopted in all subsequent editions and translations, notably those by T. L. Heath, P. Ver Eecke, E. J. Dijksterhuis and C. Mugler. Indeed, Ver Eecke pronounced it to be of all possible orderings "le plus rationnel". What began as merely a philological concern to keep strictly to the sequence of the manuscript sources has thus given rise to the astonishing view that this ordering has intrinsic rational merit, despite such patent incongruities as the placing of the *Sand Reckoner* and the *Quadrature of the Parabola* and others to be discussed below.

This may, first of all, serve as a nice reminder of the pre-eminent position of Heiberg in our contemporary reading of Archimedes. Further, I am not quite clear as to what 'patent incongruities' Knorr meant. Clearly his interest lay with the chronological sequence, and as such the order of the *Opera Omnia* makes no sense. It is not a random order, though, and its significance should be pondered.

Here is the order of Heiberg's second edition:

SC I – SC II – DC – CS – SL – PE I – PE II – Aren. – QP – FB I – FB II – Stom. – Meth. – Book of Lemmas – Bov. – Fragments (in reality, Testimonia).

Up to QP, inclusive, this follows (as explained by Knorr) the order of codex A (which was the only order available to Heiberg, on manuscript authority, for his first edition). The works extant on the Palimpsest follow in the order FB – Stom. – Meth. (perhaps designed to keep the *Method* till later?), and then follow several works from diverse sources: the Book of Lemmas from the Arabic, the *Cattle Problem* from a different line of transmission altogether, and then of course the Testimonia from sources other than Archimedes himself. One should note the outcome, that Heiberg foregrounded the works in which he detected most interpolations. This is not a paradox: the works foregrounded by Heiberg were the elementary works in pure geometry, and the detection of many interpolations could have meant to Heiberg an indication of the significance such works had for Archimedes' ancient and medieval readers.

While Heiberg's principle was purely philological, he followed manuscripts that, themselves, made rational choices (so that Ver Eecke's judgement is not *necessarily* false). The system underlying A is quite clear. A sequence of five works in pure geometry (SC I, SC II, DC, CS, SL) is followed by a sequence of four works that refer in some way or another to the physical order (PE I – PE II – Aren. – QP; this is followed in codex A by Eutocius' commentaries, and then by a treatise by Hero on Measures). Such an arrangement is suggestive of a previous 'canonical' selection of 'top five Archimedean geometrical rolls', 'top four Archimedean physical rolls', perhaps representing a previous arrangement of rolls by baskets, perhaps of some majuscule codices with only four to five works each.[15] In each sequence, the internal order is roughly from the simpler to the more complex.

It so happens that the works preserved via traditions other than codex A tend to be less focused on pure geometry. Three of the works preserved via C – FB I, FB II, Meth. – have a marked 'physical' character. The *Stomachion*, also preserved via C, may be a unique study in geometrical combinatorics.[16] And while the Book of Lemmas does touch on pure geometry, the *Cattle Problem* is an arithmetical work. The fragments, finally, refer to such diverse topics as astronomy, optics or the arithmetico-geometrical study of semi-regular solids reported by Pappus.[17] In short, the emphasis on pure geometry – very natural based on codex A alone – is less faithful to the corpus as a whole as recognized today. Or indeed as recognized by some other past traditions. For the order of codex C was distinct:

PE I (?)[18] – PE II – FB I – FB II – Meth. – SL – SC I – SC II – DC – Stom.

This has five works referring to the physical world (PE I–II, FB I–II, *Method*) followed by five works of a non-physical character (SL, SC I–II, DC, *Stomachion*). Once again, the origin in some earlier arrangement is likely, and the main classificatory principle is the same – referring, or failing to refer, to an outside physical reality. The striking difference is that codex C chose to position the physical works prior to the non-physical ones.

At issue is a fundamental question regarding Archimedes' scientific character. Was he primarily a pure geometer, who indulged in some exercises of a more physical or non-geometrical character? Or was he primarily an author of 'mixed' works, so that the more purely geometrical works – such as *Sphere and Cylinder* – should be seen as no more than one further option in the spectrum of possible Archimedean variations? A very different Archimedes would emerge if we were to order his works, say, as follows:

[15] These two options, of course, do not rule each other out. See Blanchard 1989 for some suggestive comparisons.

[16] Netz *et al.* 2004.

[17] Hultsch 1876: 350–8.

[18] The beginning of the Archimedes portion of the Palimpsest appears to be lost. The text begins towards the end of PE II. There could be works prior to PE I, or the manuscript could start with PE II only. Either option, however, is less likely than that the manuscript started with PE I.

Semi-Regular Solids[19]
Stomachion
Book of Lemmas
Measurement of the Circle
Method
Conoids and Spheroids
Sphere and Cylinder I
Sphere and Cylinder II
Cattle Problem
Planes in Equilibrium I
Planes in Equilibrium II
Spiral Lines
Arenarius
Quadrature of Parabola
Floating Bodies I
Floating Bodies II

What would such a counterfactual order suggest? Above all, a certain lack of order, and the sense of an author who reveled in variety. This, indeed, may not be too far of the mark. But notice how different this is from the impression made by Heiberg's order chosen for the *Opera Omnia*! For his sober-minded Teubner edition, based on the authority of the sober-minded scribe of A, Heiberg has produced a sober-minded Archimedes – one who was above all a pure geometer. This, once again, may possibly be historically correct. But then again, perhaps it is not. The one thing clear is that the order forms *an editorial decision*: a different ordering of the works would have given us perhaps a less sober, perhaps even a less geometrical Archimedes.

The dialect of Archimedes' works

The very language in which Archimedes' works should be read forms a genuine philological puzzle. I do not think we are ready to solve this puzzle, yet, and so I merely outline here the problem, expanding somewhat the discussion of this problem from pp. 179–80 above and focusing on the significance of Heiberg's approach to it.

---

[19] While not extant, Archimedes' work on semi-regular solids is known through a report in Book v of Pappus' *Collection*. I am envisaging how Archimedes' works would have looked had a work such as this appeared first.

Some of the manuscripts that give evidence for Archimedes' works contain a significant presence of Doric dialect forms, in particular ποτι for Koine προς, ειμεν for Koine ειναι, εσσειται for εσται as well as certain phonological variations, predominantly the use of long α for Koine η. Such dialect forms are very common in the manuscript evidence for PE i, CS, QP, *Arenarius* (A alone), FB i (C alone) and SL (both A and C). The dialect forms are much less common, or totally missing, in SC i, SC ii, DC, PE ii (both A and C), FB ii, *Stomachion* and *Method* (C alone). Heiberg's comment on this last work (ii.xviii) is telling: 'And even though I do not doubt that this work, too, was written in Doric by Archimedes, I dare not reinstate the dialect that was so diligently removed by the interpolator.'[20] In other words, Heiberg sees the Koine dialect as a kind of interpolation, inserted into the text of SC i, SC ii and DC (works that Heiberg would anyway consider heavily mediated by their readers) as well as some other works.

While SC i, SC ii and DC are completely free of Doric dialect, all the other works display a certain mixture of Doric and Koine, more Doric in such works as SL, much more Koine in works such as *Method*. Heiberg's edition removes this sense of gradation, introducing instead a clear bifurcation. SC i, SC ii, DC and *Method* are printed mostly in pure Koine, *no mention made* in the critical apparatus for the (rather few) cases where Doric forms are present. PE i, PE ii, CS, QP, *Arenarius*, FB i, FB ii and SL are printed in pure Doric, *no mention made* in the critical apparatus for the (rather many) cases where Koine forms are present.[21] Notice that Heiberg imposed Doric on PE ii and FB ii, *against* the manuscripts – which he avoided doing for *Method* – presumably because of a desire to preserve their continuity with PE i and FB i, respectively. Underlying this simple bifurcation is an even simpler monolithic image of Archimedes' language. As Heiberg said plainly, his position was that Archimedes wrote in Doric and in Doric alone.

Heiberg, ever the philologer, did produce an explicit survey of the dialect variation. This however he did not in the critical apparatus itself, but inside a dedicated index of manuscript variations, positioned as the major component of the introduction to the second volume. This doubly marginalizes the importance of the dialect variations. First, by taking them away from the critical apparatus, and second, by positioning them in the second

---

[20] 'et quamquam non dubito, quin hoc quoque opus Dorice scripserit Archimedes, dialectum de industria ab interpolatore remotam restituere ausus non sum.'

[21] The *Stomachion* – preserved in fragmentary form and therefore more tactfully handled – is the only work for which Heiberg simply prints, without comments, the form of the manuscript (according to Heiberg's readings), allowing a 'mixed' dialect.

volume, rather than in the third and final volume (which is where critical editions typically present their major philological observations).

In this case as in the case of excisions (to which the question of dialect is after all closely related, as Heiberg's excisions, as we saw, centred on what he defined as Koine-only treatises) Heiberg could well be right. We could never tell for sure whether Heiberg was indeed right on dialect, but his position is indeed plausible. What Heiberg did achieve however is to obscure the very question which, to my knowledge, has not been addressed at all to date. Which dialect(s) did Archimedes write in, and what was the significance of such choice? I do not have the expertise required to solve such questions, but I wish to emphasize that these questions have yet even to be posed. Would a choice to write in Doric, or in Koine, carry specific cultural meanings? It is very intriguing that a late source tells us that Archytas is the model for Doric prose.[22] Archytas of course was primarily a scientific author, indeed known for his contribution to the exact sciences. Was there a cultural value attached to Doric as a marker of scientific prose? (Eudoxus, from the Doric-speaking island of Cnidus, could have written in Doric as well; for certain, he did not write in Koine which was not yet available in his time.)[23] Clearly, dialectal choice was, in Archimedes' time, a charged generic marker. Hellenistic authors were keenly aware of their position as heirs to a rich literary tradition, varied by genre and by dialect – the two often going hand in hand. Elegy would be written in (a specific variety of) Ionic, epic poetry in the Homeric dialect (which in itself was a *Kunstsprache*, an ad-hoc amalgamation of several layers of Greek that never served together in any actually spoken Greek).[24]

Heiberg's implicit claim was that the question of dialect was minor, because it was unmarked: what would Archimedes write in, if not his native language? Even deeper lies the assumption that a mathematician's language does not matter. Archimedes would write in Doric, the unmarked

---

[22] Gregory of Corinth, *On Dialects*. (A6g in Huffman 2005: 279–80). This – Byzantine – source mentions Archytas and Theocritus as the models of Doric, Archytas clearly intended therefore as the model of Doric *prose*. While late, it is difficult to see how such a statement could emerge based on anything other than solid ancient testimony from the time that Archytas' works were still widespread.

[23] Nor should we think in terms of a monolithic 'Doric' opposed to a monolithic 'Koine'. It is completely unclear to me, for instance, whether the Doric prose of Archimedes' usage could not have allowed των, instead of ταν, more often than Heiberg assumes (there are about twenty cases of such variation in each of SL and *Arenarius*, where Heiberg always prints ταν).

[24] The locus classicus for an interpretation of this traditional observation is an essay by Parry from 1932, 'Studies in the epic technique of oral verse-making. II. The Homeric language as the language of an oral poetry', most conveniently available as chapter 6 of Parry 1971.

form he would speak anyway, since he would not even think about which language to use: the contents matter, and not their verbal form. Such is the image projected by Heiberg's editorial choice to minimize the question of dialect and to assume a purely Doric Archimedes. I am not sure this is true, and so I suspect that there is an open question as to the cultural significance of Archimedes' choice of dialect. This question is elided by Heiberg's editorial choices.[25]

Once again: I do not condemn Heiberg. I point, instead, to the significance of Heiberg's move away from the manuscripts, regardless of how close this may or may not have brought him to the 'original text'. The main consequence of Heiberg's move was to make the verbal texture of the text appear much more consistent than it was in the manuscript evidence. The main implication of that would be to minimize the very significance of verbal texture: to make Archimedes, once again, into a pure geometer – one who cares about his mathematics and not at all about his style.

The format of Archimedes' works

If Heiberg's Archimedes ignores questions of verbal shape, this Archimedes certainly pays attention to mathematical shape or format. In the critical edition, the text is articulated throughout by a systematic arrangement based on two dualities: that of the introductory text as against the sequence of propositions; and, inside the propositions, that of the general statement as against the particular proof. Both are determined by the major feature of the format, namely the sequence of numbers of propositions inside each work. The first numeral, preceding the first proposition, marks the transition from introduction to the sequence of propositions; from then onwards, each numeral is followed by a single paragraph written out without diagrammatic labels, which is the general statement preceding the main proof.

This format has basis in the manuscripts' authority and may to some extent reflect Archimedes himself. In some ways, however, Heiberg tends to emphasize the regularity of this format and even to insert it against the manuscripts' authority.

The layout itself is significant. Heiberg has the proposition numerals written inside the block of printed text with clear spaces preceding and

[25] All of this is closely parallel to the question of dialect in Theocritus – another third-century Syracusan extant, mostly, in some form of Doric, poetic in this case – and even though the analogous problem has been researched for the case of Theocritus, scholars are far from consensus (see Abbenes 1996).

following them, serving in this way to articulate the writing in a highly marked form. Following that, Heiberg writes out his text in accordance with the clear paragraph arrangement dictated by modern conventions, with the general statement always occupying a separate paragraph. The Byzantine manuscripts followed a somewhat different layout. Numerals for propositions – where present – are marginal notes that do not break the sequence of the writing (this articulation is provided, however, by the diagrams, as a rule positioned at the end of their respective propositions). Division into paragraphs is less common in Byzantine manuscripts (where it is performed by spacing inside the line of writing, where the break is to take place, together with an optional bigger initial in the *following* line, positioned outside the main column of writing). Typically, general statements do not form in this sense a paragraph apart, such division into paragraphs being reserved for more major divisions in the text – typically for the very beginning of a proposition or, occasionally, in such major transitions as the passage from the 'greater' to the 'smaller' cases in the Method of Exhaustion (so, for instance, codex C in SL 25, I 96.30). It is likely that Archimedes' original papyrus' rolls were, if anything, less articulated than that.[26] Not that this impugns Heiberg's use of paragraphs: modern editions universally ignore such questions of layout, imposing modern conventions, and even though the layout of the manuscripts, as of Archimedes himself, did not possess Heiberg's visible articulation, it is fair to say that the two divisions – of introduction from main propositions, and of general statements from proofs – are genuinely part of Archimedes' style.

However, because Heiberg is committed to a *visible* layout, he is also forced to set clear-cut divisions where the original may be less clearly defined.

First, even though the Archimedean text does operate between the polarities of discursive prose and mathematical proposition, it is not as if the transition between the two is typically handled as a break in the text. Rather, Archimedes negotiates the transition in varied ways that make it much smoother. To take a few examples: following the main introductory sequence in CS (I 246–258.18), Archimedes moves on to a passage (I 258.19–260.24) where several simple claims are either asserted without argument, or are accompanied by a minimal argument without diagrammatic labels (e.g. Archimedes explains that when a plane cuts both sides of a cone, it produces either a circle or an ellipse). Only following that, at I 260.25, Archimedes moves on to a longer and more complicated

---

[26] On early papyrus practices of articulation of text, see Johnson 2000.

proposition that also calls for a diagram. Codex A also marked this proposition with the marginal numeral A. Heiberg prints the entire sequence I 246–260.24 preceding 'proposition 1' as a single paragraphed block of text, that is the 'introduction', followed by the sequence of 'propositions' starting at I 260.25. But clearly Archimedes' intention was to create a smooth transition mediated by the passage I 258.19–260.24, which does not fall easily under either 'introduction' or 'propositions'.

Very similar transitions are seen in SC I, SC II, QP and PE I, with Heiberg making different choices: in SC I and SC II the transitional material is incorporated into the 'introduction'; in QP and PE I it is incorporated into the 'propositions'. Further, while the first proposition of the *Method* has a complex argument that calls for a diagram, Archimedes rounds it off with a second-order comment that makes it appear rather like part of the 'introduction' (II 438.16–21). Heiberg, very misleadingly, prints this comment as if it formed part of proposition 2: clearly Archimedes' point was to smooth, once again, the transition from introduction to propositions. If we bear in mind that the complex interplay of introduction and propositions is typical of the *Arenarius*, and that FB II, PE II and DC do not possess an introduction at all, we discover that Heiberg's neat dichotomy of introduction divided from text is found in SL alone!

Heiberg's clear articulation of the text into 'propositions' falling into paragraphs tends to obscure, once again, the variety of formats found in the corpus. Quite often, the text relapses into briefer arguments set in a general language that does not call for a diagram. Heiberg marks such passages off and heads them as 'corollaries' or *porisma*, but this is done against the manuscripts' evidence where, instead, such passages form part of the unbroken flow of the text. This happens twenty times in the corpus. Heiberg systematically introduces the title *porisma* into the printed text, noting in the apparatus that the manuscripts 'omit' this title! For instance PE I: Heiberg prints πορισμα α in II 130.22 and πορισμα β in II 132.4, with the following apparatus: 130.22 *om.* AB Πο D, 132.4 *om.* AB. That is: one copy of A introduced, in the first case, a marginal mark anticipating Heiberg's own intrusion. But the original text had no such headings. The important consequence is that the original text allowed stretches of text, inside the main flow of 'propositions', where no detailed, diagrammatic argument was required – and without segregating such passages by a title such as 'corollary'.

The variety of the original is wider than that. Thus, for instance, some propositions have a complex internal structure not neatly captured by the simple division into general statement and particular proof (such as the analysis-and-synthesis pairs typical of SC II, as well as the extraordinarily complex internal structures – punctuated by several diagrams – of FB II.8–10). Other propositions do not even display this simple division: for instance, several key propositions of SC I, starting with 23, take the form of a 'thought experiment' where a certain operation is carried out followed by an observation. Such propositions do not call for a general statement. Further, many of the propositions of QP do not have a general statement and start instead directly with diagrammatic labels. Now, Heiberg does report correctly the contents of such deviant propositions, but his overall system of articulating the text by explicit numerals tends to force the readings of all propositions into a single mould. More, indeed, can be said for the case of QP. The manuscripts do mark numerals for the first four propositions (the first three of which, however, defy easy counting, as they form the transitional material from introduction to propositions). Then, from proposition 5 onwards, no numerals are present. Heiberg dutifully notes this fact but in a misleading fashion (analogous to his treatment of the title 'corollary'): he goes on printing the numerals, noting in the critical apparatus to proposition 5 that from this point onwards the numerals are 'omitted' by the manuscripts.

This is not a unique case: the manuscripts for DC and *Method* never contain numerals for proposition numbering; Heiberg introduces the numbering and then makes the apparatus report their 'omission'.

A similar pattern can be seen inside the introductory material. There, Archimedes often includes material of substantive axiomatic import – certain assumptions, or definitions, that he requires later on for his argument. Typically, Heiberg introduces titles to head such passages (that, in the original, belong directly to the flow of the introduction), and then numbers the individual claims made in such passages. Thus, Heiberg's introduction of SC I is divided (following Torelli) into three parts: a general discussion proper (I 2–4), αξιωματα or 'definitions', so headed and numbered 1–6 (I 6), λαμβανομενα or 'postulates', so headed and numbered 1–5 (I 8). Titles and numbers are not in the original. Similar systematizations of the axiomatic material take place in *Method*, SL (inside the later axiomatic passage, II 44.16–46.21) and PE I.

Heiberg's position must have been that all such titles and numerals were required and so would have been lost only through some textual corruption. Otherwise, he could at the very least have marked off such editions by, say, pointed brackets, or, at the very least, commenting in the apparatus *add.* for 'I added' instead of *om.* for 'the manuscripts omitted…' This position blinded Heiberg to the serious textual question regarding the origins of such numerals in general. While the manuscripts do usually possess numerals for proposition numbers, there seems to be some occasional disagreement between the manuscripts as to *which* numerals to attach. This disagreement is typically between the various copies of codex A, and so carries little significance (aside from signalling to us that the scribes may have felt a certain freedom changing those numbers). In the few cases (SL, SC i, SC ii) where Heiberg could compare the numbering reconstructed for codex A with that reconstructed for codex C, the numbers were indeed the same. However, it is interesting to observe that codex C has the number 11 for what Heiberg titles (based on codex A) PE ii.10.[27] Heiberg almost certainly was unable to read this number but, once this evidence is considered, we find a remarkable fact: the two early Byzantine manuscripts for PE ii numbered their propositions differently. This of course raises the possibility that such numbers are indeed not part of the original text but are rather (as their marginal position suggests) a late edition by Late Ancient or Byzantine readers. Here, remarkably, Heiberg may have failed to be critical enough. The possibility that the numbering was not authorial apparently did not even cross his mind.

This phenomenon of systematization by titles and numerals is quite out of keeping with Heiberg's overall character as an editor. There must have been a major reason for Heiberg to intervene in the text so radically, and so blindly. This fact complements the evidence we have seen for Heiberg's treatment of Archimedes' verbal style. Just as Heiberg considered Archimedes indifferent to his verbal style, so we see Heiberg imputing to Archimedes meticulous attention to mathematical style. And this, even though such an imputation flies in the face of the evidence. Whereas Archimedes' text shows a great variety of forms of presentation, a gradation between more or less formal, more or less general, and a merely discursive arrangement, Heiberg produces a text marked by the dichotomies of introductory and formal, general and particular, throughout producing a neatly signposted text. This is a consistent Archimedes – and a consistently formal one.

A close-up on the *Method*

Archimedes' *Method* forms a special case. First, Heiberg faced here a task somewhat different from elsewhere: he needed not only to judge a text, but also, to a certain extent, to formulate it himself. Much of the text of the Palimpsest was illegible to him and so much had to be supplied. Second,

---

[27] The Archimedes Palimpsest 14r col. 1, margins of line 11.

here we can test Heiberg's judgement. Heiberg's decisions elsewhere – that this or that was by Archimedes himself, this or that was by an interpolator – will probably never be verified or refuted. But whenever we can now read passages of the Palimpsest that were illegible to Heiberg, we thereby test a conjecture. The issue of course is not to see how good Heiberg was as a philologer. He was a superb one and, indeed, the new readings of the Palimpsest often corroborate Heiberg's guesses to the letter. I shall now concentrate, however, on three false guesses – which together form a systematic whole, characteristic of Heiberg's overall approach to the text of Archimedes.

This is also a good example of the enormous sway Heiberg's edition had over Archimedes' destiny through the twentieth century. Heiberg's edition was careful and prudent: pointed brackets surrounding passages that he fully guessed, dots to mark lacunae that he could not read at all (often with remarks in the apparatus asserting the length of such lacunae), dots underneath doubtful characters. It is true that today we find that a number of characters Heiberg printed with confidence were wrong, but this is a natural phenomenon in a palimpsest where the overlaying text occasionally creates the illusion of false characters. All of this was accompanied by a Latin translation – as was Heiberg's practice elsewhere – where doubtful passages were carefully marked by being printed in italics. In short, any careful reader could tell which part of the text was Heiberg's, and which was Archimedes'. And yet, Heiberg's influence was such that all later editors, translators and readers operated, as it were, on the basis of Heiberg's Latin translation, largely speaking ignoring the difference between the Latin printed in Roman characters (which Heiberg read confidently) and the Latin printed in italics (which Heiberg merely guessed or supplied). Here, more than anywhere else, Heiberg's text supplanted that of Archimedes. This had real consequences, subtle but consistent – so as to change the overall texture of the treatise.

(1) The first case is the most clear-cut. We now recognize *Method* proposition 14 (to follow Heiberg's misleading numerals) as one of the most important proofs ever written by Archimedes, but this is on the strength of a new reading, illegible to Heiberg. As read by Heiberg, this proposition is a mere variation on themes developed elsewhere in the *Method*, of little deep value.

The *Method* typically operates by the combination of two principles: a method of indivisibles (conceiving an $n+1$-dimensional object as constituted by a continuity of n-dimensional objects), and the application of results from geometrical mechanics for the derivation of results in pure geometry. This is often done by obtaining a common centre of gravity to all pairs, suitably defined, of the *n*-dimensional objects; assuming that the centre of gravity is then inherited by a pair of *n*+1-dimensional objects constituted by the *n*-dimensional objects; and finally applying the results that follow from the geometrical proportions inherent in the Law of the Balance. This is illustrated by Archimedes through a variety of results arranged by Heiberg as propositions 1–11. As Archimedes clarifies in the introduction, his intent is to provide also 'classical' or purely geometrical proofs for a couple of new results, measuring the volumes of (a) the intersection of a cylinder and a triangular prism, (b) the intersection of two orthogonally inclined cylinders. Nothing survives of the proofs for (b), but we have considerable evidence for no fewer than three proofs for (a). The first, arranged by Heiberg as the two propositions 12–13, is a proof based on both a method of indivisibles as well as geometrical mechanics. The second is proposition 14, on which more below; the third – called by Heiberg 'proposition 15' – survives in fragmentary form, but it is clear beyond reasonable doubt that this forms, indeed, a 'classical' proof based on standard geometrical principles applied elsewhere. This is in fact a proof based on the method of exhaustion.

Proposition 14 therefore occupies a middle ground between the special procedures of the *Method*, and the standard geometrical principles applied elsewhere. Indeed, it uses only one part of the procedures of the *Method*. It makes no use of geometrical mechanics, based instead on indivisibles alone. Archimedes considers a certain proportion obtained for any arbitrary slice in the solid figures – so that a certain triangle A is to another triangle B as a certain line segment C is to another line segment D. The set of all triangles A constitutes the triangular prism; the set of all triangles B constitutes the intersection of cylinder and triangular prism that Archimedes sets out to measure; the set of all line segments C constitutes a certain rectangle; the set of all line segments D constitutes a parabolic segment enclosed by that rectangle.

Heiberg's readings reached this point, and then Heiberg hit what was, for him, a lacuna in his readings. He picked up the thread of the argument as follows. It is assumed that, since the proportion holds between all *n*-dimensional figures, it will also hold between all *n*+1-dimensional figures. We therefore have the proportion: a triangular prism to the intersection of a cylinder and a triangular prism, as rectangle to parabolic segment. Since the ratio of a rectangle to the parabolic segment it contains is known, and since the triangular prism is measurable, the intersection of the triangular prism and the cylinder is measured as well.

All this makes sense and we can therefore even understand why Heiberg was content: his reading, though lacunose, was mathematically sound. He did remark on the lacuna 'Quid in tanta lacuna fuerit dictum, non exputo'[28] – 'I do not guess what were to be written in such a long lacuna'. This comment may be prudent, but it accompanies a text that, otherwise, is meant to be read as mathematically meaningful. In other words, the implication would be that the missing lacuna was no more than ornament that does not impinge on the mathematical contents of proposition 14, and it was certainly in this way that proposition 14 was read through the twentieth century.[29]

The upshot of this reading is indeed to make the proposition less important, because it contains nothing new. It applies the method of indivisibles – previously applied in the *Method* – by assuming that a certain property obtained for n-dimensional objects is inherited by the $n+1$-dimensional objects they constitute. It differs from the previous propositions in a merely negative way – it does not apply geometrical mechanics – and therefore it makes no contribution to our understanding of Archimedes' mathematical procedures.

This understanding of proposition 14 was revolutionized by the readings of Netz *et al.* (2001–2), where the lacuna was finally read. It is clear that this lacuna adds much more than ornament. Indeed, it forms the mathematical heart of the proof. Archimedes applies certain results concerning the summation of sets of proportions developed elsewhere, results that call for counting the number of objects in the sets involved, with the number of objects in this set equal to the number of objects in that set. And this – even though the sets involved are infinite! Thus, Archimedes does no less than count (by the statement of numerical equality) infinite sets. The proof is therefore not a mere negative variation on the previous proofs; to the contrary, it opens up a unique avenue, completely unlike anything else extant from Greek mathematics. Heiberg's minimal interpretation of the text is thus refuted. Though, of course, this is not to blame Heiberg: what else could he do?

(2) The next example comes from the final, fragmentary proposition 15. The first page of this proposition survives on fos. 158–9 of the

---

[28] Heiberg 1913: 499, n. 1.

[29] See in particular Sato 1986, Knorr 1996, texts rare for paying any attention to proposition 14, both assuming that the text extant in Heiberg can be taken to represent Archimedes' own reasoning.

Palimpsest, in a form which was mostly illegible to Heiberg. There follows a gap in the text extant in the Palimpsest, followed by four considerable fragments extant on fo. 165 of the Palimpsest. Two of those fragments were nearly fully read by Heiberg, and they formed a basis for an interpretation of the proof as a whole, one which the much fuller reading we possess today corroborates on the whole. Its main feature is the following. In this, purely geometrical proof, Heiberg makes Archimedes follow a route comparable to that used in the measurement of conoids of revolution in CS. A sequence of prisms is inscribed inside the curvilinear object; the difference between the sequence of prisms and the curvilinear object is made smaller than any stated magnitude; and the assumption that the curvilinear figure is *not* of the volume stated then leads to contradiction. All of this is well known from elsewhere in Archimedes and Heiberg had many patterns to follow – especially from CS itself – in his reconstruction of the text of fos. 158–9 beginning the proof.

In contrast to proposition 14, where the lacuna unread by Heiberg – no more than about half a column of writing – proved to be much richer in mathematical meaning than Heiberg imagined, here, fos. 158–9 contain three and a half columns of writing, mostly unread by Heiberg, and they contain practically no mathematical significance. Here the surprise is the opposite to that of proposition 14. Heiberg in his reconstruction rather quickly establishes the geometrical construction required for inscribing prisms inside the curvilinear object. Archimedes himself, however, went through what may have been the most detailed construction in his entire corpus. The construction is much slower than that of the analogous proofs in CS. At the end of these three and a half columns of writing, Archimedes had not yet reached the explicit conclusion that the difference between the curvilinear object and the inscribed prisms is smaller than any given magnitude. It appears that in making the transition from the unorthodox procedures of propositions 1–14, to the 'classical' procedure of proposition 15, Archimedes made a deliberate effort to make proposition 15 as 'classical' as possible – as explicit and precise as possible. (One of course is reminded of how Heiberg tends, elsewhere, to doubt passages where Archimedes is especially explicit and transparent. Would he have excised a good deal of proposition 15, had he been able to read more of it?)

Archimedes' motives are difficult to judge but the effect most certainly was to emphasize the gap between the two parts of the treatise, the unorthodox and the orthodox. This gap was somewhat smoothed over in Heiberg's reconstruction though, once again, let this not be construed as a criticism of Heiberg: for, once again, there was no way for him to guess how different Archimedes' construction here was from that of Heiberg's models in CS.

(3) A final example is from proposition 6. Here Archimedes determines the centre of gravity of a hemisphere – as it appears from the beginning of the proposition, the relatively legible verso side of fo. 163. Heiberg thus knew what this proposition was about. The text then moves on to the recto side of fo. 163, which was barely legible to Heiberg, fo. 170 – mostly illegible in 1906 and one of the three leaves to have disappeared since – and the recto of 157, completely unread by Heiberg. As mentioned, we have meanwhile lost fo. 170 but, at the same time, through modern technologies, we have recovered practically the entire text of fos. 163 (recto) and 157 (recto) As a result, we now know that Heiberg's reconstruction of the parts he could not read was wrong.

Heiberg's modus operandi here was straightforward. While proposition 6 was mostly illegible, proposition 9 was mostly easy to read, especially in the well preserved (then) fos. 166–7 and 48–41. This proposition 9 dealt with finding the centre of gravity of *any* segment of the sphere, i.e. proposition 6 can be seen as a special case of proposition 9. What Heiberg did, then, was to reconstruct proposition 6 on the basis of proposition 9. In proposition 9, Archimedes constructs an auxiliary cylinder MN, whose various centres of gravity balance with certain cones related to the segments of the sphere. This cylinder is then imported by Heiberg into proposition 6 itself. But there is no need of such an auxiliary construction in proposition 6. Indeed, the finding of the centre of gravity of a hemisphere is much simpler than that of finding the centre of gravity of a general segment (which is not all that surprising as this happens often: a special case may have properties that make it easier to accomplish). The position of the centre of gravity along the axis is found, in an elegant manner, by considering just the cone which is already contained by the hemisphere. Heiberg's reconstruction of proposition 6 made it appear as if it were a precise copy of proposition 9, merely plugging in the special properties of the hemisphere. But it appears that Archimedes took two different routes, a more direct and elegant one for finding the centre of gravity of the hemisphere, and an indirect one for finding the centre of gravity of a general segment.

Once again, we can hardly blame Heiberg. He played it safe, reconstructing a passage difficult to read on the basis of a closely related passage that was easier to read – just as he reconstructed proposition 15 on the basis of CS, and proposition 14 on the basis of propositions 1–11. How else would you reconstruct, if not on the basis of what you have *available*? But this immediately suggests that the act of reconstruction has, automatically, a significant consequence: if reconstruction is necessarily based on what one has available, reconstruction necessarily tends to *homogenize* the text. Hence 14 appears like 1–11; 15 appears like CS; 6 appears like 9. The *Method* as a whole loses something of its internal variety and of its difference from other parts of the corpus.

In truth, of course, the *Method* is all about difference. It is different from the rest of the corpus; it highlights internal variety, where the original procedure contrasts with 'classical', geometrical approaches. After all, what is the point of supplying three separate proofs of the same result (propositions 12–13, proposition 14, proposition 15) if not to highlight the difference between all of them? This can be seen at all levels. I have concentrated on the global forms of marking difference, but one can find such forms at a more local level. We may return to proposition 14 to take a closer look at its unfolding. The proposition falls into three parts: (a) a geometrical passage showing that a certain proportion holds, (b) a proportion theory passage showing that this proportion may be summed up for sets of infinite multitude and (c) an arithmetical passage calculating the numerical value of the segment of the cylinder measured. Heiberg did not read (b) at all, and had to reconstruct large parts of (a). The only part he could read in full was (c), which is indeed surprisingly careful and detailed. Heiberg's reconstruction ignored (b), and produced a careful and detailed development of (a). In Heiberg's reading, therefore, the proposition unfolded in an uninterrupted progression of careful geometrical argument, followed by a transition based directly on the method of indivisibles (and thus merely reduplicating propositions 1–11) leading to another careful, arithmetical argument.

Following Netz *et al.* (2001–2), we now know that the structure of the proof is much more unwieldy. Remarkably, passage (a) hardly possesses any argument. The difficult and remarkable geometrical conclusion required by Archimedes is thrust upon the reader as a given. This is then followed by the subtle and difficult argument of (b), leading finally to the much simpler passage (c) which now, in context, is truly startling in its slow development of such an obvious claim. Archimedes first states a difficult result as obvious, then outlines the most difficult claim imaginable, and then finally develops in full a sequence of mere arithmetical equivalences. This proposition 14 forms a microcosm of the *Method* as a whole: its fundamental principle of composition is *sharp difference*. Heiberg could hardly have guessed this, staring as he did at the nearly illegible pages of the Palimpsest. Perhaps he should have been more forthcoming in revealing his ignorance. Perhaps it would have been best to avoid all those passages translated in Latin printed in italics, so as to broadcast in all clarity the lacunose nature of Heiberg's own reading. But then again, the temptation to reproduce, in full, the mathematical contents of the *Method* was irresistible and the remarkable fact, after all, is that Heiberg came so close to achieving this reproduction. Where he erred, that was in the spirit of the text more than in its mathematical contents. And so he did reconstruct, mostly, the mathematical contents of the *Method* – transforming along the way the texture of Archimedes' writings.

The texture of Archimedes' writings: summary

We have seen several ways in which Heiberg manipulated the evidence of the manuscripts, transforming it to produce his text of Archimedes and, through that transformation, projecting his image of Archimedes. The manuscripts' diagrams were ignored, producing an image of Archimedes whose arguments were *textually explicit*. The bracketing of suspected inter-polations produced an image of Archimedes whose arguments were *less immediately accessible*. As for Heiberg's overall conventions of presentation, these would serve to make the argument appear *more consistent* than it really was – visible most clearly in Heiberg's reconstruction of the *Method*. There, obviously, Archimedes used a wide variety of approaches – which Heiberg tended to narrow down. This drive towards consistency marked Heiberg's project as a whole.

All in all, then, Heiberg's interventions make Archimedes to be textually explicit, non-accessible and consistent. Now, it is not as if Heiberg, through-out, adopted this editorial policy. The practices adopted for the edition of Archimedes display Heiberg's assumptions concerning Archimedes himself. Thus, Vitrac shows, in his analysis of Heiberg's edition of Euclid, that, with the latter, Heiberg's policies were quite different, emphasizing transparency – nearly the opposite of those of Archimedes.

Very likely, this editorial policy reveals, therefore, a certain image of mathematical *genius*. Heiberg could well make his Euclid transparent and accessible; Archimedes had to be difficult. While perfectly explicit and consistent, the mathematical genius is also remote and difficult. This, of course, is no more than guesswork, ascribing to Heiberg motives he may never have formulated explicitly for himself. I shall not linger on such possibilities. And, indeed, let us not forget: Heiberg could well be *right*. There are probably grounds for saying that Euclid was easier to read than Archimedes, that on the whole Euclid took more pains to make his text accessible.

The one point I would like to stress, finally – and the one which Heiberg almost inevitably would tend to obscure – is the *variety* of Archimedes' writings. Heiberg's editorial policy is in itself consistent, and it can't help reflecting a single image Heiberg entertained of the texture of Archimedes' writings. But in truth, the major feature of the corpus is that so many of its constituent works are unlike the others. Some are extant in Doric, some in Koine. Is this an artefact of the transmission alone? Perhaps. But the argument for that is yet to be made. The *Arenarius* stands apart: it is written in discursive prose. The *Cattle Problem* stands apart – it is written in poetic form. The *Method* stands apart – it deals with questions of procedure, putting side by side various approaches. Even *Sphere and Cylinder* II stands apart – it is the only work dedicated to problems alone. Many works diverge from the imaginary norm of pure geometry. Some works are heavily invested in numerical values – not only the *Measurement of the Circle*, but also the *Arenarius* and (in part) *Spiral Lines*, *Planes in Equilibrium* I and *Quadrature of Parabola* (as well as the no longer extant treatise on semi-regular solids and, likely, the *Stomachion*). Some works are heavily invested in physical considerations, such as *Planes in Equilibrium* I–II, *Floating Bodies* I–II and *Quadrature of Parabola*. Even a book with the straightforward theme and methods of *Sphere and Cylinder* I becomes marked by the very striking format of presentation, with the polygons represented by series of curved lines (surely one of the most striking features to arrest the attention of the original treatise – if indeed this convention is due to Archimedes himself). Which work by Archimedes remains 'typical'? Perhaps *Conoids and Spheroids*...

Inside many works, again, Archimedes plays throughout with variety: with putting side by side the physical and the geometrical, twice, in *Quadrature of Parabola* as well as *Method*; with putting side by side the numerical and the geometrical, in *Spiral Lines*, *Planes in Equilibrium*, *Quadrature of Parabola*, *Semi-Regular Solids* and *Stomachion*.

And so, is it so unlikely, finally, that Archimedes should, on occasion, be more explicit, on occasion, more opaque? If the answer is positive, then much of the argument for Heiberg's excisions – his major editorial intervention in the text of Archimedes – disappears.

Perhaps the answer should be negative; perhaps Heiberg was right in his reconfiguration of the Archimedean text. But this article serves as a note of caution: authors possess complex individual styles, and it is always hazardous to revise them on the basis of any single editorial policy. Which, once again, reminds us that we should not blame Heiberg: is it fair to ask anyone to make himself, deliberately, inconsistent? Such is the editor's plight: forever limping upon his crutches of a single method – gasping, out of breath, as he tries to catch up with an author who flies upon the wings of a creative mind.

Bibliography

Abbreviations used in this chapter

SC *Sphere and Cylinder*
DC *Measurement of the Circle*
CS *Conoids and Spheroids*
SL *Spiral Lines*
PE *Planes in Equilibrium*
Aren. *Arenarius*
QP *Quadrature of Parabola*
FB *Floating Bodies*
Meth. *Method*
Stom. *Stomachion*
Bov. *Cattle Problem*

Abbenes, J. G. J. (1996) 'The Doric of Theocritus: a literary language', in *Theocritus*, ed. M. A. Harder, R. F. Regtuit and G. C. Wakker. Groningen: 1–19.

Blanchard, A. (1989) 'Choix antiques et codex', in *Les débuts du codex*, ed. A. Blanchard. Turnhout: 181–90.

Czwallina-Allenstein, A. (1922–5) *Archimedes / Abhandlungen*. Leipzig.

Heiberg, J. L. (1879) *Quaestiones Archimedeae*. Copenhagen.
    (1880) *Archimedes, Opera Omnia*, 1st edn. Leipzig.
    (1910–15) *Archimedes, Opera Omnia*, 2nd edn. Leipzig.

Hultsch, F. (1876–8/1965) *Pappus, Collectio*, 3 vols. Berlin.

Johnson, W. A. (2000) 'Towards a sociology of reading in Classical antiquity', *American Journal of Philology* 121: 593–627.

Knorr, W. R. (1978) 'Archimedes and the *Elements*: proposal for a revised chronological ordering of the Archimedean corpus', *Archive for History of Exact Sciences* 19: 211–90.

(1996) 'The method of indivisibles in ancient geometry', in *Vita Mathematica: Historical Research and Integration with Teaching*, ed. R. Calinger. Washington, D.C.: 67–86.

Mugler, C. (1970–2) *Les oeuvres d'Archimède* 4 Vols. Paris.

Netz, R., Acerbi, F. and Wilson, N. (2004) 'Towards a reconstruction of Archimedes' *Stomachion*', *Sciamus* **5**: 67–100.

Netz, R. Tchernetska, N. and Wilson, N. 2001–2. 'A new reading of *Method* Proposition 14: preliminary evidence from the Archimedes Palimpsest', *Sciamus* **2**: 9–29 and **3**: 109–25.

Parry, M. (1971) *The Collected Papers of Milman Parry*. Oxford.

Poincaré, H. (1913) *Dernières Pensées*. Paris.

Sato, T. (1986) 'A reconstruction of *The Method* Proposition 17, and the development of Archimedes' thought on quadrature', *Historia Scientiarum* **31**: 61–86 and **32**: 61–90.

Spang-Hanssen, E. (1929) *Bibliografi over J. L. Heibergs skrifter*. Copenhagen.

Stamatis, E. S. (1970–4) *Archimedous Hapanta*. Athens.

Toomer, G. J. (1990) *Apollonius,* Conics v–vii. New York.

Ver Eecke, P. (1921) *Archimède, Les oeuvres complètes*. Paris.

Weitzmann, K. (1947) *Illustrations in Roll and Codex*. Princeton, N.J.

Whittaker, J. (1990) *Alcinous, Enseignement des doctrines de Platon*. Paris.

4 | John Philoponus and the conformity of mathematical proofs to Aristotelian demonstrations

ORNA HARARI

One of the central issues in contemporary studies of Aristotle's *Posterior Analytics* is the conformity of mathematical proofs to Aristotle's theory of demonstration. The question, it seems, immediately arises when one compares Aristotle's demonstrative proofs with the proofs in Euclid's *Elements*. According to Aristotle, demonstrative proofs are syllogistic inferences of the form 'All A is B, all B is C, therefore all A is C', whereas Euclid's mathematical proofs do not have this logical form. Although the discrepancy between mathematical proofs and Aristotelian demonstrations seems evident, it is only during the Renaissance that the conformity of mathematical proofs to Aristotelian demonstrations emerges as a controversial issue.[1] The absence of explicit discussions of the conformity of mathematical proofs to Aristotelian demonstrations in the earlier tradition seems puzzling from the perspective of contemporary studies of Aristotle's theory of demonstration. The formal discrepancies between Aristotelian demonstrations and mathematical proofs seem so obvious to us that it is difficult to understand how the conformity between mathematical proofs and Aristotelian demonstrations was ever taken for granted. In this chapter I attempt to bring to light the presuppositions that led ancient thinkers to regard the conformity of mathematical proofs to Aristotelian demonstrations as self-evident.

Neither an outright rejection nor an explicit approval of the conformity of mathematical proofs to Aristotelian demonstrations is found in the extant sources from late antiquity; however, two approaches to this issue can be detected. According to one approach, found in Proclus' commentary on the first book of Euclid's *Elements*, the conformity of

---

[1] The first Renaissance thinker to reject the conformity of mathematical proofs to Aristotelian demonstrations is Alessandro Piccolomini. His treatise *Commentarium de certitudine mathematicarum disciplinarum*, published in 1547, initiated the debate known as the *Quaestio de certitudine mathematicarum*, in which other Renaissance thinkers, such as Catena and Pereyra, sided with Piccolomini in stressing the incompatibility between mathematical proofs and Aristotelian demonstrations, whereas other thinkers, such as Barozzi, Biancani, and Tomitano, attempted to reinstate mathematics in the Aristotelian model. I discuss this debate and its ancient origins in the conclusions.

certain mathematical proofs to Aristotelian demonstrations is questioned.[2] According to the other approach, found in Philoponus' commentary on Aristotle's *Posterior Analytics*, the conformity of mathematical proofs to Aristotelian demonstrations is taken for granted.[3] Nevertheless, these thinkers did not address the same question that Aristotle's contemporary interpreters discuss. Whereas contemporary studies focus on the discrepancy between the formal requirements of Aristotelian demonstrations and mathematical proofs, the ancient thinkers focused on the non-formal requirements of the theory of demonstration – namely, the requirements that demonstrations should establish essential relations and ground their conclusions in the cause.

In view of this account, I attempt to explain why the question whether mathematical proofs meet these non-formal requirements does not arise within the context of Philoponus' interpretation of Aristotle's theory of demonstration. Regarding the requirement that demonstrative proofs should establish essential relations, I show that Philoponus considers it nonproblematic in the case of all immaterial entities including mathematical objects. I show further that Philoponus' assumption that mathematical objects are immaterial renders the requirement that the middle term should serve as a cause irrelevant for mathematical demonstrations, since according to Philoponus causes are required only to explain the realization of form in matter. Accordingly, the dependence of mathematical proofs on definitions is sufficient, in Philoponus' view, to guarantee their conformity to Aristotelian demonstrations. In substantiating this conclusion, I then discuss Proclus' argument to the effect that certain mathematical proofs do not conform to Aristotelian demonstrations. I show that within the context of Proclus' philosophy of mathematics, in which geometrical objects are conceived of as realized in matter, consideration of the question whether mathematical proofs meet the two non-formal requirements – a question which Philoponus ignores with regard to mathematical demonstrations – led Proclus to argue for the non-conformity of certain mathematical proofs to

---

[2] Proclus' commentary on the first book of Euclid's *Elements* was translated into Latin in 1560 by Barozzi and it played an instrumental role in the debate over the certainty of mathematics. For the reception of Proclus' commentary on the *Elements* in the Renaissance, see Helbing 2000: 177–93.

[3] Philoponus' commentary on the *Posterior Analytics* has been hardly studied; hence it is difficult to assess its direct or indirect influence on the later tradition. Nevertheless, it seems that the several traits of Philoponus' interpretation of the *Posterior Analytics* are found in the medieval interpretations of Aristotle's theory of demonstrations, such as the association of demonstrations of the fact with demonstrations from signs which is found in Averroes (see n. 38) and the identification of the middle term of demonstration with real causes (see n. 27).

Aristotelian demonstrations. As a corollary to this discussion, I conclude my chapter with an attempt to trace the origins of contemporary discussions of the conformity of mathematical proofs to Aristotelian demonstrations to the presuppositions underlying Philoponus' and Proclus' accounts of this issue. I thereby outline a possible explanation for how concerns regarding the ontological status of mathematical objects and the applicability of Aristotle's non-formal requirements to mathematical proofs evolved into concerns regarding the logical form of mathematical and demonstrative proofs.

Philoponus on mathematical demonstrations

In the *Posterior Analytics* 1.9, Aristotle states that if the conclusion of a demonstration 'All A is C' is an essential predication, it is necessary that the middle term B from which the conclusion is derived will belong to the same family (*sungeneia*) as the extreme terms A and C (76a4–9). This requirement is tantamount to the requirement that the two propositions 'All A is B' and 'All B is C', from which the conclusion 'All A is C' is derived, will also be essential predications. The example that Aristotle presents in this passage for an essential predication is 'The sum of the interior angles of a triangle is equal to two right angles'. In his comments on this discussion Philoponus tries to show that the attribute 'having the sum of its interior angles equal to two right angles' is indeed an essential attribute of triangles. He does so by arguing that Euclid's proof meets the requirements of Aristotelian demonstrations:

For having [its angles] equal to two right angles holds for a triangle in itself (*kath' auto*). And [Euclid] proves this [theorem] not from certain common principles, but from the proper principles of the knowable subject matter. For instance, he proves that the three angles of a triangle are equal to two right angles, by producing one of the sides and showing that the two right angles, the interior one and its adjacent exterior angle, are equal to the three interior angles,[4] so that such a syllogism is produced: the three angles of a triangle, given that one of its sides is produced, are equal to the two adjacent angles. The two adjacent angles are equal to two right angles. Therefore the angles of a triangle are equal to two right angles. And that the two adjacent angles are equal to two right angles is proved from the [theorem] that two adjacent angles are either equal to two right angles or are two right angles. Whence [do we know] that adjacent angles are either equal to two right angles or

---

[4] The proof that Philoponus describes is not identical to Euclid's proof. Philoponus' reference to 'two right angles' implies that he envisages a right-angled triangle, whose base is extended so as to create two adjacent right angles. Euclid's proof refers to an arbitrary triangle. This discrepancy does not affect Philoponus' reasoning, as he states in the sequel that two adjacent angles are either equal to two right angles or are two right angles.

are two right angles? We know it from the definition of right angles, [stating] that when a straight line set up on a straight line makes the adjacent angles equal to each other, the two equal angles are right. Well, having brought [the conclusion] back to the definition and the principles of geometry, we no longer inquire further, but we have the triangle proved from geometrical principles.[5]

In showing that Euclid's proof conforms to the Aristotelian model of demonstration, Philoponus focuses on two issues: (1) he presents Euclid's proofs in a syllogistic form, and (2) he grounds the proved proposition in the definition of right angle. The notion of first principles, on which Philoponus' account is based, includes only one of the characteristics of Aristotelian first principles – namely, their being proper to the discipline. In Philoponus' view, the dependence of Euclid's geometrical proof on geometrical first principles, rather than on principles common to or proper to other disciplines, is sufficient to establish that this proof conforms to the Aristotelian model. Two other characteristics of Aristotelian first principles are not taken into account in this passage. First, Philoponus does not raise the question whether the middle term employed in this proof is related essentially to the subject of this proof; that is, he does not consider the question whether a proposition regarding an essential attribute of adjacent angles can by any means serve to establish the conclusion that this attribute holds essentially for triangles.[6] Nor does he express any reservations concerning the auxiliary construction, in which the base is extended and two adjacent angles are produced. Second, Philoponus does not mention Aristotle's requirement that the first principles should be explanatory or causal; he does not raise the question whether the middle term in his syllogistic reformulation of Euclid's proof has a causal or explanatory relation to the conclusion. Thus Philoponus' account of the conformity of Euclid's proofs to Aristotelian demonstrations raises two questions: (1) why Philoponus ignores the question whether mathematical propositions state essential relations; and (2) why the causal role of the principles of demonstration is not taken into account. The following two sections answer these questions respectively.

Essential predications

Philoponus addresses the question whether mathematical proofs establish essential predications in his comments on the *Posterior Analytics* 1.22. He

---

[5] 116. 7–22, Wallies. All translations are mine.
[6] For Philoponus' syllogistic reformulation to be a genuine Aristotelian demonstration, one has to assume that adjacent angles and triangles are related to each other as genera and species. This assumption is patently false.

formulates this question in response to Aristotle's contention that sentences whose subject is an attribute, such as 'the white (*to leukon*) is walking' or 'the white is a log' cannot feature in demonstrations, because they are not predicative in the strict sense (*Posterior Analytics* 83a1–21). This contention jeopardizes, in Philoponus' view, the status of geometrical proofs. The subject matter of geometry, according to Philoponus, is shapes and their attributes. Hence, Aristotle's narrow conception of predication may imply that proofs that establish that certain attributes belong to shapes are not demonstrative because they prove that certain attributes, such as having the sum of the interior angles equal to two right angles, belong to other attributes, such as triangles (239.11–14).[7] Philoponus dismisses this implication saying:

Even if these [attributes] belong to shapes accidentally, they are completive [attributes] of their being (*symplērōtika tēs ousias*) and like *differentiae* that make up the species they are [the attributes] by which [shapes] are distinguished from other things.[8] ... Just as 'being capable of intellect and knowledge' or 'mortal' or any of the [components] in its definition do not belong to 'man' as one thing in another, but [man] is completed from them, so the circle is also contemplated (*theōreitai*) from *all* the attributes which are observed in it. Similarly, also the triangle would not be something for which 'having three angles equal to two right angles' or 'having the sum of two sides greater than the third' do not hold, but if one of these [attributes] should be separated, immediately the being of a triangle would be abolished too.[9]

This account does not answer Philoponus' original query; it does not tackle the question whether proofs that establish predicative relations between two attributes are demonstrative. Instead, Philoponus focuses here on the question whether the attributes that geometry proves to hold for shapes are essential, arguing that mathematical attributes like *differentiae* are parts of the definitions of mathematical entities. However, the analogy between the *differentiae* of man and mathematical propositions is not as obvious as Philoponus formulates it. The attributes 'capable of knowledge' and 'mortal' distinguish men from other living creatures; the former distinguishes human beings from other animals and the latter distinguishes

---

[7] Philoponus presupposes here Aristotle's categorical scheme, in which terms belonging to the nine non-substance categories are attributes of terms belonging to the category of substance. According to Aristotle's *Categories* the term 'shape' belongs to the category of quality. Hence, Philoponus claims that geometry studies attributes of attributes.

[8] The term 'completive attributes' (*symplērōtikos*) refers in the neo-Platonic tradition to attributes without which a certain subject cannot exist. On these attributes and their relation to *differentiae*, see De Haas 1997: 201 and Lloyd 1990: 86–8.

[9] 239.14–25, Wallies.

them from divine entities, which are also capable of knowledge but are not mortal. By contrast, the geometrical attributes that Philoponus mentions in this passage do not distinguish triangles or circles from other shapes. Admittedly, the attribute 'having the sum of the interior angles equal to two right angles' holds only for triangles, yet, unlike 'having three sides', it is not the feature that distinguishes triangles from other shapes. It seems, then, that in accounting for the essentiality of mathematical attributes, Philoponus expands the notion of *differentia*, so as to include all the attributes of mathematical entities. He does not distinguish between attributes that enter into the definition of an entity and necessary attributes; he concludes from the statement that a triangle will cease to be a triangle if one of its attributes were separated from it that these attributes are essential. Thus, rather than explaining why mathematical attributes are essential in Philoponus' view, this passage reflects his assumption that the essentiality of mathematical attributes is evident. This assumption, I surmise, can be understood in light of Philoponus' interpretation of the principles of demonstration.

In his comments on the *Posterior Analytics* ii.2,[10] Philoponus accounts for the distinction between indemonstrable premises and demonstrable conclusions in terms of the distinction between composite and incomposite entities. Incomposite entities, according to this discussion, are simple or intelligible substances such as the intellect or the soul, which are considered (*theōroumenon*) without matter.[11] In the case of such entities, Philoponus argues, the defining attribute is not different from the definable object and therefore propositions concerning such entities are indemonstrable or immediate. Another characterization of indemonstrable premises is found in Philoponus' interpretation of Aristotle's discussion of the relationship between definitions and demonstrations in the *Posterior Analytics* ii.2–10. In addressing the question whether it is possible to demonstrate a definition, Philoponus draws a distinction between two types of definition: formal and material. Formal definitions are the indemonstrable principles of demonstration that define incomposite entities; they include, according to Philoponus, the essential attributes (*ousiodōs*) of the defined object. Material definitions, by contrast, serve as demonstrative conclusions and

---

[10] The editor of Philoponus' commentary on the *Posterior Analytics*, M. Wallies, doubted the attribution of the commentary on the second book of the *Posterior Analytics* to Philoponus (v–vi). The authenticity of the commentary on the second book does not affect my argument, because all the references I make here to the commentary on the second book accord with views expressed in Philoponus' other commentaries.

[11] 339. 6–7, Wallies.

include the attributes that are present in matter.[12] In this interpretation, then, the ontological distinction between incomposite and composite entities accounts for two characteristics of the principles of demonstration: their indemonstrability and their essentiality. The question whether certain propositions meet Aristotle's requirements is not answered by an examination of their logical characteristics, but by the ontological status of their subjects.

It follows from this discussion that from Philoponus' viewpoint the immateriality of the subject of predication is sufficient to guarantee the essential relation between a subject and its attributes.[13] This assumption may explain Philoponus' approach to the issue of the essentiality of mathematical propositions. Mathematical objects, according to Philoponus, are abstractions from matter[14] – that is, they belong to the class of incomposite objects that serve as the subjects of formal definitions. Thus, in light of Philoponus' characterization of these definitions, it plausible to regard all attributes of mathematical objects as essential, because the immateriality of these objects seems to entail, in Philoponus' view, the essentiality of their attributes. In what follows, I show that the ontological distinction between incomposite and composite entities also explains why the causal role of the middle term is not taken into account in Philoponus' discussion of the conformity of Euclid's proofs to Aristotelian demonstrations.

Causal demonstrations

In his commentary on Aristotle's *Physics* ii.2, Philoponus examines the tenability of Aristotle's criticism of the theory of Forms, which involves, according to Aristotle, separation from matter of the objects of physics, although they are less separable than mathematical objects. In so doing, Philoponus draws a distinction between separability in thought and separability in existence, claiming that he agrees with Aristotle that the forms

---

[12] 364.16–18, Wallies.

[13] Two reasons may explain why Philoponus does not consider the possibility that immaterial entities have accidental attributes. First, it is commonly held in the ancient tradition that only individuals have accidental attributes, which belong to their matter. Second, Philoponus' notion of essential predication is more formal than Aristotle's. In characterizing essential predications Philoponus appeals to extensional, rather than intensional, considerations. In his view, attributes that belong to all members of a species and only to them are essential (e.g., *In An. Post.* 63.14–20, Wallies; *In DA* 29.13–30.1, Hayduck; *In Cat.* 64.9, Busse).

[14] For Philoponus' conception of mathematical objects, see (e.g.) *In Phys.* 219.10; *In DA*, 3.7–11. For a discussion of this view, see Mueller 1990: 465–7.

of natural things cannot be separated in existence from matter, but he disagrees with Aristotle's view if it implies that these forms cannot be separated
by reason and in thought.[15] Although Philoponus' account of the indemonstrability of the principles of demonstration presupposes the possibility
of separating the definitions of both mathematical and physical entities,
the ontological difference between these classes of objects is nevertheless
maintained. In his commentary on Aristotle's *De anima*, Philoponus draws
a distinction between physical and mathematical definitions, arguing that
physical definitions should refer to the matter of physical substance, their
form and the cause by virtue of which the form is realized in matter.[16]
Mathematical definitions, by contrast, refer only to the form:

The mathematician gives the definitions of abstracted forms in themselves, without
taking matter into account, but he gives these [definitions] in themselves. For this
reason he does not mention the cause in the definition; for if he defined the cause,
clearly he would also have taken the matter into account. Thus, since he does not
discuss the matter he does not mention the cause. For example, what is a triangle?
A shape contained by three lines; what is a circle? A shape contained by one line.
In these [definitions] the matter is not mentioned and hence neither is the cause
through which this form is in this matter. Unless perhaps he gives the cause of those
characteristics holding in themselves for shapes, for instance, why a triangle has its
angles equal to two right angles.[17]

Philoponus' distinction between physical and mathematical definitions
has two related consequences for the methods employed in physics and
mathematics. First, although both physical and mathematical demonstrations are based on indemonstrable formal definitions, these definitions
adequately capture the nature of mathematical objects but they fail to
exhaust the nature of physical objects. In the case of physical demonstrations, the formal definition captures only one aspect of the object: its
form. Full-fledged knowledge of physical objects requires reference also
to the matter of this object and the cause of the realization of the form
in matter. Indeed, in both the commentary on Aristotle's *De anima* and
the commentary on the *Posterior Analytics*, Philoponus considers formal
definitions of physical objects deficient. In the commentary on *De anima*,
Philoponus argues that definitions that do not include all the attributes

---

[15] 225.4–11, Vitelli. For the relationship between Philoponus' discussion of separability in
thought of physical definitions and his analysis of demonstrations in the natural sciences, see
De Groot 1991: 95–111.
[16] 55.31–56.2, Hayduck.
[17] 57.35–58.6, Hayduck.

of an object are not physical definitions, but are dialectical or empty. His example of such an empty definition is the formal definition of anger: 'anger is a desire for revenge'. The adequate definition of anger, according to Philoponus, is 'anger is boiling of the blood around the heart caused by a desire for revenge'.[18] This definition refers to the form, the matter and the cause. Similarly, in the commentary on the *Posterior Analytics*, Philoponus claims that neither the formal nor the material definition is a definition in the strict sense; only the combination of these two yields an adequate definition.[19] This conception of definition is evidently inapplicable to mathematics. Mathematical objects are defined without reference to matter or to their cause, hence formal definitions provide an exhaustive account of these objects.

The second consequence of Philoponus' distinction between physical and mathematical definitions concerns the explanatory or causal relations in demonstrative proofs. Although in the above-quoted passage Philoponus contends that the cause is also studied in mathematics when a relation between a mathematical object and its attributes is proved, it seems that this cause is different from the one studied in physics. According to the above passage, physics studies the cause of the realization of form in matter, but since mathematics does not deal with the matter of its objects, its explanations do not seem to be based on this type of cause. Furthermore, Philoponus' analysis of physical demonstrations in terms of the distinction between formal and material definitions gives rise to a problem that has no relevance for mathematical demonstrations. This interpretation gives rise to the question of how the material aspect of a physical entity, which is a composite of form and matter, can be demonstratively derived from the formal definition, given that this definition does not exhaust the nature of the composite entity. Stating this question differently, how, in Philoponus' view, can a proposition regarding a substance taken with matter be demonstratively derived from a proposition regarding its form, which is considered in separation from matter? Evidently this question does not arise in the mathematical context. Mathematical definitions do not refer to matter; hence, they give an exhaustive account of mathematical objects. In what follows, I show that Philoponus answers this question by appealing to extra-logical considerations. More specifically, I show that the causal role of the middle term in demonstrations provides Philoponus with the means of bridging the gap between formal definitions and material definitions.

[18] 43.28–44.8, Hayduck.
[19] 365.1–13, Wallies.

In his comments on the *Posterior Analytics* II.2, Philoponus presents the following explanation for Aristotle's remark that the questions 'what it is' (*ti esti*) and 'why it is' (*dia ti*) are the same:

For if the 'what it is' and the 'why it is' are different, it is insofar as the former is sought with regard to simple [entities] and the latter with regard to composite [entities]. Yet these [questions] are the same in substrate, but different in their mode of employment. Both the 'what it is' and the 'why it is' are studied in the case of the eclipse being an affection of the moon. And we use these, the 'what it is' and the 'why it is', differently. But if we take an eclipse itself by itself, we seek what is the cause of an eclipse, and we say that it is a privation of the moon's light due to screening by the earth. But if we seek whether an eclipse exists (*hyparkhei*) in the moon, namely why it exists, we take the 'what it is' as a middle term, namely privation of the moon's light coming about as a result of screening by the earth.[20]

Although this passage is presented to account for the identity between the questions 'what it is' and 'why it is', Philoponus dissociates these two questions. The distinction he draws here is based on the ontological distinction between simple and composite entities. The question 'what it is' is asked with regard to simple entities, whereas the question 'why it is' is asked with regard to composite entities. In the case of composite entities, Philoponus argues, 'what it is' and 'why it is' are different questions. The definition of an eclipse and the cause of its occurrence are not identical. The exact significance of Philoponus' distinction between these questions is not clear from this passage. The examples presented by Philoponus seem to blur his distinction between an eclipse considered in the moon and an eclipse considered in separation from the moon, as the accounts given for both cases are identical – 'privation of the moon's light due to screening by the earth'. This difficulty in understanding Philoponus' distinction between 'what it is' and 'why it is' may stem from his attempt to accommodate his view, which dissociates these questions, with Aristotle's claim that these questions are identical. As a result, Philoponus follows Aristotle in exemplifying the answers to these questions by one and the same account. However, according to Philoponus' other discussions of the definitions of entities, which are considered in separation from matter, the account for the eclipse taken in separation from the moon should be the formal definition 'screening by the earth', whereas 'privation of the moon's light due to screening by the earth' is the full definition, resulting from a demonstration that relates the formal definition to the material definition.[21] Despite the difficulty in

[20] 339.20–9, Wallies.
[21] 371.19–25, Wallies.

understanding the distinction made in this passage, Philoponus clearly does not follow Aristotle here in assimilating definitions with explanations. This conclusion finds further support in Philoponus' comments on the *Posterior Analytics* I.4.

In the *Posterior Analytics* I.4, Aristotle presents four senses in which one thing is said to hold for another 'in itself'. The first two senses are predicative and they constitute Aristotle's account for the predicative relations that the premises of demonstration should express. According to the first sense, a predicate holds for a subject in itself if it is a part of the definition of the subject. According to the second sense, a predicate holds for a subject in itself if the subject is a part of the definition of the predicate. The third sense distinguishes substances that exist in themselves from attributes, which depend on substances, by virtue of their being said of them. The fourth sense distinguishes a causal relation between events from an incidental relation between events. In his comments on this fourfold distinction Philoponus argues that only the first two senses of 'in itself' contribute to the demonstrative method,[22] yet he also regards the fourth sense (i.e. the causal sense) as relevant to the theory of demonstration. According to Philoponus, the causal sense of 'in itself', though it does not contribute to the formation of the premises of demonstration, contributes to the 'production of the whole syllogism'.[23] More precisely, Philoponus argues that the causal sense of 'in itself' expresses the relation between the cause, taken as the middle term of demonstration, and the conclusion. The example Philoponus presents of this contention is the following syllogism: The moon is screened by the earth. The screened thing is eclipsed. Therefore, the moon is eclipsed. Commenting on this syllogism, Philoponus remarks that the fact that screening by the earth is the cause of the eclipse of the moon is not expressed in the premises of this demonstration, but its causal force becomes evident from its role as a middle term.[24] In this discussion, then, Philoponus employs two different senses of 'in itself' in accounting for the relations expressed in the premises of demonstration and the relation between the middle term and the conclusion. The premises of demonstration, according to Philoponus, are 'in itself' in one of the two first senses delineated by Aristotle. That is, their predicate is either a part of the definition of the subject or their subject is a part of the definition of the predicate. By contrast, the middle

---

[22] 65.10–11, Wallies.
[23] 65.15, Wallies.
[24] 65.16–19, 65.20–3, Wallies.

term and the conclusion of a demonstration are related according to the fourth sense of 'in itself' – that is, they are related as cause and effect.[25] So, according to Philoponus, the derivation of the demonstrative conclusion is not solely based on the transitivity of the predicative relation stated in the premises. In addition to the transitivity of the predicative relation, the demonstrative derivation is based on causal relations between the middle term and the conclusion. Such a distinction between logical relations and extra-logical or causal relations is explicitly drawn at the beginning of Philoponus' introduction to his commentary on the second book of the *Posterior Analytics*:

In the first book of the *Apodeiktike* (i.e. the *Posterior Analytics*), he showed how there is a demonstration and what is a demonstration and through what premises it has come about, and he showed further how a demonstrative syllogism differs from other syllogisms and that in other syllogisms the middle term is the cause of the conclusion and not of the thing and in demonstrative syllogism the middle term is the cause both of the conclusion and of the thing.[26]

It follows from this discussion that Philoponus' ontological distinction between physical and mathematical entities yields different accounts for physical and mathematical demonstrations. The distinction between the three facets of physical entities – i.e. the form, the matter and the cause for the realization of form in matter – is reflected in Philoponus' interpretation of the theory of demonstration. In this interpretation, demonstrations, like physical entities, have three components: indemonstrable premises, regarded as formal definitions, demonstrative conclusions, which are material definitions, and the middle term, which serves as the cause that relates the formal definition to the material definition. Philoponus' distinction between the form of a physical entity and the cause of the realization of form in matter finds expression in the distinction he draws between the formal definition considered in itself and that formal definition in its role as the middle term in demonstration. This distinction implies that

[25] The analysis of demonstrative derivation in causal terms is widespread in Philoponus' commentary on the *Posterior Analytics* (e.g., 24.22–4; 26.9–13; 119.19–21; 173.14–20; 371. 4–19). The causal analysis of demonstrative derivation underlies Philoponus' introduction of a second type of demonstration, called 'tekmeriodic demonstration', in which causes are deduced from effects (*In An. Post.* 33.11; 49.12; 169.8; 424.13, Wallies; *In Phys.* 9.9–10.21, Vitelli). On Philoponus' notion of tekmeriodic proofs and its reception in the Renaissance, see Morrison 1997: 1–22.

[26] 334.1–8, Wallies. The distinction between the middle term as the cause of the thing and the middle term as the cause of the conclusion is also found in the Latin medieval tradition of interpreting the *Posterior Analytics*. See De Rijk 1990.

demonstrative derivation rests on two relations: the transitivity of the pre-dicative relation that the premises state and the causal relation between the middle term and the conclusion. This distinction is applicable to physical demonstrations, for which the cause of the realization of form in matter is sought. The demonstrative derivation in these demonstrations is based not only on logical relations but also on causal relations. Mathematical enti-ties, by contrast, have only one facet: the form. Accordingly, Philoponus' account of the conformity of mathematical demonstrations to Aristotelian demonstrations focuses only on the formal requirements of the theory of demonstration. The conformity of mathematical demonstrations to Aristotelian demonstrations is guaranteed if the conclusions can be shown to depend on the definitions of mathematical entities. Since mathematical objects have no matter, mathematical demonstrations can be based only on logical derivation; the question whether the middle term is the cause of the conclusion does not arise in this context, as the separation from matter renders superfluous questions concerning causes.[27]

The analysis of Philoponus' interpretation of Aristotle's theory of dem-onstration reveals the importance of the ontological distinction between simple and composite entities for his account of conformity of mathemati-cal proofs to Aristotelian demonstrations. The assumption that mathemati-cal objects are analogous to simple entities by being separated in thought from matter does not give rise to two questions that may undermine the conformity of mathematical proofs to Aristotelian demonstrations. The first question is whether mathematical predications are essential; the second is whether the middle term in mathematical proofs is the cause of the conclusion. The first question does not arise because the separation from matter implies that only the essential attributes of entities are taken into consideration. The second does not arise because causal considerations are relevant only with regard to composite entities, as it is only in their case that the cause of the realization of form in matter can be sought. Hence, given the assumption that mathematical entities are separated in thought from matter, the question whether mathematical proofs conform to the non-formal requirements of Aristotle's theory of demonstration does not arise. This conclusion gains further support from Proclus' discussion of the conformity of mathematical proofs to Aristotelian demonstrations.

---

[27] This conclusion may explain Proclus' otherwise curious remark that the view in which geometry does not investigate causes is originated in Aristotle (*In Eucl.* 202.11, Friedlein). If this explanation is correct, Philoponus' conception of mathematical demonstrations seems to reflect a widespread view in late antiquity.

Proclus on the conformity between mathematical proofs and Aristotelian demonstrations

Proclus' philosophy of geometry is formulated as an alternative to a conception whereby mathematical objects are abstractions from material or sensible objects.[28] According to Proclus, mathematical objects do not differ from sensible objects in their being immaterial, but in their matter. Sensible objects, in Proclus' view, are realized in sensible matter, whereas mathematical objects are realized in imagined matter. In Proclus' philosophy of geometry, then, mathematical objects are analogous to Philoponus' physical objects; they are composites of form and matter. Proclus' philosophy of mathematics is at variance not only with Philoponus' views regarding the ontological status of geometrical objects but also with Philoponus' views regarding the conformity of Euclid's proofs to Aristotelian demonstrations.[29] In his discussion of the first proof of Euclid's *Elements* in the commentary on the first book of Euclid's *Elements*, Proclus questions the conformity of *certain* mathematical proofs to the Aristotelian model:

We shall find sometimes that what is called 'proof' has the properties of demonstration, in proving the sought through definitions as middle terms – and this is a perfect demonstration – but sometimes it attempts to prove from signs. This should not be overlooked. For, although geometrical arguments always have their necessity through the underlying matter, they do not always draw their conclusions through demonstrative methods. For when it is proved that the interior angles of a triangle are equal to two right angles from the fact that the exterior angle of a triangle is equal to the two opposite interior angles, how can this demonstration be from the cause? How can the middle term be other than a sign? For the interior angles are equal to two right angles even if there are no exterior angles, for there is a triangle even if its side is not extended.[30]

In this passage, Proclus claims that Euclid's proof that the sum of the interior angles of a triangle is equal to two right angles (*Elements* I.32) does not conform to Aristotle's model of demonstrative proofs. In so doing, he focuses on the causal role of the middle term in Aristotelian demonstrations. Proclus argues that Euclid's proof does not conform to the Aristotelian model because it grounds the equality of the sum of the interior angles of a triangle to two right angles in a sign rather than in a cause.

---

[28] *In Eucl.* 50.16–56.22, Friedlein.

[29] A discussion of the relationship between Proclus' philosophy of geometry and his analysis of mathematical proofs is beyond the scope of this paper. For this issue, see Harari 2006.

[30] 206.12–26, Friedlein.

Proclus' reason for regarding this Euclidean proof as based on signs rather than on causes concerns the relationship between the auxiliary construction employed in this proof and the triangle. According to Proclus, the extension of the triangle's base is merely a sign and not a cause of the equality of the triangle's angles to two right angles because 'there is a triangle even if its side is not extended'. The exact force of this statement is clarified in Proclus' discussion of the employment of this auxiliary construction in another Euclidean proof – the proof that the sum of any two interior angles of a triangle is less than two right angles (*Elements* i.17). In this discussion, Proclus claims that the extension of the triangle's base cannot be considered the cause of the conclusion since it is contingent: the base of a triangle may be extended or not, whereas the conclusion that the sum of any two interior angles of a triangle is less than two right angles is necessary.[31] Hence, in questioning the conformity of certain Euclidean proofs to Aristotelian demonstrations, Proclus raises the two questions that Philoponus ignores in the case of mathematical demonstrations. Unlike Philoponus, Proclus asks whether the middle term in Euclid's proofs is the cause of the conclusion and whether it is essentially related to the triangle.

Furthermore, Proclus' attempt to accommodate Euclid's proofs of the equality of the sum of the interior angle of a triangle to two right angles with Aristotle's requirement that demonstrations should establish essential relations indicates that he shares with Philoponus the assumption that demonstrations regarding material entities require an appeal to causal considerations. In concluding his lengthy discussion of Euclid's proof that the sum of the interior angles of a triangle is equal to two right angles, Proclus says:

We should also say with regard to this proof that the attribute of having its interior angles equal to two right angles holds for a triangle as such and in itself. For this reason, Aristotle in his treatise on demonstration uses it as an example in discussing essential attributes ... For if we think of a straight line and of lines standing in right angles at its extremities, then if they incline so that they generate a triangle we would see that in proportion to their inclination, so they reduce the right angles, which they made with the straight line; the same amount that they subtracted from these [angles] is added through the inclination to the angle at the vertex, so of necessity they make the three angles equal to two right angles.[32]

The procedure described in the passage, in which a triangle is generated from two perpendiculars to a straight line that rotate towards each other

---

[31] 311.15–21, Friedlein.
[32] 384.5–21, Friedlein.

up to their intersection point, is also presented by Proclus in his comments on propositions 1.16 and 1.17 of the *Elements*. In both cases, he regards this procedure – and not Euclid's auxiliary construction in which the triangle's base is extended – as the true cause of the conclusion.[33] Proclus' appeal to this procedure in searching for the true cause of these conclusions indicates that in attempting to accommodate Euclid's proofs with Aristotle's requirement that demonstrations should establish essential relations, he grounds mathematical conclusions in causal relations rather than in logical relations. Proclus considers the proposition that the sum of the interior angles of a triangle is equal to two right angles essential not because it is derived from the definition of a triangle, as Aristotle's theory of demonstration requires, but because the proposition is derived from the triangle's mode of generation. Viewed in light of Philoponus' interpretation of Aristotle's theory of demonstration, Proclus' attempt to accommodate Euclid's proof with Aristotelian demonstrations seems analogous to Philoponus' account of physical demonstrations. In both cases, causal considerations are employed in rendering proofs concerning material objects compatible with Aristotelian demonstrations.

This examination of the presupposition underlying Philoponus' and Proclus' views regarding the conformity of mathematical proofs to Aristotelian demonstrations has led to the following conclusions.

(1) The pre-modern formulation of the question of the conformity of mathematical proofs to Aristotelian demonstrations concerns the applicability of the non-formal requirements of the theory of demonstration to mathematical proofs. More specifically, this formulation concerns the questions whether mathematical attributes are proved to belong essentially to their subjects and whether the middle term in mathematical proofs serves as the cause of the conclusion.

(2) The emergence or non-emergence of the question of the conformity of mathematical proofs to Aristotelian demonstration is related to assumptions concerning the ontological status of mathematical objects. This question does not arise in a philosophical context in which mathematical objects are conceived of as separated in thought from matter, whereas it does arise when mathematical objects are conceived of as realized in matter.

(3) Demonstrations concerning composites of form and matter were understood in late antiquity as based on causal relations, viewed as additional to the logical necessitation of conclusions by premises.

---

[33] 310.5–8, 315.15, Friedlein.

Causal considerations are employed with regard to mathematical demonstrations, when mathematical objects are considered material; they
are not employed when mathematical objects are considered separated
in thought from matter.

Conclusions

In concluding this chapter, I examine the relationship between the modern
formulation of the question of the conformity of mathematical proofs
to Aristotelian demonstrations and its formulation in late antiquity. The
modern discussions of the relationship between Aristotle's theory of demonstration and mathematical proofs focus on Aristotle's formal requirement
that demonstrations should be syllogistic inferences from two universal
predicative propositions, which relate the subject and predicate of the conclusion to a third term, called the 'middle term'.

The disagreement among Aristotle's modern commentators concerns
whether mathematical proofs can be cast in this logical form. For instance,
Ian Mueller, who says they cannot, argues that in a syllogistic reformulation
of Euclidean proofs the requirement that the inference should have only
three terms is not always met, because the mathematical proofs depend
on the relations between mathematical entities and not on their properties
taken in isolation from other entities.[34] The possibility of expressing mathematical relations in syllogistic inferences is also central in modern attempts
to render Aristotle's theory of demonstration compatible with mathematical proofs. Henry Mendell, for instance, shows that Aristotle's theory of
syllogism does have the formal means that make possible syllogistic formulations of mathematical proofs. In so doing, he argues that the relation
of predication, which is formulated by Aristotle as 'x belongs to y', can be
read flexibly so that it also accommodates two-place predicates, such as 'x
equals y', or 'x is parallel to y'.[35] Mendell's argument, like Mueller's, focuses
on the possibility of expressing relations within the formal constraints of
the theory of syllogism. The extra-logical consequences of the expansion
of the theory of syllogism to relational terms and their compatibility with
Aristotle's theory of demonstration are not at the centre of either Mendell's
or Mueller's argument. More specifically, they do not address the question
of whether relational terms or mathematical properties can be proved to

[34] Mueller 1975: 42.
[35] Mendell 1998.

be essential predicates of their subjects.[36] This question, as I showed, was central in the discussions of the conformity of mathematical proofs to Aristotelian demonstrations in late antiquity.

The non-formal requirements of the theory of demonstration were also central in the Renaissance debate over the certainty of mathematics.[37] Piccolomini's objective in his *Commentarium de certitudine mathematicarum disciplinarum* was to refute what he presents as a long-standing conviction that mathematical proofs conform to the most perfect type of Aristotelian demonstration, called in the Renaissance *demonstratio potissima*. The classification of types of demonstrations that underlies Piccolomini's argument is based on Aristotle's distinction between demonstrations of the fact (*hoti*) and explanatory demonstrations or demonstration of the reasoned fact (*dioti*). This distinction has been further elaborated by Aristotle's medieval commentators and it appears in the Proemium of Averroes' commentary on Aristotle's *Physics* as a tripartite classification of demonstrations into *demonstratio simpliciter, demonstratio propter quid* and *demonstratio quid est*. It is in this context that Averroes claims that mathematical proofs conform to the perfect type of demonstration, in his terminology *demonstratio simpliciter*.[38] According to this classification, the different types of demonstration differ in the epistemic characteristics of their premises, hence in the epistemic worth of the knowledge attained through them. Following this tradition, Piccolomini's argument for the inconformity of mathematical proofs to Aristotelian demonstrations focuses on these characteristics. According to Piccolomini *potissima* demonstrations are demonstrations in which knowledge of the cause and of its effects is attained simultaneously; the premises of such demonstrations are prior and better known than the conclusion; their middle term is a definition, it is unique and it serves as the proximate cause of the conclusion. Mathematical demonstrations, so Piccolomini and his followers argue, fail to meet these requirements. The importance of the non-formal requirements of the theory of demonstration for the Renaissance debate over the certainty of mathematics comes to the fore in the following passage from Pereyra's *De communibus omnium rerum naturalium principiis et affectionibus*:

---

[36] This question is not utterly ignored in modern interpretations of the *Posterior Analytics*. See McKirahan 1992; Goldin 1996; Harari 2004.

[37] For a general discussion of the *Quaestio de certitudine mathematicarum*, see Jardine 1998. For the influence of this debate on seventeenth-century mathematics, see Mancosu 1992 and 1996.

[38] *Aristotelis opera cum Averrois commentariis*, vol. IV, 4.

Demonstration (I speak of the most perfect type of demonstration) must depend upon those things which are *per se* and proper to that which is demonstrated; indeed, those things which are accidental and in common are excluded from perfect demonstrations ... The geometer proves that the triangle has three angles equal to two right ones on account of the fact that the external angle which results from extending the side of that triangle is equal to two angles of the same triangle which are opposed to it. Who does not see that this medium is not the cause of the property which is demonstrated? . . . Besides, such a medium is related in an altogether accidental way to that property. Indeed, whether the side is produced and the external angle is formed or not, or rather even if we imagine that the production of the one side and the bringing about of the external angle is impossible, nonetheless that property will belong to the triangle; but what else is the definition of an accident than what may belong or not belong to the thing without its corruption?[39]

Pereyra's argument for the inconformity of mathematical proofs to Aristotelian demonstrations is similar to Proclus' argument. Like Proclus, Pereyra focuses on the question whether mathematical proofs meet the non-formal requirements of the theory of demonstration. More specifically, he raises the two questions that were at the centre of Proclus' discussion of this issue: (1) Do the premises of mathematical proofs state essential or accidental relations? (2) Are Euclid's proofs, which are based on auxiliary constructions, explanatory? These questions are viewed in this passage as interrelated; real explanations are provided when the relation between a mathematical entity and its property is proved to be essential. This requirement is met if the premises on which the mathematical proof is based state essential relations. The only allusion to the syllogistic form of inference made in this passage is to the middle term in syllogistic demonstrations. However, like Proclus, Pereyra considers the middle term only in its role as the cause of the conclusion. Its formal characteristics, such as its position, are not discussed here. Thus, pre-modern and modern discussions of the conformity of mathematical proofs to Aristotelian demonstrations concern different facets of the theory of demonstration. Whereas the modern discussions focus on the formal structure of Aristotelian demonstrations, pre-modern discussions concern its non-formal requirements. Accordingly, the questions asked in these discussions are different. The modern question is whether syllogistic inferences can accommodate relational terms whereas the pre-modern question is whether mathematical proofs establish essential relations.

---

[39] The translation is based on Mancosu 1996: 13. The complete Latin text appears on p. 214, n. 12 of Mancosu's book.

Nevertheless, when the pre-modern discussion of the conformity of mathematical proofs to Aristotelian demonstrations is viewed in light of its underlying ontological presuppositions, a conceptual development leading to the modern formulation of this question may be traced. Discussions of the conformity of mathematical proofs to Aristotelian demonstrations in late antiquity were associated with discussions of whether mathematical objects are immaterial or material;[40] that is, whether they are conceptual or real entities. This ontological distinction is reflected in different accounts of the relation of derivation, on which demonstrations are based. Whereas demonstrations concerning immaterial objects are based on definitions and rules of inference alone, demonstrations concerning material objects require the introduction of extra-logical considerations, such as the causal relations between form and matter. Thus, the question of the ontological status of mathematical objects reflects the epistemological question: whether extra-logical considerations have to be taken into account in mathematics. When discussions of the conformity of mathematical proofs to Aristotelian demonstrations in late antiquity are viewed in isolation from ontological commitments, they seem to be conceptually related to modern discussions of the nature of mathematical knowledge. The need to take into account extra-logical considerations when mathematical objects are considered material is equivalent to Kant's statement that mathematical propositions are synthetic *a priori* judgements. Developments in modern logic led to a reformulation of Kant's statement in terms of logical forms. Kant's contention that mathematical knowledge cannot be based on definitions and rules of inference alone was regarded by Bertrand Russell as true for Kant's time. According to Russell, had Kant known other forms of logical inference than the syllogistic form, he would not have claimed that mathematical propositions cannot be deduced from definitions and rules of inference alone.[41] In light of this account, the modern discussions of the conformity of mathematical proofs to Aristotelian demonstrations, which focus on whether syllogistic inferences can accommodate relational terms, may be understood as evolving from the pre-modern discussions of whether mathematical proofs establish essential relations, and to establish this conclusion, two conceptual developments have to be traced: the process by which the question whether mathematical propositions are

---

[40] This assumption seems to underlie the Renaissance discussions of this issue as well. In the eleventh chapter of his treatise Piccolomini attempts to reinstate the status of mathematics as a science by claiming that mathematical objects are conceptual entities, existing in the human mind.

[41] Russell 1992: 4–5.

essential has become dissociated from questions concerning the ontological status of mathematical objects, and the process leading to the development of modern logic.

Bibliography

Editions

Philoponus, *In Aristotelis Categorias commentarium*, ed. A. Busse, CAG 13/1, Berlin 1898.

Philoponus, *In Aristotelis De anima commentaria*, ed. M. Hayduck, CAG 15, Berlin 1897.

Philoponus, *In Aristotelis Physicorum libros commentaria*, ed. H. Vitelli, CAG 16, Berlin 1897.

Philoponus, *In Aristotelis Analytica posteriora commentaria*, ed. M. Wallies, CAG 13/3, Berlin 1909.

Proclus, *In primum Euclidis elementorum librum commentarii*, ed. G. Friedlein, Hildesheim 1969.

Studies

De Groot, J. (1991) *Aristotle and Philoponus on Light*. New York.

De Haas, F. A. J. (1997) *John Philoponus' New Definition of Prime Matter: Aspects of Its Background in Neoplatonism and the Ancient Commentary Tradition.* Leiden.

De Rijk, L. M. (1990) 'The *Posterior Analytics* in the Latin West', in *Knowledge and the Sciences in Medieval Philosophy: Proceedings of the Eighth International Congress of Medieval Philosophy*, ed. M. Asztalos, J. E. Murdoch and I. Niiniluoto. *Acta Philosophica Fennica* **48**: 104–27.

Goldin, O. (1996) *Explaining an Eclipse: Aristotle's* Posterior Analytics *2.1–10*. Ann Arbor, MI.

Harari, O. (2004) *Knowledge and Demonstration: Aristotle's* Posterior Analytics. Dordrecht.

(2006) '*Methexis* and geometrical reasoning in Proclus' commentary on Euclid's *Elements*', *Oxford Studies in Ancient Philosophy* **30**: 361–89.

Helbing, M. O. (2000) 'La fortune des Commentaires de Proclus sur le premier livre des *Eléments* d'Euclide à l'époque de Galilée', in *La Philosophie des mathématiques de l'antiquité tardive*, ed. G. Bechtle and D. J. O'Meara. Fribourg: 177–93.

Jardine, N. (1988) 'Epistemology of the sciences', in *The Cambridge History of Renaissance Philosophy*, ed. C. Schmitt, Q. Skinner and E. Kessler. Cambridge: 685–711.

Lloyd, A. C. (1990) *The Anatomy of Neoplatonism*. Oxford.

Mancosu, P. (1992) 'Aristotelian logic and Euclidean mathematics: seventeenth century developments of the *Quaestio de certitudine mathematicarum*', *Studies in History and Philosophy of Science* 23: 241–65.

(1996) *Philosophy of Mathematics and Mathematical Practice in the Seventeenth Century*. Oxford.

McKirahan, R. (1992) *Principles and Proofs: Aristotle's Theory of Demonstrative Science*. Princeton, NJ.

Mendell, H. (1998) 'Making sense of Aristotelian demonstration', *Oxford Studies in Ancient Philosophy* 16: 169–78.

Morrison, D. (1997) 'Philoponus and Simplicius on tekmeriodic proofs', in *Method and Order in Renaissance Philosophy of Nature: The Aristotle Commentary Tradition*, ed. D. A. Di Liscia, E. Kessler and C. Methuen. Aldershot: 1–22.

Mueller, I. (1975) 'Greek mathematics and Greek logic', in *Ancient Logic and Its Modern Interpretation*, ed. J. Corcoran. Dordrecht: 35–70.

(1990) 'Aristotle's doctrine of Abstraction in the Commentators', in *Aristotle Transformed: The Ancient Commentators and Their Influence*, ed. R. Sorabji. Ithaca, NY: 463–80.

Russell, B. (1992) *Principles of Mathematics* (first edn 1903). London.

5 | Contextualizing Playfair and Colebrooke
    on proof and demonstration in the Indian
    mathematical tradition (1780–1820)

DHRUV RAINA

The social shaping of representations of so called non-Western astronomy
and mathematics in eighteenth- and nineteenth-century European scholarship has been of recent scholarly interest from the perspective of the politics
of knowledge.[1] A principal concern has been the changing estimation of
non-Western mathematical traditions by European mathematicians and
historians of mathematics between the end of the last decades of the eighteenth century and the early decades of the nineteenth century; that is from
the heyday of the Enlightenment to the post-Enlightenment period. While
these studies have been informed by Said's *Orientalism*,[2] they have sought
to examine the question whether the history of mathematics (the least likely
case) is also inscribed within the frame of European colonial adventure and
enterprise, as happened in the arts, literature and social sciences.[3]

It has been suggested that the European scholarship on the sciences of
India reveals fractures along national lines, which in turn reflected the
diversity of educational and institutional contexts of the world of learning.[4] This chapter examines the relationship between the histories of Indian
astronomy and mathematics produced by French astronomers and the
translation from the Sanskrit of works on Indian algebra undertaken by a
colonial administrator and British Indologist, Henry Thomas Colebrooke.
The contrast revealed the divergent disciplinary orientations of the interpreters themselves. Second, in elaborating upon the canonization of a very
important translation of Indian mathematical works by Colebrooke,[5] I shall
argue that the standard European depiction of the Indian mathematical

---

[1] Charette 1995; Raina 1999.
[2] Said 1978.
[3] Assayag *et al.* 1997.
[4] Raina 1999.
[5] Sir Henry Thomas Colebrooke was the son of the Chairman of the East India Company
Directors, and arrived in India as an official of the Company in 1782–3. In India he acquired
a proficiency in Sanskrit literature and commenced writing on Hindu law, the origins of
caste, etc. As a result he was appointed Professor of Hindu Law and Sanskrit at the College
of Fort William, Calcutta (Buckland 1908: 87–8). His translation of texts of Bhaskara and
Brahmagupta became classics of nineteenth-century history of Indian mathematics.

tradition as devoid of proof went contrary to the spirit of Colebrooke's translation and the large number of proofs and demonstrations therein contained. In other words, this chapter elaborates upon how the Indian tradition of mathematics came to be constructed as one that was devoid of the idea of proof. While this characterization acquired stability in the nineteenth century, the construction itself was prefigured in the eighteenth century. However, in the second half of the nineteenth century there were historians of mathematics who held that specific kinds of proof were encountered in Indian mathematical texts.

It could be suggested that the concerns possibly giving the several contributions in the present volume a thematic unity is the focus upon the empirical reality of mathematical practices, which perhaps suggests that mathematical traditions the world over, in the past as in the present, were and are characterized by several cultures of proof. Furthermore, studies on the culture(s) of proving among contemporary mathematicians, pure and applied, appear to indicate that rather than there being a unique criterion of what constitutes a proof there exist several mathematical subcultures.[6] This view pushes in the direction of a sociological view of proof, amounting to a consensus theory of proof. Clearly this runs contrary to the formal verificationist idea that proofs are pinioned on their 'intrinsic epistemic quality'.[7] This naturally raises the question as to how and when will these issues surface in the efforts of historians of mathematics. For if, as is suggested, it was not until the middle of the nineteenth century that proof became the sole criterion of validating mathematical statements,[8] then its reflection is to be found in the constructions of histories of mathematics as well.

In order to look at the more technical mathematical writing it is first necessary to briefly describe the optic through which Europeans turned their gaze on India during this period and the tropes that defined their literary production on India during these decades. The eighteenth century has been considered the formative period for the emergence of the discourse on colonialism, but this discourse was not yet 'monolithic or univocal'. European writing on India comprised a network of intersecting and contending representations.[9] The representations of India in this writing are naturally very 'diverse, shifting, historically contingent, complex and competitive'. The texts themselves are shaped often by 'national and religious rivalries, domestic concerns', and the cognitive or intellectual cultures of

[6] Heinz 2000; MacKenzie 2001; Heinz 2003.
[7] Heinz 2003: 234–5.
[8] Heinz 2003: 938.
[9] Teltscher 1995: 2.

the respective interlocutors.[10] Critical studies on oriental scholarship have sought to situate these texts in national and religious contexts and to identify the elements they share.[11] It has been argued that until the eighteenth century it was possible to speak of a European tradition of writing about India that differentiated into several national traditions by the middle of the eighteenth century. The birth of a specifically British tradition is put around 1765 when the East India Company was granted rights to collect land revenues and administer civil justice in Bengal.[12] With the founding of the Asiatic Society, British writing on India especially from the 1780s onwards was marked by the impulse of British writers to 'foreground the textual nature of their activity', in other words to anchor their writings on India in the specific study of classical texts produced in India.[13]

The French missionaries who came to India in the late seventeenth century were the first to have spoken of India's scientific past. French Indology, according to Jean Filliozat, emerged in the early decades of the eighteenth century, when the King's librarian requested Etienne Fourmont, of the Collège Royal, to draw up a list of works of note from India and Indo-China, to be purchased for the King's library. By 1739, a catalogue of Sanskrit works had been prepared, and copies of Vedas, epics, philosophical and linguistic texts and dictionaries had been procured.[14] Curiously enough there were very few, if any, scientific texts that were included in the cargo to the King's library.[15] The Jesuit astronomers were the first to study the Indian astronomical systems that Filliozat considers 'the first scientific or even cultural achievements of India studied by Europeans'.[16] Kejariwal goes so far as to suggest that the 'history of French Orientalism is also the history of the rediscovery of ancient Indian astronomy in the modern period'.[17]

A fruitful approach into this archive of scientific texts and not just literary or religious texts is to pay attention to moments where the standard cultural descriptions characterizing the early European writing on India are challenged or unsettled through the textual analysis of similar and different forms of reasoning.[18] In examining these mathematical texts, it is thereby essential for our purpose to be alert to those moments and descriptions of

---

[10] Teltscher 1995: 2; Raina 1999; Jami 1995.
[11] Inden 1990; Zupanov 1993.
[12] Teltscher 1995: 3.
[13] Teltscher 1995: 6.
[14] Filliozat 1955: 1–3.
[15] Raina 1999.
[16] Filliozat 1957.
[17] Kejariwal 1988: 17.
[18] Teltscher 1995: 14.

mathematical results and procedures encountered within Sanskrit texts that were not accompanied by demonstrations or proof or exegesis. The British mathematician and geologist John Playfair (1748–1819) in introducing the Indian astronomy broadly speaking to an English speaking audience was to write:

The astronomy of India is confined to one branch of the science. It gives no theory, nor even any description of the celestial phenomena, but satisfies itself with the calculation of certain changes in the heavens . . . The Brahmin . . . obtains his result with wonderful certainty and expedition; but having little knowledge of the principles on which his rules are founded, and no anxiety to be better informed, he is perfectly satisfied, if, as it usually happens, the commencement and duration of the eclipse answer, within a few minutes, to his prediction.[19]

There are four ideas that are evident in this passage, and that run constantly throughout the construction of Indian astronomy and mathematics. Inasmuch as Indian astronomy is a science it differs from modern astronomy in that (a) it lacks a theoretical basis, (b) it does not provide a description of celestial phenomena, and (c) it is not methodologically reflective ('little knowledge of the principles on which his rules are founded'), which in turn amounts to the idea that (d) the Indian astronomer computes but does so blindly. In other words these computations were performed blindly by the Indian astronomers. On account of the predictive accuracy of the astronomy it merited the stature of a science, and the Indian astronomers were concerned no more with it than in this instrumental context.

The origins of British Indology: different starting points, different concerns

British studies on Indian astronomy and mathematics may be said to lie at the conjuncture of two different historiographies: French and British. One of the earliest British Indologists to speak of the distinctive tradition of Indian algebra was Reuben Burrow (1747–92), a mathematician and a one-time assistant to Maskelyne, the Astronomer Royal in Greenwich. The prior French tradition of the history of science had been preoccupied with the origins of Indian astronomy. Burrow centred the question about the origins of Indian mathematics. This will become evident further ahead. That Burrow had a different optic from the French is evident in his 'Hints concerning the Observatory at Benaras':

---

[19] Playfair 1790 (1971): 51.

Notwithstanding the prejudices of the Europeans of the last century in favour of their own abilities, some of the first members of the royal society were sufficiently enlightened to consider the East Indies and China & c, as new worlds of science that remained undiscovered . . . had they not too hastily concluded that to be lost, which nothing but the prejudice of ignorance and obstinacy, had prevented being found, we might at this time [be] in possession of the most finished productions of Asia as well as Europe; the sciences might, in consequence, have been carried to a much higher degree of perfection with us than they are at present; and the elegance and superiority of the Asiatic models might have prevented the neglect and depravity of geometry, and that inundation of Algebraic barbarism which has ever since the time of Descartes, both vitiated taste, and overrun the publications, of most of the philosophical societies in Europe.[20]

The encounter with other non-European scientific traditions was encouraged by the ideological impulse to advance the frontiers of knowledge. In that sense Burrow's philosophy of science resonated with that of the Enlightenment thinkers. The most striking feature of the above passage is that the Indian tradition for Burrow is still not characterized as algebraic or geometric. In fact, at this point the characterization is the very reverse of the late nineteenth century where Indian mathematics is constituted as one that is algebraic in spirit at the expense of geometry. This nineteenth-century portraiture of Indian mathematics depicted the traditions as algebraic or algorithmic, and as one where the geometric side of mathematics was underdeveloped. Modern European mathematics since Descartes, in Burrow's words, had been overwhelmed by *algebraic barbarism*. An exposure to Asiatic models would then have prevented the neglect of geometry that marked contemporary sciences. I do not know if one could interpose the suggestion that there may have been some Anglo-French rivalry at stake. But then that is not immediately germane to the construction. The relevant concern here is that *until the end of the eighteenth century some British Indologists still entertained the hope that they would discover Indian geometrical texts that would unveil to them the foundations of an Indian geometrical tradition.* Thus Playfair would in 1792 pose six questions to the researchers of the Asiatic Society, the first of which was: 'Are any books to be found among the Hindus, which treat professedly of Geometry?'[21] Playfair was thus asking if it were possible to identify elements of a corpus of knowledge albeit in a different disguise that could be considered geometry in the sense in which it was conceived in Europe. For one it could be

[20] Burrow 1783 (1971): 94–5.
[21] Playfair 1792: 151.

said that the question that the geometry of the Hindus could have a different basis from the Greek ones is implied by the 'professedly' in the question. That this is what Playfair meant might be inferred from his elaboration upon the question he posed:

I am led to propose this question, by having observed, not only that the whole of the Indian Astronomy is a system constructed with great geometrical skill, but that the trigonometrical rules given in the translation from the *Surya Siddhanta*, with which Mr. Davis[22] has obliged the world, point out some very curious theorems, which must have been known to the author of that ancient book.[23]

According to Playfair, as he engages with Davis' translation of the *Surya Siddhanta* the 'trigonometrical canon' of Indian astronomy is constructed on the basis of a theorem. The theorem is stated as:

If there be three arches[24] of a circle in arithmetical progression, the sum of the sines of the two extremes arches is to twice the sine of the middle arch as the cosine of common difference of the arches to the radius of the circle.[25]

Though the theorem was not known to Europe before Viete, Playfair continues, the method was employed by the Indian astronomers for constructing trigonometrical tables, and was based on the simpler procedure of calculating sines and arcs than through the use of methods that were based on extracting square roots.[26] The immediate task for Playfair appears to have been to identify those mathematical works where the theorem on which the trigonometrical rule employed in astronomy is first laid out. This brings us back to Burrow's concern with the origins of Indian mathematics.

Contrasting approaches: sifting the mathematical from the astronomical rexts

In the late eighteenth century it would have been possible to differentiate between the efforts of the British Indologists and those of their French counterparts studying Indian astronomy and mathematics on two counts. Methodologically speaking, while the British Indologists were busy

---

[22] Samuel Davis (1760–1819) was a judge in Bengal and produced one of the first translations of the *Surya Siddhanta*.
[23] Playfair 1792: 151.
[24] An 'arc of a circle' is what is meant here. I have kept the original spelling.
[25] Playfair 1792: 152.
[26] Playfair 1792: 152.

underlining the textual nature of their enterprise, the French astronomer-savants relied a great deal on proto-ethnographic descriptions of the mathematical and astronomical practices of India. Secondly, the histories of Indian astronomy of Bailly and Le Gentil are preoccupied with the astronomy of India and the origins of Indian astronomy.[27] Even Montucla's history of mathematics relies extensively upon the proto-ethnographic sources employed by Le Gentil and Bailly and draws inferences concerning Indian mathematics from them.[28] The British Indological tradition, on the other hand, engaged with specific texts and from the astronomical rules presented there made a claim that these rules must be based on a mathematical system, and proceeded to discover mathematical texts. Their focus thus shifts from the origins of astronomy to the origins of Indian mathematics, in particular Indian algebra and arithmetic. What were the rules encountered and what were the claims made? The shift was precipitated by the desire to craft a history of mathematics independently of the history of astronomy. As scholars approached the corpus of Indian astronomical texts, they encountered a corpus of knowledge recognizable to them as algebra and arithmetic. Consequently, John Playfair was later to insist upon the need to search for a geometrical tradition.

Reuben Burrow was probably amongst the earliest of the British Indologists to engage with the textual tradition of Indian mathematics, although this search was prompted through his exposure to and study of astronomy, including Indian astronomy. This does not mean that these texts did not relate in any way to the histories of Le Gentil and Bailly. Actually, the texts of the former provided an initial frame for approaching the differences between the Indian and Modern traditions. For Burrow the study of the procedures employed by Indian astronomers in calculating eclipses would advance the progress of modern astronomy as well: 'and the more so as our methods of calculation are excessively tedious and intricate'.[29] The sentiment echoes that of Le Gentil and Bailly; and it is certain that he was acquainted with the work of Le Gentil,[30] though it is not possible to say the same of Bailly's *Traité de l'astronomie indienne et orientale*. This fascination with the computational procedures employed in astronomy led Burrow to infer in 1783 the existence of an advanced algebraic tradition:

---

[27] Bailly 1775; Le Gentil 1781.
[28] Montucla 1799.
[29] Burrow 1783 (1971): 101.
[30] Burrow 1783 (1971): 116.

It is also generally reported that the Brahmins calculate their eclipses, not by astro-nomical tables as we do, but by rules . . . If they (the rules) be as exact as ours, . . . it is a proof that they must have carried algebraic computation to a very extraordinary pitch, and have well understood the doctrine of 'continued fractions', in order to have found those periodical approximations . . .[31]

The rules for computing eclipses employed by the Brahmins were not only different, but their complexity varied with the requisite degree of exactness:

. . . which entirely agrees with the approximation deduced from algebraic formulae and implies an intimate acquaintance with the Newtonian doctrine of series . . . and therefore it is not impossible for the Brahmins to have understood Algebra better than we do.[32]

This was to become the central point from which in subsequent papers Burrow would build his argument for the existence of an advanced algebra among the Indians. The problem was taken up again by Colebrooke dis-cussed below, and in a paper published slightly later by Edward Strachey, 'On the early history of algebra'.[33] The paper emphasized the originality and importance of algebra among the Hindus and contained extracts that were translated from the *Bija-Ganita* and *Lilavati*.[34] These extracts were translations into English from Persian translations of the original Sanskrit texts.[35] But Burrow admits that these extracts were translated in 1784, but he deferred publishing them till a full text was obtained.[36] But he prizes the moment: 'when no European but myself . . . even suspected that the Hindoos had any algebra'.[37] The rationale provided for the existence of treatises on algebra in India in Burrow's 1790 paper on the knowledge of the binomial theorem among the Indians is the same as that suggested in the earlier one (1783). Many of the approximations used in astronomy were 'deduced from infinite series; or at least have the appearance of it'.[38] These included finding the sine from the arc and determining the angles of a

---

[31] Burrow 1783 (1971): 101.

[32] Burrow 1783 (1971): 101.

[33] Strachey 1818.

[34] These works were authored by the twelfth-century mathematician Bhaskara II, and while the first of these deals with problems in algebra and the solution of equations, the latter focuses more on arithmetic.

[35] Strachey's paper will not be discussed here, since the focus will be on the translation of versions of Sanskrit texts into English and not the manner in which these Sanskrit texts were reported in translations of Persian and Arab mathematical works.

[36] Burrow 1790.

[37] Burrow 1790: 115.

[38] *Ibid.*

right-angled triangle given the hypotenuse and sides without recourse to a table of sines, etc.

The urgency of the moment was then to discover those texts before they perished. Burrow thus emphasized the need for the collection of available astronomical and mathematical texts that till then had not been the focus of attention of the French Académiciens. The idea that the existing tradition was probably algebraic was being insinuated: 'That many of their books are depraved and lost is evident, because there is now not a single book of geometrical elements to be met and yet that they had elements not long ago, and apparently more extensive than those of Euclid is obvious from some of their works of no great antiquity.'[39] At this liminal moment it appears as if the issue whether the geometric tradition prevailed over the algebraic or vice versa in India had not been settled. It cannot be decisively be said that Burrow had a fixed view on the subject. But certainly the texts he encountered were not of a 'geometric' nature. But the trigonometrical calculations gave cause for belief that the semblance of such a system was in existence. And while Burrow promised to publish translations of *Lilavati* and the *Bija-Ganita*, the promise was not fulfilled during his life. Inspired by Burrow's research, Colebrooke embarked on a study of Sanskrit in order to probe some of the issues raised by Burrow more deeply.

It was left to Samuel Davis to publish the first translation and analysis of an Indian scientific work from the Sanskrit into a European language, this being a translation of the *Surya Siddhanta*.[40] This translation was based on the reading of an original version of the text procured by Sir Robert Chambers in 1788. Davis encountered a number of obscure technical terms and had to rely upon a *teeka* or commentary procured by Jonathan Duncan.[41] In fact, if you examine the structure of Davis' paper, it appears as a *teeka* on the *Surya Siddhanta*, with passages translated from the text and Davis' explanation intercalated between the translated passages.

Davis begins by contesting the portrait of Indian astronomy and astronomers projected by Le Gentil and Bailly,[42] without naming either of them.

---

[39] *Ibid.*

[40] Davis 1789.

[41] *Ibid.*

[42] More than Bailly and Le Gentil, Davis was refuting Sonnerat's constructions of Indian astronomy:

> ... my present intention, which is to give a general account only of the method by which the Hindus compute eclipses, and thereby to show, that a late French author was too hasty in asserting generally that they determine by set forms couched in enigmatical verses &c. So far are they from deserving the reproach of ignorance, which Mons. Sonnerat has implied,

The first idea that he rejected was that this astronomical tradition was disfigured over the years by idolatry and that the gems of Indian astronomy had been irretrievably lost over the centuries, in the absence of a textual tradition. The second idea was that the Brahmins had shrouded their astronomy in mystery such that it was impossible to arrive at a cogent account of it. Further, they loathed sharing their ideas with others. Davis set out to show that:

> . . . numerous treatises in Sanskrit on astronomy are procurable, and that the Brahmins are willing to explain them . . . I can farther venture to declare, from the experience I have had, that Sanskrit books in this science are more easily translated than almost any others, when once the technical terms are understood: the subject of them *admitting neither of metaphysical reasoning nor of metaphor*, but being delivered in plain terms *and generally illustrated with examples in practice*, . . .[43]

The British Indologists were departing from the reading of Académiciens grounded in Jesuit proto-ethnography, by textually locating their work. This textual grounding would revise the portrait of the French savants. A hundred years later in a review of the history of the history of Indian astronomy Burgess was to write: 'Mr. Davis' paper, however, was the first analysis of an original Hindu astronomical treatise, and was a model of what such an essay ought to be.'[44] It appears then, as has been argued elsewhere, that the French savants in India were unable to establish trust with their Indian interlocutors, in total contrast to the first generation of British Indologists such as William Jones,[45] and if one takes Davis' account literally then Davis himself. Two papers of William Jones followed closely on the heels of Davis' papers and a cursory glance at them reveals that they mutually respected and supported each other's enterprise.[46] And yet they both were in agreement with Bailly's thesis of the independent origins of the Indian zodiac, differing very strongly with Montucla on this count:

> that on inquiry, I believe the Hindu science of astronomy will be found as well known now as it ever was among them, although perhaps, not so generally, by reason of the little encouragement men of science at present meet with . . . (Davis 1789: 177).

Evidently, Sonnerat unlike Davis could not enter the world of the Hindu astronomers on account of his inability to abandon a hermeneutic of suspicion. Pierre Sonnerat was a French naval official who travelled to India towards the last decades of the eighteenth century and published a book *Voyages aux Indes Orientales et à la Chine* in 1782 which discussed the history, religion, languages, manners, arts and science of the regions he visited.

[43] Davis 1790: 175 (emphasis added).
[44] Burgess 1893: 730–1.
[45] Raj 2001.
[46] An eighteenth-century Indian scholar who worked closely both with Jones and along with his associates with Colebrooke was Radhakanta Tarkavagisa (Rocher 1989).

I engage to support an opinion (which the learned and industrious M Montucla seems to treat with extreme contempt) that the Indian division of the zodiac was not borrowed from the Greeks or Arabs, but having been known in this country from time immemorial and being the same in part with other nations of the old Hindu race . . .[47]

But then they were also gradually transforming and refining the portrait Bailly had left behind. Thus Jones recognized that in Davis' translation resided the hope that it would 'convince M. Bailly that it is very possible for an European to translate and explain the *Surya Siddhanta*.'[48]

Playfair's programme and Colebrooke's recovery of Indian algebraic texts

In order to recapitulate a point made earlier, the French Jesuits of the seventeenth and eighteenth centuries were the inaugurators of a tradition, which was to inspire the histories of Le Gentil and Jean-Sylvain Bailly.[49] Bailly's history inspired the work of the British mathematician John Playfair and provided a stimulus to subsequent generations of British Indologists writing on Indian mathematics; though they were to disagree with the details of Bailly's *Histoire*, adding some nuance here and digressing from it in another context.[50] The antediluvian hypothesis proposed by Bailly was the source of both fascination and controversy, and was the outcome of his attempt to juxtapose observations of ancient Indian astronomy with astronomical theory of his day;[51] from which he went on to draw the inference that ancient Indian astronomy was the source of Greek astronomy.[52] However, this reading was located within Jesuit historiography which sought to accommodate Indian history within the Christian conception of time.[53]

Bailly's work was introduced to English-speaking readers through an article authored by John Playfair entitled 'Remarks on the Astronomy of the Brahmins' published in the *Transactions of the Royal Society of Edinburgh*.[54]

---

[47] Jones 1790a.

[48] Jones 1790b.

[49] Raina 1999.

[50] Raina 2001a.

[51] According to this hypothesis astronomy originated among the Indians, but the Indians in turn had received it from an even more ancient people. The traces of this exchange had been lost in antiquity.

[52] Bailly 1775.

[53] Raina 2003.

[54] Playfair 1790.

The article draws extensively, need I say almost exclusively, upon the *Mémoirs* of Le Gentil published by the Académie des Sciences, Paris and Bailly's *Astronomie Indienne*.[55] This article of Playfair's was of prime importance for Indologists working on the history of Indian astronomy for the next four decades.

Playfair's central contribution resided in re-appropriating Bailly's *Traité* in the light of the contributions of Davis and Burrow and proposing a set of tasks that could well be considered a research programme for the Asiatic Society. These included: (a) to search for and publish works on Hindu geometry, (b) to procure any books on arithmetic and to ascertain those arithmetical concerns whose trace is not to be found among the Greeks, (c) to complete the translation of the *Surya Siddhanta* as initiated by Samuel Davis, (d) to compile a *catalogue raisonné*, with a scholarly account of books on Indian astronomy, (e) to examine the heavens with a Hindu astronomer in order to determine their stars and constellations, (f) to obtain descriptions and drawings of astronomical buildings and instruments found in India.[56]

If Bailly had stirred a hornet's nest in his time by suggesting that the origins of astronomy were in India, albeit that this astronomy was inherited by the Indians from an even more ancient people, Burrow's paper did the same with the origins of algebra. It is at this time difficult to separate the discussion on the history of astronomy from the history of algebra; for both the Académiciens and the Indologists often turn to the history of astronomy to evoke computational procedures that were analysed mathematically. This programme of the recovery of the mathematical literature from the astronomical literature was taken up by Colebrooke, who may be seen as providing translations from the Sanskrit into English of the first texts supposedly dedicated solely to algebra and arithmetic. I say supposedly because portions of some of the texts Colebrooke discovered for the English-speaking world were essentially the mathematical sections of larger astronomical canons of the Indian tradition.

We come now to Colebrooke's translation practices. In order to describe them we need to understand how Colebrooke identified an authenticated version of the texts that he set out to translate. It needs to be pointed out that at the very outset no final version of the three texts, from which only portions were translated, was readily available to him. Consequently, he worked with his Brahmin interlocutors and collected and collated

---

[55] Le Gentil 1789; Bailly 1787.
[56] Playfair 1792: 152–5.

fragments of the works of Bhaskara and Brahmagupta before proceeding to finalize versions of the three texts translated. But the enormous task was to finalize and authenticate a version as the version of these texts. The central question then was: how were the fragments of the texts to be ordered into a sequence or other fragments spliced into appropriate sections of the sequence of fragments in order to complete the collation of the text. His native interlocutors were thus assigned the task of providing him with an exhaustive commentary(ies) on these texts and most certainly worked with him through the process of translation. The larger the set of commentaries available on a given text, say the *Lilavati*, the greater the importance of the text within the canon. The commentaries themselves served two exceedingly important functions. In the first instance the commentaries were employed to identify the missing portions of the fragments available, and to fix the sequence of chapters. In other words it is through the commentaries that the text was finalized. Second, the commentaries were employed to illustrate and explain semantically and technically obscure portions and procedures expounded in the main text.

A typical page of Colebrooke's translation thus comprises an upper half or two-thirds that are translations from the Sanskrit of finalized versions of the texts of Bhaskara and Brahmagupta, while the lower half or third comprises: (1) Colebrooke's explication of the text when need be, with references to other texts, which is done with footnotes, (2) translations from one or several commentaries that clarify the meaning of a term or terms or procedures mentioned in the portion of the text on the upper portion of the page, but at no point in Colebrooke's text is the entire commentary translated. In fact the text comprises translations from portions of several commentaries, and it is Colebrooke who decided which part of one of several commentaries or portions of several commentaries best elaborates or clarifies a portion of the master text being translated. But the commentaries are internally paired off against each other in order to arrange chronologically the commentaries and thus provide a diachronic relation between them.

Colebrooke drew upon a rich commentarial tradition while working on his translation of the *Lilavati*. The first of these was a commentary by Gangādhara dated AD 1420. The commentary was limited to the *Lilavati*, but as Colebrooke informs us, it authenticated an important chapter from the *Bija-Ganita*.[57] Further, Suryadasa's *Ganitámrita* dated AD 1538 was a commentary on the *Lilavati* and the *Surya-pracāsa* was a commentary

---

[57] C1817: xxv.

on the *Bija-Ganita* that contained a clear interpretation of the text with a concise explication of the arithmetical rules.[58] The other important composition was Ganesa's *Buddhivilasini* (*c.* AD 1545), comprising a copious exposition of the text with demonstration of the rules. However, Ganesa had not written a commentary on the *Bija-Ganita* and Colebrooke drew on the work of Krishna which explained the rules with a number of demonstrations. In addition to which two other commentaries were used, namely that of Ramakrishna Deva entitled *Manoranjana*, a text of uncertain date, and finally the *Ganitakaumud*, which was known through the works of Suryadasa and Ranganatha.[59]

A brief recapitulation is required before we proceed to the translations of Colebrooke, for his work certainly marks a departure in the study of the history of Indian mathematics. Two main historiographic currents in the eighteenth century oriented the study of the history of the mathematics and astronomy of India. The first approach was that pursued by the Jesuit savants in India, who were observing the astronomical and computational procedures circulating among Indian astronomers. Their audience did not merely comprise the devout back in France, but the Académiciens and astronomers, two of whom transcribed these proto-ethnographic accounts into a history of Indian astronomy. Administrator–scholars, who studied texts, collated fragments of texts and published translations with critical editions and commentaries, while indebted to the first, pursued another approach. In the late eighteenth century, Sanskrit commentaries and canonized astronomical or mathematical works were considered the key to obscure technical terms and texts. What needs to be examined is whether by the late nineteenth century commentaries shared the same destiny as some of the Vedic texts. For it has been pointed out that by the second half of the nineteenth century some Sanskritists belittled, marginalized and removed 'explicit references to the intermediary process of transmission and exegesis of texts without which they would not have had access to them'.[60] The status of proofs in the Indian tradition is related to how these commentaries on mathematical texts were read.

---

[58] C1817: xxvi. The term explication involves two different tasks when applied to literary texts and scientific texts. In the case of literary texts explication means to unfold; or to offer a detailed explanation of a story. In the case of a scientific text or procedure, explication involves the transformation of the explicandum by the explicatum. However, explication in Colebrooke does not possibly conform to the notion that the explicandum is pre-scientific and inexact, while the explicatum is exact. The explicandum and explicatum are related to each other in their difference and not in a hierarchy of exact/inexact.

[59] C1817: xxvii–xxviii.

[60] Vidal 1997: 25.

The point needs some reaffirmation since both Colebrooke and Davis, who worked with commentaries of canonized astronomical and mathematical texts respectively, do mention the existence of demonstrations, and rules in the texts they discuss. In Colebrooke's introduction to his *Algebra with Arithmetic and Mensuration, from the Sanscrit of Brahmegupta and Bhascara*, there are four terms of concern to us here, namely demonstration, rule, proof and analysis, that come up often, but it is only the last of these that Colebrooke clarifies. Further, as will be noticed in the next section the terms demonstration and proof are used interchangeably by Colebrooke. Noted by its absence in the title is the term 'geometry', as a systematized science; on the contrary, the translation does allude to mensuration as discussed in the books he translates. The crucial problematic for Colebrooke was, as with Burrow before him, to determine the origins of Indian algebra. Inspired, as it were, by the textual exemplars of Davis and Burrow, and guided by the research programme John Playfair had drawn up for the researchers of the Asiatic Society, Colebrooke highlighted the pathway to his own work:

In the history of mathematical science, it has long been a question to whom the invention of algebraic analysis is due, among what people, in what region was it devised, by whom was it cultivated and promoted, or by whose labours was it reduced *to form and system.*[61]

The subsequent narrative focuses upon establishing that 'the imperfect algebra of the Greeks', that had through the efforts of Diophantus advanced no further than solving equations with one unknown, was transmitted to India. The Indian algebraists, through their ingenuity, advanced this 'slender idea' to the state of a 'well arranged science'.[62] In his reading, Colebrooke shares a fundamental historiographic principle, disputed by current scholarship, with Burrow, one that enjoyed currency among historians of mathematics into the twentieth century. In this historiographic frame: '. . . the Arabs themselves scarcely pretend to the discovery of Algebra. *They were not in general inventors but scholars*, during the short period of their successful culture of the sciences.'[63]

The science of 'algebraic analysis', a term Colebrooke would later expand upon, existed in India before the Arabs transmitted it to modern Europe.[64] The evidence for these claims resided in the translations of

---

[61] C1817: ii (emphasis added).
[62] C1817: xxiv.
[63] C1817: ii (emphasis added).
[64] *Ibid.*

the *Bija-Ganita* and *Lilavati* of Bhaskara,[65] as well as Brahmagupta's (Colebrooke: 'Brahmegupta') *Ganitadhyaya* and *Kuttakadhyaya* (the chapter entitled 'The pulveriser') (Colebrooke: *Cuttacadhyaya*), the last two as their name suggests being the mathematical sections of Brahmagupta's *Brahmasphutasiddhanta*. Without focusing too much on the antiquity of these texts, Colebrooke saw his oeuvre as disclosing that the:

modes of analysis, and in particular, *general methods for the solution of indeterminate problems* both of the first and second degrees, are taught in the Vija-Ganita, and those for the first degree repeated in the Lilavati, which were unknown to the mathematicians of the west until invented anew in the last two centuries by algebraists of France and England.[66]

The terrain of historical studies on Indian mathematics was being transformed into a polemical one, with Colebrooke surreptitiously introducing categories that the French Indologists had denied the Indian tradition: typically for the first time he speaks of 'modes of analysis', or the 'general methods for the solution of indeterminate problems'. The historians of astronomy had previously advanced the idea that the Indians had no idea of the generalizability of the methods they employed. In the absence of such generalizability, how could it have been possible to extend the idea of generalized methods dedicated to solving classes of problems in order to extract the different 'modes of analysis'? The intention here is not to paint Colebrooke's construction as the diametrical opposite of that of the French historians of science that provided a context to his effort. On the contrary, Colebrooke's project is naturally marked by a deep ambivalence. The ambivalence arises from the fact that he attempted to draw the characterization of Indian mathematics away from the binary typologies of the history of science that were already set in place. According to these typologies Indian mathematics was characterized as algebraic and pragmatic while European mathematics was geometric and theoretical (deductive). Since the British Indologists were not mathematicians by profession they lacked mathematical legitimacy amongst the network of historians of mathematics and deterred his ability to create a new vocabulary. This also explains why Playfair was so important to the Indological enterprise. He was a mathematician of repute who endowed the Indological accounts with authority.

---

[65] I have given here the contemporary English spellings of the names of Sanskrit books and scholars and removed the diacritics. Colebrooke himself spelled the *Bija-Ganita* as *Vija-Ganita* and *Bhaskaracharya* as *Bhascara Acharya*.

[66] C1817: iv (emphasis added).

Colebrooke begins by pointing out that Aryabhata was the first of the Indian authors known to have treated of algebra. As he was possibly a contemporary of Diophantus, the issue was important for drawing an arrow of transmission from Alexandria to India or vice versa. Colebrooke leaves the issue of the invention of algebra open by suggesting that it was Aryabhata who developed it to the high level that it attained in India;[67] this science he called an 'analysis'.[68] It is here for the first time that a portion of the Indian mathematical tradition is referred to as analysis, and it is important to get to the sense in which he employs the term.

It is noticed that the use of a notation and algorithms is crucial to this algebraic practice; which Colebrooke then proceeds to elaborate upon, subsequently stating the procedures not merely for denoting positive or negative quantities, or the unknowns but of manipulating the symbols employed.[69] An important feature of this algebra is that all the terms of an equation do not have to be set up as positive quantities, there being no rule requiring that all the negative quantities be restored to the positive state. The procedure is to operate an equal subtraction (*samasodhana*) 'for the difference of like terms'. This operation is compared with the *muqabalah* employed by the Arab algebraists.[70] The presence of this 'analytic art' among the Indians was apparent from the mathematical procedures evident in the variety of mathematical texts that were becoming available to the Indologists.

The analytic art comprised procedures that included, according to Colebrooke, the arithmetic of surd roots, the cognizance that when a finite quantity was divided by zero the quotient was infinite, an acquaintance with the procedure for solving second degree equations and 'touching upon' higher orders, solving some of these equations by reducing them to the quadratic form, of possessing a general solution of indeterminate equations in the first degree. And finally, Colebrooke finds in the *Brahmasphutasiddhanta* (§18:29–49) and *Bija-Ganita* (§75–99) a method for obtaining a 'multitude' of integral solutions to indeterminate second-degree equations starting from a single solution that is plugged in. It was left to Lagrange to show that problems of this class would have solutions that are whole numbers.[71] The analytic art of the Indians or algebraic

---

[67] The high level of attainment was ascribed to the ability of the Indian algebraists to solve equations involving several unknowns; and of possessing a general method of solving indeterminate equations of the first degree (C1817: x).

[68] C1817: ix.

[69] C1817: x–xi.

[70] C1817: xiv.

[71] C1817: xiv–xv.

analysis is then for Colebrooke: '*calculation attended with the manifestation of its principles*'. This is manifest in the Indian mathematical texts being discussed since they intimate to the reader a '*method aided by devices*, among which symbols and literal signs are conspicuous'.[72] In this sense Indian algebra bears an affinity with D'Alembert's conception of analysis as the 'method of resolving mathematical problems by reducing them to equations'.[73] Delambre and Biot would subject these views of Colebrooke to trenchant criticism, but that is another subject.[74] The issue at stake here is that Colebrooke had insinuated the idea that Indian mathematics was not lacking in methodological reflection or generality, a feature that had hitherto been denied.

Did Colebrooke's view of algebraic analysis provide for demonstrations or proofs of its rules or procedures? Citing specific sutras from the *Brahmasphutasiddhanta*, the *Bija-Ganita* and the *Lilavati*, Colebrooke moves to a characterization of Indian algebra, just as Diophantus is evoked to characterize early Greek algebra. Thus, we are informed that these Indian algebraists applied algebraic methods both in astronomy and geometry, and in turn, geometric methods were applied to '*the demonstration of algebraic rules*'. Obviously, Colebrooke was construing the visual demonstrative procedures employed by Bhaskara to which we come as exemplifying geometrical demonstration. Further, he goes on to state that:

In short, they cultivated Algebra much more, and with greater success than geometry; as is evident in the comparatively low state of their knowledge in the one, and the high pitch of their attainments in the other.[75]

This passage came to be quoted ever so often in subsequent histories of science, and in the writings of mathematicians as evidence of the algebraic nature of Indian mathematics.[76] The power of its imagery resides in its ability to draw the boundary between different civilizational styles of mathematics. In this contrast between Western and Indian mathematics it could be suggested that Colebrooke's qualification concerning the 'comparatively

---

[72] C1817: xix–xx.

[73] *Ibid.*

[74] Raina 1999.

[75] C1817: xv.

[76] The nineteenth-century British mathematician Augustus De Morgan, a self-proclaimed aficionado of Indian mathematics, wrote a preface to the book of an Indian mathematician punctuated with aperçus from Colebrooke's introduction. The introduction in fact provides him the ground to legitimate the work of the Indian mathematician for a British readership (Raina and Habib 1990).

low' state of one and 'high pitch' of the other was lost sight of and the contrast between the two traditions came to be subsequently accentuated.

This leads me to conjecture that Colebrooke's translation is a watershed in the occidental understanding of the history of Indian mathematics on a second count as well, this being that it inadvertently certified the boundary line drawn between Indian algebra and Greek geometry. This was not Colebrooke's intention at all, but a consequence of the comparative method he had adopted. Colebrooke's particular comparative method consisted in displaying where India's specific contributions to mathematics resided, and he always contrasted these contributions with the Greek and Arab traditions of mathematics.[77] This attempt to accentuate the contrast certainly revealed the differences, but with the loss of the context of the contrast, it was first transformed into a caricature and then stabilized as a characterization. The boundary lines had however been marked out before Colebrooke's time. This passage is crucial because it is followed by a discussion of some procedures of demonstration in Indian algebra that I shall briefly lay out.

Thus the specific areas in which 'Hindu Algebra appears particularly distinguished from the Greek' are four.[78] Some of these have been mentioned above. The additional one that has not been mentioned concerns the application of algebra to 'astronomical investigation and geometrical demonstration', in other words algebra is applied to the resolution of geometrical questions. In the process the Indian algebraists, Colebrooke suggests, developed portions of mathematics that were reinvented recently. This last statement of his prompted a very severe reaction. He then takes up three instances, which he considers 'anticipations of modern discoveries' from the texts he discusses and lays out their procedures of demonstration. There is nothing in the subsequent portion of the introduction to suggest that he did not consider these as demonstrations.

Proofs and demonstrations in Colebrooke's translations of Indian algebraic work

Colebrooke's *Algebra with Arithmetic and Mensuration* was completed shortly after his departure from India for England in 1814. The volume comprises the translation of four Sanskrit mathematical texts, namely the *Bija-Ganita* and *Lilavati* of Bhaskara, and the *Ganitadhyaya* and *Kuttakadhyaya* of Brahmagupta. These translations were undertaken during

[77] Going by his text alone, he appears to have been totally oblivious of Chinese mathematics.
[78] C1817: xvi.

his homeward voyage – we are informed of this through the biography of Colebrooke written by his son.[79] Further, Colebrooke's interest, as pointed out earlier, in the subject was aroused by Reuben Burrow's paper that appeared in the second volume of the *Asiatic Researches*. Colebrooke's son, Sir T. E. Colebrooke, writes:

It must be admitted that the utmost learning which may be employed on this abstruse subject leaves the question open to some doubt, and resembles in this respect, one of those indeterminate problems which admit a variety of solutions. The treatises which have come down to us are variants of arithmetical and algebraical science, of whose antiquity few would venture to suggest a doubt. They exhibit the science in a state of advance which European nations did not attain till a comparatively recent epoch. *But they contain mere rules for practice, and not a work on the path by which they are arrived at.* There is nothing of the rigour . . .[80]

This biography of Colebrooke was published more than half a century after Colebrooke's work had appeared, by which time the standard representation of Indian mathematics was more or less in place as evident from the emphasis in the quotation.[81] However, as I shall argue below, this understanding was quite at variance with the spirit and content of Colebrooke's translation, which, not without ambivalence, made a strong case for the idea of analysis and demonstration in the Indian mathematical tradition. A point to be noted here is that when Colebrooke the son comments on the Indian mathematical tradition in the 1870s the historiographical context has totally changed and he writes about Indian mathematics and the absence of proof in a spirit quite at variance with his father who wrote in the early decades of the nineteenth century. The change in the historiographical context is evident in Haran Chandra Banerji's publication of the first edition of Colebrooke's translation of the *Lilavati* in 1892 and in the second edition that appeared in 1927.[82]

---

[79] Colebrooke, T. E. 1873: 303.

[80] Colebrooke, T. E. 1873: 309.

[81] Colebrooke's son also raises the question of the reception of Colebrooke's *Algebra with Arithmetic and Mensuration* by Delambre. In his work on the history of astronomy of the middle ages Delambre based his remarks on Colebrooke based on a review of the work by Playfair (Colebrooke, T. E. 1873: 310). Delambre's critique of Colebrooke's work has been discussed in Raina 2001b. Re J. S. Mill who wrote the manual of imperial history of India, Colebrooke the son notes, '. . . in his laboured pleading against the claims of the Hindus to be regarded as a civilized race, devotes some space to an examination of Mr. Colebrooke's work, and then does little more than repeat the doubts of Delambre whose criticisms on the weakness of the external proof he repeats almost verbatim' (Colebrooke, T. E. 1873: 311). Evidently Colebrooke the son wishes to disabuse his readers of the prejudiced criticism of Colebrooke the father's work.

[82] Banerji 1927.

The really interesting feature is the convergence in the reading of Colebrooke the son and Banerji concerning the mathematical style of Bhaskara. In the introduction to this translation Banerji was to write about Bhaskara: 'The author does not state the reasons for the various rules given by him. I have tried to supply the reasons as simply and shortly as they occurred to me; but still some cases . . . and shorter demonstrations may possibly be given.'[83] Banerji proceeded to edit Colebrooke's translation of these mathematical works by keeping those demonstrations given chiefly by Ganesa and Suryadasa 'which are satisfactory and instructive' and omitting those which 'are obscure and unsatisfactory'.[84] In other words Banerji exercises his editorial prerogative and omits some proofs or demonstrations, insisting that the omitted geometrical proofs for these formulas were given in Euclid II.5 and 9. The reason he offers for omitting the 'proofs' of Ganesa is because Banerji clarified that he had introduced these proofs to facilitate calculations required in §134 of the *Lilavati*.[85] Whatever may be the reason, it is obvious that Banerji's reading of these texts is located within the 'historiography of the absence of proof'.[86]

Colebrooke's magnum opus was published in 1817 and the introduction to the work is hereafter referred to as the 'dissertation', which is what it is titled in any case. Very briefly, I shall just mention the chapterization of this work. The first chapter consists of the definitions of technical terms. Drawing upon these definitions the second chapter deals with numeration and the eight operations of arithmetic, which included rules of addition and subtraction, multiplication, division, obtaining the square of a quantity and its square root, the cube and the cube root. The discussion up to Chapter 6 comprises the statement and exemplification of arithmetical rules for manipulating integers, and fractions. The examples provided illustrate the different operations. It is in Chapter 6 that we come to the plane figures and it is here that §134 states the equivalent of the Pythagorean Theorem.[87]

The discussion below will centre around rule §135 of the *Lilavati* in Colebrooke's translation, where Colebrooke suggests that Ganesa had

---

[83] Banerji 1927: vi.

[84] Banerji 1927: xv.

[85] Banerji 1927: xvi.

[86] An equally insightful exercise would be to see how and where Banerji's text differs from that of Colebrooke; on which portions of the text does Banerji find it necessary to comment upon Colebrooke's translation and interpretation; and at what points does he insert his own commentary and replace that of Colebrooke. This would be a separate project, sufficient though it be to point out that Banerji is more of a practising mathematician than Colebrooke.

[87] C1817: 59.

offered both algebraic and geometrical proofs. In a contemporary idiom these rules are stated as:

$$2ab + (a-b)^2 = a^2 + b^2 \qquad\qquad \text{I}$$
$$(a+b)(a-b) = a^2 - b^2 \qquad\qquad \text{II}$$

§134 of the *Lilavati* is translated from Sanskrit as:

The square root of the sum of the squares of those legs is the diagonal. The square root, extracted from the difference of the squares of the diagonal and side is the upright; and that extracted from the difference of the squares of the diagonal and upright, is the side.[88]

§135 that follows is translated as:

Twice the product of two quantities, added to the square of their difference, will be the sum of their squares. The product of their sum and difference will be the difference of their squares: as must be everywhere understood by the intelligent calculator.[89]

And this theorem came in for much discussion from the 1790s when Playfair first wrote about it in his discussion of Davis' translation of the *Surya-Siddhanta*.

Now §135 is marked with two footnotes: the one indicates that §135 is a stanza of six verses in the anustubh metre and the next importantly indicates that Ganesa the commentator on Bhaskara's *Lilavati* provides both an 'algebraic and geometrical proof' of the latter rule, the one marked as II above (my labelling), and an algebraic demonstration of the first marked as I above (my labelling). Colebrooke is not just translating from Bhaskara II's *Lilavati*: in the footnotes he intercalates a translation of Ganesa's commentary. The latter demonstration is taken from the *Bija-Ganita* §148; and it is in §147 that the first of the rules is given and demonstrated.[90] Colebrooke renders the term *Cshetragatopapatti* as geometrical demonstration and *Upapatti avyucta-criyaya* as proof by algebra.[91] We come to one of the geometrical demonstrations of rule labelled II as given in the *Bija-Ganita* §148 and §149 of Bhaskara to which Colebrooke refers as such.

§148: Example: Tell me friend, the side, upright and hypotenuse in a [triangular] plane figure, in which the square-root of three less than the side, being lessened by one, is the difference between the upright and the hypotenuse.[92]

---

[88] *Ibid.*
[89] *Ibid.*
[90] C1817: 222–3.
[91] C1817: 59.
[92] C1817: 223.

In modern language this could be translated as $\sqrt{a\text{-}3} - 1 = c - b$, where Bhaskara immediately suggests taking $c-b$ as 2. In this demonstration the difference between one of the sides (upright) and the hypotenuse is assumed as 2.

(a) The square of that added to one to which 3 is added: $(2+1)^2 + 3 = 12$ – this is the side.
(b) $12^2 = 144$ – this is the difference between the squares of the hypotenuse and side (upright).
By the rule the difference of the squares is equal to the product of the sum and difference
Which means $a^2 - b^2 = (a+b)(a-b)$.

It is in this context that here Bhaskara includes a proof of the rule, to which Colebrooke refers. This proof as is evident is based on a form of reasoning that draws upon figures with particular dimensions. The text then gives the square of 7 as 49 represented as below (Figure 5.1):

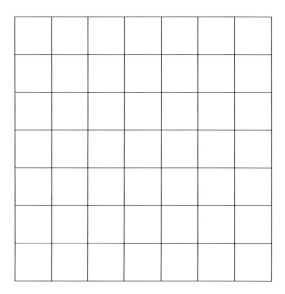

Figure 5.1   The square a^2.

From this square of 7×7 subtract a square of 5, which is 25.
This gives the following (Figure 5.2).
We are left with a remainder of 24.
$a-b=2$ and $a+b=12$ and the product consists of 24 equal cells (Figure 5.3).

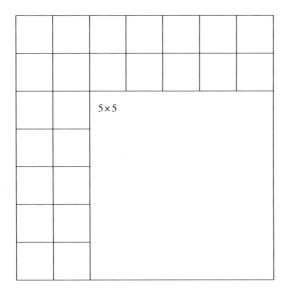

Figure 5.2   The square a^2 minus the square b^2.

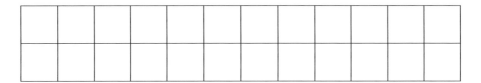

Figure 5.3   The rectangle of sides $a+b$ and $b-a$.

The text reads: 'thus it is demonstrated that the difference of the squares is equal to the product of the sum and the difference'.[93] The text then proceeds on the basis of this example to construct other Pythagorean triples.

Similarly, another visual demonstration follows for §149.

§149 Rule: The difference between the sum of the squares of two quantities whatsoever, and the square of their sum, is equal to twice their product; as in the case of two unknown quantities.[94]

The demonstration is worked out on the basis of a particular case, and provides a procedure thus for any two sets of numbers. Colebrooke's translation of Bhaskara's demonstration reads: 'For instance, let the quantities be 3 and 5. Their squares are 9 and 25. The square of their sum is 64. From this taking away the sum of the squares the remainder is 30.'[95] And then in the

93   C1817: 223.
94   C1817: 224.
95   C1817: 30.

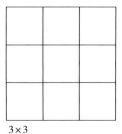

3×3

Figure 5.4 The square a^2.

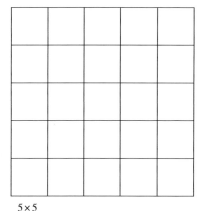

5×5

Figure 5.5 The square b^2.

translation Bhaskara exhorts his reader to 'See' the illustration that follows (see Figures 5.4–5.6). Thus $(3+5)^2 = 64 \ldots, (a+b)^2$

From this subtract $3^2 + 5^2 \ldots a^2 + b^2$

Which makes $64 - 34 = 30 \ldots (a+b)^2 - (a^2 + b^2)$

The left-over square cells are seen to be equal to twice the product (Figure 5.7). After which Bhaskara concludes: 'Here square compartments, equal to twice the product are apparent, and (the proposition) is proved.'[96]

We have here two cases of visual demonstration (Colebrooke calls them geometrical demonstrations) though in his translations he vacillates between the terms proofs and demonstrations. But clearly both are demonstrations from particular cases formulated within the framework of particular cases treated in a general way.

Furthermore, Colebrooke briefly discusses two different demonstrations of the Pythagorean theorem in Bhaskara's *Bija-Ganita* (§146). The first of

[96] C1817: 224.

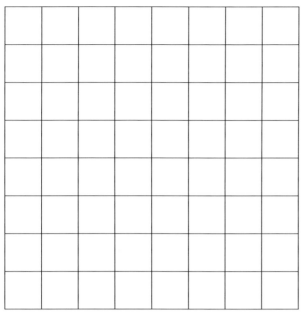

8×8

Figure 5.6 The square $(a+b)^2$.

In other words, from Figure 5.6, delete the sum of the squares: which is 3×3 and 5×5.

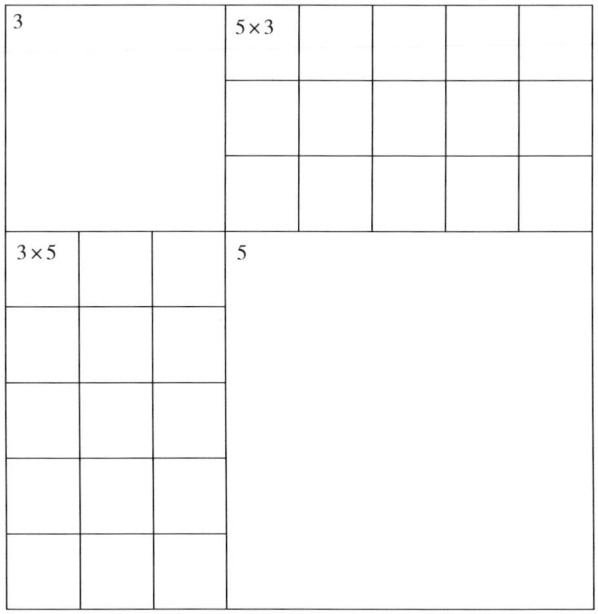

3

5×3

3×5

5

Figure 5.7 The area $(a+b)^2$ minus the squares a^2 and b^2 equals twice the product ab.

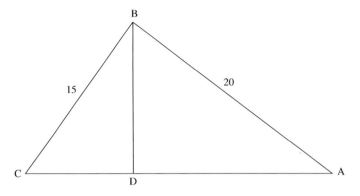

Figure 5.8   A right-angled triangle ABC and its height BD.

these demonstrations, we are reminded, is similar to Wallis' demonstration that appeared in the treatise on angular sections. Colebrooke sets Wallis' and Bhaskara's demonstrations side by side, such that Bhaskara's method is apprehended in Wallis' idiom (Figure 5.8).[97]

Wallis	Bhaskara
In a rectangular triangle, C and D designate the sides and B the hypotenuse. The segments are χ and δ.	Using the same symbols for the sides and segments, Bhaskara's demonstration
$B:C::C:\chi$	$B:C::C:\chi$
$B:D:D:\delta$	$B:D:D:\delta$
Therefore	Therefore
$C^2 = B\chi$	$\chi = C^2/B$
$D^2 = B\delta$	$\delta = D^2/B$
Therefore	Therefore
$C^2 + D^2 = (B\chi + B\delta) = B(\chi + \delta) = B^2$	$B = \chi + \delta = C^2/B + D^2/B$
	$B^2 = C^2 + D^2$

We shall now try to illustrate Bhaskara's procedure above as it appears in Colebrooke's translation, but I shall adopt a contemporary form of the argument. The problem that Bhaskara poses in §146 of the *Bija-Ganita* is: 'Say what is the hypotenuse in a plane figure, in which the side and upright are equal to 15 and 20? And show the demonstration of the received mode of composition.'[98] So consider a right-angled triangle ABC whose sides are 15 and 20 and rotate the figure as above. Drop a perpendicular to the side AC and let $AD = \chi$ and $DA = \delta$. Now AC is the hypotenuse of the triangle ABC and BC and AD of triangles BCD and DBA respectively.

[97]   C1817: xvi–xvii.
[98]   C1817: 220.

Bhaskara then posits the ratios:

$$\frac{AC}{BC} = \frac{BC}{CD} \text{ and } \frac{AC}{AB} = \frac{AB}{AD}$$

$$\chi = \frac{(BC)^2}{AC} \text{ and } \delta = \frac{(AB)^2}{AC}$$

$$\text{Now } (\chi + \delta) = \frac{(BC)^2}{AC} + \frac{(AB)^2}{AC}$$

$$\text{Or } (AC)^2 = (BC)^2 + (AB)^2$$

And thus the value of AC is computed, and from this the value of BD.[99]

Thus the procedure is reasoned again for a particular case with the sides of 15 and 20, but clearly the procedure is applicable for any set of numbers that constitute the sides of a right-angled triangle. It needs to be pointed out here that Colebrooke highlights the fact that Bhaskara 'gives both modes of proof' when discussing the solution of indeterminate problems involving two unknown quantities.

The instances Colebrooke has selected in his dissertation are 'conspicuous' as he says, for as pointed out earlier his method is to accentuate the contrast to destabilize as it were the then received picture within the binary typologies of the history of mathematics mentioned earlier.[100] But the task is undertaken with a great deal of caution. The next example chosen is that of indeterminate equations of the second degree, wherein, according to Colebrooke, Brahmagupta provided a general method, in addition to which he proposes rules to resolve special cases. It is well known that Bhaskara solved the equation $ax^2 + 1 = y^2$ for specific values of the variable a. But Colebrooke went on to suggest that Bhaskara proposed a method to solve all indeterminate equations of the second degree that were 'exactly the same' as the method developed by Brouncker. In effect, Colebrooke appeared to be suggesting that Bhaskara's method was generalizable, that he was aware of the problem and its 'general use', a feature for whose discovery modern Europe had to await the arrival of Euler on the stage of European mathematics.[101]

---

[99] C1817: 220–1.

[100] C1817: xviii.

[101] A contemporary mathematical review of the solution of Pell's equation indicates that the 'Indian or English method of solving the Pell equation is found in Euler's Algebra'. However, it is subsequently clarified that Euler, and his Indian or English predecessors, assumed that the method always produced a solution, whereas the contemporary understanding is that if a solution existed the method would find one. Further, Fermat had probably proved that there was a solution for each value of a, and the first published proof was that of Lagrange (Lenstra 2002: 182).

On reading of the early responses from a French savant to the work of Colebrooke, it is possible to discern that Delambre for one uses a very fine comb in rebutting several of the points taken up by Colebrooke. While Colebrooke himself does not draw a very fine distinction between the use of the terms 'proof' and 'demonstration' in his reading, he does distinguish between algebra and analysis; and as mentioned earlier he specifies wherein the Indian tradition could be characterized as an algebraic analysis. A study of the reception of Colebrooke's translations of the works on Indian arithmetic and algebra is a matter for a separate study. The curious question to be examined by such a study is that despite its canonical status in Western scholarship on the history of Indian mathematics and algebra, neither Colebrooke nor Davis ever insinuated that it was a tradition devoid of proof or demonstration. And yet, as the nineteenth-century historiography of Oriental mathematics evolved, a theory of the absence of proof would become one of its salient elements. The strong criticism of Colebrooke's work at the time was possibly provoked by Colebrooke's method of taking up those demonstrations from Indian mathematics for which equivalents existed in eighteenth-century European mathematics. This would have vitiated both the claims of novelty and originality, both very important features of the new sciences. Second, up to the end of the eighteenth century British Indologists still believed that they could discover the origins of an Indian geometry and the later work of the Indologist G. Thibaut may be seen to be in continuity with that tradition. But by the end of the nineteenth century the binary typologies of the history of mathematics, that portrayed the West as geometric and the East as algebraic, were well in place in the standard picture.

Acknowledgements

I thank the participants at the Workshop on the History and Historiography of Proofs in Ancient Traditions, Paris, for their questions, comments and suggestions, and more recently Karine Chemla for a very close reading of the text. The usual disclaimer applies.

Bibliography

Assayag, J., Lardinois, R. and Vidal, D. (1997) *Orientalism and Anthropology: From Max Mueller to Louis Dumont*. Pondy Papers in Social Sciences. Pondicherry.

Bailly, J.-S. (1775) *Histoire de l'astronomie ancienne depuis son origine jusqu'à l'établissement de l'école d'Alexandrie*. Paris.

Bailly, J.-S. (1787) *Traité de l'astronomie indienne et orientale*. Paris.

Banerji, H. C. (1927) *Colebrooke's Translation of the Lilavati with notes by Haran Chandra Banerji*, 2nd edn. Calcutta.

Buckland, C. E. (1908) *Dictionary of Indian Biography*. New York.

Burgess, J. (1893) 'Notes on Hindu astronomy and our knowledge of it', *Journal of the Royal Asiatic Society*: 717–61.

Burrow, R. (1783) 'Hints concerning the Observatory at Benaras', in *Warren Hastings Papers*, ff. 263–76, British Museum. (Reprinted in Dharampal 1971: 94–112.)

Charette, F. (1995) 'Orientalisme et histoire des sciences: L'historiographie des sciences islamiques et hindoues, 1784–1900', MA thesis, Department of History, University of Montreal.

Colebrooke, H. T. (1873) *Miscellaneous Essays by H. T. Colebrooke with Notes by E. B. Coswell*, 2 vols. London.

Colebrooke, T. E. (1873) *The Life of H. T. Colebrooke*. London.

Davis, S. (1790) 'On the early astronomical computations of the Hindus', *Asiatic Researches* 2: 225–87.

Dharampal (ed.) (1971) *Indian Science and Technology in the Eighteenth Century: Some Contemporary Accounts*. Delhi.

Filliozat, J. (1951) 'L'Orientalisme et les sciences humaines', *Extrait du Bulletin de la Société des études Indochinoises*, 26: 4.

(1955) 'France and Indology', *Bulletin of the Ramakrishna Mission Institute of Culture*, Transactions No. 12.

(1957) 'Ancient relations between India and foreign astronomical systems', *The Journal of Oriental Research – Madras*, 25 (I–IV): 1–8.

Heinz, B. (2000) *Die Innenwelt der Mathematik: Zur Kultur und Praxis einer beweisenden Disziplin*. Vienna.

(2003) 'When is a proof a proof', *Social Studies of Science* 33(6): 929–43.

Holwell, J. Z. (1767) 'An account of the Manner of Inoculating for the smallpox in the East Indies', addressed to the President and Members of the College of Physicians in London.

Inden, R. (1990) *Imagining India*. Oxford.

Jami, C. (1995) 'From Louis XIV's Court to Kangxi's Court: an institutional analysis of the French Jesuit mission to China (1688–1712)', in *East Asian Science: Tradition and Beyond*, ed. K. Hashimoto, C. Jami and L. Skar. Osaka: 493–9.

Jones, W. (1790a) 'On the antiquity of the Indian Zodiac', *Asiatic Researches* 2: 289–306.

Jones, W. (1790b) 'A supplement to the essay on Indian chronology', *Asiatic Researches* ii: 389–403.

Kejariwal, O. P. (1988) *The Asiatic Society of Bengal and the Discovery of India's Past 1784–1838*. Oxford.

Le Gentil, G. H. J. B. (1779–81) *Voyages dans les mers de l'Inde, fait par ordre du roi, à l'occasion du passage du Vénus, sur le disque du soleil, le 6 Juin 1761 & le 3 du même mois 1769*, 2 vols. Paris.

——— (1785) 'Mémoires sur l'origine du zodiaque', in *Mémoires de M. Le Gentil de l'Académie des sciences*, Publié dans le volume de cette Académie pour les années 1784 et 1785.

Lenstra, H. W. (2002) 'Solving the Pell equation', *Notices of the AMS* **49**(2): 182–92.

MacKenzie, D. (2001) *Mechanizing Proof: Computing, Risk, and Trust.* Cambridge, MA.

Montucla, J. E. (1799–1802) *Histoire des mathématiques* 4 vols. Paris. (Republished by Librairie Scientifique et Technique Albert Blanchard.)

Murr, S. (1986) 'Les Jésuites et l'Inde au XVIIIe siècle: Praxis, utopie, préanthropologie', *Revue de l'Université d'Ottawa* **56**: 9–27.

Playfair, J. (1790) 'Remarks on the astronomy of the Brahmins', *Transactions of the Royal Society of Edinburgh*, **2**, part I: 135–92. (Reprinted in Dharampal 1971: 48–93.)

Playfair, J. (1792) 'Questions and remarks on the astronomy of the Hindus', *Asiatic Researches* IV: 151–5.

Raina, D. (1999) 'Nationalism, institutional science and the politics of knowledge: ancient Indian astronomy and mathematics in the landscape of French Enlightenment historiography', PhD thesis, University of Göteborg.

——— (2001a) 'Jean-Sylvain Bailly's antediluvian hypothesis: the relationship between the *lumières* and the British indologists', Table ronde: *L'Orientalisme: un héritage en débat*, Paris: La Villette, 18 May 2001.

——— (2001b) 'Disciplinary boundaries and civilisational encounter: the mathematics and astronomy of India in Delambre's *Histoire* (1800–1820)', *Studies in History* **17**: 175–209.

——— (2003) 'Betwixt Jesuit and Enlightenment historiography: the context of Jean-Sylvain Bailly's *History of Indian Astronomy*', *Revue d'Histoire des mathématiques* **9**: 253–306.

Raina, D., and Habib, S. I. (1990) 'Ramchundra's treatise through the haze of the golden sunset: the aborted pedagogy', *Social Studies of Science* **20**: 455–72.

Raj, K. (2001) 'Refashioning civilities, engineering trust: William Jones, Indian intermediaries and the production of reliable legal knowledge', *Studies in History* **17**: 175–209.

Rocher, R. (1989) 'The career of Rādhākānta Tarkavāgīśa, an eighteenth-century pandit in British employ', *Journal of the American Oriental Society* **109**: 627–33.

Said, E. W. (1978) *Orientalism*. London.

Sonnerat, P. (1782) *Voyage aux Indes Orientales et à la Chine, fait par ordre du Roi, depuis 1774 jusqu'en 1781*. Paris.

Strachey, E. (1818) 'On the early history of algebra', *Asiatic Researches* **12**: 160–85.

Teltscher, K. (1995) *India Inscribed: European and British Writing on India 1600–1800*. Oxford.

Vidal, D. (1997) 'Max Müller and the theosophist: the other half of Victorian orientalism', in *Orientalism and Anthropology: From Max Mueller to Louis Dumont*, ed. J. Assayag, R. Lardinois and D. Vidal. Pondicherry: 18–27.

Županov, I. G. (1993) 'Aristocratic analogies and demotic descriptions in the seventeenth-century Madurai Mission', *Representations* **41**: 123–47.

6 | Overlooking mathematical justifications in the Sanskrit tradition: the nuanced case of G. F. W. Thibaut

AGATHE KELLER

Introduction

Until the 1990s, the historiography of Indian mathematics largely held that Indians did not use 'proofs' in their mathematical texts.[1] Dhruv Raina has shown that this interpretation arose partly from the fact that during the second half of the nineteenth century, the French mathematicians who analysed Indian astronomical and mathematical texts considered geometry to be the measure of mathematical activity.[2] The French mathematicians relied on the work of the English philologers of the previous generation, who considered the computational reasonings and algorithmic verifications merely 'practical' and devoid of the rigour and prestige of a real logical and geometrical demonstration. Against this historiographical backdrop, the German philologer Georg Friedrich Wilhelm Thibaut (1848–1914) published the oldest known mathematical texts in Sanskrit, which are devoted only to geometry.

These texts, *śulbasūtras* (sometimes called the *sulvasūtras*) contain treatises by different authors (Baudhāyana, Āpastamba, Kātyāyana and Mānava) and consider the geometry of the Vedic altar.[3] These texts were written in the style typical of aphoristic *sūtras* between 600 and 200 BCE. They were sometimes accompanied by later commentaries, the earliest of which may be assigned to roughly the thirteenth century. In order to understand the methods that he openly employed for this corpus of texts, Thibaut must be situated as a scholar. This analysis will focus on Thibaut's historiography of mathematics, especially on his perception of mathematical justifications.

---

[1] Srinivas 1990; H1995.

[2] See Raina 1999: chapter VI.

[3] I will adopt the usual transliteration of Sanskrit words, which will be marked in italics, except for the word Veda, which is found in English dictionaries.

Thibaut's intellectual background

Thibaut's approach to the *śulbasūtra*s combines what half a century before him had been two conflicting traditions. As described by Raina and by Charette, Thibaut was equal parts acute philologer and scientist investigating the history of mathematics.

A philologer

Thibaut trained according to the German model of a Sanskritist.[4] Born in 1848 in Heidelberg, he studied Indology in Germany. His European career culminated when he left for England in 1870 to work as an assistant for Max Müller's edition of the Vedas. In 1875, he became Professor of Sanskrit at Benares Sanskrit College. At this time, he produced his edition and studies of the *śulbasūtra*s, the focus of the present article.[5] Afterwards, Thibaut spent the following twenty years in India, teaching Sanskrit, publishing translations and editing numerous texts. With P. Griffith, he was responsible for the *Benares Sanskrit Series*, from 1880 onwards. As a specialist in the study of the ritualistic *mimāṃsa* school of philosophy and Sanskrit scholarly grammar, Thibaut made regular incursions into the history of mathematics and astronomy.

Thibaut's interest in mathematics and astronomy in part derives from his interest in *mimāṃsa*. The authors of this school commented upon the ancillary parts of the Vedas (*vedāṅga*) devoted to ritual. The *śulbasūtra*s can be found in this auxiliary literature on the Vedas. As a result of having studied these texts, between 1875 and 1878,[6] Thibaut published several articles on Vedic mathematics and astronomy. These studies sparked his curiosity about the later traditions of astronomy and mathematics in the Indian subcontinent and the first volume of the *Benares Sanskrit Series*, of which Thibaut was the general scientific editor, was the *Siddhāntatattvaviveka* of Bhaṭṭa Kamalākara. This astronomical treatise written in the seventeenth century in Benares attempts to synthesize the reworkings of theoretical astronomy made by the astronomers under the patronage of Ulug Begh with the traditional Hindu *siddhānta*s.[7]

Thibaut's next direct contribution to the history of mathematics and astronomy in India was a study on the medieval astronomical treatise the

---

[4] The following paragraph rests mainly on Stache-Rosen 1990.

[5] See Thibaut 1874, Thibaut 1875, Thibaut 1877a, Thibaut 1877b.

[6] The last being a study of the *jyotiṣavedāṅga*, in Thibaut 1878.

[7] See Minkowski 2001 and *CESS*, vol. 2: 21.

Pañcasiddhānta of Varāhamihira. In 1888, he also edited and translated this treatise with S. Dvivedi and consequently entered into a heated debate with H. Jacobi on the latter's attempt to date the Veda on the basis of descriptions of heavenly bodies in ancient texts. At the end of his life, Thibaut published several syntheses of ancient Indian mathematics and astronomy.[8] His main oeuvre, was not in the field of history of science but a three-volume translation of one of the main *mimāṃsa* texts: Śaṅkarācārya's commentary on the *Vedāntasūtras*, published in the *Sacred Books of the East*, the series initiated by his teacher Max Müller.[9] Thibaut died in Berlin at the beginning of the First World War, in October 1914.

Among the *śulbasūtra*s, Thibaut focused on Baudhāyana (*c.* 600 BCE)[10] and Āpastamba's texts, occasionally examining Kātyāyana's *śulbapariśiṣṭa*. Thibaut noted the existence of the *Mānavasulbasūtra* but seems not to have had access to it.[11] For his discussion of the text, Thibaut used Dvārakānātha Yajvan's commentary on the Baudhāyana *sulbasūtra* and Rāma's (*fl.* 1447/9) commentary on Kātyāyana's text.[12] Thibaut also occasionally quotes Kapardisvāmin's (*fl.* before 1250) commentary of Āpastamba.[13] Thibaut's introductory study of these texts shows that he was familiar with the extant philological and historical literature on the subject of Indian mathematics and astronomy. However, Thibaut does not refer directly to any other scholars. The only work he acknowledges directly is A. C. Burnell's catalogue of manuscripts.[14] For instance, Thibaut quotes Colebrooke's translation of *Līlāvatī* but does not refer to the work explicitly.[15] Thibaut also reveals some general reading on the history of mathematics. For example, he implicitly refers to a large history of attempts to square the circle, but his sources are unknown.

His approach to the texts shows the importance he ascribed to acute philological studies.[16] Thibaut often emphasizes how important commentaries are for reading the treatises: 'the *sūtra*-s themselves are of an

[8] Thibaut 1899, Thibaut 1907.
[9] Thibaut 1904.
[10] Unless stated otherwise, all dates refer to the *CESS*. When no date is given, the *CESS* likewise gives no date.
[11] For general comments on these texts, see Bag and Sen 1983, in *CESS*, vol 1: 50; vol 2: 30; vol 4: 252. For the portions of Dvārakānātha's and Venkateśvara's commentaries on Baudhāyana's treatise, see Delire 2002.
[12] Thibaut 1875: 3.
[13] Thibaut 1877: 75.
[14] Thibaut 1875: 3.
[15] Thibaut 1875: 61.
[16] See for instance Thibaut 1874: 75–6 and his long discussions on the translations of *vṛddha*.

enigmatical shortness . . . but the commentaries leave no doubt about the real meaning'.[17]

The importance of the commentary is also underlined in his introduction of the *Pañcasiddhānta*: 'Commentaries can be hardly done without in the case of any Sanskrit astronomical work . . .'[18]

However, Thibaut also remarks that because they were composed much later than the treatises, such commentaries should be taken with critical distance:

Trustworthy guides as they are in the greater number of cases, their tendency of sacrificing geometrical constructions to numerical calculation, their excessive fondness, as it might be styled, of doing sums renders them sometimes entirely misleading.[19]

Indeed, Thibaut illustrated some of the commentaries' 'mis-readings' and devoted an entire paragraph of his 1875 article to this topic. Thibaut explained that he had focused on commentaries to read the treatises but disregarded what was evidently their own input into the texts. Thibaut's method of openly discarding the specific mathematical contents of commentaries is crucial here. Indeed, according to the best evidence, the tradition of 'discussions on the validity of procedures' appears in only the medieval and modern commentaries.[20] True, the commentaries described mathematics of a period different than the texts upon which they commented. However, Thibaut valued his own reconstructions of the *śulbasūtras* proofs more than the ones given by commentaries.

The quote given above shows how Thibaut implicitly values geometrical reasoning over arithmetical arguments, a fact to which we will return later. It is also possible that the omission of mathematical justifications from the narrative of the history of mathematics in India concerns not only the conception of what counts as proof but also concerns the conception of what counts as a mathematical text. For Thibaut, the only real mathematical text was the treatise, and consequently commentaries were read for clarification but not considered for the mathematics they put forward.

In contradiction to what has been underlined here, the same 1875 article sometimes included commentators' procedures, precisely because the method they give is 'purely geometrical and perfectly satisfactory'.[21]

---

[17] Thibaut 1874: 18.

[18] Thibaut 1888: v.

[19] Thibaut 1875: 61–2.

[20] These are discussed, in a specific case, in the other chapter in this volume I have written; see Chapter 14.

[21] This concludes a description of how to transform a square into a rectangle as described by Dvārakaṅtha in Thibaut 1875: 27–8.

Thus there was a discrepancy between Thibaut's statements concerning his methodology and his philological practice.

Thibaut's conception of the Sanskrit scholarly tradition and texts is also contradictory. He alternates between a vision of a homogeneous and a historical Indian society and culture and the subtleties demanded by the philological study of Sanskrit texts.

In 1884, as Principal of Benares Sanskrit College (a position to which he had been appointed in 1879), Thibaut entered a heated debate with Bapu Pramadadas Mitra, one of the Sanskrit tutors of the college, on the question of the methodology of scholarly Sanskrit pandits. Always respectful to the pandits who helped him in his work, Thibaut always mentioned their contributions in his publications. Nonetheless, Thibaut openly advocated a 'Europeanization' of Sanskrit studies in Benares and sparked a controversy about the need for pandits to learn English and the history of linguistics and literature. Thibaut despaired of an absence of historical perspective in pandits' reasonings – an absence which led them often to be too reverent towards the past.[22] Indeed, he often criticized commentators for reading their own methods and practices into the text, regardless of the treatises' original intentions. His concern for history then ought to have led him to consider the different mathematical and astronomical texts as evidence of an evolution.

However, although he was a promoter of history, this did not prevent him from making his own sweeping generalizations on all the texts of the Hindu tradition in astronomy and mathematics. He writes in the introduction of the *Pañcasiddhānta*:

these works [astronomical treatises by Brahmagupta and Bhāskarācarya] claim for themselves direct or derived infallibility, propound their doctrines in a calmly dogmatic tone, and either pay no attention whatever to views diverging from their own or else refer to such only occasionally, and mostly in the tone of contemptuous depreciation.[23]

Through his belief in a contemptuous arrogance on the part of the writers, Thibaut implicitly denies the treatises any claim for reasonable mathematical justifications, as we will see later. Thibaut attributed part of the clumsiness which he criticized to their old age:

---

[22] See Dalmia 1996: 328–30.

[23] Thibaut 1888: vii. I am setting aside here the fact that he argues in this introduction for a Greek origin of Indian astronomy. The square brackets indicate the present author's addenda for the sake of clarity.

Besides the quaint and clumsy terminology often employed for the expression of very simple operations (. . .) is another proof for the high antiquity of these rules of the cord, and separates them by a wide gulf from the products of later Indian science with their abstract and refined terms.[24]

After claiming that the treatises had a dogmatic nature, Thibaut extends this to the whole of 'Hindu literature':

The astronomical writers . . . therein only exemplify a general mental tendency which displays itself in almost every department of Hindu Literature; but mere dogmatic assertion appears more than ordinarily misplaced in an exact science like astronomy . . .[25]

Thibaut does not seem to struggle with definitions of science, mathematics or astronomy, nor does he discuss his competency as a philologer in undertaking such a study. In fact, Thibaut clearly states that subtle philology is not required for mathematical texts. He thus writes at the beginning of the *Pañcasiddhānta*:

texts of purely mathematical or astronomical contents may, without great disadvantages, be submitted to a much rougher and bolder treatment than texts of other kinds. What interests us in these works, is almost exclusively their matter, not either their general style or the particular words employed, and the peculiar nature of the subject often enables us to restore with nearly absolute certainty the general meaning of passages the single words of which are past trustworthy emendation.[26]

This 'rougher and bolder treatment' is evident, for instance, in his philologically accurate but somewhat clumsy translation of technical vocabulary. He thus translates *dīrghacaturaśra* (literally 'oblong quadrilateral') variously; it is at some times a 'rectangular oblong', and at others an 'oblong'.[27] The expression 'rectangular oblong' is quite strange. Indeed, if the purpose is to underline the fact that it is elongated, then why repeat the idea? The first of Thibaut's translations seems to aim at expressing the fact that a *dīrghacaturaśra* has right angles, but the idea of orthogonality is never explicit in the Sanskrit works used here, or even in later literature. Thibaut's translation, then, is not literal but coloured by his own idea of what a *dīrghacaturaśra* is. Similarly, he calls the rules and verses of the treatises, the Sanskrit *sūtras*, 'proposition(s)', which gives a clue to what he expects of a

---

[24] Thibaut 1875: 60.
[25] Thibaut 1888: vii.
[26] Thibaut 1888: v.
[27] See for instance Thibaut 1875: 6.

scientific text, and thus also an inkling about what kind of scientific text he suspected spawned the *śulbasūtras*.

Thibaut's historiography of science

For Thibaut, 'true science' did not have a practical bent. In this sense, the science embodied in the *śulbas*, which he considered motivated by a practical religious purpose, is 'primitive':

> The way in which the *sūtrakāra*-s [those who compose treatises] found the cases enumerated above, must of course be imagined as a very primitive one. Nothing in the *sūtra*-s [the aphorisms with which treatises are composed] would justify the assumption that they were expert in long calculations.[28]

However, he considered the knowledge worthwhile especially because it was geometrical:

> It certainly is a matter of some interest to see the old *ācārya*-s [masters] attempting to solve this problem [squaring of the circle], which has since haunted so m[an]y unquiet minds. It is true the motives leading them to the investigation were vastly different from those of their followers in this arduous task. *Theirs was not the disinterested love of research which distinguishes true science*, nor the inordinate craving of undisciplined minds for the solution of riddles which reason tells us cannot be solved; theirs was simply the earnest desire to render their sacrifice in all its particulars acceptable to the gods, and to deserve the boons which the gods confer in return upon the faithful and conscientious worshipper.[29]

Or again:

> . . . we must remember that they were interested in geometrical truths only as far as they were of practical use, and that they accordingly gave to them the most practical expression.[30]

Conversely, the practical aspect of these primitive mathematics explains why the methods they used were geometrical:

> It is true that the exclusively practical purpose of the *Śulvasūtra*-s necessitated in some way the employment of practical, that means in this case, geometrical terms, . . .[31]

---

[28] Thibaut 1875: 17.
[29] Thibaut 1875: 33. The emphasis is mine.
[30] Thibaut 1875: 9.
[31] Thibaut 1875: 61.

This geometrical basis distinguished the *śulbasūtra*s from medieval or classical Indian mathematical treatises. Once again, Thibaut took this occasion to show his preference for geometry over arithmetic:

Clumsy and ungainly as these old *sūtra*-s undoubtedly are, they have at least the advantage of dealing with geometrical operations in really geometrical terms, and are in this point superior to the treatment of geometrical questions which we find in the *Līlāvatī* and similar works.[32]

As is made clear from the above quotation, Thibaut was a presentist historian of science who possessed a set of criteria which enabled him to judge the contents and the form of ancient texts. In another striking instance, Thibaut gives us a clue that Euclid is one of his references. Commenting on rules to make a new square of which the area is the sum or the difference of two known squares, Thibaut states in the middle of his own translation of Baudhāyana's *śulbasūtra*s:

Concerning the methods, which the *Śulvasūtras* teach for *caturasrasamāsa* (sum of squares) and *caturasranirhāra* (subtraction of squares), I will only remark that they are perfectly legitimate; they are at the bottom the same which Euclid employs.[33]

Contemptuous as he may be of the state of Indian mathematics, Thibaut did not believe that the *śulbasūtra*s were influenced by Greek geometry.[34]

For Thibaut, history of mathematics ought to reconstruct the entire deductive process from the origin of an idea to the way it was justified. Although later commentaries may include some useful information, they do not give us the key to understanding how these ideas were developed at the time when the treatises were composed. This lack of information provoked Thibaut to complain about Indian astronomical and mathematical texts.

Thibaut clearly considered the texts to have been arranged haphazardly because the order of the rules do not obey generative logic. He thus defined his task: 'I shall extract and fully explain the most important *sūtra*-s (. . .) and so try to exhibit in some systematic order the knowledge embodied in these ancient sacrificial tracts.'[35] Here, Thibaut assumed that these works – not treatises but 'tracts' (presumably with derogatory connotations) – are not clear and systematic. Further, Thibaut felt the need to disentangle ('extract') the knowledge they contain.

---

[32] Thibaut 1875: 60.
[33] Thibaut 1877: 76. Translations within brackets are mine.
[34] Thibaut 1875: 4. This however was still being discussed as late as Staal 1999.
[35] Thibaut 1875: 5.

In his view, this knowledge might be quite remarkable but it was ill presented. Thus commenting a couple years later on the *Vedāṅgajyotiṣa*, he remarked:

The first obstacle in our way is of course the style of the treatise itself with its enigmatical shortness of expression, its strange archaic forms and *its utter want of connection between the single verses.*[36]

He thus sometimes remarked where the rules should have been placed according to his logic. All the various texts of the *śulbasūtras* start by describing how to construct a square, particularly how to make a square from a rectangle.

However, Thibaut objected: 'their [the rules for making a square from a rectangle] right place is here, after the general propositions about the diagonal of squares and oblongs, upon which they are founded'.[37] Consequently, Thibaut considered the *śulbasūtras* as a single general body of text and selected the scattered pieces of the process he hoped to reconstruct from among all the *sūtras* composed by various authors. At the same time, he distinguished the different authors of the *śulbasūtras* and repeatedly insisted that Āpastamba is more 'practical' than Baudhāyana, whom he preferred. For instance, an example of his method:

Baudhāyana does not give the numbers expressing the length of the diagonals of his oblongs or the hypotenuses of the rectangular triangles, and I subjoin therefore some rules from Āpastamba, which supply this want, while they show at the same time the practical use, to which the knowledge embodied in Baudhāyana's *sūtra* could be turned.[38]

When alternating among several authors was insufficient for his purposes, Thibaut supplied his own presuppositions.

Indeed, Thibaut peppered his text with such reconstructions:

The authors of the *sūtra*-s do not give us any hint as to the way in which they found their proposition regarding the diagonal of a square; but we may suppose . . . The question arises: how did Baudhāyana or Āpastamba or whoever may have the merit of the first investigation, find this value? . . . I suppose that they arrived at their result by the following method which accounts for the exact degree of accuracy they reached . . . Baudhāyana does not state at the outset what the shape of his wheel will be, but from the result of his rules we may conclude his intention . . .[39]

---

[36] Thibaut 1877: 411; the emphasis is mine.
[37] Thibaut 1875: 28.
[38] Thibaut 1875: 12.
[39] Thibaut 1875: 11, 18, 49.

Because he had an acute idea of what was logically necessary, Thibaut thus had a clear idea of what was sufficient and insufficient for reconstructing the processes. As a result, Thibaut did not deem the arithmetical reasoning of Dvārakānātha adequate evidence of mathematical reasoning.

The misunderstandings on which Thibaut's judgements rest are evident. For him, astronomical and mathematical texts should be constructed logically and clearly, with all propositions regularly demonstrated. This presumption compelled him to overlook what he surely must have known from his familiarity with Sanskrit scholarly texts: the elaborate character of a *sūtra* – marked by the diverse readings that one can extract from it – enjoyed a long Sanskrit philological tradition. In other words, when a commentator extracts a new reading from one or several *sūtra*s, he demonstrates the fruitfulness of the *sūtra*s. The commentator does not aim to retrieve a univocal singular meaning but on the contrary underline the multiple readings the *sūtra* can generate. Additionally, as Thibaut rightly underlined, geometrical reasoning represented no special landmark of correctness in reasoning to medieval Indian authors.

Because of these expectations and misunderstandings Thibaut was unable to find the mathematical justifications that maybe were in these texts. Let us thus look more closely at the type of reconstruction that Thibaut employed, particularly in the case of proofs.

Practices and readings in the history of science

It is telling that the word 'proof' is used more often by Thibaut in relation to philological reasonings than in relation to mathematics. Thus, as we have seen above, the word is used to indicate that the clumsiness of the vocabulary establishes the *śulbasūtras*' antiquity.

No mathematical justifications in the *śulbasūtras*

However, for Thibaut, Baudhāyana and probably other 'abstractly bent' treatise writers doubtlessly wanted to justify their procedures. More often than not, these authors did not disclose their modes of justification. Thus, when the authors are silent, Thibaut developed fictional historical procedures. For instance:

The authors of the *sūtra*-s do not give us any hint as to the way in which they found their proposition regarding the diagonal of a square [e.g. the Pythagorean proposition in a square]; but we may suppose that they, too, were observant of the fact that the square on the diagonal is divided by its own diagonals into four triangles, one of which is equal to half the first square. This is at the same time an immediately convincing proof of the Pythagorean proposition as far as squares or equilateral rectangular triangles are concerned . . . But how did the *sūtrakāra*-s [composers of treatises] satisfy themselves of the general truth of their second proposition regarding the diagonal of rectangular oblongs? Here there was no such simple diagram as that which demonstrates the truth of the proposition regarding the diagonal of the square, and other means of proof had to be devised.[40]

Thibaut thus implied that diagrams were used to 'show' the reasoning literally and thus 'prove' it. This method seems to hint that authors of the medieval period of Sanskrit mathematics could have had some sort of geometrical justification.[41] Concerning Āpastamba's methods of constructing fire altars, which was based on known Pythagorean triplets, Thibaut stated:

In this manner Āpastamba turns the Pythagorean triangles known to him to practical use . . . but after all Baudhāyana's way of mentioning these triangles as proving his proposition about the diagonal of an oblong is more judicious. It was no practical want which could have given the impulse to such a research [on how to measure and construct the sides and diagonals of rectangles] – for right angles could be drawn as soon as one of the *vijñeya* [determined] oblongs (for instance that of 3, 4, 5) was known – but the want of some mathematical justifications which might establish a firm conviction of the truth of the proposition.[42]

So, in both cases, Thibaut represented the existence and knowledge of several Pythagorean triplets as the result of not having any mathematical justification for the Pythagorean Theorem. Thibaut proceeded to use this fact as a criterion by which to judge both Āpastamba's and Baudhāyana's use of Pythagorean triplets. Thibaut's search for an appropriate geometrical mathematical justification in the *śulbasūtra*s may have made him overlook a striking phenomenon.

Two different rules for the same result

Indeed, Thibaut underlined that several algorithms are occasionally given in order to obtain the same result. This redundancy puzzled him at times.

---

[40] Thibaut 1875: 11–12.

[41] See Keller 2005. Bhāskara's commentary on the *Āryabhaṭīya* was not published during Thibaut's lifetime, but I sometimes suspect that either he or a pandit with whom he worked had read it. The discussion on *viṣamacaturaśra* and *samacaturaśra*, in Thibaut 1875: 10, thus echoes Bhāskara I's discussion on verse 3 of Chapter 2 of the *Āryabhaṭīya*. Thibaut's conception of geometrical proof is similar to Bhāskara's as well.

[42] Thibaut 1875: 17.

For instance, Thibaut examined the many various *caturaśrakaraṇa* – methods to construct a square – given by different authors.[43] Āpastamba, Baudhāyana and Kātyāyana each gave two methods to accomplish this task. I will not expound these methods here; they have been explained amply and clearly elsewhere.[44] Thibaut also remarked that in some cases, Baudhāyana gives a rule and its reverse, although the reverse cannot be grounded in geometry. Such is the case with the procedure to turn a circle into a square:

Considering this rule closer, we find that it is nothing but the reverse of the rule for turning a square into a circle. It is clear, however, that the steps taken according to this latter rule could not be traced back by means of a geometrical construction, for if we have a circle given to us, nothing indicates what part of the diameter is to be taken as the *atiśayatṛtīya* (i.e. the segment of the diameter which is outside of the square).[45]

I am no specialist in *śulba* geometry and do not know if we should see the doubling of procedures and inverting of procedures as some sort of 'proofs', but at the very least they can be considered efforts to convince the reader that the procedures were correct. The necessity within the *śulbasūtras* to convince and to verify has often been noted in the secondary literature, but has never fully or precisely studied.[46] Thibaut, although puzzled by the fact, never addressed this topic. Similarly, later historians of mathematics have noted that commentators on the *śulbasūtras* sought to verify the procedures while setting aside the idea of a regular demonstration in these texts. Thus Delire notes that Dvārakānātha used arithmetical computations as an easy method of verification (in this case of the Pythagorean Theorem).[47] The use of two separate procedures to arrive at the same result, as argued in another chapter in this volume,[48] could have been a way of mathematically verifying the correctness of an algorithm – an interpretation that did not occur to Thibaut.

---

[43] Thibaut 1875: 28–30.
[44] Thibaut 1875: 28–30; Bag and Sen 1983 in *CESS*, vol. 1; Datta 1993: 55–62; and finally Delire 2002: 75–7.
[45] Thibaut 1875: 35.
[46] See for instance Datta 1993: 50–1.
[47] Delire 2002: 129.
[48] See Keller, Chapter 14, this volume.

Conclusion

Thibaut, as we have thus seen, embodied contradictions. On the one hand, he swept aside the Sanskrit literary tradition and criticized its concise *sūtras* as obscure, dogmatic and following no logic whatsoever. On the other hand, as an acute philologer, he produced nuanced studies on the differences among the approaches of different authors. Through his naive assumption of a practical mind of the 'Hindu astronomers', his fruitless search for proper visual demonstrations in an algorithmic tradition, and a disregard of commentaries in favour of the treatises, Thibaut envisioned a tradition of mathematics in India blind to the logic that could have been used to justify the algorithms which he studied. Such arguments could have been perceived through the case of the 'doubled' procedures in the *śulbasūtras*, and maybe even through the arithmetical readings of these geometrical texts found in later commentaries.

Acknowledgement

I would like to thank K. Chemla and M. Ross for their close reading of this article. They have considerably helped in improving it.

Bibliography

CESS (1970–94) *Census of the Exact Sciences in Sanskrit*, ed. D. Pingree, 5 vol. Philadelphia, PA.

Dalmia (1996) 'Sanskrit scholars and pandits of the old school: The Benares Sanskrit College and the constitution of authority in the late nineteenth century', *Journal of Indian Philosophy* **24**: 321–37.

Datta, B. (1993) *Ancient Hindu Geometry: The Science of the Sulba*. New Delhi.

Delire, J. M. (2002) 'Vers une édition critique des śulbadīpikā et śulbamīmāṃsā commentaires du Baudhāyana śulbasūtra: Contribution à l'histoire des mathématiques Sanskrites', PhD thesis, Université Libre de Bruxelles.

Keller, A. (2005a) 'Making diagrams speak, in Bhāskara I's commentary on the *Āryabhaṭīya*', *Historia Mathematica* **32**: 275–302.

Minkowski, C. (2001) 'The pandit as public intellectual: the controversy over virodha or inconsistency in the astronomical sciences', in *The Pandit: Traditional Scholarship in India*, ed. A. Michaels. New Delhi: 79–96.

Raina, D. (1999) 'Nationalism, institutional science and the politics of knowledge; ancient Indian astronomy and mathematics in the landscape of French Enlightenment historiography', PhD thesis, University of Göteborg.

Srinivas, M. D. (1990) 'The methodology of Indian mathematics and its contemporary relevance', in *History of Science and Technology in India*, ed. S. Prakashan, vol. II, Chapter 2. New Delhi.

Staal, F. (1999) 'Greek and Vedic geometry', *Journal of Indian Philosophy* **27**: 105–27.

Stache-Rosen, V. (1990) *German Indologists: Biographies of Scholars in Indian Studies Writing in German, with a Summary of Indology in German*, 2nd edn. New Delhi.

Thibaut, G. F. (1874). 'Baudhayānaśulbasūtra' , in *The Pandit*. Reprinted and re-edited in Chattopadhyaya, D. (1984) *Mathematics in the Making in Ancient India*. Delhi. (Page numbers refer to this edition.)

(1875) 'On the Sulvasutras', in *Journal of the Asiatic Society of Bengal*. Reprinted and re-edited in Chattopadhyaya, D. (1984) *Mathematics in the Making in Ancient India*. Delhi. (Page numbers refer to this edition.)

(1877a) 'Baudhayānaśulbasūtra', in *The Pandit*. Reprinted and re-edited in Chattopadhyaya, D. (1984) *Mathematics in the Making in Ancient India*. Delhi. (Page numbers refer to this edition.)

(1877b) 'Contributions to the explanation of the Jyotishavedānga', *Journal of the Asiatic Society of Bengal* **46**: 411–37.

(1880) 'On the Sūryaprajapti', *Journal of the Asiatic Society of Bengal* **49**: 107–27 and 181–206.

(1882) 'Katyayana śulbapariśiṣṭa with the commentary of Ràma son of Sùryadasa', *The Pandit* n.s. **4**: 94–103, 328–39, 382–9 and 487–91.

(1884) 'Notes from Varāha Mihira's Pañchasiddhāntikā', *Journal of the Asiatic Society of Bengal* **53**: 259–93.

(1885) 'The number of stars constituting the several Nakṣatras according to Brahmagupta and Vriddha-Garga', *Indian Antiquary* **14**: 43–5.

(1894) 'On the hypothesis of the Babylonian origin of the so-called lunar zodiac', *Journal of the Asiatic Society of Bengal* **63**: 144–63.

(1895) 'On some recent attempts to determine the antiquity of Vedic civilization', *Indian Antiquary* **24**: 85–100.

(1899) *Astronomie, Astrologie und Mathematik*. Strasburg.

(1904) *Vedānta sūtras with the commentary by Shaṅkarācarya*, translated by George Thibaut. Delhi.

(1907) 'Indian astronomy', *Indian Thought* **1**: 81–96, 313–34 and 422–33.

Thibaut, G. F. and Dvivedi (1888) *Pañcasiddhāntika*. Chowkhamba Sanskrit Studies vol. LXVIII. Varanasi. (Reprinted 1968.)

7 | The logical Greek *versus* the imaginative
Oriental: on the historiography of 'non-Western'
mathematics during the period 1820–1920

FRANÇOIS CHARETTE

What makes Greek mathematics distinctive?

In 1841, in an essay–review of Jean Jacques Sédillot's (1777–1832) partial
translation of a comprehensive thirteenth-century Arabic treatise on spherical astronomy and instrumentation written for the use of practical astronomers, and published posthumously by his son Louis Amélie (1808–75) in
1834–5 under the title *Traité des instruments astronomiques des Arabes*, the
French physicist Jean-Baptiste Biot (1774–1862) made the following bold-
sounding statement:

One finds [in this book] renewed evidence for this peculiar habit of mind, following
which the Arabs, as the Chinese and Hindus, limited their scientific writings to the
statement of a series of rules, which, once given, ought only to be verified by their
applications, without requiring any logical demonstration or connections between
them: this gives those Oriental nations a remarkable character of dissimilarity,
I would even add of intellectual inferiority, comparatively to the Greeks, with
whom any proposition is established by reasoning, and generates logically deduced
consequences.[1]

Apart from the very ill-founded nature of Biot's judgement – which, incidentally, is contradicted on the very next page when he concedes that the
book under review is not a representative work of Arabic astronomy, but
rather a practical treatise for 'vulgar' use – this is nonetheless a clear formulation of the idea that is at the core of the present investigation. For sure,
such an opinion was not new. But the undeviating boldness and precision of
Biot's statement is really remarkable. I will thus take it as the starting point
of my inquiry into the historiography of the mathematical demonstration

---

[1] '. . . on y trouve une nouvelle preuve de cette singulière habitude de l'esprit, en vertu de laquelle
les Arabes, comme les Chinois et les Hindous, bornaient leurs compositions scientifiques à
l'exposition d'une suite de règles, qui, une fois posées, devaient se vérifier par leurs applications
mêmes, sans besoin de démonstration logique, ni de connexion entre elles: ce qui donne à
ces nations orientales un caractère remarquable de dissemblance, et j'ajouterai d'infériorité
intellectuelle, comparativement aux Grecs, chez lesquels toute proposition s'établit par
raisonnement, et engendre des conséquences logiquement déduites.' Biot 1841: 674–5.

by labelling it the 'forthright formulation' of the ideology under scrutiny. But a few words on Biot are in order here to put his essay–review in context. Already in 1834, L. A. Sédillot had stridently claimed the originality of Arabic science, basing his argument on his alleged finding that a tenth-century Arab astronomer had discovered the third inequality of the moon, 600 years before Tycho Brahe. Biot soon became a passionate opponent of Sédillot in an unending debate that occupied the Paris Academy of Science for more than 40 years. Biot, who in his polemic pieces against Sédillot revealed a profoundly anti-Arab ideology, was more candid with regard to Chinese and Indian science, about which he wrote numerous essays collected at the end of his life in his *Études sur l'astronomie indienne et sur l'astronomie chinoise* (Paris, 1862). His son Edouard (1803–50), who had abandoned a liberal career for the study of sinology, was probably the first European who, after the Jesuits, made available new sources on Chinese mathematics; he published three papers on this topic between 1835 and 1841. Together with K. L. Biernatzki's famous paper on Chinese arithmetic and algebra printed in Crelle's *Journal für reine und angewandte Mathematik* in 1856 (and based entirely on various newspaper articles by the Protestant missionary in China Alexander Wylie), E. Biot's contributions constituted the very few fragments of Chinese mathematics available to European histo-rians until the beginning of the twentieth century.[2] For Indian mathematics, Biot senior could rely on the widely available publications of British Sanskritists such as Henry Thomas Colebrooke (1765–1837), as well as on an increasing secondary literature based on them. This, of course, put J. B. Biot in a position of authority to judge Oriental science.

Before examining in more details the contexts and the evolution of the idea so precisely enunciated by Biot, let us contrast it with the view of a German historian of mathematics, Siegmund Günther (1848–1923), who, in 1908, nicely summarized the researches of the second half of the nine-teenth century on the matter. In a chapter devoted to Indian mathematics, Günther wrote the following:

But this [Indian] mathematics has such a peculiar character, that a study thereof is assured to guarantee the highest lure. In particular, one can only be fascinated by the fundamental opposition between the Indian and Greek ways of thinking and of looking at things. The Greek is – with a few exceptions confirming the rule – a rigid synthetician, whose emphasis lies fully on rigorous demonstrations and who lives so much in spatial considerations that he will almost invariably attempt to cloth even arithmetical things into geometrical garments. Conversely, the Indian, being exceptionally gifted for everything computational, has very little appeal to

---

[2] Martzloff 1997: 4–5.

demonstrations: 'look at the figure' he says, allowing nothing but illustrative demonstrations [*Anschauungsbeweise*], whereas he could not have any feeling for the impressive but often awkward efforts of a Euclid or an Archimedes to really impose on reluctant [readers] the conviction of the validity of a theorem.[3]

Günther's judgement is obviously more respectful and nuanced than that of Biot. I shall analyse the genealogy of the ideas expressed by Günther in the second half of this chapter.

First it is necessary to proceed towards the source of Europe's knowledge of Indian mathematics. The efforts of Strachey (1813) and Taylor (1816) for making Bhāskara's mathematical works available in English translation were very soon rendered obsolete by Colebrooke's authoritative annotated translation of the mathematical parts of the works of Bhāskara and Brahmagupta in 1817. The same year, the Scottish mathematician John Playfair (1748–1819), who had been noted for his interest in the history of Indian astronomy, contributed an essay–review of Colebrooke to the *Edinburgh Review*. Playfair noted the absence of demonstrations in the *Lilavati* and the *Bīja-Gaṇita*, but acknowledged that Bhāskara's fifteenth- and sixteenth-century commentators, such as Gaṇeśa, supplied demonstrations of the rules in several instances. He had to concede, however, that those occasional demonstrations were 'often obscure, from the want of reference to a figure; for, though the figure be constructed on the margin, there is no reference to it by letters'.[4] After having presented a survey of the most important results achieved by Bhāskara, Playfair made the following observation:

But in the midst of these curious results, there is a subject of regret that almost continually presents itself. When such rules are laid down as the preceding, they are usually given without any analysis whatever, and even without any synthetic demonstration, so that the means by which the knowledge was obtained, remains quite unknown . . . In consequence of this, a mystery still hangs over the mathematical

---

[3] 'Und doch ist diese Mathematik von so auszeichnender Eigenart, daß die Beschäftigung mit ihr den höchsten Reiz gewähren muß. Insonderheit fesselt den Beschauer der grundsätzliche Gegensatz zwischen indischer und griechischer Denk- und Betrachtungsweise. Der Grieche ist – und die wenigen Ausnahmen bestätigen nur die Regel – strenger Synthetiker, der auf rigorose Beweisführung das größte Gewicht legt und so durchaus in räumlichen Vorstellungen lebt, daß er selbst arithmetische Dinge fast ausschließlich in ein geometrisches Gewand zu kleiden bestrebt ist. Umgekehrt liegt dem für alles Rechnerische ausnehmend befähigten Inder sehr wenig an der Demonstration; "siehe die Figur" sagt er und läßt keine anderen als Anschauungsbeweise zu, während er für die imponierenden, aber oft unbehilflichen Anstrengungen eines Euclides und Archimedes, die Überzeugung von der Richtigkeit eines Satzes förmlich einem Widerstrebenden aufzuzwingen, gar keinen Sinn haben konnte.' Günther 1908: 178.

[4] Playfair 1817: 158.

knowledge of the East; and it is much to be feared that the means of removing it no longer exist.[5]

Playfair regretted the absence of demonstrations, because he mainly expected them to illuminate the mechanisms of mathematical discovery among ancient authors.

His interest in the innate heuristic patterns of mathematical creation thus stands in remarkable contrast to the usual strict concern for *results*, which is characteristic of most nineteenth-century writings on history of mathematics (however naive it might be to hope that demonstrations would necessarily provide clues for understanding the underlying patterns of discovery).

Concerning a particular geometrical theorem, he further remarks that it 'is demonstrated in a very ingenious and palpable manner, not altogether according to the rigour of the Greek geometry, but abundantly satisfactory to those who are pleased with an argument when it is sound, though it be not dressed in the *costume* of science'.[6] Another proof he sees as revealing 'ingenious and simple' reasoning that must stem from 'a system of geometrical demonstration that was not very refined, or very scrupulous about introducing mechanical considerations'.[7] But even in those cases when demonstration was wanting, Playfair nevertheless believed that there existed an original procedure of demonstration, no longer extant.[8] In passing we must note the belief expressed by Playfair that science, as for every other civilizational aspect of India, was 'immoveable' and deprived of progress.

Three comparative views on Greek and Oriental mathematics: Hankel, Cantor and Zeuthen

I now come to the major part of my inquiry, in which I offer a detailed analysis of the comparative views of three eminent historians of mathematics, Hankel, Cantor and Zeuthen, on Greek versus 'Oriental' (Indian, Chinese, Islamic) mathematics.

---

[5] Playfair 1817: 151.
[6] Playfair 1817: 159–60.
[7] Playfair 1817: 160.
[8] See on p. 159 the remarks on the theorem that in a circumscribed [this condition is not specified in the Sanskrit text] quadrilateral with sides a, b, c, d and diagonals g, h we have $ac + bd = gh$, a theorem 'by no means very easy to be demonstrated' and which 'argues for a very extensive knowledge of elementary trigonometry, and such as is by no means easily acquired'.

Contexts and predecessors

In France, the geometer Michel Chasles (1793–1880) and the exiled Italian mathematician Guglielmo Libri (1803–69) stirred interest in the history of mathematics among fellow mathematicians. The first published in 1837 a remarkable book entitled *Aperçu historique sur l'origine et le développement des méthodes en Géométrie, particulièrement de celles qui se rapportent à la Géométrie moderne*, in which historical studies sought to inform and inspire the renewal of modern geometry. The second, whose scientific contributions are today completely forgotten, united patriotic feelings with a liberal and enlightened historical erudition that found its expression in his four-volume *Histoire des sciences mathématiques en Italie*. These two works certainly represent the finest pieces of scholarship in mathematical historiography from the first half of the nineteenth century.

In Germany, some men combined a command of science and of classical and orientalist philology which helped them produce remarkable works of historical erudition. We can mention Ludwig Ideler (1766–1846) in Berlin (astronomy and mathematical chronology) or, more importantly for us, Georg Heinrich Nesselmann in Königsberg (1811–81) who may have been the first to offer lectures on the history of mathematics on a regular basis, which resulted in a much-praised history of Greek algebra (1842). Another important figure for our present concerns is the Heidelberg professor of mathematics Arthur Arneth (1802–58), author of a now forgotten *Geschichte der reinen Mathematik in ihrer Beziehung zur Entwicklung des menschlichen Geistes* (Stuttgart, 1852), in which he clearly enunciated the fundamental opposition between the Greek and Indian styles of practising mathematics. We shall return to his ideas below.

The works of Libri, Arneth, Nesselmann and Chasles impressed the three most important writers on history of ancient and medieval mathematics in the late nineteenth century mentioned above. The distinguished Danish geometer and historian of mathematics Hieronymus Georg Zeuthen (1839–1920) was a pupil of Chasles in Paris and he himself conceded how Chasles's influence had been decisive for his historical works. Moritz Cantor (1829–1920) also went to Paris where he met Chasles, whose historico-mathematical studies inspired an equally strong fascination in him.

But another mathematician produced a very influential book some years before Cantor and Zeuthen would publish their major works. Hermann Hankel was born in 1839, the same year as Cantor. His essay on ancient and medieval mathematics originated from the lectures he gave at the University of Tübingen from the year of his appointment in 1869 until his premature death in 1873. It was published posthumously the next year by his father, who was Professor of Physics in Leipzig. In spite of its being unfinished, this book can be rightly qualified as the most original and refreshing view on the topic to have been offered in print up to its day. Hankel was notable for including an up-to-date summary – the only one available to date, especially for Arabic mathematics – of the findings of Colebrooke, Woepcke and other orientalists on the mathematics of the Hindus and Muslims. With his numerous thought-provoking interpretations, Hankel's history represented a compelling source of inspiration for the forthcoming generation of 'professional' historians of mathematics, among whom we mention the names of Cantor, Bretschneider, Zeuthen, Tannery, Heiberg, Eneström, Allman, von Braunmühl, Günther, Loria, Hultsch, Curtze, Suter, etc.[9]

The *éminence grise* among them was undoubtedly Moritz Cantor, who enjoyed the privilege of studying mathematics in Göttingen with Carl Gauss and others. But another Göttingen professor, Moritz Stern, instilled in him the taste for historical studies. Arneth's lectures on the history of mathematics in Heidelberg, which Cantor heard in 1848, are also said to have exerted a strong influence on him.[10] Cantor's 'antiquarian' style of scholarship – with its erudite, detailed and comprehensive narrative of every single episode of mathematical history within its own specific context – is evident in his monumental *Vorlesungen über Geschichte der Mathematik*, whose first volume appeared in 1880. This style is often contrasted with the 'presentist' and Platonic approach of H. G. Zeuthen, who insisted on the necessity to select the most significant episodes of the history of mathematics in order to illuminate our understanding of the development of mathematics from a modern perspective, a vision embodied in his highly original and influential historical essay on the theory of the conics in antiquity (published in Copenhagen in 1885 and in German translation the next year). His introductory *Geschichte der Mathematik im Altertum und Mittelalter* (1896) of didactic intent (the intended readership were the future teachers of mathematics in Denmark) had nevertheless a scope and depth similar to Hankel's history, and remained for several decades the best work of its genre.

India's illogical lure

Playfair's essay on Indian mathematics provided the inspiration for Arthur Arneth's 'cultural' history of mathematics, in which we find the first

[9]   On those historians of mathematics, see the biographical notices in Part II of Dauben and Scriba 2002.
[10]   See Hofmann 2008; Folkerts in Dauben and Scriba 2002: 387–91, on 387.

precise formulation of the idea opposing the apodictic rationality of Greek mathematical practice to the more intuitive one of the Indians. He contended that whereas the Greeks were trying to recognize that which is given (*das Gegebene*) and has a form (*das Gestaltete*), the Indians were *creating* forms (*Gestaltungen*) through active research, satisfying themselves to know that something exists, without concern for knowing *how* it is so.[11] Both styles were one-sided, but necessary. The rapid development of modern mathematics, according to Arneth, owed much to the mingling of these two contrasting styles of mathematical practice.

Let us turn our attention to Hankel, Cantor and Zeuthen's writings. Hankel's original views on mathematical demonstration contrast with the coarse dogmatism of Biot, on the one side, and the more sophisticated conservatism of Cantor, on the other.[12] Hankel devoted thirteen pages to the Greek concepts and practice of analysis and synthesis, presenting a competent and inspiring survey of the topic.[13] For him, the painstaking care associated with analysis and synthesis and the 'dry dogmatic syllogism' so peculiar to Greek mathematicians was not a 'useless burden' to them; in fact, he says, 'for their mental strength, this form, so annoying to us, was the appropriate one'.[14]

Hankel's account of Indian mathematics is still permeated with the German romantic fascination for India and its philosophy. Like Playfair, he noted the occasional and partial use of certain forms of demonstration in Indian mathematical texts: 'There is also little to find among the Indians of . . . a practice of proof. Only here and there does a commentator add some remarks to the rules and theorems, which can pave the way to their derivation.'[15] Indian geometry, radically different from that of the Greeks, was also characterized by the absence of demonstration in the traditional (Greek) sense; there is simply a reference to a figure accompanied by the exclamation 'Look!' This kind of 'illustrative demonstration' (*Anschauungsbeweis*), as we have seen in our previous quotation of Günther, strongly fascinated historians of mathematics. Cantor saw this as a typically Indian mode of thought: 'This form of demonstration, which does not appear in Brahmagupta, must certainly be considered as (typically) Indian. Combined with the algebraic

---

[11] Arneth 1852: 141.
[12] Cantor's views are analysed further below.
[13] Hankel 1874: 137–50.
[14] Hankel 1874: 208.
[15] 'Von solcher Entwickelung und Beweisführung ist nun auch bei den Indern nicht eben so viel zu finden. Nur hie und da fügt ein Commentator zu den Regeln und Sätzen einige Bemerkungen, welche den Weg zu deren Ableitung geben können.' Hankel 1874: 182–3.

form of demonstration, it is tremendously characteristic for the mental capacity of those geometers. To compute with almost endless possibilities, they never go beyond that.'[16] Compare Zeuthen: 'In all cases they do not give such justifications in words, but satisfy themselves to make a drawing and, with the word "look!", refer to the figure, which, for the Greeks, forms the starting point of the actual demonstration.'[17] However, in a commentary on the geometry of Brahmagupta, Hankel found a more promising kind of demonstration: 'If we except the strange form of the expression, we do find in this passage the idea of the demonstration, briefly it is true, but hinted at with absolute clarity . . . But how different is this derivation from a Euclidean one!'[18]

But why was Indian mathematical practice so different from the Greek one? Hankel was convinced that the reasons lay in Indian philosophy: 'The Brahmans [have] an essentially different way of thinking than the Greeks; for them the reasons are less important than the results, the why less important than the how; they operate more with ideas and imaginations than with concepts. The sharpness and certainty they thereby lose is compensated by increased depth and breadth.'[19] And he then offered as an explanatory example the case of grammar: whereas the Greeks have a *logical* and *syntactical* grammatical system, Indian grammar – epitomized by Pāṇini – is *empirical* and *etymological*.[20] But these aspects of Pāṇini's system he considered fruitful, for we are dealing with a 'unique and absolutely scientific grammar'. The formal constraints imposed on scientific writings, however, namely the use of compact versified rules, he sees as an obvious obstacle to the formulation of theorems and their logical proofs. This negative remark notwithstanding, Hankel did not consider the Indian

[16] 'Diese Beweisform, welche bei Brahmagupta nirgend auftritt, muss wohl als indisch betrachtet werden. Sie ist mit der algebraischen Beweisform verbunden ungemein charakteristisch für die Fassungskraft jener Geometer. Rechnen in nahezu unbegrenzter Möglichkeit, darüber kommen sie nicht hinaus.' Cantor 1894: 614. In the third edition (1914: 656), the word 'Fassungskraft' is replaced by 'Darstellungsweise' (mode of representation).

[17] 'Jedenfalls geben sie solche Begründungen nicht in Worten wieder, sondern sie begnügen sich damit zu zeichnen und durch das Wort 'Siehe! ' auf die Figur hinzuweisen, die der wirklichen Beweisführung der Griechen zu Grunde lag.' Zeuthen 1896: 261.

[18] 'Sehen wir von der fremdartigen Form des Ausdruckes ab, so finden wir in dieser Stelle die Idee des Beweises zwar kurz, doch völlig klar angedeutet. . . . Wie verschieden aber ist diese Ableitung von einer nach Art des Euklid!' Hankel 1874: 208.

[19] 'Die Brahmanen [haben] eine von den Griechen wesentlich verschiedene Art zu denken; sie legen weniger Werth auf die Begründung, als auf das Resultat, weniger auf das Warum als das Wie; sie operieren mehr mit Ideen und Vorstellungen, als mit Begriffen. Was sie dadurch an Schärfe und Bestimmtheit verlieren, gewinnen sie wieder durch größere Tiefe und Weite.' Hankel 1874: 173.

[20] Pāṇini (*c.* fifth century BCE) is the author of the fundamental grammar of classical Sanskrit.

style as being intrinsically an impediment to mathematical progress, for he went as far as declaring that a combination of Indian ideas (imagination!) and Greek principles (logic!) would improve the contemporary teaching of geometry, by giving students a sharper mathematical intuition. Such a combination, he maintained, could also have helped to advance mathematical progress, but *logic*, in the end, *was wanting amongst the Indians*.

A very pervasive dogma among nineteenth-century historians of mathematics proclaimed the essentially geometrical character of the Greek mind, in contrast to that of the Orientals (Indian and Chinese), more akin to computational and algebraical operations. One consequence of this ideological assumption led Cantor to assume rigidly that all geometrical notions attested in India are necessarily influenced by the Greeks, because 'we should not and cannot expect a non-geometrical nation to have made essential progresses [in geometry]'.[21] For the *śulbasūtras*, Cantor had first postulated an influence through Hero of Alexandria,[22] but he had to retract his opinion in view of the evidence, put forward by Indologists, for the chronological impossibility of such a transmission.[23] He later postulated a possible influence from Mesopotamia.[24] The Greek influence on the geometry of Brahmagupta, for example, he considered certain, and again he had less a 'rigorous Euclid' in mind than a 'calculator' like Hero.[25] Cantor's mostly anti-Indian and Hellenocentrist attitude is evident in a letter to Paul Tannery dated 6 June 1880. Concerning an arithmetical method employed by Āryabhaṭa, which, although similar, differs from that of the Greek Thymaridas, he wrote: 'the matter is that Āryabhaṭa uses the method "epanthem of Thymaridas", which proves indeed that those scientific bandits of India did not content themselves with Greek geometry, but also appropriated Greek algebra, to which, it is true, they have added much'.[26]

Zeuthen's interpretation of Indian mathematical history stood closer to Hankel's views than those of Cantor. He agreed with both of them that it was only through Greek influence that the Indian computing skills (*Rechenfertigkeit*) could lead to real mathematical progress. What they

---

[21] 'Wesentliche Fortschritte dürfen und können wir von einem nicht geometrisch angelegten Volksgeiste nicht erwarten.' Cantor 1894: 612.

[22] Cantor 1894: 603–4.

[23] See Chapter 6 by Agathe Keller in this volume on the work of Thibault.

[24] 'Erinnern wir uns, wie vieles an Babylon mahnt!' Cantor 1907: 645 [3rd edn of Cantor 1894].

[25] Cantor 1894: 615; 1907: 657.

[26] 'C'est qu' Āryabhaṭa emploie la méthode dite «épanthème de Thymaridas», ce qui prouve bien que ces bandits scientifiques de l'Inde ne se contentaient guère de la géométrie grecque, mais qu'ils s'emparèrent encore de l'algèbre grecque, à laquelle, il est vrai, ils ajoutèrent beaucoup.' Tannery 1950: XIII 314; cf. Cantor 1894: 583–4.

inherited from the Greeks they developed in this direction without being burdened by the logical circumspection that characterizes the Greeks. In this manner, they could appropriate new rules and methods without necessarily understanding the underlying reason for their validity. The Indians could also go beyond Diophantus especially 'because of their less sensitive (*feinfühlig*) logic',[27] which made the transfer of existing rules from rational to irrational numbers easier than it would have been to a Greek.

Another example of Indian improvement over the Greeks is their use of negative numbers. In contrast to the limitations a 'cautious Greek' had to deal with, the 'calculating Indian' could take calculations 'just as they present themselves', as Zeuthen writes, without caring as to whether or not a quantity was positive or not; the Indians 'arranged themselves' with such negative quantities, simply qualifying them as 'debts'.[28] One sees here a notable example of the Hellenocentrist tendency to systematically distort the interpretation of non-Greek mathematical thought by reducing the associated cognitive processes to irrational fortuities.

Excursus: Hero and Diophantus – two 'orientalized' Greeks?

Another problematic aspect encountered by historians of mathematics was related to their interpretation of two 'anomalous' Greek mathematicians, Hero and Diophantus, whose styles, methods and preoccupations profoundly diverged from those of classical Greek mathematics.

The tone is set very clearly by Hankel when he writes about Diophantus that 'if his works were not written in Greek, it would occur to nobody to think that he sprang from Greek culture; his mind and spirit is too far away from that which revealed itself during the classical period of Greek mathematics.'[29] Hankel sees Diophantus' *Arithmetica*, from a historical point of view, as counting among the most significant mathematical works of Greek antiquity; he even added the surprising (over)statement that, in terms of originality and independence, his contributions stand perhaps higher than those of any other Greek mathematician![30] Hankel enthusiastically argued for the dependence of Diophantus on Indian sources which would have

[27] Zeuthen 1896: 279.
[28] Zeuthen 1896: 180.
[29] 'Wären seine Schriften nicht in griechischer Sprache geschrieben, niemand würde auf den Gedanken kommen, dass sie aus griechischer Cultur entsprossen wären; so weit ist sein Sinn und Geist von dem entfernt, der sich in der klassischen Zeit griechischer Mathematik geoffenbart hatte.' Hankel 1874: 157.
[30] Hankel 1874: 170.

been circulating in Alexandria before his lifetime.[31] With the decline of Hellenism, the rigidly systematical spirit of classical geometry was supplanted by a definitely *orientalized* form of mathematics exemplified by Diophantus' *Arithmetica*.

Siegmund Günther, whom we mentioned above, saw in Diophantus a 'double nature'. In his earlier works, such as the *Porismata*, it was possible to detect purely Hellenistic demonstration practices which had obliged him to employ laborious roundabouts. But by the time of composing the *Arithmetica*, Diophantus had experienced a true *emancipation* from his predecessors, notably in his use of symbolism and by his use of 'clever tricks', his 'boldness' and his 'skilfulness'.[32]

Zeuthen implicitly followed Hankel by refusing to exclude an Indian influence on Diophantus. Conversely, he wrote, later Indian authors may also have been influenced by the Greek algebraist. For this statement Zeuthen harvested the criticism of his friend Tannery:

> Mr. Zeuthen shows a strong tendency to go back to Hankel's thesis: the Greeks, wonderfully gifted in geometry, had no talent whatsoever for arithmetic. The composition of a work such as that of Diophantus can only be explained by supposing the influence, in Hellenized Egypt, of a race particularly apt to numerical computations, such as that of the Hindus.[33]

Tannery, in this case, shared the opinion of Cantor, to whom he wrote in 1885: 'As for the sources I assume for Diophantus, I would not want you to think that I am close to Hankel; I have always believed that Diophantus was exclusively Greek.'[34]

Compare Cantor: 'He belonged to his own time and to his own nation.'[35] Note that Nesselmann in 1842 had expressed views similar to those of Cantor and Tannery, and rejected Bombelli's (1579) earlier assumption of an Indian influence, to which he was led by mistaking a scholion of Maximus Planudes in a Vatican manuscript for a part of Diophantus' work.[36] It was

---

[31] Hankel 1874: 204–5.

[32] Günther 1908: 163–8.

[33] 'M. Zeuthen accuse une propension assez marquée à revenir à la thèse de Hankel: les Grecs, merveilleusement doués pour la Géométrie, ne l'étaient nullement pour l'Arithmétique; la rédaction d'un ouvrage comme celui de Diophante ne peut s'expliquer qu'en supposant l'influence, dans l'Egypte hellénisée, d'une race particulièrement apte aux calculs numériques, comme celle des Hindous.' Tannery 1950: xii 219.

[34] 'Quant aux sources où je crois que puisait Diophante, je ne voudrais pas un seul instant que vous pensiez que je me rapproche de Hankel; j'ai toujours cru que Diophante était exclusivement grec.' Tannery 1950: xiii 328.

[35] 'Er stand . . . innerhalb seiner Zeit, innerhalb seines Volkes.' Cantor 1894: 450.

[36] Nesselmann 1842: 284–5.

the Indologist Edward Strachey (1813, 1818) who first positively formulated the thesis that Hindu algebra had influenced Diophantus, a contention repeated, albeit in a much more nuanced fashion, by Colebrooke.[37]

The case of Hero of Alexandria – with his imaginative and practical
problem-solving approach without emphasis on demonstrations – was less
problematic.[38] Cantor had argued for Old Egyptian influence, a hypothesis
– already insinuated by Hankel[39] – that nobody took the trouble to challenge.[40] In any case, there was a certain uneasiness in interpreting Hero and
Diophantus. The reason for our excursus is connected with the following: if
Greek mathematics can be essentially opposed to an Oriental style, how can
it be that two important Greek authors are basically 'oriental' in style? This
observation could not really undermine the main thesis: both authors were
simply given a status of exceptions . . .

Excursus 2: Cantor on inductive demonstrations in Ancient Egypt

A similar pattern is discernible in Cantor's speculations about the geometrical knowledge supposedly acquired by Thales in Ancient Egypt,
and the peculiar deductive shaping he, as a Greek, immediately conferred
on the primitive rules and demonstrations of the Egyptians. Cantor had
collaborated with Eisenlohr in his efforts to decipher the Rhind Papyrus,
a translation of which was published in Leipzig in 1877.

In the geometrical problems of Ahmes, formulae are given as such,
without derivation. But we are dealing with a book of exercises, Cantor
says, so we should not ask for something which cannot be contained in
it, namely derivations (*Ableitungsverfahren*) of the formulae. Ahmes must
have taken these derivations from another, now lost, theoretical textbook.[41]
This hypothetical 'theoretical' textbook on geometry Cantor imagines to
have contained primitive inductive demonstrations or even illustrative
demonstrations (*Beweisführung durch Anschauung*), as with the Indians.[42]
But to assume strict geometrical demonstrations is not necessary in the
context of Egyptian mathematics.[43]

---

[37] C1817.
[38] Günther 1908: 217.
[39] Hankel 1874: 85. Hankel, who only had access to a summary description of the Rhind Papyrus
by Birch (1868), recognized the similarities with Hero but was not sure whether the papyrus
was older than the Alexandrian's lifetime or not.
[40] Cantor 1894: 365–7.
[41] Cantor 1894: 53; 1907: 91, 113.
[42] Cantor 1907: 113.
[43] Cantor 1907: 106.

Thus Egyptian theory is inductive, and Greek theory is deductive. Thales, when he obtained his geometrical knowledge in Egypt, must have offered different kinds of demonstration than the Egyptians did (for example, the theorem stating that the diameter divides the circle in two equal parts), for the simple reason that he had a Greek mind! Cantor puts it as follows:

As a Greek he generalized, as a pupil of Egypt he grasped through the senses what he then made comprehensible to the Greeks. It was an ethnic characteristic [*Stammeseigentümlichkeit*] of the Greeks to get to the bottom of all things, and, starting from practical needs, to reach speculative explanations. Nothing of the sort with the Egyptians.[44]

With the Egyptians, Cantor speculates, either the figure sufficed for the proof, or it was done through computation of the areas of both semicircles according to the same, possibly uncomprehended, rule.

The problematic status of Islamic mathematics

The confrontation with Arabic mathematical writings and the bibliographical information about it forced historians of mathematics to adopt a different approach than with Indian mathematics. First it became increasingly obvious that a large number of Greek mathematical works, including virtually all major ones, had been not only translated into Arabic but also studied, commented upon, adapted and transformed. Greek mathematics had been thoroughly assimilated within Islamic culture. On the other hand, Indian influences were obvious in several works, such as the arithmetic of al-Khwārizmī, or (it was presumed) in the treatise on practical geometrical constructions by Abū al-Wafāʾ. How was it possible, then, to treat Islamic mathematics within the category 'Oriental'? Which status did historians of mathematics grant to Arabic mathematics? Another, related problem was of course the question of its originality. In this respect late nineteenth-century historians of mathematics proved surprisingly severe, in spite of the excellent works of Franz Woepcke.

The question of originality

Although he presented an excellent summary of the available evidence (mostly thanks to Woepcke's works), Hankel claimed at the outset that the Arabs had added little to what they had received from the Greeks and the

---

[44] 'Als Grieche hat er verallgemeinert, als Schüler Aegyptens sinnlich erfasst, was er dann den Griechen wieder fassbarer gemacht hat. Es war eine griechische Stammeseigentümlichkeit, den Dingen auf den Grund zu gehen, vom praktischen Bedürfnisse zu speculativen Erörterungen zu gelangen. Nicht so den Aegyptern.' Cantor 1894: 140.

Indians. Of course, it was no longer possible, at the end of the nineteenth century, to maintain the old myth of preservation. But this myth was replaced by another version that was as economical as possible: Cantor formulated it this way: '[The Arabs] have been capable not only to preserve, but also to expand the treasures entrusted to them.'[45] These intellectual treasures, however, were regarded by Cantor as *fundamentally foreign* elements, which could only live in the artificial milieu of the princely courts.[46]

Symptomatically, Hankel, Cantor and Zeuthen found only few examples of original and independent contributions by the Arabs. Zeuthen, indeed, introduced his chapter on Arabic mathematics by mentioning that he 'would have liked to emphasize the full extent and value of the mathematical works of the Arabs, in order to avoid negative conclusions from the relatively few positive results achieved beyond those known to the Greeks'.[47] This fact, he says, provides the very reason for restricting his presentation to a few selected examples of the kinds of works the Arabs did. In this connection we should mention that, in 1888, Zeuthen had offered to the readers of *Bibliotheca Mathematica* a question that implicitly sought to undermine Woepcke's view of the originality of Islamic contributions to algebra (especially the application of conic sections to the resolution of algebraic equations).[48] Zeuthen suspected that the Greeks had already applied these techniques to the same algebraic problems, thereby raising serious doubts as to whether the Arabs had really been innovative in this regard.

The obsessive search for influences

Otherwise, Hankel and especially Cantor were animated by a desire to identify in Islamic mathematics as many foreign influences they could, even on the basis of tenuous similarities. Thus Hankel did not hesitate to assign to the Indians a proof of a certain identity involving geometric series recorded by al-Karajī, even though Woepcke had been unable to detect any Indian influence on al-Karajī in general.[49] In the same manner, he saw nothing in the indeterminate analysis of al-Karajī that went beyond Diophantus.[50]

---

[45] '[Die Araber] haben das Ihnen anvertraute Gut nicht nur zu bewahren, auch zu vermehren gewusst.' Cantor 1894: 771.
[46] Cantor 1894: 741–2; 1907: 786–7.
[47] Zeuthen 1896: 297.
[48] Zeuthen 1888.
[49] Woepcke 1853: 61–2; Hankel 1874: 42.
[50] Hankel 1874: 270.

Identifying the origin of al-Khwārizmī's algebra presented more serious difficulties, since it differed from both the Greek and Indian algebraic traditions. But for Cantor, Islamic algebra could under no circumstances be autochthonous: it could only feature Greek and Indian elements, so he assumed an amalgam of both traditions. In general, however, Cantor was convinced that there existed two separate schools in Islamic mathematics, bringing about a fundamental opposition between the disciples of Indian methods and those, more numerous, who strictly adhered to the Greek tradition.[51] Cantor's entire section on Islamic mathematics shows precisely his constant concern for associating every single mathematician or result within one of the two groups.

How did the Arabs handle the Greek axiomatic–deductive methods?

Now we come to the more crucial question: were the 'Arabs' up to dealing with Greek thought? How did 'Oriental' mathematicians come to terms with the Euclidean axiomatic–deductive method? Hankel described the nature of Euclid's influence on Islamic mathematical practice with the following words:

In the same way, one zealously occupied himself with the logical analysis of his (Euclid's) method, his definitions and axioms, and one used his demonstrations for the exemplification of the rules of formal logic in a similarly pedantic manner as what our German logicians still liked to do almost until our century.[52]

Thus the 'Greek oversubtlety', as Hankel says (*griechische Spitzfindigkeit*), was a level too high for the Arabs. Its perversion he exemplified with [pseudo-]Ṭūsī's vain attempt to prove Euclid's postulate of parallels.[53] To this observation Hankel adds the following statement concerning the status and use of demonstrations in Arabic treatises:

Despite their even doctrinary acquaintance with the demonstrative method [of the Greeks], the Arabs, most of the time, have refrained from providing the demonstrations, and have dogmatically strung the theorems and rules together, exactly as the

---

[51] Cantor 1894: 718–19.

[52] Hankel 1874: 272.

[53] The Arabic text of a recension of Euclid's *Elements* wrongly attributed to Naṣīr al-Dīn al-Ṭūsī had been printed in Rome in 1586 and was available through Wallis' analysis thereof in his history of algebra, his interpretation being possible thanks to the collaboration of orientalist Pococke. See Molland 1994 and Stedall 2001.

Indians used to do in their siddhantas. Were they motivated by a concern for the shortness and corresponding cheapness of their books?[54]

Cantor's judgement was not as severe as Hankel's, but he was nevertheless convinced that the practice of demonstration had almost a character of exception among Muslim mathematicians.[55] Confronted with a highly original treatise of practical geometry by Abū al-Wafā' (then known only through a mutilated Persian version which Woepcke had summarized), Cantor had no recourse to contextualization to explain the absence of demonstrations – as he did in the case of the geometrical part of the Rhind Papyrus, where he accepted it precisely because of the practical nature of the work. For him Abū al-Wafā''s treatise recalled Indian geometry, so that 'one would almost expect as a proof [of the validity of a particular construction] the request "look!", with which Indian geometers are satisfied to conclude their construction procedures.'[56] Thus for him there was no doubt that this work was an example of *Anschauungsgeometrie*, so thoroughly Indian in style that no deductive demonstrations, even on the part of one of the best Muslim mathematicians, could be possibly assumed.

Epilogue

For Zeuthen, the breakthrough in the history of mathematics occurred with the resolution of third-degree equations by means of roots (Cardano and Tartaglia), an achievement that closes the medieval periodization of mathematics and announces the rapid advances made thereafter, modelled on and inspired by a close study of Greek mathematics. Zeuthen's periodization explains why nearly three-quarters of his book (245 pages out of 332 in the first German edition) is devoted to Greek mathematics.

In view of this, it is probably erroneous to assume that Zeuthen and his colleagues saw the practice of mathematical demonstration as the key to mathematical progress. The Muslims had been competent and respectful

---

[54] 'Trotz dieser selbst doktrinären Bekanntschaft mit der demonstrativen Methode haben die Araber sich meistens aller Beweise enthalten und Lehrsätze wie Regeln dogmatisch aneinandergereiht, nicht anders als es die Inder in ihren Siddhanten zu thun pflegen. Hat sie dazu die Rücksicht auf Kürze und entsprechend grössere Wohlfeilheit ihrer Bücher bewogen?' Hankel 1874: 273.

[55] Commenting on an original geometrical problem solved by al-Kūhī in which the latter inserted a rigorous proof with diorismos, Cantor noted that 'in general the imitators of the Greeks – Arabs not excluded – considered [this practice] by no means with the same regularity' ['... was die Nachahmner der Griechen im allgemeinen – die Araber nicht ausgeschlossen – keineswegs mit gleicher Regelmässigkeit zu beachten pflegten']. Cantor 1894: 705.

[56] Cantor 1894: 700; cf. 709–10.

students of the Greeks, and, although relatively very little was known around 1900, their works revealed – even to the least interested historians such as Tannery – a sophisticated mathematical practice within which demonstration, closely following the Greek model, played an important role. Yet, it was thought, this assimilation of Greek mathematical thinking and practice did not instil much progress among them; the Arabs' contributions, however extensive and honest they may have been, did not bring about any major breakthrough, nothing comparable to what would happen in sixteenth- and seventeenth-century Europe. For the 'Arabs' were implicitly considered as immature custodians of a higher knowledge, who could not properly deal with it; being mere imitators of a foreign tradition, they were unable to reach the critical level beyond which real progress could have been initiated. For Zeuthen, the Eastern Arabs had been unable to emancipate themselves from the rigid geometrical approach of the Greek; and the Western Arabs, who supposedly did liberate themselves from this approach, still remained 'too reverential' toward the Greeks.[57]

On the other hand, the Indians, in spite of the supposed laxness and lack of rigour of their mathematical practice and the primitiveness of the few demonstrations revealed in their works, had indeed achieved results superior to those of the Arabs in arithmetic and algebra. Some authors even went as far as comparing this 'Indian' style of mathematical practice with the intuitive works of certain modern mathematicians, probably because it was realized that absolute rigour had not played a fundamental role in early modern Europe.[58] Few believed that a stringent axiomatic–deductive system was a necessary condition for mathematical discovery. Nevertheless, historians of mathematics unanimously insisted that it was precisely *the lack of a logical, rigorous system* of mathematical thought similar to the Greek one that prohibited any further progress in India. Imagination alone could at best generate haphazard discoveries. The refusal of systematic rationality to the Orientals was saved whenever one encountered anything ingenious in their mathematics by explaining it through their having recourse to 'tricks, dodges' (*Kunstgriffe*), as in the case of al-Bīrūnī's solution of the chessboard problem.[59] For Tannery, theory provided with demonstration was the

---

[57] Zeuthen 1896: 314.

[58] Günther (1908: 127) says of Hero that he is a sort of 'antique Euler'. Hankel (1874: 202–3) compares Bhāskara's numerical methods, especially in his solution of the so-called Pell equation, with those of modern mathematicians. On the relatively unimportant role of mathematical proofs (compared to the concern for 'exactness of contructions') in early modern Europe, see Bos 2001: 8.

[59] Cantor 1894: 713–14.

distinguishing feature between pre-scientific and scientific mathematics;[60] but Indian mathematics, although categorized under the 'scientific' genus by all historians of mathematics, featured only primitive, indeed pre-scientific, kinds of proofs. This is an apparent paradox. Had 'Oriental' mathematics a special status? Tannery certainly perceived it this way. In fact, he and his colleagues were convinced that no civilization other than the Greek ever attained the scientific level autonomously. Thus, the pre-scientific mathematics of India only became scientific after it had been nurtured by Greek influence. Indian mathematics, however, remained stigmatized with a special and incomplete status of scientificity, because it had only imperfectly assimilated the Greek model.

Concluding remarks

Nineteenth-century historians of mathematics did not claim the practice of demonstration only for the Greeks, but they insisted on its character of exception in 'Oriental' mathematics. (Consequently, much of twentieth-century historiography simply disregarded the evidence already available, and returned to the simplified view that a concern for proof and rigour never existed outside of ancient Greece and modern Europe – perhaps with the exception of medieval Islam.) The criterion that really allowed a separation of 'Western' from 'non-Western' science was one of *style*: systematic and axiomatic–deductive in one case, intuitive (at best inductive), illustrative and unreflected in the other.[61] The ideology associated with this fundamental separation, even though its roots could be traced back to the Renaissance, did not crystallize until late in the nineteenth century. I will now conclude with a short sketch of the ideological landscape that favoured its dogmatic formulation.

   With the accomplishment of the imperialist enterprise and the general confidence that space, people and nature could be successfully dominated, Western Europeans acquired the ultimate certainty of their superiority over the rest of the world. It is no wonder, then, that the Romantic and Orientalist enthusiasm, omnipresent in the first half of the century, was quickly annihilated. Dismissing previous attempts to proclaim the originality of 'Oriental' science and consolidating the integrity of 'Western'

---

[60] Tannery 1950: x 25.

[61] This idea is still common today; a massive argumentation in favour of the distinctiveness of the Western scientific style can be found in Crombie 1994. For a critical view, see Hart 1999.

science was, indeed, a major characteristic of scholarship in the history of science during the last quarter of the nineteenth century. The views became increasingly and consensually Helleno- and Eurocentrist, not in the ingenuous and instinctive manner of previous generations, but in systematic and dogmatic ways. In this context we can mention the influence of Comtian positivism, and the rise, in some milieus, of racist and antisemitic theories. The famous lecture 'L'Islam et la science' delivered by Ernest Renan at the Sorbonne in 1883 proclaimed the scientific inferiority of Semitic races as opposed to Indo-Aryan ones, and emphasized the essentially antagonistic nature of the Islamic faith toward science.[62] The works of Pierre Duhem on ancient Greek and medieval Latin cosmology promulgated the relative insignificance of extra-European science.[63] Even the Arabist Bernard Carra de Vaux, a close collaborator of Tannery, found recognition mainly for his work on Greek technological works preserved only in Arabic, and contributed an appendix to Tannery's *Recherches sur l'histoire de l'astronomie ancienne* in which he misinterpreted one of the most interesting chapters of Islamic planetary theory by reducing it to an example of the way in which, when it attempted to be original, Islamic science revealed only 'weakness' and 'pettiness'.[64] Such was indeed the dominant perspective in Europe around 1900 when the discipline of history of science was established as an international network of scholars under the aegis of Paul Tannery. History of science sought to and succeeded in promoting and defending the values and uniqueness of Western civilization.[65]

Bibliography

Arneth, A. (1852) *Geschichte der reinen Mathematik in ihrer Beziehung zur Entwicklung des menschlichen Geistes.* Stuttgart.

Biot, J.-B. (1841) [Review of] '*Traité des instruments astronomiques des Arabes,* traduit par J. J. Sédillot', *Journal des Savants* 1841: 513–20, 602–10 and 659–79.

Bos, H. (2001) *Redefining Geometrical Exactness: Descartes' Transformation of the Early Modern Concept of Construction.* New York.

Cantor, M. (1894) *Vorlesungen über Geschichte der Mathematik, vol. I, Von den ältesten Zeiten bis zum Jahre 1200 n. Chr,* 2nd edn. Leipzig.
      (1907) = 3rd edn of Cantor 1894.

---

[62] Renan 1883. Cf. Tannery 1950: x 391.
[63] On Duhem's historiography of Islamic science, see Ragep 1990.
[64] Carra de Vaux 1893: 338.
[65] See Pyenson 1993.

Carra de Vaux B., (1893) 'Les sphères célestes selon Nasîr-Eddîn Attûsî', in *Recherches sur l'histoire de l'astronomie ancienne*, ed. P. Tannery. Paris: 337–61.

Crombie, A. (1994) *Styles of Scientific Thinking in the European Tradition: The History of Argument and Explanation Especially in the Mathematical and Biomedical Sciences and Arts*, 3 vols. London.

Dauben, J. W. and C. J. Scriba (eds.) (2002) *Writing the History of Mathematics: Its Historical Development*. Basel.

Günther, S. (1908) *Geschichte der Mathematik, vol. 1, Von den ältesten Zeiten bis Cartesius*. Leipzig.

Hankel, H. (1874) *Zur Geschichte der Mathematik im Alterthum und Mittelalter*. Leipzig.

Hart, R. (1999) 'Beyond science and civilization: a post-Needham critique', *East Asian Science, Technology, and Medicine* **16**: 88–114.

Hofmann, J. E. (2008) 'Cantor, Moritz Benedict', in *Complete Dictionary of Scientific Biography*, www.encyclopedia.com.

Martzloff, J.-C. (1997) *A History of Chinese Mathematics*. Berlin.

Michaels, A. (1978) *Beweisverfahren in der vedischen Sakralgeometrie: Ein Beitrag zur Entstehungsgeschichte von Wissenschaft*. Wiesbaden.

Molland, G. (1994) 'The limited lure of Arabic mathematics', in *The 'Arabick' Interest of the Natural Philosophers in Seventeenth-Century England*, ed. G. A. Russell. Leiden: 215–23.

Nesselmann, G. H. F. (1842) *Versuch einer kritischen Geschichte der Algebra der Griechen*. Berlin.

Playfair, J. (1817) 'On the algebra and arithmetic of the Hindus' [Review of C1817], *Edinburgh Review* **39**: 141–63.

Pyenson, L. (1993) 'Prerogatives of European intellect: historians of science and the promotion of Western civilization', *History of Science* **31**: 289–315.

Ragep, J. (1990) 'Duhem, the Arabs, and the history of cosmology', *Synthèse* **83**: 201–14.

Renan, E. (1883) 'L'islamisme et la science', in *Oeuvres complètes*, ed. H. Psichari (1947–61), 10 vols., vol. ɪ (1947). Paris: 945–60.

Stedall, J. (2001) 'Of our own nation: John Wallis's account of mathematical learning in medieval England', *Historia Mathematica* **28**: 73–122.

Tannery, P. (1912–50) *Mémoires scientifiques*, 17 vols. Toulouse.

Zeuthen, H. G. (1888) 'Question 20', *Bibliotheca Mathematica* **2**: 63.
  (1896) *Geschichte der Mathematik im Altertum und Mittelalter*. Copenhagen.

8 | The pluralism of Greek 'mathematics'

G. E. R. LLOYD

Greek *mathēmatikē*, as has often been pointed out, is far from being an exact equivalent to our term 'mathematics'. The noun *mathēma* comes from the verb *manthanein* that has the entirely general meaning of 'to learn'. A *mathēma* can then be any branch of learning, or anything learnt, as when in Herodotus (1 207) Croesus refers to the *mathēmata* – what he has learnt – from his own bitter experiences. So the *mathēmatikos* is, strictly speaking, the person who is fond of learning in general, as indeed it is used in Plato's *Timaeus* at 88c where the point at issue is the need to strike a balance between the cultivation of the intellect and that of the body, the principle that later became encapsulated in the dictum '*mens sana in corpore sano*'. Yet Plato also recognizes certain special branches of the *mathēmata*, as when in the *Laws* at 817e the Athenian Stranger speaks of those that are appropriate for free citizens as those that relate to numbers, to the measurement of lengths, breadths and depths, and to the study of the stars, in other words, very roughly, arithmetic, geometry and astronomy. In Hellenistic Greek *mathēmatikos* is used more often of the student of the heavens in particular (whether what we should call the astronomer or the astrologer) than of the mathematician in general in our sense.

Whether we should think of either what we call mathematics or what we call philosophy as well-defined disciplines before Plato is doubtful. I have previously discussed the problems so far as philosophy is concerned.[1] Those whom modern scholars conventionally group together as 'the Presocratic philosophers' are a highly heterogeneous set of individuals, most of whom would not have recognized most of the others as engaged in the same inquiry as themselves. Their interests spanned in some, but not all, cases what we call natural philosophy (the inquiry into nature), cosmology, ontology, epistemology, philosophy of language and ethics, but the ways in which those interests were distributed among the different individuals concerned varied considerably.

It is true that we have one good fifth-century BCE example of a thinker most of whose work (to judge from the very limited information we have

[1] Lloyd 2006b.

about that) related to, or used, one or other branch of mathematics, namely Hippocrates of Chios. He was responsible not just for important particular geometrical studies, on the quadrature of lunules, but also, maybe, for a first attempt at systematizing geometrical knowledge, though whether he can be credited with a book entitled (like Euclid's) *Elements* is more doubtful. Furthermore in his other investigations, such as his account of comets, reported by Aristotle in the *Meteorology*, he used geometrical arguments to explain the comet's tail as a reflection.

Yet most of those to whom both ancient and modern histories of pre-Euclidean Greek mathematics devote most attention were far from just 'mathematicians' in either the Greek or the English sense. Philolaus, Archytas, Democritus and Eudoxus all made notable contributions to one or other branches of *mathēmatikē*, but all also had developed interests in one or more of the studies we should call epistemology, physics, cosmology and ethics. A similar diversity of interests is also present in what we are told of the work of such more shadowy figures as Thales or Pythagoras. The evidence for Thales' geometrical theorems is doubtful, but Aristotle (who underlines the limitations of his own knowledge about Thales) treats him as interested in what he, Aristotle, termed the material cause of things, as well as in soul or life. Pythagoras' own involvement in geometry and in harmonics has again been contested,[2] and the more reliably attested of his interests relate to the organization of entities in opposite pairs, and, again, to soul.

These remarks have a bearing on the controversy on the question of whether deductive argument, in Greece, originated in 'philosophy' and was then exported to 'mathematics',[3] or whether within mathematics it was an original development internal to that discipline.[4] Clearly when neither 'philosophy' nor 'mathematics' were well-defined disciplines, it is hard to resolve that issue in the terms in which it was originally posed, although, to be sure, the question remains as to whether the Eleatic use of *reductio* arguments did or did not influence the deployment of arguments of a similar type by such figures as Eudoxus.

If we consider the evidence for the investigation of what Knorr, in other studies,[5] called the three 'traditional' mathematical problems, of squaring the circle, the duplication of the cube and the trisection of an angle, those who figure in our sources exhibit very varied profiles. Among the ten or so individuals who are said to have tackled the problem of squaring the circle

---

[2] Burkert 1972.
[3] Szabó 1978.
[4] Knorr 1981.
[5] Knorr 1986.

it is clear that ideas about what counts as a good, or even a proper, method of doing so differed.[6] At *Physics* 185a16–17 Aristotle distinguishes between fallacious quadratures that are the business of the geometer to refute, and those where that is not the case. In the former category comes a quadrature 'by way of segments' which the commentators interpret as lunules and forthwith associate with the most famous investigator of lunules, whom I have already mentioned, namely Hippocrates of Chios. Yet even though there is another text in Aristotle that accuses Hippocrates of some mistake in quadratures (*On Sophistical Refutations* 171b14–16), it may be doubted whether Hippocrates committed any fallacy in this area.[7] In the detailed account that Simplicius gives us of his successful quadrature of four specific types of lunules, the reasoning is throughout impeccable. Quite what fallacy Aristotle detected then remains somewhat of a mystery.

But two other attempts are also referred to by Aristotle and dismissed either as 'sophistic' or as not the job of the geometer to disprove. Bryson is named at *On Sophistical Refutations* 171b16–18 as having produced an argument that falls in the former category: according to the commentators, it appealed to a principle about what could be counted as equals that was quite general, and thus far it would fit Aristotle's criticism that the reasoning was not proper to the subject-matter.

Antiphon's quadrature by contrast is said not to be for the geometer to refute (*Physics* 185a16–17) on the grounds that it breached the geometrical principle of infinite divisibility. It appears that Antiphon proceeded by inscribing increasingly many-sided regular polygons in a circle until – so he claimed – the polygon coincided with the circle (which had then been squared). The particular interest of this procedure lies in its obvious similarity to the so-called but misnamed method of exhaustion introduced by Eudoxus in the fourth century. This too uses inscribed polygons and claims that the difference between the polygon and the circle can be made as small as one likes. It precisely does *not* exhaust the circle. If Antiphon did indeed claim that after a *finite* number of steps the polygon coincided with the circle, then that indeed breached the continuum assumption. But of course later mathematicians were to claim that the circle could nevertheless be treated as identical with the infinitely-sided inscribed rectilinear figure. Other solutions were proposed by other figures, by a certain Hippias for instance and by Dinostratus. Whether the Hippias in question is the famous sophist of that name has been doubted, precisely on the grounds that the

---

[6] Mueller 1982 gives a measured account.
[7] Lloyd 2006a reviews the question.

device attributed to him, the so-called quadratrix, is too sophisticated for the fifth century.

Although much remains obscure about the precise claims made in different attempts at quadrature, it is abundantly clear first that different investigators adopted different assumptions about the legitimacy of different methods, and second that those investigators were a heterogeneous group. Some were not otherwise engaged in mathematical studies at all, at least to judge from the evidence available to us. An allusion in Aristophanes (*Birds* 1001–5) suggests that the topic of squaring the circle had by the end of the fifth century become a matter of general interest, or at least the possible subject of anti-intellectual jokes in comedy.

Among those I have mentioned in relation to quadratures several are generally labelled 'sophists', this too a notoriously indeterminate category and one that evidently cannot be seen as an alternative to 'mathematician'. As is well known Plato does not always use the term pejoratively, even though he certainly has severe criticisms to offer, both intellectual and moral, of several of the principal figures he calls 'sophists'. Yet Plato himself provides plenty of evidence of the range of interests, both mathematical and non-mathematical, of some of those he names as such. As regards the Hippias he calls a sophist, those interests included astronomy, geometry, arithmetic, but also, for instance, linguistics: however, whether the music he also taught related to the mathematical analysis of harmonics or was a matter of the more general aesthetic evaluation of different modes is unclear. Again, the fragments that are extant from Antiphon's treatise *Truth* deal with questions in cosmology, meteorology, geology and biology.[8] Protagoras, who is said by Plato to have been the first to have taught for a fee, famously claimed, according to Aristotle *Metaphysics* 998a2–4, that the tangent does not touch the circle at a point, a meta-mathematical objection that he raised against the geometers.

Thus far I have suggested some of the variety within what the Greeks themselves thought of as encompassed by *mathēmatikē* together with some of the heterogeneity of those who were described as engaged in 'mathematical' inquiries. But in view of some persistent stereotypes of Greek mathematics it is important to underline the further fundamental disagreements (1) about the classification of the mathematical sciences and the hierarchy within them, (2) about the question of their usefulness, and

---

[8] The identification of the author of this treatise with the Antiphon whose quadrature is criticized by Aristotle is less disputed than the question of whether the sophist is identical with the author called Antiphon whose *Tetralogies* are extant.

especially (3) on what counts as proper, valid, arguments and methods. Let me deal briefly with the first two questions before exemplifying the third a little more fully.

(1) Already in the late fifth and early fourth centuries BCE a divergence of opinion is reported as between Philolaus and Archytas. According to Plutarch (*Table Talk* 8 2 1, 718e) Philolaus insisted that geometry is the primary mathematical study (its 'metropolis'). But Archytas privileged arithmetic under the rubric of *logistikē* (reckoning, calculation, Fr. 4). The point is not trivial, since how precisely geometry and arithmetic could be considered to form a unity was problematic. According to the normal Greek conception, 'number' is defined as an integer greater than 1. In this view, arithmetic dealt with discrete entities. But geometry treated of an infinitely divisible continuum. Nevertheless both were regularly included as branches of 'mathematics', sister branches, indeed, as Archytas called them (Fr. 1). The question of the status of other studies was more contested. For Aristotle, who had, as we shall see, a distinctive philosophy of mathematics, such disciplines as optics, harmonics and astronomy were 'the more physical of the *mathēmata*' (*Physics* 194a7–8). The issue of 'mechanics' was particularly controversial. According to the view of Hero, as reported by Pappus (*Collection* Book 8 1–2), mechanics had two parts, the theoretical which consisted of geometry, arithmetic, astronomy and physics, and the practical that dealt with such matters as the construction of pulleys, war machines and the like. However, a somewhat different view was propounded by Proclus (*Commentary on Euclid's Elements* 41.3 – 42.8) when he included what we should call statics, as well as pneumatics, under 'mechanics'.

(2) That takes me to my next topic, the issue of the usefulness of mathematics, howsoever construed. Already in the classical period there was a clear division between those who sought to argue that mathematics should be studied for its practical utility, and those who saw it rather as an intellectual, theoretical discipline. In Xenophon's *Memorabilia* 4 7 2–5 Socrates is made to insist that geometry is useful for land measurement, astronomy for calendar regulation and navigation, and so on, and he there dismissed the more theoretical or abstract aspects of those subjects. Similarly Isocrates too distinguished the practical and the theoretical sides of mathematical studies and in certain circumstances favoured the former (11 22–3, 12 26–8, 15 261–5). Yet Plato of course took precisely the opposite view. It is not for practical, mundane, reasons that mathematics is worth studying, but rather as a training for the soul in abstract thought. But even some who emphasized practical utility sometimes defined that very broadly. It is striking that

in the passage just quoted from Pappus he included both the construction of models of planetary motion and that of the marvellous gadgets of the 'wonder-workers' among 'the most *necessary* of the mechanical arts from the point of view of the needs of life'. Meanwhile the most ambitious claims for the all-encompassing importance of 'mathematics' were made by the neo-Pythagorean Iamblichus at the turn of the third and fourth centuries CE. He argued in *On the Common Mathematical Science* (ch. 32: 93.11–94.21) that mathematics was the source of understanding in *every* mode of knowledge, including in the study of nature and of change.

(3) From among the many examples that illustrate how the question of the proper method in mathematics was disputed let me select just five.

(3.1) In a famous and influential passage in his *Life of Marcellus* (ch. 14, cf. *Table Talk* 8 2 1, 718ef) Plutarch interprets Plato as having banned mechanical methods from geometry on the grounds that these corrupted and destroyed the pure excellence of that subject, and it is true that Plato had protested that to treat mathematical objects as subject to movement was absurd. The first to introduce such degenerate methods, according to Plutarch, were Eudoxus and Archytas. Indeed we know from a report in Eutocius (*Commentary on Archimedes Sphere and Cylinder* 2, 3 84.12–88.2) that Archytas solved the problem of finding two mean proportionals on which the duplication of a cube depended by means of a complex three-dimensional kinematic construction involving the intersection of three surfaces of revolution, a right cone, a cylinder and a tore. Plutarch even goes on to suggest that Archimedes himself agreed with the Platonic view (as Plutarch represents it) that the work of an 'engineer' was ignoble and vulgar. Most scholars are agreed first that that most probably misrepresents Archimedes, and secondly that few practising mathematicians would have shared Plutarch's expressed opinion as to the illegitimacy of mechanical methods in geometry.

(3.2) My second example comes from Archimedes himself and concerns precisely how he endorsed the usefulness of mechanics, as a method of discovery at least. In his *Method* (2 428.18–430.18) he sets out what he describes as his 'mechanical' method which depends first on an assumption of indivisibles and then on imagining geometrical figures as balanced against one another about a fulcrum. The method is then applied to get the area of a segment of a parabola, but while Archimedes accepts the method as a method of discovery, he puts it that the results have thereafter to be demonstrated rigorously using the method of exhaustion standard throughout Greek geometry. At the same time the method *is* useful 'even for the proofs of the theorems themselves' in a way he explains (*Method*

428.29–430.1): 'it is of course easier, when we have previously acquired, by the method, some knowledge of the questions, to supply the proof, than it is to find it without any previous knowledge'. We should note that what is at stake is not just the question of admissible methods, but that of what counts as a proper demonstration.

(3.3) For my third example I turn to Hero of Alexandria.[9] Although he frequently refers to Archimedes as if he provided a model for demonstration, his own procedures sharply diverge, on occasion, from his. In the *Metrica*, for instance, he sometimes gives an arithmetized demonstration of geometrical propositions, that is he includes concrete numbers in his exposition. Moreover in the *Pneumatica* especially he allows exhibiting a result to count as a proof. Thus at 1 16.16–26 and at 26.25–28 he gives what we would call an empirical demonstration of propositions in pneumatics, expressing his own clear preference for such by contrast with the merely plausible reasoning used by the more theoretically inclined investigators. In both respects his procedures breach the rules laid down by Aristotle in the *Posterior Analytics*, both in that he permits 'perceptible' proofs and does not base his arguments on indemonstrable starting points and in that he moves from one genus of mathematics to another. If we think of precedents for his procedures, then they have more in common with the suggestion that Socrates makes to the slave-boy in Plato's *Meno* (84a), namely that if he cannot give an account of the solution to the problem of doubling the square, he can point to the relevant line.

(3.4) Fourthly there is Ptolemy's redeployment of the old dichotomy between demonstration and conjecture in two contexts in the opening books of the *Syntaxis* and of the *Tetrabiblos*. In the former (*Syntaxis* 1 1, 1 6.11–7.4) he discusses the difference between *mathēmatikē*, 'physics' and 'theology'. The last two studies are conjectural, 'physics' because of the instability of what it deals with, 'theology' because of the obscurity of its subject. *Mathēmatikē*, by contrast, which here certainly includes the mathematical astronomy that he is about to expound in the *Syntaxis*, alone of these three is demonstrative, since it is based on the incontrovertible methods of geometry and arithmetic. Whatever we may think about the difficulties that Ptolemy himself registers, in practice, in living up to this ideal when it comes, for instance, to his account of the movements of the planets in latitude, it is clear what his ideal is. Moreover when in the *Tetrabiblos* (1 1, 3.5–25, 1 2, 8.1–20) he speaks of the other branch of the study of the heavens, that which engages not in the prediction of the movements of the

---

[9] Cf. Tybjerg 2000: ch. 3.

heavenly bodies, but in that of events on earth on their basis – astrology, in other words, on our terms – that study is downgraded precisely on the grounds that it cannot deliver demonstration. It is conjectural, though he would claim that it is based on tried and tested assumptions.

(3.5) Fifthly and finally there are Pappus' critical remarks, in the opening chapters (1–23) of Book 3 of his *Collection*, on certain procedures based on approximations that had been used in tackling the problem of finding two mean proportionals in order to solve the Delian problem, of doubling the cube.[10] Although certain stepwise approximations can yield a result that is correct, they fall short, in Pappus' view, in rigour. Pappus himself distinguishes between planar, solid and linear problems in geometry and insists that each has its own procedures appropriate for the subject matter in question.

What we find in all of the cases I have taken is a sensitivity not just to the correctness of results or the truth of conclusions, but to the appropriateness or otherwise of the methods used to obtain them. It is not enough just to know the truth of a theorem: nor is it enough to have *some* means of justifying the claim to such knowledge. No: what is required is that the method of justification be the correct one for the field of inquiry concerned according to the particular standards of correctness of the author in question. That is the recurrent demand: yet it is clearly not the case that all Greek investigators who would have considered themselves *mathēmatikoi* agreed on what is appropriate in each type of case or had uniform views on what counts as a demonstration.

Similar second-order disputes recur in most other areas of inquiry that the Greeks engaged in, and this too is worth illustrating since it suggests that the phenomenon we have described in mathematics is symptomatic of more general tendencies in Greek thought. Sometimes we find such disagreements *within* what is broadly the same discipline, sometimes *across* different disciplines. In medicine the Hippocratic treatise *On Ancient Medicine* provides examples of both kinds. The author first castigates other doctors who try to base medical practice on what he calls 'hypotheses', arbitrary postulates such as 'the hot', 'the cold', 'the wet', 'the dry' and anything else they fancy (*CMG* 1 1, 36.2–21). In this author's view, that is wrong-headed since medicine is and has long been based on experience. The investigation of what happens under the earth or in the sky may be forced to rely on such postulates, but they are a disaster in medicine, where they have the result of narrowing down the causal principles of diseases. While that drives a wedge between medicine and 'meteorology', he goes on in chapter 20 (51.6–18)

---

[10] I may refer to the detailed analysis in Cuomo 2000: ch. 4.

specifically to attack the importation into medicine of methods and ideas
that he associates with 'philosophy', by which he here means speculative
theories about such topics as the constitution of the human body. For good
measure he insists that if one were to engage in that study, the proper way
of doing so would be to start from medicine.

Medicine provides particularly striking examples of second-order
debates parallel to those in mathematics: indeed in the Hellenistic period
the disagreements among the medical sects were as much about methods
and epistemology as they were about medical practice. But other fields too
exhibit similar fundamental divisions between competing approaches. In
music theory, Barker has explored the analogous disputes first between
practitioners on the one hand, and theoretical analysts on the other, and
then, among the latter, between those who treated musical sound in geometrical terms, as an infinitely divisible continuum, and those who adopted
an analysis based rather on arithmetic.[11] Further afield I may simply remark
that the methods and aims of historiography are the subject of explicit
comment from Herodotus onwards. His views were criticized, implicitly,
by his immediate successor Thucydides, who contrasts history as enter-
tainment with his own ambition to provide what he calls a 'memorial for
eternity' (1 21). But to achieve that end depended, of course, on the critical
evaluation of eyewitness accounts, as well as an assumption that certain
patterns of behaviour repeat themselves thanks to the constancy of human
nature.

With the development of both the practice and the teaching of rhetoric –
the art of public speaking – goes a new sense of what it takes to persuade an
audience of the strength of your case – and of the weakness of your rivals'
position. Both the orators and the statesmen deployed a rich vocabulary of
terms, such as *apodeiknumi*, *epideiknumi* and cognates, to express the claim
that they have proved their point, as to the facts of the matter in question, as
to the guilt or innocence of the parties concerned, or as to the benefits that
would accrue from the policies they advocated.

Yet that very same vocabulary was taken over first by Plato and then
by Aristotle to *contrast* what they claimed to be strict demonstrations on
the one hand with the arguments that they now downgraded as merely
plausible or persuasive, such as were used in the law courts and political
assemblies – and this takes us back to mathematics, since it provides the
essential background to the claims that some, but not all, mathematicians
made about the strictest mode of demonstration that they could deliver.

---

[11] Barker 1989, 2000.

Aristotle was, of course, the first to propose an explicit definition of rigorous demonstration, which must proceed by way of valid deductive argument from premises that are not just true, but also necessary, primary, immediate, better known than, prior to and explanatory of the conclusions. Furthermore Aristotle draws up a more elaborate taxonomy of arguments than Plato had done, distinguishing demonstrative, dialectical, rhetorical, sophistic and eristic reasoning according first to the aims of the reasoner (which might be the truth, or victory, or reputation) and secondly to the nature of the premises used (necessary, probable, or indeed contentious). Yet while the ideal that Aristotle sets for philosophy and for mathematics is rigorous, axiomatic–deductive, demonstration, he not only allows that the rhetorician will rely on what he calls rhetorical demonstration, but concedes that in philosophy itself there may be stricter and looser modes, appropriate to different subject matter.[12]

The goal the philosophers set themselves was certainty – where the conclusions reached were, supposedly, immune to the types of challenges that always occurred in the law courts and assemblies. Yet from some points of view the best area to exemplify this was not philosophy itself (ontology, epistemology or ethics) but, of course, mathematics. However, the attitudes of both Plato and Aristotle themselves towards mathematics were distinctly ambivalent – not that they agreed on the status of that study. For Plato, the inquiries the mathematician engages in are inferior to dialectic itself: they are part of the prior training for the philosopher, but do not belong to philosophy itself. The grounds for this that he puts forward in the *Republic* are twofold, that the mathematician uses diagrams and that he takes his 'hypotheses' for granted, as 'clear to all'.[13] So although mathematics studies intelligible objects and so is superior to any study devoted to perceptible ones, it is inferior to dialectic which is purportedly based ultimately on an 'unhypothesised starting point', the idea of the Good.

Aristotle, by contrast, clearly accepts that mathematical arguments can meet the requirements of the strictest mode of demonstration, since he privileges mathematical examples to illustrate that mode in the *Posterior*

---

[12] Lloyd 1996: ch. 1.

[13] The interpretation of the expression 'as clear to all', *hōs panti phanerōn*, in the *Republic* 510d1, is disputed. My own view is that Plato is unlikely not to have been aware that many of the hypotheses adopted by the mathematicians were contested (including for example the definitions of straight line and point). When Socrates says that the mathematicians give no account to themselves or anyone else about their starting-points, it would seem that this is their *claim*, rather than (as it has generally been taken) their *warrant*. Burnyeat (2000: 37), however, has argued that there is no criticism of mathematics in this text, but simply an observation of an inevitable feature of their methods.

Analytics. But mathematics suffers from a different shortcoming, in his view, which relates to the ontological status of the subject matter it deals with. Unlike Plato, who suggested that mathematics studies separate intelligible objects that are intermediate between the Forms and sensible particulars, Aristotle argued that mathematics is concerned with the mathematical properties of physical objects.[14] While physical objects meet the requirements of substance-hood, what mathematics studies belongs rather to the category of quantity than to that of substance.

While Plato and Aristotle disagreed about the highest mode of philosophizing, 'dialectic' in Plato's case, 'first philosophy' in Aristotle's, they both considered philosophy to be supreme and mathematics to be subordinate to it. Yet mathematics obviously delivered demonstrations, and exemplified the goal of the certainty and incontrovertibility of arguments, far more effectively than metaphysics, let alone than ethics. Once Euclid's *Elements* had shown how virtually the whole of mathematical knowledge could be represented as a single, comprehensive system, derived from a limited number of indemonstrable starting points, that model exerted very considerable influence as an ideal, not just within the mathematical disciplines, but well beyond them.[15] Euclid's own *Optics*, like many treatises in harmonics, statics and astronomy, proceeded on an axiomatic–deductive basis, even though the actual axioms Euclid invoked in that work are problematic.[16] More remarkably Galen sought to turn parts of medicine into an axiomatic–deductive system just as Proclus did for theology in his *Elements of Theology*.[17] The prestige of proof 'in the geometrical manner', *more geometrico*, made it the ideal for many investigations despite the apparent difficulties of implementing it.

The chief problem lay not with deductive argument itself, but with its premisses. Aristotle had shown that strict demonstration must proceed

[14] Lear 1982.

[15] As noted, the question of whether Hippocrates of Chios had a clear notion of ultimate starting-points or axioms in his geometrical studies is disputed. In his quadratures of lunes he takes a starting-point that is itself proved, and so not a primary premiss. Ancient historians of mathematics mention the contributions of Archytas, Eudoxus, Theodorus and Theaetetus leading up to Euclid's own *Elements*, but while the commentators on that work identify particular results as having been anticipated by those and other mathematicians, the issue of how systematic their overall presentation of mathematical knowledge was remains problematic.

[16] Thus one of Euclid's definitions in the *Optics* (def. 3, 2.7–9: cf. Proposition 1, 2.21–4.8) states that those things are seen on which visual rays fall, while those are not seen on which they do not. That seems to suggest that visual rays are not dense, a conception that conflicts with the assumption of the infinite divisibility of the geometrical continuum. See Brownson 1981; Smith 1981; Jones 1994.

[17] Lloyd 2006c.

from premises that are themselves indemonstrable – to avoid the twin flaws of circular argument and an infinite regress. If the premises could be proved, then they should be, and that in turn meant that they could not be considered ultimate, or primary, premises. The latter had to be self-evident, *autopista*, or *ex heautōn pista*. Yet the actual premises we find used in different investigations are very varied. To start with, the kinds or categories of starting points needed were the subject of considerable terminological instability. Aristotle distinguished three types, definitions, hypotheses and axioms, the latter being subdivided into those specific to a particular study, such as the equality axiom, and general principles that had to be presupposed for intelligible communication, such as the laws of non-contradiction and excluded middle. Euclid's triad consisted of definitions, common opinions (including the equality axiom) and postulates. Archimedes in turn begins his inquiries into statics and hydrostatics by setting out, for example, the postulates, *aitēmata*, and the propositions that are to be granted, *lambanomena*, and elsewhere the primary premises are just called starting points or principles, *archai*.

As regards the actual principles that figure in different investigations, they were far from confined to what Aristotle or Euclid would have accepted as axioms. In Aristarchus' exploration of the heliocentric hypothesis, he set out among his premises that the fixed stars and the sun remain unmoved and that the earth is borne round the sun on a circle, where that circle bears the same proportion to the distance of the fixed stars as the centre of a sphere to its surface. Archimedes, who reports those hypotheses in the *Sand-Reckoner* 2 218.7–31, remarks that strictly speaking that would place the fixed stars at infinite distance. The assumption involves, then, what we would call an idealization, where the error introduced can be discounted. But in his only extant treatise, *On the Sizes and Distances of the Sun and Moon*, Aristarchus' assumptions include a value for the angular diameter of the moon as 2°, a figure that is far more likely, in my view, to have been hypothetical in the sense of adopted purely for the sake of argument, than axiomatic in the sense of accepted as true. Meanwhile outside mathematics, we find Galen, for example, taking the principles that nature does nothing in vain, and that nothing happens without a cause, as indemonstrable starting points for certain deductions in medicine. In Proclus, the physical principles that natural motion is from, to, or around the centre, are similarly treated as indemonstrable truths on which natural philosophy can be based.

The disputable character of many of the principles adopted as axiomatic is clear. Euclid's own parallel postulate was attacked on the grounds that it should be a theorem proved within the system, not a postulate at all, although attempts to provide a proof all turned out to be circular. Yet the controversial character of many primary premisses in no way deterred investigators from claiming their soundness. The demand for arguments that are unshakeable or immovable, unerring or infallible, inflexible in the sense of not open to persuasion, indisputable, irrefutable or incontrovertible is expressed by different authors with an extraordinary variety of terms. Among the most common are *akinēton* (immovable), used for example by Plato at *Timaeus* 51e, *ametapeiston* or *ametapiston* (not subject to persuasion), in Aristotle's *Posterior Analytics* 72b3 and Ptolemy's *Syntaxis* 1 1 6.17–21, *anamartēton* (unerring), in Plato's *Republic* 339c, *ametaptōton* (unchanging) and *ametaptaiston* (infallible), the first in Plato's *Timaeus* 29b and Aristotle's *Topics* 139b33, and the second in Galen, K 17(1) 863.3, and especially the terms *anamphisbētēton*, incontestable (already in Diogenes of Apollonia Fr. 1 and subsequently in prominent passages in Hero, *Metrica* 3 142.1, and in Ptolemy, *Syntaxis* 1 1 6.20 among many others) and *anelegkton*, irrefutable (Plato, *Apology* 22a, *Timaeus* 29b, all the way down to Proclus in his *Commentary on Euclid's Elements* 68.10).[18]

The pluralism of Greek mathematics thus itself has many facets. The actual practices of those who in different disciplines laid claim to the title of *mathēmatikos* varied appreciably. They range from the astrologer working out planetary positions for a horoscope, to the arithmetical proofs and use of symbolism discussed by Mueller and Netz in their chapters, to the proof of the infinity of primes in Euclid or that of the area of a parabolic segment in Archimedes. There was as much disagreement on the nature of the claims that 'mathematics' could make as on their justification. One group asserted the pre-eminence of mathematics on the grounds that it achieved certainty, that its arguments were incontrovertible. Many philosophers and quite a few mathematicians themselves joined together in seeing this as the great pride of mathematics and the source of its prestige. But the disputable nature of the claims to indisputability kept breaking surface, either in general or in relation to particular results. Moreover while there was much deadly serious searching after certainty, there was also much playfulness, the 'ludic' quality that Netz has associated with other aspects of the

---

[18] It is striking that the term *anamphisbētēton* may mean indisputable or undisputed, just as in Thucydides (1 21) the term *anexelegkton* means beyond refutation (and so also beyond verification). In neither case is there any doubt, in context, as to how the word is to be understood. That is less clear in the case of the chief term for 'indemonstrable', *anapodeikton*, which Galen has been seen as using of what has not been demonstrated (though capable of demonstration) although in Aristotle it applies purely to what is incapable of being demonstrated (see Hankinson 1991).

aesthetics that began to be cultivated in the Hellenistic period.[19] In the case of mathematics, there were occasions when its practitioners delighted in complexity and puzzlement for their own sakes.

From a comparative perspective what are the important lessons to be learnt from the material I have thus cursorily surveyed in this discussion? The points made in my last paragraph provide the basis for an argument that tends to turn a common assumption about Greek mathematics on its head. While one image of mathematics that many ancients as well as quite a few modern commentators promoted has it that mathematics is the realm of the indisputable, it is precisely the disputes about both first-order practices and second-order analysis that mark out the ancient Greek experience in this field. Divergent views were entertained not just about what 'mathematics' covered, but on what its proper aims and methods should be. The very fluidity and indeterminacy of the boundaries between different intellectual disciplines may be thought to have contributed to the construction of that image of mathematics as the realm of the incontrovertible – contested as that image was. But we may remark that that idea owed as much to the ruminations of the philosophers – who used it to propose an ideal of a 'philosophy' that could equal and indeed surpass mathematics – as it did to the actual practices of the mathematicians themselves.

It may once have been assumed that the development of the axiomatic–deductive mode of demonstration was an essential feature of the development of mathematics itself. But as other studies in this volume amply show, there are plenty of ancient traditions of mathematical inquiry that got on perfectly well, grew and flourished, without any idea of the need to define their axiomatic foundations. In Greece itself, as we have seen, it is far from being the case that all those who considered themselves, or were considered by others, to be mathematicians thought that axiomatics was obligatory.

This raises, then, two key questions with important implications for comparativist studies. First how can we begin to account for the particular heterogeneity of the Greek mathematical experience and for the way in which the axiomatic–deductive model became dominant in some quarters? Second what were the consequences of the hierarchization we find in some writers on the development and practice of mathematics itself?

In relation to the first question, my argument is that there was a crucial input from the side of philosophy, in that it was the philosopher Aristotle who first explicitly defined rigorous demonstration in terms of valid deductive argument from indemonstrable primary premisses – an ideal

---

[19] Netz 2009.

that he promoted in part to create a gap between demonstrative reasoning and the merely plausible arguments of orators and others. Whether or how far Aristotle was influenced by already existing mathematical practice is a question we are in no position to answer definitively. But certainly his was the first explicit definition of such a style of demonstration, and equally clearly soon afterwards Euclid's *Elements* exemplified that style in a more comprehensive manner than any previously attempted.

From this it would appear that it was the particular combination of cross-disciplinary and interdisciplinary rivalries in Greece that provided an important stimulus to the developments we have been discussing. Elsewhere in other mathematical traditions there was certainly competition between rival practitioners. It is for the comparativist to explore how far the rivalries that undoubtedly existed in those traditions conformed to or departed from the patterns we have found in Greece.

Then on the second question I posed of the consequences of the proposal by certain Greeks themselves of a hierarchy in which axiomatic–deductive demonstration provided the ideal, we must be even-handed. On the one hand we can say that with the development of axiomatics there was a gain in explicitness and clarity on the issue of what assumptions needed to be made for conclusions that could claim certainty. On the other there was evidently also a loss, in that the demand for incontrovertibility could detract attention from heuristics, from the business of expanding the subject and obtaining new knowledge. This is particularly evident when Archimedes remarks that conclusions obtained by the use of his Method had thereafter to be proved rigorously using the standard procedures of the method of exhaustion. If we can recognize – with one Greek point of view – that there was good sense in the search for axioms insofar as that identified and made explicit the foundations on which the deductive structure was based, we should also be conscious – with another Greek opinion indeed – of a possible conflict between that demand for incontrovertibility and the need to get on with the business of discovery.

Bibliography

Barker, A. D. (1989) *Greek Musical Writings*, vol. II. Cambridge.
   (2000) *Scientific Method in Ptolemy's* Harmonics. Cambridge.
Brownson, C. D. (1981) 'Euclid's optics and its compatibility with linear
   perspective', *Archive for History of Exact Sciences* 24: 165–94.

Burkert, W. (1972) *Lore and Science in Ancient Pythagoreanism*. Cambridge, MA.

Burnyeat, M. F. (2000) 'Plato on why mathematics is good for the soul', in *Mathematics and Necessity*, ed. T. Smiley. Oxford: 1–81.

Cuomo, S. (2000) *Pappus of Alexandria and the Mathematics of Late Antiquity*. Cambridge.

(2001) *Ancient Mathematics*. London.

Hankinson, R. J. (1991) 'Galen on the foundations of science', in *Galeno: Obra, Pensamiento e Influencia*, ed. J. A. López Férez. Madrid: 15–19.

Jones, A, (1994) 'Peripatetic and Euclidean theories of the visual ray', *Physis* **31**: 47–76.

Knorr, W. R. (1981) 'On the early history of axiomatics: the interaction of mathematics and philosophy in Greek antiquity', in *Theory Change, Ancient Axiomatics and Galileo's Methology*, ed. J. Hintikka, D. Gruender and E. Agazzi. Dordrecht: 145–86.

(1986) *The Ancient Tradition of Geometric Problems*. Boston, MA.

Lear, J. (1982) 'Aristotle's philosophy of mathematics', *Philosophical Review* **91**: 161–92.

Lloyd, G. E. R. (1996) *Aristotelian Explorations*. Cambridge.

(2006a) 'The alleged fallacy of Hippocrates of Chios', in G. E. R. Lloyd, *Principles and Practices in Ancient Greek and Chinese Science*. Aldershot: ch. VII. (Originally published in 1987 in *Apeiron* 20: 103–83.)

(2006b) 'The pluralism of intellectual life before Plato', in G. E. R. Lloyd, *Principles and Practices in Ancient Greek and Chinese Science*. Aldershot: ch. X. (originally published as 'Le pluralisme de la vie intellectuelle avant Platon', in *Qu'est-ce que la philosophie présocratique?*, ed. A. Laks and C. Louguet (2002). Lille: 39–53.)

(2006c) 'Mathematics as model of method in Galen', in G. E. R. Lloyd, *Principles and Practices in Ancient Greek and Chinese Science*. Aldershot: ch. V. (Originally published in *Philosophy and the Sciences in Antiquity*, ed. R. W. Sharples (2005). Aldershot: 110–30.)

Mendell, H. (1998) 'Making sense of Aristotelian demonstration', *Oxford Studies in Ancient Philosophy* **16**: 161–225.

Mueller, I. (1982) 'Aristotle and the quadrature of the circle', in *Infinity and Continuity in Ancient and Medieval Thought*, ed. N. Kretzmann. Ithaca, NY: 146–64.

Netz, R. (1999) *The Shaping of Deduction in Greek Mathematics*. Cambridge.

(2004) *The Transformation of Mathematics in the Early Mediterranean World*. Cambridge.

(2009) *Ludic Proof*. Cambridge.

Smith, A. M. (1981) 'Saving the appearances of the appearances: the foundations of classical geometrical optics', *Archive for History of Exact Sciences* **24**: 73–99.

Szabó, Á. (1978) *The Beginnings of Greek Mathematics*, trans. A. M. Ungar. Budapest. (Originally published as *Anfänge der griechischen Mathematik*. Munich (1969).)

Tybjerg, K. (2000) 'Doing philosophy with machines: Hero of Alexandria's rhetoric of mechanics in relation to the contemporary philosophy', PhD thesis, University of Cambridge.

Generalizing about polygonal numbers
in ancient Greek mathematics

IAN MUELLER

Introduction

The main source for our information about the Greek handling of what are
called polygonal numbers is the *Introduction to Arithmetic* of Nicomachus
of Gerasa (*c.* 100 CE).[1] Heath says of the *Introduction* that "Little or nothing
in the book is original, and, except for certain definitions and refine-
ments of classification, the essence of it evidently goes back to the early
Pythagoreans."[2] I am not interested in this historical claim, the evidence
for which is very slight; indeed I am not interested in chronology at all but
only in certain features of Nicomachus' treatment of polygonals, which I
discuss in Section 1, and in the general argumentative structure of a short
treatise by Diophantus called *On Polygonal Numbers*,[3] which I discuss in
Section 2.

1. Nicomachus of Gerasa

In the *Introduction* Nicomachus makes a contrast between the standard
Greek way of writing numbers, in which, e.g., 222 is written σκβ, where σ
represents 200, κ 20, and β 2, and what he says is a more natural way:

II.6.2 First one should recognize that each letter with which we refer to a number . . .
signifies it by human convention and agreement and not in a natural way; the
natural, direct (*amethodos*), and consequently simplest way to signify numbers
would be the setting out of the units in each number in a line side by side . . . :

---

[1] Greek text: Hoche 1866; English translation: D'Ooge 1926; French translation: Bertier 1978.
There is material parallel to Nicomachus' presentation in Theon of Smyrna (Hiller 1878). For
dates of individuals I use Toomer's articles in *The Oxford Classical Dictionary* (Hornblower and
Spawforth 1996).

[2] Heath 1921: I 99.

[3] Greek text: T1893: 450,1–476,3; French translation: Ver Eecke 1926. I do not discuss the final
part of the treatise (476,4–480,2), a broken-off and inconclusive attempt to show how to find
how many kinds of polygonal a given number is. *The Oxford Classical Dictionary* locates
Diophantus in the interval between 150 BCE and 280 CE. Heath 1921: II 448 says that "he
probably flourished A.D. 250 or not much later."

unit	α,
two	αα,
three	ααα,
four	αααα,
five	ααααα,

and so on.

Nicomachus' "natural" representation of numbers would seem to break down the customary Greek contrast between the numbers and the unit, but Nicomachus insists that it does not:

II.6.3 Since the unit has the place and character of a point, it will be a principle (*arkhê*) . . . of numbers . . . and not in itself (*oupô*) . . . a number, just as the point is a principle of line or distance and not in itself a line or distance.

We find a close analog of Nicomachus' "natural" representation of numbers in the account of finitary number theory in Hilbert and Bernays' great work *Grundlagen der Mathematik*, except that in the *Grundlagen* the alphas are replaced by strokes. As that work makes clear, this representation provides a basis for developing all of elementary arithmetic, including everything known to the Greeks. Much the most important feature of the representation in this regard is the treatment of the numbers as formed from an initial object (the unit or one) by an indefinitely repeatable successor operation which always produces a new number. This treatment validates definition and proof by mathematical induction, the core of modern number theory. The finitary arithmetic of Hilbert and Bernays rests essentially on the intuitive manipulation of sequences of strokes (units) together with elementary inductive reasoning.[4] It is difficult for me to see any substantial difference between the manipulation of sequences of strokes or alphas and the manipulation of lines and figures in what is frequently called cut-and-paste geometry; the objects are different, but the reasoning seems to me to be in an important sense the same.

I mention this modern form of elementary arithmetic only to provide a contrast with its ancient forebears. Nicomachus relies heavily on the notion of numbers as multiplicities of units and the representation of them as collections of alphas, but, after he has introduced his natural representation, it by and large vanishes in favor of a much more clearly geometric or configurational representation in which three is a triangular number, four a square number, and five a pentagonal number (Figure 9.1).

---

[4] In this paper I use words like "inductive" and "induction" only in connection with mathematical induction.

Figure 9.1 Geometric representation of polygonal numbers.

Nicomachus also mentions hexagonal, heptagonal, and octagonal numbers, and there is no question that he has the idea of an *n*-agonal number, for any *n*, but he only expresses this with words like "and so on forever in the direction of increase" (*aei kata parauxêsin houtôs*; ii.11.4). It is clear that Nicomachus intends to make some kind of generalization, but it is not at all clear what, if any, theoretical or mathematical ideas underlie it. Any connection between what he says and the natural representation of numbers is at best indirect. Nicomachus is relying on the idea that the numbers go on forever, but much more central to his account of polygonal numbers is the geometric fact that an *n*-agon is determined by the *n* points which are its vertices. If induction lies behind the reasoning, it is not made at all explicit.

I turn now to some further features of what Nicomachus says. The first sentence of his description of triangular numbers is quite opaque, but it is clearly intended to bring out their configurational aspect. I quote it in the translation of d'Ooge:

II.8.1 A triangular number is one which, when it is analyzed into units, shapes into triangular form the equilateral placement of its parts in a plane. Examples are 3, 6, 10, 15, 21, 28, and so on in order. For their graphic representations (*skhêmatographiai*) will be well-ordered and equilateral triangles . . . .

Here again we have the thought of continuing indefinitely. Nicomachus now indicates the arithmetical procedure for generating these triangular numbers, again insisting on the distinction between the unit and a number even though leaving it aside would simplify his description.

And, proceeding as far as you wish, you will find triangularization of this kind, making the thing which consists of a unit first of all most elementary, so that the unit may also appear as *potentially* a triangular number, with 3 being *actually* the first.

ii.8.2 The sides <of these numbers> will increase by consecutive number, the side of the potentially first being one, that of the actually first (i.e., 3) two, that of the actually second (i.e., 6) three, that of the third four, of the fourth five, of the fifth six, and so on forever.

If we ignore the distinction between a unit and a number,[5] we may express Nicomachus' claim here as:

The side of the *n*th (actual or potential) triangular number is *n*.

Nicomachus now turns to deal more explicitly with the question of the relationship between the sequence of triangular numbers and the "natural" numbers:

> II.8.3 Triangular numbers are generated when natural number is set out in sequence (*stoikhêdon*) and successive ones are always added one at a time starting from the beginning, since the well-ordered triangular numbers are brought to completion with each addition and combination. For example, from this natural sequence

$$1, 2, 3, 4, 5, 6, 7, 8, 9, 10, 11, 12, 13, 14, 15,$$

> if I take the very first item I get the potentially first triangular number, 1:

$$\alpha$$

> then, if I add to it the next term, I get the actually first triangular number, since 3 is 2 and 1, and in its graphic representation it is put together as follows: two units are placed side by side under one unit and the number is made a triangle:

$$\alpha$$

$$\alpha \quad \alpha$$

> And then, following this, if the next number, 3, is combined with this and spread out into units and added, it gives and also graphically represents 6, which is the actually second triangular number:

$$\alpha$$

$$\alpha \quad \alpha$$

$$\alpha \quad \alpha \quad \alpha$$

Nicomachus continues in this vein for the first seven (potential and actual) triangular numbers, essentially showing that:

The *n*th triangular number is the sum of the first *n* "natural" numbers.

---

[5] As I shall sometimes do, without – I hope – introducing any confusion or uncertainty.

He proceeds to show in the same way that:

The *n*th square number is the sum of the first *n* odd numbers and its side is *n*.

but in this case the odd numbers are added so as to preserve the square shape (Figure 9.2).

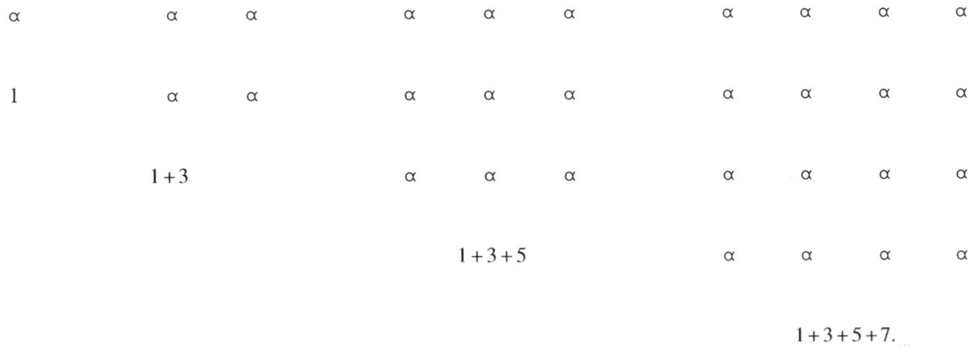

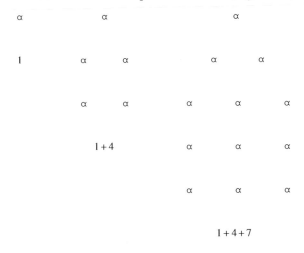

Figure 9.2 The generation of square numbers.

The formulation corresponding to the presentation of the pentagonal numbers is:

The *n*th pentagonal number is the sum of the first *n* numbers $x_1, x_2, \ldots, x_n$ which are such that $x_{i+1} = x_i + 3$, and its side is *n*.

The first three are represented below (Figure 9.3).

Figure 9.3 The generation of the first three pentagonal numbers.

We are not given a graphic representation of the the next pentagonal number 22, but its representation would certainly be the following (Figure 9.4):

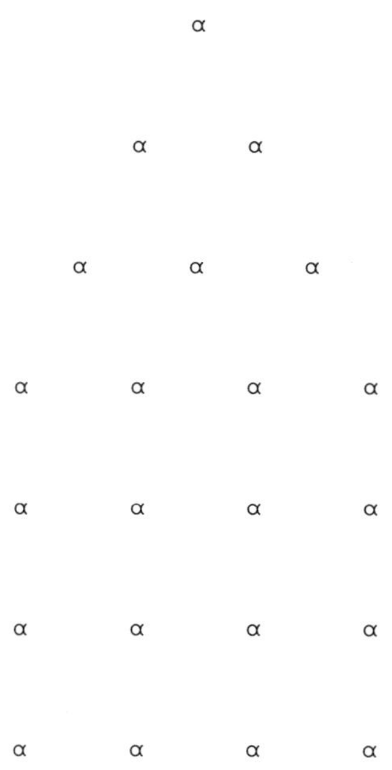

α

α   α

α   α   α

α   α   α   α

α   α   α   α

α   α   α   α

α   α   α   α

$1 + 4 + 7 + 10$

Figure 9.4 The graphic representation of the fourth pentagonal number.

Nicomachus proceeds through the octagonal numbers without figures, making clear that:

[Nic*]. The sum of the first n numbers $x_1, x_2, \ldots, x_n$ which are such that $x_{i+1} = x_i + j$ is the nth $j+2$-agonal number and its side is n.

He then turns to showing that his presentation of polygonal numbers is in harmony with geometry (<hê> *grammikê* <*didaskalia*>), something which he says is clear both from the graphic representation and from the following considerations:

II.12.1 Every square figure divided diagonally is resolved into two triangles and every square number is resolved into two consecutive triangulars and therefore is composed of two consecutive triangulars. For example, the triangulars are:

1, 3, 6, 10, 15, 21, 28, 36, 45, 55, etc.,

and the squares are:

1, 4, 9, 16, 25, 36, 49, 64, 81, 100.

If you add any two consecutive triangulars whatsoever you will always produce a square, so that in resolving any square you will be able to make two triangulars from them. And again if any triangle is joined to any square figure[6] it produces a pentagon, for example if the triangular 1 is joined to the square 4, it makes the pentagonal 5, and if the next <triangular>, that is 3, is added to the next <square> 9 it makes the pentagonal 12, and if the following <triangular> 6 is added onto the following <square> 16, it gives the following <pentagonal> 22, and 25 added to 10 gives 35, and so on forever.

Nicomachus states similar results for adding triangulars to pentagonals to get hexagonals, to hexagonals to get heptagonals, and to heptagonals to get octagonals, "and so on *ad infinitum*." He introduces a table (Table 9.1) as an aid to memory:

Table 9.1:

Triangles	1	3	6	10	15	21	28	36	45	54
Squares	1	4	9	16	25	36	49	64	81	100
Pentagons	1	5	12	22	35	51	70	92	117	145
Hexagons	1	6	15	28	45	66	91	120	153	190
Heptagons	1	7	18	34	55	81	112	148	189	235[7]

and describes some of the relevant sums, results which we might formulate as:

The $n+1$th square number is the nth triangular number plus the $n+1$th triangular number;
The $n+1$th pentagonal number is the nth triangular number plus the $n+1$th square number,

or, generally,

The $n+1$th $k+1$-agonal number is the nth triangular number plus the $n+1$th k-agonal number.

　　At this point I would like to introduce some of Heath's remarks about Nicomachus' *Introduction*:

It is a very far cry from Euclid to Nicomachus. Numbers are represented in Euclid by straight lines with letters attached, a system which has the advantage that, as in algebraical notation, we can work with numbers in general without the necessity of giving them specific values.... Further, there are no longer any proofs in the proper sense of the word; when a general proposition has been enunciated, Nicomachus regards it as sufficient to show that it is true in particular instances; sometimes we are left to infer the proposition by induction from particular cases which are alone given.... probably Nicomachus, who was not really a mathematician, intended his

---

[6] Here some exaggeration, since the triangle and the square have to "fit together."
[7] Apparently the octagons are missing.

Introduction to be, not a scientific treatise, but a popular treatment of the subject calculated to awaken in a beginner an interest in the theory of numbers . . . . Its success is difficult to explain except on the hypothesis that it was at first read by philosophers rather than mathematicians . . ., and afterwards became generally popular at a time when there were no mathematicians left, but only philosophers who incidentally took an interest in mathematics.[8]

Heath's remarks here are aimed at the whole of the *Introduction*, but I wish only to consider them in relation to Nicomachus' treatment of polygonal numbers. There is no question that, as Heath also notes, Nicomachus' flowery and imprecise language is a "far cry" from Euclid's sparse, formal formulations. But the representation of polygonal numbers by straight lines would obliterate their configurational nature. Nicomachus shows how triangular configurations of units can be generated as the series 1, 1+2, 1+2+3, etc. But I do not see what he could do to "prove" this fact and, therefore, how he could "prove" any fact about polygonal numbers as configurations. Of course, we know how to prove things about polygonal numbers, namely by eliminating all geometric content and transforming Nic*, which for Nicomachus expresses an arithmetical fact about configurations, into an arithmetical definition in which the geometrical terminology is at most a convenience, perhaps as follows:

[$\text{Def}_{\text{geo/arith}}$]. p is the nth $j+2$-agonal number with side n if and only if $p=x_1+x_2+\cdots+x_n$, where $x_{i+1}=x_i+j$ and $x_1=1$.

I assume that Fowler had something of this kind in mind when he advanced the hypothesis that lying behind Nicomachus' presentation were ancient proofs using mathematical induction.[9] I doubt this very much, but the more important point for me is that, unless something like $\text{Def}_{\text{geo/arith}}$ is used to eliminate the configurational aspect of polygonal numbers, anything like a Euclidean foundation for the theory of them lies well beyond the scope of Greek mathematics.

2. The argument of Diophantus' *On Polygonal Numbers*

In Tannery's edition of *On Polygonal Numbers* there are four propositions. The propositions are purely arithmetical and in none of them is there a mention of polygonals.[10] I quote them and give algebraic representations

---

[8] Heath 1921: I 97–9.

[9] Fowler 1994: 258.

[10] When I say that these propositions are purely arithmetical, I only mean to point out the absence of the notion of polygonality from the formulations and proofs of the propositions.

of their content; in footnotes I give simple algebraic proofs of the results in order to show that the results are correct. Diophantus' arguments are cumbersome and roundabout.

[452,2] [Dioph 1] If three numbers exceed one another by an equal amount, then eight times the product of the greatest and the middle one plus the square on the least produces a square the side of which is equal to the sum of the greatest and twice the middle one.

$$\text{if } x=y+k \text{ and } y=z+k, \text{ then } 8xy+z^2=(x+2y)^2.[11]$$

[454,6] [Dioph 2] If there are numbers in any multitude in equal excess, <the excess> of the greatest over the least is their excess multiplied by one less than the multitude of numbers set out.

$$\text{if } x_1, x_2, \ldots x_{n+1} \text{ are such that } x_{i+1}=x_i+j \text{ then } x_{n+1} - x_1=nj.[12]$$

[456,2] [Dioph 3] If there are numbers in any multitude in equal excess, the sum of the greatest and least multiplied by their multitude makes a number which is double of the sum of the numbers set out.

$$\text{if } x_1, x_2, \ldots x_n \text{ are such that } x_{i+1}=x_i+j \text{ then}$$
$$(x_n+x_1)n=2(x_1+x_2+\cdots+x_n).[13]$$

[460,5] [Dioph 4] If there are numbers in any multitude in equal excess starting from the unit, then the sum multiplied by eight times their excess plus the square of two less than their excess is a square of which the side minus 2 will be their excess

---

I do not mean to suggest, nor do I believe, that Diophantus' reasoning does not include geometric elements of the kind we find in the so-called geometric algebra of Book 2 of Euclid's *Elements*. But discussion of that issue would require a detailed examination of Diophantus' proofs, a task which I cannot undertake here.

[11] Proof: Let $x=z+2k$ and $y=z+k$. Then we should prove that:

$$8(z+2k)(z+k)+z^2=((z+2k)+2(z+k))^2.$$

But

$$8(z+2k)(z+k)+z^2=8(z^2+3zk+2k^2)+z^2=9z^2+24zk+16k^2=$$
$$(3z+4k)^2=((z+2k)+2z+2k)^2=((z+2k)+2(z+k))^2.$$

[12] Dioph 2 is sufficiently obvious that there is really nothing to prove, the basic idea being that $x_2=x_1+j, x_3=x_2+j=x_1+2j, x_4=x_3+j=x_1+3j$, and so on.

[13] We give an inductive proof of Dioph 3. For $n=1$ the theorem says that $x_2-x_1=1\cdot j$. Suppose $(x_1+x_n)n=2(x_1+x_2+\ldots+x_n)$. We wish to show that:

$$(x_1+x_{n+1})(n+1)=2(x_1+x_2+\cdots+x_{n+1}).$$

But:

$$(x_1+x_{n+1})(n+1)=(x_1+x_n+j)(n+1)$$
$$=(x_1+x_n)n+x_1+x_n+(n+1)j=2(x_1+x_2+\cdots+x_n)+x_1+nj+x_n+j$$
$$=2(x_1+x_2+\cdots+x_n)+x_{n+1}+x_{n+1}=2(x_1+x_2+\cdots+x_{n+1}).$$

(That $x_{n+1}=x_1+nj$ is a trivial reformulation of Dioph 2.)

multiplied by a certain number which, when a unit is added to it, is double of the multitude of all the numbers set out with the unit.

$$\text{if } p=x_1+x_2+\cdots+x_n, \text{ where } x_{i+1}=x_i+j \text{ and } x_1=1, \text{ then}$$
$$p8j+(j-2)^2=((2n-1)j+2)^2 \ [=((n+n-1)j+2)^2].$$

It is easy to prove Dioph 4 using Dioph 2 and 3,[14] as Diophantus does, although his argument is cumbersome. Here I wish only to present the very beginning of his argument and a diagram, provided by me, representing it.

[460,13] For let AB, CD, EF be numbers in equal excess starting from the unit.[15] I say that the proposition results. For let there be as many units in GH as the numbers set out with the unit. And since the excess by which EF exceeds a unit is the excess by which AB exceeds a unit multiplied by GH minus 1,[16] if we set out each unit, AK, EL, GM, we will have that LF is KB multiplied by MH. So LF is equal to the product of KB, MH. And if we set out KN as 2, we will investigate whether, if the sum is multiplied by 8 KB (which is their excess) and the square of NB (which is less than their excess by 2) is added, the result is a square of which the side minus 2 produces a number which is their excess (KB) multiplied by GH,HM together (Figure 9.5).

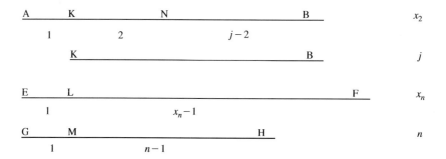

Figure 9.5 Diophantus' diagram, *Polygonal Numbers*, Proposition 4.

[14] Since:

$$((2n-1)j+2)^2 - (j-2)^2$$
$$= 4n^2j^2 - 4nj^2 + j^2 + 8nj - 4j + 4 - j^2 + 4j - 4$$
$$= 4n^2j^2 - 4j^2n + 8nj = 4j(n^2j - jn + 2n),$$

to prove Dioph 4 we need only prove:

$$2(x_1+x_2+\cdots+x_n)=n^2j-jn+2n,$$

or, by Dioph 3:

$$(x_n+x_1)n=n^2j-jn+2n, \text{ that is } x_n+x_1=nj-j+2.$$

[15] Note that AB, CD, and EF are numbers, not the unit.
[16] Cf. Dioph 2.

As I have said, the material described thus far in this section is purely arithmetical. However, if one accepts Def$_{geo/arith}$, what Diophantus has shown is that:

[Dioph 4$_{geo/arith}$] if p is the nth $j+2$-agonal number, then
$$p8j+(j-2)^2=((2n-1)j+2)^2.$$

It is clear from Diophantus' initial less specific statement of what he will show that he does think that he can establish this :

[450,11] Here it is established (*edokimasthê*) that if any polygonal is multiplied by a certain number (which is a function (*kata tên analogian*) of the multitude of angles in the polygonal) and a certain square number (again a function of the multitude of angles in it) is added, the result is a square.

if p is a $j+2$-agonal number, there are functions f and c such that
$$f(j+2)p+c(j+2) \text{ is a square number.}$$

After announcing this result Diophantus states the goal of the treatise:

[450,16] We will establish this and indicate how one can find a prescribed polygonal with a given side and how the side of a given polygonal can be taken.

That is,

how to find (1) the $j+2$-agonal p with side n and (2) the side of a $j+2$-agonal p.

This last subject is the concern of the final part of the treatise (472,21–476,3). Nic* allows one to solve these in a slightly cumbersome mechanical way, but what Diophantus proves enables him to give what amounts to formulae for the solutions:

(1) $\quad p = \dfrac{((2n-1)j+2)^2 - (j-2)^2}{8j}$,

(2) $\quad n = \dfrac{1}{2}\left(\dfrac{\sqrt{p8j+(j-2)^2}-2}{j}+1\right)$.

This last material is quite mundane, and I shall not discuss it. My major concern will be with the material immediately following the presentation of the arithmetical results Dioph 1 to 4. For those four propositions are purely arithmetical; they do not say anything about polygonal numbers and certainly do not establish anything about spatial configurations of units. It is in the remainder of the treatise that Diophantus tries to establish a general truth corresponding to Nic*, but as I have indicated, I believe that it is impossible to prove this truth within the confines of Greek mathematics.

What I will try to explain is the specific reason why Diophantus' attempt to do so fails, emphasizing that, although his reasoning is mathematically much more elaborate than Nicomachus', his handling of generalization is essentially the same, namely the presentation of examples which make the general truth "obvious."

Before turning to that material I want to signal the very first statement in *On Polygonal Numbers*, which concerns the first (actual) polygonal number of each kind:

[450,1] Each of the numbers starting from three which increase by one is a first polygonal after the unit. And it has as many angles as the multitude of units in it. Its side is the number after the unit, i.e., 2. 3 is triangular, 4 square, 5 pentagonal, and so on.

This is, I think, the only application of $Def_{geo/arith}$ that Diophantus takes for granted, i.e., he takes for granted that:

the first $j+2$-agonal (after 1) has side 2 and is $j+2$.

After making a remark about the ordinary conception of square numbers,[17] Diophantus gives (450,11 and 16) the announcement of what he is going to prove, which I have already quoted, and proves his four arithmetical propositions. It is at this point that he first reintroduces the notion of a polygonal number in his announcement of what he intends to prove next, which is tantamount to $Def_{geo/arith}$:

[468,14] These things being the case, we say that if there are numbers starting from the unit in any multitude and in any excess, the whole is polygonal. For it has as many angles as the number which is greater than the excess by 2, and the number of its sides is the multitude of the numbers set out with the unit.

He now invokes Dioph 4:

[470,1] For we have shown that the sum of all the numbers set out multiplied by 8 KB plus the square of NB produces the square of PK.

Here Diophantus is working with a figure in which the line AKNB of Figure 6 for Dioph 4 is extended to the right so that PK is a representation of $(2n-1)j+2$.[18] But to get a representation of $j+2$ he also extends AKNB to the left (Figure 9.6):

[470,4] But also if we posit AO as another unit, we will have KO as two, and KN is similarly two.

---

[17] [450,9] "It is immediately clear that squares have arisen because they come to be from some number being multiplied by itself."
[18] This specification of PK occurs at 466,1–2.

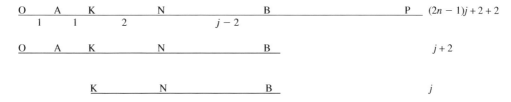

Figure 9.6 Diophantus' diagram, *Polygonal Numbers*.

But now Diophantus is only interested in OB ($j+2=1+(1+j)$), KB (j), and BN ($j-2$), and, in his only application of Dioph 1, he says:

[470,6] Therefore OB, BK, BN will exceed one another by an equal amount. Therefore, 8 times the product of the greatest OB and the middle BK plus the square of the least BN makes a square the side of which is the sum of the greatest OB and 2 of the middle BK. Therefore OB multiplied by 8 KB plus the square of NB is equal to the square of OB and 2KB together.

$$(j+2)8j+(j-2)^2=(j+2+2j)^2.$$

This is, of course, just the special case of Dioph 4 in which $n=2$. To make this point clear Diophantus argues that $j+2+2j=(2\cdot2-1)j+2$:

[470,13] And the side minus two (OK) leaves 3 KB, which is KB multiplied by three. But three plus one is 2 multiplied by 2.

Diophantus underlines the analogy with Dioph 4 and then points out that OB ($j+2$) is the first $j+2$-agonal number:

[470,17] ... the sum of the numbers set out with the unit produces (*poiei*) the same problem as OB, but OB is a chance number and is the first polygon {of its kind} after the unit (since AO is a unit and the second number is AB), and {OB} has two as side.

So, in addition to proving Dioph 4, Diophantus has proved a special case of it in which $n=2$, a case for which he has asserted that p is the first $j+2$-agonal number. These two propositions by themselves do not imply that whenever the conditions of Dioph 4 hold, p is a $j+2$-agonal number with side n. But this is precisely what Diophantus asserts:[19]

[470,21] Therefore also the sum of all the numbers set out is a polygon with as many angles as OB and having as many angles as it is greater by 2 (i.e., by OK) than the excess, KB; and it has as side GH, which is the number of the numbers set out with the unit.

---

[19] Commentators have standardly approved this "reasoning," or at least not raised any doubts about it. See Poselger 1810: 34–5; Schulz 1822: 618; Nesselmann 1842: 475; Heath 1885: 252; Wertheim 1890: 309; Massoutié 1911: 26; and Ver Eecke 1926: 288.

There is no more basis for this generalization than for the generalizations we have seen in Nicomachus; indeed, in a sense there is even less since Diophantus has considered only first polygonals and shown that they satisfy Dioph 4. Like Nicomachus, he clearly could show the same thing for any particular example, but that hardly proves his claim or the next one:

[470,27] And what is said by Hypsicles in a definition[20] has been demonstrated, namely:

> If there are numbers in equal excess in any multitude starting from the unit, then, when the excess is one the whole is triangular, when it is two, square, three, pentagonal. The number of angles is said to be greater than the excess by two, and its sides are the multitude of numbers set out with the unit.

It is not clear exactly what the definition of Hypsicles was.[21] In Diophantus' representation he said something about the first three polygonals, but it seems reasonable to suppose that he at least intended a generalization and so can be credited with Def$_{geo/arith}$.[22] But we have no information about how he used it – if he did. In any case Diophantus would have been on firmer footing had he made the definition the basis of his treatise rather than purporting to do the impossible, namely demonstrate it. Had he done this he would not have had to worry about Dioph 1 and the special case of it which he invokes to deal with first $j+2$-agonal numbers.

Diophantus now applies Hypsicles' definition and his own results to triangular numbers.

[472,5] Hence, since triangulars result when the excess is one and their sides are the greatest of the numbers set out, the product of the greatest of the numbers set out and the number which is greater by one than it is double the triangular indicated.

$$\text{If } p=x_1+x_2+\ldots+x_n \text{ with } x_{i+1}=x_i+1 \text{ and } x_1=1, \text{ then } p \text{ is a triangular}$$
$$\text{with side } x_n \text{ and } x_n(x_n+1)=2p.\text{[23]}$$

Diophantus returns again to first polygonal numbers. He recalls the application of Dioph 1 at 470,6.

[472,9] And since OB has as many angles as there are units in it, if it is multiplied by 8 multiplied by what is less than it by two (that is by the excess; that will be

---

[20] D'Ooge 1926: 246 endorses Gow's (1884: 87) suggestion that *en horôi* might mean "in a book called *Definition*." In itself this suggestion seems to me unlikely, but the recurrences of the word *horos* in 472,14 and especially 472,20 seem to me to rule it out completely.

[21] Standard *floruit*: *c.* 150 BCE.

[22] Contrast Nesselmann 1842: 463.

[23] Proof: It follows from Hypsicles' definition that $x_1+x_2+\ldots+x_n$ is a triangular number p with side n. But by Dioph 2 $x_n=(n-1)\cdot1+1=n$. And by Dioph 3 $2(x_1+x_2+\ldots+x_n)=n(x_n+x_1)=x_n(x_n+1)$.

8 × KB) <and> the square of what is less than it by 4 is added (that is NB), it produces a square.

> $j+2$ is a $j+2$-agonal and $(j+2)8j+(j-2)^2$ is a square.

This, too, is immediately generalized with no justification.

[472,14] And this will be a definition (*horos*) of polygonals:

> Every polygonal multiplied by 8 multiplied by what is less by two than the
> multitude of its angles plus the square of what is less than the multitude of
> angles by 4 makes a square.

> If p is $j+2$-agonal, $p8j+(j-2)^2$ is a square.

[472,20] In this way we have demonstrated simultaneously this definition of polygonals and that of Hypsicles.

In this case the truth which Diophantus purports to establish as a definition is not a definition in the standard sense at all, since $n8j+(j-2)^2$ can be
a square even when n is not a $j+2$-agonal; $2\cdot8\cdot3+(3-2)^2=7^2$, but 2 is not
pentagonal.[24] And his claim to have demonstrated it is just as weak as his
claim to have established Def$_{geo/arith}$.

Conclusion

It is certainly not surprising that Diophantus' treatise on polygonal numbers
shows great mathematical skill. And it is perhaps also not surprising that its
sense of logical rigor is at times not superior to that of Nicomachus. Within
the limits of Greek mathematics there can be no mathematical demonstration of an arithmetical characterization of configurationally conceived
polygonal numbers. Within those limits Aristotle (*Posterior Analytics* 1.6
(Ross)) was correct to insist that the generic difference between arithmetic
and geometry cannot be breached.

---

[24] This shortcoming is already pointed out in the *editio princeps* of the Greek text of Diophantus
(Bachet 1621: 21 of the edition of *On Polygonal Numbers*). What Diophantus says at 472,14
could serve as a definition for triangulars and squares. For, ignoring complications that would
arise if one tried to avoid "numbers" less than 1, it is easy to prove that:

> $p=1+2+\cdots+n$ (i.e., p is a triangular) if and only if $p8\cdot1+(3-4)^2$ is a square (i.e., if and only
> if $8p+1$ is a square);
> $p=1+3+\cdots+2n-1$ (i.e., p is a square) if and only if $p8\cdot2+(4-4)^2$ is a square (i.e., if and
> only if $16p$ is a square, i.e., if and only if p is a square).

It is tempting to think, although it cannot be proved, that Diophantus was misled by the
truth of these biconditionals to the false notion that Dioph 4 was the basis of a definition of
polygonality in general.

Bibliography

Bachet, C. (ed. and trans.) (1621) *Diophanti Alexandrini Arithmeticorum Libri Sex et De Numeris Multangulis Liber Unus*. Paris.

Bertier, J. (trans.) (1978) *Nicomaque de Gérase:* Introduction Arithmétique. Paris.

D'Ooge, M. L. (trans.) (1926) *Nicomachus of Gerasa:* Introduction to Arithmetic. University of Michigan Studies, Humanistic Series, vol. 16. New York.

Fowler, D. (1994) 'Could the Greeks have used mathematical induction? Did they use it?', *Physis* **31**: 253–65.

Gow, J. (1884) *A Short History of Greek Mathematics*. Cambridge.

Heath, T. (1885) *Diophantus of Alexandria: A Study in the History of Greek Algebra*. Cambridge.

  (1921) *A History of Greek Mathematics* (2 vols.) Oxford.

Hilbert, D., and Bernays, P. (1934) *Grundlagen der Mathematik*, vol. i. Berlin.

Hiller, E. (ed.) (1878) *Theonis Smyrnaei Philosophi Platonici* Expositio Rerum Mathematicarum ad Legendum Platonem Utilium. Leipzig.

Hoche, R. (ed.) (1866) *Nicomachi Geraseni Pythagorei* Introductionis Arithmeticae Libri ii. Leipzig.

Hornblower, S., and Spawforth, A. (eds.) (1996) *The Oxford Classical Dictionary*, 3rd edn. Oxford.

Massoutié, G. (trans.) (1911) *Le traité des nombres polygones de Diophante d'Alexandrie*. Macon.

Nesselmann, G. H. F. (1842) *Die Algebra der Griechen*. Berlin.

Poselger, F. T. (trans.) (1810) *Diophantus von Alexandrien über die Polygonzahlen*. Leipzig.

Ross, W. D. (ed.) (1964) *Aristotelis* Analytica Priora *et* Posteriora. Oxford.

Schulz, O. (trans.) (1822) *Diophantus von Alexandria Arithmetische Aufgaben nebst dessen Schrift über die Polygonzahlen*. Berlin.

Ver Eecke, P. (trans.) (1926) *Diophante d'Alexandrie, les six livres arithmétiques et le livre des nombres polygones*. Bruges.

Wertheim, P. (trans.) (1890) *Die Arithmetik und die Schrift über Polygonalzahlen des Diophantus von Alexandria*. Leipzig.

10 | Reasoning and symbolism in Diophantus: preliminary observations

REVIEL NETZ

In memoriam D. H. F. Fowler

1. Introducing the problem

This chapter raises two separate questions, one dealing with the role of reasoning in Diophantus, the other with the role of symbolism.[1] Needless to say, this discussion of symbolism and reasoning in Diophantus is of philosophical interest, as the nature of symbolic reasoning is central to modern philosophy of mathematics. My main interest, for this philosophical question, is to underline our need to consider the demonstrative function of symbolism *cognitively* and *historically*. The promise of symbolic reasoning was often seen as a transition into a mode of reasoning where the subjective mind is excluded, and an impersonal machine-like calculation takes its place.[2] But in reality, of course, the turn into symbolic proof must have involved the transition from one kind of subjective operation to another, from one set of cognitive tools to another. The abstract question, concerning the role of formalism as such in mathematics, may blind us to the actual cognitive functions served by various formal tools in different historical constellations. This chapter, then, may serve as an example for this kind of cognitive and historical investigation.

The specific question concerning symbolism and reasoning in Diophantus is especially difficult and interesting. Ever since the work of Nesselmann

---

[1] The central idea of this article – that Diophantine symbolism should be primarily understood against the wider pattern of scribal practices – was first suggested to me in a conversation with David Fowler. I will forever remember, forever miss, his voice.

[2] The locus classicus for that is Wittgenstein's *Tractatus* (Wittgenstein 1922) e.g. 6.126: 'Whether a proposition belongs to logic can be calculated by calculating the logical properties of the *symbol* . . .' (italics in the original); 6.1262: 'Proof in logic is only a mechanical expedient to facilitate the recognition of tautology, where it is complicated.' Probably, though, even the Wittgenstein of the *Tractatus* would not have denied the possibility of studying the cognitive and historical conditions under which a certain 'mechanical expedient' in fact 'facilitates the recognition of tautology'. But the thrust of the philosophy of mathematics suggested by Wittgenstein's *Tractatus* was to turn attention away from the proving mind and hand and on to the proof's symbols.

(1842), it has been widely recognized that Diophantus' symbols are not the same as those of modern algebra: his was a *syncopated*, not a *symbolic* algebra, the so-called symbols being essentially abbreviations (for a fuller account of what that means, see Section 2 below). Building on this understanding, we need to avoid the Scylla and Charybdis of Diophantus studies. One, which may be called the great-divide-history-of-algebra, stresses that abbreviations are not symbols: Diophantus is not Vieta, and Diophantus' symbols have no role in his reasoning.[3] The other, which may be called the algebra-is-algebra-history-of-algebra, stresses that symbols (even when abbreviations in character) are symbols: Diophantus is a symbolic author and his writings directly prepare the way for modern algebra (this is assumed with different degrees of sophistication in many general histories of mathematics).[4] In this chapter, I shall try to show how Diophantus' symbols derive from his specific historical context, and how they serve a specific function in his own type of reasoning: the symbols are neither purely ornamental, nor modern.

So I do believe that Diophantus' use of symbolism has a functional role in his reasoning. But, even apart from any such function, it is interesting to consider the two together. This combination may serve to characterize Diophantus' work. First, the work stands out from its predecessors in the Greek mathematical tradition, indeed in the Greek literary tradition, by its foregrounding of a special set of symbols. This foregrounding is apparent not only in that the work in its entirety makes use of the symbols, but also in that the introduction to the work – uniquely in Greek mathematics – is almost entirely dedicated to the presentation of the symbolism.[5] Second, the work stands out from its predecessors in the Mediterranean tradition of numerical problems in its foregrounding of demonstration (in a sense that we shall try to clarify below). The text takes the form of a set of arguments leading to clearly demarcated conclusions, throughout organized

---

[3] For this, see especially Klein 1934–6, a monograph that makes this claim to be the starting point of an entire philosophy of the history of mathematics.

[4] See e.g. Bourbaki 1991: 48; Boyer 1989: 204; besides of course being a theme of Bashmakova 1977). Bourbaki is laconic and straightforward (Bourbaki 1991: 48): 'Diophantus uses, for the first time, a literal symbol to represent an unknown in an equation.' Boyer is balanced and careful. Noting Nesselmann's classification, and stating that Diophantus was 'syncopated', he goes on to add that (Boyer 1989: 204) 'with such a notation Diophantus was in a position to write polynomials in a single unknown almost as concisely as we do today', however, 'the chief difference between the Diophantine syncopation and the modern algebraic notation is in the lack of special symbols for operations and relations, as well as of the exponential notation.'

[5] The introduction is in Tannery I.2–16, of which I.4.6–12.21 is organized around the presentation of the symbolism.

by such connectors as 'since', 'therefore', etc. Since the text is at the intersection of the Greek mathematical tradition with the Mediterranean tradition of numerical problems, it follows that these two characteristics – foregrounding symbolism and foregrounding reasoning – may be taken to define it.

This chapter follows on some of my past work in the cognitive and semiotic practices of Greek mathematics. I bring to bear, in particular, three strands of research. I extend the theoretical concepts of deuteronomy (Netz 2004) and analysis as a tool of presentation (Netz 2000), arguing that Diophantus was primarily a deuteronomic author – intent on rearranging, homogenizing and extending past results – employing the format of analysis as a tool of presentation that highlights certain aspects of his practice. I further contrast Diophantus' use of symbolism with the geometrical practice of formulaic expressions (N1999, ch. 4), arguing that Diophantus' use of symbolism is designed to display the rationality of transitions inside the proof and that this display is better supported, in the case of Diophantus' structures, by symbols as opposed to verbal formulae. In short: because Diophantus is deuteronomic, he uses analysis; because he uses analysis, he needs to display the rationality of transitions; because he needs to display the rationality of transitions, he uses symbols.[6]

Further, Diophantus needs to display rationality in a precise way: both allowing quick calculation of the relationship between symbols, as well as allowing a synoptic – as well as semantic – grasp of the contents of the terms involved. To do this, he uses symbols in a precise way, which I call bimodal. The symbols are simultaneously verbal and visual, and in this way they provide both quick calculation and a semantic grasp. What finally makes Diophantus' symbols have this property? This, I argue, derives from the nature of the symbolism as used in scribal practice in pre-print Greek civilizations. This involves the one main piece of empirical research underlying this chapter. I have studied systematically a group of Diophantine manuscripts, and consulted others, to show a result which is mainly negative: it must be assumed that, in the manuscript tradition, the decision whether to employ a full word or its abbreviation was left to the

---

[6] By 'Diophantus' I mean – as we typically do – 'the author of the *Arithmetica*'. I have no firm views on the authorship of *On Polygonal Numbers*, a work closer to the mainstream of Greek geometrical style. If indeed the two works had the same author (as the manuscripts suggest) we will find that, for different purposes, Diophantus could deploy different genres – not a trivial result – but neither one to change our understanding of the genre of the *Arithmetica*. But we are not in a position to make even this modest statement so that it is best to concentrate on the *Arithmetica* alone.

scribe's discretion, and no pattern was assumed at the outset. The two – full word and its abbreviation – acted as *allographs*. This may be seen as a consequence of the scribal culture within which Diophantus operated. The upshot of this chapter, then, is to situate Diophantus historically in terms of a precise deuteronomic, scribal culture, and within the context of practices available to him from elite Greek mathematics.

2. Notes on symbolism in Diophantus

We recall Nesselmann's observation: Diophantus belongs to the category of 'syncopated algebra', where the text is primarily arranged as discursive, natural language (if of course in the rigid style typical of so much Greek mathematics), with certain expressions systematically abbreviated.[7] In this, it is generally understood to constitute a stepping stone leading from the rhetorical algebra of, say (if we allow ourselves such heresy), *Elements* Book II, to the fully symbolic algebra of the moderns.

As a first approximation, let us take a couple of sentences printed in Tannery's edition (prop. I.10, T1893, I. 28.13–15):

(1) Τετάχθω ὁ προστιθέμενος καὶ ἀφαιρούμενος ἑκατέρῳ ἀριθμῷ ϛΑ. κἂν μὲν τῷ Κ προστεθῇ, γίνεται ϛΑ Μ°Κ.

Let the <number> which is added and taken away from each number <sc. of the two other given numbers> be set down, <namely> ϛΑ <:Number 1>. And if it is added to 20, result: ϛΑ Μ°Κ <:number 1 Monads 20>.

We see here the most important element in Diophantus' symbolism: a special symbol for 'number', ϛ. We also see a transparent abbreviation for 'monads', Μ°. To these should be added especially: two transparent abbreviations, for 'dunamis' (effectively, 'square'), Δ^υ, and for 'cube', Κ^υ. Symbols for higher powers exist and are made by combining symbols for the low powers, e.g. ΔΚ^υ, dunamis–cube, or the fifth power. An appended ^{χ} turns such a power into its related unit fraction: a dunamis, Δ^υ, can become a dunamiston, Δ^{υχ}, or the unit fraction correlated with a dunamis. (The symbol itself is reminiscent in form especially of the standard scribal symbols for case endings.) Finally we should mention a special symbol for

---

[7] For a previous, brief characterization of Diophantus' symbolism in practice, see Rashed 1984: lxxxi–lxxxii, whose position I follow here. Heath 1885: 57–82 may still be read with profit. In general, many of the claims made in this section were made by past scholars already, and my apology for going through this section in detail is that the point is worth repeating – and should be seen in detail as an introduction to the following and much more speculative discussion.

'lacking', roughly an upside-down Ψ (I shall indeed represent it in what follows by Ψ, for lack of better fonts. Note that this is to be understood as a 'minus' sign followed by the entirety of the remaining expression – as if it came equipped with a set of following parentheses.) Together with Greek alphabetic numerals (A, B, I, K, P, Σ for 1, 2, 10, 20, 100, 200...) one has the main system with which complex phrases can be formed of the type, e.g.

(2) KᵘBΔᵘA ₅B MᵒΓ Ψ Kᵘ A ΔᵘΓ ₅Δ MᵒA

Most of all, Diophantine reasoning has to do with manipulation of such phrases.

Syntactically, note that such phrases have a fixed order: one goes through the powers in a fixed sequence (although in terms of Greek syntax, any order could be natural). The numeral, also, always follows the unit to which it refers (this, however, can be explained as natural Greek syntax). Finally, there is a fixed order relative to the 'lacking' symbol: the subtrahend is always to the right of the symbol. This of course follows from the very meaning of 'lacking'.

Semantically, we may say that the 'number' functions rather like an 'unknown', on which the 'dunamis' or the 'cube' depend as well (a single 'number' multiplied by itself results in a single 'dunamis' which, once again multiplied by a 'number', yields a 'cube'). The monads, on the other hand, are independent of the 'number'.

Let us consider the wider context. When we discuss symbolism in Diophantus, we need to describe it at three levels. First, there is the symbolism which Diophantus had explicitly introduced in the preface to his treatise. Second, Diophantus has a number of fairly specialized symbols which he did not explicitly set out. Third, we should have a sense of the entire symbolic regime of the Diophantine page, bringing everything together – the markedly Diophantine, and the standard symbolism of Greek scribal practice.

The symbols explicitly introduced by Diophantus are those mentioned above (in the order in which Diophantus introduces them): Δᵘ, Kᵘ, ΔᵘΔ, ΔKᵘ, Kᵘ K, ₅, Mᵒ, ˣ, Ψ. These then unmistakably belong to the phrases such as those of example (2), serving further to underline the importance of this type of expression.

Beyond that, the manuscripts display a variety of further symbols. Tannery systematically represents symbolically in his edition such symbols as he feels, apparently, to be markedly Diophantine (on the other hand, he always resolves standard scribal abbreviations; more on this below). The following especially are noticeable among the markedly Diophantine:

The alphabetic numerals themselves. While Greek numbers are very
often written out by alphabetic numerals, they are more frequently
spelled out in Greek writing as the appropriate number words – just
as we have to decide between '5' and 'five'. The avoidance of number
words and the use of alphabetical numerals, instead, is therefore a
decision involving a numerical code.

□, for 'square' (used here in the meaning of 'a square number').

⊥, for 'the right sides', in a right-angled triangle. Here they are studied
as fulfilling Pythagoras' theorem and therefore offering an arena for
equalities for square numbers. Strangely, Tannery does not print this
symbol.

A′, B′, Γ′, etc. for 'first', 'second', 'third', etc. This is used in the important
context where several numbers are involved in the problem, e.g. what
we represent by '$n_1 + n_2 = 3n_3$' which, for Diophantus, would be 'the
first and the second are three times the third', with 'first', 'second', etc.
used later on systematically to refer to the same object. Of course,
such symbols are not to be confused with their respective numerals
and they are differently written out.

B^{πλ}, Γ^{πλ}, for 'two times', 'three times', etc. This symbolism is based on the
alphabetic numerals, tucking on to them a transparent abbreviation
of the Greek form of 'times'.

E^{ιΓ}: this is an especially dramatic notation whereby Diophantus refrains
from resolving the results of divisions into unit fractions, and instead
writes out, like in the example above, 'five thirteenths' in a kind of
superscript notation. Tannery further transforms this notation into
a sort of upside-down modern notation. As long as we do not mean
anything technical by the word, we may refer to this as Diophantus'
'fraction symbolism'.

The last few mentioned symbols (with the possible exception of the fraction symbolism) are not unique to Diophantus, but for obvious reasons the
text has much more recourse to such symbols than ordinary Greek texts so
that, indeed, they can be said to be markedly Diophantine.

One ought to mention immediately that many words, typical to
Diophantus, are not abbreviated. These fall into two types. First, several
central relations and concepts – 'multiply', 'add', 'given', etc. – are written
in fully spelled out forms. In other words, Diophantus' abbreviations are
located within the level of the noun-phrase, and do not touch the structure
of the sentence interrelating the noun-phrases. 'Lacking' is the exception to
the rule that relations are not abbreviated, but it serves to confirm the rule
that abbreviations are located at the level of the noun-phrase. The 'lacking'

abbreviation is used inside the noun-phrase of the specific form of example (2) above, when a quantitative value is set out statically. The relation of subtraction holding dynamically *between* such noun-phrases – when one engages in the *act* of subtracting a value from a quantitative term – this operation is referred to by a different verb, 'take away' (*aphairein*), which is not abbreviated.

Further, the logical signposts marking the very rigid form of the problem, such as 'let it be set down', 'to the positions', etc., are fully written out. In other words, just as symbolism does not reach the level of the sentence, so it does not reach the level of the paragraph. The rule is confirmed: abbreviations are confined to the level of the noun-phrase. I shall return to discuss the significance of this limitation in Section 4 below. For the time being, I note the conclusion, that Diophantus' marked use of symbolism is not co-extensive with Diophantus' marked use of language.

Over and above Diophantus' marked use of symbolism, it should be mentioned that Greek manuscripts, certainly from late antiquity onwards, used many abbreviations for common words such as prepositions, connectors, etc.: our own '&', for instance, ultimately derives from such scribal practices. There are also many abbreviations of grammatical forms, especially case markings, so that the Greek nominal root is written, followed by the abbreviation for 'ov', 'ois', etc. as appropriate. Such abbreviations are of course in common use in the manuscripts of Diophantus. Most (but not all) of such symbols were transparent abbreviations and in general they could be considered as a mere aid to swift writing. Their use is as could be predicted: the more expensive a manuscript was, the less such abbreviations would be used; they are more common in technical treatises than in literary works; humanists, proud of their mastery of Greek forms, would tend to resolve abbreviations, while Byzantine scribes – often scrambling to get as much into the page as possible – would also often tend to abbreviate.

We should mention one scribal abbreviation, which is not at all specific to Diophantus, but which is especially valuable to him: the one for the sound-sequence /is/. It so happens that this common sound-sequence is the lexical root for 'equal' in Greek. Since it is a very common sound-sequence, it naturally has a standard abbreviation, so that Diophantus has 'for free' a symbol for this important relation.

How are such symbols understood? That is, what is the relationship between Diophantus' symbols, and the alphabetically written words that they replace? The first thing to notice, as already suggested above, is that the symbols are most often a transparent abbreviation of the alphabetical form. Diophantus' own strategy of choice in the symbols he had himself coined was to clip the word into its first syllable (especially when this is a simple, consonant–vowel syllable), which he then turned into a symbol by placing the vowel as a superscript on the consonant: Kᵘ, Δᵘ, Mᵒ. The symbols result from two reductions – a word into its initial syllable, a syllable into its consonant. All of this makes sense in terms of natural language phonology so that, in such cases, Diophantus' symbolism may be tied to the heard sound and not just to the visible trace. (It may be relevant that in all three words – monas, dunamis, kubos – the stress falls indeed on the first syllable.) With arithm- and leipsei this simple strategy fails. The symbols, in both cases, are more complex: perhaps some combination of the alpha and the rho of the arithmos (but this is a well-known palaeographic puzzle), certainly some reference to the psi of the leipsei. This is in line with the standard symbolism, e.g. for prepositions: these are often rendered by a combination of their consonants ('pros', e.g., becoming a ligature of the pi and the rho).

Note also that while alphabetical numerals do not directly represent the sounds of the number-words they stand for, the system as a whole is isomorphic to spoken numerals (two-number words, 'two and thirty' become two number-symbols, ΛB). In this, the alphabetical numeral system differs from its main alternative in Greek antiquity, the acrophonic system where each symbol had, directly, a sound meaning (Π for pente, five, Δ for deka, ten, etc.: the only exception is the use of a stroke for the unit), but the acrophonic number symbolism as a whole was equivalent to the Roman system with which we are familiar and was no longer isomorphic to spoken numerals: not ΛB, but ΔΔΔΙΙ. The latter clearly is not meant to be pronounced as 'deka-deka-deka-click-click'. In fact, it is no longer a pronounced symbol: the trace has become free of the sound. In the alphabetical system, everything can be understood as symbols standing for sounds in natural Greek: I believe this may be the reason why this system was finally preferred for most ordinary writing.

With this in mind, we can see that Diophantus' marked symbols are at least potentially spoken: the numbers, as explained above, as well as the symbols based upon them. A stroke turns a numeral into its dependent ordinal or unit-fraction (identical in sound, as in symbol: compare English 'third', 'fourth', etc.). Further, ordinals are sometimes rendered in an even more direct phonological system, e.g. Δᵉᵘ, abbreviating δευτερος, for 'second'. (Thus the system for ordinals has three separate forms: the fully written-out word, the phonologically abbreviated form and the alphabetic numeral-based form. This is important, given the role of ordinals as a kind of unknown-mark in expressions such as 'the first number'.) The ×-times symbolism, too, merely adds the onset consonants of the abbreviated words: Bᵖᵃ for 'double'.

The symbols for square, and for sides in a right-angled triangle, are the exception, then. There the trace, and not the sound, becomes the vehicle of meaning. The reason for this is clear, as the trace here has indeed such an obvious connotation. The sign and the signified are isomorphic. Even so, note that the understanding is that □ stands not just for the concept 'square' but also and perhaps primarily for the sequence 'tetragon', as witnessed by the fact that the symbol is often followed by case marking: □ᵒⁱˢ for 'tetragonois', 'by the squares'. The most interesting exception is the form □ □, sometimes used to represent 'squares', the plural marked not by the sound of the case ending, but by the tracing of duplication (compare our use of 'pp.', for instance, for 'pages'; notice also that the same also happens occasionally with the 'number' symbol).

Speaking generally for Greek writing in manuscripts, the phonological nature of abbreviation symbolism becomes most apparent through the rebus principle. To provide an example: there is a standard scribal abbreviation for the Greek word 'ara', 'therefore'. There is also an important preposition, 'para', meaning, roughly, 'alongside'. The letter pi, followed by the symbol for 'ara', may be used to represent the preposition 'para'. Such rebus writing is common in Greek manuscripts and shows that the symbol for 'ara' stands not merely for the concept 'therefore' but, perhaps more fundamentally, for the sound-sequence 'ara'.

Obviously, Diophantus' symbolism does not lend itself to such rebus combinations. One can mention, however, an important close analogue. We recall Diophantus' symbol for 'number', meaning, effectively, the 'unknown'. This may be said to be the cornerstone of Diophantus' symbolism: on it ride the higher powers; it is the starting point for investigation in each problem. It is thus, perhaps, not inappropriate that this symbol is the least transparently phonological. It is, so to speak, Diophantus' cipher. Crucially, it is also clearly defined by Diophantus in his introduction: 'That which possesses none of these properties [such as dunamis, cube, etc.] and has in it an indeterminate number of monads, is called a number and its symbol is ς' (Tannery 6.3–5). Thus the symbol is, strictly speaking, only to be used for the indeterminate, or unknown, goal of the problem. It should be used in such contexts as 'Let the <number> which is added and taken away from each number <sc. of the two other given numbers> be set down, <namely> ςA <:Number 1>.' Notice the two occurrences of 'number' in this phrase. The first is 'number' in its standard Greek meaning (which therefore, one would think, should not be abbreviable into the symbol ς). In the phrase 'from each number', the word 'number' does not stand for an unknown number, but just for 'number'. It is only the second number – the one counted as '1' - which serves as an unknown in this problem. Only this, then, by Diophantus' explicit definition, counts as a ς; appropriately, then, Tannery prints the first 'number' as a fully spelled-out word and the second as a symbol. But as the reader may guess by now, there are many cases in the manuscripts where 'number' of the first type is abbreviated, as well, using Diophantus' symbol ς.[8] Thus the symbol is understood, at least by Diophantus' scribes, to range not across a semantic range (the unknown number), but across a phonological or orthographic range (the representation of the sound, or trace, 'arithm-'). It would indeed be surprising if it were otherwise, given that scribal symbolism, as a system, was understood in such phonological or orthographic terms.

The text in example (1) above followed closely (with some variation of orthography) Tannery's edition. It is clearly punctuated and spaced (as it is not in the manuscripts, not even the Renaissance ones). It has accents and aspiration marks (like the Renaissance manuscripts, but most probably unlike Diophantus' text in late antiquity). It also sharply demarcates the two kinds of writing: explicit and markedly Diophantine symbols, which, in the proof itself, Tannery systematically presents in abbreviated form, on the one hand; and standard scribal abbreviations, which Tannery systematically resolves (as, indeed, philologers invariably do).

As Tannery himself recognized, his systematization of the symbolism was not based on manuscript evidence. I shall not say anything more on the unmarked symbolism, such as the case markings, whose usage indeed differs (as one expects) from one manuscript to another. They should be mentioned, so that we keep in mind the full context of Diophantus' symbols. But even more important is that Diophantus' own marked symbolism is not systematically used in the manuscripts. The symbols described above are often interchanged with fully written words. This is as much as can be expected. Both Δ^{υ} and Δυναμις stand for exactly the same thing – the sound pattern or trace /dunamis/ – and so there is no essential reason to use one and not the other. Thus a free interchangeability is predicted.

Notice first the form of example (1) in *all* the Paris manuscripts, comparing the (translated) form of Tannery's text to that of the manuscripts:

---

[8] This was pointed out already by Nesselmann 1842: 300–1. Indeed, my impression is that awareness of such quirks of Diophantus' text was more widespread prior to Tannery: following the acceptance of his edition, knowledge of the manuscripts (as well as of the early printed editions – whose practices, I note in passing, are comparable to those of the manuscripts) became less common among scholars of Diophantus' mathematics.

Tannery: Let the <number> which is added and taken away from each number <sc. of the two other given numbers> be set down, <namely> ςΑ <:Number 1>. And if it is added to 20, result: ςΑ M°K <:number 1 Monads 20>.

Manuscripts: Let the <number> which is added and taken away from each number <sc. of the two other given numbers> be set down, <namely> One number. And if it is added to 20, result: One number, 20 Monads.

Here we see Tannery's most typical treatment of the manuscripts: abbreviating expressions which, in the manuscripts, are resolved, within the problem itself. Note the opposite, inside enunciations. For example, the enunciation to III.10 which, in Tannery's form, may be translated:

Tannery: To find three numbers so that the <multiplication> by any two, taken with a given number, makes a square.

Compare this with, e.g., Par. Gr. 2379:

Manuscript: To find three numbers so that the <multiplication> by any two, taken with a given ς, makes a □.

Tannery, we recall, followed a rational system: inside the proof, all markedly Diophantine symbols were presented in abbreviated form, while in the enunciation no symbolism was used. We find that the manuscripts sometimes have abbreviated forms where Tannery has fully written words, and sometimes have fully written words where Tannery has abbreviations. In other words, Tannery's rational system does not work. I had systematically studied the marked Diophantine symbols through the propositions whose number divide by ten, in Books I to III, in all the Paris manuscripts. These are only eight propositions, but the labour, even so, was considerable: essentially, I was busy recording noise. As a consequence of this, I gave up on further systematic studies, merely confirming the overall picture described here, with other manuscripts.

One notices perhaps a gradual tendency to introduce more and more abbreviated forms as the treatise progresses (do the scribes become tired, in time?): Par. Gr. 2378, for instance, has no symbolism in my Book I specimens at all, while they are frequent in Book III. The ordinal numbers, with their three separate forms (fully spelled out, phonologically abbreviated, alphabetical numeral based), are especially bewildering. Consider once again III.10, once again in Par. Gr. 2378. I plot the sequence of ordinals, using N for the alphabetic numeral, P for phonological abbreviation and F for the full version:

NNNNPPFFFFFFFFNFFFFPFNNFFFPF.

Tannery has all as alphabetical numerals. The most we can say is that, in the manuscripts, there is an overall tendency to prefer using the same form within a single phrase, though exceptions to this are found as well. Here we see Tannery homogenizing, turning numbers into numerals. But we may also find the opposite, e.g. in 1.20, an expression we may translate as

Tannery: Let the two <numbers> be set down as ςϛ3
τετάχθωσαν οἱ δύο ςϛ3
Par. Gr. 2485: Let the 2 <numbers> be set down as Numbers, Three.
τετάχθωσαν οἱ Β ἀριθμοὶ τρεῖς

Tannery has spelled out the word 'two', to signal that it functions here in a syntactic, not an arithmetical way. But it is neither syntactic nor arithmetical, it is phonological/orthographic. In the manuscripts, we have the phonological/orthographic object /duo/ which may be represented, as far as the scribes are concerned, by either B or δύο: both would do equally well.

Significantly, it is difficult to discern a system even in the symbols introduced by Diophantus himself. Consider Par. Gr. 2380, inside 11.10: ς ενος μοναδων Γ, that is 'ς one, monads 3' (I quote this as an elegant example where both Diophantus' special symbols, as well as numerals, are interchanged with fully spelled out words). Very typical are expressions such as Par. Gr. 2378, 11.20: Δ^{υ} Δ αριθμους E M°, that is 'Δ^{υ} 4, numbers 5, M°1'. The 'numbers' – alone in the phrase – are spelled out. In general, one can say that monads appear to be abbreviated more often than anything else in Diophantus' symbolism: this may be because they are so common there. But the main fact is not quantitative, but qualitative: one finds, in all manuscripts, the full range from Diophantine phrases fully spelled out in natural Greek, through all kinds of combinations of symbols and full words, to fully abbreviated phrases.

My conclusion is that symbols in Diophantus are *allographs*: ways of expressing precisely the same things as their fully spelled out equivalents. And once this allography is understood, the chaos of the manuscripts becomes natural. For why should you decide in advance when to use this or that, when the two are fully equivalent?

One should now understand Tannery's plight. That he systematized his printed edition is natural: what else should he have done? I am not even sure we should criticize him for failing to provide a critical apparatus on the symbols. The task is immense and its fruits dubious. In particular, given Tannery's goal – of reconstructing, to the best of his ability, Diophantus' original text – a critical study of the abbreviations seems indeed hopeless. The interrelationships between manuscripts, in terms of their choice of abbreviation as against a fully spelled out word, are tenuous. Sometimes one discerns affinities: the same sequence of symbols is sometimes used in a group of manuscripts, suggesting a common origin (and why shouldn't a scribe be influenced by what he has in his source?). But such cases are rare while, on the whole, patterns are more often found *inside* a single manuscript: a tendency to avoid abbreviations for a stretch of writing, then a tendency to put them in . . .

However, Tannery did not make appeal to this argument – which would have put his edition in the uncomfortable position of being, in a central way, Tannery's rather than Diophantus'. So he made appeal to another argument. When criticized by Hultsch (1894) for his failure to note scribal variation for symbolism in his apparatus, Tannery replied that he had found that tedious,[9] because – so he had implied – Diophantus had purely abbreviated forms, that is in line with Tannery's edition – which then were corrupted by the manuscript tradition. This question merits consideration.

In the handful of thirteenth-century manuscripts we possess (the earliest), symbolism is more frequent. Thus the tendency of scribes, *during the historical stretch for which we have direct evidence*, was to resolve abbreviations into words. The simplest hypothesis, then, would be that of a simple extrapolation: throughout, *scribes tend to resolve abbreviations* – hence, Diophantus himself must have produced a strict abbreviated text.

This is false, I think, for the following reasons. First, the relevant consideration is not that of Diophantus' manuscript tradition alone, but that of scribal practice in general. We may then witness a peak in the use of abbreviations in Byzantine technical manuscripts of the relevant period of the twelfth and thirteenth centuries – which are in general characterized by minute writing aiming to pack as much as possible into the page. Early minuscule manuscripts, and of course majuscule texts, often are more of luxury objects and have fewer abbreviations; humanist manuscripts, again, for similar reasons, tend to have fewer abbreviations. Thus the evidence of the process of resolution of abbreviations, from the thirteenth to the sixteenth centuries, may not be extended into the past, as an hypothetical series of resolution stretching all the way from as far back as the fourth century CE.

Second, I find it striking that the Arabic tradition knows nothing of Diophantus' symbols. There are of course good linguistic reasons why Arabic (as well as Syriac and Hebrew) would not rely as much on the kind of abbreviation typical to the Greek and Latin tradition. Indeed, to continue with the linguistic typology, symbolism is also independently

---

[9] T1893/5: xxxiv–xlii.

used in Sanskrit mathematics.[10] Indo-European words are a concatenation of prefixes, roots and suffixes. Each component is phonologically autonomous, so that it is always possible to substitute some by alternative symbols. A written word can thus naturally become a sequence concatenating symbols, or alphabetic representations, for prefixes, roots and suffixes. Semitic words, on the other hand, are consonantal roots inside which are inserted patterns of vocalic infixes. The components cannot be taken apart in the stream of speech, so that it is no longer feasible to substitute a word by a concatenation of symbols, each standing for a root or a grammatical element. Quite simply, the language does not function in terms of such concatenations. Arab translators, then, had naturally resolved standard Greek abbreviations into their fully spelled out forms. But they did respect some symbols: for instance, magical symbols, similar in character to those known from Greek-era Papyri (though not derived from the Greek), are attested in the Arabic tradition;[11] most famously, the Arabs had gradually appropriated Indian numeral symbols. In such cases, the symbols were understood primarily not as phonological units, but as written traces. I suggest that, had Diophantus' use of symbolism been as consistent as Tannery makes it, an astute mathematical reader would recognize in it the use of symbolism which goes beyond scribal expediency, and which is based on the written trace – especially, given Diophantus' own, explicit introduction of the symbols. The Arab suppression of the symbolism in Diophantus suggests, then, that they saw in it no more than the standard scribal abbreviation they were familiar with from elsewhere in Greek writing.

I conclude with two comments, one historical, and the other cognitive. Historically, we see that Diophantus' symbols are rooted in a certain scribal practice. This should be seen in the context of the long duration of Greek writing. In antiquity, Greek writing was among the simplest systems in use anywhere in human history: a single set of characters (roughly speaking, our upper case), used with few abbreviations. Through late antiquity to the early Middle Ages, the system becomes much more complex: the use of abbreviations becomes much more common, and a new set of characters (roughly speaking, our lower case) is introduced while the old set remains in use in many contexts. In other words, the period is characterized by an explosion in allography.[12] This may be related to the introduction of the

---

[10] See the lucid discussion in H1995: 87–90.

[11] Canaan 1937–8/2004, especially 2004: 167–75.

[12] It is difficult to find precise references for such claims that are rather the common stock of knowledge acquired by palaeographers in their practice. The best introduction to the practices of Greek manuscripts probably remains Groningen 1955. For abbreviations in early Greek script, see McNamee 1982.

codex, and with the overall tenor of the culture with which it is associated: a culture where writing as such becomes the centre of cultural life, with much greater attention to its material setting. It is in this context that Diophantus introduces his symbols: they are the product of the same culture that gave rise to the codex.

Cognitively, we see that those symbols introduced by Diophantus are indeed allographs. That is: they do not suppress the verbal reading of the sign, but refer to it in a different, visual way. It was impossible for a Greek reader to come across the symbol M° and not to have suggested to his mind the verbal sound-shape 'monad'. But at the same time, the symbol itself would be striking: it would be a very common shape seen over and over again in the text of Diophantus and nowhere else. It would also be a very simple shape, immediately read off the page as a single visual object. Thus, alongside the verbal reading of the object, there would also be a visual recognition of it, both obligatory and instantaneous. I thus suggest that what is involved here is a *systematic bimodality*. One systematically reads the sign both verbally and visually. One reads out the word; but is also aware of the sign.

To sum up, then, Diophantus' symbolism gives rise to a bimodal (verbal and visual) parsing of the text (at the level of the noun-phrase). I shall return to analyse the significance of this in Section 4 below, where I shall argue that this bimodality explains the function of Diophantus' symbols within his reasoning. Before that, then, let us acquaint ourselves with this mode of reasoning.

3. Notes on reasoning in Diophantus

A sample of Diophantus

The following is a literal translation of Diophantus' I.10. I follow Tannery's text, with the difference that, for each case where a symbol is available (including alphabetical numerals which, when symbolic, I render by our own Arabic numerals), I toss a couple of coins to decide whether I print it as symbol or as resolved word. (25% I make to be full words, which is what I postulate, for the sake of the exercise, might have been the original ratio.) The translation follows my conventions from the translation of Greek geometry,[13] including the introduction of Latin numerals to count steps of construction and Arabic numerals to count steps of reasoning.

---

[13] See Netz 2004.

To two given ςς: to add to the smaller of them, and to take away from the greater, and to make the resulting <number> have a given ratio to the remainder.

Let it be set forth to add to 20, and to take away from 100 the same ς, and to make the greater 4-times the smaller.

(a) Let the <number> which is added and taken away from each ς <sc. of the two given numbers> be set down, <namely> number, one. (1) And if it is added to twenty, results: ς1 M°20. (2) And if it is taken away from 100, results: M°100 lacking number 1. (3) And it shall be required that the greater be 4-^{tms} the smaller. (4) Therefore four-^{tms} the smaller is equal to the greater; (5) but four-^{tms} the smaller results: M°400 Ψ ς4; (6) these equal ς1 M°20

(7) Let the subtraction be added <as> common, (8) and let similar <terms> be taken away from similar <terms>. (9) Remaining: numbers, 5, equal M°380. (10) And the ς results: monads, 76.

To the positions. I put the added and the taken away on each ς, ς 1; it shall be M°76. And if M°76 is added to 20, result: monads, 96; and if it is taken away from 100, remaining: monads, 24. And the greater shall stand being 4-^{tms} the smaller.

Diophantus the deuteronomist: systematization and the general

To understand the function of the text above, I move on to compare it with three other, hypothetical texts. I argue that all were possible in the late ancient Mediterranean. However, only the first two had existed, while the third remained as a mere logical possibility, never actualized in writing.

Text 1:
A: I have a hundred and a twenty. I take away a number from the greater and add it to the smaller. Now the smaller has become four times that which was greater. How much did I take away and add?
B: ?
A: Seventy six! Check for yourself.

Text 2:
Hundred and twenty. I took away from the greater and added the same to the smaller, and the smaller became four times that which had been greater.
Take the greater, a hundred. Its four times is four hundred. Take away the smaller, twenty. Left is three hundred eighty. Four plus one is five. Divide three hundred eighty by five: seventy six. Seventy six is the number taken away and added.

Text 3:

Given two numbers, the first greater than the second, and given the ratio of a third number to unity, to find a fourth number so that, added to the second and removed from the first, it makes the ratio of the second to the first equal to the given ratio of the third number to unity.

Let the fourth have been found. Since the second number together with the fourth has to the first lacking the fourth the ratio of the third to unity, make a fifth number which is the third multiplied by the first lacking the third multiplied by the fourth. This fifth number is equal to the second together with the fourth. So the third multiplied by the first lacking the third multiplied by the fourth is equal to the second with the fourth.So the third multiplied by the first is equal to the second with the fourth with the third multiplied by the fourth, or to the second with the fourth taken the third and one times. That is, the third multiplied by the first, lacking the second, is equal to the fourth taken the third and one times. Multiply all by the third and one fraction. Thus the third multiplied by the first, multiplied by the third and one fraction, lacking the second multiplied by the third and one fraction, is equal to the fourth taken the third and one times, multiplied by the third and one fraction, which is the fourth. So the third multiplied by the first, multiplied by the third and one fraction, lacking the second multiplied by the third and one fraction, is equal to the fourth.

So it shall be constructed as follows. Let one be added to the third to make the sixth. Let the seventh be made to be the fraction of the sixth. Let the third be multiplied by the first and by the seventh to make the eighth.

Again, let the second be multiplied by the seventh to make the ninth.

Now let the ninth be taken away from the eighth, to make the fourth. I say that the fourth produces the task.

[Here it is straightforward to add an explicit synthesis, showing that the ratio obtains; for brevity's sake, I omit this part.]

I suggest that we see Diophantus' text with reference to texts 1 and 2 – of which it must have been aware – and with reference to text 3 – which it deliberately avoided.[14] Based on Høyrup's work,[15] I assume that texts such as text 1 were widespread in Mediterranean cultures from as far back as

[14] Text 3 is my invention; perhaps not the most elegant one possible. All I did was to try to write, in an idiom as close as possible to that of Diophantus, a general analysis of the problem, following a line of reasoning hewing closely to the steps of the solution in Diophantus' own solution. (This is not a mechanical translation: obviously, a particular solution such as Diophantus' underdetermines the general analysis from which it may be derived, since any particular term may be understood as the result of more than one kind of general configuration.)

[15] See, for instance, H2002: 362–7. It is fair to say that my summary is based not so much on this reference from the book, as on numerous discussions, conference papers and preprints from

the third millennium BCE (if not earlier), surviving, arguably, into our own time. They persisted almost exclusively as an oral tradition (sometimes, perhaps, taking a ride for a couple of centuries on the back of written traditions of the type of text 2, and then proceeding along in the oral mode). Such texts are called by Høyrup 'lay algebra'.

Occasionally, lay algebra gets written and systematized (to a certain extent) in an educational context. It then typically gets transformed into texts such as text 2: the mere question-and-answer format of text 1 is transformed into a set of indicative and imperative sentences put forward in the rigid, authoritarian style typical of most written education prior to the twentieth century. This is school algebra which has appeared several times in Mediterranean cultures. One can mention especially its Babylonian (early second millennium BCE), Greek (around the year zero) and Italian (early second millennium CE) forms. The Babylonian layer is important as the first school algebra of which we are aware; the Greek layer is important, for our purposes, as providing, possibly, a context for Diophantus' work; the Italian layer is important, for our purposes, as providing a context for the interest in Diophantus in the Renaissance.

The historical relationship between various school algebras is not clear and it may be that they depend on the persistence of lay algebra no less than on previous school algebras. It should be said that, while essentially based on the written mode, this is a use of writing fundamentally different from that of elite literary culture. Writing is understood as a local, ad-hoc affair. The difference between the literacy of school algebra and the oralcy of lay algebra is huge, in terms of their *archaeology*: clay tablets, papyri and *libri d'abbaco* often survive, spoken words never do. But the clay tablets, papyri and *libri d'abbaco* of school algebra do not belong to the world of Gilgamesh, Homer or Dante. They are not faithfully copied and maintained, and the assumptions we have for the stability of written culture need not hold for them.

What would happen when such materials become part of elite literate culture itself? One hypothetical example is text 3: a reworking of the same material, keeping as closely as possible to the features of elite literate Greek mathematics (which was developed especially for the treatment of geometry). This may be called, then – just so that we have a term – Euclidean algebra.[16] When transforming the materials of lay and school algebra into

the author, and that as such summaries go it is likely to deviate in some ways from the way in which Høyrup himself would have summed up his own position.

[16] I use the term 'Euclidean' to refer to elite, literate mathematical practices. It is true that Euclid – especially Books I and II – could have been occasionally part of ancient education (the three papyrus as fragments P. Mich. 3. 143, P. Berol. Inv 17469 and P. Oxy. 1.29, with definitions

elite-educated, literate form, Diophantus chose to produce not Euclidean algebra, but Diophantine algebra.

I note in passing that the character of Diophantus – as intended for elite literate culture – is in my view not in serious doubt. The material does not conform to elementary school procedures; it is ultimately of great complexity, suitable only for a specialized readership. It had survived only inside elite literate tradition; and, as is well known, it quickly obtained the primary mark of elite literate work – having a commentary dedicated to it (that of Hypatia).[17]

In other words, I suggest that Diophantus is engaged primarily in the rearrangement of previously available material into a certain given format, of course then massively extending it to cover new grounds that were not surveyed by school algebra itself. This is very much the standard view of Diophantus, and I merely wish to point out here what seem to me to be its consequences. Let us agree that Diophantus is engaged in the refitting of previous traditions into the formats of elite writing sanctioned by tradition. Then it becomes open to suggest that he belongs to the overall practice of late antiquity and the Middle Ages which I have elsewhere called deuteronomic: the production of texts which are primarily dependent upon some previous texts.[18] Typically, deuteronomic texts emphasize consistency, systematicity and completion. There is an attention to the manner of writing of the text. This means that they bring together various elements that might have been originally disparate. The act of trying to bring disparate

of Book I, Propositions I.8–10 and II.5, respectively – most likely derive from a classroom context). However, the bulk of papyri finds with mathematical educational contents are different in character, involving basic numeracy and measuring skills or, in more sophisticated examples, coming closer to Hero's version of geometry. The impression is that, in antiquity itself, Euclid was fundamentally a cultural icon, which occasionally got inducted into the educational process.

[17] The evidence is the flimsiest imaginable – a mere statement in the Suidas (Adler IV:644.1–4: Υπατια . . . εγραψεν υπομνημα εις Διοφαντον) which, however, if not proving beyond doubt that *Hypatia* wrote a commentary on Diophantus, makes it at least very likely that *someone* did.

[18] Virtually everyone, from Tannery to Neugebauer onwards, has agreed that Diophantus was acquainted with many arithmetical problems deriving from earlier Mediterranean traditions and was therefore at least to some extent a systematizer. Some, such as Heath, had thought that Diophantus' systematization of earlier problems may not have been the first in the Greek world, making comparison with Euclid as the culmination of a tradition of writing *Elements* (I doubt this for Euclid and find it very unlikely for Diophantus). The dates are fixed, based on internal evidence, as –150 to +350. What else is argued concerning Diophantus' dates is based on scattered, late Byzantine comments which are best ignored. The *e silentio*, together with Diophantus' very survival, suggest – no more – a late date. (The silence is not meaningless, as it encompasses authors from Hero to the neo-Platonist authors writing on number.) A late date was always the favourite among scholars (not surprisingly, then, the thesis of an early

components into some kind of coherent unity then would lead to a certain transformation.

The way this applies to Diophantus is obvious. He brings together previously available problems. He arranges them in a relatively clear order, ranging from the simple to the complex. He classifies, creating clear units of text, for instance the Greek Book VI, all dedicated to right-angled triangle problems. In the introduction he discusses his way of writing down the problems, and introduces a special manner of writing for the purpose.

The structuring involves large-scale and small-scale transformations. The large-scale transformation is a product of the arrangement of the disparate problems in a rational structure. The problems often become combinatorial variations on each other, e.g. II.11–13:

11. To add the same number to two given numbers, and to make each a square.
12. To take away the same number from two given numbers, and to make each of the remainders a square.
13. To take away from the same number two given numbers, and to make each of the remainders a square.

In such cases, it seems clear that Diophantus had used the rational structure as a guide, actively searching for more problems, bringing completion to his much more fragmentary sources. The huge structure – thirteen books, of which, in some form or another, ten survive, with perhaps four hundred problems solved – was built on the basis of such rational, combinatorial completion.

The small-scale transformation involves each and every problem, which is presented, always, in the form above. It is immediately obvious that, in this respect, Diophantus consciously strove to imitate elite literate Greek mathematics though (as suggested by the examples above) this in itself would not determine the form of his text. Quite simply, there was more than a single way of producing numerical problems in elite literate Greek

---

date was defended by Knorr 1993). I shall assume such a late date, while realizing of course the hypothetical nature of the argument: the dating of Diophantus is the first brick of speculation in the following, speculative edifice. I would like to question, though, the very habit of treating the post quem and the ante quem as defining a homogeneous chronological segment. One's attitude ought to be much more probabilistic – and should appreciate the fact that not all centuries are alike. Here are two probabilistic claims:
(1) the first century BCE, and the first century CE, both saw less in activity in the exact sciences; the second century CE, as well as the first half of the fourth century CE, saw more.
(2) The e silentio is more and more powerful, the further back in time we go. I think it is therefore correct to say that Diophantus most likely was active either in the second century CE or the first half of the fourth century CE.

format - not a single monolith to start with. In fitting his text into the established elite Greek mathematical format, Diophantus had a certain freedom.

The first decision made by Diophantus was to keep the basic dichotomy of presentation from standard Greek mathematics, with an arrangement of a general statement followed by a particular proof. This indeed would appear as one of the most striking features of the Greek mathematical style. But most important, this arrangement is essential to the large-scale transformation introduced by Diophantus. To produce a structure based on rational completion, Diophantus needed to have something to complete rationally: a set of general statements referring to each problem in terms transcending the particular parameters of the problem at hand.

I therefore argue that Diophantus' general statements can be understood, at two levels, as a function of his deuteronomic project. He needs the general statements so as to conform to the elite form of presentation he sets out to emulate. Even more important, he needs them to provide building blocks for his main project of systematization. The upshot of this is that Diophantus does *not* need the general statements for the logical flow of the individual problem. This is indeed obvious from an inspection of the problems, where the general statements play no role at all.

This observation may shed some light on the major *mathematical* question regarding Diophantus, that is, did he see his project in terms of providing *general solutions*? In some ways he clearly did. The clearest evidence is in the course of the propositions (extant in Arabic only) vii.13–14. We are given a square number N which is to be divided into any three numbers (i.e. N=a+b+c) so that either N+a, N+b, N+c are all squares (vii.13), or N–a, N–b, N–c are all squares (vii.14). It is not surprising that, in both cases, we reach a point in the argument where we are asked to take a given square number and divide it into two square numbers[19] – the famous Fermatian problem ii.8. Now, Diophantus (or his Arabic text) explicitly says that this is possible for 'It has been seen earlier in this treatise of ours how to divide any square number into square parts.'[20] There, of course, the divided square is a particular number, 16. (The particular number chosen as example in vii.13–14 is 25.) This reference is hardly a late gloss, as the very approach taken to the problem is predicated upon the reduction into ii.8. Indeed, the natural assumption on the part of any reader familiar with elite Greek

---

[19] By iteration, this allows us to divide a square number into any number of square numbers; Diophantus, in fact, requires a division into three parts. Note however that even the basic operation of iteration itself calls for a generalization of the operation of ii.8.

[20] Sesiano 1982: 166.

geometry would be that results should be transferable from one set of numerical values to any other soluble set, on the analogue of the transferability of geometrical results from one diagram to another: this would be the implication of picking a mode of presentation which is so suggestive of that of elite geometry.

It is also likely that the very exposure to certain quasi-algebraic practices (basically those of additions or subtractions of terms until one gets a simple equation of species) as well as the choice of simple parameters would instil the skills required for the finding of solutions with different numerical values from those found by Diophantus himself, so that the text of Diophantus, taken as a whole, does teach one how to find solutions in terms more general than those of the particular numerical terms chosen for an individual Diophantine solution.[21] Having said that, however, the fundamental point remains that Diophantus allows his generality, such as it is, to emerge *implicitly* and from *the totality of his practice*. There is no effort made to make the generality of an individual claim *explicit* and visible *locally*. He does not solve the problem of dividing a square number into two square numbers in terms that are in and of themselves general – which he could have done by pursuing such problems *in general terms*.

Why doesn't he do that? There are three ways of approaching this. First, readers' expectations on how generality is to be sustained would have been informed with their experience in elite Greek geometry. There, generality is not so much explicitly asserted, as it is implicitly suggested.[22] It is true that the nature of Greek geometrical practice – based on the survey of a finite range of diagrammatic configurations – does not map precisely into Diophantus' practice. Greek geometry allows a rigorous, even if an implicit, form of generality, which Diophantus' technique does not support. This mismatch, in fact, may serve as partial explanation for the emerging gap in Diophantus' generality.

Second, if indeed I am right and Diophantus' goals were primarily completion and homogeneity, and that the general statement may have been introduced in the service of such goals, than our problem is to a large extent diffused. Diophantus did not provide explicit grounds for his generality, but this is because he was not exactly looking for them. He did not introduce general statements for the reason that he was looking for general solutions. Rather, he introduced general statements because he perceived such statements to be an obligatory feature of a systematic arrangement

---

[21]   This, if I understand him correctly, is the claim of Thomaidis 2005.
[22]   As argued in N1999: ch. 6 (a comparison also made by Thomaidis 2005).

of mathematical contents. Of course, I imagine that he would still prefer a general proof to a particular one – but only as long as other, no less important characteristics of the proof were respected as well. But this, I suggest, was not the case. I will try to show why in the next section.

Even before that, let us mention the third and most obvious account for why Diophantus did not present a more general approach. An argument that comes to mind immediately is that Diophantus did not produce more general arguments because he did not possess the required symbolism. Fundamentally, what we then do is to put side by side our symbolism and that of Diophantus so as to observe the differences and then to pronounce those differences as essential for a full-fledged argument producing a general algebraical conclusion. Of course, the differences are there. In particular, Diophantus has explicit symbols for a single value in each power: a single 'number' (a single x), a single 'dunamis' (a single x^2), a single 'cube' (a single x^3), etc. There is thus no obvious way of referring even to, say, two unknowns such as x and y. This is a major limitation, and of course it does curtail Diophantus' expressive power. Some scholars come close to suggesting that this, finally, is why Diophantus does not produce explicit general arguments.[23] But by now we can see how weak this argument is, and this for two reasons.

First, it is perfectly possible to express a general argument without the typographic symbolism expressing several unknowns, by the simple method of using natural language (over whose expressive power, after all, typographic symbols have no advantage). This is the upshot of text 3 above. Of course, even though a text such as text 3 does prove a general claim, it does so in an opaque form that does not display the rationality of the argument. But this helps to locate the problem more precisely: it is not that, with Diophantus' symbolism, it was impossible to prove general claims; rather, it was impossible to prove general claims *in a manner that makes the rationality of the argument transparent*.

Second, and crucially, note that it was perfectly possible for Diophantus to make the rather minimal extensions to his system so as to encompass multiple variables. Indeed, since the most natural way for him of speaking of several unknowns was to speak of 'the first number', 'the second number', etc., he effectively had the symbolism required – all he needed was to make the choice to put together the less common symbol for 'number' together with the standard abbreviation for numerals: α ʹ ς would be 'the first number', β ʹ ς would be 'the second number', etc. A bit more cumbersome than

---

[23] See e.g. Heath 1885: 80–2.

x and *y*, for sure, a confusing symbolism, as well (one would need to develop procedures to differentiate 'two numbers' from 'the second number') – but an effective symbolism nonetheless. Why did Diophantus not use it? *Because he had no use for it.* The task Diophantus set himself did not call for multiple symbols for multiple unknowns. He did not set out to produce general proofs but rather to solve problems, where (with few exceptions) a *single* unknown was to be found. Diophantus' project aimed not to obtain the generality of Euclidean theorems, but rather to solve problems, in a manner expressing the rationality of the solution. This task defined, for Diophantus, his choice of symbolism.

So let us then reframe accordingly our interpretation of Diophantus' symbolism: not as a second-rate tool for the task of modern algebra, but, instead, as the perfect tool for the task Diophantus set himself. I proceed to discuss this task.

Diophantus the analyst: choosing a mode of persuasion

Over and above the rigid structure of general enunciation followed by particular problem, Diophantus follows a rigid form for each of the problems. We should now explain Diophantus' motivations in choosing this particular form (that he chose some rigid form – instead of allowing freely varying forms for setting out problems – is of course natural given his deuteronomic project).

The basic structure of the Diophantine proposition, as is well known, is that of analysis: that is, Diophantus assumes, for each proposition, that it has already been solved. Typically, he then terms the hypothetically found element 'number' (the ς with which we are familiar) and notes the consequences of the assumption that the conditions of the problem are met (in the case quoted above: 20, together with the number, is four times 100, lacking the number). This is then manipulated by various 'algebraic' operations (roughly, indeed, those later used by al-Khwarizmi, in his algebra) until the number comes to be defined as monads. This then is quickly verified in a final statement where the terms are put 'in the positions'. In the Arabic Diophantus, besides the quick verification one also has a formal synthesis, repeating the argumentation of the analysis *backwards* so that one sees that, given the solution, the terms of the problem cannot fail to hold. Sesiano believes this may be due to Hypatia; alternatively, this could be due to some Arabic commentator. In any case, the systematic addition of the synthesis may serve as another example of how deuteronomic texts seek the goal of *completion*.

It is natural that, among the models available to him from elite literate Greek mathematics, Diophantus would choose that of analysis. While not the most common form of presenting propositions, it is very markedly associated with problems rather than with theorems – i.e. with those situations where one is faced not with a statement, whose truth is to be corroborated, but with a task which is to be fulfilled.[24] This is of course the nature of the material Diophantus had available to him. And, since he set out to produce a systematic, monolithic work, it is natural that he would use the same form of presentation throughout – resulting in a unique text among the extant Greek works, consisting of analysis and nothing else.

The choice of the analytic form has important consequence for the nature of the reasoning. Now, it is often suggested that analysis is a method of discovery: that is, it is a way by which Greek mathematicians came to know how to solve problems. I have written on this question before, in an article called 'Why did Greek mathematicians publish their analyses?' I shall not repeat in detail what I had to say there, but the title itself suggests the main argument.[25] Whatever heuristic contribution the analytic move – of assuming the task fulfilled – may have had, this cannot account for *writing the analysis down*. The written-down analysis most certainly is not a *protocol* of the discovery of the solution. It must serve some other purpose in the context of presentation, which is what I was trying to explain in my article. Like most authors on Greek geometry, I had completely ignored Diophantus in that previous article of mine, but in fact here is a clear case for my claim: no doubt, Diophantus in general knew the values solving his tasks, as part of his tradition. The analysis, for him, was not a way of finding those values, but of presenting them.

What is the contribution of analysis in the context of presentation? I have suggested the following: when producing solutions to problems (unlike the case where one sets out proofs of theorems) one faces a special burden of showing the preferability of the offered solution to other, alternative solutions. This, indeed, was a standard arena of polemic in Greek mathematics:

---

[24] This is the main theme of Knorr 1986. In general, for the nature of ancient analysis, the best starting-point today is the *Stanford Encyclopedia of Philosophy* entry, with its rich but well-chosen bibliography: http://plato.stanford.edu/entries/analysis/, by M. Beaney. Otte and Panza 1997 are the best starting point in print. I will state immediately my position, that much of the discussion of ancient analysis is vitiated by paying too much attention to Pappus' pronouncements on the topic (*Collectio* VII.1–2): while Pappus was not an unintelligent reader of his sources, it is most likely that he presents not so much any earlier theory but rather his own interpretation, so that his authority on the subject is that of a *secondary* source.

[25] The selective discussion in that article may be supplemented by my comments on a few analyses by Archimedes, in Netz 2004: 207, 217–18.

are problems solved in the most appropriate way? The task, then, is to show how the offered solution to the problem comes out naturally, given the terms themselves. This is what the analysis does: it reaches the solution to the problem, as a demonstrative consequence of the terms that the problem had set out. Thus analysis need not discover a solution, nor prove its truth (though this is a by-product of a successful analysis). Its aim may simply be to display how the solution emerges naturally out of the conditions set out by the problem. The aim of the proof in an analysis is not in its conclusion, but in the process itself: it lays down a rational bridge leading from the terms of the problem, to the solution offered.

If this is true, then Diophantus should have similar expectations from his own analyses. But in fact this goal of the analyses emerges from his choice of the form itself. He avoided schoolroom algebraical presentations with their take-it-or-leave-it approach: probably, within the overall expectations of elite literate Greek mathematics, this could not do. Such texts were driven by a culture whose central mode was persuasion, and the text therefore had to display a rational, persuasive structure. But neither did Diophantus aim primarily to show *the reason why*. He could easily have chosen to adopt a strictly theoretical approach to numerical problems, as, one may perhaps say, certain Arabic mathematicians did much later; his fluency in extending numerical problems and solving quite complex ones suggest that, in sheer terms of mathematical intelligence, he was quite capable of such a theoretical approach. But he did not aim at such. He understood his task in a more limited way – not so much to open up a new field of theoretical inquiry, but rather to arrange a field inherited from the past. The only constraint was that this field should display a rational, persuasive structure: Diophantus' analyses served just that. Instead of the take-it-or-leave-it of lay and school algebra, Diophantus would have rational bridges leading from the terms of the problems to their solutions. Thus he would show that the solutions are not arbitrary, but arise naturally given the terms set out by the problems.[26]

---

[26] It is interesting to notice in this context the cases where Diophantus departs from the strict analytic presentation. This happens, in particular, where he has to make some arbitrary choices of numerical values. Then he sometimes takes us into his confidence, explaining the rational basis for his next move. For example in v.2: 'but 16 monads are not some arbitrary number, but are a square which, added to 20 monads, makes a square as well. So I am brought to investigate: which square has a fourth bigger than 20 monads, and taken together with twenty monads makes a square. So the square results to be bigger than 80. But 81 is a square bigger than 80. . .' – this entire discussion is there to explain why, in an arbitrary move, Diophantus picks the numerical value 9 and none else. The choice is arbitrary; but Diophantus shows that it is not irrational, and is somehow suggested by the values at hand.

My interpretation of Diophantus thus relies on two theoretical contexts I developed elsewhere: *deuteronomy*, and *analysis as a tool of presentation*. What is Diophantus' project? I interpret this within the theoretical context of what I call deuteronomy: it is to systematize and complete previously given materials, making them all conform with some ideal standard. This systematic structure is two-dimensional. Horizontally, all units should conform to each other. Vertically, all units should conform to the ideals of Greek elite mathematics. How does Diophantus then fulfil his project? I interpret this within the theoretical context of analysis as a tool of presentation. If all the units are to be the same, then the most natural format to take is that of a problem. And to make those problems conform to the ideals of Greek elite mathematics, the method of analysis is deployed, so as to display the rationality of each of the moves made through the text.

This, finally, I suggest, is the function of reasoning in Diophantus: to build a rational bridge leading from the terms of the problem, to the solution. I now need to show how Diophantus' symbols may serve this function.

Diophantus' symbolism and the display of rationality

My basic thesis is that the reasoning in Diophantus is designed, primarily, to display a rational bridge leading from the terms of the problem to the solution. Two questions arise: (1) How does symbolism such as that used by Diophantus help with this goal? (2) Why would it help with such a goal here, and not elsewhere in Greek mathematics?

Let me first discuss the appropriateness of Diophantus' symbolism for his goal.

Diophantus' goal, as I reconstruct, is in one sense limited, in another sense ambitious. The goal is limited, because he does not aim at powerful, general theoretical insight into numerical problems. He merely aims at classifying and completing them as a system. The goal is ambitious, because each solution, at each step, has to clear a high cognitive hurdle. It has to display, step by step, its rationality.

Both the limit and the ambition explain why a general, theoretical approach such as text 3 above would not be appropriate. It is not called for, because of the limited ambition; and it is undesirable because, with the prolix phrases and the difficulty of fixing the identity of the entities involved, it becomes impossible to survey, step by step, the rationality of the argument as it unfolds. Note that in a text with theoretical goals, local obscurity can be tolerated: the reader is then expected to *work* his or her way through the text. It is quite feasible to have valid arguments expressed in roundabout, extremely subtle, or even paradoxical fashion, so that it is only by reading them several times over – effectively, producing a commentary – that one comes to see their validity. Indeed, such writing is very typical of the Western *philosophical* tradition. Diophantus' world had also people reading, say, Stoic metaphysics, which is as opaque (and as precise) as text 3 above. But Stoic metaphysics is the product of a professional community of specialists who pride themselves in their fluency in a complex language. Its subject matter is perceived to have enormous inner significance. Thus readers prefer the theoretical power of an argument to its apparent rationality: it is more important to derive a truth than to show that that truth arises naturally (indeed, there is a premium in a difficult-to-parse argument, in whose production and parsing both author and reader may take pride). On the other hand, because the author offers *solutions* he is under a special obligation, as argued above, to display the rationality of the solution as it unfolds, to show that it is not a contrived solution but instead derives naturally from the terms of the problem.[27]

This immediately suggests a function for Diophantus' symbolism. Obviously, it makes the parsing easier: it abbreviates overall, and it brings about clear visual signposts with which the text is structured and its entities identified.

But let us be more precise: just what is being more easily parsed, and how? To repeat the conclusion of Section 2 above: we see that Diophantus' symbolism gives rise to a systematic bimodal reading, visual and verbal, at the level of the noun-phrase. This, I argue, directly serves the goal of constructing a rational bridge leading from the terms of the problem to its solution.

For what is a rational bridge like? It is a structure where everything is meaningfully present to the mind, and is also under the mind's control. The relationships are all calculated and verified, but they are perceived as meaningful relationships and not as mere symbolic structures lacking in meaning. In modern terms, we may say that Diophantus needs to have a semantic derivation; it also ought to be cognitively computable.

Since the derivation must be semantic, a bimodal reading is preferable to a strictly visual one. For Diophantus, it appears important that the derivation refers directly to numbers and monads, and does not make use of some opaque symbols. The derivation should be conducted throughout at the level of the meanings: the signified – and not only the signs – should never

---

[27] I follow an explanatory mode comparable to that of Chemla 2003. Considering the closely analogous case of the use of particular examples in Chinese mathematics, Chemla argues that these were used because the authors were seeking *generality above abstraction*. My analogous argument is that Diophantus sought *transparency above generality*.

be lost out of sight, for otherwise the derivation would appear as a con-
jurer's trick out of which the solution happened to have emerged – precisely
the opposite effect of the rational bridge Diophantus aims to construct.

At the same time, the visual component of the bimodal reading serves in
the computation of the expression. The eye glances quickly to the correct
spot in the phrase, finding the correct value. Even more important, perhaps:
the mind is trained to look for the expressions, so that a visual–spatial
arrangement for the phrase comes to aid the purely verbal computation.
This is a speculative statement: I believe it to be true. Let me explain. First
of all, independently of how a particular phrase may be spelled out, through
abbreviations or through fully written-out words, it is certainly read by a
mind that is already acquainted with the fixed structure of the phrase on
the page, and with its limited arsenal of symbols. Thus the reader would
have triggered in him or her not only the verbal response, but also the visual
response. In other words, it appears to me that, just as the mind involuntarily creates a verbal representation of a Diophantine abbreviation, so it
involuntarily creates a visual representation of a Diophantine spelled-out
word. Thus the reader has three resources available: (1) the actual trace of
the page, (2) the verbal representation of the contents, kept by the mind's
working memory of phonological representations, (3) the visual representation of the contents, kept by the mind's working memory of visual
representations. Resource (1) would then serve to stabilize and keep in
place both resources (2) and (3). It is obvious that the presence of a visual
resource, over and above the verbal resource, helps in the computation of
the expression: I shall return to explain this in more detail below.

What is involved in the computation? The reader, above all, verifies that a
certain relation holds, in the rational bridge, leading from one statement to
the next. In other words, what we need is to have a tool for operating upon
phrases expressing arithmetical values. We need to verify that the product
of an operation on the expression X is indeed the expression Y. So we can
see why the operations themselves do not call for symbolism: they may be
fully spelled out, instead. What we need is symbolism for the arithmetical
values on which the operations operate. We can thus see why Diophantine
symbolism stops at the level of the noun-phrase and does not reach the
level of the sentence.

The computation is thus local to the level of the noun-phrase. Indeed, it
is clear that the resources (2) and (3) – the verbal and visual representation
of expressions in the reader's working memory – are limited in capacity and
duration. In fact, all that they allow is the verification of the relation in a
single stage of the argument – the rational bridge is built one link at a time.
We can now return to I.10 and consider the verification in action:

(1) And if it is added to twenty, results: ϛ1 M°20. (2) And if it is taken away from 100, results: M°100 lacking number 1. (3) And it shall be required that the greater be 4-^{tms} the smaller. (4) Therefore four-^{tms} the smaller is equal to the greater; (5) but four-^{tms} the smaller results: M°400 Ψ ϛ 4; (6) these equal ϛ1 M°20

(7) Let the subtraction be added <as> common, (8) and let similar <terms> be taken away from similar <terms>. (9) Remaining: numbers, 5, equal M°380. (10) And the ϛ results: monads, 76.

This – the entirety of the argumentative part of the proposition – all revolves around a single verification, the one connecting the statement of steps 5–6 taken as a whole, and the statement of step 9. The operation to be verified is contained in steps 7–8; steps 1–5 (which are very simple, but somewhat convoluted) make sense as soon as their purpose becomes clear: to bring the two expressions of steps 5–6 into close proximity, in preparation for the verification of the operation. Finally, step 10 is a very simple consequence of step 9 and calls for no cognitive effort.

Note, then, that steps 7–8 are fully spelled out: they do not include any of Diophantus' symbolic terms. The operation itself is fully verbal and semantic: the meaning of the operation is directly told to the reader. On the other hand, the substratum for the operation – the phrases of steps 5, 6 and 9 – is presented in the bimodal form of abbreviations. One knows throughout what one talks about: these are not abstract symbols, but 'numbers' and 'monads'. On the other hand, the computations can relatively easily be carried out: a 'lacking' in the one can be translated into an addition to the other, which easily leads to 5; 400 with 20 taken away easily leads to 380; each result is attached to the correct rubric, 'number' in the first case, 'monads' in the second. In all of this, the simplification introduced by a fixed visual structure to which objects can be added or removed is of obvious help.

This, then, is my suggestion for the role of symbolism in Diophantus' reasoning. As Diophantus transformed the lay and school algebra material at his disposal, into the argumentative form of Greek mathematical analysis, he added in a tool which served in this analytic form – making the argument display the rationality of the passage from the terms of the problem to the terms of its solution.[28] We can see why the transition from lay and school algebras, to elite literate algebra, would encourage Diophantus to introduce the type of symbolism he uses. But we should also consider the second transition leading to Diophantus' text. His text differs not only from

[28] An analogous account can perhaps be provided for Diophantus' fraction symbolism. With fractions, as well, Diophantus does not develop a symbolic operation that allows him to calculate directly on fractions (e.g. from $a/b*c/d$ to get $a*b/c*d$). Thus the validity of the operations is left for the reader to verify explicitly. However, the symbolism – whose essence

previous lay and school algebras, but also from the established elite literate Greek mathematics Diophantus was familiar with. This mathematics had included no such symbolism as Diophantus'. Why would Diophantus introduce such a symbolism, then? In other words, what is the function served by symbolism, in the case of the problems studied by Diophantus – but which is not required in the case of the problems studied by previous elite literate Greek mathematicians?

The question can be put precisely: why are Greek geometrical relations easily computable without symbolism, while Diophantus' numerical relations are not? The question is cognitive, and so we should look for a cognitive divide between the character of geometrical and numerical relations. To begin with, then, let us remind ourselves of how Greek geometrical relations are expressed.

As described in Chapter 4 of N1999, Greek geometrical texts are written in a system of formulaic expressions, the most important of which is the family of ratio-expressions, e.g. 'the ratio of A to B is the same as the ratio of C to D' (typically, the slots A, B, C and D are filled by spelled-out formulae for geometrical objects, e.g. 'the [two letters]', the standard formulaic representation of a line). One may then bring in further information, always expressed within the same system of formulaic expressions, e.g. that 'C is equal to E', or that 'the ratio of C to D is the same as the ratio of G to H'. Extra information of the first kind would license a conclusion such as 'the ratio of A to B is the same as the ratio of E to D', while extra information of the second kind would license a conclusion such as 'the ratio of A to B is the same as the ratio of G to H'.

To repeat, the system is based on formulaic expressions – all within natural Greek grammar. No special symbolism is involved and the text is spelled out in ordinary alphabetical writing, so that the mind doubtless first translates the written traces into verbal representation and then computes the validity of the argument on the basis of such verbal representations.

Note now that the formulaic expressions of Greek geometry are characterized by a hierarchical, generative structure. Typically, a formulaic expression has, as constituent elements subordinate to its own structure, several smaller formulaic expressions, all ultimately governing the characters of the alphabet indicating diagrammatic objects. Thus in 'the ratio of A

---

is that divisions are not represented as unit fractions but are left 'in the raw' – makes such a verification possible. It is one thing to be told that 6 divided by 8 is 4^3 (where you directly verify that 8^6 is the same as 4^3); another, to be told that 6 divided by 8 is $2'4'$ (where the verification depends on a relatively complex, separate calculation – usually, much more complex than in this simple example).

to B is the same as the ratio of C to D' one can detect three levels: the level of the proportion statement, which is in turn a structure of two ratio statements, each of which in turn is a structure of two object descriptions (which, in the Greek original form, would refer through characters of the alphabet indicating diagrammatic objects). The structure is hierarchical in that its constituents are related to each other in relations of syntactic subordination; it is generative in that such constituents can be added and substituted at will.

This substitution is in fact one of the two bases of the computation of the validity of the geometrical argument in Greek mathematics – the other being the diagram, which we may ignore here. It is feasible precisely because the formulaic expression is hierarchical and generative. Mathematical computation here is parasitic upon syntactic computation. The mind is equipped with a tool for computing substitutions on hierarchic, generative syntactic structures. It is thus a matter of immediate inspection that, from the two expressions 'the ratio of A to B is the same as the ratio of C to D' and 'C is equal to E', the expression 'the ratio of A to B is the same as the ratio of E to D': one unfailingly knows where to affix the correct substitution, based on one's structural grasp of the expression 'the ratio of A to B is the same as the ratio of C to D'. Since natural language syntax is the mental tool brought to bear when computing the validity of such arguments, it is only natural that they are represented verbally and not visually.

We see then that, to the extent that expressions possess a hierarchic structure, they may be effectively computed through natural language tools. And it is important to notice that Greek geometrical formulae are indeed characterized by such hierarchic structures, with proportion as the central operation in this type of mathematics.

Not all expressions in natural language, however, have this hierarchic structure based on subordination. Alongside subordinate structure, natural language uses another structural principle, that of paratactic arrangement, i.e. the concatenation of phrases to create larger phrases without introducing an internal structure of dependency. This is the difference between expressions of the type 'The A of the B of the C' and expressions such as 'A and B and C'. Expressions of the first kind contain, in their syntactic representation, internal structure, which the mind can use in manipulating them. Expressions of the second kind are syntactically represented as mere concatenation lacking internal structure, so that there is nothing syntactic computation can latch onto.

My suggestion, then, is obvious: the central Diophantine expression – the phrase representing the sums of, e.g., dunamis, number and monads – is paratactic and not subordinate in structure. It thus essentially differs from expressions such as 'the ratio of A to B is the same as the ratio of C to D'. For this reason, purely verbal representations of the Diophantine phrase are of limited value, and Diophantus naturally was led to look for further tools for easing computation, in the principle of allography present in his scribal culture.

I find it striking that the same seems to be true of numerical expressions in natural language as a whole. It seems that numerical expressions tend to be paratactic, rather than subordinate: this may be because they are essentially open-ended in character, 'A and B and C and D'. Thus they always offer incentives for non-verbal representation in which their computation is aided by more than natural language syntax. Number symbolism itself is the primary example. For after all the earliest and most central case of symbolic argument is precisely that – the algorithm, manipulating number-symbolism via a translation of numbers from natural language into a visual code.[29]

4. Summary

The suggestion of this article can now be put forward as follows. Involved in the deuteronomic project of fitting in previously available texts within established forms, Diophantus set himself the task of presenting lay and school algebra within the format – and expectations – of Greek geometrical analysis. This entailed the task of constructing a rational bridge leading from the setting of the problems to their solutions. Since the expressions involved were numerical in character (rather than standing for qualitative relations), their structure was not subordinate, but paratactic. As a consequence, the syntax of natural language no longer helped in their computation and could not support the task of constructing a rational bridge. Instead, Diophantus reached for the tool available to him in his culture – allography – to construct expressions whose visual structure could support the same task. These two features of Diophantus' context – deuteronomy and allography – both may have to do, ultimately, with the material history of writing in late antiquity. And so, the relationship between reasoning and symbolism in Diophantus is found to be dependent upon the very specific historical conditions of late antiquity.

The complex, many-dimensional nature of the account sketched here is in itself significant. Why does Diophantus use his particular symbolism?

---

[29] Allard 1992.

Because he has a particular task, and particular tools, all reflecting a complex historical setting. Everything argued here is tentative but of one thing I am certain: the history of mathematical symbolism is not linear. Let us discard the notion of a single linear trajectory from 'natural language' to 'symbolic algebra', a gradual transition from the concrete to the abstract, from the less expressive to the more expressive, a simple teleological route leading to an ever more perfect science. In truth, mathematics never did rely on natural language: from its very inception it expressed itself, in its various cultural traditions, through different complicated formulaic languages, using various specialized traces for numerical values or for diagrams. History then takes off in a non-linear fashion. Symbolism is invented and discarded, employing this or that set of cognitive tools, inventing this or that form of writing, in the service of changing goals: nothing is predetermined. Symbolism – just as mathematics itself – is contingent. The same, finally, must be true of our own (various uses of) symbolism: they should be seen not as the 'natural' achievement of precise abstraction but as a historical artefact. We should therefore study the precise cognitive tools our symbolism employs, the precise tasks that such symbols are made to achieve, and the precise historical route that brought us to the use of such symbols. The modern equation is not the 'natural' outcome of a mathematical history destined to reach its culmination in the nineteenth century; it is a culturally specific form. This article, sketching a speculative account of Diophantus' symbolism, offered one chapter from the historical route leading to that equation.

Bibliography

Allard, A. (1992) *Al-Khwarizmi / Le Calcul Indien (Algorismus)*. Namur.

Bashmakova, I.G. (1997) *Diophantus and Diophantine Equations*. Washington, DC. (Trans. of Bashmakova 1972: Moscow.)

Bourbaki, N. (1991) *Elements of the History of Mathematics* (tr. J. Meldrum). New York.

Boyer, C. B. (1989) *A History of Mathematics* (rev. U. C. Mertzbach). New York.

Canaan, T. (1937–8) 'The decipherment of Arabic talismans, Part I', *Berytus* **4**: 69–110; 'Part II', *Berytus* **5**: 141–51. (Reprinted in ed. E. Savage-Smith (2004) *Magic and Divination in Early Islam*. Trowbridge: 125–77.)

Chemla, K. (2003) 'Generality above abstraction: the general expressed in terms of the paradigmatic in mathematics in ancient China', *Science in Context* **16**: 413–58.

Groningen, B. A. van (1955) *Short Manual of Greek Palaeography*. Leiden.

Heath, T. (1885) *Diophantus of Alexandria: A Study in the History of Greek Algebra*. Cambridge.

Hultsch, F. (1894) 'Diophanti Alexandrini Opera, ed. Tannery, vol. i [Rezension]', *Berliner Philologische Wochenschrift* **14**(26): 801–7.

Klein, J. (1934–6) *Greek Mathematical Thought and the Origins of Algebra*. Cambridge, MA. (Reprinted 1968.)

Knorr, W. R. (1986) *The Ancient Tradition of Geometric Problems*. Boston, MA.
  (1993) '"Arithmetike stoicheiosis": on Diophantus and Hero of Alexandria', *Historia Mathematica* **20**: 180–92.

McNamee, K. (1981) *Abbreviations in Greek Literary Papyri and Ostraca*. Chico, CA.

Nesselmann, G. H. F. (1842) *Versuch einer kritischen Geschichte der Algebra*. Berlin.

Netz, R. (2000) 'Why did Greek mathematicians publish their analyses?', in *Ancient and Medieval Traditions in the Exact Sciences*, ed. P. Suppes, J. M. Moravcsik and H. Mendell. Stanford, CA: 139–57.
  (2004) *The Works of Archimedes*, vol. i. Cambridge.

Otte, M. and Panza, M. (1997) *Analysis and Synthesis in Mathematics*. Dordrecht.

Rashed, R. (1984) *Diophante / Les Arithmétiques*. Paris.

Sesiano, J. (1982) *Books iv to vii of Diophantus'* Arithmetica *in the Arabic Translation attributed to Qusta Ibn Lūqā*. New York.

Thomaidis, Y. (2005) 'A framework for defining the generality of Diophantos' methods in *Arithmetica*', *Archive for History of Exact Sciences* **59**: 591–641.

Wittgenstein, L. (1922) *Tractatus Logico-Philosophicus*. London.

11 | Mathematical justification as non-conceptualized practice: the Babylonian example

JENS HØYRUP

Speaking about and doing – doing without speaking about it

Greek philosophy, at least its Platonic and Aristotelian branches, spoke much about demonstrated knowledge as something fundamentally different from opinion; often, it took mathematical knowledge as the archetype for demonstrated and hence certain knowledge – in its scepticist period, the Academy went so far as to regard mathematical knowledge as *the only* kind of knowledge that could really be based on demonstrated certainty.[1]

Not least in quarters close to Neopythagoreanism, the notion of mathematical demonstration may seem not to correspond to our understanding of the matter; applying our own standards we may judge the homage to demonstration to be little more than lip service.

Aristotle, however, discusses the problem of finding principles and proving mathematical propositions from these in a way that comes fairly close to the actual practice of Euclid and his kin. Even though Euclid himself only practises demonstration and does not discuss it we can therefore be sure that he was not only making demonstrations but also explicitly aware of doing so in agreement with established standards. The preface to Archimedes' *Method* is direct evidence that its author knew demonstration according to established norms to be a cardinal virtue – the alleged or real heterodoxy consisting solely in his claim that discovery without strict proof was also valuable. Philosophical commentators like Proclus, finally, show beyond doubt that they too saw the mathematicians' demonstrations in the perspective of the philosophers' discussions.

As to Diophantus and Hero we may find that their actual practice is not quite in agreement with the philosophical prescriptions, but there is no doubt that even *their* presentation of mathematical matters was

A preprint version of this article appeared in *HPM 2004: History and Pedagogy of Mathematics*, Fourth Summer University History and Epistemology of Mathematics, ICME 10 Satellite Meeting, Uppsala 12 17 July 2004. Proceedings Uppsala: Universitetstryckeriet, 2004. I thank Karine Chemla for questions and commentaries which made me clarify the final text on various points.

[1] See, e.g., Cicero, *Academica* II.116–17 (ed. Rackham 1933).

meant to agree with such norms as are reflected in the philosophical prescriptions.

Justification unproclaimed – or absent

But is it not likely that mathematical demonstration has developed as a practice in the same process as created the norms, and thus before such norms crystallized and were hypostasized by philosophers? And is it not possible that mathematical demonstration – or, to use a word which is less loaded by our reading of Aristotle and Euclid, *justification* – developed in other mathematical cultures without being hypostasized?

A good starting point for the search for a mathematical culture of this kind might be that of the Babylonian scribes – if only for the polemical reason that 'hellenophile' historians of mathematics tend to deny the existence of mathematical demonstration in this area. In Morris Kline's (relatively moderate) words,[2] written at a moment when non-specialists tended to rely on selective or not too attentive reading of popularizations like Neugebauer's *Science in Antiquity* (1957) and *Vorgriechische Mathematik* (1934) or van der Waerden's *Erwachende Wissenschaft* (1956):

Mathematics as an organized, independent, and reasoned discipline did not exist before the classical Greeks of the period from 600 to 300 B.C. entered upon the scene. There were, however, prior civilizations in which the beginnings or rudiments of mathematics were created

. . .

The question arises as to what extent the Babylonians employed mathematical proof. They did solve by correct systematic procedures rather complicated equations involving unknowns. However, they gave verbal instructions only on the steps to be made and offered no justification of the steps. Almost surely, the arithmetic and algebraic processes and the geometrical rules were the end result of physical evidence, trial and error, and insight.

The only opening toward any kind of demonstration beyond the observation that a sequence of operations gives the right result is the word 'insight', which is not discussed any further. Given the vicinity of 'physical evidence' and 'trial and error' we may suppose that Kline refers to the kind of insight which makes us understand in a glimpse that the area of a right-angled triangle must be the half of that of the corresponding rectangle.

[2] Kline 1972: 3, 14.

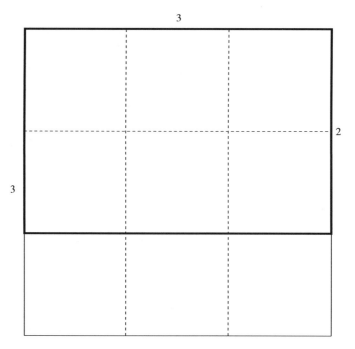

Figure 11.1 The configuration of VAT 8390 #1.

Evident validity

In order to see how much must be put into the notion of 'insight' if Kline's characterization is to be defended we may look at some texts.[3] I shall start by problem 1 from the Old Babylonian tablet VAT 8390 (see Figure 11.1) (as also in following examples, an explanatory commentary follows the translation): [4]

Obv. i

1. [Length and width] I have made hold:[5] 10` the surface.[6]
2. [The length t]o itself I have made hold:

---

[3] I use the translations from H2002 with minor corrections, leaving out the interlinear transliterated text and explaining key operations and concepts in notes at their first occurrence – drawing for this latter purpose on the results described in the same book. In order to facilitate checks I have not straightened the very literal ('conformal') translations. The first text (VAT 8390 #1) is translated and discussed on pp. 61–4.

[4] The Old Babylonian period covers the centuries from 2000 BCE to 1600 BCE (according to the 'middle chronology'). The mathematical texts belong to the second half of the period.

[5] To make the lines *a* and *b* 'hold' or 'hold each other' (with further variations of the phrase in the present text) means to construct ('build') the rectangular surface ⊏ ⊐(*a,b*) which they contain. If only one line *s* is involved, the square □ (*s*) is built.

[6] I follow Thureau-Dangin's system for the transliteration of sexagesimal place value numbers, where `, ``, ... indicate increasing and ′, ″, ... decreasing sexagesimal order of magnitude,

3. [a surface] I have built.
4. [So] much as the length over the width went beyond [7]
5. I have made hold, to 9 I have repeated: [8]
6. as much as that surface which the length by itself
7. was [ma]de hold.
8. The length and the width what?
9. 10` the surface posit,[9]
10. and 9 (to) which he has repeated posit:
11. The equalside[10] of 9 (to) which he has repeated what? 3.
12. 3 to the length posit
13. 3 t[o the w]idth posit.
14. Since 'so [much as the length] over the width went beyond
15. I have made hold', he has said
16. 1 from ₁3 which t]o the width you have posited
17. tea[r out:] 2 you leave.
18. 2 which yo[u have l]eft to the width posit.
19. 3 which to the length you have posited
20. to 2 which ⟨to⟩ the width you have posited raise,[11] 6.

and where 'order zero' when needed is marked ° (I omit it when a number of 'order zero' stands alone, thus writing 7 instead of 7°). 5`2°10´ thus stands for $5 \cdot 60^1 + 2 \cdot 60^0 + 10 \cdot 60^{-1}$. It should be kept in mind that absolute order of magnitude is not indicated in the text, and that `, ´ and ° correspond to the merely mental awareness of order of magnitude without which the calculators could not have made as few errors as actually found in the texts. The present problem is homogeneous, and therefore does not enforce a particular order of magnitude. I have chosen the one which allows us to distinguish the area of the surface (10`) from the number 1/6 (10´).

[7] The text makes use of two different 'subtractive' operations. One, 'by excess', observes how much one quantity *A* goes beyond another quantity *B*; the other, 'by removal', finds how much remains when a quantity *a* is 'torn out' (in other texts sometimes 'cut off', etc.) from a quantity *A*. As suggested by the terminology, the latter operation can only be used if *a* is part of *A*.

[8] 'Repetition to/until *n*' is concrete, and produces *n* copies of the object of the operation. *n* is always small enough to make the process transparent, $1 < n < 10$.

[9] 'Positing' a number means to take note of it by some material means, perhaps in isolation on a clay pad, perhaps in the adequate place in a diagram made outside the tablet. 'Positing *n* to' a line (obv. ɪ 12, etc.) is likely to correspond to the latter possibility.

[10] The 'equalside' *s* of an area *Q* is the side of this area when it is laid out as a square (the 'squaring side' of Greek mathematics). Other texts tell that *s* 'is equal by' *Q*.

[11] 'Raising' is a multiplication that corresponds to a consideration of proportionality; its etymological origin is in volume determination, where a prismatic volume with height *h* cubits is found by 'raising' the base from the implicit 'default thickness' of 1 cubit to the real height *h*. It also serves to determine the areas of rectangles which were constructed previously (lines ɪ 20 and ɪɪ 7), in which case, e.g., the 'default breadth' (1 'rod', *c.* 6 m) of the length is 'raised' to the real width. In the case where a rectangular area is constructed ('made hold'), the arithmetical determination of the area is normally regarded as implicit in the operation, and the value is stated immediately without any intervening 'raising' (thus lines ɪɪ 7 and 10).

21. Igi 6^{12} detach: 10′.

22. 10′ to 10` the surface raise, 1`40.

23. The equalside of 1`40 what? 10.

Obv. II

1. 10 to 3 wh[ich to the length you have posited]

2. raise, 30 the length.

3. 10 to 2 which to the width you have po[sited]

4. raise, 20 the width.

5. If 30 the length, 20 the width,

6. the surface what?

7. 30 the length to 20 the width raise, 10` the surface.

8. 30 the length together with 30 make hold: 15`.

9. 30 the length over 20 the width what goes beyond? 10 it goes beyond.

10. 10 together with [10 ma]ke hold: 1`40.

11. 1`40 to 9 repeat: 15` the surface.

12. 15` the surface, as much as 15` the surface which the length

13. by itself was made hold.

This problem about a rectangle exemplifies a characteristic of numerous Old Babylonian mathematical texts, namely that the description of the procedure already makes its adequacy evident. In Obv. I 4–5 we are told to construct the square on the excess of the length of the rectangle over its width and to take 9 copies of it, in lines I 6–7 that these can fill out the square on the length. Therefore, these small squares must be arranged in square, as in Figure 11.1, in a 3×3 pattern (lines I 11–13). But since the side of the small square was defined in the statement to be the excess of length over width (I 14–15, an explicit quotation), removal of one of three rows will leave the original rectangle, whose width will be 2 small squares.[13] In this unit, the area of the rectangle is $2 \cdot 3 = 6$ (I 18–20); since the rectangle is already there, there is no need for a 'holding' operation. Because the area measured in standard units (square 'rods') was 10`, each small square must be $\frac{1}{6} \cdot 10` = 1`40$ and its side $\sqrt{1`40} = \sqrt{100} = 10$ (I 21–23). From this it follows that the length must be $3 \cdot 10 = 30$ and the width $2 \cdot 10 = 20$ (II 1–3).

---

[12] 'Igi n' designates the reciprocal of n. To 'detach igi n', that is, to find it, probably refers to the splitting out of one of n parts of unity. 'Raising a to igi n' means finding $a \cdot 1/n$, that is, to divide a by n.

[13] In our understanding, 2 times the side of the small square. However, the Babylonian term for a square configuration (*miṭḫartum*, literally '[situation characterized by a] confrontation [between equals]'), was numerically identified by and hence with its side – a Babylonian square (primarily thought of as a square frame) 'was' its side and 'had' an area, whereas ours (primarily thought of as a square-shaped area) 'has' a side and 'is' an area.

The one who follows the procedure on the diagram and keeps the exact (geometrical) meaning and use of all terms in mind will feel no more need for an explicit demonstration than when confronted with a modern step-by-step solution of an algebraic equation,[14] in particular because numbers are always concretely identified by their role ('3 which to the length you have posited', etc.). The only place where doubts might arise is why 1 has to be subtracted in I 16–17, but the meaning of this step is then duly explained by a quotation from the statement (a routine device). There should be no doubt that the solution *must be* correct.

None the less a check follows, showing that the solution is valid (II 5 onwards). This check is very detailed, no mere numerical control but an appeal to the same kind of understanding as the preceding procedure: as we see, the rectangle is supposed to be already present, its area being found by 'raising'; the large and small squares, however, are derived entities and therefore have to be constructed (the tablet contains a strictly parallel problem that follows the same pattern, for which reason we may be confident that the choice of operations is not accidental).

A similar instance of evident validity is offered by problem 1 of the text BM 13901 (Figure 11.2),[15] the simplest of all mixed second-degree problems (and by numerous other texts, which however present us with the inconvenience that they are longer):

Obv. I

1. The surfa[ce] and my confrontation[16] I have accu[mulated]:[17] 45′ is it. 1, the projection,[18]
2. you posit. The moiety[19] of 1 you break, [3]0′ and 30′ you make hold.

---

[14] For instance,

$$3x + 2 = 17$$
$$\Rightarrow 3x = 17 - 2 = 15$$
$$\Rightarrow x = \tfrac{1}{3} \cdot 15 = 5.$$

[15] Translation and discussion in H2002: 50–2.

[16] The *mitḫartum* or '[situation characterized by the] confrontation [of equals]', as we remember from n. 13, is the square configuration parametrized by its side.

[17] 'To accumulate' is an additive operation which concerns or may concern the measuring numbers of the quantities to be added. It thus allows the addition of lengths and areas, as here, in line 1, and of areas and volumes or of bricks, men and working days in other texts. Another addition ('appending') is concrete. It serves when a quantity *a* is joined to another quantity *A*, augmenting thereby the measure of the latter without changing its identity (as when interest, Babylonian 'the appended', is joined to *my* bank account while leaving it as mine).

[18] The 'projection' (*wāṣītum*, literally something which protrudes or sticks out) designates a line of length 1 which, when applied orthogonally to another line *L* as width, transforms it into a rectangle ⊏⊐(*L*,1) without changing its measure.

[19] The 'moiety' of an entity is its 'necessary' or 'natural' half, a half that could be no other fraction – as the circular radius is by necessity the exact half of the diameter, and the area of a triangle is

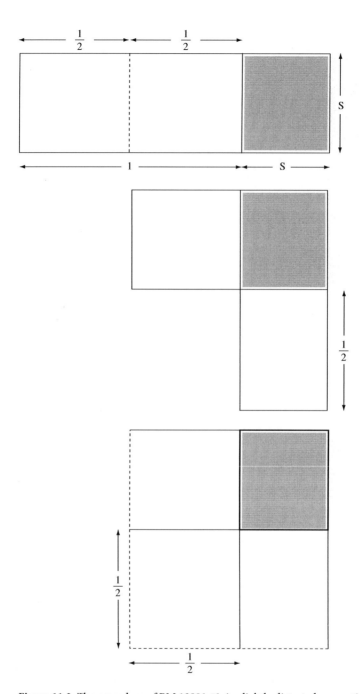

Figure 11.2 The procedure of BM 13901 #1, in slightly distorted proportions.

3. 15′ to 45′ you append: ₁by] 1, 1 is equal. 30′ which you have made hold

4. in the inside of 1 you tear out: 30′ the confrontation.

The problem deals with a 'confrontation', a square configuration identified by its side *s* and possessing an area. The sum of (the measures of) these is told to be 45′. The procedure can be followed in Figure 11.2: the left side *s* of the shaded square is provided with a 'projection' (ɪ 1). Thereby a rectangle ⊏ ⊐(*s*,1) is produced, whose area equals the length of the side *s*; this rectangle, together with the shaded square area, must therefore also equal 45′. 'Breaking' the 'projection 1' (together with the adjacent rectangle) and moving the outer 'moiety' so as to make the two parts 'hold' a small square □(30′) does not change the area (ɪ 2), but completing the resulting gnomon by 'appending' the small square results in a large square, whose area must be 45′ + 15′ = 1 (ɪ 3). Therefore, the side of the large square must also be 1 (ɪ 3). 'Tearing out' that part of the rectangle which was moved so as to make it 'hold' leaves 1–30′ for the 'confrontation', [the side of] the square configuration.

As in the previous case, once the meaning of the terms and the nature of the operations is understood, no explanation beyond the description of the steps seems to be needed.

In order to understand *why* we may compare to the analogous solution of a second-degree equation:

$$x^2 + 1 \cdot x = \tfrac{3}{4}$$
$$\Leftrightarrow \quad x^2 + 1 \cdot x + (\tfrac{1}{2})^2 = \tfrac{3}{4} + (\tfrac{1}{2})^2$$
$$\Leftrightarrow \quad x^2 + 1 \cdot x + (\tfrac{1}{2})^2 = \tfrac{3}{4} + \tfrac{1}{4} = 1$$
$$\Leftrightarrow \quad (x + \tfrac{1}{2})^2 = 1$$
$$\Leftrightarrow \quad x + \tfrac{1}{2} = \sqrt{1} = 1$$
$$\Leftrightarrow \quad x = 1 - \tfrac{1}{2} = \tfrac{1}{2}$$

We notice that the numerical steps are the same as those of the Babylonian text, and this kind of correspondence was indeed what led to the discovery that the Babylonians possessed an 'algebra'. At the same time, the terminology was interpreted from the numbers – for instance, since 'making ½ and ½ hold' produces ¼, this operation was identified with a numerical multiplication; since 'raising' and 'repeating' were interpreted in the same way, it was impossible to distinguish them.[20] Similarly, the two additive

---

found by raising exactly the half of the base to the height. It is found by 'breaking', a term which is used in no other function in the mathematical texts.

[20] Actually, both Neugebauer and Thureau-Dangin knew that this was not the whole truth: none of them ever uses a wrong operation when reconstructing a damaged text. On one occasion Neugebauer (1935–7: ɪ 180) even observes that the scribe uses a wrong multiplication. However,

operations were conflated, etc. All in all, the text was thus interpreted as a numerical algorithm:

Halve 1: ½.
Multiply ½ and ½: ¼.
Add ¼ to ½: 1.
Take the square root of 1: 1.
Subtract ½ from 1: ½.

A similar interpretation as a mere algorithm results from a reading of the symbolic solution if the left-hand side of all equations is eliminated. It is indeed this left-hand side which establishes the identity of the numbers appearing to the right, and thereby makes it obvious that the operations are justified and lead to the solution. In the same way, the geometric reference of the operational terms in the Babylonian text is what establishes the meaning of the numbers and thereby the pertinence of the steps.

Didactical explanations

Kline wrote at a moment when the meaning of the terms and the nature of the operations was *not* yet understood and where the text was therefore usually read as a mere prescription of a numerical algorithm; his opinion is therefore explainable (we shall return to the fact that this opinion of his also reflects deeply rooted post-Renaissance scientific ideology). How this understanding developed concerns the history of modern historical scholarship.[21] But how did Old Babylonian students come to understand these matters? (Even we needed some explanations and some training before we came to consider algebraic transformations as self-explanatory.)

Neugebauer, fully aware that the complexity of many of the problems solved in the Old Babylonian texts presupposes deep understanding and not mere glimpses of insight, supposed that the explanations were given in oral teaching. In general this will certainly have been the case, but after Neugebauer's work on Babylonian mathematics (which stopped in the late 1940s) a few texts have been published which turn out to contain exactly the kind of explanations we are looking for.

---

they never made this insight explicit, for which reason less brilliant successors did not get the point. For instance, Bruins and Rutten 1961 abounds in wrong choices (even when Sumerian word signs are translated into Akkadian).

[21] See Høyrup 1996 for what evidently cannot avoid being a partisan view.

Most explicit are some texts from late Old Babylonian Susa: TMS VII, TMS IX, TMS XVI.[22] Since TMS IX is closely related to the problem we have just dealt with, whereas TMS VII investigates non-determinate linear problems and TMS XVI the transformation of linear equations, we shall begin by discussing TMS IX (Figures 11.3 and 11.4). It falls in three sections, of which the first two run as follows:

#1

1. The surface and 1 length accumulated, 4[0′. ᵎ30, the length,ʳ 20′ the width.]²³
2. As 1 length to 10′ ⌊the surface, has been appended,]
3. or 1 (as) base to 20′, [the width, has been appended,]
4. or 1°20′ [ᵎis positedʳ] to the width which together ⌈with the length ᵎholdsʳ] 40′
5. or 1°20′ toge⟨ther⟩ with 30′ the length hol[ds], 40′ (is) [its] name.
6. Since so, to 20′ the width, which is said to you,
7. 1 is appended: 1°20′ you see. Out from here
8. you ask. 40′ the surface, 1°20′ the width, the length what?
9. [30′ the length. T]hus the procedure.

#2

10. [Surface, length, and width accu]mulated, 1. By the Akkadian (method).
11. [1 to the length append.] 1 to the width append. Since 1 to the length is appended,
12. [1 to the width is app]ended, 1 and 1 make hold, 1 you see.
13. [1 to the accumulation of length,] width and surface append, 2 you see.
14. [To 20′ the width, 1 appe]nd, 1°20′. To 30′ the length, 1 append, 1°30′.²⁴
15. [ᵎSinceʳ a surf]ace, that of 1°20′ the width, that of 1°30′ the length,
16. [ᵎthe length together withʳ the wi]dth, are made hold, what is its name?
17. 2 the surface.
18. Thus the Akkadian (method).

Section 1 explains how to deal with an equation stating that the sum of a rectangular area $\sqsubset\!\sqsupset(l,w)$ and the length l is given, referring to the situation that the length is 30′ and the width 20′. These numbers are used as identifiers, fulfilling thus the same role as our letters l and w. Line 2 repeats the

---

[22] All were first published by Bruins and Rutten 1961 who, however, did not understand their character. Revised transliterations and translations as well as analyses can be found in H2002: 181–8, 89–95 and 85–9 (only part 1), respectively. A full treatment of TMS XVI is found in Høyrup 1990: 299–302.

[23] As elsewhere, passages in plain square brackets are reconstructions of damaged passages that can be considered certain; superscript and subscript square brackets indicate that only the lower or upper part respectively of the signs close to that bracket is missing. Passages within ᵎ...ʳ are reasonable reconstructions which however may not correspond to the exact formulation that was once on the tablet.

[24] My restitutions of lines 14–16 are somewhat tentative, even though the mathematical substance is fairly well established by a parallel passage in lines 28–31.

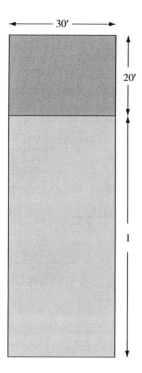

Figure 11.3 The configuration discussed in TMS IX #1.

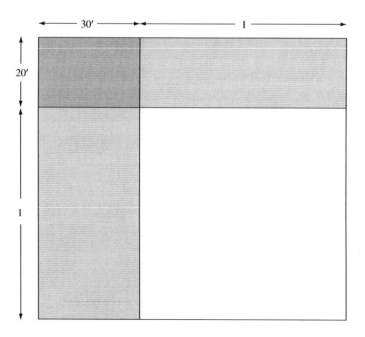

Figure 11.4 The configuration of TMS IX #2.

statement but identifying the area as 10′. In line 3, this is told to be equivalent to adding 'a base' 1 to the width, as shown in Figure 11.3 – in symbols, $\sqsubset\sqsupset(l,w)+l=\sqsubset\sqsupset(l,w)+\sqsubset\sqsupset(l,1)=\sqsubset\sqsupset(l,w+1)$; the 'base' evidently fulfils the same role as the 'projection' of BM 13901. Line 4 tells us that this means that we get a (new) width 1°20′, and line 5 checks that the rectangle contained by this new width and the original length 30′ is indeed 40′, as it should be. Lines 6–9 sum up.

Section 2 again refers to a rectangle with known dimensions – once more $l=30′$, $w=20′$. This time the situation is that both sides are added to the area, the sum being 1. The trick to be applied in the transformation is identified as the 'Akkadian method'. This time, both length and width are augmented by 1 (line 11); however, the resulting rectangle $\sqsubset\sqsupset(l+1,w+1)$ contains more than it should (cf. Figure 11.4), namely beyond a quasi-gnomon representing the given sum (consisting of the original area $\sqsubset\sqsupset(l,w)$, a rectangle $\sqsubset\sqsupset(l,1)$ whose measure is the same as that of l, and a rectangle $\sqsubset\sqsupset(1,w)=w$), also a quadratic completion $\sqsubset\sqsupset(1,1)=1$ (line 12). Therefore, the area of the new rectangle should be $1+1=2$ (line 13). And so it is: the new length will be 1°30′, the new width will be 1°20′, and the area which they contain will be $1°30′·1°20′=2$ (lines 15–17).

Since extension also occurs in section 1, the 'Akkadian method' is likely to refer to the quadratic completion (this conclusion is supported by further arguments which do not belong within the present context).

After these two didactical explanations follows a problem in the proper sense. In symbolic form it can be expressed as follows:

$$\sqsubset\sqsupset(l,w)+l+w=1\,,\quad \tfrac{1}{17}(3l+4w)+w=30′$$

The first equation is the one whose transformation into

$$\sqsubset\sqsupset(\lambda,\omega)=2$$

($\lambda=l+1$, $\omega=w+1$) was just explained in Section 2. The second is multiplied by 17, thus becoming

$$3l+21w=8°30′.$$

and further transformed into

$$3\lambda+21\omega=32°30,$$

whereas the area equation is transformed into

$$\sqsubset\sqsupset(3\lambda,21\omega)=2′6.$$

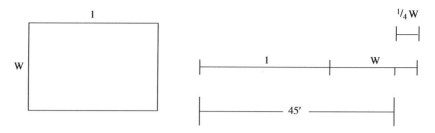

Figure 11.5 The situation of TMS xvi #1.

Thereby, the problem has been reduced to a standard rectangle problem (known area and sum of sides), and it is solved accordingly (by a method similar to that of BM 13901 #1).

The present text does not explain the transformation of the equation 1/17 $(3l + 4w) + w = 30'$, but a similar transformation is the object of Section 1 of TMS xvi (Figure 11.5):

1. [The 4th of the width, from] the length and the width to tear out, 45′. You, 45′
2. [to 4 raise, 3 you] see. 3, what is that? 4 and 1 posit,
3. [50′ and] 5′, to tear out, ˺posit˹. 5′ to 4 raise, 1 width. 20′ to 4 raise,
4. 1°20′ you ⟨see⟩, 4 widths. 30′ to 4 raise, 2 you ⟨see⟩, 4 lengths. 20′, 1 width, to tear out,
5. from 1°20′, 4 widths, tear out, 1 you see. 2, the lengths, and 1, 3 widths, accumulate, 3 you see.
6. Igi 4 de[ta]ch, 15′ you see. 15′ to 2, the lengths, raise, [3]0′ you ⟨see⟩, 30′ the length.
7. 15′ to 1 raise, [1]5′ the contribution of the width. 30′ and 15′ hold.[25]
8. Since 'The 4th of the width, to tear out', it is said to you, from 4, 1 tear out, 3 you see.
9. Igi 4 de⟨tach⟩, 15′ you see, 15′ to 3 raise, 45′ you ⟨see⟩, 45′ as much as (there is) of [widths].
10. 1 as much as (there is) of lengths posit. 20, the true width take, 20 to 1′ raise, 20′ you see.
11. 20′ to 45′ raise, 15′ you see. 15′ from 3015′ [tear out],
12. 30′ you see, 30′ the length.

Even this explanation deals formally with the sides l and w of a rectangle, although the rectangle itself is wholly immaterial to the discussion. In symbolic translation we are told that

$$(l + w) - \tfrac{1}{4}w = 45'.$$

[25] This 'hold' is an ellipsis for 'make your head hold', the standard phrase for retaining in memory.

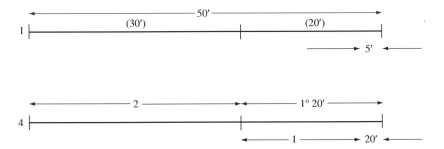

Figure 11.6 The transformations of TMS xvi #1.

The dimensions of the rectangle are not stated directly, but from the numbers in line 3 we see that they are presupposed to be known and to be the same as before, 50′ being the value of $l + w$, 5′ that of ¼w – cf. Figure 11.6.

The first operation to perform is a multiplication by 4. 4 times 45′ gives 3, and the text then asks for an explanation of this number (line 2). The subsequent explanation can be followed on Figure 11.6, which certainly is a modern reconstruction but which is likely to correspond in some way to what is meant by the explanation. The proportionals 1 and 4 are taken note of ('posited'), 1 corresponding of course to the original equation, 4 to the outcome of the multiplication. Next 50′ (the total of length plus width) and 5′ (the fourth of the width that is to be 'torn out') are taken note of (line 3), and the multiplied counterparts of the components of the original equation (the part to be torn out, the width, and the length) are calculated and described in terms of lengths and widths (lines 3–4); finally it is shown that the outcome (consisting of the components $1 = 4w - 1w$ and $2 = 4l$) explains the number 3 that resulted from the original multiplication (lines 4–5).

Now the text reverses the move and multiplies the multiplied equation that was just analysed by ¼. Multiplication of 2 ($= 4l$) gives 30′, the length; multiplication of 1 gives 15′, which is explained to be the 'contribution of the width'; both contributions are to be retained in memory (lines 6–7). Next the contributions are to be explained; using an argument of false position ('if one fourth of 4 was torn out, 3 would remain; now, since it is torn out of 1, the remainder is 3 · ¼'), the coefficient of the width ('as much as (there is) of widths') is found to be 45′. The coefficient of the length is seen immediately to be 1 (lines 1–10).

Next (line 10) follows a step whose meaning is not certain; the text distinguishes between the 'true length' and the 'length' *simpliciter*, writing however the value of both in identical ways. One possible explanation (in my opinion quite plausible, and hence used in the translation) is that the 'true width' is the width of an imagined 'real' field, which could be 20 rods (120 m), whereas the width *simpliciter* is that of a model field that can be drawn in the school yard (2 m); indeed, the normal dimensions of the fields dealt with in second-degree problems (which are school problems without any practical use) are 30′ and 20′ rods, 3 and 2 m, much too small for real fields but quite convenient in school. In any case, multiplication of the value of the width by its coefficient gives us the corresponding contribution once more (line 11), which indeed has the value that was assigned to memory. Subtracting it from the total (which is written in an unconventional way that already shows the splitting) leaves the length, as indeed it should (lines 11–12).

Detailed didactical explanations such as these have only been found in Susa; once they have been understood, however, we may recognize in other texts rudiments of similar explanations, which must have been given in their full form orally,[26] as once supposed by Neugebauer.

These explanations are certainly meant to impart *understanding*, and in this sense they are demonstrations. But their character differs fundamentally from that of Euclidean demonstrations (which, indeed, were often reproached for their opacity during the centuries where the *Elements* were used as a school book). Euclidean demonstrations proceed in a linear way, and end up with a conclusion which readers must acknowledge to be unavoidable (unless they find an error) but which may leave them wondering where the rabbit came from. The Old Babylonian didactical texts, in contrast, aim at building up a tightly knit conceptual network in the mind of the student.

However, conceptual connections can be of different kinds. Pierre de la Ramée when rewriting Euclid replaced the 'superfluous' demonstrations by explanations of the practical uses of the propositions. Numerology (in a general sense including also analogous approaches to geometry) links mathematical concepts to non-mathematical notions and doctrines; to this genre belong not only writings like the ps-Iamblichean *Theologoumena arithmeticae* but also for some of their aspects, Liu Hui's commentaries to *The Nine Chapters on Mathematical Procedures*, which cannot be understood in isolation from the *Book of Changes*.[27] Within this spectrum, the Old Babylonian expositions belong in the vicinity of Euclid, far away from Ramism as well as numerology: the connections that they establish all belong strictly within the same mathematical domain as the object they discuss.

---

[26] Worth mentioning are the unpublished text IM 43993, which I know about through Jöran Friberg and Farouk al-Rawi (personal communication), and YBC 8633, analysed from this perspective in H2002: 254–7.

[27] According to Chemla 1997.

Justifiability and critique

Whoever has tried regularly to give didactical explanations of mathematical procedures is likely to have encountered the situation where a first explanation turns out on second thoughts – maybe provoked by questions or lacking success of the explanation – not to be justifiable without adjustment. While didactical explanation is no doubt one of the sources of mathematical demonstration, the scrutiny of the *conditions under which* and the *reasons for which* the explanations given hold true is certainly another source. The latter undertaking is what Kant termed *critique*, and its central role in Greek mathematical demonstration is obvious.

In Old Babylonian mathematics, critique is less important. If read as demonstrations, explanations oriented toward the establishment of conceptual networks tend to produce circular reasoning, in the likeness of those persons referred to by Aristotle 'who . . . think that they are drawing parallel lines; for they do not realize that they are making assumptions which cannot be proved unless the parallel lines exist'.[28] In their case, Aristotle told the way out – namely to 'take as an axiom' (ἀξιόω) that which is proposed. This is indeed what is done in the *Elements*, whose fifth postulate can thus be seen to answer metatheoretical critique.

However, though less important than in Greek geometry, critique is not absent from Babylonian mathematics. One instance is illustrated by the text YBC 6967,[29] a problem dealing with two numbers *igûm* and *igibûm*, 'the reciprocal and its reciprocal', the product of which, however, is supposed to be 1˹ (that is, 60), not 1:

Obv.
1. [The *igib*]*ûm* over the *igûm*, 7 it goes beyond
2. [*igûm*] and *igibûm* what?
3. Yo[u], 7 which the *igibûm*
4. over the *igûm* goes beyond
5. to two break: 3°30′;
6. 3°30′ together with 3°30′
7. make hold: 12°15′.
8. To 12°15′ which comes up for you
9. [1˹ the surf]ace append: 1˹12°15′.
10. [The equalside of 1˹]12°15′ what? 8°30′.
11. [8°30′ and] 8°30′, its counterpart,[30] lay down.[31]

---

[28] *Prior Analytics* II, 64ᵇ34–65ᵃ9, trans. Tredennick 1938: 485–7.
[29] Transliterated, translated and analysed in H2002: 55–8.
[30] The 'counterpart' of an equalside is 'the other side' meeting it in a common corner.
[31] Namely, lay down in writing or drawing.

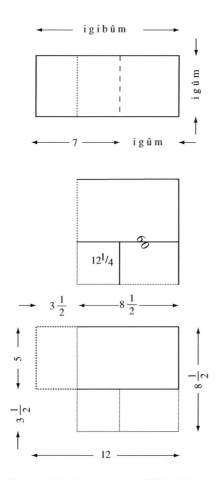

Figure 11.7 The procedure of YBC 6967.

Rev.
1. 3°30′, the made-hold,
2. from one tear out,
3. to one append.
4. The first is 12, the second is 5.
5. 12 is the *igibûm*, 5 is the *igûm*.

The procedure can be followed in Figure 11.7; the text is another instance of self-evident validity, and only differs from those discussed under this perspective in having the sides and the area of the rectangle *represent* numbers and not just themselves. The interesting point is found in Rev. 2–3. In cases where there is no constraint on the order, the Babylonians always speak of addition before subtraction. Here, however, the 3°30′ that is to be added to the left of the gnomon (that is, to be put back in its original position) must first be at disposition, that is, it must already have been torn out below.

This compliance with a request of concrete meaningfulness should not be read as evidence of some 'primitive mode of thought still bound to the concrete and unfit for abstraction'; this is clear from the way early Old Babylonian texts present the same step in analogous problems, often in a shortened phrase 'append and tear out' and indicating the two resulting numbers immediately afterwards, in any case never respecting the norm of concreteness. This norm thus appears to have been introduced precisely in order to make the procedure justifiable – corresponding to the introduction in Greek theoretical arithmetic of the norm that fractions and unity could be no numbers in consequence of the explanation of number as a 'collection of units'.[32]

But the norm of concreteness is not the only evidence of Old Babylonian mathematical critique. Above, we have encountered the 'projection' and the 'base', devices that allow the addition of lines and surfaces in a way that does not violate homogeneity, and the related distinction between 'accumulation' and 'appending'. Even these stratagems turn out to be secondary developments. A text like AO 8862 (probably from the early phase of Old Babylonian mathematics, at least within Larsa, its local area) does not make use of them. Its first problem starts thus:

1. Length, width.[33] Length and width I have made hold:
2. A surface have I built.
3. I turned around (it). As much as length over width
4. went beyond,
5. to inside the surface I have appended:
6. 3`3. I turned back. Length and width
7. I have accumulated: 27. Length, width, and surface w[h]at?

As we see, a line (the excess of length over width) is 'appended' to the area; 'accumulation' also occurs, but the reason for this is that 'appending' for example the length to the width would produce an irrelevant increased width and no symmetrical sum (cf. the beginning of TMS XVI, above, which first creates a symmetrical sum and next removes part of it).

This 'appending' of a line to an area does not mean that the text is absurd. In order to see that we must understand that it operates with a notion of 'broad lines', lines that carry an inherent virtual breadth. Though not made

---

[32] See Høyrup 2004: 148f.

[33] That is, the object of problem is told to be the simplest configuration determined solely by a length and a width – namely, according to Babylonian habits, a rectangle.

explicit, this notion underlies the determination of areas by 'raising';[34] it is widespread in pre-modern practical mensuration, in which 'everybody' (locally) would measure in the same unit, for which reason it could be presupposed tacitly[35] – land being bought and sold in consequence just as we are used to buying and selling cloth, by the yard and not the square yard. However, once didactical explanation in school has taken its beginning (and once it is no longer obvious which of several metrological units should serve as standard breadth), a line which at the same time is 'with breadth' and 'without breadth' becomes awkward. In consequence, critique appears to have outlawed the 'appending' of lines to areas and to have introduced devices like the 'projection' – the latter in close parallel to the way Viète established homogeneity and circumvented the use of broad lines of Renaissance algebra.[36]

All in all, mathematical demonstration was thus not absent from Old Babylonian mathematics. Procedures were described in a way which, once the terminology and its use have been decoded, turns out to be as transparent as the self-evident transformations of modern equation algebra and in no need of further explicit arguing in order to convince; teaching involved didactical explanations which aimed at providing students with a corresponding understanding of the terminology and the operations; and mathematical concepts and procedures were transformed critically so as to allow coherent explanation of points that may initially have seemed problematic or paradoxical. No surviving texts suggest, however, that all this was ever part of an explicitly formulated programme, nor do the texts we know point to any thinking about *demonstration as a particular activity*. All seems to have come as naturally as speaking in prose to Molière's Monsieur Jourdain, as consequences of the situations and environments in which mathematics was practised.

Mathematical Taylorism: practically dubious but an effective ideology

Teachers, in the Bronze Age just as in modern times, may have gone beyond what was needed in the 'real' practice of their future students, blinded by the fact that the practice they themselves knew best was that of their own

---

[34] Cf n. 11 above.

[35] See Høyrup 1995.

[36] Namely the 'roots', explained by Nuñez 1567: fos. 6r, 232r to be rectangles whose breadth is 'la unidad lineal'.

trade, the teaching of mathematics. None the less, the social *raison d'être* of Old Babylonian mathematics was the training of future scribes in practical computation, and not deeper insight into the principles and metaphysics of mathematics. Why should this involve demonstration? Would it not be enough to teach precisely those *rules* or algorithms which earlier workers have found in the texts and which (in the shape of paradigmatic cases) also constitute the bulk of so many other pre-modern mathematical hand-books? And would it not be better to teach them precisely as rules to be obeyed without distracting reflection on problems of validity?

That 'the hand' should be governed in the interest of efficiency by a 'brain' located in a different person but should in itself behave like a mindless machine is the central idea of Frederick Taylor's 'scientific management' – 'hand' and 'brain' being, respectively, the worker and the planning engineer. In the pre-modern world, where craft knowledge tended to constitute an autonomous body, and where (with rare exceptions) practice was not derived from theory, Taylorist ideas could never flourish.[37] In many though not all fields, autonomous practical knowledge survived well into the nine-teenth, sometimes the twentieth century; however, the *idea* that practice should be governed by theory (and the ideology that practice is derived from the insights of theory) can be traced back to the early modern epoch. Already before its appearance in Francis Bacon's *New Atlantis* we find something very similar forcefully expressed in Vesalius' *De humani corpo-ris fabrica*, according to which the art of healing had suffered immensely from being split into three independent practices: that of the theoretically schooled physicians, that of the pharmacists, and that of vulgar barbers supposed to possess no instruction at all; instead, Vesalius argues, all three bodies of knowledge should be carried by the same person, and that person should be the theoretically schooled physician.

In many fields, the suggestion that material practice should be the task of the theoretically schooled would seem inane; even in surveying, a field which was totally reshaped by theoreticians in the eighteenth century, the scholars of the *Académie des Sciences* (and later Wessel and Gauss), even when working in the field, would mostly instruct others in how to perform the actual work and control they did well. Such circumstances favoured the development of views close to those of Taylorism – why should those who merely made the single observations or straightened the chains be bothered

---

[37] Aristotle certainly thought that master artisans had insight into 'principles' and common workers not (*Metaphysics1*, 981b1–5), and that slaves were living instruments (*Politics* I.4); but reading of the context of these famous passages will reveal that they do not add up to anything like Taylorism.

by explanations of the reasons for what they were asked to do? If the rules used by practitioners were regarded in this perspective, it also lay close at hand to view these as 'merely empirical' if not recognizably derived from the insights of theoreticians.

Such opinions, and their failing in situations where practitioners have to work on their own, are discussed in Christian Wolff's *Mathematisches Lexikon*:

> It is true that performing mathematics can be learned without reasoning mathematics; but then one remains blind in all affairs, achieves nothing with suitable precision and in the best way, at times it may occur that one does not find one's way at all. Not to mention that it is easy to forget what one has learned, and that that which one has forgotten is not so easily retrieved, because everything depends only on memory.[38]

Wolff certainly identified 'reasoning mathematics' (also called '*Mathesis theorica*' or '*speculativa*') with established theoretical mathematics, but none the less he probably hit the point not only in his own context but also if we look at the conditions of pre-modern mathematical practitioners: without insight into the reasons why their procedures worked they were likely to err except in the execution of tasks that recurred so often that their details could not be forgotten.[39] Even the teaching of practitioners' mathematics through paradigmatic cases exemplifying rules that were or were not stated explicitly will always have involved some level of explanation and thus of demonstration – and certainly, as in the Babylonian case, internal mathematical rather than philosophical or otherwise 'numerological' explanation. Whether critique would also be involved probably depended on the level of professionalization of the teaching institution itself.

But those mathematicians and historians who were not themselves involved in the teaching of practitioners were not forced to discover such subtleties. For them, it was all too convenient to accept Taylorist ideologies (whether *ante litteram* or *post*) and to magnify their own intellectual standing by identifying the appearance of explicit or implicit rules with mindless rote learning (if derived from supposedly *real* mathematics) or blind

---

[38]   Wolff 1716: 867 (my translation).

[39]   The 'rule of three', with its intermediate product deprived of concrete meaning, only turns up in environments where the problems to which it applies were really the routine of every working day – notwithstanding the obvious computational advantage of letting multiplication precede division. Its extensions into 'rule of five' and 'rule of seven' never gained similar currency. A more recent example, directly inspired by Adam Smith's theory of the division of labour, is Prony's use of 'several hundred men who knew only the elementary rules of arithmetic' in the calculation of logarithmic and trigonometric tables (McKeon 1975).

experimentation (if not to be linked to recognizable theory). Such ideologies did not make opinions such as Kline's necessary and did not engender them directly, but they shaped the intellectual climate within which he and his mental kin grew up as mathematicians and as historians.

Bibliography

Bruins, E. M., and Rutten, M. (1961) *Textes mathématiques de Suse*. Mémoires de la Mission Archéologique en Iran vol. xxxiv. Paris.

Chemla, K. (1997) 'What is at stake in mathematical proofs from third-century China', *Science in Context* **10**: 227–51.

Høyrup, J. (1990) 'Algebra and naive geometry: an investigation of some basic aspects of Old Babylonian mathematical thought', *Altorientalische Forschungen* **17**: 27–69 and 262–354.

(1995) 'Linee larghe: Un'ambiguità geometrica dimenticata', *Bollettino di Storia delle Scienze Matematiche* **15**: 3–14.

(1996) 'Changing trends in the historiography of Mesopotamian mathematics: an insider's view', *History of Science* **34**: 1–32.

(2004) 'Conceptual divergence – canons and taboos – and critique: reflections on explanatory categories', *Historia Mathematica* **31**: 129–47.

Kline, M. (1972) *Mathematical Thought from Ancient to Modern Times*. New York.

McKeon, R. M. (1975) 'Prony, Gaspard-François-Clair-Marie Riche de', in *Dictionary of Scientific Biography*, vol. xi. New York: 163–6.

Neugebauer, O. (1934) *Vorlesungen über Geschichte der antiken mathematischen Wissenschaften, vol.* i, *Vorgriechische Mathematik*. Berlin.

(1935–7) *Mathematische Keilschrift-Texte*, vols. i–iii. Berlin.

(1957) *The Exact Sciences in Antiquity*, 2 edn. Providence, RI.

Nuñez, P. (1567) *Libro de Algebra en Arithmetica y Geometria*. Anvers.

Rackham, H. (ed. and trans.) (1933) *Cicero*: De natura deorum. Cambridge, MA.

Tredennick, H. (ed. and trans.) (1938) *Aristotle*: Prior Analytics, in *Aristotle: The Categories, On Interpretation and Prior Analytics*, ed. and trans. H. P. Cook and H. Tredennick. Cambridge, MA.

van der Waerden, B. L. (1956) *Erwachende Wissenschaft: Ägyptische, babylonische und griechische Mathematik*. Basel.

Wolff, C. (1716) *Mathematisches Lexicon*. Leipzig.

12 | Interpretation of reverse algorithms in several Mesopotamian texts

CHRISTINE PROUST, TRANSLATION MICAH ROSS

Is it possible to discuss proofs in texts which contain only numbers and no verbal element? I propose to analyse a Mesopotamian tablet containing a long series of reciprocal calculations, written as numeric data in sexagesimal place value notation. The provenance of this tablet, which today is conserved at the University Museum in Philadelphia under the number CBS 1215, is not documented, but there are numerous parallels from the scribal schools of southern Mesopotamia, notably Nippur and Ur, all from the Old Babylonian period (beginning two millennia before the Christian era). Thus, one might suppose that it shares in the scribal tradition inherited from the southern Sumero-Akkadian culture.[1] The text is composed of only two graphemes: vertical wedges (ones) and *Winkelhaken* (tens).[2] The limited number of graphemes is clearly not due to the limited knowledge of writing possessed by the author of the text. The tablet was composed at the time when 'the scribal art' (*nam-dub-sar*, in Sumerian) achieved its most refined developments, not only in the domains of mathematics and Sumerian or Akkadian literature, but also in the consideration of writing, language and grammar.[3] Hence, my hypothesis is that this text contains an original mathematical contemplation and that a close analysis of the tablet and its context yields the keys to understanding the text.[4]

Purely numeric texts are not rare among cuneiform documentation, but, with the exception of the famous tablet Plimpton 322 which has inspired an abundant literature, such texts have drawn relatively little attention from historians.[5] Indeed, the numeric tablets do not contain information written in

---

[1] According to A. Sachs who published it, the tablet CBS 1215 is part of a collection called 'Khabaza 2', purchased at Baghdad in 1889. He thought it hardly possible that it came from Nippur, making reference to the intervening disputes among the team of archaeologists at Nippur (Sachs 1947: 230 and n. 14).

[2] See the copy by Robson 2000: 23, and an extract of this copy in Table 12.3 below.

[3] Cavigneaux 1989.

[4] I thank all those who, in the course of seminars or through critical readings, have participated in the collective work of which this article is the result, beginning with Karine Chemla, whose remarks have truly improved the present version of the text.

[5] On the subject of Plimpton 322, a tablet probably from the Old Babylonian period perhaps from Larsa, which presents a list of fifteen Pythagorean triplets in the form of a table, see

384

verbal style (in Sumerian or in Akkadian language) and then numeric tablets are less explicit than other types of tablets in the intentions and the methods of their authors. It is generally admitted that numeric tablets are some sort of collection of exercises destined for pedagogical purposes. However, the content and context of the tablets show that the purposes of a text such as that of tablet CBS 1215 were greater than simple pedagogy. In particular, I would like to show in this chapter that the text is organized in order to stress the operation of the reciprocal algorithm and to show why the series of steps on which it is founded leads effectively to the desired reciprocal.

Before I go too far into the analysis, let me give a brief description of the tablet. The text is composed of 21 sections. (See the transcription in Appendix 1.) The entries of the sections are successively 2.5, 4.10, 8.20, ..., 10.6.48.53.20, namely the first 21 terms of a geometric progression for an initial number 2.5 with a common ratio of 2. (Details on the cuneiform notation of numbers and their transcription appear later.) Other than the absence of any verbal element in its writing, the text possesses some obviously remarkable properties (see Table 12.3 and Appendix 1).

(1) In each section, the numbers are set out in two or three columns. Thus, the spatial arrangement of the numeric data is an important element of the text.

(2) The sections are increasingly long and, as will be seen, the result appears to be the application of iterations.

(3) In each section, the last number is identical to the first. The procedure progresses in such a fashion that its point of arrival corresponds exactly with its point of departure. The text, therefore, reveals the phenomena of reciprocity.

What do these three properties (spatial arrangement, iteration and reciprocity) reveal to us? Do they disclose the thoughts of the ancient scribes about the mathematical methods which constitute the reciprocal algorithm, particularly about the topic of its validity? In order to respond to these questions, it will be necessary not only to analyse the text in detail, but also to compare and contrast it with other texts.

Reciprocal algorithms are not known only by their numeric form. In particular, a related tablet, VAT 6505, contains a list of instructions composed

notably Robson 2001a; Friberg 2007: Appendix 7; Britton *et al.* 2011. Among the other analyses of numeric texts, outside that which bears upon the tablet studied here, one may cite those which concern the tables from the first millennium, such as the large table of reciprocals from the Seleucid period AO 6456 – for example Bruins 1969 and Friberg 1983, and several other tables from the same period (Britton 1991–3; Friberg 2007: Appendix 8).

Table 12.1 Principal texts studied here

	Museum number	Provenance	Contents	Style
A	CBS 1215	Unknown	Reciprocal	Numeric
B	VAT 6505	Unknown	Reciprocal	Verbal
C	UET 6/2 222	Ur	Square Root	Numeric
D	IM 54472	Unknown	Square Root	Verbal

in Akkadian. Sachs has shown that these instructions refer to calculations found in the numeric tablet CBS 1215.[6] Thus, we have both a numeric text and a verbal text related to the same algorithm. These two texts both refer to the reciprocal algorithm in widely different manners. They neither employ the same means of expression, nor do they deliver exactly the same type of information. Thus there is a shift between the different texts and the practices of calculation to which they refer.

In addition, some properties of the tablet CBS 1215, notably those which concern spatial arrangement and reciprocity, are likewise manifested in calculations of square roots. Such is notably the case for the tablet UET 6/2 222, which is an Old Babylonian school exercise from Ur (see Table 12.1). Also, in the case of the square root algorithm just as for the reciprocal algorithm, both numeric and verbal texts are attested. In fact, J. Friberg has shown that tablet IM 54472, composed in Akkadian, contains instructions which relate to calculations found in the numeric tablet UET 6/2 222.[7]

In order to facilitate the reading of the following sections, which alternate between different tablets, I have designated the tablets by the letters A to D. The concordance between these letters, their museum numbers and provenance is presented in Table 12.1.[8]

In addition, many other parallels to Tablet A exist. In some cases, entire sections of the text are identically reproduced. Such reproductions and citations occur principally in the texts from the scribal schools which operated

---

[6] Sachs 1947.

[7] Friberg 2000: 108–12.

[8] The tablets of Table 12.1 have been published in the following articles and works. A = CBS 1215 in Sachs 1947 for the transliteration and interpretation; Robson 2000: 14, 23–4 for the hand copy and several joins ; B = VAT 6505 in Neugebauer 1935–7: I 270, II pl. 14, 43; C = UET 6/2 222 in Gadd and Kramer 1966: 248; D = IM 54472 in Bruins 1954. Other than the tablet from Ur, the tablets come from illicit excavations. VAT 6505 may come from the north because of its orthographic and grammatical properties (H2002: 331, n. 383); according to Friberg 2000: 106, 159–60, it may come from Sippar. IM 54472 likewise may come from the north, perhaps from Shaduppum (Friberg 2000: 110).

in Nippur, Ur and elsewhere.[9] The school texts yield precious information about the context of the use of the reciprocal algorithm and will be used on a case-by-case basis to supplement the small, essential body of texts presented in Table 12.1.[10]

The historical problem posed by relationships that may have existed between the authors of different texts is difficult to resolve because the provenance is usually unknown and the dating is uncertain. Some available information seem to indicate that the numeric texts and their pedagogical parallels may pertain to the southern tradition (Ur, Uruk, Nippur), and the verbal texts, notably Tablet B which may come from Sippar, belong to the northern tradition of Old Babylonian Mesopotamia.[11] The possible historic opposition between the north and the south, however, did not exclude certain forms of communication, since the two traditions were not isolated and the scribes from different regions had contact with one another through numerous exchanges, notably circulating schoolmasters.[12] Even though uncertainty about the sources does not permit the establishment of a clear geographic distribution, it is entirely possible that the two types of texts existed in the same contexts. Regardless of the relationship between the authors of these different styles of texts, it is possible to hypothesize two points of view about the same algorithm. The important point, whether or not these two points of view emanate from the same scribal context, is that they clearly have different objectives. The verbal texts are series of instructions, which appear to have been intended to help someone execute the algorithm. Some portion of the numeric tables are school exercises intended for the training of student scribes. The function of Tablet A seems to have been of a different nature.

Tablet A does not conform to the typology of a school tablet, even though it was used in an educational context, as was probably the case with all the mathematical texts of the Old Babylonian period. Through a comparison of Tablet A with parallel or similar texts, I would like to provide more detailed

[9] What are called 'school tablets' in Assyriology are the products of students in scribal schools. These tablets generally have a standardized appearance and contents, and because of this fact are easily recognizable, at least in the case of those that date from the Old Babylonian period.

[10] This documentation may be specified further: the list of parallels with A is presented in Table 12.6; the other tablets containing reciprocals are assembled in Table 12.7; those which contain calculations of square and cubic roots are in Table 12.8.

[11] The provenances of different tablets and their parallels are detailed in the notes relative to Tables 12.1, 12.6, 12.7 and 12.8. In the case of Mari, it is interesting to note that the tablets from this northerly site seem more akin to the tablets of the south than those of the north. Thus, if different scribal traditions were confirmed, they would clearly reveal complex trans-regional phenomena of communication, and not only local peculiarities.

[12] Charpin 1992; Charpin and Joannès 1992.

responses to the questions concerning its function. Is Tablet A only a collection of exercises, from which the school exercises were extracted? What is the tablet's relationship to pedagogical practice? How does the information differ from the information presented in the verbal texts? What specific significance may be determined from its structure or its layout? These questions, as will be seen, are connected in the way that Tablet A corresponds with the operation of the reciprocal algorithm and with its justification.

Place-value notation and reciprocals

Since numeric texts are constructed of numbers written in the sexagesimal place value notation characteristic of Mesopotamian mathematical texts, let us review the key principals of this notation. With the base being 60, there are 59 'digits'. (Zero is not found in the Old Babylonian period.) These 59 digits are represented by the repetition of the signs 1 (a vertical wedge) and 10 (the *Winkelhaken*) as many times as necessary.[13]

Examples: $\mathsf{Y\!Y}$ (2) $\langle\mathsf{Y\!Y\!Y}$ (13) $\langle\!\langle$ (20)

According to the positional principle, each unit in a given place represents 60 units of the preceding place (at its right). For the transcription of numbers, I have followed the modern notation proposed by F. Thureau-Dangin, wherein the sexagesimal digits are separated by dots.[14]

Example: $\mathsf{Y\!Y}\langle\mathsf{Y\!Y\!Y}\langle\!\langle$ is rendered as 2.13.20

In cuneiform texts, no place is marked as being that of the units, thus the numbers have no value; they are determined to a factor 60^n (where n is some whole positive or negative number), which, after a fashion, resembles 'floating decimal' notation. For example, the numbers $1, 60, 60^2$ and $1/60$ are all written in the same way, with a vertical wedge: the scribes did not make use of any special signs such as commas or zeros in the final places similar to those we use in modern Indo-Arabic numerals. In the texts studied here, the operations performed on the numbers are multiplications and the determination of reciprocals and square roots, namely operations which do not require that the magnitudes of the numbers be fixed. In the transcriptions, translations and interpretations presented here, I have therefore not

---

[13] The word 'digit' here indicates each sexagesimal place. These 'digits' are written in additive decimal notation.

[14] Other authors prefer to separate the sexagesimal places by a blank space or a comma (such is the case of Sachs, as will be seen later).

restored the orders of magnitude, in keeping with the indeterminacy of the value in the cuneiform writing. However, in these circumstances, might it be possible to establish 'equalities' between numbers, although their values are not specified? Even though the sign '=' might be considered an abuse of language (and an anachronism), I use it in the commentary. This convenience seems acceptable to me insofar as we bear in mind that the sign '=' denotes not a relationship of equality between quantities, but rather an equivalence between notations. For example, $2 \times 30 = 1$ signifies that the product of 2 and 30 is noted as 1.

How were these sexagesimal numbers used in calculations? The great number of school tablets discovered in the refuse heaps of the scribal schools present relatively accurate information about both the way in which place-value notation was introduced in education in the Old Babylonian period and also its use. The course of the scribes' mathematical education is particularly well documented at Nippur, the principal centre of teaching in Mesopotamia.[15] At Nippur, and undoubtedly in the other schools, the first stage of mathematical apprenticeship consisted of memorizing many lists and tables: metrological lists (enumerations of measures of capacities, weights, areas and lengths), metrological tables (tables of correspondence between different measures and numbers in place-value notation) and numerical tables (reciprocals, multiplications and squares).[16] After having memorized these lists, the apprentice scribes used these tables in calculation exercises which chiefly concerned multiplication, the determination of reciprocals and the calculation of areas. Documentation shows that place-value notation came at precise moments in the educational curriculum. Place-value notation does not occur among the expression of measurements which appeal to other numerations, based on the additive principle. They appear in the metrological tables, where each measure (a value written in additive numeration followed by a unit of measure) is placed in relation to an abstract number (a number in place-value notation, not followed by a unit of measure). Moreover, the abstract numbers are found exclusively in the numeric tables and in exercises for multiplication and advanced calculations of reciprocals.[17] The calculation of areas necessitates the transformation of measures into abstract numbers and back again, transformations assured by the metrological tables.[18]

---

[15] Robson 2001b; Robson 2002; Proust 2007.

[16] These tables are described in detail in Neugebauer 1935–7: I ch. I.

[17] In the following pages, 'abstract numbers' will refer to the numbers written in sexagesimal place value notation.

[18] For more details about these mechanisms, see Proust 2008.

Table 12.2 Standard reciprocal table

N	inv(N)	N	inv(N)	N	inv(N)
2	30	15	4	36	1.40
3	20	16	3.45	40	1.30
4	15	18	3.20	45	1.20
5	12	20	3	48	1.15
6	10	24	2.30	50	1.12
8	7.30	25	2.24	54	1.6.40
9	6.40	27	2.13.20	1.4	56.15
10	6	30	2	1.21	44.26.40
12	5	32	1.52.30		

Let us return to the topic of the determination of reciprocals, which is the subject of Tablet A. A small list of reciprocal pairs was memorized by the apprentice scribes in the course of their elementary education. These pairs form a standard table, found in numerous sources at Nippur and also in the majority of Mesopotamian educational centres. That table is as shown in Table 12.2. Obviously, the entries of the standard reciprocal table are the reciprocals of regular sexagesimal single-place numbers, plus two reciprocals for numbers in two places (1.4 and 1.21).[19]

The determination of a reciprocal is an important operation for the scribes because the operation that corresponds with our division was effected through multiplication by the reciprocal. Two consequences result from this conceptualization of 'division'. First, it privileges the regular numbers, which, in fact, are omnipresent in the school texts. Next, division is not properly identified as an operation. In order to effect a division, first a reciprocal is found, then a multiplication is made.[20] In this way, division has

---

[19] Two numbers form a reciprocal pair if their product is written as 1. A regular number in base-60 is a number for which the reciprocal permits a finite sexagesimal expression (numbers which may be decomposed into the product of factors 2, 3 or 5, the prime divisors of the base). The oldest reciprocal tables contain not only the regular numbers, but also the complete series of numbers in single place (1 to 59). In these tables, the irregular numbers are followed by a negation: 'igi 7 nu', meaning '7 has no reciprocal'; see for example the two Neo-Sumerian reciprocal tables known from Nippur, HS 201 in Oelsner 2001 and Ni 374 in Proust 2007: § 5.2.2. It may be said that although the Sumerian language contains no specific term to indicate the regular numbers, it nonetheless contains an expression for the irregular numbers: 'igi … nu'.

[20] The concept of division presented here is that which was taught in the scribal schools and the one used most often in mathematical texts, particularly in those texts discussed in the present chapter. However, this is not the only extant conceptualization. For example, divisions by irregular numbers occur sometimes, but they are formulated as problems: find the number, which, when multiplied by some number, returns some other number (H2002: 29). Likewise, among the mathematical texts, there exist slightly different usages of 'reciprocals', somewhat closer to our concept of fractions. In certain texts, the goal is to take the fraction 1/7 or 1/11

no name in Sumerian, contrary to the determination of a reciprocal (*igi*, in Sumerian) and multiplication (*a-ra$_2$*, in Sumerian).

The determination of the reciprocal of a regular number is thus a fundamental objective of Babylonian positional calculation. The standard tables furnish the reciprocals of the ordinary regular numbers. In what follows, I call the numbers that appear in Table 12.2 'elementary regular factors'. For the other regular numbers which do not appear in the standard table, the scribes had recourse to a reciprocal algorithm, which is precisely what Tablet A addresses.

Sachs identified the reciprocal algorithm thanks to the verbal text of Tablet B (VAT 6505).[21] First, I present the way in which Sachs understood this algorithm and described it in an algebraic formula. Then, I will analyse the way in which Tablets A and B both refer to the same algorithm and the ways in which they differ. This contrast will indirectly permit some of the particular objectives pursued in Tablet A to be clarified.

Sachs' formula

The colophon of Tablet B indicates that the text is composed of twelve sections. The entries are the first twelve terms of a geometric progression for an initial number 2.5 with a common ratio of 2 – the same terms which constitute the beginning of Tablet A. In fact, only five sections are even partially preserved but these remains allowed Sachs to reconstitute the entirety of the original text. The well-preserved entry of the seventh section is 2.13.20, that is 2.5 after six doublings. The text may be translated as follows:[22]

1. 2,[13],20 is the *igûm*.[What is the *igibûm*?]
2. [As for you, when you] perform (the operations),
3. take the reciprocal of 3,20; [you will find 18]
4. Multiply 18 by 2,10; [you will find 39]
5. Add 1; you will find 40.
6. Take the reciprocal of 40; [you will find] 1,30.
7. Multiply 1,30 by 18,
8. you will find 27. The *igibûm* is 27.
9. Such is the procedure.

of a number (see, for example, the series of problems such as A 24194). Finally, in rare cases, approximations for the reciprocals of irregular numbers are found (H2002: 29, n. 50).

[21] Sachs 1947.

[22] B Section 7, translation by Sachs 1947: 226. Damaged portions of text are placed in square brackets. *igûm* and *igibûm* are Akkadian words for pairs of reciprocals.

According to Sachs, whose notations I have reproduced,[23] the algorithm is based on the decomposition of the initial number c as the sum $a + b$, this decomposition is summarized by the following formula (in which the reciprocal of a number n is denoted by $\bar{n}$):

$$\bar{c} = \overline{a+b} = \bar{a} \cdot \overline{\left(1 + b\bar{a}\right)}$$

Applied to the data in B Section 7, this formula leads to the following reconstruction:[24]

$$c = 2,13;20$$
$$c = a + b = 3;20 + 2,10$$
$$\bar{a} = \overline{3;20} = 0;18$$
$$\bar{ab} = 0;18 \times 2,10 = 39$$
$$1 + \bar{ab} = 1 + 39 = 40$$
$$\overline{1 + \bar{ab}} = \overline{40} = 0;1,30$$
$$\bar{c} = \bar{a} \times \overline{1 + \bar{ab}} = 0;18 \times 0;1,30 = 0;0,27$$

On the one hand, the 'Sachs formula' allows us to follow the sequence of calculations by the scribe and on the other hand it establishes for us the validity of the algorithm according to modern algebra. Moreover, it provides historians with a key to understanding Tablet A and its numerous parallels. In fact, as indicated above, the first twelve sections of Tablet A contain the same numeric data as their analogues in Tablet B. For example, the transcription of Section 7 of Tablet A is as follows:

[2.]13.20	18
40	1.30
[27]	2.13.20

In Tablet A Section 7 are found, in the same order, the numbers which appear in the corresponding section of Tablet B. Clearly, the numeric Tablet A refers to the same algorithm as the verbal text of Tablet B. Until now, the 'Sachs formula' has provided a suitable explanation of the reciprocal algorithm. This formula is generally reproduced by specialists in order to explain texts referring to this algorithm in numeric versions (Tablet A and its school

---

[23] In *translations*, like Neugebauer, Sachs used commas to separate sexagesimal digits, but unlike Neugebauer, he did not use 'zeros' and semicolons to indicate the order of magnitude of the numbers. He used these marks only in the mathematical commentaries and interpretations of the sources.

[24] Sachs 1947: 227.

parallels) as well as in verbal version (Tablet B) (see Tables 12.6, 12.7 and 12.8 below). However, in my estimation, this formula does not permit us to explain the differences between the Tablets A and B, nor to grasp specific objectives pursued by them in referring to the algorithm. The principal shifts that I note between the 'Sachs formula' and the texts that it supposedly describes are the following:

(1) The tools employed by Sachs in his interpretation (algebraic notation, using semicolons and zeros) are not those used by the Old Babylonian scribes. The 'Sachs formula' leaves unclear the actual practices of calculation to which the texts of Tablets A and B make reference.
(2) The text of Tablet B, just like the remains of Tablet A, does not refer to the algorithm in an abstract manner but in a precise manner, with a series of particular numbers, namely 2.5 and its successive doublings. The algebraic formula does not explain the choice of these particular numbers.
(3) None of the properties of Tablet A (spatial arrangement, iteration and reciprocity) are found in Tablet B. The 'Sachs formula' does not allow the stylistic differences that separate Tablets A and B to be described or interpreted.

I would like to draw attention to the fact that Tablet A tells us much more than an algebraic formula in modern language can convey. What information is conveyed by the text of Tablet A but not contained by the 'Sachs formula?' Answering this question will help us understand the original process of the ancient scribes and their methods of reasoning. In that attempt, I will concentrate for now on the particular properties of the text of Tablet A, then on the particular numbers found therein.

Spatial arrangement

Using Sachs' interpretation as a starting point, I am ready to detail the algorithm of determining a reciprocal to which Tablet A refers. I rely on the numeric data in Tablet A Section 7, which are presented above and in Appendix 1:

- the number 2.13.20 terminates with 3.20, which appears in the reciprocal table, thus 3.20 is an elementary regular factor[25] of 2.13.20;
- the reciprocal of 3.20 is 18; 18 is set out on the right;

[25] As indicated above, I call any factor which appears in the standard reciprocal table (that is, Table 12.2) an 'elementary regular factor'.

- the product of 2.13.20 by 18 is 40; 40 is therefore a second factor and it is regular; 40 is set out on the left and its reciprocal 1.30 is set out on the right;
- the number 2.13.20 is therefore factored into the product of two elementary regular factors: 3.20 and 40;
- the reciprocal of 2.13.20 is the product of the reciprocals of these two factors, namely the numbers set out on the right: 1.30 and 18;
- the product of 1.30 by 18 is 27
- 27 is the desired reciprocal.

Then, the reciprocal of this result is found, leading back to 2.13.20, the same number as the initial data. For the time being, let us put aside this last step in order to comment on the reciprocal algorithm, as I have reconstituted it in the steps above.

Essentially, the algorithm is based on two rules. On the one hand, a regular number can always be decomposed into the product of elementary regular factors – that is, into the product of numbers appearing in the standard reciprocal table.[26] On the other hand, the reciprocal of a product is the product of reciprocals. These rules correspond to the spatial arrangement of the numbers into two columns.

The factorization of 2.13.20 appears in the left column:
$2.13.20 = 3.20 \times 40$
The factorization of the reciprocal appears in the right column:
$18 \times 1.30 = 27$

Let us note an interesting difference between Tablets A and B in their manner of executing the procedure. No addition appears in Tablet A, but one instance appears in Tablet B (line 5). This addition may be interpreted as being a step in the multiplication of 2.13.20 by 18. The number 2.13.20 is decomposed into the summation of 2.10 and 3.20. Then each term is multiplied separately by 18, and finally the two partial products are added. This method of multiplication is economical. With one of the partial products being obvious (3.20×18 is equal to 1 by construction), the multiplication is reduced to 2.10×18. This decomposition of multiplication may draw on the practices of mental calculation or the use of an abacus. It therefore seems that the instructions of text B refer not only to the steps of the algorithm, but also to the execution of multiplications. Text A, on the contrary, makes reference only to the steps of the algorithm. The execution of multiplication

---

[26] Naturally, this decomposition is not unique. The choices made by the scribes will be analysed later.

seems to be outside the domain of text A. I will return later to this external aspect of multiplication in relation to the analysis of errors.

Finally, let us underscore that the spatial arrangement of the text on Tablet A does not correspond to the normal rules of formatting tablets in the scribal tradition. When the scribes wrote on tablets, they were accustomed to starting the line as far left as possible and ending it as far right as possible, even if it meant introducing large spaces into the line itself. This method of managing the space on the tablet is found in all genres of texts – administrative, literary and mathematical. The example on the obverse of tablet Ni 10241 (see the copy in Appendix 2) is a good illustration of this. In this tablet, the last digit of the number contained in each line is displaced to the right and a large space separates the digits 26 and 40 in the number 4.26.40. The same happens with the digits 13 and 30 in the number 13.30. This space has no mathematical value. It corresponds to nothing save the rules of formatting. The management of spaces in Tablet A, and likewise the reverse of Tablet Ni 10241, is different. The spaces there have a mathematical meaning, since they allow columns of numbers to appear. The areas of writing to the left, centre and right have a function with respect to the algorithm.

Thus in Tablet A appear the principles of the spatial arrangement of numbers which have a precise meaning in relation to the execution of the reciprocal algorithm. In each section, certain numbers (the factors of the number for which the reciprocal is sought) are placed to the left; others (the factors of the reciprocal) are set out on the right; and still others (the products of the factors) are located in the central position. A simple description of these principles of spatial arrangement suffices to account for the basic rules on which it is based. Every regular number may be decomposed into products of elementary regular factors, and the reciprocal of a product is the product of the reciprocals. More than an algebraic formula, this explanation of the principles of spatial arrangement allows us to understand the working of the algorithm and to reveal some elements of what might have been the actual practices of calculation.

The calculations to which the different results appearing in the columns correspond are multiplications. There is, in this text, a close relationship between the floating place-value notation and multiplication, just as in the body of school documentation. However, if the text records the results of multiplications, it bears no trace of the actual execution of these operations, whereas such traces seem detectable in the verbal text of Tablet B as said above. In Tablet A, in contrast, the steps of the algorithm and the execution of multiplication are dissociated.

Table 12.3 Transcription and copy of Section 20

Line	Transcription		Copy Robson 2000: 23
1	5.3.24.**26.40**	[9]	
2	45.30.**40**	1.30	
3	1.8.**16**	3.45	
4	**4.16**	3.45	
5	**16**	3.45	
6	14.3.45		
7	5[2.44].3.45		
8	1.19.6.5.37.30		
9	11.51.54.50.37.**30**	2	
10	23.43.49.41.**15**	4	
11	1.34.55.18.**45***	16	
12	25.18.**45***	16	
13	**6.45**	1.20	
14	**9**	6.[40]	
15	8.53.20		
16	2.22.13. 20		
17	37.55.33.20		
18	2.31.42.13.20		
19	5.3.24.26.40		

Even though the texts of the Tablets A and B refer to the same algorithm, some features distinguish them. In the first case, the text is two-dimensional: the spatial arrangement of the numbers plays a critical role, referring to the steps of calculation but not to the manner of carrying out the multiplications. In the second case, the text concerns a linear continuation of the instructions, which refer not only to the algorithm, but also to the execution of the multiplications. Another difference appears in Section 5. When the numbers for which the reciprocal is determined reach a certain size, the phenomenon of iteration appears in Tablet A, but not in Tablet B (so far as the preserved portion allows us to judge).

Iteration

Let us consider Section 20, of which the transcription and the copy are given in Table 12.3. (The bold type and underscoring have been added.) First, I will explain the first part of the section, concerning the reciprocal of 5.3.24.26.40 (lines 1 to 9).

The idea of determining the reciprocal through factorization is used with more force here. The number for which the reciprocal is sought is

5.3.24.26.40. The first factor chosen is 6.40, the last part of the number. Its reciprocal is 9 (written to the right). The product of 5.3.24.26.40 and 9 is 45.30.40 (written to the left). The reciprocal of this number is not given in the standard reciprocal tables, thus once again the same sub-routine is applied. The process continues until an elementary regular number is obtained. In the fourth iteration, 16 is finally obtained. With the reciprocals having been written down in the right-hand column at each step, it suffices to multiply these numbers to arrive at the desired reciprocal. The multiplication is carried out term by term,[27] in the order of the group of intermediate products in the central column. In other words, 3.45 is multiplied by 3.45. The result (14.3.45) is multiplied by 3.45. Then that result is multiplied by 1.30; and that result is multiplied by 9. Thus for 11.51.54.50.37.30 the desired reciprocal is obtained.

In modern terms, the algorithm may be explained by two products:

The factorization of 5.3.24.26.40 appears in the left-hand column (or, more precisely, in the last part of the numbers in the left-hand column):
$5.3.24.26.40 = 6.40 \times 40 \times 16 \times 16 \times 16$.
Likewise, the factorization of the reciprocal appears in the right-hand column:
$9 \times 1.30 \times 3.45 \times 3.45 \times 3.45 = 11.51.54.50.37.30$.

Since the sub-routine is repeated, the usefulness of the rules for spatial arrangement of the text becomes clear. The factors of a number for which the reciprocal is sought are on the left. The factors of the reciprocal are on the right and the partial products are in the centre. The spatial arrangement of the text probably corresponds with a practice allowing an automatic execution of the sequence of operations. Such an arrangement displays the power of the algorithm and demonstrates possibilities of the spatial organization of the writing – possibilities that the linear arrangement of a verbal text like Tablet B does not include.

Reverse algorithms

Now let us consider the entirety of Section 20 of Tablet A (Table 12.3 above). Lines 1–9 show step by step that the reciprocal of 5.3.24.26.40 is 11.51.54.50.37.30. This number, in turn, is set out on the left and subjected to the same algorithm: 11.51.54.50.37.30 ends with 30; the reciprocal of 30, which is 2, is set out on the right, etc. As in the other examples, the number

---

[27] In the cuneiform mathematical texts, multiplication is an operation which has no more than two arguments.

11.51.54.50.37.30 is decomposed into the product of elementary regular factors. The reciprocals of these factors are set out on the right, and finally the reciprocal is obtained by multiplying term by term the factors set out on the right. The result is, naturally, the initial number, 5.3.24.26.40. It is the same in all the sections: after having 'released'[28] the reciprocal in terms of a quite long calculation, the scribe undertakes the determination of the reciprocal of the reciprocal by the same method and returns to the point of origin. Each section is thus composed of two sequences: the first sequence, which I will call the direct sequence, and the second sequence, the reverse of the first (in the sense that it returns to the point of departure). In what way did this scribe execute the algorithm in the reverse sequence? What interest did he have in systematically undoing what he had done?

To execute the reverse sequence, the scribe would have been able to use the results of the direct sequence, which provided him with decomposition into elementary regular factors. It was enough for him to consider the factors set out on the right in the first part of the algorithm. For example in Section 20, to find the reciprocal of 11.51.54.50.37.30, he was able to select the factors 3.45, 3.45, 3.45, 1.30 and 9 which appeared in the first part, but this simple repetition of factors was not what he did. He applied the algorithm in its entirety, and as in the direct sequence, the factors were provided by the final part of the number. (In 11.51.54.50.37.30, the first elementary factor is 30, then 15, etc.) This same algorithmic method is applied in the direct sequence and in the reverse sequence of each section. I will elaborate on this point later, particularly when analysing the selection of factors in the whole text. Already this remark suggests a first response to the question of the function of the reverse sequence. It might be supposed that the reverse sequence is intended to verify the results of the direct sequence, but if such were the case, it would be expected that the scribe would choose the most expedient method, and the most economic in terms of calculations. Clearly, he did not search for a short cut. He did not use the results provided from his previous calculations, which could have been done in several ways. As has just been seen, he could have used the factors already identified in the direct sequence. It would also have been simple for him to use the reciprocal pairs calculated in the preceding section. Section 19 establishes that the reciprocal of 2.31.42.13.20 is 23.43.49.41.15. However, several texts attest to the fact that the scribes knew perfectly well that when doubling a number, the reciprocal is divided by 2 (or, more exactly, its reciprocal is multiplied

---

[28] The Sumerian verb which designates the act of calculating a reciprocal is du_8 (release) and the corresponding Akkadian verb is *paṭārum*; F. Thureau-Dangin translates this verb as '*dénouer*', and J. Høyrup as 'to detach'.

by 30).[29] In verifying the result of Section 20, it was therefore sufficient to multiply 23.43.49.41.15 by 30. Proceeding in another way, the scribe could have multiplied together the initial number and its reciprocal in order to verify the fact that the product was equal to 1. These simple methods show that it was unnecessary to reapply the reciprocal algorithm. In fact, the reverse sequence does not seem to have had the verification of the result of the direct sequence as a primary purpose. The fact that, in the second part, the algorithm was used in its entirety provokes speculation that if it were a verification, it concerns the algorithmic method itself and not merely the results that it produced.

Another important aspect of the algorithm is the selection of particular numbers. This aspect appears in comparison between Tablets A and B. Both use the same geometric progression. The particular role of this series, omnipresent in all Mesopotamian school exercises of the Old Babylonian period, is one of the first points that ought to be made clearer. A second point is connected to the algorithm itself. Given that the decomposition into the product of elementary regular factors is not unique, one wonders if some rule governed the scribes' choice of one factor over another. This question invokes another question, even more interesting in light of the questions discussed in this article: did the scribes apply different rules to select factors in the direct and reverse sequences? Does this selection clarify the function of the reverse sequences?

Numeric repertory

As has been seen, the entries in the sections of Tablet A, as with those of B, are the terms of the geometric progression for an initial number 2.5 with a common ratio of 2. What information did the scribe obtain in each of these sections? After the reciprocal of 2.5 has been obtained by factorization, it is possible to find all the other reciprocals by more direct means, as has been explained above. For example, in each section, the reverse sequence could repeat the calculations of the direct sequence, since it leads back to the point of departure, but this is not the case. The repeated application of the recip-rocal algorithm does not produce any new result (other than the reciprocal of 2.5). From the perspective of an extension of the list of reciprocal pairs,

---

[29] Some texts containing lists of reciprocal pairs founded on this principle are known: beginning with a number and its reciprocal, they give the following doublings and halvings. For example the tablet from Nippur N 3958 gives the series of doublings/halvings of 2.5 / 28.48 (Sachs 1947: 228).

this text is useless. Thus, what is the function of the repetition of the same algorithm forty-two times (in 21 sections, each one containing a direct sequence and a reverse sequence), since it returns results already seen?

First of all, why has the scribe chosen the number 2.5, the cube of 5, as the initial number of the text? This selection undoubtedly has some importance, because the entry 2.5 and the terms of the dyadic series which result provide the majority of numeric data in exercises found in the school archives of Mesopotamia. An initial explanation could be drawn from the arithmetic properties of this number. It has been seen previously that the list of entries in the standard reciprocal table (Table 12.2) is composed of regular numbers in a single place, followed by two more numbers in two places, 1.4 and 1.21. However, we note that 1.4, 1.21 and 2.5 are respectively powers of 2, of 3 and of 5 ($1.4 = 2^6$; $1.21 = 3^4$; $2.5 = 5^3$). Better yet, if the list of all the regular numbers in two places is set in the lexicographic order,[30] the first number is the first power of 2, that is, 1.4; the first power of 3, that is, 1.21, comes next, and the first power of 5, 2.5, comes thereafter. Thus, in some ways, 2.5 is the logical successor in the series 1.4, 1.21. Even if this explanation is thought too speculative, one must admit the privileged place accorded to the numbers 1.4, 1.21 and 2.5. The importance of the powers of 2, of 3 and of 5 perhaps indicates the manner by which the list of regular numbers (and their reciprocals) were obtained. Beginning with the first reciprocal pairs, the other pairs can be generated by multiplications by 2, by 3 and by 5 (and their reciprocals by multiplication by 30, 20 and 12 respectively). This process theoretically would allow the entire list of regular numbers in base-60 and their reciprocals to be obtained.[31] The importance of the series of doublings of 2.5 in the school documentation could also be explained by its pedagogical advantages. I will return to this point later.

For now, let us try to draw some conclusions by analysing the selection of factors in the factorization procedure. The execution of the factorization depends, at each step, on the determination of the factors for the number for which the reciprocal is sought. Does the selection of these factors correspond to fixed rules? First of all, let us note that in all of Tablet A, the same choices of the factors correspond to identical numbers. For example, the number 1.34.55.18.45 appears several times, and in each case, the factor chosen is 3.45. Let us now examine these selections, by distinguishing between the case of the direct sequences (Table 12.4) and the reverse

[30] The numbers cannot be arranged according to magnitude, since this is not defined. The school documentation shows that in some cases the scribes used a lexicographical order. See for example the list of multiplication tables. Here, reference is made to this lexicographical order. The numbers are set out in increasing order by the left-most digit, then following, etc.

[31] I think that reciprocal tables such as the one found in the large Seleucid tablet AO 6456 were constructed in this way. A similar idea is developed by Bruins 1969.

Table 12.4 Selection of factors in the direct sequences

Number to factor	Section	Factor chosen	Reciprocal of factor	Largest elementary regular factor	
2.5	1	5	12		
4.10	2	10	6		
4.16	18, 20, 21	16	3.45		
1.8.16	20, 21	16	3.45		
8.20	3	20	3		
10.40	11, 12	40	1.30		
2.50.40	15	40	1.30		
45.30.40	20	40	1.30		
42.40	13, 14	2.40	22.30	40	
11.22.40	18	2.40	22.30	40	(1)
3.2.2.40	21	2.40	22.30	40	
33.20	5	3.20	18		
2.13.20	7	3.20	18		
8.53.20	9	3.20	18		
35.33.20	11	3.20	18		
2.22.13.20	13	3.20	18		
9.28.53.20	15	3.20	18		
10.6.48.53.20	21	3.20	18		
16.40	4	6.40	9		
1.6.40	6	6.40	9		
4.26.40	8	6.40	9		
17.46.40	10	6.40	9		
1.11.6.40	12	6.40	9		
4.44.26.40	14	6.40	9		
18.57.46.40	16	6.40	9		
1.15.51.6.40	18	6.40	9		
5.3.24.26.40	20	6.40	9		

sequences (Table 12.5). The factorizations that present irregularities (in a meaning to be specified later) are shown in grey and numbered at the right of the tables. The factorizations are ordered according to column 3, which contains the factors chosen in the different decompositions. Column 5 gives the largest elementary regular factor if it is different from the factor chosen by the scribe. Column 2 specifies the section to which the appropriate decomposition belongs (I considered only sections well enough preserved to permit a safe reconstitution of the text).

Tables 12.4 and 12.5 show that the chosen factor is determined by the last digits of the number to be factored. In so doing, the scribes made use of an arithmetical property of the base-60 place value notation – that is, the numbers to be factorized are all regular and thus they always end with

Table 12.5 Selection of factors in the reverse sequences

Number to factor	Section	Factor chosen	Reciprocal of factor	Largest elementary regular factor	
7.**12**	3	12	5		
1.41.**15**	11	15	4	1.15	(2)
23.43.49.41.**15**	19	15	4	1.15	
2.**15**	5	15	4		(2′)
14.**24**	2	24	2.30		
3.22.**30**	10	30	2	2.30	
12.39.22.**30**	14	30	2	2.30	
47.27.39.22.**30**	18	30	2	2.30	(3)
50.37.**30**	12	30	2	7.30	
11.51.54.50.37.**30**	20	30	2	7.30	
13.**30**	8	30	2		(3′)
3.**36**	4	36	1.40		
6.**45**	9	45	1.20		
1.**48**	5	48	1.15		
28.**48**	1	48	1.15		
25.18.**45**	13	3.45	16	45	
1.34.55.18.**45**	17	3.45	16	45	(4)
5.55.57.25.18.**45**	21	3.45	16	45	

a sequence of digits which form a regular number.[32] All that is needed is to adjust for a suitable sequence. (In the case of 2.13.20, we may take 20, or 3.20, or even 13.20.) In practice, the final part, insofar as it is an elementary regular number, is likely to be a factor. (For 2.13.20, the factor might be 20, or 3.20.) In the majority of cases, the scribe chose, from among the possible factors, the 'largest' (3.20 rather than 20), in order to render the algorithm faster.[33] Thus, in general, the selected factor is the largest elementary

[32] This property is the result of a more general rule: for a given base, the divisibility of an integer by the divisors of the base is seen in the last digits of the number. For a discussion of the particular problems resulting from divisibility in 'floating' base-60 cuneiform notation, a system in which there is no difference between whole numbers and sexagesimal fractions, see Proust 2007: §6.2.

[33] The word 'large' has nothing to do with the *magnitude* of the abstract numbers, since magnitude is not defined, but with their *size*. A two-place number is 'larger' than a single-place number; for numbers with the same number of digits, the 'larger' number is the last in the lexicographical order. The speed of the algorithm depends on the size of the numbers thus defined: the 'larger' the factors are, the fewer factors there will be and thus fewer iterations. Let us specify that the order according to the size of the numbers is different from the lexicographical order mentioned above. The two orders appear in cuneiform sources. The order according to the size appears in the Old Babylonian reciprocal tables, and the lexicographical order occurs in the Seleucid reciprocal tables such as AO 6456, as well as in the arrangement of the multiplication tables in the Old Babylonian numerical tables.

regular number formed by the terminal part of the number.[34] Nevertheless, this rule allows four exceptions (cases numbered in the last column of Tables 12.4 and 12.5), that need to be considered.

(1) The selected factor, 2.40, does not appear in the standard reciprocal tables, and it is the factor 40 which ought to have been chosen. Nonetheless let us note that the reciprocal of 2.40 is 22.30, which is a common number that figures among the principal numbers of the standard multiplication tables. (The table of 22.30 is one of those learned by heart in the primary level of education, especially at Nippur.) Thus, 2.40 is 'nearly' elementary, and its reciprocal was undoubtedly committed to memory – so case (1) does not truly constitute an irregularity.

(2) and (3) In case (2), the largest elementary factor is 1.15, but the factor 15, the entry of (2'), is used instead. In case (3), the selected factor could be either 2.30 or 7.30, but the factor 30, the entry of (3'), is used instead. This choice occurred as if the scribe sought to restrict the factors used in the calculation. The general rule of the 'largest elementary regular factor', regularly applied in the direct sequences, is, in the reverse sequences, opposed by another rule restricting the numeric repertory.

(4) In this case, the factor might have been 45, but the scribe has obviously tried to use a larger factor. However, the numbers derived from the last two sexagesimal places (18.45 or 8.45) are not regular. Thus, 8 is decomposed into the summation 5+3, and the final part of the number selected as a factor is 3.45.

Several general conclusions may be drawn from these observations. First, the number of factors occurring in the decompositions is limited. They are principally 3.20 and 6.40 (less frequently 10, 16, 25, 40 and 22.30) for the direct sequences and principally 30 (less frequently 12, 15, 24, 36 and 45, 48 and 3.45) for the reverse sequences. This limited number of factors is explained by the way in which the list of entries was constructed – namely, 2.5, a power of 5, is multiplied by 2 repeatedly, giving rise to a series of numbers for which the final sequences describe regular cycles. However, the scribes' choices intervene. On the one hand, the direct sequences obey the 'greatest elementary regular factor' rule. On the other hand, the reverse sequences present numerous irregularities in regard to this rule. The number of factors used in the calculations is reduced. Finally, an interesting point to emphasize is that although the direct and reverse sequences

---

[34] For this reason, Friberg 2000: 103–5 designates this procedure the 'trailing part algorithm'.

refer to the same algorithm, they do not seem to share in the same way the liberty permitted by the fact that the decomposition of numbers into regular factors is not unique. How do these two different ways of choosing the decomposition clarify the function of the reverse algorithm for us? Part of the answer is found in the school documentation. I will return to this question after analysing the parallels with Tablet A.

The observation of errors appearing in this tablet brings something else to light. The fact that these errors are not numerous shows the high degree of erudition of the author of the text. Appearing in the transcription of A. Sachs and the copy of E. Robson, these errors are as follows:

Section 4: the scribe has written 15.40 in place of 16.40.
Section 5: the scribe has written 9 in place of 8.
Section 11: the scribe has written **35.33**.20 in place of **36.23**.20.
Section 19: the scribe has written 19 in place of 18.

The errors are all of the same type: forgotten or superfluous signs. The absence of a vertical wedge in certain instances, for example in Section 4, may be the result of the deterioration of the surface of the tablet, not an error. In fact, in clay documents, signs are frequently hidden by particles of dirt or salt crystals, or flakes of clay have been broken off due to both ancient and modern handling.[35] Whatever the case may be, if the errors exist, they are not the result of errors in calculation, but simple faults in writing. Moreover, and this detail has great significance, the errors are not propagated in the following sequence of calculations.[36] The arithmetic operations themselves, namely the multiplications, are then carried out in another medium in which the error had not occurred. The text proceeds as if it does nothing but receive and organize the results of calculations computed in this external medium. For example, the fact that, in the number 36.23.20 of Section 11, the scribe has transformed one ten in the middle place into a unit in the left-hand place may be explained as an error in transferring a result from some sort of abacus. Quite probably, some of the multiplications, particularly those which appear in the last sections and involve big numbers, required outside assistance, probably in the form of a physical instrument (such as an abacus).

[35] See the description of the state of this tablet by Sachs 1947: 230.
[36] It is not always the case in this genre of text. For example, in the tablet MLC 651, a school tablet in which the reciprocal is determined of 1.20.54.31.6.40 (a term from the series of doublings of 2.5; see Table 12.4), an error appears in the beginning of the algorithm and propagates throughout the following text. The error is a real error in calculation, which arose in the course of the execution of one of the multiplications.

Computing reciprocals in school texts

Tablet A possesses numerous parallels, nearly all of which appear in the characteristic form of tablets called Type IV by Assyriologists. Scribes used these Type IV tablets to train in numeric calculation. The copy presented in Appendix 2 is typical of these small lenticular or square tablets. Consideration of these parallels allows us to establish our tablet in the context of the scribal schools. This corpus in particular will allow us to determine the elements that relate directly to the school education to be detected, as well as those which do not seem to be connected to purely pedagogical purposes. From these comparisons, hypotheses about the function of the tablet, the reciprocal algorithm, and most notably the direct and reverse sequences may be put forth.

Let us consider all the known Old Babylonian tablets containing non-elementary reciprocal pairs (other than those which figure in the standard tables). To my knowledge, this set comprises a small group of about thirty tablets, listed in Tables 12.6 and 12.7 below.[37] In the first table, I have gathered the parallels of Tablet A. In the second table are found the other texts; they also contain reciprocal pairs extracted from geometric progression. The different columns of the tables provide information about the following points:

(1) The inventory number and type of school tablet.
(2) The provenance.
(3) Reciprocal pairs contained in the tablet; when there are several pairs, the entries are always the terms of a geometric progression with a common ratio of 2; I have indicated only the number of pairs and the first pair.
(4) The format of the text, indicated by numbers: (1) if the text appears as a simple list of reciprocal pairs; (2) if the presence of a factorization algorithm is noted; (3) if the presence of direct and reverse sequences of the factorization algorithm is noted.[38]
(5) In Table 12.6, a supplementary column indicates the corresponding section of Tablet A. Sections which have more than twenty doublings

---

[37] The tablets cited in the Tables 12.4 and 12.5 have been published in the following articles and works. CBS 10201 in Hilprecht 1906: no. 25; N 3891 in Sachs 1947: 234; 2N-T 500 in Robson 2000: 20; 3N-T 362 in Robson 2000: 22; Ni 10241 in Proust 2007: §6.3.2; UET 6/2 295 in Friberg 2000: 101; MLC 651 in Sachs 1947: 233; YBC 1839 in Sachs 1947: 232; VAT 5457 in Sachs 1947: 234; TH99-T192, TH99-T196, TH99-T584, TH99-T304a are unedited tablets, soon to be published by A. Cavigneaux *et al.*; MS 2730, MS 2793, MS 2732, MS 2799 in Friberg 2007: §1.4. (Note: among the tablets of the Schøyen Collection published in this last work are found other reciprocal pairs, but their reading presents some uncertainty.)

[38] For example, format (1) is found on the obverse of the tablet Ni 10241, and format (2) on its reverse (see the Appendix).

Table 12.6 Parallels with Tablet A

Number, type	Provenance	Contents			A
		Reciprocal pairs	Format		
2N-T 496, IV	Nippur	16.40 / 3.36	(1)		Section 4
3N-T 605, IV	Nippur	4.26.40 / 13.30	(1)		Section 8
2N-T 115, IV	Nippur	9.28.53.20 / 6.19.41.15	(1)		Section 15
Ni 10244, IV	Nippur	1.15.51.6.40 / 47.27.39.22.30	(1)		Section 18
Ni 10241, IV	Nippur	4.26.40 / 13.30	(1) and (2)		Section 8
2N-T 500, IV	Nippur	17.46.40 / 3.22.30	(1) and (2)		Section 10
CBS 10201	Nippur	8 pairs : 2.5 / 28.48, etc.	(2)		Section 1–8
N 3891, IV	Nippur	8.53.20 / 6.45	(1) and (3)		Section 9
3N-T 362, IV	Nippur	17.46.40 / 3.22.30	(3)		Section 10
UET 6/2 295, IV	Ur	2.5 / 28.48	(2)		Section 1
W 16743ay, IV	Uruk	10.6.48.53.20 / 5.55.57.25.18.45	(1)		Section 21
TH99-T196, IV	Mari	5.55.57.25.18.45 / 10.6.48.53.20	(1)		Section 20 (reverse sequence)
TH99-T192, IV	Mari	1.9.26.40 / 51.50.24 Note: 1.9.26.40 = 8.20 ×	(1)		Section 3 (indirectly)
		8.20 and 8.20 is the entry of A #3.			
FLP 1283, IV	Unknown	Obverse: proverb; reverse: 2.5 / 28.48	(1)		Section 1
YBC 10802, IV	Unknown	2.22.13.20 / 25.18.45	(1)		Section 13
BM 80150	Unknown	Numeric table; 13 pairs: 2.5 / 28.48, etc.	(1)		Sections 1–13
MLC 651, IV	Unknown	1.20.54.31.6.40 / 44.29.40.39.50.37.30	(2)		Section 23 (extrapolation)
		(with an error in calculation)			
YBC 1839, IV	Unknown	4.26.40 / 13.30	(2)		Section 8
MS 2799, IV	Unknown	2.41.49.2.13.20 / 22.14.50.19.55.18.45	(1)		Section 24 (extrapolation)

Table 12.7 Reciprocal exercises not appearing in Tablet A

Number	Provenance	Reciprocal pairs	Contents	Format
UM 29–13–021	Nippur	30 pairs: 2.5 / 28.48 etc. 6 pairs: 2.40 / 22.30 etc. 10 pairs: 1.40 / 36 etc. 8 pairs: 1.4 / 56.15 etc. 9 pairs: 4.3 / 14.48.53.20 etc.		(1)
TH99-T584, iv	Mari	1.4 / 56.15		(1)
TH99-T304a, iv	Mari	4.16 / 14.3.45	$(4.16 = 1.4 \times 2^2)$	(1)
VAT 5457, iv	Unknown	9.6.8 / 6.35.30.28.7.30	$(9.6.8 = 1.4 \times 2^9)$	(2)
MS 2730, iv	Unknown	4.51.16.16 / 12.21.34.37.44.3.45	$(4.51.16.16 = 1.4 \times 2^{14})$	(2)
MS 2793, iv	Unknown	41.25.30.48.32 30 / 1.26.54.12.51.34.11.22.<1.52.30>	$(41.25.30.48.32\ 30 = 1.4 \times 2^{23})$	(1)
MS 2732, iv	Unknown	1.9.7.12 / 52.5	$(1.9.7.12 = 4.3 \times 2^{10})$	(2)

of 2.5 are called 'extrapolations'. Since Tablet A is limited to twenty doublings, these sections do not appear there.

Tables 12.6 and 12.7 show that a strong relation exists between Tablet A and the school texts. Nearly all the direct parallels (Table 12.6) or indirect parallels (Table 12.7) are Type IV school tablets. Each concerns a single reciprocal calculation. The tablets that are not of Type IV contain lists of reciprocals, all like Tablet A. These tablets are UM 29–13–021 and CBS 10201, from Nippur, as well as BM 80150, of unknown origin.

The majority of school exercises use the data found in Tablet A. Two exercises from Nippur are reproductions identical to Sections 9 and 10 of Tablet A, including the reverse sequence. When the factorization method is employed in the exercises, it uses the factors chosen in Tablet A, except in one case.[39] The tablets in Table 12.7 that do not use the geometric progression with a common ratio of 2 and an initial number 2.5 still have links with Tablet A. Specifically, they use a geometric progression with a common ratio of 2, but with an initial term of 1.4 (and in one case 4.3), as found for example in the tablet UM 29–13–021 from Nippur.

These observations could indicate that the tablets such as Tablet A and the other tablets which are not Type IV school exercises (CBS 10201, UM 29–13–021, BM 80150) were the work of schoolmasters and that one of the purposes of their authors was the collection of exercises for the education of scribes. The link between Tablet A and teaching is incontestable, but does this signify that Tablet A is a 'teacher's textbook' from which the exercises were drawn? Several arguments fit with this hypothesis, but it also raises serious objections. Beginning with what is now known about the school context and proceeding more specifically to Tablet A and its parallels I will present arguments for and against this text's being a 'teacher's textbook'.

The structure of school documents of an elementary level speaks in favour of the hypothesis. Lists of exercises can be considered a 'teacher's textbook' if we consider them only on this level. Exercises from the elementary level are extracts of texts written on tablets of a particular type, called Type I by Assyriologists.[40] This relationship between a 'teacher's textbook' and pedagogical extracts appears both for the mathematical texts and also for the lexical texts. However, as far as the advanced school texts are concerned,

---

[39] In tablet CBS 1020, the factorization of 16.40 uses the factor 40 in place of 6.40. It is not, however, a Type IV school text, but a tablet containing a list of eight reciprocals, the function of which is closer to the function of Tablet A.

[40] Some authors think that the Type I tablets from Nippur are perhaps the product of students who have finished their elementary education, undergoing some type of examination (Veldhuis 1997: 29–31).

whether they are lexical or mathematical like the reciprocal exercises, the situation is different and far from simple. The exercises are not formulaic like those of an elementary level. If the documentation regarding the elementary level is composed of numerous duplicata, the documentation at an advanced level is composed only of unique instances, and this is true for the lexical texts and for the mathematical texts. Duplicata occur neither among the advanced school exercises nor among the most erudite texts to which they are connected. The school documentation at an advanced level thus does not present as clear and regular a structure as that at an elementary level, and it cannot be relied on to identify the nature of the relationship that connects Tablet A with the school exercises.

Nevertheless, the important fact remains that Tablet A has a large number of pedagogical parallels. Moreover, the known school exercises about reciprocal calculations all bear upon a number connected with the data in Tablet A, whether directly (one of the terms of the series of doublings of 2.5), or indirectly (one of the terms of the series of doublings of another number such as 1.4 or 4.3). These instances have a unique relationship with the direct sequences on Tablet A. On the other hand, reverse sequences are rarely found in the school exercises. They appear only in two tablets from Nippur, which reproduce exactly Sections 9 and 10 of Tablet A, and in a tablet from Mari (TH99-T196). Again, in the two cases from Nippur, the reverse sequences are not isolated, but associated with the direct sequences. Thus, it is not the data from the reverse sequences that provide the material for the school exercises, but rather the data from the direct sequences. In general, the reverse sequences provide a very small contribution to the prospective 'collection of exercises' for teaching, and yet they constitute half the text of tablet A.

The pedagogical interest in the series of doublings of 2.5 must also be considered because this series allows the repetition of the same algorithm many times, under conditions where it provides only results known in advance, with a gradually increasing level of difficulty. In fact, this argument relates to the educational value of the geometric progression with a common ratio of 2 and an initial term of 2.5, not to Tablet A in its entirety. Tablet A is constructed around the idea of reciprocity, a notion clearly fundamental to its author and hardly present in the ordinary exercises about reciprocal calculations.

These considerations lead to the notion that it is possible that the relationship between Tablet A and the school exercises is exactly the opposite of what is usually believed. Tablet A does not seem to be the source of school exercises: rather it seems derived from the school materials with which the scribes of the Old Babylonian period were familiar. In this case, the material was developed, systematized and reorganized with different objectives than the construction of a set of exercises.[41]

The function of the reverse sequence seems to be the key to understanding the whole text. It has been suggested above that the reverse sequence might play a role in relation to the functional verification of the algorithm. The question that arises concerns, more precisely, the nature of the relationship between the direct sequence and the reverse sequence. In order to advance this inquiry, we turn to other cases in the cuneiform documentation which present direct and reverse sequences. As emphasized in the introduction, these cases appear in several tablets containing calculations of square roots. Thus let us examine these calculations.

Square roots

Sources presently known to contain calculations of square roots are not so numerous as those concerning reciprocals. Nonetheless, they present interesting analogies with what we have just considered. First of all, texts in both a numeric and verbal style are found for the same algorithm. Additionally, the fundamental elements of the reciprocal algorithm – factorization, spatial arrangement in columns (in the case of the numeric texts) and the presence of reciprocity – appear in these texts. This small collection of texts allows us to consider some of the problems raised above from other angles: the nature of the reciprocal algorithm, the connections between the direct and reverse sequences, the specificity of numeric texts with respect to verbal texts and the nature of the links that the different types of texts have with education.

Table 12.8 gives the list of tablets containing the calculations of square roots (I recall in column 1 the letters indicated in Table 12.1).[42] I have likewise included those which contain calculations of cube roots, though

---

[41] This process may be compared to that described by Friberg for the various Mesopotamian and Egyptian texts under the name of 'recombination texts'. For him, this type of compilation is tightly connected with educational activity (Friberg 2005: 94).

[42] The tablets of Table 12.8 have been published in the following articles and works: C = UET 6/2 222 in Gadd and Kramer 1966: no. 222 – see Table 12.1; YBC 6295 in Neugebauer and Sachs 1945: 42; VAT 8547 in Sachs 1952: 153; D = IM 54472 in Bruins 1954: 56 – see Table 12.1; TH99-T3 is an unedited tablet, soon to be published by A. Cavigneaux *et al.*; Si 428 in Neugebauer 1935–7: ı 80; HS 231 in Friberg 1983: 83; 3N-T 611 in Robson 2002: 354; YBC 6295 in Neugebauer and Sachs 1945: text Aa, this tablet is believed to have come from Uruk, in the south of Mesopotamia according to Neugebauer 1935–7: ı 149 and to H2002: 333–7; VAT 8547 in Sachs 1952: 153.

Table 12.8 Calculations of square and cube roots

Tablet	Number, type	Provenance	Calculation	Style
C	UET 6/2 222, IV	Ur	Square root of 1.7.44.3.45 (result: 1.3.45)	Numeric
	3N-T 611, IV	Nippur	Square root of 4.37.46.40 (result: 16.40)	Numeric
	HS 231, IV	Nippur	Square root of 1.46.40 (result: 1.20) (uncertain reading)	Numeric
	TH99-T3, IV	Mari	Square root of 2.6.33.45 (result: 11.15)	Numeric
	Si 428, IV	Sippar	Square root of 2.2.2.2.5.5.4 (result: 1.25.34.8)	Numeric
D	IM 54472	Unknown	Square root of 26.0.15 (result: 39.30)	Verbal
	YBC 6295	Unknown	Cube root of 3.22.30 (result: 1.30)	Verbal
	VAT 8547	Unknown	Cube roots of 27, 1.4, 2.5 and 3.36 (results: 3, 4, 5, 6 respectively)	Verbal

no numeric version occurs with cube root calculations. This absence poses an interesting question: is this the result of chance in preservation or a significant fact?

Tablet D, of unknown origin, contains a text composed in Akkadian which concerns the procedure of calculating the square root of 26.0.15. For a detailed analysis, see the various publications on the subject of this text.[43] Two interesting points should be highlighted here. The first is the presence of the factorization algorithm, in the form of instructions wherein the terms are quite similar to those in Tablet B regarding reciprocals. The second is the last phrase: '39.30 is the side of your square. 26.0.15 is the result (of the product of 39.30 by 39.30).' The tablet thus ends with a verification of the result.

Tablet C is a small lenticular school tablet, the transcription and copy of which are shown in Table 12.9.[44] The process of calculation by factorization occurs in the case of Tablet C, as Friberg has remarked. The number 1.7.44.3.45 ends with 3.45, which is selected as an elementary regular factor.

---

[43] Chemla 1994: 21; Muroi 1999: 127; Friberg 2000: 110. Because no copy of the text has yet been published, it is not known if the presence of zero in the middle place is indicated on the tablet by a blank space, as sometimes happens in cuneiform texts, particularly those of the first millennium.

[44] Copy: Gadd and Kramer 1966; transcription: Friberg 2000: 108. See also Robson 1999: 252.

Table 12.9 Tablet C

Transcription		Calculations	Copy
	1.3.45	$1.3.45 \times 1.3.45 = 1.7.44.3.45$	
	1.3.45		
15	1.7.44.3.45 16	inv(3.45) = 16; sq.rt.(3.45) = 15	
15	18.3.45 16	inv(3.45) = 16; sq.rt.(3.45) = 15	
17	4.49	sq.rt.(4.49) = 17	
	3.45	$15 \times 15 = 3.45$	
	1.3.45	$3.45 \times 17 = 1.3.45$	

UET 6/2 222 reverse

The number 16, its reciprocal, is set out on the right; on the same line, the number 15, its square root, is set out on the left; the product of 1.7.44.3.45 by 16 (which gives a second factor) is placed on the centre of the following line. The process is repeated until a number for which the square root is given by the standard tables is found.[45] The desired square root is the product of the numbers recorded on the left.

It should be noted that this small text, like those found in the sections of Tablet A, begins and ends with the same number, and as before, the calculation forms a loop. It starts with an arithmetical operation (the square of 1.3.45), then it proceeds by a sequence which carries out the reverse operation (the square root of the resulting number, 1.7.44.3.45). Here, the direct sequence and the reverse sequence rely on algorithms of a different nature, even though in the cases involving reciprocals, they rely on the same algorithm. Could it be said that the calculation of the square of 1.3.45 is a simple verification of the result of the calculation of the square root? In this case, it would be logical that the verification should come at the end of the calculation (as is the case in the verbal Tablet D) and not at the beginning. The text thus illustrates something else, which seems to relate to the fact that the square and the square root are reciprocal operations. This 'something else' is perhaps akin to what the author of Tablet A illustrated with the reverse sequences.

The algorithm for calculating square roots is based on the same mechanism of factorization as that for determining the reciprocal. In the numeric versions, the rules concerning the layout are analogous: the factors are

---

[45] As in the case of the reciprocals, the calculations of the squares and square roots rely on a small stock of basic results memorized by the scribes during their elementary education. The tables of squares and square roots are largely found in the school archives. See, notably, Neugebauer 1935–7: i ch. I.

placed in the central column; the reciprocals of these are placed to the right; a supplementary column appears on the left, in which are placed the square roots of the factors. This supplementary column shows us that the algorithm in fact has two components: a factorization (right-hand column) and square root (left-hand column). In the case of the reciprocal's algorithm, the right-hand column provides the factors which serve all at once as the factorization and the determination of the reciprocals. Thus the two components merge. However, the method of application of the factorizations presents a particular mathematical problem for the square roots. In effect, the algorithm for finding a reciprocal is, by definition, applied to the regular numbers. The factorizations are always possible, and lead mechanically to the result. Alternately, perfect squares can quite easily be the product of irregular numbers, and in this case, factorization by the standard method is impossible. The important point to note is that, even though the algorithms for the determination of the reciprocal and the extraction of a square root diverge from one another in their components and even though they present different mathematical problems as their topic, they are presented in the texts in a parallel fashion.

The specificity of the numeric texts with regard to the verbal texts thus appears more clearly. For the square roots, the layout of the numeric texts observes the same rules regarding arrangement in columns as for the determination of reciprocals. This spatial arrangement facilitates control of the calculation. In fact, it is enough, when finding the desired number, to multiply all those that are set out on the right in the case of reciprocals, and those on the left in the case of roots. It is notable that, in the case of reciprocals as well as square and cube roots, the verbal versions contain only numbers of a small size, which do not demand recourse to iteration. The numeric versions contain numbers of large size, and the arrangement in columns shows that it is possible to develop the iterations without limit, which confers power on the process. The verbal and numeric versions of the calculations of square roots refer nonetheless to the same algorithms. In fact, the verbal texts contain instructions which detail how to 'place' certain numbers 'beneath' others, in a way which corresponds with the spatial arrangement of the numeric texts.

What is the place of square roots in the education of the scribes? The format of the tablets containing the calculation of square roots, which are all of Type ɪv for the numeric versions, shows that they were school exercises. However, in this case the exercises are much less standardized than the calculation of reciprocals. For square roots, the numeric repertory offers no regularity, whereas for the reciprocals, the repertory is homogeneous (as seen above, it is based principally on the doublings of 2.5). Moreover, the group of tablets containing the calculations of square roots is small, whereas the group of exercises of the calculation of reciprocals is numerically important. The great frequency of calculations of reciprocals is undoubtedly explained by the importance of this technique in calculation, but another reason may be postulated. In the reciprocal, the two components (factorization and the determination of reciprocals) are superimposed. The algorithm for the determination of a reciprocal by factorization puts the mechanism of factorization first. The determination of a reciprocal by factorization is thus a fundamental procedure,[46] essential to other algorithms, even though it is applied in a less general way for the roots than for the reciprocals. Consequently, the reciprocal exercises probably occupy a more elementary educational level than those that contain square roots. The calculations of square roots may be situated between the work of beginning scribes and works of scholars, in a grey area that has left us few traces.

What, then, of the cube roots? They appear in two verbal texts, wherein they are treated in a manner identical to the square roots, except for the verifications, which do not appear in either case.[47] No numeric version is known for these calculations. It cannot be excluded that the absence of a numeric version of the calculation of a cube root is due to the chances of preservation but other explanations are possible. Indeed, tables of squares, square roots and cube roots are known to us from the preserved numeric tablets, but tables of cubes are unknown. The absence of a table of cubes is undoubtedly linked to the fact already mentioned that multiplication is an operation with two arguments. Consequently, the cube root has no reverse operation in the Mesopotamian mathematical tradition. This fact would explain why it has not been found in a numeric format, which is founded on the notion of reciprocity.

This analysis of the calculation of square roots also emphasizes by contrast the fact that the reciprocal algorithm is a combination of two different components (factorization and the determination of a reciprocal). In addition, it may be seen that the numeric texts have an approach

---

[46] The Akkadian term *makṣarum* probably has some link with the process of factorization. It appears in two texts, in slightly different senses: it appears in the *incipit* of tablet YBC 6295 cited in Table 12.6 ([*ma*]-*ak-ṣa-ru-um* šaba-si = the *makṣarum* of the cube root); it designates an enlargement in tablet YBC 8633.

[47] Note also the following curious detail: in VAT 8547, all the entries appear in the standard tables of cube roots, and the application of the reciprocal algorithm to these numbers leads to a complication of the situation. Thus, 27 is decomposed according to a somewhat artificial manner as the product of 7.30 and 3.36. It is clear that in this case, as in that of Tablet A, the purpose is not to obtain a new result.

relatively unified with that of the reciprocal algorithm. The function of the reverse algorithm seems the same in all cases. It does not enact a verification of the result, or even a verification of the algorithm itself in the case of the square roots, since the direct and reverse sequences do not rely on the same algorithm. Their presence seems to indicate something else with respect to the nature of the operations themselves. It stresses the fact that the reverse operation of a square is the square root, and the reverse operation of the reciprocal is the reciprocal itself.

Conclusion

I can now reconsider several questions left aside from the preceding discussion. The function of the tablet is at the heart of these questions, and I will treat these questions before returning to the ways of reasoning we can detect in the text.

It has been seen that the content of Tablet A is connected with the context of teaching but that it cannot be interpreted as a simple collection of data intended to provide exercises for the education of young scribes. I have suggested that its relationship with the school exercises could be the reverse of what is generally supposed. It might not be a 'teacher's textbook' from which the school exercises were taken but rather a text constructed and developed from existing school material. Indeed the relationships between school exercises and scholarly texts were probably not so unidirectional and the two relations could well be combined. However, the point which interests us here is that Tablet A appears in the form of an original inquiry and its purpose seems to have been communication between erudite scribes. Seen from this perspective, the same piece of text takes on another dimension. The way in which the text is organized and arranged, and the repertory of numeric data on which it is built, are essential components of the text. In a certain way, these components constitute the means of expression by which Tablet A refers to the reciprocal algorithm.

But what is the relationship between Tablet A and the algorithm for reciprocals? Is it a practical text in the sense that the text executes concretely the operations necessary for the determination of a reciprocal? It is not certain that the writing of a text was essential to the execution of the algorithm, since the known texts obviously record only part of the series of actions that allow the result to be obtained. On the one hand, the multiplications are probably executed elsewhere. On the other hand, by the standards of school practices, the written traces are incomplete. They often state only the first step of the process of factorization, as is notably the case in the tablets of the Schøyen Collection published by Friberg listed in Table 12.7. The tablet does not refer to all the steps necessary to execute the algorithm. Tablet A is not a simple set of instructions for execution of the reciprocal algorithm.

What does tablet A say about this algorithm and how? First of all, the author of Tablet A expresses himself by means of numbers arranged in a precise way, not by means of a linear continuation of the instructions, as is done in the verbal texts. The numeric texts refer to the same algorithms as the verbal texts, but they do it in a different way. The spatial arrangement of the writing has its own properties and emphasizes certain functions of the algorithm. The arrangement into columns renders the process of determining a reciprocal transparent. Indeed, to find the desired number, it is enough to multiply the numbers on the right in the case of the reciprocals and the numbers on the left in the case of the roots. The arrangement into columns certainly recalls the practices of calculation external to the text, but the fact that this arrangement was set in writing clearly emphasizes the principles of the function of the algorithm – that is, the fact that it is possible to factorize the regular numbers into the product of regular numbers and the fact that the reciprocal of a product is the product of the reciprocals. Moreover, the spatial arrangement of the text underscores the power of the procedure of developing the iterations without limitation. On this topic, let us recall the striking fact that the recourse to iteration does not appear in the verbal texts, which limit themselves to numbers of a small size, whereas the iteration expands in a rather spectacular way in Tablet A, and in a more modest way in the numeric versions of the calculations of the square roots. For the ancient reader, the spatial arrangement of the numbers in Tablet A serves the functions that Sachs' formula does for the modern reader: it shows why the algorithm works. The layout says more than the formula in showing not only why, but also *how* it operates and what its power is.

Tablet A is constructed on the repetition of the doublings of 2.5. The educational value of this series in the instruction of the factorization algorithm has been underscored above, but perhaps the essence lies elsewhere. The fact that the scribes limited themselves to the geometric progression with an initial number 2.5 and a common factor of 2 guarantees the regularity of the entries. This series assures the calculator that the result remains in the domain of regular sexagesimal numbers, a condition necessary for the existence of a sexagesimal reciprocal (with finite expression) and for the operation of the algorithm. It undoubtedly did not escape the scribes that it was possible to choose other series (in tablet UM 29–13–021 are found series based on other initial terms, such as 2.40, 1.40, 4.3). However, the series of doublings of 2.5 is a typical example which allows the scribes to refer to the algorithm by specific numeric data. In other words, this series plays the role of a paradigm. It is possible that the choice of 2.5 comes from the previously noted fact that this number is a logical continuation of the standard reciprocal tables in which the last entries are 1.4 and 1.21.

Fundamentally, Tablet A is built on reciprocity. What expresses the systematic presence of the reverse sequences? It has been shown that the purpose was not the verification of the results because such a matter could have taken a much simpler form. It could have had a role in the verification of the algorithm itself and thus ensured the validity of the mechanism. However, as suggested above, the significance of the reverse sequences could have been above all to express a mathematical rule: 'The reverse of the reverse is itself.' Whatever the case may be, it is clear that in the reverse sequences, the author abandons the stereotypical patterns found in the direct sequences of the text (and found also in the school exercises) and plays with the freedom remaining to him in the choice of factors for the decomposition into elementary regular factors. The reverse sequences thus highlight another important mathematical aspect: the multiplicity of decompositions.

The purpose of the text on Tablet A is thus clearly the algorithm itself, its operation and its justification. The text refers to the algorithm not in a verbal manner, but by an interpretable spatial arrangement, the exploitation of a paradigm well known to the scribes, and the recourse to the reverse sequences in a systematic way. Tablet A therefore bears witness to the reflection of the ancient Mesopotamian scribes on some of the fundamental principles of numeric calculation: the possibility of decomposing the regular numbers into two or more (through iteration) elementary regular factors, the freedom which the multiple valid decompositions offer to the calculator (given that the direct and reverse sequences show two different strategies for the selection of factors), the stability of the multiplication for reciprocal (the reciprocal of a product is the product of reciprocals of the factors) and the involutive character of the determination of a reciprocal (given the fact that this operation is its own reverse operation).

Appendix I | Tablet A (CBS 1215)

Sachs 1947: 237; Robson 2000: 23. The asterisks refer to the remark which follows the transcription. I have added the elements of the appearance to facilitate the reading: the final part of the number which plays a role as a factor is set in bold; the final result of the calculation is underlined; the format reproduces the layout of the tablet.

Obverse

Column I 1–8		Column II 9–13		Column III 13–16	
2.5	12	8.53.20	18	6.45	1.20
25	2.24	2.40	22.30	9	[6.40]
28.48	1.15	6.45	1.20		8.53.20
36	1.40	9	6.40		[2.2]2.13.[20]
	2.5		8.53.20		
4.10	6	17.46.40	9	4.44.26.40	[9]
25	2.24	2.40	22.30	42.40	2[2.30]
14.24	2.30	3.22.30	2	16	3.[45]
36	1 .40	6.45	1.20		1.24.22.30
	4.10	9	6.40	[12.3]9.22.30	[2]
			8.53.20	[25.18].45*	[16]
8.20	3		17.46.40	[6.45]	[1.20]
25	2.24			[9]	[6.40]
7.12	5	36^{sic}.2^{sic}3.20	18		[8].53.20
36	1.40	10.40	1.[30]		[2.22.13. 20]
	8.20	[16]	3.4[5]		[4.44.26.40]
16.40	9		5.37.30	[9.28].53.[20]	[18]
2.30	24	[1.41.1]5	4	2.50.40	[1.30]
3.[36]	[1.40]	[6.45]	1.20	[4.16]	[3.45]
6	10	[9]	6.40	[16]	[3.45]
	15^{sic}.40		[8.53].20		14.3.[45]
			[35.33].20		[2]1.5.3[7.30]
33.20	18	[1].11.6.[40]	9	[6.19.4]1.15	[4]
10	6	10.40	1.[30]	[25.18.45]*	[16]
1.48	1.15	16	3.4[5]	[6.45]	[1.20]
2.15	4		5.37.30	[9]	[6.40]
8^{sic}	6.40	50.37.30	2		[8.53.20]
	26.40	1.41.15	4		2.[22.13.20]
	33.20	6.4[5]	1.20		9.[28.53.20]
1.6.40	9	9	6.40	18.57.[46.40]	[9]
10	6		[8.5]3.[20]	[2.50.40]	[1.30]
54	1.6.40		35.33.20	4.[16]	[3.45]
			1.11.6.40	16	[3.45]
[2].13.20	18				[14].3. [45]
[40]	1.30	2.22.13.20	[18]		[21.5.37.30]
[27]	2.13.20	42.40	22.30	[3.9.50.37.30]	[2]
		16	3.45	[6.19.41.15]	[4]
4.26.40	9		1.24.22.30		
40	1.30	25.18.45*	[16]	(continued on the reverse)	
13.30	2				
27	2.13.20				
	4.26.40				

(continued on the reverse)

Reverse (on the reverse of the tablet, the columns run from right to left, as is customary)

Column III 21		Column II 19–20		Column I 16–18	
10.6.48.**53.20**	18	[2.31.42.**13.20**	18]	(continued)	
3.2.2.**40**	22.[30]	[45.30.**40**	1.30]	[25.18.**45***	16]
1.8.**16**	3.4[5]	[1.8.**16**	3.45]	[6.**45**	1.20]
4.**16**	3.[45]	[4.**16**	3.45]	[9	6.40]
16	3.[45]	**16**	[3.45]	[8.53.20]	
1[4.3.4]5		14.[3.45]		[2.22.13.20]	
52.44.[3.4]5		5[2.44.3.45]		[9.28.53.20]	
19.46.31.24.22.[30]		1.18^{sic}.6.[5.37.30]		[18.57.46.40]	
5.55.57.25.18.4[5]	16	23.43.49.[41.15]	[4]	[37.55.**33.20**	18]
1.34.55.18.**45***	16	1.[3]4.55.18.**45***	[16]	[11.**22.40**	22.30]
25.18.**45***	[16]	[25].18.**45**ˣ	1[6]	[4.**16**	3.45]
6.**45**	[1.20]	[6].**45**	1.[20]	[16	3.45]
9	[6.40]	[9]	6.40	[14.3.45]	
8.53.20		8.53.20		[5.16.24.22.30]	
2.22.13. 20		2.22.13.20		[1.34.55.18.**45***	16]
37.55.33.20		37.55.3[3.20]		[25.18.**45***	16]
10.6.48.53.20		2.31.42.13.[20]		[6.**45**	1.20]
				9	[6.40]
		5.3.24.**26.40**	[9]	[8.53.20]	
		45.30.**40**	1.30	2.22.13.[20]	
		1.8.**16**	3.45	37.55.33.[20]	
		4.**16**	3.45		
		16	3.45		
		14.3.45			
		5[2.44].3.45			
		1.19.6.5.37.30			
		11.51.54.50.**37.30**	2	1.15.51.**6.40**	9
		23.43.49.41.**15**	4	11.**22.40**	22.30
		1.34.55.18.**45***	16	4.**16**	3.45
		25.18.**45***	16	**16**	[3.45]
		6.**45**	1.20	14.[3.45]	
		9	6.[40]	5.16.[24.22.30]	
		8.53.20		47.27.[39.22.**30**	2]
		2.22.13. 20		[1.34.55.18.**45***	16]
		37.55.33.20		[25.18.**45***	16]
		2.31.42.13.20		[6.**45**	1.20]
		5.3.24.26.40		[9	6.40]
				8.[53.20]	
				2.2[2.13. 20]	
				37.55.[33.20]	
				1.15.51.[6.40]	

Notes are on p. 420

Notes to pp. 418–19
Section 4: Read 16.40 in place of 15.40.
Section 5: Read 9 in place of 8.
Section 11: Read 35.33.20 in place of 36.23.20.
Section 19: Read 19 in place of 18.
*Section 13 to Section 21: The factor chosen is 3.45 (from the reciprocal 16). I could not set it in bold type because it does not obviously constitute the final part of the number, as in the other cases. However, if 8 is decomposed into the sum 5+3, the factor 3.45 is scarcely hidden. (For more precise details, see the part of the article devoted to the analysis of the entirety of this text.)

Appendix ii | Ni 10241

Old Babylonian school tablet from Nippur, conserved in Istanbul, copy Proust 2007.

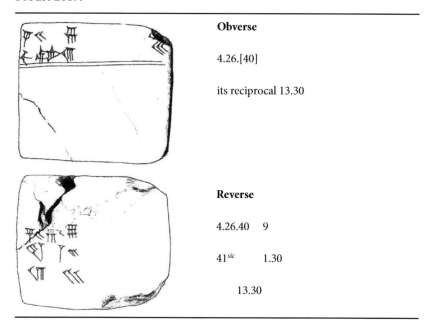

Obverse

4.26.[40]

its reciprocal 13.30

Reverse

4.26.40   9

41[sic]   1.30

13.30

Bibliography

Britton, J. P. (1991–3) 'A table of 4th powers and related texts from Seleucid Babylon', *Journal of Cuneiform Studies* **43–5**: 71–87.
Britton, J. P., Proust, C. and Schnider, S. (2011) 'Plimpton 322: a review and a different perspective', *Archive for History of Exact Sciences* **65**: 519–66.

Bruins, E. (1954) 'Some mathematical texts', *Sumer* **10**: 55–61.

(1969) 'La construction de la grande table de valeurs réciproques AO 6456', *Proceedings of the 17th Rencontre Assyriologique Internationale.* Bruxelles: 99–115.

Cavigneaux, A. (1989) 'L'écriture et la réflexion linguistique en Mésopotamie', in *Histoire des idées linguistiques*, vol. I, *La naissance des métalangages en Orient et en Occident*, ed. S. Auroux. Liège: 99–118.

Charpin, D. (1992) 'Les malheurs d'un scribe ou de l'inutilité du sumérien loin de Nippur', in *Nippur at the Centennial*, Papers read at the 35th Rencontre Assyriologique Internationale, Philadelphia, 1988, ed. M. deJong Ellis. Philadelphia, PA: 7–27.

Charpin, D., and Joannès, F. (eds.) (1992) *La circulation des biens, des personnes et des idées dans le Proche-Orient ancien*, Proceedings of the 38th Rencontre Assyriologique Internationale, Paris.

Chemla, K. (1994) 'Nombres, opérations et équations en divers fonctionnements', in *Nombres, astres, plantes et viscères, sept essais sur l'histoire des sciences et des techniques en Asie Orientale*, ed. I. Ang and P.-E. Will. Paris: 1–36.

Friberg, J. (1983) 'On the big 6-place tables of reciprocals and squares from Seleucid Babylon and Uruk and their Old Babylonian and Sumerian predecessors', *Sumer* **42**: 81–7.

(2000) 'Mathematics at Ur in the Old Babylonian period', *Revue d'Assyriologie* **94**: 98–188.

(2005) *Unexpected Links Between Egyptian and Babylonian Mathematics.* Singapore.

(2007) *A Remarkable Collection of Babylonian Mathematical Texts: Manuscripts in the Schøyen Collection – Cuneiform Texts*, vol. I. New York.

Gadd, C. J., and Kramer, S. N. (1966) *Literary and Religious Texts, Second part.* Ur Excavations Texts vol. VI/2. London.

Hilprecht, H. V. (1906) *Mathematical, Metrological and Chronological Tablets from the Temple Library of Nippur*. Babylonian Expedition vol. XX/1. Philadelphia, PA.

Muroi, K. (1999) 'Extraction of square roots in Babylonian mathematics', *Historia Scientiarum* **9**: 127–32.

Neugebauer, O. (1935–7) *Mathematische Keilschrifttexte*, vols. I–III. Berlin.

Neugebauer, O., and Sachs, A. J. (1945) *Mathematical Cuneiform Texts.* New Haven, CT.

Oelsner, J. (2001) 'Eine Reziprokentabelle der Ur III-Zeit', in *Changing Views on Ancient Near Eastern Mathematics*, ed. J. Høyrup and P. Damerow. Berlin: 53–8.

Proust, C. (2007) *Tablettes mathématiques de Nippur*, Part I, *Reconstitution du cursus scolaire*, Part II, *Édition des tablettes conservées à Istanbul*. Istanbul.

(2008) 'Quantifier et calculer: usages des nombres à Nippur', *Revue d'histoire des mathématiques* **14**: 143–209.

Robson, E. (1999) *Mesopotamian Mathematics, 2100–1600 BC: Technical Constants in Bureaucracy and Education*. Oxford.

(2000) 'Mathematical cuneiform tablets in Philadelphia. Part 1 : problems and calculations', *SCIAMVS* **1**: 11–48.

(2001a) 'Neither Sherlock Holmes nor Babylon: a reassessment of Plimpton 322', *Historia Mathematica* **28**: 167–206.

(2001b) 'The Tablet House: a scribal school in Old Babylonian Nippur', *Revue d'Assyriologie* **95**: 39–66.

(2002) 'More than metrology: mathematics education in an Old Babylonian scribal school', in *Under One Sky: Astronomy and Mathematics in the Ancient Near East*, ed. J. M. Steele and A. Imhausen. Münster: 325–65.

Sachs, A. J. (1947) 'Babylonian mathematical texts I', *Journal of Cuneiform Studies* **1**: 219–40.

(1952) 'Babylonian mathematical texts II: Approximations of reciprocals of irregular numbers; III: The problem of finding the cube root of a number', *Journal of Cuneiform Studies* **6**: 151–6.

Veldhuis, N. (1997) 'Elementary education at Nippur: the lists of trees and wooden objects', PhD thesis, University of Groningen.

13 | Reading proofs in Chinese commentaries: algebraic proofs in an algorithmic context

KARINE CHEMLA

The earliest Chinese text devoted to mathematics that has been handed down through the written tradition, *The Nine Chapters on Mathematical Procedures* (*Jiuzhang suanshu*), was probably compiled on the basis of older documents and completed in the form in which we have it today in the first century CE.[1] Until recently, there was no evidence indicating the nature of the documents that may have been used in composing *The Nine Chapters*. However, in 1984, in a tomb that had been sealed *c.* 186 BCE at Zhangjiashan (today in the Hubei Province), archaeologists found a text entitled the *Book of Mathematical Procedures* (*Suanshushu*) which may have been used for this purpose.[2] Like this book that was brought to light thanks to archaeological excavations but did not survive through written transmission, *The Nine Chapters* is mainly composed of particular problems and algorithms for solving them, without displaying any apparent interest in establishing

---

[1] In what follows, the title is abbreviated as *The Nine Chapters*. The full title would be more accurately translated as 'Mathematical procedures in nine chapters/patterns'. However, to avoid confusion with titles of other Chinese mathematical books, the English translation of which is quite close to that of *The Nine Chapters*, I give a translation that does not diverge from the usual English title given to the book. In this volume, A. Volkov (see Chapter 15, Appendix 2) chooses to translate the title as *Computational Procedures of Nine Categories*. In the earliest document that was handed down and that outlines the history of *The Nine Chapters* as a book, i.e. the third-century commentator Liu Hui's preface, the process of compilation is sketched and mentioned as having lasted more than a century. In the introduction to Chapter 6 in CG2004, I gather the evidence on the basis of which I consider the book to have been completed in the first century CE. In this chapter, unless otherwise stated, I follow the critical edition of *The Nine Chapters* given in CG2004. The reader can find in this book a complete French translation of the Classic and its traditional commentaries; see below. Other translations of the same texts have appeared in recent years: some into modern Chinese (Shen Kangshen 1997; Guo Shuchun 1998; Li Jimin 1998), one other into English (Shen, Crossley and Lun 1999, based on Shen 1997). It is impossible, within the framework of this chapter, to comment on all the differences between the translation given here and these other translations. The interested reader can compare the various interpretations.

[2] The first critical edition of this text can be found in Peng Hao 2001. Two translations into English have already appeared (Cullen 2004; Dauben 2008). *The Nine Chapters* and the *Book of Mathematical Procedures* have a number of similarities. For example, they deal with the same concept of fractions, conceived of as composed of a numerator and a denominator. Moreover, they contain similar algorithms to compute with fractions. In addition to testifying to the fact that these elements of mathematical knowledge existed in China before 186 BCE, the *Book of Mathematical Procedures* provides additional information that will prove useful for us below.

the correctness of the algorithms provided.[3] However, soon after its completion, the book became a 'Classic' (*jing*) and retained this status in the subsequent centuries, which accounts for the specific fate it had not only in China, but also in Korea and Japan. On the one hand, as is clear from the references made to it, the book remained a key reference work for practitioners of mathematics in China until at least the fourteenth century, and this fact most probably explains why it is the earliest extant text to have been handed down through the written tradition. On the other hand, commentaries on it were regularly composed, two of which were perceived as so essential to the reading of the text that they were handed down with the Classic itself. In fact, no ancient edition of *The Nine Chapters* has survived that does not contain the commentary completed by Liu Hui in 263 and the explanations added to it by a group of scholars under the supervision of Li Chunfeng.[4] This detail of textual preservation indicates how closely linked to each other these texts became, to the extent that, at some point in history, they constituted, for Chinese readers, an integrated set of texts that were no longer dissociated. As a consequence, if we, as contemporary exegetes, are to understand how *The Nine Chapters* was approached in ancient China, it is important that we, like Chinese readers, read the text of the Classic in relation to that of its commentaries.

This relationship proves important in several respects. On the one hand, through the commentaries, one can establish that even though the problems contained in *The Nine Chapters* all appear to be particular statements, they were read by the earliest readers whom we can observe as general statements. The commentators exhibit the expectation that the algorithm linked to a problem should solve not simply this problem, but the category of problems for which the problem, taken as paradigm, stood.[5] On the other hand, the commentators make explicit some theoretical dimensions that

[3] In Chemla 1991 and 1997/8, I have given several hints indicating that the situation is not so simple. However, since the focus of this chapter lies elsewhere, I shall not dwell on this question. The reason why this issue is crucial for us here will become clear in Part II of this chapter. Let us stress that the title of *The Nine Chapters* contains the character *shu* 'procedure' which introduces the statement of the algorithms contained in both books.

[4] Below, for the sake of simplicity, we refer to this layer of the text by the expression of 'Li Chunfeng's commentary'. In fact, the situation is less simple than is presented here. There are problems in distinguishing between the two layers of commentaries (I have summarized the state of our present knowledge on the topic in CG2004: 472–3). In the present chapter, I have attempted to deal with my topic in a way that is not jeopardized by this difficulty.

[5] In fact, this presentation of *The Nine Chapters* is simplified. An algorithm can be given after a set of problems. Moreover, there are cases when an algorithm is given outside the context of any problem, or constitutes an instantiation of such an algorithm. However, this does not invalidate the main thesis.

were driving the inquiry into mathematics in ancient China. For instance, they reveal that generality was a key theoretical value and that finding out the most general operations was an aim pursued by the practitioners of mathematics.[6] However, a crucially important fact for us lies elsewhere: after the description of virtually every algorithm presented in *The Nine Chapters*, or between the sentences prescribing its successive operations, the commentators set out to prove its correctness. These texts thus provide the earliest evidence available today regarding the practice of mathematical proof in ancient China, and this is the reason why, in this chapter, we shall concentrate on them.

In contrast to what can be found in ancient Greek geometrical sources, where statements are proved to be true, the Chinese commentators systematically strove to establish the correctness of algorithms.[7] It can hence be assumed that the commentaries bear witness to a practice of mathematical proof that, as a practice, developed independently from what early Greek sources demonstrate. However, we shall not dwell on this issue here. Instead, and as a prerequisite to tackling this question in the future, we shall aim at better understanding this practice of proof. Thereby, we may hope to cast light more generally on some of the fundamental operations required when proving the correctness of algorithms – a section of the history of mathematical proof that, to my knowledge, has been so far almost entirely neglected.

Even though it constitutes an oversimplification to be refined later, let us say, for the present, that an algorithm consists of a list of operations that can be applied to some data in order to yield a desired magnitude. In this context, proving that such an algorithm is correct involves establishing that the obtained result corresponds to the desired magnitude. It can be shown that, when fulfilling this task, the commentators systematically made use of some key operations. Moreover, they employed specialized terms to refer to concepts related to these operations.[8] These facts disclose that, far from being ad-hoc developments, these proofs complied with norms familiar to the actors, since they devised technical terms related to them. The way in

---

[6] Chemla 2003 establishes these points. Below, we shall find additional evidence supporting these theses.

[7] It can be shown that this is how the commentators themselves conceive of the aim of their reasonings. See Chapter A in CG2004: 26–8. I do not come back to this point here. Note that the commentators leave some of the most basic algorithms without proof. Guo 1992: 301–20 stressed this fact, emphasizing that this feature meant that the commentators were shaping an architecture of algorithms, the proofs of which depended on algorithms proved previously. From another angle, one can argue that reduction to fundamental algorithms, and not to simple problems, is also a key point at stake in the proofs carried out by the commentators.

[8] Chapter A of CG2004: 26–39 sketches these points.

which the reflection *about* proof developed in ancient China still awaits further study. In this chapter, I shall focus on further highlighting and analysing two key operations that are fundamental constituents of the practice of proof documented by our commentators. The first part presents in some detail an example illustrating the two features on which we shall concentrate: on the one hand, determining the 'meaning' of a computation or of a sub-procedure; on the other hand, carrying out what I called an 'algebraic proof within an algorithmic context' – what I mean by this expression will become clear with the example. In the case of the former feature, our analysis will provide an opportunity to examine the modalities according to which the 'meaning' of a sequence of computations can be determined. As for the latter feature, after having brought to light fundamental transformations characteristic of this part of the proof, I shall present evidence in favour of the hypothesis that there existed an interest in ancient China regarding what could guarantee the validity of these transformations. In particular, in Part II of this chapter, I shall explain why the commentaries on the algorithms carrying out the arithmetical operations on fractions can be read as related to this concern. This explanation will lead us to examine the algorithms that *The Nine Chapters* contains for multiplying and dividing fractions. Beyond the fact that the proof of their correctness further illustrates how the commentators proceeded in their proofs, we shall show why they can be considered as belonging to the set of fundamental ingredients grounding the 'algebraic proof in an algorithmic context'. Bringing this point to light will require that we view algorithms from the two distinct perspectives by which they were worked out in ancient China. Not only should we read algorithms, as the commentators did, as pure sequences of operations yielding a magnitude, but we should also consider them as prescriptions of computations, carried out on the surface, on which the calculations were executed, and yielding a value.[9] In conclusion, we shall be in a position to raise some questions on the nature and history of algebraic proof.

I Two key operations for proving the correctness of algorithms

The setting and the first key components of the proofs

The main example in the framework of which we shall follow the third-century commentator Liu Hui in his proof of the correctness of an algorithm deals with the volume of the truncated pyramid with circular

[9] On this opposition, see Chemla 2005.

base (see Figure 13.1 below).[10] The problem in which *The Nine Chapters* introduces this topic reads as follows:[11]

(5.11) SUPPOSE ONE HAS A TRUNCATED PYRAMID WITH CIRCULAR BASE, THE CIR-CUMFERENCE OF THE LOWER CIRCLE OF WHICH IS 3 *ZHANG*, THE CIRCUMFERENCE OF THE UPPER CIRCLE OF WHICH IS 2 *ZHANG*, AND THE HEIGHT OF WHICH IS 1 *ZHANG*. ONE ASKS HOW MUCH THE VOLUME IS. ANSWER: 527 *CHI* 7/9 *CHI*.

Note the numerical values attached to the particular solid considered: the circumference of the circle forming the base is 3 *zhang*. This detail will prove important below. Let us stress the fact that *The Nine Chapters* uses throughout the ratio of 3 to 1 for that of the circumference of a circle to its diameter. Liu Hui opens his commentary by putting forward the hypothesis that these were also the values used when the examined procedure was shaped. He states: 'This procedure presupposes that the circumference is 3 when the diameter is 1.'

Elsewhere, the commentator designates such values as *lüs*, thereby indicating that they can be multiplied or divided by a same number without their relative meaning, which is to represent a relationship between the circumference and the diameter of the circle, being affected. We shall meet this concept again below. To go back to problem 5.11 in *The Nine Chapters*,

---

[10]   I translate the Chinese term *yuanting* as 'truncated pyramid with a circular base' on the basis of an analysis of the structure of a system of terms designating solids in *The Nine Chapters*. In the terminology of solids, three pairs of names work in a similar fashion: each of these pairs contains two terms formed by prefixing either *fang* (square, rectangle) or *yuan* (circle) to the name of a given body. The designated solids correspond to each other, in that they belong to the same genus. They differ only in that they have, respectively, either square or circular sections. The relation between the terms in Chinese expressed a relation between the designated solids. I hence translated these pairs as such, reproducing, in English, the structure of the terminology of the Chinese. This leads to an interpretation of the second term as designating a general kind of solid, two species of which are considered: the one with square base and the one with circular base. Since *fangting* designates the 'truncated pyramid with square base', *yuanting* was translated as 'truncated pyramid with circular base'. For more details, see Chapter D in CG2004: 103–4. On previous occasions (Chemla 1997/8; Chapter A in CG2004: 36–8), I have already discussed this passage of *The Nine Chapters* and the commentaries. The critical edition and the translation into French can be found in CG2004: 424–7. I come back to it again in this chapter to cast light on the proof from a new angle. LD1987: 73, Li Jimin 1990: 327–8 and Guo 1992: 137–8 present an outline of Liu Hui's proof.

[11]   A problem of *The Nine Chapters* is indexed by a pair of numbers: the first number indicates the chapter in the Classic in which the problem is placed. The second number indicates its position in the sequence of problems of the chapter. We shall always translate the text of the Classic in upper-case letters, in contrast to the commentaries, which are translated in lower-case ones. In addition to indicating clearly to which part of the text a given passage belongs, this convention imitates the way in which the different types of text are presented in the earliest extant documents.

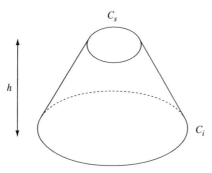

Figure 13.1   The truncated pyramid with circular base.

if such is the case, as a consequence, the diameter of the lower circle of the solid to be considered is consequently equal to its height. The truncated pyramid dealt with can thus be inscribed into a cube.

In the Classic, the outline of the problem is immediately followed by an algorithm allowing the reader to rely on the data provided to determine the desired volume. It reads as follows:

THE CIRCUMFERENCES OF THE UPPER AND LOWER CIRCLES BEING MULTIPLIED BY ONE ANOTHER, THEN MULTIPLIED EACH BY ITSELF, ONE ADDS THESE (THE RESULTS); ONE MULTIPLIES THIS BY THE HEIGHT AND DIVIDES BY 36.

To expound the argument on proof that I have in view, I shall need to make use of a representation of the algorithm as list of operations. To this end, let us note, as on Figure 13.1, C_s(resp. C_i) the circumference of the upper (resp. lower) circle and h the height of the solid. With these notations, the algorithm can be represented in a synoptic way, as follows:

Multiplications	Multiplication	Division
sum	by h	by 36

$$C_i \longrightarrow C_i C_s + C_i^2 + C_s^2 \longrightarrow (C_i C_s + C_i^2 + C_s^2)h \longrightarrow (C_i C_s + C_i^2 + C_s^2)h/36$$
$$C_s$$

In what follows, I shall regularly employ such representations for lists of operations.

Immediately after the statement of the algorithm as given by the Classic, in the first section of his exegesis, the commentator sets out to establish its correctness within the framework of the hypothesis that *The Nine Chapters* made use of a ratio between the circumference and the diameter of the circle equivalent to taking $\pi = 3$. His proof proceeds along three interwoven lines of argumentation. The first line consists of establishing an algorithm, for which Liu Hui proves that it yields the desired volume. The second line amounts to transforming this algorithm *as such* into the algorithm the correctness of which is to be proved. For this, Liu Hui applies valid transformations to the algorithm taken as list of operations, thereby modifying it progressively into other lists of operations, without affecting its result. In the following, we shall make clear what such transformations can be. Third, in doing so, the commentator simultaneously accounts for the form of the algorithm as found in *The Nine Chapters*, by making explicit the motivations he lends to its author for not stating the algorithm as he or she most probably first obtained it, but instead changing it.

This whole process provides an analysis of the reasons underlying the algorithm. The analysis is not developed merely for its own sake. It also yields a basis on which the commentators devise new algorithms for determining the volume of the truncated pyramid with circular base. Accordingly, in a second shorter section of his exegesis, Liu Hui can make use of the values he employs for the relationship between the circumference and the diameter of the circle (314 and 100) to offer new algorithms. Later on, Li Chunfeng will similarly rely on the values he selects for these magnitudes to do the same. However, our analysis will concentrate on the first section of Liu Hui's commentary.

Interestingly enough, a reasoning that has exactly the same structure and the same wording is developed to account for the algorithm that *The Nine Chapters* gives for the volume of the cone, after problem 5.25. On the one hand, this similarity indicates that the text of the commentary analysed here is reliable. On the other hand, such a fact shows that the proofs of the correctness were established by the commentators in relation to other proofs and not developed independently. Other phenomena lead to the same conclusion.[12] This similarity relates to the fact that the proof had a certain kind of generality – an issue to which we shall come back later. Let us for now concentrate on how Liu Hui deals with the truncated pyramid with circular base.

The first step in Liu Hui's reasoning is to make use of an algorithm for which the correctness was established in the section placed immediately before this one. Provided after problem 5.10, this algorithm allows the computation of the volume of the truncated pyramid with square base when one knows the sides of the upper square (D_s) and lower square (D_i) as well as the height h (see Figure 13.2).[13]

---

[12]　See Chemla 1991 and 1992, for example.
[13]　The proof is analysed in Li Jimin 1990: 304ff., Chemla 1991 and Guo Shuchun 1992: 132–5.

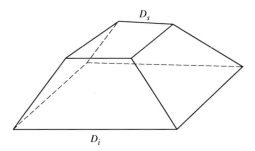

Figure 13.2 The truncated pyramid with square base.

Using the same notations for algorithms as above, it can be represented as follows:

Multiplications	Division
sum	by 3
Multiplication by h	

$$D_i \xrightarrow{\hspace{2cm}} (D_iD_s + D_i^2 + D_s^2)h \xrightarrow{\hspace{2cm}} (D_iD_s + D_i^2 + D_s^2)h/3$$
$$D_s$$

On this basis, Liu Hui states a first algorithm (algorithm 1) which determines the volume of the truncated pyramid with square base circumscribed to the truncated pyramid with circular base which is considered. Quoting the algorithm of the Classic verbatim – a fact that I indicate by using quotation marks in the translation – his commentary reads:

This procedure presupposes (*yi'*) that the circumference is 3 when the diameter is 1. One must hence divide by 3 the circumferences of the upper and lower circles to make the upper and lower diameters respectively. 'Multiplying them by one another, then multiplying each of them by itself', adding, 'multiplying this by the height and dividing by 3' makes the volume of the truncated pyramid with square base.

The only transformation (transformation 1) needed to make use of the algorithm quoted in this new context is to prefix its text with two divisions by 3. These operations change the given circumferences into the corresponding diameters, the lengths of which are respectively equal to the lengths of the sides of the upper and lower circumscribed squares.[14] Algorithm 1 can be represented as follows:

[14]   Incidentally, this proposition is stated in the *Book of Mathematical Procedures* (slips 194–5, Peng Hao 2001: 111).

Divisions by 3   Multiplications, sum,   Division by 3
                     Multiplication by h

$$C_i \longrightarrow D_i = C_i/3 \longrightarrow \left[\frac{C_i}{3}\frac{C_s}{3} + (\frac{C_i}{3})^2 + (\frac{C_s}{3})^2\right].h \longrightarrow \left[\frac{C_i}{3}\frac{C_s}{3} + (\frac{C_i}{3})^2 + (\frac{C_s}{3})^2\right].h/3$$

$$C_s \qquad D_s = C_s/3$$

To determine the 'meaning' of the result, that is, that one obtains the volume of the truncated pyramid with square base, Liu Hui has to rely on both the algorithm established earlier and values corresponding to a value of π. Such an operation of 'interpretation' corresponds to a key concept used by the commentators in the course of proving the correctness of algorithms: they refer to the 'intention' of an operation or a procedure, or its 'meaning', by the specific term of *yi*. In what follows, we shall pay particular attention to the ways in which such a 'meaning' is determined.

The first step in Liu Hui's proof of the correctness of the investigated algorithm belonged to what I have called above the 'first line of argumentation'. The next step goes along both the second and the third lines. This step makes us encounter the aspect of proof that is the main focus in this chapter. I shall hence examine it in great detail.

After having obtained the algorithm just examined, Liu Hui considers a case:

Suppose that, when one simplifies the circumferences of the upper and lower circles by 3, none of the two is exhausted, . . .

Here, as is the rule elsewhere, the term 'simplifying' has to be interpreted as meaning 'dividing'.[15] In all extant mathematical documents from ancient China, the result of a division is given in the form of an integer to which, if the dividend is not 'exhausted' by the operation, a fraction is appended. The numerator and denominator consist of the remainder of the dividend and the divisor, respectively, both possibly simplified when this was possible. As a consequence, more generally, in these texts, fractions are always smaller than 1.

With respect to the algorithm he has just established, Liu Hui then considers the case in which, after dividing the circumferences by 3, *neither* of them yields an integer. In such cases, the next step of the algorithm would lead to multiplying quantities composed of an integer and a fraction with each

[15] To obtain evidence supporting this claim, the reader is referred to the glossary of Chinese terms I composed (CG2004: 897–1035). Unless otherwise mentioned, all glosses of technical terms rely on the evidence published in this glossary.

other. This operation implies inserting at this point the algorithm that *The Nine Chapters* gave for multiplying not only such quantities, but also any two quantities – integers, fractions, integers with fractions – the correctness of which has been established in the first of *The Nine Chapters*. Let us examine this algorithm in detail before considering the modalities of its insertion.

The general procedure for multiplying

This algorithm, like the others, has two faces. On the one hand, it is a list of operations, the text of which is recorded in *The Nine Chapters*. On the other hand, the operations it prescribes were carried out on a surface on which quantities were represented with counting rods in ancient China.[16] For the sake of my argument, it will prove useful to have some knowledge about the way in which computations were physically handled on this surface. At first sight, it may seem strange that such details are necessary, since we deal with proofs and not with actual computations. However, the relation between the two will become clearer below.

On the surface, the execution of division and multiplication started from the basis of a fixed layout of their operands, which evolved throughout the flow of computations. At the beginning of a multiplication, the multiplicand was set in the lower row of the space in which the operation was executed, while the multiplier was placed in its upper row. At the end of the computation, the multiplier had disappeared, leaving the result in the middle row of the surface and the multiplicand in the lower row. In contrast, division started with the dividend placed in the middle row, in opposition to the divisor, put in the lower row. At the end of the computation, the quotient had been obtained in the upper row. Under the quotient, either the place of the dividend had been left empty, which indicated that the result was an integer, or there was its remainder, in which case the result had to be read as integer (upper row) plus numerator (middle row) over denominator (lower row). Let us illustrate this description by what the computations for the algorithm yielding the volume of the circumscribed truncated pyramid must have looked like. Figure 13.3 shows a sequence of three successive states of the surface for computing. We indicate a separation between the rows for the sake of clarity. In fact, we have no idea whether or not there were marks on this surface. In the first state, on the left-hand side, the circumfer-

---

[16] Although they do refer to the fact that computations were carried out on such a surface, the earliest extant texts discussed in this chapter contain very little information regarding how these computations were handled. The argumentation supporting the way in which I suggest recovering them is provided in Chemla 1996.

C_s		C_s Dividend 3 Divisor	a_s integer b_s numerator 3 denominator
	Dividing by 3		
C_i		C_i Dividend 3 Divisor	a_i integer b_i numerator 3 denominator

Figure 13.3 The layout of the algorithm up to the point of the multiplication of fractions.

ences of the upper and lower bases were displayed, respectively in the upper and lower rows of the surface. The reason for this is that numbers derived from them would soon enter into a multiplication. Before that multiplication, the algorithm prescribes that both circumferences be divided by 3. These divisions were to be set up and carried out in the upper and lower spaces, with the row in which the numbers had been placed becoming in turn a space in which a computation was executed according to the same rules of presentation. For instance, the upper row was split into three sub-rows, with the dividend C_s occupying the middle sub-row and the divisor 3 the lower sub-row (second state of the surface in Figure 13.3).[17] In the situations considered by Liu Hui, once the divisions were completed, none of the dividends in the upper and lower spaces would have vanished, the result of each division being of the form of an integer increased by a fraction (third state in Figure 13.3). These, then, are the quantities to be multiplied according to the next step of the algorithm ('Multiplying them by one another, then multiplying each of them by itself'). This feature of hierarchical organization, according to which a space in which a number is placed can become a sub-space, in which an operation is performed according to the same rules at any level, is, in my view, one of the most important characteristics of this system of computation. This feature ensures that the successive computations required by an algorithm will be articulated with each other spatially, instead of being dissociated and carried out independently of each other.

The right-hand part of Figure 13.3 shows the state of the surface for computing, at the point where the algorithm requires inserting the algorithm for multiplying quantities that consist of an integer and a fraction. Let us

[17] In LD1987: 16–18, the reader can find descriptions of how the computations of a multiplication and a division were carried out on the surface for computing.

a_s	integer						'parts
b_s	numerator	$3a_s$	b_s	$3a_s+b_s$			of the
3	denominator	3		3	3 ·		product'
					$(3a_s+b_s).(3a_i+b_i)$	$(3a_s+b_s).(3a_i+b_i)$	dividend
						9	divisor
a_i	integer						
b_i	numerator	$3a_i$	b_i	$3a_i+b_i$	$3a_i+b_i$	$3a_i+b_i$	
3	denominator	3		3	3	3	

Figure 13.4   The execution of the multiplication of fractions on the surface for computing.

read what is called in *The Nine Chapters* the 'PROCEDURE FOR THE FIELD WITH THE GREATEST GENERALITY', which fulfils this task.

PROCEDURE: THE DENOMINATORS OF THE PARTS RESPECTIVELY MULTIPLY THE INTEGER CORRESPONDING TO THEM; THE NUMERATORS OF THE PARTS JOIN THESE (THE RESULTS); MULTIPLYING [THE RESULTS] BY EACH OTHER MAKES THE DIVIDEND. THE DENOMINATORS OF THE PARTS BEING MULTIPLIED BY EACH OTHER MAKE THE DIVISOR. ONE DIVIDES THE DIVIDEND BY THE DIVISOR.

If we represent the successive states of the surface for computing when this sequence of operations is used from left to right, we obtain the result shown in Figure 13.4.[18]

The same algorithm can be found in the *Book of Mathematical Procedures*. The description here, while slightly more specific regarding the display of the arrays of numbers on the surface, can be interpreted along the same lines. Liu Hui's commentary on the first step of the procedure contains two elements that prove quite interesting for our purpose.

The first element relates to the conception of the movements effected on the surface by the computations. Liu Hui offers a slight rewriting of the way in which the first step should be carried out: the products of the denominators by the corresponding integers are, in his words, 'made to enter the (corresponding) numerators'. This does not change anything in the resulting configuration (column 3). However, this first sequence of operations prescribed by the 'procedure for the field with the greatest generality'

---

[18]   Perhaps, the layout of the first step should be restored in a different way. The middle row of the upper and lower spaces could be divided into two sub-rows: one in which the result of the multiplication would be placed – that is, in the middle as usual – and a second one in which the numerator would remain. Thereafter, the two sub-rows would again fuse into a unique row, with the numerator joining the product.

thereby appears as an operation of multiplication carried out on the three lines that are the array of numbers yielded by the previous division. The operation multiplies the content of the upper row by that of the lower row, progressively adding the results to the middle row, where, in the end, the final result is to be read. This point is quite important. First, it reveals the continuity between an array of positions read as a quantity $(a + b/3)$ and the configuration on which a computation is carried out on the surface. In the same vein, an array of two lines will regularly be considered as a quantity (a fraction) or as an operation (a division). We shall come back to this feature on several occasions below. Second, this point shows the material articulation between the operations of multiplication and division on the surface for computing. Each of the operations can be applied to the configuration at which the other operation ends. The management of positions on the surface hence appears to be highly sophisticated and carefully planned to allow forms of articulation between the different computations.

It is from this point of view that we can best understand Li Chunfeng's interpretation of the name of the operation carried out by the procedure: 'Field with the greatest generality'.[19] What explains such a name, in his view, is that, in contrast to previous algorithms, this procedure unifies the three algorithms for multiplying either integers, or fractions, or even quantities composed of integers and fractions. If we interpret integers as being numbers of the type $a + 0/n$ (for any number n), fractions as of the type $0 + b/n$, the 'procedure for the field with the greatest generality' can be uniformly applied to multiply any type of numbers. Furthermore, the 'procedure for multiplying fractions' is embedded in it. Note that the procedure is quite complex in the case of multiplying integers. However, uniformity, as stressed by Li Chunfeng, seems to be preferred over simplicity.[20] These remarks will prove useful below. In case the procedure Liu Hui devised for

[19] In fact, Li Chunfeng explains the name 'the greatest generality', which is actually the name given to the same operation in the *Book of Mathematical Procedures*. It may well be the case that the original name of the procedure in *The Nine Chapters* was 'the greatest generality'. We shall see that the generality of the procedure is precisely the key point Li Chunfeng stresses in his comment. The critical edition and the translation of this piece of commentary can be found in CG2004: 172–3.

[20] It is from this angle that one may understand why the description of an algorithm given in the introduction of this chapter is oversimplified. An algorithm may cover several types of cases and include branchings to deal with them. In relation to this, practitioners of mathematics in ancient China seem to have valued generality in algorithms, which led to writing algorithms of which the text may be less straightforward than our first description at the beginning of this chapter. See Chemla 2003.

the circumscribed truncated pyramid dealt only with integers or fractions, other procedures could be used to multiply. However, given the fact that there are cases in which 'none of the circumferences is exhausted' by the division by 3, the most general procedure must be used.

The second element important for us in Liu Hui's commentary on the first step of the 'procedure for the field with the greatest generality' is the intention he reads in the fact that the operation be used. Multiplying an integer by the corresponding denominator, as he interprets, intends to 'make' the integers 'communicate' (*tong*) with the numerators. In other words, the units of the integer *a* and those of the numerator (expressed by the denominator) are made equal, which allows adding up the transformed integer and the numerator. As is often the case, the reason brought to light for employing an operation is expressed in the form of an operation ('make communicate'). The former operation can be prescribed by directly making use of the latter name, which thus refers to both the operation to be carried out and the intention motivating its use. The result, in our case $3a + b$, is designated as the 'parts of the product' (*jifen*). It is 'parts', here a number of 'thirds', in that it is composed of units, the size of which is defined by a denominator. In what follows, we shall meet with these terms again.[21]

We are now in a position to go back to the list of operations established by Liu Hui for computing the volume of the truncated pyramid circum-scribed to the one considered in problem 5.11.

Inserting an algorithm: a key operation for proof

As Liu Hui envisaged, it is possible that none of the upper and lower circumferences is 'exhausted' by the division by 3. Thus, in order to carry out the various multiplications required by algorithm 1, one needs to make use of the 'procedure for the field with the greatest generality'. The insertion of this procedure in algorithm 1 (transformation 2) yields algorithm 2, which, *qua* list of operations, can be represented by the following list of operations:

---

[21]   For the interpretation of the terms, see my glossary (CG2004). In fact, *jifen* 'parts of the product' refers to the numerator in our sense, when its value is greater than that of the denominator. One may view the numerator as a dividend, when looking at it from an operational point of view, and as 'parts of the product', when considering it as constituting a quantity. To be more precise, the commentator introduces the expression of 'parts of the product' (*jifen*) in relation to the operation of 'making communicate', when the latter is first used in *The Nine Chapters*, that is, when commenting on the procedure for dividing between quantities with fractions. We shall analyse this operation and the commentary on it below.

Divisions by 3	Multiplying integers by corresponding denominator, incorporating the numerator	Multiplications, sums,

$$C_i \xrightarrow{\hspace{1cm}} D_i = b_i \dfrac{a_i}{3} \; [[[\xrightarrow{\hspace{1cm}} \; 3a_i + b_i \xrightarrow{\hspace{1cm}} \; (3a_i + b_i)^2 +$$

$$(3a_i + b_i)(3a_s + b_s) +$$

$$C_s \qquad D_s = b_s \dfrac{a_s}{3} \; [[[\qquad 3a_s + b_s \qquad (3a_s + b_s)^2$$

Multiplying denominators, dividing by the result, 9,]]], multiplying by h, dividing by 3

The way in which Liu Hui describes this process is highly interesting for our purpose. Here is how his text reads (my emphasis):

Suppose that, when one simplifies the circumferences of the upper and lower circles by 3, none of the two is exhausted, then, *backtracking*, one *makes them communicate, as a consequence they are taken respectively as upper and lower diameters.*

In terms of computation, the first operation for multiplying quantities with fractions is prescribed by means of the operation expressing its intention – 'make communicate' – which yields, respectively, $3a_i + b_i$ and $3a_s + b_s$. However, *in this context*, Liu Hui states, this computation carries out a *backtracking*. This term captures two nuances. First, it refers to the fact that one goes in a direction opposite to the one just followed. Second, it implies that one goes back to the starting point: $3a_i + b_i$ restores C_i, whereas $3a_s + b_s$ restores C_s. Two facts allow this conclusion. On the one hand, 'making communicate' turns out to be the operation inverse to the division by 3, carried out just before – and we saw how that was displayed on the counting surface. On the other hand, since the results of division are given in the form of an integer increased by a fraction, they are exact. This is a key fact for ensuring that the application of the multiplication opposite to a given division restores the original numbers – and even restores the original set-up of the division as column 3 in Figure 13.4 shows.[22] We meet with the importance of this key fact here for the first time. We shall stress its relevance for our topic on several occasions below.

[22] The fact that the divisor is 3 is important to ensure that one goes back to the numbers one started with. If simplification of the remaining fraction in the result could occur, the operation of 'making communicate' would not amount to applying the inverse operation.

Why backtrack, one may ask, when discussing these two operations, if it leads us to start from where, in any case, our starting point already was? Liu Hui's next sentence makes clear where the relevance for this 'detour' lies. Indeed if the *value* obtained is the same, the sequence of two opposed operations provides it with a new *meaning* (*yi*): C_i and C_s no longer represent the circumferences, but as results of the operation of 'making communicate', they are now interpreted as representing the diameters, disregarding denominators, that is, with reference to other algorithms. This passage reveals the importance the commentator grants to interpreting the meaning of operations.

Cancelling opposed operations: another key operation for proof

Let us now consider the consequences of these remarks for algorithm 2 when considered as a list of operations. What was just analysed implies that the first section of the list of operations can be transformed (transformation 3):

Division by 3   Make communicate   Multiplications, sums, etc.

$$C_i \xrightarrow{\hspace{1.5cm}} D_i = b_i \xrightarrow{\quad a_i \quad} 3a_i + b_i = C_i -(\dots) \xrightarrow{\hspace{1.5cm}}$$
$$\phantom{C_i \xrightarrow{\hspace{1.5cm}} D_i = } \frac{a_i}{3}$$

$$C_s \qquad\qquad D_s = \frac{a_s}{b_s} \qquad\qquad 3a_s + b_s = C_s$$
$$ 3$$

is transformed into:

Multiplications, sums, etc.

$$C_i \xrightarrow{\quad} (\dots\dots\dots) \xrightarrow{\quad}$$
$$C_s$$

The first two operations cancel each other, since their sequence amounts to returning to the original values – and to the original set-up. Deleting both operations from the list of operations does not change the value yielded by algorithm 2, nor does this transformation change the meaning of the final result. This is the first transformation of a list of operations *qua* list that we encounter and it belongs to what I called the second line of argumentation. We shall meet with other transformations of this kind below. This particular transformation is valid for the reasons stressed above. Taken as a whole, algorithm 2, which computed the volume of the truncated pyramid

with square base circumscribed to one with a circular base in case quantities with fractions occurred, can hence be transformed into algorithm 2′,
without altering the result:

Multiplications
Sums
$$C_i \longrightarrow C_i^2 + C_i \cdot C_s + C_s^2$$
$$C_s$$

Multiplying the denominators, dividing by the result 9, multiplying
the result by h, dividing by 3

The essential point now is that algorithm 2′ shares the same initial list of
operations with the algorithm for the truncated pyramid with circular base
as described in *The Nine Chapters*. The reason why this fact is important is
that the arguments outlined above allow the interpretation of the 'meaning',
namely, the 'intention' (*yi*) of the first part of the algorithm, the correctness
of which is to be established. Liu Hui writes (my emphasis):

If one multiplies by one another the upper and lower diameters, then multiplies
each by itself respectively, then adds these and multiplies by the height, this gives
the *parts of the product (jifen) of 3 truncated pyramids with square base*.

Again, this statement is worth analysing in detail. Note, first, that Liu
Hui refers to C_i and C_s as 'diameters'. This is the meaning of the initial values
entered in the algorithm that was established by bringing to light the pair
of deleted, opposed operations. These values are diameters, with respect to
the denominators. Such an analysis corresponds to the fact that the result
of the first section of the algorithm is interpreted as 'parts of the product' in
reference to the 'procedure for the field with the greatest generality'. More
generally, it is by reference to algorithm 2′, itself obtained from a combination of three algorithms, that the interpretation of the result of the first part
of the algorithm is made explicit. Algorithm 2′ has been shown to yield the
volume of the circumscribed truncated pyramid. To state the meaning of
the result of its first part as the 'parts of the product (*jifen*) of 3 truncated
pyramids with square base', two of its final computations had to be dropped
(dividing the result by 9 and dividing by 3). Each computation relates to
a different algorithm among the algorithms that are combined, and the
structure of the statement highlights the different statuses of the factors
which are left out. The proof of the correctness of the algorithm for the
truncated pyramid with square base had established that the first part of its
computations yielded the value of 3 pyramids. The proof of the correctness

of the 'procedure for the field with the greatest generality' shows that, before dividing by the product of the denominators, the resulting 'dividend' corresponds to the 'parts of the product'.[23] Note, however, that the order of the division by the product of the denominators and the multiplication by the height was implicitly inverted so that the meaning of the result could be stated in this way. This transformation is valid. Its validity again rests on the fact that the results of divisions are exact. Here too, this transformation is one that may be applied to the list of operations as such in order to change it into another list. In other passages, Liu Hui brings to light and comments on this inversion, which he calls by the name of '*fan*' (inversion). However, here the inversion is carried out tacitly. We shall come back to it later. In conclusion, we see the operations involved here in determining the 'meaning' (*yi*) of the result of the first part of the algorithm, the correctness of which is to be established. They depend in an essential way on relying on the meaning of previously established algorithms.

The discussion above highlights an interesting fact. If we concentrate on the first section of the algorithm determining the volume of the truncated pyramid with circular base, we can view it from two angles. When seeking to uncover its 'meaning', it is necessary to restore the opposed operations that cancel each other and consider algorithm 2. However, when using the section as a list of operations for computing, it is more rational to delete the unnecessary operations, as in algorithm 2'. Although both algorithms yield the same result, the algorithm for computing differs from the algorithm for shaping the meaning (*yi*) of the result. This is a crucial fact for proving the correctness of procedures. Sometimes, the two algorithms coincide, in which case the algorithm is transparent concerning the reasons for which it is correct. The main reason for which it may not be transparent is due precisely to the very transformations that are applied to the list of operations as such, and which interest us in relation to the second line of argumentation.

At this point of our argument, several remarks can be made on the way in which Liu Hui deals with the algorithms found in *The Nine Chapters*. First,

---

[23] Here, an element of argumentation can be retrospectively added to what was said earlier. The 'procedure for the field with the greatest generality' is not referred to by the name of the operation in the commentary we are analysing. Three elements lead us, nevertheless, to the conclusion that such is the procedure that is inserted. First, the situation described is exactly the one for which the procedure was made: multiplying in general and multiplying integers increased by fractions in particular. This is clearly the case envisaged by Liu Hui. In addition, the list of operations to be followed corresponds exactly to that of the 'procedure for the field with the greatest generality'. However, other procedures could be used, as is demonstrated by the 'procedure for more precise *lü*' (CG2004: 194–7). Lastly, the terms *tong* 'make communicate' and *jifen* 'parts of the product' are specifically attached to the arithmetical procedures given in *The Nine Chapters* to deal with integers increased by fractions.

the commentator aims at accounting for the algorithm as described in the Classic – this is part of what we called the third line of argumentation and is interwoven with the first two lines. For instance, in this case, he seems to be attempting to account for the reason why the algorithm does not begin with a division by 3, or, more directly, for why the algorithm is not transparent, in the sense just introduced.[24] This question will lead him to formulate motivations which explain the transformation of the algorithm he obtained into the algorithm actually provided by *The Nine Chapters*, which yields the same result.

Second, the reason Liu Hui adduces for that is the possibility that the division by 3 *may* introduce results with fractions. Here this detail reveals a key dimension in his expectations towards *The Nine Chapters*. If we recall the data of problem 5.11, the circumference of the lower circle is 3 *zhang*. However, the case Liu Hui considers, to reconstitute the motivations of the author(s) of the procedure, is one in which 'none' of the two circumferences is 'exhausted' by the division by 3. This indicates that he believes the authors considered other cases than that of the problem in *The Nine Chapters* in order to shape the procedure. Hence the commentator does not imagine that the Classic provides algorithms for solving only the particular problem after which they are given. He expects the algorithm to have been generally established and consequently he accounts for the correctness of the general algorithm as well as its form.[25] To be more precise, Liu Hui seems to be considering that, in their shaping of the procedure, the author(s) of the procedure took into account all cases in which the data for the circumferences would be integers. His reasoning would otherwise have been formulated in a different way. Such hints regarding the types of numbers that may constitute data for a given algorithm would be extremely important to gather if we want to understand better what generality meant in ancient China and how the possibility of covering cases with different types of numbers was handled. It would be all the more important in the context of the argument I want to make in this chapter, for establishing a link between the 'algebraic proof in an algorithmic context' and the reflection about numbers.

Third, it appears that the commentator believes that, when possible, the author(s) of procedures avoided unnecessarily complex computations, in particular computations with fractions. He regularly repeats this hypothesis

---

[24] On the basis of additional evidence, Chemla 1991 argues in favour of the hypothesis that Liu Hui seeks to read reasons accounting for its correctness in the statement of an algorithm. He succeeds in doing so for the algorithm which computes the volume of the truncated pyramid with square base.

[25] This is also what is shown by other passages of his commentary; see Chemla 2003.

about their motivations, when he accounts for why the order of a division and a multiplication was inverted with regard to the order given by the reasoning he offered. The rewriting of lists of operations that the author(s) of procedures undertook may hence be motivated, in his view, by the actual handling of computations. This is how Liu Hui explains the form of the beginning of the procedure. As we shall discuss below, several specific features of the mathematics of ancient China can be correlated with this concern. In our case, the fact which the commentator brings to light in this respect is that the procedure offered by *The Nine Chapters* has the property of working uniformly for all the data. As mentioned above, this property was stressed by Li Chunfeng as characterizing the 'procedure for the field with the greatest generality'. It would then be transferred to the algorithm for determining the volume of the examined truncated pyramid. Note that, in contrast to the former, for which uniformity was obtained at the expense of simplicity, in the latter case, no artificial step is necessary to guarantee a uniform treatment of all the possible data. It is to be noted, however, that uniformity is not a property shared by all the algorithms in *The Nine Chapters*. The procedure given for dividing between quantities having fractions, which will be discussed below, is a counterexample, in which the latter cases are reduced to the former ones.

These remarks lead to an observation that is essential for the argument made in this chapter. If we observe the transformation between the first part of algorithm 1 and that of algorithm 2′, what was carried out was an inversion in the order of divisions and multiplications. This transformation, accomplished in the algorithm as a list of operations, was actually carried out and accounted for through a procedure dealing with quantities with fractions. A link is thereby established between a transformation that operates on lists of operations as such and an algorithm for executing arithmetical operations on quantities with fractions. This link will be more generally the focus of Part II of this chapter. Furthermore, as has already been stressed, this decomposition of the transformation that leads from the first section of algorithm 1 to that of algorithm 2′ highlighted the necessity of relying on the possibility of cancelling two opposed operations that were placed one after the other. This is how the transformation appears to be carried out in Liu Hui's view. In Part II, we shall also come back to this point.

Without entering into all the details, let us give a sense of what the flow of computations on the surface for computing looks like for the algorithms considered. We can represent the main structure of the initial section of algorithm 1 – which amounts to that of algorithm 2 – as the following sequence of states (Figure 13.5).

Dividing   Multiplying by one another

(Procedure for the field with the greatest generality)

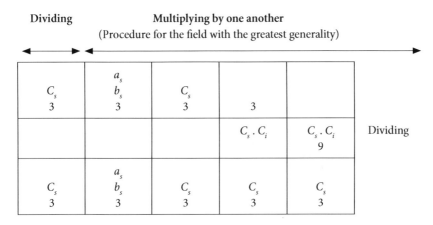

Figure 13.5 The basic structure of algorithms 1 and 2, for the truncated pyramid with square base.

Multiplying by one another   Dividing

C_s		
	3	
	$C_s \cdot C_i$	$\dfrac{C_s \cdot C_i}{9}$
C_i	$\dfrac{C_i}{3}$	$\dfrac{C_i}{3}$

Dividing

Figure 13.6 The basic structure of algorithm 2′, which begins the computation of the volume sought for.

The beginning of algorithm 2′ would instead yield Figure 13.6.

Postfixing operations to an algorithm within the context of the proof

Let us now return to Liu Hui's commentary on the algorithm determining the volume of the truncated pyramid with circular base and read its following section. The commentator's interpretation of the result of the first section of the algorithm as 'parts of the product (*jifen*) of 3 truncated pyramids with square base' produces a foundation upon which his reasoning can be built. He writes (transformation 4):

Here, one must multiply the denominators, 3, by one another – hence one obtains 9 – to make the divisor, and divide by this. If, in addition to this, one divides by 3, one obtains the volume of the truncated pyramid with square base.

The first division ends the 'procedure for the field with the greatest generality'. The reason underlying its correctness is not mentioned here. The second division ends the algorithm for computing the volume of the truncated pyramid with square base. Mentioning the two divisions in succession allows making sense of the operations step by step, and hence, globally, of the result. Moreover, this will prove important for the following part of the reasoning.[26]

As a consequence, by successive transformations of algorithm 1, the following algorithm (algorithm 3) is obtained for determining the volume of the truncated pyramid with square base circumscribed to the desired truncated pyramid with circular base:

Multiplications	Division	Division
Sum	by 9	by 3
Multiplication by h		

$$C_i \longrightarrow (C_iC_s + C_i^2 + C_s^2)h \longrightarrow (C_iC_s + C_i^2 + C_s^2)h/9 \longrightarrow [(C_iC_s + C_i^2 + C_s^2)h/9]/3$$
$$C_s$$

The appending of two operations to yield algorithm 3 belonged to the first line of argumentation, as does the next transformation to be effected. Indeed, once he has obtained an algorithm for the truncated pyramid with square base, Liu Hui turns to considering how to derive the volume of the truncated pyramid with circular base on the basis of the volume of the circumscribed pyramid. It is by a fifth transformation of the obtained list of operations that he achieves this goal: operations are to be postfixed to the former sequence to get an algorithm yielding the volume of the truncated pyramid with circular base inscribed in the obtained pyramid with square base. Liu Hui first makes a geometrical statement (my emphasis):

To *look for* the volume of the truncated pyramid with circular base, when knowing the truncated pyramid with square base, is *also* like to look for the surface of the circle at the centre of the surface of the square.

Two words deserve some attention here, which is why I emphasized them. The first one is 'to look for' (*qiu*). It regularly introduces the task that

---

[26] Below, we shall meet with cases in which Liu Hui combines two divisions that follow each other. The fact that he does in some cases and does not in others relates clearly to the argument he is making. This feature highlights how carefully the relationship between shaping a procedure and arguing for the correctness of a procedure is handled.

the outline of a problem asks to fulfil. This detail indicates that, in ancient China, algorithms may have been conceived as composed by combining a sequence of algorithms which carry out a sequence of tasks, the completion of which was identified as leading to the solution of a given kind of problem. This corresponds quite well to the kind of reasoning Liu Hui has been developing so far in the commentary we are reading.

The second word to be stressed is 'also'. It refers to the fact that the same argument was given earlier in the commentary, after problem 5.9, when Liu Hui was deriving the algorithm for the volume of the cylinder from that of the volume of the parallelepiped. This 'also' thus indicates that the proofs are not carried out in isolation from each other, but rather in parallel with each other – a fact that we have already stressed above.

In fact, after problem 1.33, devoted to computing the area of a circle, Liu Hui had derived the values of 3 to 4 as corresponding *lüs* for the area of the circle and that of the circumscribed square, respectively, from the values of 3 to 1 for expressing the relationship between the circumference of the circle and its diameter. In the commentary on problem 5.9, these values were declared to allow the transformation of the volume of a cylinder into that of the circumscribed parallelepiped. The same statement is made here, and the geometrical assertion is followed by its translation into algorithms (transformation 5): the same multiplication by 3 and division by 4 ensure the transformation from the truncated pyramid with square base into the truncated pyramid with circular base. As Liu Hui puts it:

Hence, if one multiplies by the *lü* of the circle, 3, and divides by the *lü* of the square, 4, one obtains the volume of the truncated pyramid with circular base.

As a consequence, at this point of his commentary, Liu Hui has determined a correct algorithm yielding the volume of the desired truncated pyramid, which ends the first line of argumentation. Algorithm 4 correctly yields the value of the desired magnitude.

Multiplications	Division	Division	**Multiplication by 3**
Sum	by 9	by 3	
Multiplication by h			

$C_i \longrightarrow (C_iC_s + C_i^2 + C_s^2)h \longrightarrow [(C_iC_s + C_i^2 + C_s^2)h/9]/3 \longrightarrow [[(C_iC_s + C_i^2 + C_s^2)h/9]/3].3$

C_s

Division by 4

$\longrightarrow [[[(C_iC_s + C_i^2 + C_s^2)h/9]/3].3]/4$

Transforming algorithms as lists of operations

The goal, from this point onwards, is the transformation of this algorithm 4, *qua algorithm*, into the one for which the correctness is to be established, that is, the one provided by *The Nine Chapters* for the volume of the truncated pyramid with circular base. Liu Hui hence resumes reasoning along the second line of argumentation. Considering the list of operations obtained by the last transformation (5), he remarks:

> But, earlier, in order to look for the volume of the truncated pyramid with square base, we had divided by 3. Now, in order to look for the volume of the truncated pyramid with circular base, one must also multiply by 3. Since the two *denominators* are equal, hence they *compensate* each other.

Before clarifying the italicized terms, let us observe the argument made here. The commentator clearly considers the operations that follow each other as a *list* and carries out a transformation of this list as such. The algorithm yielding the circumscribed truncated pyramid with square base, he remarks, ended by a division by 3, whereas transformation 4 first appended to it a multiplication by 3.[27] Liu Hui thus suggests deleting both from the list of operations, thereby carrying out transformation 6. It can be represented as follows (Figure 13.7):

Multiplications / Sum / Multiplication by h — Division by 9 — ~~Division by 3~~ — ~~Multiplications by 3~~

$C_i, C_s \longrightarrow (C_i C_s + C_i^2 + C_s^2)h \longrightarrow [(C_i C_s + C_i^2 + C_s^2)h/9]$~~$/3 \longrightarrow [(C_i C_s + C_i^2 + C_s^2)h/9]/3.3$~~

Division by 4 $\longrightarrow [(C_i C_s + C_i^2 + C_s^2)h/9]/4$

Figure 13.7 Algorithm 5: cancelling opposed multiplication and division.

Transformation 6 modifies the list of operations without altering the meaning or the value of the result. We meet here with the same phenomenon as above. Bringing to light the opposed multiplication and division was crucial to interpreting the meaning (*yi*) of the result. However, when viewing the list of operations as a means for computing, the two operations appear unnecessary. This is how Liu Hui progressively accounts for the shape of the algorithm found in the Classic.

[27] Let us stress, in the previous quotation, the use of the same term when referring to the two algorithms: 'to look for' (*qiu*). This confirms the part played by problems in decomposing the task to be fulfilled into sub-tasks conceived of as problems.

Although the transformation seems comparable to transformation 3 discussed earlier, it is worth noticing that Liu Hui refers to the two in different terms. Earlier, the commentator spoke of 'backtracking' and in correlation with this he stressed the fact that the values of the circumferences had been restored while their meaning had changed. In contrast to this, Liu Hui stresses here the fact that the two operations 'compensate each other' (*xiang zhunzhe*). The emphasis is placed on the cancellation of their effects as operations. This gives a hint of the subtlety of the formulation of the reasoning.

The validity of this transformation is not to be taken for granted. It is again guaranteed by the fact that, in ancient China, the result of a division was given exactly, that is, as an integer increased by a fraction. We shall show below that the commentator links these two facts.

The quoted sentence makes use of another expression, which requires further analysis: the argument given for establishing the conclusion that the two operations 'compensate each other' is formulated in the form that 'the two *denominators* are equal'. Why is the word 'denominator' (*mu*) used here? There appears no reason explaining in which sense the '3' with which one multiplies can be considered as a 'denominator'. Let us stress that, in the other passage in which the same reasoning is developed, after problem 5.25, the same term recurs, which indicates that this is not due to an error in the transmission of the text. These occurrences seem to imply that this term *mu* has another technical meaning that I was unable to elucidate. This is why, before it is found out, I translate the term in the usual way. However, consequently, a very striking fact must be noted: in the commentaries, there is only one other occurrence of this term with exactly this same use, and this usage is found in the commentary establishing the correctness of the algorithm for multiplying fractions.[28] This hint again links the line of argumentation we are examining with the algorithms for carrying out arithmetical computations with fractions. The point is worth noting, in relation to the argument to be developed in Part II of this chapter.

Another detail casts some light on the way in which Liu Hui operates. If we observe the list of operations that Liu Hui is transforming, we can see that it first enumerates a division by 9, where the '3's' involved stand for π; second, a division by 3 corresponding to the computation of the volume of the circumscribed pyramid; and, thirdly, a multiplication by 3, where the '3' again stands for π. One might have expected that the proof would cancel a multiplication and a division by 3 that would both be linked to π.[29] The

---

[28] See *mu* 'denominator' in my glossary, CG2004.
[29] I am indebted to Anne Michel-Pajus for this remark.

expectation is all the more natural when we know that in a second part of his commentary, Liu Hui relies on his proof to yield a new algorithm that makes use of his own values for π. However, such is not the case. The commentator cancels operations that follow each other. This seems to indicate that he takes care not to modify arbitrarily the order in which the reasoning led to establishing the operations constituting an algorithm. Such a detail reinforces the hypothesis that he is working on lists of operations as such, being careful to make explicit the transformations applied to them and the motivations for using them.[30] There is, however, another way of accounting for this detail, i.e. that Liu Hui thinks that he recovers the reasoning followed by the author(s) of the Classic.

By transformation 6, a list of operations was remodelled into another list, equivalent in that it yielded the same result. Transformation 7 continues along the second line of argumentation, even though it consists of applying a different operation to algorithm 5. Liu Hui goes on as follows:

We thus only multiply the *lü* of the square, 4, by the denominator 9, hence we obtain 36, and we divide at a stroke.

Liu Hui designates the two factors by which one should still divide to end algorithm 5, i.e. 4 and 9, by the part they were shown to play in the reasoning (*lü* of the square, denominator). Instead of carrying out the divisions successively, transformation 7 suggests 'dividing in combination' (*lianchu*), which I translated as 'dividing at a stroke'. This implies transforming the end of algorithm 5 into the multiplication of the two divisors by each other and dividing by the product.

With the expression of 'dividing at a stroke', we meet with a technical term that recurs regularly in the commentaries but is not to be found in *The Nine Chapters*. We may account for this by noticing that it is a designation of the division typical of the mode of proving the correctness of algorithms on which the chapter concentrates.

Two successive divisions were accounted for, each being shown to be necessary for its own reasons. As above, Liu Hui had to dissociate them to bring to light the meaning of the result of the algorithm he shaped. However, viewing the list of operations as a means for computing leads to modifying the way of carrying them out, namely, by transforming the end of algorithm 5. Liu Hui thereby accounts for the form of the algorithm given by *The Nine Chapters*, by highlighting that the two operations were

---

[30] This conclusion should be nuanced by the remark made above concerning the change in the order of the multiplication by *h* and the division by 9.

grouped into a unique division. The technical term chosen for this division refers to the motivation of the effected transformation. As a consequence, algorithm 5

$$C_p C_s \longrightarrow (C_i C_s + C_i^2 + C_s^2)h \longrightarrow (C_i C_s + C_i^2 + C_s^2)h/9 \longrightarrow [(C_i C_s + C_i^2 + C_s^2)h/9]/4$$

is transformed into the algorithm

$$C_p C_s \longrightarrow (C_i C_s + C_i^2 + C_s^2)h \longrightarrow (C_i C_s + C_i^2 + C_s^2)h/36$$

which is equivalent to it and identical to the desired algorithm. This was what was to be obtained: the correctness of the procedure provided by *The Nine Chapters* is established. The way in which the proof was conducted highlights in the best way possible how the activities of shaping an algorithm and proving the correctness are intertwined.

Such is the type of proof that I suggest designating as 'algebraic proof in an algorithmic context'. It is characterized by the articulation of the three lines of argumentation I distinguished. However, clearly, the second line of argumentation is the one that is specific to it. Several points need to be made clear to explain the expression by which I suggest referring to this kind of proof.

First, to justify the fact that I speak here of an 'algorithmic context', it will be useful to compare what we analysed with a translation in modern terms. The reasoning we followed can be rewritten as the following sequence of steps:

$$V = \frac{\left[\dfrac{C_i C_s}{3 \cdot 3} + \left(\dfrac{C_i}{3}\right)^2 + \left(\dfrac{C_s}{3}\right)^2\right].h}{3} \cdot \frac{3}{4}$$

$$= \frac{\left[\dfrac{C_i C_s + C_i^2 + C_s^2}{9}\right].h}{3} \cdot \frac{3}{4}$$

$$= \frac{\left[C_i C_s + C_i^2 + C_s^2\right].h}{9} \cdot \frac{1}{4}$$

$$= \frac{\left[C_i C_s + C_i^2 + C_s^2\right].h}{36}$$

The first line encapsulates the first line of reasoning, which establishes an algorithm fulfilling the task required by the terms of the problem. In the following lines, corresponding to the second line of argumentation, equalities are reshaped, whereas, in the commentaries, what is rewritten are instead algorithms.[31] In correlation with this, in the latter case, intermediary sequences of operations are provided with an interpretation

Second, why do I speak of an 'algebraic proof'? I take it as a typical element of this kind of proof that it involves transforming lists of operations *as such* – the second line of argumentation – and that the validity of these transformations should be addressed. If we observe the transformations leading from one line to the next one in the modern version of the reasoning, sequences of operations are reshaped, with complete generality, and this leads to transforming a correct equality in a correct way into an equality that is equivalent and was desired. I claim that, although in a different form, the same mathematical work is carried out on the basis of algorithms in the commentary we analysed. This is the element that I recognize to be present in the ancient Chinese text and for which I retain the expression under discussion. This interpretation implies a use of the term 'algebraic' in relation to operating on the operations themselves.

Let us, at this point, recapitulate the transformations that we identified by means of our analysis and that were carried out on a list of operations. We had:

- I. Eliminating inverse operations that follow each other

$$
\begin{array}{llll}
\text{Division by 3} & \text{Make communicate} & \text{Multiplications, sums, etc.} \\
C_i \xrightarrow{} D_i = b_i = \dfrac{a_i}{3} \xrightarrow{} & 3a_i + b_i = C_i \xrightarrow{} (\ldots\ldots\ldots) \xrightarrow{} \\
C_s \qquad\quad D_s = b_s = \dfrac{a_s}{3} & 3a_s + b_s = C_s
\end{array}
$$

$$\text{has been transformed into}$$

Multiplications, sums, etc.
$$
\begin{array}{l}
C_i \xrightarrow{} (\ldots\ldots\ldots) \xrightarrow{} \\
C_s
\end{array}
$$

---

[31] In an algebraic proof of a more general type, transformations can be applied to both sides of the sign of equality in parallel, that is, to two lists of operations simultaneously. The formulas used recall those stated by Li Ye in his *Sea-Mirror of the Circle Measurements* (1248), where formulas express the fact that different operations on different entities lead to the same result.

- II. Inverting the order of divisions and multiplications

Dividing by 9   Multiplying by h

$$C_p\,C_s \text{——}(\ldots)\text{——}> (C_iC_s + C_i^2 + C_s^2)/9 \text{————}> [(C_iC_s + C_i^2 + C_s^2)/9]\cdot h$$

has been transformed into

Multiplying by h Dividing by 9

$$C_p\,C_s \text{——}(\ldots)\text{——}> (C_iC_s + C_i^2 + C_s^2)h \text{————}> (C_iC_s + C_i^2 + C_s^2)h/9$$

We saw that this very inversion had been carried out tacitly in the commentary we examined but it is made explicit in other commentaries and referred to by the technical term *fan*.[32] Moreover, I underlined the fact that the transformation between algorithm 1 and algorithm 2′ could be conceived of as belonging to this type.

- III. Combining divisions

Dividing by 9   Dividing by 4

$$(C_iC_s + C_i^2 + C_s^2)h \text{——}> (C_iC_s + C_i^2 + C_s^2)h/9 \text{——}> [(C_iC_s + C_i^2 + C_s^2)h/9]/4$$

has been transformed into

Dividing by 36

$$(C_iC_s + C_i^2 + C_s^2)h \text{——}> (C_iC_s + C_i^2 + C_s^2)h/36$$

Now, several questions present themselves with respect to these transformations, which appear to be the fundamental transformations needed to argue along the line of argumentation examined. First, how were they conceived of? Moreover, what guaranteed their validity? Furthermore, did the commentators consider this question and in which ways? Addressing these issues is essential to determine in which sense, in these commentaries, we may have an 'algebraic proof in an algorithmic context'. As announced in the introduction, I shall argue that a link was established in ancient China between the validity of these fundamental transformations and the kind of numbers with which one operated. Moreover, in what follows, I intend to show that the commentaries on the algorithms provided by *The Nine Chapters* for carrying out arithmetical operations on numbers containing fractions can be interpreted as addressing the question of the validity of the fundamental transformations, in the ways in which these transformations

---

[32] See the commentaries on the 'procedure of suppose' (rule of three), at the beginning of Chapter 2; the procedure for unequal sharing, at the beginning of Chapter 3; the procedures following problems 5.21 and 5.22.

were conceived. These suggestions seem to be natural on the basis of the previous discussion. Indeed, on several occasions, we observed the connection between transformations applied to a list of operations and algorithms carrying out arithmetical operations on quantities with fractions. We now need to focus on the latter procedures to analyse this connection systematically.

II Grounding the validity of the fundamental transformations of lists of operations

The first hint that the commentators link the validity of the fundamental transformations to the kinds of numbers used in them is found when Liu Hui accounts for why, in his view, *The Nine Chapters* introduces quadratic irrationals. We shall hence follow him in his argumentation.

Eliminating inverse operations that follow each other

After problem 4.16, *The Nine Chapters* describes a general and abstract 'procedure for extracting the square root'.[33] In a first part of the procedure, an algorithm is provided for determining the root of an integer digit by digit. It is followed, in a second part, by a procedure dealing with quantities containing fractions, which reduces the problem to the case dealt with in the first part. The commentary in which we are interested discusses a statement that concludes the first part of the procedure and asserts:

IF, BY EXTRACTION, THE (NUMBER) IS NOT EXHAUSTED, THAT MEANS THAT ONE CANNOT EXTRACT THE (ITS) ROOT, HENCE, ONE MUST NAME IT (i.e., the number) WITH 'SIDE'.

Three historians, independent from each other, have established that, here, *The Nine Chapters* was addressing the case when the number N, the root of which is sought, was not exhausted when one had reached the digit for the units in the square root. All concluded that *The Nine Chapters* was prescribing, for such cases, that the result be given as 'side of N', which is to be interpreted as meaning 'square root of N'.[34]

---

[33] It relies on a numeration system that is place-valued and decimal. The introduction to Chapter 4 in CG2004: 322–35 analyses its main features. The critical edition and the translation of the piece of commentary discussed can be found in CG2004: 364–6.

[34] Volkov 1985; Li Jimin 1990. As for me, references can be found in Chemla 1997/8 or CG2004. Note that the Classic states, without providing any argument in favour of this assertion, that in these cases the extraction cannot be carried out.

The reason Liu Hui adduces for explaining why it was necessary to give the result in the form of quadratic irrationals, when necessary, is fundamental for our purpose. The commentator first considers a way of providing the result as a quantity of the type integer increased by a fraction but discards it as impossible to use. This leads him to make explicit the constraints that, in his view, the result should satisfy. He writes (my emphasis):

Every time one extracts the root of a number-product[35] to make the side of a square, *the multiplication of this side by itself must in return (huan) restore (fu)* (this number-product).

This sentence is essential: the kind of result to be used is the one that guarantees a property for a sequence of opposed operations. A link is thereby established between the kinds of numbers to be used as results and the possibility of transforming a sequence of two opposed operations. More precisely, the result of the square root extraction must ensure that the sequence of two opposed operations annihilates their effects and restores the original data: their sequence can thereby be deleted.

Why is this important? To suggest answers to this question, one may observe how the results of actual extractions are given in the commentaries. It turns out that, when a commentator is seeking to establish a value, the results of square root extraction are given as approximations.[36] However, the fact that the operation inverse to a square root extraction *restores (fu)* the original number and the meaning of the magnitude to which the extraction was applied is used precisely in the context of an 'algebraic proof in an algorithmic context'.[37] This confirms the link we suggested between the

---

[35] The type of number for which one can extract the square root is a number that, from a conceptual point of view, is a 'product'. This corresponds to a specific concept in Chinese, *ji*, which can designate a number-product, an area, or a volume.

[36] This is the case when the commentator discusses new values for expressing the relationship between the circumference of the circle and its diameter. See the commentary after problem 1.33, CG2004: 178–85. However, this statement must be nuanced. There is a context in which Liu Hui uses quadratic irrationals as such in computations. This is in fact the passage that allows interpretation of the obscure sentence by which *The Nine Chapters* introduces quadratic irrationals. In it, the commentator seeks to assess with precision the ratio between the sphere and the circumscribed cube that Zhang Heng (78–142) derived from his approximation for π, which states that the square on the circumference is to the square on the diameter as 10 is to 1. As I suggested, the use of the irrationals here is driven by the aim of highlighting that Zhang Heng's algorithms were worse than that of *The Nine Chapters*. In the end, Liu Hui introduces an approximation of a square root in the form of an integer to conclude the evaluation. See Chemla and Keller 2002.

[37] The text in question, that is, the commentary after problem 5.28, is discussed in Chemla 1997/8. An outline is provided below, in note 39.

introduction of certain kinds of numbers and the line of proof that made use of transformations carried out on lists of operations.

In fact, the commentary further bears witness to the fact that the link is not merely established for such quantities. Once Liu Hui has introduced the constraint that the result of a square root extraction must satisfy for the cases in which the number N is not exhausted, he examines more closely two results for root extraction in the form of an integer increased by a fraction – one by defect and one by excess. It is revealing that his analysis of the values concerns how they behave when one applies the inverse operation to them but this is not what is most important for us here. The statement by which he concludes his investigation is essential for the comparison it establishes. Liu Hui writes:

One cannot determine its value (i.e. the value of the root). Therefore, it is only when 'one names it (i.e. the number N) with "side"' *that one does not make any mistake (or, that there is no error). This is* analogous to *the fact, when one divides 10 by 3, to take its rest as being 1/3,* one is hence again able to restore (fu) its value. *(My emphasis)*

The mention of this other 'restoring' in the context of the commentary on square root extraction reveals that for quantities of the type of an integer increased by a fraction, it was a property that was also deemed essential. Indeed, the comparison made here between square root extraction and division further confirms the link I seek to document. In his commentary, Liu Hui manifests his understanding that, as kinds of numbers, quadratic irrationals and integers with fractions differ.[38] However, he stresses here the analogy between them *precisely* from the point of view that introducing them as results in both cases allows two opposed operations applied in succession to cancel their effects. In Part I of this chapter, we saw how this cancelling led to deleting such a sequence of operations from the algorithm that was being shaped. It is hence tempting to conclude that, as with quadratic irrationals, Liu Hui linked the introduction of fractions to possibilities of transforming lists of operations as such.

This hypothesis is supported by the fact that the 'restoring' made possible by the introduction of fractions is also evoked and used within the context of 'algebraic proofs' of the type we study. This is easily established by noticing that the concept of *fu* 'restoring' introduced here occurs only in such contexts. This fact confirms, if it were necessary, the correlation between this property shared by various kinds of numbers and the conduct of such

---

[38] See Chemla and Keller 2002.

types of proof.[39] The introduction of such quantities is hence related to a specific perspective on lists of operations as such.

In conclusion, Liu Hui interprets the necessity of introducing fractions and quadratic irrationals as deriving from the necessity of restoring the original value when applying the inverse operation to the result of an operation – this is the only motivation he brings forward. In other words, for the results of divisions or square root extractions – which are conceived

[39] Compare the discussion of the commentary placed after problem 5.28, mentioned above. In it, the commentator successively applies the operation inverse to the last of the operations to the results of a sequence of algorithms. This operation, he states, restores the meaning and value of the last intermediary step. If we represent the sequence of operations as above, we have the following pattern of reasoning. The algorithm known to be correct is the following one:

$$C \xrightarrow{\text{multiplying by itself}} C^2 \xrightarrow{\text{multiplying by } h} C^2 h \xrightarrow{\text{dividing by 12}} V$$

The question is to determine the meaning of the following sequence of operations applied to V:

$$V \xrightarrow{\text{multiplying by 12}} \xrightarrow{\text{dividing by } h} \xrightarrow{\text{extracting the square root}} ?$$

The meaning of the result of the first two steps can be determined as follows:

$$C \xrightarrow{\text{multiplying by itself}} C^2 \xrightarrow{\text{multiplying by } h} C^2 h \xrightarrow{\text{dividing by 12}} V \xrightarrow{\text{multiplying by 12}} C^2 h$$

then

$$C \xrightarrow{\text{multiplying by itself}} C^2 \xrightarrow{\text{multiplying by } h} C^2 h \xrightarrow{\text{dividing by } h} C^2$$

This is correct, because multiplying by 12 restores that to which the division by 12 had been applied. Thereafter, dividing by h restores that to which multiplying by h had been applied. Now, because of the property of square root discussed, we have

$$C \xrightarrow{\text{multiplying by itself}} C^2 \xrightarrow{\text{extracting the square root}} C$$

and the meaning of the result of the following algorithm is established

$$V \xrightarrow{\text{multiplying by 12}} \xrightarrow{\text{dividing by } h} C^2 \xrightarrow{\text{extracting the square root}} \sqrt{12V/h} = C$$

This is how the correctness of the inverse algorithm is established. In the case of problem 5.28, the inverse operations successively applied are a multiplication, a division and a squaring. At each step, the commentator stresses that 'restoring' was achieved. Note that the reasoning implicitly put into play to express the meaning of the first part of algorithm 2' as 'the parts of the product of 3 truncated pyramids with square base' in the passage discussed above can be seen as similar to the one just described. These examples show the relationship of the property of numbers which permits restoration and the conduct of the second line of argumentation with the operation of establishing the meaning (*yi*) of the result of a list of operations.

as a kind of division – the fact that they are exact guarantees that inverse operations which follow each other can be deleted from an algorithm.[40] Yielding exact results perhaps matters less to computations than to proofs: it grounds the validity of one of our three fundamental transformations. Such is the link that is established between the numbers with which one works and the transformations that can be applied to sequences of operations. Because the evidence relating to quadratic irrationals is far less abundant than the evidence involving fractions, for the remaining part of my argumentation, I shall hence focus mainly on the latter.

So far, we can establish that the commentator Liu Hui ascribes the motivation in question to *The Nine Chapters*, thereby demonstrating that he himself makes the connection between the use of some quantities and the validity of a transformation. Can we follow Liu Hui and attribute the same idea to the author(s) of the Classic? The argumentation is delicate and difficult to conclude with certainty. It is true that quantities such as fractions and quadratic irrationals date to the time when *The Nine Chapters* was compiled. In fact, only fractions occur in the *Book of Mathematical Procedures*. As for using such quantities in relation to proofs, so far, our *terminus ante quem* is 263, when Liu Hui completed his commentary. The occurrences of the term 'restoring' or 'returning to' (*fu*) the original value provide interesting clues. The concept is not to be found in *The Nine Chapters*. However, it is attested to in the *Book of Mathematical Procedures*, in contexts where similar concerns can be perceived. Interestingly enough, there, *fu* occurs *only* after the statement of an algorithm for carrying out division or root extraction. After these algorithms, a procedure is then prescribed that aims at 'returning to' the original value. By contrast, *fu* never occurs in a procedure solving a problem. It is always appended to another algorithm and carries out the inverse operation. This is complementary to the idea one may derive from the commentaries on *The Nine Chapters* that there is a link between the way in which the results of division and root extraction are given and an interest in the possibility of restoring the original value.[41] Even

[40] Note that, so far, the link has been established only for multiplications and divisions by integers. The more general case still awaits consideration.

[41] See *fu* in my glossary (CG2004: 924–5). In the *Book of Mathematical Procedures*, one occurrence of *fu* is to be found in the context of the operation of 'detaching the length', which asks to determine the length of a rectangle when its area and its width are given (slips 160–3, Peng Hao 2001: 114). There, the first procedure deals with the case when both the area of the rectangular field and its width are integers. The inverse procedure distinguishes the case when the result is an integer from the one in which it has a fraction. A second procedure considers the case when both data are pure fractions. The algorithm that returns to the original value is that of multiplying fractions. When the width consists of an integer increased by a set of fractions, the operation called 'small width' is carried out by a general procedure,

more interesting is that, although in the *Book of Mathematical Procedures* the aim of restoring is achieved for division, the results of which are always exact, this requirement is not fulfilled for root extraction. The procedure provided for the latter operation gives only approximate results. In other words, we reach an interesting conclusion: the concern for 'restoring', which is explicit for both division and root extraction in the *Book of Mathematical Procedures*, that is, already as early as the second century BCE, apparently existed *before* the solution satisfying it did for root extraction. This seems to indicate that the need for 'restoring' motivated the introduction of a new algorithm for root extraction and the introduction of quantities that would ensure that the result be always exact, as we find them in *The Nine Chapters*, and not the converse. These remarks thus lend support to Liu Hui's thesis that, in *The Nine Chapters*, the introduction of quadratic irrationals and fractions aimed at ensuring that opposed operations cancel each other.

We see how the evidence from the *Book of Mathematical Procedures* helps to avoid misinterpreting the fact that neither the concept of 'returning to' (*fu*) the original value nor the related one of 'backtracking' (*huan*) occur in *The Nine Chapters*. This absence cannot be explained by the fact that these concerns appear only at a later date. Nor, in fact, should the absence be explained by the hypothesis that *The Nine Chapters* was merely a set of recipes without any interest in accounting for the correctness of the algorithms. I have already alluded to the fact that the commentator regularly manifests his expectation that the procedures given by *The Nine Chapters* be transparent on the reasons underlying them.[42] In addition to this, with respect to the point under discussion, if the term *fu* 'restoring' does not occur in *The Nine Chapters*, the Classic makes use of a technical expression that clearly belongs to a set of cognate terms and betrays the same concern: *baochu* 'dividing in return'.[43] For a division to be prescribed in this way indicates the *reason* why it is carried out: the expression points out the

---

again followed by an algorithm explicitly aiming at 'returning to' the original value. In this context, there are several occurrences of *fu* (slips 165–6, Peng Hao 2001: 116). However, the text of the procedure for doing so appears to be corrupted. The last occurrence of *fu* is the most interesting for us. It is to be found in the *Book of Mathematical Procedures*, after a procedure giving approximations for extracting square roots (slips 185–6, Peng Hao 2001: 124–5). The case considered in the paradigm to which the procedure is attached is that of an integer that is not a perfect square. The result is given as an approximation by an integer increased by a fraction. However, it is asked to return to the original value. The end of the slip reads: 'one restores it like in the procedure for detaching the width'. In other words, not only is the concern of *fu* common to the two contexts of division and root extraction, but also the procedures for carrying it out.

42   See notes 3 and 24.

43   See, for instance, the second part of the algorithm for square root extraction.

fact that a value was used earlier in the flow of computations, that it was interpreted as having been expanded by an unnecessary factor, and that the 'division in return' compensates for this by cancelling the factor. In dealing with the proof of the correctness, the commentary usually brings to light a pattern in the way in which the algorithm is accounted for, thereby echoing the formulation of the procedure in the Classic. Such divisions highlight an interesting point, suggesting a hypothesis to account for why *fu* does not occur in *The Nine Chapters*.

So far, we have shown that Liu Hui establishes a link between the introduction of kinds of numbers expressing the results of divisions and root extractions, on the one hand, and the fact that the sequence of a division and the multiplication inverse to it restored the original value, on the other hand. This link coordinated perfectly with situations we met in the example analysed in Part I of this chapter, where this property was twice used to explain why pairs of operations were deleted from the final algorithm. However, situations in which one 'divides in return' reveal other ways in which the annihilation of the effects of a pair of two opposed operations by each other can be put into play in an algorithm. In such cases, the two operations do not both disappear from the algorithm. This is precisely why, when prescribing one of them, *The Nine Chapters* can refer to the reason for using it. By contrast, since the operation of 'restoring' is disclosed when one accounts for an algorithm but not when one describes it, the fact may explain why the term *fu* does not occur in the Classic.

Establishing the validity of fundamental operations and the arithmetical operations on parts

In fact, one of the divisions examined in Part I of the chapter is of the kind of a 'division in return'. When, in algorithm 3, a division by 9 is prescribed, it echoes the fact that earlier in the computations, instead of multiplying diameters, the algorithm multiplied their triple.[44] Liu Hui does not use specific terminology that would indicate its nature as a 'division in return'. Like *The Nine Chapters*, he more generally indicates the point only occasionally. However, in this case, the division by 9 is part of the 'procedure for the field

---

[44] Perhaps the distinction between the two types of situation is grasped by the distinction which Liu Hui introduces between 'backtracking' (*huan*) and 'compensating each other' (*xiang zhunzhe*). If this is the case, a relation would be introduced between various types of cancellation of opposed multiplication and division. In any event, although the distinction is important, the fundamental reason underlying the fact that the effects of the operations eliminate each other is the same: it relies on the premiss that the exact results of division are given.

with the greatest generality'. And the nature of the division as being 'in return' is highlighted in the commentaries, precisely when they establish the correctness of this other algorithm.

This brings us back to the thesis that we aim at establishing here: that is, that the reasoning which accounts for the validity of the fundamental transformations identified in Part I may have to be read from the commentaries on the procedures for carrying out arithmetical operations on numbers with fractions. We saw that the simple fact of introducing fractions was essential to accounting for the validity of the first fundamental transformation. Computing with fractions proves essential for the validity of the other two transformations.

When introducing transformation II, I already stressed the link between transforming sequences of operations (in that case, inverting the order of division and multiplication) and describing algorithms for computing with quantities having fractions (inserting the 'procedure for the field with full generality'). In the remaining part of this chapter, I shall argue for my main thesis by showing that the validity of transformations II and III can be interpreted as being treated in the commentaries dealing with the correctness of algorithms given for multiplying and dividing between quantities having fractions, respectively. To do so, we shall discuss them in the order in which they are presented in *The Nine Chapters*, since, interestingly enough, it appears to be also the relevant order of the underpinning reasons. We shall hence deal first with division in relation to transformation III, and then turn to multiplication in relation to transformation II. Note that all the procedures that allow the execution of arithmetical operations with fractions are systematically provided in Chapter 1 of *The Nine Chapters*.

One point will appear to be central in this discussion: the relationship between the pair numerator and denominator and the pair dividend and divisor.[45] Let us then examine further this relationship as a preliminary to the following subsections of this chapter. In Part I, we recalled that, in ancient China, fractions, conceived of as a pair of a numerator and a denominator, were introduced as the result of division. As we showed in Figure 13.3, dividend and divisor were arranged in an orderly fashion on the surface for computing and, at the end of the division, what remained in the position of the dividend and the divisor were read, respectively, as numerator and denominator. The continuity between the two pairs of objects is hence manifest from the point of view of the surface for computing. One can choose to read the two lower lines on the surface either as the

---

[45] In his discussion on fractions, Li Jimin 1990: 62–91 stresses this relationship and discusses the algorithms for dividing and multiplying that we analyse below.

dividend and divisor of a division to be carried out, or as the numerator and denominator of a completed division. Both interpretations will be used in the commentaries examined below. The fact that the operation of division and the expression of a fraction are set up in the same way evokes the identity of their representations in modern notations. However, two differences should be stressed. First, in ancient China, the fundamental concept of quantity was not that of a general fraction – a rational number, if you will – but that of an integer increased by a fraction smaller than 1, which is precisely the result of a division on the surface. Fractions were just a component of them. Second, in our case, we do not have, on the surface, notations for 'objects', but rather 'operational notations', i.e. notations on which operations are carried out. The continuity just emphasized derives from the fact that, following the flow of a division, we go from one to the other and back again. Indeed, the application of the inverse multiplication to the final configuration of a division restores the division one started with, exactly as it was originally set up (see Figure 13.4). But, in the case of adding up fractions, the corresponding numerator and denominator are placed on the same line horizontally, in such a way that, in the end, the result of the addition is yielded in three lines consisting of an integer, a numerator and a denominator.[46]

Seen from another angle, a numerator and a denominator compose a quantity and are essentially dependent on each other. In ancient China, they were both conceived of as constituted of the same 'parts' *fen* of a unit, which could either be abstract or not.[47] The size of the part was determined by the denominator, which amounted to the number of parts into which the unit was cut. As for the numerator, it was understood as consisting of a multiplicity of such parts. In contrast to this, a dividend and a divisor are, to start with, separate entities, which happen to be brought into relation when they become functions in the same operation of division. This operation of bringing entities into relation with each other seems to have been deemed essential in ancient China, as we shall see below. As regards the entities considered, at that point, they become linked in a way that makes them share properties with the pair of a numerator and a denominator. This parallel is regularly stressed by the commentaries.

The first example of this kind is found in the commentary glossing the name of the operation of 'simplifying parts' – the first operation on

---

[46] Compare Li Jimin 1982b: 204–5, especially; Chemla 1996, where I reconstruct operational notations in a different way.

[47] When the fraction was appended to an integer, its numerator and denominator were made of parts of the smallest unit used in the expression of the integer.

fractions discussed in *The Nine Chapters*. There, the commentary discusses the reasons why, once fractions are introduced, it is a valid operation to divide – or to multiply – both the numerator and the denominator by the same number to transform the expression of the fraction. This property is required in order for the 'procedure for simplifying parts' to be correct. The validity of the operation is approached from the perspective that the numerator and the denominator are constituted of parts of the same size. Multiplying them by the same number *n* is interpreted as a dissection of each part into *n* finer and equal parts – a process called 'complexification', and the operation opposite to the 'simplification' that the commentator introduces. Conversely, a simultaneous division of the numerator and the denominator by *n* leads to uniting the parts composing them, *n* at a time, and getting coarser parts. This does not change the quantity as such, but just its inner structuring and its expression. Thus the commentary can conclude: 'Although, hence, their expressions differ, when it comes to making a quantity, this amounts to the same.'[48] Note that, from the point of view of the operations involved, the reasoning establishes the validity of another mode of inserting a multiplication and a division opposed to each other in the course of an algorithm.

What is important is that, immediately afterwards, this question of multiplying and dividing conjointly numerator and denominator is extended to the case of dividend and divisor. The commentator writes: 'Dividend and divisor are deduced one from the other.' Once the two entities are placed in relation to each other, as functions of a division, the same reasoning then applies. One can break up or assemble units in the same way. However, the difference between the case of the fraction and the general case is that dividend and divisor 'often have (parts) that are of different size'. The dividend, for instance, may have an integer and a fraction. Its expression would then include at least two types of units. Both terms of the division may also have different fractions. 'This is why', the commentator concludes, 'those who make a procedure (a procedure generalizing simplification?) first deal with all the parts.' This will require a technique, introduced immediately afterwards, related to the adding up of fractions. On this basis, the question will be taken up again in the context of dividing between quantities having fractions, for which all the necessary ingredients will be available. Thereby, the parallel between the pair of numerator and denominator and the pair of dividend and divisor will be completed.

[48] To be precise, part of the above discussion is held in the commentary on the algorithm following the 'procedure for simplifying parts', i.e. the 'procedure for gathering parts', which allows adding up fractions. Compare, respectively, CG2004: 156–7, 158–61.

We can now turn to examining in greater detail the relationship between proving the correctness of procedures dealing with fractions and establishing the validity of transformations II and III. To do so, we shall have to analyse new samples of proof contained in our Chinese sources. This will give us the opportunity to describe further the specificities of the practice of proof to which our documents bear witness.

Proving the correctness of the general algorithm for division

Let us examine the way in which, in his commentary, Liu Hui establishes that the 'procedure for directly sharing' is correct, before considering why this argument can be interpreted as related to the validity of transformation III.[49] *The Nine Chapters* introduces the algorithm for dividing between quantities with fractions after the two following problems:

(1.17) Suppose one has 7 persons sharing 8 units of cash and 1/3 of a unit of cash. One asks how much a person gets.
Answer: a person gets 1 unit of cash 4/21 of unit of cash.
(1.18) Suppose again one has 3 persons and 1/3 of a person sharing 6 units of cash, 1/3 and 3/4 of a unit of cash. One asks how much a person gets.
Answer: a person gets 2 units of cash 1/8 of unit of cash.

In the first problem, the quantity that is to become the dividend contains one fraction, whereas the second problem leads to both the dividend and the divisor having fractions. The fact that the dividend even contains two fractions is remarkable. Interestingly enough, such quantities, in which an integer is followed by a sequence of fractions, occur only in problems related to similar divisions.[50] We shall see that this is linked to the fact that Liu Hui uses the operations introduced in his commentary on the addition of fractions for his proof.

These two problems are in fact the first ones in Chapter 1 for which the data are neither pure integers nor pure fractions. Moreover, they are the first problems in which the fractions derive from sharing a unit that is not abstract. Furthermore, problem 1.18 mixes together fractions of different

---

[49] The critical edition and the translation of this piece of commentary can be found in CG2004: 166–9.

[50] In addition to the situation examined here, this also designates problems linked to the 'procedure for the small width', which opens Chapter 4. The procedure provides another way of carrying out the division. For comparison, I refer the reader to the introduction to Chapter 4 in CG2004. The interpretation of the 'procedure for directly sharing' requires an argumentation that I developed in Chemla 1992 (I do not repeat the bibliography given in this earlier publication).

kinds of units – cash and persons. In correlation with these changes, the algorithm described is of a type that breaks with previous procedures.[51] Let us translate how it reads before providing an interpretation:

DIRECTLY SHARING.
PROCEDURE: ONE TAKES THE QUANTITY OF PERSONS AS DIVISOR, THE QUANTITY OF UNITS OF CASH AS DIVIDEND AND ONE DIVIDES THE DIVIDEND BY THE DIVISOR. IF THERE IS ONE TYPE OF PART, ONE MAKES THEM COMMUNICATE. (here comes a commentary by Liu Hui that we shall analyse below) IF THERE ARE SEVERAL TYPES OF PARTS, ONE EQUALIZES THEM AND HENCE MAKES THEM COMMUNICATE. (second part of Liu Hui's commentary)

The procedure hence presents itself as one that covers all possible (rational) cases for the data. The organization of the set of problems distinguishes between cases when the data are both integers (case 1), cases when they both contain only one type of denominator (case 2), and cases where there appear several distinct denominators (case 3; problem 1.18 illustrates which situations may occur in this case).

The fundamental case is case 1. It is solved by the first operation prescribed by the procedure: a simple division.

For problems falling in the category of case 2 (that of problem 1.17), the data can be of the type either $(a + b/c)$ and d, or $(a + b/c)$ and $(d + e/c)$. In the second case, the procedure suggests applying the operation of 'making communicate'. Let us stress that the operation of 'making communicate' is used here for the first time by *The Nine Chapters*. In Part I of this chapter, we encountered the operation in the context of Liu Hui's commentary. There, we saw that this operation was applied to quantities such as $(a + b/c)$ and ensured that a and b shared the same units, thus transforming $(a + b/c)$ into $ac + b$. For the case considered here, it transforms the units of the two integers a and d accordingly, so that the number of units obtained (ac and dc, respectively) share the same size as the corresponding numerators. The quantities $(a + b/c)$ and either d or $(d + e/c)$ are thereby transformed into $ac + b$ and cd (or $cd + e$). The problem is thus reduced to the first case, and the procedure is concluded by a division. In modern symbolism, the procedure can be represented as follows:

$$(a + \frac{b}{c}) / d = (ac + b) / dc$$

$$(a + \frac{b}{c}) / (d + \frac{e}{c}) = (ac + b) / (dc + e)$$

[51] The previous procedures all prescribed operations involving numerators and denominators to yield the result. Clearly the description of the procedure to come is of a different style.

One should not forget, however, that the modern symbolism erases the fact that the two fractions are fractions of units that are of a different nature.

The final case (case 3) is, in turn, reduced to the previous one by the operation of 'equalizing', *tong*.[52] This operation relates to the fractional parts of the quantities, making them share the same denominator ('equalizing them' in terms of parts). The resulting transformation for cases such as that of problem 1.18 can be represented as follows:

$$(a + \frac{b}{c}) / (d + \frac{e}{f} + \frac{g}{h}) = (a + \frac{bfh}{cfh}) / (d + \frac{ech + gfc}{cfh})$$

Once all fractions share the same denominator, we are brought back to case 2, and the problem is solved as above, by 'making' integers and fractions 'communicate'. Such is the complete procedure, the correctness of which Liu Hui sets out to establish in his commentary. Note that the procedure for solving case 3 contains that for solving case 2 which, in turn, embeds that for solving the fundamental case. Liu Hui develops the proof with respect to the whole procedure, that is, the one solving case 3, addressing the operations in the order in which they are carried out in this case.

In the first section, Liu Hui thus addresses the operation that occurs last in the text, i.e. that of 'equalizing'.

He does so by reference to the algorithm for adding up fractions, which he has discussed previously (after problem 1.9). The commentator quotes the first steps of this other procedure for computing *bfh, ech, gfc*, on the one hand, and *cfh* on the other hand, thereby providing a translation of 'equalizing' into operational terms. It thus appears that, to divide in case 3, the operations to be applied first are the same as those by which one starts adding up fractions. In parallel, Liu Hui recalls his interpretation of the 'meaning' of these steps: he had shown that the latter computed a denominator equal for all fractions whereas the former homogenized the numerators so that the value of the original fractions might be preserved. Liu Hui thereby refers the discussion for establishing the 'meaning' of the operation that *The Nine Chapters* calls here 'equalizing' to this other commentary of his, where he showed how the corresponding steps ensured that one 'makes' parts corresponding to different denominators 'communicate'. The algorithms for adding up fractions, on the one hand, and dividing in case 3,

---

[52] To make things simpler, I mark the transcription of the term in pinyin with an apostrophe, to distinguish it from the term that has the same pronunciation *tong* 'make communicate'. For all these terms, I refer the reader to my glossary in CG2004. I argue there that the operation to which 'equalizing' corresponds differs slightly, whether one considers *The Nine Chapters* or its commentaries.

on the other hand, share a common sub-procedure and, in the context of division, which comes second in *The Nine Chapters*, the commentator states the conclusions of his previous analysis without developing the reasoning again.

This stands in contrast to the luxury of details with which Liu Hui discusses the second operation to be considered within the context of division in the following sentences. *The Nine Chapters* prescribes this operation with the same term of 'making them communicate' as the one we discussed above. The term is encountered here for the first time in the Classic proper. However, although the name is the same as the term already discussed, it corresponds here to the prescription of different computations. Following Liu Hui in his analysis, we shall be able to make clear which prescription is meant and why the same term can refer to different operations according to the context.

As above, Liu Hui translates what, in this context, 'making them communicate' amounts to in operational terms. He then brings to light the 'meaning' of the operation in terms of parts. He writes:

With the help of the denominator[53] 'making them communicate' is multiplying by the denominator of the parts the integers (or: integral parts of the quantities) and incorporating these (the results) into the numerators. By multiplying, one disaggregates the integers, thus making the parts of the product (*jifen*). The parts of the product and the numerators hence communicate with each other, this is why one can make them join each other.

Liu Hui hence makes explicit what the operation of 'making them communicate' means for the quantities at hand. In terms of computations, $(a + b/c)$ and $(d + e/c)$ are transformed into $(ac + b)$ and $(dc + e)$, respectively. We recognize the result of the operation as indicated in Part I of this chapter. However, in contrast to that previous occurrence, here the commentator decomposes this transformation into elementary operations and interprets their effects in such a way that he brings to light why *The Nine Chapters* may refer to it as 'make communicate'.

The first operation consists of multiplying the integers a and d by c, thereby transforming them into ac and dc. These quantities are what is first designated here as 'parts of the product', or parts yielded by a multiplication.[54]

---

[53] Note that, whether one is within the context of case 2 or after the equalization in case 3, only a single value remains for all denominators.

[54] We have already discussed the expression *jifen* in Part I of this chapter. In this new context, *jifen* could also be understood as 'accumulated parts', which would give *ji* an ordinary meaning. As we suggested above, *jifen* may be interpreted as referring to what, for us, would be a numerator, in a situation in which the numerator is larger than the denominator. In the

Whatever the literal interpretation of this expression may be, there is no doubt that the result is understood as being of the kind of 'parts', that is, as sharing the same identity as the numerator and the denominator – both of which are a collection of 'parts'. This identification derives from interpreting the 'meaning' of the multiplication, in terms of the situation in which it is applied, as a disaggregation.

As we alluded to above, Liu Hui had already discussed the link between multiplying and disaggregating parts in the context of the addition of fractions. There, after the numerator and denominator were both multiplied by the same number n – an operation he called a 'complexification' – the fraction obtained was interpreted as composed of parts that were n times finer. Moreover, in this other context, different 'sets of parts' (a/b, c/d, . . .) were 'complexified' jointly, that is, in correlation with each other, in such a way that their denominators became equal to (bd . . .) and the parts composing them were identical. Liu Hui interpreted this joint transformation as 'making the parts communicate' and thereby allowing them to be added to each other.

The same link between multiplication and disaggregation recurs here, but in a slightly different way. Through the multiplication, the units composing the integers are interpreted to be dissociated into parts of the same size as the fractional parts. This dissymmetric transformation of the integers alone ensures that the parts forming the two elements of a quantity of the type $a + b/c$ are 'made to communicate' and can be added to each other. It will prove interesting to distinguish here two dimensions in the interpretation of the effect of the operation. On the one hand, with the disaggregation, Liu Hui brings to light a 'material meaning' of the multiplication. On the other hand, he recognizes in this transformation the operation of 'making entities communicate'. In different contexts, the way in which this formal result is achieved may differ. However, from a formal point of view, the action is the same. This is what accounts for the fact that the same name can be used to refer to different actual computations.

In fact, so far, the commentator has considered the operation of 'making entities communicate', prescribed by the Classic for case 2 of the division, only from the point of view of each quantity of the type $a + b/c$ taken separately. As above, each quantity is transformed by the operation into an integral number of parts. However, in case 2 of the 'procedure for directly

case under discussion, the numerator consists of an accumulation of layers of parts equal in number to the denominator, in contrast to the state in which, after the division is carried out, these layers are each transformed into a unit. The glossary in CG2004 discusses why the technical term *jifen* can refer, in some circumstances, to ac and, in others, to $ac + b$.

sharing', this transformation is carried out on the dividend and the divisor *jointly* and the denominators *c* will both be forgotten. The correctness of the procedure can only be established after this other aspect has been accounted for. In the next section of the commentary, Liu Hui turns to address the transformation. Again, it will be dealt with in terms of 'making communicate' and this expression will take on new concrete meanings. Indeed, the argument will show why communication is established not only between components of the same quantity (*a* and *b*/*c*; *d* and *e*/*c*) but also between the dividend and the divisor, contained in the middle and lower parts of the surface for computing. This is how the procedure can be concluded by a division between integers. This remark suggests that, in so doing, Liu Hui is still deploying his interpretation of the meanings he reads in the term 'making communicate', a phrase used here by *The Nine Chapters*.

The correlative transformation of the dividend and the divisor recalls the commentary on the 'procedure for simplifying parts'. We noted above that, in this commentary, Liu Hui had compared the two situations from the point of view that first numerator and denominator, and then dividend and divisor could be transformed in relation to each other. Pointing out a contrast between the two pairs, the commentator had stressed that dividend and divisor could involve 'parts' of different size. We highlighted the fact that, in the context of the addition of fractions, he showed how to transform distinct fractional parts into parts of the same size. However, one aspect of the difference between the two situations has not yet been discussed. We meet it here for the first time, and it appears that it is precisely this difference that Liu Hui addresses now. Following him, we can explain the difference as follows. The simplification or complexification of a fraction implies considering the quantities expressed with respect to the same part jointly. However, the terms of a division can have parts that differ not only in size, but also in nature. In our case, the dividend contains parts of cash while the divisor has parts of persons. It is interesting that, for the operations discussed previously (adding up, subtracting, comparing, computing the average), the data of the problems were all abstract and, in correlation with this, these operations can be applied only to terms that are homogeneous with each other in this respect – they only need to be homogenized with regard to their size. For division, in contrast, the terms can furthermore be of a different nature.[55] This is what the problem shows and what is dealt with from a theoretical and, most importantly, general point of view now.

[55] Li Chunfeng's commentary on the name of the operation, 'directly sharing', may address this difference. We shall come back to it below. Note that the same remark holds true for 'multiplying parts'.

The key point that Liu Hui stresses is that by the very fact that these quantities are taken as dividend and divisor, they are 'put in relation'. By this act, a relationship is established between them, which has operational consequences. Here, the commentator first introduces the concept of *lü* which precisely characterizes the situation created: 'Whenever quantities are given/put in relation with each other, one calls them *lü*.'

In the case we examine, dividend and divisor are 'put' in relation, as quantities of given, but distinct, units. It is the context of an operation that shapes this relationship. The values expressing the relation between the circumference and the diameter of a circle are also *lüs*. However, by contrast to the former quantities, they are rather 'given' in relation with each other. In this case, it is a situation that brings them into relation. Liu Hui, meeting here with a phenomenon that, from a formal point of view, will turn out to be quite widespread, discusses it from a much more general angle, which will thus prove useful and relevant in several other sections of his commentary. This is a recurring and important feature of the commentator's proofs and one that makes them difficult to interpret: he systematically brings to a given context a more general outlook from which to address the correctness of a given operation, and thereby introduces a concept and an argument that will be shown to recur in different contexts.[56] In fact, the concept of *lü* had already been introduced by *The Nine Chapters* in relation to the prescription of the rule of three, at the beginning of Chapter 2. The commentary will regularly, and more generally, bring to light in all kinds of mathematical situations that quantities are *lüs* and use this property for establishing the correctness of a procedure.

Once the concept is introduced, Liu Hui states the consequence for the entities that it qualifies: '*Lüs*, being by nature in relation to each other, communicate.' We hence meet with a second occurrence of the term 'communicate' in the context of the commentary on the 'procedure for directly sharing', an occurrence which echoes the wording of the procedure itself. This time, it refers to the fact that the dividend and divisor are brought into communication, even though this operation is grasped from a more general point of view.

---

[56] On this feature of proofs, see Chemla 1991. The same phenomenon is shown to happen for the operations of 'homogenizing' and 'equalizing', which are introduced in the commentary on adding up fractions. We saw above another dimension of the relationship between the conduct of a proof and the search for generality when we stressed the parallel between the proofs of the correctness of the algorithms for the truncated pyramid with circular base and the cone, respectively. On the concept of *lü*, see Li Jimin 1982a, Guo Shuchun 1984, Li Jimin 1990: 136–61, Guo Shuchun 1992: 142–99, and the entry in the glossary in CG2004.

The consequences of such a state are made explicit in the commentary following problem 3.17, in which Liu Hui asserts:

Every time one obtains *lüs*, that is that, since when one refines (the units in which they are expressed), one refines them all and, when one makes them coarser, one makes them all coarser, the two quantities are transformed in relation to each other (literally, interact with each other) and that is all.[57]

Once the relationship is set, for instance, in our case, by the fact that 'dividend' and 'divisor' are 'put in relation to each other' as quantities of given units, any modification of the value of one that comes from a systematic dissection of its units – or a reunion of them – must be reflected in a dissection – or reunion – for the units of the other for the relationship to be maintained.[58] This is where the property of numerator and denominator is seen in a more general perspective. This is also the point where a parallel is established between the commentary on the 'procedure for simplifying parts' and our context. The next sentence of Liu Hui's commentary on the 'procedure for directly sharing' states the same property with respect to *lüs*: 'If there are parts, one can disaggregate; if parts are reiterated superpositions, one simplifies.'

However, in contrast to the former statement, this quote makes precise in which circumstances one may find it useful to 'disaggregate' the units of both terms, or 'simplify' them – that is, carry out a systematic aggregation of their units. The disaggregation is to be used when the values put in communication have 'parts', that is, contain fractions. Previously, being in communication allowed the integer and the fractions to enter together into the same operation of addition. Here, being in communication further implies that, when modified, the values are transformed simultaneously. This latter property is used to transform the values of the *lüs* into integers

---

[57] See CG2004: 306–7, 797, n. 73. In that case, the commentary brings to light that, in order to account for the procedure, one must understand that the *lüs* chosen to express the relationship between two different kinds of silk are given in different units of weight. By virtue of their quality of being *lüs*, they nevertheless change in relation to each other. Note that there can be more than two quantities, the set of which constitutes *lüs*. In Chemla 2006, I discuss source material from the *Book of Mathematical Procedures* which documents the process of introduction of the concept of *lü*, as encapsulating parallel sequences of computations carried out on quantities that occur within a dividend and a divisor. The way in which the transformations encapsulated are described echoes in many ways Liu Hui's commentary here.

[58] Since the *lüs* express this relationship, the nature of the units of the quantities involved can be forgotten, even though this is by no means mandatory. This corresponds to what is found in the text, where in most cases, the values of *lüs* are expressed by abstract numbers. In some sense, introducing the concept of *lü* is a way of addressing the possibility of carrying out an abstraction with respect to units.

in correlation with each other. In the case of a division, by a simultaneous dissection of the units of the dividend and the divisor, one may get rid of the fractions.

Just as in the context of problem 3.17, Liu Hui approaches the correlative transformation of the values of *lü* with full generality, introducing the disaggregation of the basic units in parallel with the opposite operation, i.e. aggregating units. The circumstances in which the latter operation can be used are referred to by the technical expression of 'reiterated superpositions', which had been introduced earlier, in the commentary on the simplification of fractions. There, it designated the possibility that the numerator and denominator could be represented as rectangular arrangements of units – 'parts' in this case – having a side of the same length, equal to their greatest common divisor, or their 'equal number' in the terminology of ancient China.[59] As a consequence, dividing both by the 'equal number' amounted to expressing the fraction in terms of parts coarser than the original ones by a factor equal to that number. In the context of the general discussion about *lü*s in the commentary on 'directly sharing', disaggregation has been introduced. The next sentence then refers to the units as 'parts', even though they may be of a different nature, and states: 'If parts are reiterated superpositions, one simplifies.' The concept of 'reiterated parts' and the operation of simplification that it helps justify are thus imported into a new and more general context.

Once the general considerations have been developed fully, the commentary applies them to the case under discussion, namely, dividend and divisor. In a first step, following on the last statement, Liu Hui introduces the new concept of '*lü*s put in relation with each other', precisely when he identifies the first instance for it: 'Divisor and dividend, divided by the equal number (i.e. their greatest common divisor), are *lü*s put in relation with each other.'

In a second step, Liu Hui translates the properties of *lü*s discussed above for the specific case examined in this context. Dividend and divisor having both parts, one disaggregates repeatedly their units in parallel, which amounts to multiplying. The commentator writes with full generality: 'Therefore, if one disaggregates the parts, one necessarily makes the two denominators of the parts both multiply divisor and dividend.'

The general prescription of disaggregating (formulated at the level of reasons) leads, within our specific context, to specific operations (at the level of computations), namely, two multiplications. Thinking of the process in terms of disaggregating and joining, the procedure amounts to

---

[59]   On these terms, see the glossary in CG2004.

$$(a+\frac{b}{c})/(d+\frac{e}{f})=(ca+b)/(cd+\frac{ec}{f})=(fca+fb)/(fcd+ec)$$

(first multiplication) (second multiplication)

which is equivalent to the algorithm as provided in *The Nine Chapters*:

$$(a+\frac{b}{c})/(d+\frac{e}{f})=(a+\frac{bf}{cf})/(d+\frac{ec}{fc})=(fca+fb)/(fcd+ec)$$

(equalizing) (multiplying by the two denominators)

These are the operations applied to the divisor and the dividend, and this is what is meant by the prescription of 'making them communicate', if we follow Liu Hui's interpretation. The values of the dividend and the divisor are transformed correspondingly, and they both become integers, without their relationship being altered. Here the analysis of the operation of 'making communicate' is completed, and the correctness of the procedure for 'directly sharing' is established.[60]

From the previous discussion, three points are worth stressing. The first two are important for a description of the practice of proof.

First, as we already emphasized, the proof is carried out in such a way as to approach the phenomena with the greatest generality possible. In our case, this leads to the introduction of some key abstract concepts such as *lü*.

Second, through the analysis that is conducted during the proof, a simplification of the algorithm is hinted at, since it is shown that dividend and divisor can be simplified before a division is to be carried out. Again this is a recurrent feature in the commentators' proofs: they offer a basis on which to develop new algorithms.

Third, and more importantly for our purpose, the concept of *lü* that is introduced is intimately related to the theme of this chapter. This is the point where we go back to the main thesis for which we argue here.

Combining divisions that follow each other

In fact, identifying, in a given context, the property of entities to be *lüs* with respect to each other is a way of establishing the validity of introducing into the flow of computations multiplications and divisions that compensate

---

[60] In a last paragraph, the commentator describes another procedure that articulates the different cases possible in a different way; see Chemla 1992 for a discussion.

a b c	Two readings: **Dividend**/Division of $ac+b$ by c	$ac+b$	Dividend
d	**Divisor**	cd	Dividing by the product

Figure 13.8   The division between quantities with fractions on the surface for computing.

each other.[61] In the context of dividing between quantities with fractions, the last analysed sentence of Liu Hui's commentary shows how the commentator links the proposed transformation of units, the correctness of which was established, to the application to both the dividend and the divisor – both, in this case, themselves the results of a previous division – of the same sequence of multiplications. In other cases, the concept of *lü* is brought into play when accounting for an inversion in the order of a multiplication and a division is at stake.[62]

This brings us back to the main question of this subsection: what is the relationship between this development of Liu Hui's and the validity of our fundamental transformation III? To bring the link to light, let us consider one of the cases to which the 'procedure for directly sharing' can be applied:

$$(a+\frac{b}{c})/d = (ac+b)/dc$$

and let us look at this from the point of view of the surface for computing (Figure 13.8). The set-up of the dividend (column 1) shows in which ways it can be considered as the result of the division of $ac+b$ by c (column 2). The algorithm thus amounts to dividing by d the result of a division by c. On the one hand, $ac+b$ is that to which one returns when 'making communicate' the integer a and the numerator b – this property is guaranteed, as Liu Hui stressed, by the fact that the results of division are given as

---

[61]   Above, the introduction of specific quantities such as fractions or quadratic irrationals was justified by the necessity of having inverse operations cancel each other. Here, it is the introduction of a concept, that of *lü*, that is to account for cancelling opposed multiplication and division.

[62]   See, for instance, the second proof of correctness of the 'procedure for multiplying parts' or the proof of the correctness of the 'rule of three' in CG2004: 170–1, 224–5.

exact. On the other hand, as Liu Hui shows, the 'procedure for directly sharing' amounts precisely to multiplying *c* by *d* to divide *ac* + *b* by both of them at a stroke (column 3).[63]

Such a reasoning would be only the observation of an equivalence, were it not indicated by precisely the name given to the operation of division between any two quantities in *The Nine Chapters*, i.e. *jingfen*. I suggest understanding that the original meaning of this name was 'directly sharing'. There are two pieces of evidence to support this interpretation. First, the procedure for carrying out the same division in the *Book of Mathematical Procedures* has the same name, except for the fact that the character *jing* is written with a homophone that means 'directly'.[64] Secondly, when the seventh-century commentator Li Chunfeng comments on the name of the procedure in *The Nine Chapters*, his interpretation is in conformity with how the name is written in the *Book of Mathematical Procedures*. Since this interpretation is quite important for our purpose, let us read it:

DIRECTLY SHARING. Your servant, Chunfeng, and the others comment respectfully: As for 'Directly sharing', from 'Gathering parts' onwards,[65] (the procedures) all made the (quantity of) parts homogeneous with each other, but this one directly seeks the part of one person.[66]*One shares that which is shared by the number of persons*, this is why one says 'Directly sharing'.

The most important statement for us here is the one I italicized: the operation is interpreted as dividing a quantity that is understood as itself being yielded by a 'sharing' or, in other terms, a division. Li Chunfeng thus also reads the operation as we suggest doing, that is, as dealing with the succession of two divisions. He thereby links, on the one hand, dealing with operations that follow each other, and, on the other hand, how arithmetical operations are carried out on quantities having fractions. In doing so, Li Chunfeng probably seeks to account not only for the name of the operation, but also for why the style of the algorithm breaks with the description of all the others before it. However, this interpretation fits with what the *Book*

[63] It is interesting that the operation of 'making communicate' that *The Nine Chapters* prescribes is, for one part, the very operation that restores what can be interpreted as the original dividend. For another part, this reading provides an interpretation of 'dividing at a stroke' in terms of 'making communicate', which can be shown to be meaningful.

[64] Compare slip 26, Peng Hao 2001: 48.

[65] That is, all the procedures for adding up fractions, subtracting them, comparing them and determining their average. These procedures are all interpreted by the commentators as making the number of parts, that is, the numerators, homogeneous to each other, before applying the operation in question. Compare CG2004: 166–7.

[66] One may understand that the division is prescribed directly, without having made the fractions first homogeneous in any respect.

of Mathematical Procedures contains in relation to this operation, which provides a hint that this was how the situation was understood even before *The Nine Chapters* was compiled. It is important in this respect that one of the prerequisites for this interpretation – namely, that the multiplication inverse to a division restores the original number divided – appears to be a concern documented in the *Book of Mathematical Procedures*, as shown above. This completes our argument in this case.

An additional remark should be made. So far, in our argument, we have only considered the validity of transformation III with respect to integers. What about establishing its validity more generally? Two points should be added in this respect.

On the one hand, if we observe the contexts in which 'dividing at a stroke', or its synonym, 'dividing together' (*bingchu*), are used in the commentaries, it turns out that the two divisions that are joined are usually both divisions by integers.

On the other hand, if this is the case, in some situations this relates to the fact that the property of entities to be *lü* was put into play.[67] Similarly, if the capacity of the quantities involved to be transformed into integers is employed, transformation III is to be used in contexts in which they were already turned into integers. That such may have been the idea is plausible: more generally, *The Nine Chapters* exhibits a way of carrying out computations that grants a predominant part to integers, and the introduction of the concept of *lü* can be interpreted as one technique among several devised to fulfil this aim. Several hints can be given in favour of these hypotheses.

First, the commentators regularly interpret the choice of describing a procedure in a given way in *The Nine Chapters* as derived from the motivation of the authors to avoid generating fractions in the midst of computations. This is how, for instance, Liu Hui accounts for why, in the rule of three, the multiplication is prescribed before the division, and not after.[68] The commentators thus attribute to *The Nine Chapters* the intention of computing with integers wherever possible.

Second, the way in which division between quantities containing fractions is dealt with in the general case amounts precisely to getting rid of fractions. Liu Hui reads this way of proceeding as made possible by the status of the dividend and divisor as *lüs*. Third, in the procedure of *The Nine Chapters* in the context of which the concept of *lü* is introduced, that

---

[67]   See, for instance, how Liu Hui interprets the algorithm provided after problem 6.10 (CG2004: 514–15).

[68]   The validity of this operation is discussed in the next subsection.

is, the rule of three, it guarantees precisely that the number by which one multiplies and divides be an integer.[69] This leads to mixing together integers and non-integers in the computations in a dissymmetric way that is quite specific to the procedure for the rule of three described in *The Nine Chapters*.[70] The predominant role given to integers can be read in the way in which algorithms are composed and in the specific concepts that are introduced in correlation with this. To establish whether this feature actually plays a part in the proofs of correctness, as we suggested above, we would have to observe how the concept of *lü* is actually put into play in the commentaries, an issue that we leave for another publication.[71] Let us turn instead to the relationship between transformation II and multiplying between quantities containing fractions.

Inverting the order of a division and a multiplication that follow each other

We already hinted at the reasons for linking the 'procedure for the field with the greatest generality' and transformation II. It is hence natural to seek, in the commentary of the former, a proof of the validity of the latter. As in the previous subsection, we shall first examine how the correctness of the algorithm for multiplying quantities of the type $a + b/c$ is established. While doing so, we shall naturally be led to connecting this proof to that of the validity of transformation II.

Let us recall the procedure given by *The Nine Chapters*, which was already discussed in Part I of the chapter:

PROCEDURE: THE DENOMINATORS OF THE PARTS RESPECTIVELY MULTIPLY THE INTEGER CORRESPONDING TO THEM; THE NUMERATORS OF THE PARTS JOIN THESE (THE RESULTS); MULTIPLYING MAKES THE DIVIDEND. THE DENOMINATORS OF THE PARTS BEING MULTIPLIED BY EACH OTHER MAKE THE DIVISOR. ONE DIVIDES THE DIVIDEND BY THE DIVISOR.

Liu Hui establishes the correctness of the procedure in two steps, each of which relates to a step in the procedure. The commentary on the first set of operations reads as follows:

---

[69] Incidentally, it also allows that these numbers be prime with respect to each other.

[70] Such is not the case for the rule of three given by the *Book of Mathematical Procedures*. Discussing this difference exceeds the scope of this chapter and I shall deal with it elsewhere.

[71] As already indicated above, the nature of the data to which the operations of the various algorithms are applied should also be systematically observed, if we were to be more precise regarding the extension of the algorithms for which correctness is established.

If 'the denominators of the parts respectively multiply the integer corresponding to them and the numerators of the parts join these (the results)', one makes the bu[72] that are integral communicate and be incorporated in the numerator of the parts. In this way, denominators and numerators all (contribute to) make the dividends.

Above, we already alluded to the main elements of this commentary. Let us add only two remarks. First, we now see how the operation of 'making communicate' that is used in this proof is precisely one that was analysed in the commentary on 'directly sharing'. Second, in the transformation of $\begin{bmatrix} a \\ b \\ c \end{bmatrix}$ into $ac + b$, the latter is designated as 'dividend'. This is one of the several signs of the continuity, which we already stressed, between quantities of the type $a + b/c$ and division, from both a conceptual and a notational point of view. This point will prove important below. As a commentary on the remaining part of the procedure, Liu Hui states:

This is like 'multiplying parts'.

In other words, he asserts that the algorithm is, from this point onwards, analogous to the procedure for multiplying between 'pure' fractions, which, in *The Nine Chapters*, is placed just before it. As was observed above, the commentator refers the interpretation of some steps of the procedure to his previous commentary.[73] Three points are worth noting.

First, in the same way as we showed previously how the procedure for the truncated pyramid with circular base embedded, among other algorithms, the 'procedure for the field with the greatest generality', the latter is now shown to embed another procedure. This embedding is, however, to be distinguished from the one which accounts for the name of the operation, discussed in Part I of the chapter. The latter embedding related to the fact that the 'procedure for the field with the greatest generality' unified three procedures for multiplying different types of numbers: it referred to the algorithm as a list of operations. The new embedding manifests itself in the proof: it brings to light that, among the three cases covered by the algorithm, one of them is, in terms of reasons, more fundamental in that the correctness of the general procedure relies on its correctness. These two cases show that algorithms may be built by making use of other algorithms

---

72 The commentary refers to the data of the problems after which the procedure is given. They are all lengths expressed with respect to the unit of measure *bu*.

73 This conclusion is reinforced by the commentary placed after the procedure, which repeats one of the arguments given to account for the correctness of the algorithm for multiplying fractions.

a integer b numerator c denominator	$\dfrac{ca+b}{c}$	c			
		$(ca+b).(c'a'+b')$	$\dfrac{(ca+b).\,(c'a'+b')}{cc'}$	Dividend Divisor:
a' integer b' numerator c' denominator	$\dfrac{c'a'+b'}{c'}$	$\dfrac{c'a'+b'}{c'}$	$\dfrac{c'a'+b'}{c'}$	The order of the operations was inverted

Figure 13.9 The multiplication between quantities with fractions on the surface for computing.

in various ways, and the proof of the correctness of the former may as well incorporate the proof for the latter according to different modalities.

Second, interestingly enough, in their proofs, the commentaries regularly refer to the proofs of algorithms placed just before in the Classic.[74] This seems to possibly provide an interpretation of the reasons why the algorithms are presented in this order in *The Nine Chapters*.

Third, if we look at Figure 13.9, we see that the part of the algorithm that is applied to the elements placed on the surface for computations after the first step, that is, when divisions are restored, can be considered similar to the algorithm applied to fractions: this is an essential prerequisite for the proof of this section of the algorithm to be referred to that of the 'procedure for multiplying parts'. This yields yet another hint of the fact that practitioners of mathematics in ancient China saw continuity between the notation of quantities and the set-up of operations. The commentary on 'multiplying parts', to which we shall now turn, starts by discussing precisely this point.

The algorithm referred to reads as follows:

MULTIPLYING PARTS
PROCEDURE: THE DENOMINATORS BEING MULTIPLIED BY ONE ANOTHER MAKE THE DIVISOR; THE NUMERATORS BEING MULTIPLIED BY ONE ANOTHER MAKE THE DIVIDEND. ONE DIVIDES THE DIVIDEND BY THE DIVISOR.

The opening sentence of the commentary relates the pair of a numerator and a denominator to that of a dividend and a divisor. Liu Hui writes:

---

[74] The second proof of the correctness of the 'procedure for multiplying parts' refers explicitly to 'directly sharing'. See CG2004: 170–1. We shall show below that the first proof also needs to rely on 'directly sharing'.

Figure 13.10 The layout of a division or a fraction on the surface for computing.

In each of the cases when a dividend does not fill up a divisor, they hence have the names of denominator and numerator.

In other words, one may choose to read an array of two lines on the surface for computing, as in Figure 13.10, in two ways.

On the one hand, the array is the layout of an operation of division, which we shall represent as $a : b$. On the other hand, when a is smaller than b, which is precisely the case 'when a dividend does not fill up a divisor', it can be read as the quantity resulting from carrying out the operation, that is, the fraction a/b.

These dual points of view allow Liu Hui to link the fraction and the numerator operationally. Placing himself at the most general level, as we have seen him often do in proofs, he writes:

If there are parts (i.e. fractions), and if, when expanding the corresponding dividend by multiplication, then, correlatively, it (the dividend produced by the multiplication)[75] fills up the divisor, the (division) hence only yields an integer.

The application of this remark that appears relevant in the context in which it is formulated is that the sequence of a multiplication and a division like $(b \cdot a) : b$ yields a. Seen from the other point of view, this remark leads to stating that the multiplication $b \cdot a/b$ yields a as its result. The numerator can thereby be seen as a quantity that is b times larger than the fraction.

If, furthermore, one multiplies something by the numerator, the denominator must consequently divide (the product) in return (*baochu*). Dividing in return is 'dividing the dividend by the divisor'.

This is the point where Liu Hui introduces the operation of 'dividing in return', which we already mentioned above and which occurs only later in the text of *The Nine Chapters*. In terms of operations, 'dividing in return' is a simple division. However, the expression by which it is prescribed indi-

---

[75] The name of 'dividend' designates what is in the position of the 'dividend' on the surface for computing, at the moment when it is used. This is the assignment of variables typical of the description of algorithms in *The Nine Chapters*.

cates the reason why it must be used: earlier in the flow of computations, one multiplied by a magnitude which was n times larger than it ought to be – in most cases, by a numerator instead of the corresponding fraction – therefore a division by n is needed to cancel this unwarranted dilation.[76] In our case, Liu Hui's statement is an answer to the question of determining the product of a/b by 'something' (let us call this 'something' X) – one may note the generality of the question considered. The reasoning appears to be that, since $a{\cdot}X$ is equivalent to $[(b \cdot a) : b]{\cdot}X$ or $b{\cdot}a/b{\cdot}X$, then $a/b.X$ is hence equivalent to $a{\cdot}X : b$. If we pause a moment here, we can observe that what is dealt with is precisely our transformation II. A division followed by a multiplication, that is, $a/b{\cdot}X$, which Liu Hui emphasized as equivalent to $(a:b){\cdot}X$, has been replaced by a multiplication followed by a division, $a{\cdot}X:b$. The way in which the commentator discusses the issue highlights the link he reads between multiplying fractions (multiplying the result n/c by X) and what we called transformation II – transforming the sequence $(n:c){\cdot}X$ into $nX:c$.[77] In addition, the discussion has not yet specified the quantity X. Its result holds for any such quantity. This is yet another case where the proof does not limit itself to the context in which it is developed, but highlights the most general phenomenon possible.

In relation to the context in which Liu Hui develops this discussion, the next step turns to the consideration of a specific value for X, that is, the numerator c of the fraction c/d to be multiplied by a/b. He writes: 'Now, "the numerators are multiplied by one another", hence the denominators must each divide in return.'

---

[76] In all observed cases, the 'division in return' eliminates a factor that is an integer. Note that the beginning of Liu Hui's commentary can be read as addressing the validity of such a division: dividing, by a factor, a quantity that resulted from a multiplication by this very factor eliminates from it this factor.

[77] The commentary on the procedure solving problem 6.3 also stresses that the sequence of multiplying by a and dividing by b can be carried out as multiplying by a/b, that is, multiplying by a and dividing in return by b. The commentary on the procedure of 'suppose', at the beginning of Chapter 2, establishes the correctness of the algorithm carrying out the rule of three in two ways. On the one hand, after having shown that a sequence of a division and a multiplication yields the correct result, the commentator 'inverts their order' (*fan*) to obtain the algorithm as described in *The Nine Chapters*. On the other hand, he transforms the *lüs* expressing the relationship between the things to be changed one into the other, the former into 1 and the latter into a fraction, by which the reasoning shows one must multiply to carry out the task required. This, says Liu Hui, corresponds to 'with the numerator, multiplying and with the denominator, dividing in return'. A link is thereby established between the operation of 'inverting the order' *fan* of a division and a multiplication and that of multiplying by a fraction. Note how using the concept of *lü* and its operational properties is essential for bringing this link to light. The commentary on the procedure solving problem 6.10 puts into play all the elements examined so far.

The problem in *The Nine Chapters* asks to compute the product of a/b by c/d. On the basis of the previous observation, this operation is shown to amount to $a \cdot c/d$: b, which, in its turn and for the same reasons, amounts to $ac : d : b$. Liu Hui can hence interpret the 'meaning' of the first prescribed operation (computing ac) and can establish that it must be followed by two divisions for the desired result to be obtained. The commentator has thus produced an algorithm yielding the result required by the Classic. The last step needed to prove the correctness of the procedure given by *The Nine Chapters* is to transform the algorithm obtained ($a \cdot c : d : b$) into the one for which the correctness is to be proved. Such a transformation comes under the rubric of the second line of argumentation in an 'algebraic proof in an algorithmic context', which we introduced in Part I of the chapter. Liu Hui concludes his proof by transforming the former algorithm into the latter, as follows: 'Consequently, one makes "the denominators multiply each other" and one divides at a stroke (by their product) (*lianchu*).'

In other words, the commentator here applies transformation III, the validity of which was, as I argued above, dealt with in the commentary on 'directly sharing'.

Conclusions

The analysis developed in this chapter invites drawing conclusions on several levels.

First, the passages examined illustrate how the earliest known commentators on *The Nine Chapters* fulfilled the task of establishing the correctness of algorithms. As we suggested in the introduction, this branch of the history of mathematical proof has not yet been deeply explored. We see how the Chinese source material calls for its development. Two issues are at stake here. We need to understand the part played by proving the correctness of algorithms in the overall history of mathematical proof, and in particular in the history of algebraic proof. Moreover, on this basis, we must determine how we should locate Chinese sources in a world history of mathematical proof.

Whatever conclusion we may reach in this latter respect, it remains true that Liu Hui's and Li Chunfeng's commentaries provide source material for the analysis of the fundamental operations involved in proving the correctness of an algorithm not only in ancient China but also in general. In our limited survey of proofs from the Chinese source material, several fundamental operations appeared.

We saw how proofs relied on algorithms, which had already been established as correct, and how proofs articulated these algorithms as a basis for establishing the correctness of other procedures. Most importantly, the algorithms, together with the situations in relation to which they were introduced, provided means for determining the 'meaning' of an operation or a sequence of operations. This appears to be a key act for proving the correctness of algorithms, and it is noteworthy that a term (*yi* 'meaning') seems to have been specialized to designate it in ancient China.

Furthermore, as was stressed above on several occasions, the evidence provided by the commentaries seems to manifest a link – perhaps specific to ancient China – between the way in which the proof of the correctness of algorithms was conducted and a systematic interest in the dimension of generality of the situations and concepts encountered.[78] The fact that proofs often relate to each other, as we emphasized several times, can be correlated to this specificity. However, it will be only when historical studies of such proofs develop that we will be in a reasonable position to conclude whether this feature is characteristic of Chinese sources or intrinsic to proving the correctness of algorithms in general.

Finally, the second key operation in the activity of proving the correctness of algorithms that is documented in ancient China, and on which we focused in this chapter, was what I called the 'algebraic proof in an algorithmic context'. So far, I can locate it only in ancient Chinese source material, as far as ancient mathematical traditions are concerned. But again this conclusion may have to be revised in the future. Again, whatever the case may be, what can we learn from this occurrence regarding algebraic proof in general?

If we recapitulate our analysis in this respect, we have seen that several technical terms were introduced in relation to this dimension of proof: *fu* 'restoring', *huan* 'backtracking',[79] *baochu* 'dividing in return',[80] *fan* 'inverting',

---

[78]   I have dealt with this issue on several occasions, from Chemla 1991 onwards. However, given the complexity of this link, I cannot fully discuss it within the framework of this chapter. I plan to revisit the issue in another publication that would be entirely devoted to it. Note, however, that, here again, the commentators introduced a technical term in relation to this facet of the problem. In my glossary, I transcribed it as *yi'* 'meaning, signification', to distinguish it from *yi*, and the reader will find in these two entries partial discussion of the problem. *Yi'* designates a 'meaning' that captures the fundamental procedures that proofs disclose to be at stake within each algorithm dealt with.

[79]   A variant for this operation is *huan yuan* 'return to the origin'. On all these terms, the reader is referred to my glossary in CG2004.

[80]   A variant for this concept is the pair of terms *ru* 'enter'/*chu* 'go out'. See the glossary in CG2004.

lianchu 'dividing at a stroke', *bingchu* 'dividing together'.[81] These terms refer to the three fundamental transformations (those we designated by I, II and III) involved in the 'algebraic proof in an algorithmic context' as carried out for establishing the correctness of the algorithms presented in *The Nine Chapters*. In fact, the validity of these transformations rests on the fact that the results of divisions and extractions of square root are given as exact. We have seen that Liu Hui explicitly related the validity of the first fundamental transformation to this fact. Before we go further in concluding about the two other transformations, let us introduce the general remark regarding algebraic proof to which this fact leads us.

Such a type of proof can be characterized by the fact that it carries out transformations on sequences of operations as such. What appears here is that the validity of such transformations rests on the structural properties of the set of quantities to which the variables and constants involved in the formulas transformed may refer. As soon as it is stated, the remark sounds obvious. My claim is that it can be documented that a first version of this fact came to be understood in ancient China, in relation with the conduct of 'algebraic proof in an algorithmic context'. This claim, in turn, raises a historical question regarding this range of issues on which I shall conclude the chapter: how was the relationship between the validity of algebraic proof and structural properties of the set of magnitudes on which it operated historically discussed? It is clear that inquiring into this question should elucidate a fundamental dimension of the history of algebraic proof.

The second level on which I would like to focus in concluding relates to my argument regarding the validity of transformations II and III. In the chapter, I argued that there was an interest, in ancient China, in illuminating the grounds on which this validity rested. Moreover, I suggested that the question was dealt with in the commentaries on the algorithms for dividing and multiplying quantities of the type $a + b/c$. It is to be noted that fractions conceived as a pair of a numerator and a denominator, as well as quantities $a + b/c$, appeared in Asia, in the earliest known Chinese and Indian books. In China, the first extant document attesting to the arithmetic with such numbers, that is, the *Book of Mathematical Procedures*, also exhibits a concern for the problem of 'restoring' (*fu*) the original quantity that was divided, when applying the inverse operation. The main point, however, is that, to my knowledge, the pages that Chinese commentators devoted to establishing the correctness of algorithms carrying out arithmetical

---

[81] Note that, although multiplications also happen to be joined – for instance, in the commentary following problem 6.10 – no specific term was coined for this transformation. This dissymmetry between multiplication and division is remarkable.

operations with quantities containing fractions are unique to China, by contrast to other ancient traditions. If this were confirmed, there would appear to be a correlation between the latter proofs, on the one hand, and the use of 'algebraic proofs in an algorithmic context', on the other hand.

In Part II of this chapter, however, my argument was based only on internal considerations. One of the most important facts that grounded the argument was the continuity of concepts and notations on the surface for computing, such as operations like division or multiplication on the one hand and quantities such as fractions or numbers of the type $a + b/c$, on the other. The same configuration of numbers on the surface for computing could be read as the set-up of a division, or the result of a division, that is, a fraction. Moreover, applying a multiplication by c to the configuration in three lines representing $a + b/c$ – hence read as the set-up of a multiplication – could restore the division that had yielded it. The key element for this continuity is that of a position on the surface in which one could place and operate on a component of a quantity or a function of an operation. The surface served as a medium articulating these mathematical objects. In this way, arithmetical operations on fractions were transformed into sequences of operations, and the algorithms carrying them out were established on the basis of interpretations and transformations of these sequences of operations.[82] A link was thereby established between transforming lists of operations and operating on fractions.

I suggested reasons for considering that this was the way in which the commentators understood it. On the one hand, in the commentary following problem 5.11, we saw how the inversion of the order of a division and a multiplication was carried out by making use of the 'procedure of the field with the greatest generality'. On the other hand, when Li Chunfeng interprets the name of the operation for dividing between quantities of the type $a + b/c$, he refers to the division of a quantity itself yielded by a division.

There is, however, another angle from which to consider the relationship between the fundamental transformations I, II, III and the proofs of the correctness of algorithms for arithmetical operations on quantities of the type $a + b/c$. Most of the technical terms listed above, by which the commentators refer to these transformations, are introduced precisely in relation to commentaries discussing the necessity of using quantities like fractions or quadratic irrationals (*fu*), on the one hand, and establishing the algorithms

---

[82]   One example for this is how, if there are parts in the dividend and the divisor, 'directly sharing' is explained to be equivalent to 'multiplying' both quantities by the two denominators.

operating on quantities such as $a + b/c$ (*huan, baochu, lianchu*) on the other hand. In that way, these terms are introduced at the beginning of the book.[83]

These concluding remarks lead to a whole range of questions, which we shall formulate as a conclusion to the chapter. How was the correctness of algorithms for multiplying and dividing quantities with fractions approached elsewhere, and what connections did this concern have with the kind of 'algebraic proof in an algorithmic context' discussed here? Is there a historical relationship between the proofs we examined and the overall history of algebraic proofs? If there exists some relationship, did the proofs that were devised in ancient China actually play a historical part in this process? It is clear, I believe, that the history of mathematical proof still has many new territories to explore.

Acknowledgements

This chapter has benefited from the discussions of the working group 'History and historiography of mathematical proof in ancient traditions', which the research group REHSEIS convened at Columbia University in Paris, at Reid Hall, between March and June 2002 thanks to the generosity of the Maison des sciences de l'homme and Columbia University. It is a pleasure to express my gratitude to all the participants in this workshop and the sponsors who made it possible.

Bibliography

Chemla, K. (1991) 'Theoretical aspects of the Chinese algorithmic tradition (first to third century)', *Historia Scientiarum* 42: 75–98 (+ errata in the following issue).

(1992) 'Les fractions comme modèle formel en Chine ancienne', in *Histoire de fractions, fractions d'histoire*, ed. P. Benoit and J. Ritter. Basel: 188–207.

(1996) 'Positions et changements en mathématiques à partir de textes chinois des dynasties Han à Song-Yuan. Quelques remarques', *Extrême-Orient, Extrême-Occident* 18: 115–47.

(1997/8) 'Fractions and irrationals between algorithm and proof in ancient China', *Studies in History of Medicine and Science* n.s. 15: 31–54.

---

[83] Only *fan* will be introduced at the beginning of Chapter 2.

(2003) 'Generality above abstraction: the general expressed in terms of the paradigmatic in mathematics in ancient China', *Science in Context* **16**: 413–58.

(2005) 'The interplay between proof and algorithm in 3rd century China: the operation as prescription of computation and the operation as argument', in *Visualization, Explanation and Reasoning Styles in Mathematics*, ed. P. Mancosu, K. F. Jorgensen and S. A. Pedersen. Dordrecht: 123–45.

(2006) 'Documenting a process of abstraction in the mathematics of ancient China', in *Studies in Chinese Language and Culture: Festschrift in Honor of Christoph Harbsmeier on the Occasion of his 60th Birthday*, ed. C. Anderl and H. Eifring. Oslo: 169–94.

Chemla, K., and Keller, A. (2002) 'The Sanskrit *karanis*, and the Chinese *mian* (side): computations with quadratic irrationals in ancient China and India', in *From China to Paris: 2000 Years of Mathematical Transmission*, ed. Y. Dold-Samplonius, J. W. Dauben, M. Folkerts and B. van Dalen. Stuttgart: 87–132.

Cullen, C. (2004) *The Suan shu shu* 筭數書 '*Writings on reckoning': A Translation of a Chinese Mathematical Collection of the Second Century BC, with Explanatory Commentary*. Needham Research Institute Working Papers vol. I. Cambridge.

Dauben, J. W. (2008) '算數書. Suan Shu Shu (A Book on Numbers and Computations): English translation with commentary', *Archive for History of Exact Sciences* **62**: 91–178.

Guo Shuchun (1984) 'Analysis of the concept and uses of *lü* in *The Nine Chapters on Mathematical Procedures* and Liu Hui's commentary', *Kejishi Jikan* (Journal for the history of science and technology) **11**: 21–36. (In Chinese.)

(1992) *Gudai Shijie Shuxue Taidou Liu Hui* (Liu Hui, a leading figure of ancient world mathematics). Jinan. (In Chinese.)

(1998) *Yizhu* Jiuzhang suanshu (Translation and commentary on *The Nine Chapters on Mathematical Procedures*). Shenyang. (In Chinese.)

Li Jimin (1982a) '"Jiuzhang suanshu" *zhong de bilü lilun* (Ratio theory in *The Nine Chapters on Mathematical Procedures*)', In Jiuzhang Suanshu *yu Liu Hui* (The Nine chapters on mathematical procedures *and Liu Hui*), ed. Wu Wenjun. Beijing: 228–45. (In Chinese.)

(1982b) '*Zhongguo gudai de fenshu lilun* (The theory of fractions in ancient China)', in Jiuzhang Suanshu *yu Liu Hui* (The Nine Chapters on Mathematical Procedures *and Liu Hui*), ed. Wu Wenjun. Beijing: 190–209. (In Chinese.)

(1990) *Dongfang Shuxue Dianji* Jiuzhang suanshu *ji qi Liu Hui Zhu Yanjiu* (*Research on the Oriental mathematical Classic* The Nine Chapters on Mathematical Procedures *and on its Commentary by Liu Hui*). Xi'an. (In Chinese.)

(1998) Jiuzhang suanshu *daodu yu yizhu* (*Guidebook and annotated translation of* The Nine Chapters on Mathematical Procedures). Xi'an. (In Chinese.)

Peng Hao (2001) *Zhangjiashan Hanjian* «Suanshushu» *Zhushi* (*Commentary on the Book on Bamboo Rods from the Han dynasty Found at Zhangjiashan: the* Book of Mathematical Procedures). Beijing. (In Chinese.)

Shen Kangshen (1997) Jiuzhang Suanshu Daodu (*Guidebook for Reading* The Nine Chapters on Mathematical Procedures). Hankou. (In Chinese.)

Shen, K., Crossley, J. N., and Lun, A. W.-C. (1999) *The Nine Chapters on the Mathematical Art: Companion and Commentary*. Beijing.

Volkov, A. K. (1985) 'Ob odnom driévniékitaïskom matiématitchiéskom tiérminié' ('On an old Chinese mathematical term'), in *Tiézisy Konfiériéntsii Aspirantov i Molodykh Naoutchnykh Sotroudnikov IV AN SSSR* (Workshop of the PhD Students and Young Researchers of the Institute for Oriental Studies of the Academy of Science of the Soviet Union), vol. I/1. Summaries: 18–22. Moscow. (In Russian.)

14 | Dispelling mathematical doubts: assessing mathematical correctness of algorithms in Bhāskara's commentary on the mathematical chapter of the *Āryabhaṭīya*

AGATHE KELLER

Introduction

Contrary to the perception prevalent at the beginning of the twentieth century, a concern for the mathematical correctness of algorithms existed in the mathematical tradition in Sanskrit. Reflections on the systematic *upapattis* of Kṛṣṇa's (*fl. c.* 1600–25) commentary on the *Bījagaṇita*, the explorations of the Mādhava school (fourteenth–sixteenth century) or other traditions of mathematical validity have already been published.[1] Still, the variations among this tradition of justification and explanation need to be studied.

In the following sections, the *Āryabhaṭīyabhāṣya* of Bhāskara (BAB) is analysed with regard to its reasoning and vocabulary. The second chapter of *Āryabhaṭīya* (Ab) – an astronomical *siddhānta* composed in verse at the end of the fifth century – treats mathematics (*gaṇita*). Respecting the requirements of the genre, these aphoristic *āryas* usually provide the gist of a procedure, such as an essential relationship or the main steps of an algorithm. The BAB is not only the earliest known commentary on this treatise but also the oldest known text of mathematics in Sanskrit prose that has been handed down to us. The BAB thus gives us a glimpse into the reasonings used in the scholarly mathematical tradition in Sanskrit at the beginning of the seventh century.[2] Very little is known about who practised scholarly mathematics in classical India, and why scholarly texts were elaborated. The BAB provides information on the intellectual context in which both the Ab and the BAB were composed. First, the commentator's defence of Āryabhaṭa's treatise (and the commentator's own interpretations

I would like to thank Karine Chemla and Micah Ross for their attentive and helpful scrutinizing of this article.

[1] Ikeyama 2003; Jain 2001; Patte 2004; Srinivas 1990. Some of Kṛṣṇa's demonstrations are noted, among others, in the footnotes of C1817.

[2] Keller 2006: Introduction.

of the verses) will provide a backdrop for reflections on the mathematical correctness of procedures. Next, the arguments behind the algorithms of mathematical justification will be clarified. Afterwards, Bhāskara's vocabulary including explanations, proofs and verifications will be more precisely characterized.

1 Defending the treatise

Bhāskara's commentary, a prolix prose text, gives us a glimpse into the intellectual world of scholarly astronomers and mathematicians. The commentary records their intellectual debates. For the opening verse in which the author of the treatise mentions his name, Bhāskara's commentary explains:

. . . as a heroic man on battlefields, whose arms have been copiously lacerated by the strength of vile swords, having entered publicly a battle with enemies, who proclaims the following, as he kills: 'This Yajñadatta here ascended, a descendant of the Aditis, having undaunted courage in battle fields, now strikes. If someone has power, let him strike back!' In the same way, this master also, who has reached the other side of the ocean of excessive knowledge about Mathematics, Time-reckoning and the Sphere, having entered an assembly of wise men, has declared: 'Āryabhaṭa tells three: Mathematics, Time-reckoning, the Sphere.'[3]

Within this hostile atmosphere, Bhāskara's commentary attempts to convince the reader of the coherence and validity of Āryabhaṭa's treatise. To this end, the commentary dispels 'doubts' (*sandeha*) that arise in the explanations of Āryabhaṭa's verses. Thus, the analysis provides refutations (*parihāra*) to objections and establishes (*sādhya, siddha*) Bhāskara's readings of Āryabhaṭa's verse. This commentary presents mainly syntactical and grammatical discussions which debate the interpretation of a given word in the treatise. More often than not, the discussion of the meaning and use of a word defines and characterizes the mathematical objects in question. (Are squares all equal sided quadrilaterals? Do all triangles have equally halving

[3]   . . . *yastejasvī puruṣaḥ samareṣu nikṛṣṭāsitejovitānacchuritabāhuś śatrusaṅghātam prakāśam praviśya praharan evam āha 'ayam asāv udito 'ditikulaprasūtaḥ samareṣv anivāritavīryo yajñadattaḥ praharati / yadi kasyacicchaktiḥ pratipraharatvi'ti / evam asāo apy ācāryo gaṇitakālakriyāgolātiśayajñānodadhipārago vitsabhām avagāhya 'āryabhaṭas trīṇi gadati gaṇitaṃ kālakriyāṃ golam' iti uktavān /.* (Shukla 1976: 5).

Unless otherwise specified, the text follows the critical edition published in Shukla 1976. I would like to thank T. Kusuba, T. Hayashi and M. Yano for the help they provided in translating this paragraph, during my stay in Kyoto in 1997.

heights? etc.)[4] Bhāskara's commentary adopts technical words, and the specialized readings of the verses show that the Ab cannot be understood in a straightforward way. The verses need interpretation and the interpretation should be the correct one.

The search for the proper interpretation thus defines the commentator's task. The importance of interpretation becomes especially clear when Bhāskara criticizes Prabhākara's exegesis of the Ab.[5] For instance, in his comment on the rule for the computation of sines, Bhāskara explains that the expression *samavṛtta* refers to a circle, not a disk as Prabhakara understood it.[6] More crucially, through his understanding of the word *agra* (remainder) as a synonym of *saṅkhyā* (number), Bhāskara provides a new interpretation of the rule given in BAB.2.32–33:[7] the verse giving the rule for a 'pulverizer with remainder' (*sāgrakuṭṭakāra*) can now be read as giving a rule for the 'pulverizer without remainder' (*niragrakuṭṭakāra*).[8] This peculiar reading of the word *agra* is an extreme example of the technical and inventive devices commentators use for their interpretations.

Outside the syntactical discussion of a verse, Bhāskara sometimes considers the mathematical content of the procedure directly. Defending Āryabhaṭa's approximation of π against those of competing schools, he undertakes a refutation (*parihāra*) of the jaina value of $\sqrt{10}$ (*daśakaraṇī*), claiming that the value rests only on tradition and not on proof.

In this case also, it is just a tradition (*āgama*) and not a proof (*upapatti*) . . . But this also should be established (*sādhya*).[9]

The above statement should not induce a romantic vision of an enlightened Bhāskara using reason to overthrow prejudices transmitted through (religious) traditions. Although here he criticizes the reasoning which cites 'tradition' to justify a rule, in other cases Bhāskara accepts this very argument as evidence of the correctness of a mathematical statement.[10] The question nonetheless is raised: Bhāskara argues that the procedures of the *Āryabhaṭīya* are correct, but how does Bhāskara 'establish' a rule? Moreover, what does Bhāskara consider a 'proof'? The answer to these questions

---

[4] Keller 2006: Introduction.
[5] Keller 2006; BAB.2.11; BAB.2.12.
[6] Shukla 1976: 77; Keller 2006: I: 57.
[7] Shukla 1976: 77; Keller 2006: 132–3.
[8] Both rules are mathematically equivalent but do not follow the same pattern. Furthermore, the second reading also involves omitting the last quarter of verse 33. See Keller 2006: II, Appendix on BAB.2.32–3.
[9] *atrāpi kevala evāgamaḥ naivopapatiḥ / . . . cetad api sādyam eva.*(Shukla 1976: 72).
[10] Keller 2006: Introduction.

presents difficulties. Indeed, the rationale behind the fragmentary arguments that BAB sets forth is at times hard to grasp. The aim of this chapter is to show that two specific commentarial techniques, the 'reinterpretation' of procedures and establishing an alternative independent procedure, were used to ground the Ab's rules. To establish this point, a characterization of these commentarial techniques will be necessary. This characterization will be followed by a description of the different ways Bhāskara explicitly tries to establish the mathematical validity of Ab's rules.

2 'Reinterpretation' of procedures

Bhāskara, in an attempt to elucidate Āryabhaṭa's rules, gives interpretations of Āryabhaṭa's verses. He thus makes clear what are the different steps required to carry out a procedure, or the word used to define a mathematical object. In certain cases, having put forth such an interpretation, Bhāskara reinvests his understanding of the rule with an additional meaning. This is what I call a 'reinterpretation'. A 'reinterpretation' does not invalidate a previous interpretation. It is somehow like the poetic process of *śleṣa* which reads several meanings in the same compound, creating thus a poetic aura. A 'reinterpretation' adds a layer of meaning, gives depth to the interpretation of a rule. A 'reinterpretation' provides a new mathematical context for the different steps of a procedure which is not modified. Another name for this commentarial technique could be 'rereading' a procedure.

The next section describes how an 'explanation', a 'proof' or a 'verification' consisted of providing either an alternative independent procedure or a 'reinterpretation' of a given procedure via the Rule of Three or the Pythagorean theorem. In both cases, these arguments would provide a mathematical justification for what alone could appear as an arbitrary succession of operations. Before examining 'reinterpretations' of procedures in Bhāskara's commentary, the expression of the Rule of Three and the Pythagorean Theorem in BAB must be explained.

2.1 Rule of Three

The Rule of Three (*trairāśika*[11]) appears in verse Ab.2.26.

Now, when one has multiplied that fruit quantity of the Rule of Three
   by the desire quantity|

[11] For a general overview on the Rule of Three in India see Sarma 2002.

The quotient of that divided by the measure should be this fruit of desire||[12]

In other words, if M (the measure) produces a fruit F_M, and D is a desire for which the fruit F_D is sought, the verse may be expressed in modern algebraic notation as:

$$F_D = \frac{F_M \times D}{M} \qquad (1)$$

Obviously, this expression can also be understood as a statement that the ratios are equal:

$$\frac{F_D}{D} = \frac{F_M}{M} \qquad (2)$$

The procedure given in the verse provides an order for the different operations to be carried out. First, the desire is multiplied by the fruit. Next, the result is divided by the measure. This order of operations causes the procedure to appear as an arbitrary set of operations.[13] Bhāskara provides a standard expression to define the kind of problem which the Rule of Three solves. When the commentator thinks that a situation involves proportional quantities and thus the Rule of Three is (or can be) applied, he brings this fact to light by using a verbal formulation (*vāco yukti*) of the Rule of Three. This verbal formulation is a syntactically rigid question which reads as follows:

If the measure produces the fruit, then with the desire what is produced? The fruit of desire is produced.

This question, when it appears, shows that Bhāskara thinks that the Rule of Three can be applied. I believe that for Bhāskara the Rule of Three invokes proportionality.

2.2 The Pythagorean Theorem

Bhāskara, like other medieval Sanskrit mathematicians, does not use the concept of angles. In his trigonometry, Bhāskara uses lengths of arcs. As for right-angled triangles, Bhāskara distinguishes them from ordinary triangles by giving to each side a specific name. Whereas scalene, isosceles

---

[12] *trairāśikaphalarāśim tam athecchārāśinā hatam kṛtvā|*
     labdham pramāṇabhajitam tasmād icchāphalam idam syāt|| (Shukla 1976: 115–223).
[13] If the division was made first (resulting in the 'fruit' of one measure) and then the multiplication, the computation would have had a step-by-step meaning, but this is not the order adopted by Ab.

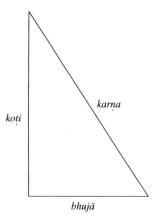

koṭi

karṇa

bhujā

Figure 14.1 Names of the sides of a right-angled triangle.

and equilateral triangles have sides (*aśra*, for all sides), flanks (*pārśva*, a synonym) and sometimes earths (*bhū*, for the base), right-angled triangles have a 'base' (*bhujā*), an 'upright side' (*koṭi*) and a 'hypotenuse' (*karṇa*), as shown in Figure 14.1. In the first half of Ab.2.17, Bhāskara states the Pythagorean Theorem:

That which precisely is the square of the base and the square of the upright side is the square of the hypotenuse.[14]

Therefore, in order to indicate that a situation involves a right-angled triangle, Bhāskara gives the names of the sides of a right-angled triangle to the segments concerned by his reasoning. Two examples of Bhāskara's 'reinterpretation' will demonstrate how he employed this theorem.

2.3 'Reinterpretation' with gnomons

The section devoted to gnomons (*śaṅku*) contains two illuminating cases.

2.3.1 A gnomon and a source of light

The standard situation is as follows: a gnomon (*śaṅku*, DE) casts a shadow (EC), produced by a source of light (A), as illustrated in Figure 14.2.

First, consider the procedure given in Ab.2.15:

The distance between the gnomon and the base, with <the height of> the gnomon for multiplier, divided by the difference of the <heights of the> gnomon and the base.|

[14] *yaś caiva bhujāvargaḥ koṭivargaś ca karṇavargaḥ saḥ* (Shukla 1976: 96).

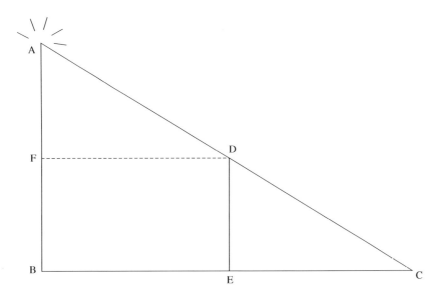

Figure 14.2 A schematized gnomon and light.

Its computation should be known indeed as the shadow of the gnomon ⟨measured⟩ from its foot.||[15]

This procedure involves a multiplication and a division. In modern algebraic notation:

$$EC = \frac{BE \times DE}{AF}$$

The procedure given in the verse appears to be an arbitrary set of operations. Bhāskara begins with a general gloss. Then, as in all his verse commentaries, Bhāskara's commentary provides a list of solved examples. These examples have a standard structure: first comes a versified problem, then a 'setting down' (*nyāsaḥ*) section, and finally a resolution (*karaṇa*).

Thus, in his 'reinterpretation' of the above procedure after a solved example, Bhāskara writes:

This computation is the Rule of Three. How? If from the top of the base which is greater than the gnomon [AF], the size of the space between the gnomon and the base, which is a shadow, [FD = BE] is obtained, then, what is obtained with the gnomon [DE]? The shadow [EC] is obtained.[16]

---

[15] *śaṅkuguṇaṃ śaṅkubhujāvivaraṃ śaṅkubhujayor viśeṣahṛtam|*
    yal labdaṃ sā chāyā jñeyā śaṅkoḥ svamūlād hi|| (Shukla 1976: 90).

[16] *etatkarma trairāśikam/ katham ? saṅkuto 'dhikāyā uparibhujāyā yadi śaṅkubhujānt-*
    arālapramāṇaṃ chāyā labhyate tadā śaṅkunā keti chāyā labhyate/ (Shukla 1976: 92.)

The standard formulation of the Rule of Three, applied to the similar triangles AFD and DEC, can be recognized here. The standard expression of the Rule of Three provides the proportional elements on which the computation is based. Here the rule indicates that the ratio of AF to FD is equal to the ratio of DE to EC. The 'reinterpretation' of the rule thus gives the arbitrary set of operations a mathematical significance. Rather than just a list of operations, the rule in Ab.2.15 becomes a Rule of Three.

2.3.2 A gnomon in relation to the celestial sphere

In the previous commented verse (BAB.2.14), Bhāskara sets out two procedures. Both rest on the proportionality of the right-angled triangle formed by the gnomon and its midday shadow with the right-angled triangle composed by the Rsine of the altitude and the zenithal distance. In the present example, one procedure uses only the Rule of Three, while the other uses the Rule of Three with the Pythagorean Theorem. Both procedures compute the same results.

Consider Figure 14.3. Here, GO represents a gnomon and OC indicates its midday shadow. The circle of radius OSu (Su symbolizing the sun) represents the celestial meridian. The radius OSu is thus equal to the radius of the celestial sphere. S'u designates the projection of the sun onto the horizon. The segment SuS'u illustrates the Rsine of altitude. Bhāskara I notes that the triangle SuS'uO is similar to GOC. Therefore the segment S'uO (that is, the Rsine of the zenithal distance) is proportional to the shadow of the gnomon at noon and the Rsine of the altitude is proportional to the length of the gnomon. This proportionality is further illustrated in Figure 14.4.

In modern algebraic notation,

$$\frac{\text{SuS'u}}{\text{GO}} = \frac{\text{S'uO}}{\text{OC}} = \frac{\text{SuO}}{\text{GC}}$$

The mathematical key to this situation is the relationship between the celestial sphere and the plane occupied by the gnomon, which Bhāskara and Āryabhaṭa call 'one's own circle' (svavṛtta). This relationship is highlighted here by a set of puns. Thus, the gnomon and the Rsine of the altitude have the same name (śaṅku), as do the shadow of the gnomon and the Rsine of zenith distance (chāya). GC is the 'half-diameter of one's own circle'.

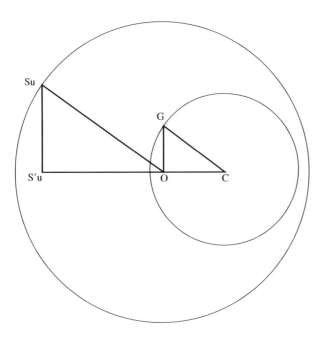

Figure 14.3 Proportional astronomical triangles.

Bhāskara states this relationship by considering the Rule of Three:[17]

In order to establish the Rule of Three – 'If for the half-diameter of one's own circle both the gnomon and the shadow ⟨are obtained⟩, then for the half-diameter of the ⟨celestial⟩ sphere, what are the two ⟨quantities obtained⟩?' In that way the Rsine of altitude and the Rsine of the zenith distance are obtained.

He also adds:[18]

Precisely these two [i.e. the Rsine of the sun's altitude and the Rsine of the sun's zenith distance] on an equinoctial day are said to be the Rsine of colatitude (*avalambaka*) and the Rsine of the latitude (*akṣajyā*).

Indeed, as illustrated in Figure 14.5, on the equinoxes the sun is on the celestial equator. At noon, the sun occupies the intersection of the celestial equator and the celestial meridian. At that moment, the zenithal distance z equals the latitude of the gnomon (φ) and the altitude (a) becomes the co-latitude ($90 - \varphi°$). Once again, the similarity of SuS′uO and OGC is underlined by a certain number of puns. Here, the Rsine of latitude (SuSu′) is called 'perpendicular' (*avalambaka*).

---

[17] *trairāśikaprasiddhyartham – yady asya svavṛttaviṣkambhārdhasya ete śaṅkuc chāye tadā gola-viṣkambhārdhasya ke iti śaṅkuc chāye labhyete* (Shukla 1976: 89).

[18] *tāv eva viṣuvati avalambakākṣajye ity ucyete/* (Shukla 1976: 89).

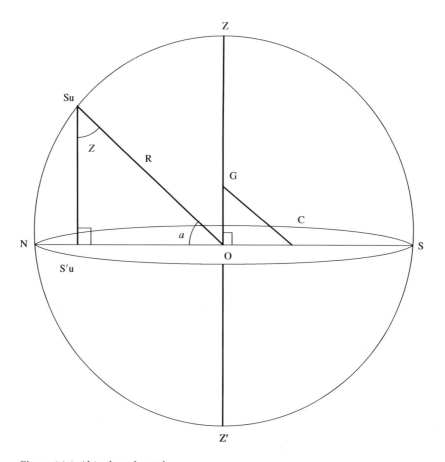

Figure 14.4 Altitude and zenith.

Now, Bhāskara considers an example for an equinox in which OG = 13, OC = 5 and the radius of the celestial sphere (SuO) is the customary 1348. Bhāskara writes:[19]

When computing the Rsine of latitude (*akṣajyā*) the Rule of Three is set down: 13, 5, 3438. What is obtained is the Rsine of latitude, 1322.[20] That is the base (*bhujā*) the half-diameter is the hypotenuse (*karṇa*); the root of the difference of the squares of the base and the hypotenuse is the Rsine of co-latitude (*avalambaka*), 3174.[21]

In this case, Bhāskara uses the fact that the triangles are both right and similar. Bhāskara then uses this similarity to compute SuS'u. Bhāskara

---

[19] *akṣajyā "nayane trairāśikasthāpanā- 13/ 5/ 3438/ labdham akṣajyā 1322/ eṣā bhujā, vyāsārdhaṃ karṇaḥ, bhujākarṇavargaviśeṣamūlam avalambakaḥ 3174.* (Shukla 1976: 90).

[20] This is an approximate value. For more on this value, see Keller 2006: BAB.2.14.

[21] This value is also an approximation.

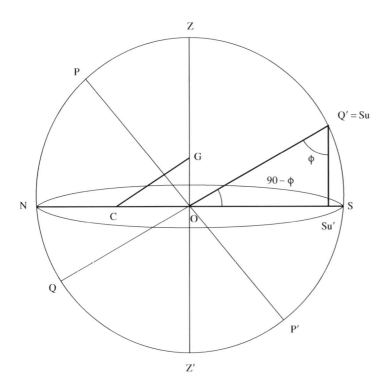

Figure 14.5 Latitude and co-latitude on an equinoctial day.

employs the Pythagorean Theorem to compute OS′u. In order to identify the right-angled triangle, Bhāskara renames the Rsine of latitude (*aksajyā*, SuS′u) as the base of a right-angled triangle (*bhujā*) and he identifies the radius of the celestial sphere as the hypotenuse. Thus, the Rsine is identi-fied with the upright side of a right-angled triangle. This identification implicitly explains how the computation is carried out. However, Bhāskara immediately adds:[22]

With the Rule of Three also 13, 12, 3438; what has been obtained is the Rsine of the colatitude, 3174.[23]

In this way, Bhāskara again computes OS′u by using the similarity of OSuSu′ and OGC. Bhāskara thus computes the same value twice, using two different methods. The most likely explanation is that he verifies the results obtained with one algorithm by using another independent process.

---

[22] *trairāśikenāpi 13/ 12/ 3438/ labdham avalambakaḥ 3174/* (Shukla 1976: 90).
[23] This value is an approximation again.

The mathematical key to both these computations is the prior relationship between the gnomon and the celestial sphere. A syntactical connection establishes the relationship between these two spaces. The invocation of the Rule of Three begins with a standard question. The naming of two of its segments identifies a right-angled triangle. This identification not only indicates one of the mathematical properties underpinning the procedure but also maps the specific astronomical problem onto a more general and abstract mathematical situation. (That is, Rsines of altitudes and zenithal distances become the legs of a simple right-angled triangle.) Since this mathematical interpretation is linked to a set of operations (first multiplication and division, then squaring the lengths with subsequent additions or subtractions of the results), the unexplained steps of the procedure are given a mathematical grounding that may serve as a justification of the algorithm itself.

This analysis thus brings to light two kinds of reasoning: the confirmation of a result by using two independent procedures and the mathematical grounding of a set of operations via their 'reinterpretation' according to the Rule of Three and/or the Pythagorean Theorem. These kinds of mathematical reasoning are also found in the parts of BAB which explicitly have a persuasive aim, attempting to convince the reader that the algorithms of the Ab are correct.

3 Explanations, verifications and proofs

Bhāskara uses specific names when referring to a number of arguments: 'explanations', 'proofs' (*upapatti*) and 'verifications' (*pratyāyakaraṇa*). These arguments do not appear systematically in each verse commentary and – as will be seen below – are always fragmentary. The following description of explanations, proofs and verifications will attempt to highlight how they are structured and the different interpretations they can be subject to.

3.1 Explanations

Bhāskara's commentary on verse 8 of the mathematical chapter of the Ab presents an example of explanation. Verse 8 describes two computations concerning a trapezoid (see Figure 14.6). The first calculation evaluates the length of two segments (*svapātalekha*, EF and FG) of the height of a trapezoid. In this case, the height is bisected at the point of intersection

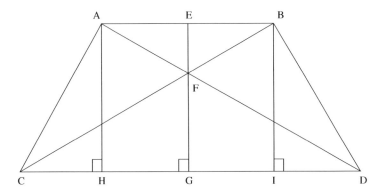

Figure 14.6 Inner segments and fields in a trapezoid.

for the diagonals. The procedure is made of a multiplication followed by a division:[24]

Ab.2.8. The two sides, multiplied by the height ⟨and⟩ divided by their sum, are the 'two lines on their own fallings'.|

When the height is multiplied by half the sum of both widths, one will know the area.||

In other words, with the labels used in Figure 14.6, we have:

$$EF = \frac{AB \times EG}{AB + CD};$$
$$FG = \frac{CD \times EG}{AB + CD}.$$

Likewise, the area $\mathscr{A}$ is:

$$A = EG \times \frac{(AB + CD)}{2}$$

On the first part of the verse, Bhāskara comments:[25]

The size of the 'lines on their own fallings' should be explained (*pratipādayitavya*) with a computation of the Rule of Three on a figure drawn by ⟨a person⟩ properly instructed. Then, by means of just the Rule of Three with both sides, a computation of ⟨the lines whose top is⟩ the intersection of the diagonals and a perpendicular ⟨is performed⟩.

This explanation consists of 'reinterpreting' the procedure – which is a multiplication followed by a division – according to the Rule of Three. The

---

[24] *āyāmaguṇe pārśve tadyogahr̥te svapātalekhe te|*
vistarayogārdhaguṇe jñeyaṃ kṣetraphalam āyāme|| (Shukla 1976: 63).

[25] *samyagādiṣṭena* (rather than *samyagānādiṣṭena* of the printed edition) *ālikhite kṣetre svapātalekhāpramāṇaṃ trairāśikagaṇitena pratipādayitavyaṃ/ tathā trairāśikenaivobhaya pārśve karṇāvalambakasampātānayanam/* (Shukla 1976: 63).

explanation contains two steps. The first step considers the proportionality in a diagram, then 'reinterprets' the set of operations of the algorithm as the application of the Rule of Three. As previously, the seemingly arbitrary set of operations is endowed with a mathematical meaning.

The second computation in verse 8 determines the area of the trapezoid. As shown in Figure 14.6, the area of the trapezoid can be broken into the summation of the areas of several triangles. Alternately, the trapezoid can be decomposed into a rectangle and two triangles.

Although no figure is explicitly drawn, Bhāskara seems to have such a diagram in mind. Indeed, he seems to refer to such a drawing when he writes:[26]

Here, with a previous rule [Ab.2.6.ab] the area of isosceles and uneven trilaterals should be shown/explained (*darśayitavya*). Or, with a rule which will be stated [Ab.2.9] the computation of the area of the inner rectangular field ⟨should be performed⟩;

Even though it has not survived, such a figure shows how areas can be added to give the area of the trapezoid. This time, a collection of already known procedures, those computing the area of triangles and rectangles, is mobilized. We do not know if they are used to 'reinterpret' the procedure or to establish an alternative independent procedure. The procedures of Ab.2.9 will be analysed below.

Both of Bhāskara's explanations in BAB.2.8 consist of:

(1) an explanation of a diagram, and
(2) either a 're-interpretation' of the procedure or exposing an independent alternative procedure. This 're-interpretation' either confirms or verifies the reasoning by looking at a diagram.

Three words refer to an explanation: *vyākhyāna*, *pradarśana* and *pratipādita*. The word *vyākhyāna* indicates that the commentary gives an explanation, but it is also used for an argument connected with a diagram:[27]

Or else, all the procedures ⟨used⟩ in the production of chords are in the realm of a diagram, and a diagram is intelligible ⟨only⟩ with an explanation (*vyakhyāna*). Therefore it has not[28] been put forth (*pratipādita*) ⟨by Āryabhaṭa in the *Āryabhaṭīya*⟩.

---

[26] *pūrvasūtreṇātra dvisamaviṣamatryaśrakṣetraphalaṃ darśayitavyam/ vakṣyamāṇasūtre-snāntarāyatacaturaśrakṣetraphalānayanam (. . .) vā/* (Shukla 1976: 63).

[27] *athavā jyotpattau yatkaraṇam tatsarvam chedyakaviṣayam, chedyakam ca vyākhyānagamyamiti [na] pratipāditam/* (Shukla 1976: 78).

[28] *na* has been added by the editor, K. S. Shukla, and is not found in the manuscripts. Another possible interpretation of the sentence reads: 'Therefore it has been put forth' ⟨by Bhāskara in his commentary⟩.

Note that this passage emphasizes that explanations belong to the genre of commentary and, at least according to Bhāskara, should not be exposed in a treatise.

The word *pradarśana* is derived from the verbal root *dr̥ś-*, 'to see'. It has a similar range of meaning as the English verb 'to show'. It is often hard to distinguish if the word refers to the visual part of an explanation or to the entirety of the explanation. For instance, in BAB.2.11, Bhāskara uses a diagram and writes:[29]

In the field drawn in this way all is to be shown/explained (*pradarśayitavya*).

Finally, the word *pratipādita* is more technical and straightforward. It commonly appears in lists of solved examples found in most of the commented verses in the mathematical part of BAB.

In the illustrations of explanations presented above, the commentator 'reinterprets' geometrical procedures according to the Rule of Three or the Pythagorean Theorem. Only geometrical procedures receive such arguments. Each time, the commentary omits a diagram to which the text seemingly refers. Among the geometrical processes, explanations are 'seen', as will be seen in the only example from the BAB in which the word 'proof' occurs.

3.2 The only two occurrences of the word 'proof'

The Sanskrit word *upapatti* refers directly to a logical argument. This word is used twice in Bhāskara's commentary, as noted by Takao Hayashi.[30] The gender of this word is feminine and it is derived from the verbal root *upa-PAD-*, meaning 'to reach'. Thus, an *upapatti* is literally 'what is reached' and has consequently been translated as 'proof'. In both instances, some ambiguity surrounds this word, and the meaning of the word is not certain.

One occurrence has been quoted above, wherein proofs (*upapatti*) are described as opposed to tradition. The other instance refers to the reasoning whereby the height of a regular tetrahedron is determined from its sides. In this case, Bhāskara understands Āryabhaṭa's rule in the second half of verse 6 of the mathematical chapter as the computation of the volume of a regular tetrahedron. Such a situation is described in Figure 14.7.

Given a regular tetrahedron ABCD, AH is the line through A perpendicular to the plane defined by the triangle BDC. AH is called the 'upward side' (*ūrdhvabhujā*). AC is called *karṇa* (literally, 'ear') because it is the

---

[29] *evam ālikhite kṣetre sarvaṃ pradarśayitavyam* (Shukla 1976: 79).
[30] H1995: 75–6.

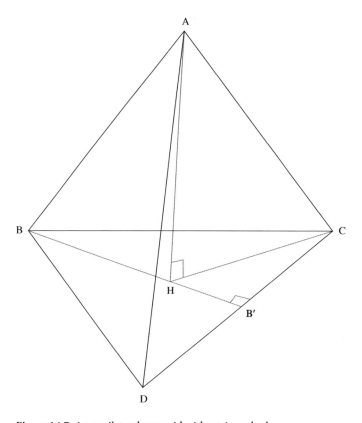

Figure 14.7 An equilateral pyramid with a triangular base.

hypotenuse of AHC. Bhāskara explains how to compute the upright side by
using the Pythagorean Theorem and the Rule of Three. The determination
of CH, from which the upright side AH may be computed, rests upon the
proportional properties of similar triangles, illustrated in Figure 14.8. The
triangles BB′C and B′CH are similar:

$$BB' : CB = CB' : CH.$$

From this relationship it is known that:

$$CH = \frac{CB \times CB'}{BB'}.$$

Bhāskara expressed this relationship as the Rule of Three. The text does
not give a precise argument, but it alludes to the properties as being clear
from a diagram. It is in this context that the word *upapatti* appears:[31]

---

[31] *trairāśikopapattipradarśanārthaṃ kṣetranyāsaḥ–* (Shukla 1976: 59).

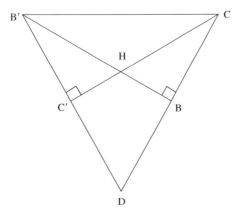

Figure 14.8 The proportional properties of similar triangles.

In order to show the proof (*upapatti*) of ⟨that⟩ Rule of Three, a field is set down.

The argument implied by this word depends on the diagram. As in the case of the explanations, the proof must have been presented orally. This situation differs from the acts of 'reinterpretation' seen above. In the present case, an argument is created, and there is no pre-existing algorithm to 'reinterpret'. However, the foundations of this new argument are set out in a diagram. Furthermore, the procedure used is the Rule of Three, as in the 'explanations' seen above. Another type of argument concerns the correctness of algorithms: verification.

3.3 Verification

Verifications are distinguished from explanations and proofs by their name, *pratyayakaraṇa*. Indeed, *pratyaya* has an etymological root in a verb meaning 'to come back', which has connotations of conviction. *Pratyayakaraṇa* thus means 'enabling to come back' or 'producing conviction'. Historians of Indian mathematics usually understand this word as a type of verification and translate it accordingly.[32]

A verification resembles an explanation in that a verification 'reinterprets' a given procedure according to another rule and establishes a mathematical grounding. The arguments that the commentator labels 'verifications' sometimes present difficulties, and currently our understanding of them is not at all certain. Below are set out several hypotheses about how these verifications can be understood.

---

[32] H1995: 73–4.

3.3.1 Verification of an arithmetical computation

Bhāskara states a verification by the Rule of Five for the rule given in Ab.2.25. Āryabhaṭa states the rule in Ab.2.25 as follows:[33]

The interest on the capital, together with the interest ⟨on the interest⟩, with the time and capital for multiplier, increased by the square of half the capital|
The square root of that, decreased by half the capital and divided by the time, is the interest on one's own capital||

This passage can be formalized as follows. Let m (*mūla*) be capital; let p_1 (*phala*) be the interest on m during a unit of time, $k_1 = 1$ (*kāla*), usually a month. Let p_2 be the interest on p_1 at the same rate for a period of time k_2. If $p_1 + p_2$, m, and k_2 are known, the rule can be expressed in modern mathematical notation as:

$$p_1 = \frac{\sqrt{mk_2(p_1 + p_2) + \left(\dfrac{m}{2}\right)^2} - \dfrac{m}{2}}{k_2}.$$

This rule is derived from a constant ratio:

$$\frac{m}{p_1} = \frac{p_1}{p_2} k_2.$$

The Rule of Five, described in BAB.2.26–27.ab, rests on the same ratio as the rule given in Ab.2.25. In the former instance though, k_1 may be a number other than 1:

$$\frac{m}{p_1} k_1 = \frac{p_1}{p_2} k_2.$$

The Rule of Five indicates an expression equal in value to p_2:

$$p_2 = \frac{p_1^2 k_2}{mk_1}.$$

The Rule of Five may therefore be used in the opposite direction to find a value for p_1.

In BAB.2.25 Bhāskara gives an example:[34]

---

[33] *mūlaphalaṃ saphalaṃ kālamūlaguṇam ardhamūlakṛtiyuktam|*
      tanmūlaṃ mūlārdhonaṃ kālahṛtaṃ svamūlaphalam|| (Shukla 1976: 114).
[34] *jānāmi śatasya phalaṃ na ca kintu śatasya yatphalaṃ saphalam |*
      māsaiś caturbhir āptaṃ ṣaḍ vada vṛddhiṃ śatasya māsotthām|| (Shukla 1976: 114).

1. I do not know the ⟨monthly-⟩ interest on a hundred. However, the ⟨monthly-⟩ ⟨interest on a hundred increased by the interest⟩|
Obtained in four months is six. State the interest of a hundred produced within a month||

This example states a case in which:

$$m = 100$$
$$k_2 = 4$$
$$p_1 + p_2 = 6$$

By the procedure given in Ab.2.25, the value of p_1 is 5.
Bhāskara then adds:[35]

Verification (*pratyayakaraṇa*) with the Rule of Five: 'If the monthly interest (*vṛddhi*)[36] on a hundred is five, then what is the interest of the interest [of value (*dhana*)-five] on a hundred, in four months?'

$$\begin{array}{cc} 1 & 4 \end{array}$$

Setting down: 100 5 The result is one. This increased by the

$$\begin{array}{cc} 5 & 0 \end{array}$$

⟨monthly⟩ interest on the capital is six *rūpa*s, 6.

Simply stated, the verification consists of knowing m, p_1 and k_2, finding p_2 and confirming that its value increased by p_1 will give the same value for $p_1 + p_2$ as stated in the problem.

The Rule of Five, as seen above, returns the value of p_2. This procedure does not deliver the same result but gives a method of inverting the procedure to check independently that the result makes sense. In this case, an independent procedure is established. The use of the Rule of Five, which Bhāskara describes as a combination of two Rules of Three, also imbues the computation with a mathematical basis in proportionality.

3.3.2 Verification of the area of plane figures

Bhāskara interprets the first half of Ab.2.9 as a way to verify procedures for areas given by Āryabhaṭa in the previous verses.

---

[35] *pratyayakaraṇam pañcarāśikena-yadi śatasya māsikī vṛddhin pañca tadā caturbhir māsaiḥ*

$$\begin{array}{cc} 1 & 4 \end{array}$$

śatavṛddheḥ [pañcadhanasya] kā vṛddhiḥ iti/ nyāsar - 100 5 *labdham 1 / etatsahitā*
śatavṛddhiḥ ṣaḍ rūpāṇi 6/ (Shukla 1976: 114–15). 5 0

[36] From now on, unless otherwise stated this is the word translated as 'interest'.

For all fields, when one has acquired the two sides, the area is their product |[37]

Bhāskara endows the verse with the goal of 'verification' – a goal nowhere explicitly appearing in the verse itself. Two steps can be distinguished in the verifications of this verse commentary, each corresponding to a diagram. The first step constructs a diagram of the figure for which an area is verified. The length and width of a rectangle with the same area as the figure are identified. This 'length' and 'width' are usually values from Āryabhaṭa's procedure for which verification is sought. For instance, to verify the area of a triangle, the length of the corresponding rectangle is identified as the height of the triangle, while the width of the rectangle is half the base of the triangle. Precisely, the area of a triangle is given elsewhere by Ab (in the first half of verse 6) as the product of half the base by the height of a triangle. The second step of the argument presents a diagram of the rectangle and computes the multiplication.

How should this argument be understood? According to one means of understanding, this argument is a formal interpretation. The reasoning would consist of considering the rule one seeks to verify as the multiplication of two quantities. Each quantity is then interpreted geometrically as either the length or width of a rectangle with the same area as the initial figure. In this way, Bhāskara calculates the length and height of the rectangle, as required by verse 9.

Another way of understanding the argument begins with the fact that the verification for a given figure *produces* a rectangle of the same area as the given figure. The fact that all figures have a rectangle with the same area would then become an implicit assumption of Sanskrit plane geometry. Takao Hayashi has interpreted this argument in such a manner.[38] The reasoning would produce a rectangle and verify that its area is equal to the area of the figure.

A third approach relies on the 'setting down' parts which contain diagrams. Such a verification consists of *constructing* a rectangle with the same area from a given figure. For instance, in the second step of the verification of the area of a triangle, Bhāskara specifies that when the parts of the area of such a triangle are rearranged (*vyasta*), they produce the rectangle which is drawn. The construction of a rectangle from the original figure is not described in Bhāskara's commentary. However, such constructions could have been known, as shown by the methods exposed in BAB.2.13. Furthermore, this process recalls the algorithms from the *śulbasūtras*, the

---

[37] *sarveṣāṃ kṣetrāṇāṃ prasādhya pārśve phalaṃ tadabhyāsaḥ|* (Shukla 1976: 66).
[38] H1995: 73.

earliest known texts of Sanskrit geometry. These algorithms produce a construction which, although not described in the text, corresponds with the discussion contained in the text. With just such a diagram, the argument in the text would arithmetically verify that the construction is correct.

These three interpretations can be combined if a verification is allowed to be simultaneously geometrical and arithmetical. Bhāskara relies on a geometrical strategy to produce a rectangle with the appropriate area, showing that he knows how to construct the corresponding rectangle from the initial figure. Because the construction is obvious, it would not be detailed, and only the lengths of the rectangle would be given. From an arithmetical perspective, this 'reinterpretation' provides a new understanding of the rule given by Āryabhaṭa. Through his arithmetical 'verification', Bhāskara explains the geometrical verification. Bhāskara explains the link between the sides of the initial figure and the lengths and widths of the rectangle with the same area as the initial figure.

Regardless of which interpretation is accepted, the verification either 'reinterprets' a first algorithm (BAB.2.9) and produces a new understanding of the procedure, or it produces a new procedure that gives the same result (BAB.2.25). In either case, the so-called 'verification' confirms the numerical results and places the procedure in a secure mathematical context. Thus, after verification, the calculations do not appear to be a set of arbitrary steps.

Conclusion

This survey of the BAB has brought to light two kinds of reasonings checking the Ab rules and seeking to convince readers of their validity. One argument exhibits an independent alternative procedure. In one case the procedure exhibited arrives at the same result as the opposite direction procedure. The second type of reasoning, which we have called 'reinterpretation', uses the Rule of Three and the Pythagorean Theorem to provide a new outlook onto the arbitrary steps of the procedure. How should the Rule of Three and the so-called Pythagorean Theorem be described in this context? They are mathematical tools which enable astronomical situations or specific problems to be 'reinterpreted' as abstract and general cases, involving right-angled triangles and proportionalities. The arbitrary steps of the procedure are thus given a mathematical explanation.

Nonetheless, the methods of reasoning are hard to understand and pin down. This difficulty may arise from their oral nature, of which Bhāskara's written text preserves only a portion. For instance, the function of diagrams in these reasonings still remains mysterious. Further detailed explorations of how Sanskrit texts explain, prove and verify mathematical algorithms will advance understanding about how the mathematical correctness of algorithms was conceptualized by mathematicians in the Indian subcontinent.

Bibliography

Ikeyama, S. (2003) 'Brāhmasphuṭasiddhānta (ch. 21) of Brahmagupta with Commentary of Pṛthudaka, critical edition with English translation and notes', *Indian Journal of History of Science* **38**: S1–308.

Jain, P. K. (2001) *The Sūryaprakāśa of Sūryadasa: A Commentary on Bhāskarācarya's Bijagaṇita*, vol. I: *A Critical Edition, English Translation and Commentary for the Chapters Upodghata, Sadvidhaprakaraṇa and Kuttakadhikara*. Vadaroda.

Keller, A. (2006) *Expounding the Mathematical Seed: Bhāskara and the Mathematical Chapter of the* Āryabhaṭīya, 2 vols. Basel.

Sarma, S. R. (2002) 'Rule of Three and its variation in India', in *From China to Paris: 2000 years of Transmission of Mathematical Ideas*, ed. Y. Dold-Samplonius, J. W. Dauben, M. Folkerts and B. Van Dalen. Stuttgart: 133–56.

Shukla, K. S. (1976) *Āryabhaṭīya of Āryabhaṭa, with the Commentary of Bhāskara I and Someśvara*. Delhi.

Srinivas, M. D. (1990) 'The methodology of Indian mathematics and its contemporary relevance', in *History of Science and Technology in India: Mathematics and Astronomy*, vol. II, ed. G. Kuppuram and K. Kumudamani. Delhi: 29–86.

15 | Argumentation for state examinations: demonstration in traditional Chinese and Vietnamese mathematics

ALEXEI VOLKOV

Introduction

Recently a number of authors have argued, once again, that a historical study of mathematical texts conducted without taking into consideration the circumstances of their production and use could be fundamentally flawed. For instance, E. Robson claimed that a large number of cuneiform Babylonian mathematical tablets were produced in the process of mathematical instruction, either by students or instructors, and therefore their interpretation as 'purely mathematical texts' would be inadequate.[1] Robson's taking into consideration the educational function of the cuneiform mathematical tablets provided additional arguments in support of a somewhat unorthodox interpretation of the mathematical tablet Plimpton 322, hitherto believed to be one of the best-studied Babylonian mathematical texts (this interpretation was originally suggested by Bruins in 1940s and 1950s and reiterated by other authors in the early 1980s).

In conventional historiography of Chinese mathematics the mathematical treatises compiled prior to the end of the first millennium CE were often tacitly assumed to be mathematical texts *per se* rather than mathematical textbooks; this assumption to a large extent shaped the approaches to their interpretation. The characteristic features of textbooks (i.e. texts composed as collections of problems often containing groups of generic problems and detailed descriptions of elementary arithmetical operations without explanations or justifications of the provided algorithms) were not allotted much attention; instead, historians often focused on singular 'mathematically significant' methods and results (such as the calculation of the value of π and the algorithm for solution of simultaneous linear equations, for instance) thus reinforcing the image of the received Chinese mathematical treatises as 'research monographs' rather than 'textbooks'.

However, even in modern mathematics a research paper can be used as teaching material, and, conversely, a mathematical statement from a

---

[1] Robson 2001: 171.

textbook can become the starting point of a professional mathematical inquiry. Similarly, it well may be possible that in a given mathematical tradition there was no wall separating texts of the two types from each other, and a special investigation of the social circumstances of the use of given mathematical texts has to be provided each time in order to avoid historiographic distortions. Unfortunately, even the most outstanding modern historians have often presented Chinese mathematical treatises as if they were research monographs; this approach to Chinese mathematical texts is found already in Mikami (1913) and certainly in Yushkevich (1955) and Needham (1959), not to mention their numerous Chinese counterparts. An attempt to classify the mathematical problems found in Chinese treatises was recently made by Martzloff,[2] yet his classification apparently reflected the seeming heterogeneity of Chinese mathematical treatises as perceived by modern historians solely on the basis of the contents of individual problems rather than the way in which mathematical treatises containing them were actually read and used in traditional China. Presumably, there may have existed social settings in which one and the same problem was treated as belonging to different categories. It can be demonstrated that the majority of the extant treatises of the late first millennium BCE to the first millennium CE were used as mathematical textbooks in state educational institutions for several centuries,[3] unlike the mathematical treatises of the Song (960–1279), Yuan (1279–1368) and Ming (1368–1644) dynasties of which the circumstances of use are often unknown. Unfortunately, all the attempts to offer a plausible reconstruction of the functioning of these texts in educational context have been thwarted by the lack of data concerning mathematics instruction in traditional China in the late first to early second millennium CE, and, in particular, by the lack of the original examination papers. To circumvent this difficulty, in what follows I will use

---

[2] Martzloff 1997: 54 suggests that the mathematical problems in Chinese treatises belonged to the four following categories: (1) 'real problems' (applicable in real-life situations); (2) 'pseudo-real problems' ('neither plausible nor directly usable'); (3) 'recreational problems'; (4) 'speculative or purely mathematical problems'. Only problems of category (2) thus may have been used in mathematical instruction, while problems of type (4) represented 'pure mathematics'. Martzloff himself (1997: 58) played down the applicability of his classification when stating that the problems of category (1) also belonged to category (4).

[3] The circumstances of the use of the recently unearthed mathematical treatise *Suan shu shu* 筭數書 (Writing on computations with counting rods) as well as the mathematical treatises and fragments found in Dunhuang caves remain unknown. Here and below I use the *pinyin* transliteration of the Chinese characters which nowadays has become a *de facto* standard in continental European sinology. I use my own translations of the titles of Chinese mathematical treatises; for the reader who may be confused by these translations I provide a list of them in Appendix II together with the translations of the titles as found in Martzloff 1997.

a 'model examination paper' found in a nineteenth-century Vietnamese mathematical treatise that turned out to be instrumental in reconstructing the role played by the commentaries on mathematical texts in the context of institutionalised mathematical instruction in traditional China and Vietnam.

Mathematics education in traditional China

In Western historiography the part played by Chinese mathematics education arguably remains underestimated, probably due to a particular stand adopted by the nineteenth-century European authors and perpetuated in the publications of influential historians of the twentieth century. A highly negative (as much as inaccurate) evaluation of mathematics education in traditional China was offered by the French sinologist Édouard Biot (1803–50) who presented mathematics education in the Mathematical College (*Suan xue* 筭學) as follows:[4] '. . . to call it a "mathematics school" would mean to praise too high the studies in this elementary [educational] institution.'[5] In this chapter I will not investigate reasons for this surprisingly low evaluation of the mathematical education in China – to do so, one probably would need to study the history of the image of China in Europe, in particular in France, created by various individuals and institutions beginning with the Jesuits.[6] Certainly, at the time when Biot was writing his lines, not much was known about the history of Chinese mathematics; Biot himself never systematically worked on Chinese mathematics and had only a partial access to the original texts.[7] It is interesting to note that Biot (mistakenly) believed that the *Jiu zhang suan shu* 九章筭術 (Computational

---

[4] In this chapter I use both the characters *suan* 筭 and *suan* 算 even though in modern editions of historical materials the former is often changed to the latter, since their original meaning, as the dictionary *Shuo wen jie zi* 說文解字 by Xu Shen 許慎 (55?–149? CE) specifies, was not the same: the character *suan* 筭 meant the counting rods, and *suan* 算, the operations performed with the instrument. In this chapter I use *suan* 筭 if it occurred in a title of a book or in a name of an institution at least once in an edition of the quoted source.

[5] '. . . le nom d'école des mathématiques donnerait une trop haute idée des études de cet établissement élémentaire. . .' (Biot 1847: 257, n. 1). In this chapter the translations from French and Chinese are mine, unless stated otherwise.

[6] Biot 1847: v–ix.

[7] Biot was familiar with three of the twelve books used for mathematics instruction in seventh-century China, namely, with the mathematical treatises *Qi gu suan jing* 緝古筭經 (Computational treatise on the continuation of [traditions of] ancient [mathematicians]) and *Sun zi suan jing* 孫子筭經 (Computational treatise of Master Sun), as well as the astronomical treatise *Zhou bi suan jing* 周髀筭經 (Computational treatise on the gnomon of Zhou [dynasty]). He was unable to identify correctly the titles of the other treatises (p. 261), and the

procedures of nine categories) compiled no later than the first century CE contained the Pascal triangle (referred to by Biot as 'binomial expansions up to the sixth degree',[8] which could hardly be seen as 'elementary', and yet argued for the inferiority of the Chinese mathematical treatises. The following phrase of Biot seemingly explains his reasons: '[The treatises] are collections of problems, the most part of them elementary, with the solutions given without demonstrations'.[9] The word 'demonstrations' might make one think that Biot meant a comparison with the European textbooks of his time written in 'Euclidean' style, as lists of theorems accompanied by proofs. This conjecture, however, lacks any supporting evidence; on the contrary, an anti-Euclidean trend was rather powerful among French educators at the moment when Biot was writing his lines, as the following quotation shows:

Whoever wishing from now on to put geometry within the reach of mind and to teach it in a rational way should, I think, present it as we just have seen it [above] and remove all that is no more than just a vague expression and pure hassle. This bothering equipment of definitions, principles, axioms, theorems, lemmas, scholia, corollaries, should be completely eliminated, as well as all other futile particularities [of the same kind], the only effect of which is that they put too heavy a burden on the [human] spirit and make it tired in its progress.[10]

Moreover, a cursory analysis of the contemporaneous French arithmetical textbooks suggests that by 'demonstrations' Biot most likely meant step-by-step explanations of numerical solutions found in a large number of French textbooks published by the mid nineteenth century, and not

---

way he approached the documents transpires from his remark on the *Zhou bi suan jing*: 'The *Zhou bi*, which has in China an immense reputation, presents several exact notions concerning the movement of the sun and the moon surrounded by strange absurdities'
(Le *Tcheou-pei*, qui a une réputation immense en Chine, présente, au milieu d'étranges absurdités, quelques notions exactes sur les mouvements du soleil et de la lune) (p. 262). Moreover, Biot did not have access to the *Jiu zhang suan shu* 九章筭術 (Computational procedures of nine categories), the cornerstone of the mathematical curriculum, and made his judgement solely on the basis of the *Suan fa tong zong* 算法統宗 (Summarized fundamentals of computational methods, 1592) by Cheng Dawei 程大位 the contents of which he believed to be identical with that of the *Jiu zhang suan shu* (*ibid.*).

[8] Biot 1847: 262.

[9] '[Les ouvrages] sont des collections de questions qui sont, pour la plupart, élémentaires, et dont la solution est donnée sans démonstration' (Biot 1847: 262).

[10] 'Quiconque voudra désormais mettre la géométrie à la portée des intelligences et l'enseigner d'une manière rationnelle, devra, je crois, la présenter telle que nous venons de la voir et en écarter tout ce qui n'est que vague expression et pure enflure. Cet attirail embarrassant de définitions, de principes, d'axiomes, de théorèmes, de lemmes, de scolies, de corollaires, doit être mis complètement de côté, ainsi que les autres distinctions futiles qui n'ont d'autre effet que de surcharger l'esprit et de le fatiguer dans sa marche' (Bailly 1857: 11–12).

deductions performed in an axiomatic system.[11] The statement of Biot as well as his reasons to claim the inferiority of Chinese textbooks certainly deserve a further investigation which, unfortunately, would lead us far beyond the scope of the present chapter.

A detailed description of mathematics instruction (once again, in the framework of a general outline of the state education in China of the Tang dynasty) was offered almost a century later by Robert des Rotours (1891–1980) who, unlike Biot, avoided any critical remarks concerning the contents and the level of the mathematical instruction in China.[12] The critique of Chinese mathematics education was back in 1959 when Needham energetically accused Ming Confucian scholarship of 'confin[ing] mathematics to the back rooms of provincial *yamens*' and the 'deadening influence' of the examination system.[13] Yet his accusations missed the target, since the Song dynasty (960–1279) algebra he praised in the same paragraph had vanished some sixty years prior to the beginning of the Ming dynasty (1368–1644) and thus certainly well before the introduction of the examination system featuring the formalized way of writing examination papers known as 'eight-legged essays' he referred to.[14] Chinese mathematics education was once again judged unsatisfactory by U. Libbrecht and J.-C. Martzloff.[15] In turn, M.-K. Siu and A. Volkov briefly addressed the critique of the latter authors, yet a full analysis of the role of the state mathematics education in traditional China remains a challenging task.[16] In this chapter I will not discuss general issues such as whether the state examinations system impeded or boosted the development of mathematics in China,[17] but shall focus instead on the changes in the interpretation and understanding of mathematical treatises which might have happened as the result of their embedding into the curriculum of the state educational institutions in the seventh century CE.

---

[11] See, for instance, P.-N. Collin, *Manuel d'arithmétique démontrée. . .*, Paris, 1828 (7th edn), which, as its very title suggests, was supposed to provide 'demonstrations'. The format of this textbook is similar to that of a large number of contemporaneous French textbooks, such as the anonymous *Abrégé d'arithmétique, à l'usage des écoles chrétiennes* (Rouen, 1810), *Abrégé d'arithmétique à l'usage des écoles primaires* (Paris, 1850), *Abrégé d'arithmétique décimale. . .* (Perpignan, 1855, actual printing 1856), among many others.

[12] Des Rotours 1932.

[13] Needham 1959: 153–4; esp. see fn. *f* on p. 153.

[14] Lee 2000: 143–4.

[15] Libbrecht 1973: 5; Martzloff 1997: 79–82.

[16] Siu and Volkov 1999.

[17] See, among others, interesting observations of Wong 2004 on the role of the 'Confucian' context in modern mathematics education.

Chinese mathematical instruction of the first millennium CE

It remains unclear when and where mathematical subjects were introduced into the curriculum of Chinese state educational institutions. Sun claims that the Mathematical College (*Suan xue* 算學) was established during the Northern Zhou dynasty (557–81) in the capital of this state, Chang'an (modern Xi'an);[18] the students of the College were called *suan fa sheng* 算法生, literally, 'students of computational methods'. Lee reports that he was unable to find any evidence confirming that the Mathematical College was indeed established under the Northern Wei dynasty (386–534), as Sun suggested.[19] However, Lee agrees that the subject had been taught officially in the North for a long time even before the Northern Wei, in particular by official historians, who excelled in calendar calculation. The system of state mathematics education established by the early seventh century in China united under the rule of the Sui (581–618) and Tang (618–907) dynasties comprised two elements: (1) the state mathematics examinations held on a regular basis, and (2) the Mathematical College operating under the control of the governmental agency called 'Supervisorate of National Youth' (*Guo zi jian* 國子監);[20] the latter was metaphorically referred to by some modern authors as the 'State University'. In Song dynasty China the Mathematical College returned under the authority of the Supervisorate of National Youth for a relatively short period of time, 1104–1131;[21] the College functioned before and after this period of time under the auspices of other governmental agencies.[22] This explains why ten out of twelve mathematical treatises used as textbooks during the Tang dynasty (618–907) were re-edited and reprinted with educational purposes in 1084 and 1200–1213. Mathematical courses also constituted a part of the curricula of the future astronomers and calendar experts instructed at the courts of the non-Chinese Jin dynasty 金 (1115–1234), and, later, Yuan 元 (1271–1368).[23]

There exist several descriptions of the instruction in the Mathematical College (*Suan xue* 算學) during the Tang dynasty; the descriptions specify the number of students, a list of the textbooks, the periods of time allotted to the study of each book, as well as other details.[24] The textbooks and the

---

[18] Sun 2000: 138.

[19] Lee 2000: 515, n. 230.

[20] Rendered 'Directorate of Education' by Hucker 1985: 299 and 'Directorate of National Youth' by Lee 2000.

[21] Li 1977: 271–9; Lee 2000: 519–20.

[22] Hucker 1985: 461.

[23] Lee 2000: 520–3.

[24] The descriptions are found in the *Tang liu dian* 唐六典 (The six codes of the Tang [dynasty]), compiled in 738, see *TLD* 21: 10b and in the *Xin Tang shu* 新唐書 (The New History of the

Table 15.1. The mathematical curriculum of the Tang State University

Number	Title	Duration of study	Programme[a]
1	*Sun zi* 孫子 (Master Sun)	One year for two treatises together	Regular
2	*Wu cao* 五曹 (Five departments)		Regular
3	*Jiu zhang* 九章 (Nine categories)	Three years for two treatises together	Regular
4	*Hai dao* 海島 (Sea island)		Regular
5	*Zhang Qiujian* 張丘建 ([Master] Zhang Qiujian)	One year	Regular
6	*Xiahou Yang* 夏侯陽 ([Master] Xiahou Yang)	One year	Regular
7	*Zhou bi* 周髀 (The gnomon of the Zhou [dynasty])	One year for two treatises together	Regular
8	*Wu jing suan* 五經筭 (Computations in the five classical books)		Regular
9	*Zhui shu* 綴術 (Mending procedures)[b]	Four years	Advanced
10	*Qi gu* 緝古 (Continuation [of traditions] of ancient [mathematicians])	Three years	Advanced
11	*Ji yi* 記遺 (Records of [things] left behind for posterity)	Not specified	Supplementary
12	*San deng shu* 三等數 (Numbers of three ranks)	Not specified	Supplementary

Notes:

[a] The terms 'regular' and 'advanced' are not found in the original descriptions; they are added for the convenience of the reader. For the explanation of these terms, see below.

[b] The meaning of the title remains unclear; see Yan 2000: 125–32.

duration of their study as specified in the *Xin Tang shu* (The New History of the Tang [dynasty]) are listed in Table 15.1.

The order of the books in Table 15.1 is that adopted in the *Xin Tang shu*; it remains unclear why the list begins with the treatises *Sun zi* and *Wu cao*, certainly less important than the treatises under numbers 3, 7 and 9, as suggested by an inspection of their extant versions listed in Table 15.2

Tang [dynasty]), compiled in 1060, see *XTS* 44: 2a. The lists of the books and the duration of their study specified in these two sources are identical. For a translation of the description found in the *Xin Tang shu*, see des Rotours 1932: 139–42, 154–5; see also Siu 1995: 226; Siu and Volkov 1999.

Table 15.2. Conventional identification of the Tang dynasty textbooks with the extant mathematical treatises

Number	Treatises listed in the *Xin Tang shu*	Identified as the following extant treatises	Author	Date of compilation
1	*Sun zi* 孫子 (Master Sun)	*Sun zi suan jing* 孫子筭經 (Computational treatise of Master Sun)	Unknown[a]	C. 400 CE (?)[b]
2	*Wu cao* 五曹 (Five departments)	*Wu cao suan jing* 五曹筭經 (Computational treatise of five departments)	Unknown[c]	Not earlier than 386 CE[d]
3	*Jiu zhang* 九章 (Nine categories)	*Jiu zhang suan shu* 九章筭術 (Computational procedures of nine categories)	Unknown[e]	Prior to the mid first century CE[f]
4	*Hai dao* 海島 (Sea island)	*Hai dao suan jing* 海島筭經 (Computational treatise [beginning with a problem] about a sea island)	Liu Hui (*fl.* 263)	C. 263 CE
5	*Zhang Qiujian* 張丘建 ([Master] Zhang Qiujian)	*Zhang Qiujian suan jing* 張丘建筭經 (Computational treatise of Zhang Qiujian)	Zhang Qiujian 張丘建	Mid fifth century CE[g]
6	*Xiahou Yang* 夏侯陽 ([Master] Xiahou Yang)	*Xiahou Yang suan jing* 夏侯陽筭經 (Computational treatise of Xiahou Yang)	Han Yan 韓延	763–79[h]
7	*Zhou bi* 周髀 (The gnomon of Zhou [dynasty])	*Zhou bi suan jing* 周髀筭經 (Computational treatise on the gnomon of Zhou [dynasty])	Unknown	Early first century CE (?)[i]

Continued

Table 15.2 *Continued*

Number	Treatises listed in the *Xin Tang shu*	Identified as the following extant treatises	Author	Date of compilation
8	*Wu jing suan* 五經筭 (Computations in the five classical books)	*Wu jing suan shu* 五經筭術 (Computational procedures [found] in the five classical books)	Zhen Luan (*fl. c.* 570 CE)	*C.* 570 CE
9	*Zhui shu* 綴術 (Mending procedures)	*Not extant*	Zu Chongzhi 祖沖之 (429–500)[j]	Second half of the fifth century CE
10	*Qi gu* 緝古 (Continuation [of the work] of ancient [authors])	*Qi gu suan jing* 緝古筭經 (Computational treatise on the continuation [traditions] of ancient [mathematicians])	Wang Xiaotong 王孝通 (*b.* ?– *d.* after 626 CE)[k]	*C.* 626 CE
11	*Ji yi* 記遺 (Records of [things] left behind for posterity)	*Shu shu ji yi* 數術記遺 (Records of the procedures of numbering left behind for posterity)	Xu Yue 徐岳 (b. before 185 – d. after 227)	*C.* 220 CE
12	*San deng shu* 三等數 (Numbers of three ranks)	*Not extant*	Dong Quan 董泉	Prior to 570 CE

Notes:

[a] A book entitled *Sun zi* 孫子 by one Sun Chao 孫綽 of the Jin dynasty (265–420) is mentioned in the lists of proscribed books of the third through the tenth century, see An and Zhang 1992: 51; it is not impossible that this was the mathematical treatise or its prototype and not the famous treatise *Sun zi bing fa* 孫子兵法 on the art of war written in *c.* fifth century BCE.

[b] Qian Baocong suggested that the treatise was compiled in *c.* 400 CE; he also believed that the extant version was altered during the Sui (581–618) and Tang (618–907) dynasties, see *SJSSa*: 275; Guo 2001: 14.

[c] In some sources the treatise credited to the authorship of Zhen Luan 甄鸞, *fl. c.* 570, see *SJSSa*: 409.

[d] The date suggested by Qian Baocong; he also suggested that the extant version of the text may have been modified in the seventh century CE, see *SJSSa*: 409, Guo

Notes: (continued)

2001: 18. Compare with the date 'fifth century? Very approximately' suggested by Martzloff 1997: 124.

[e] Liu Hui 劉徽 in his 'Preface' of 263 CE suggested that the treatise was compiled on the basis of an ancient prototype by Zhang Cang 張蒼 (?–152 BCE) and Geng Shouchang 耿壽昌 (*fl.* first century BCE), see *SJSSb*: 83; for a discussion, see CG2004: 127. The opinion of Liu Hui is one of the numerous theories concerning the date of compilation of the treatise; for an overview, see Li 1982. See also Cullen 1993a.

[f] Compare with the date '200 BCE–300 CE' suggested by Martzloff 1997: 124.

[g] Qian Baocong suggested that the treatise was completed between 466 and 485 CE (*SJSSa*: 325), while Feng Lisheng argued for the interval 431–50 (Guo 2001: 16).

[h] Guo 2001: 25. The text of the original treatise written by Xiahou Yang 夏侯陽 most probably in the first half of the fifth century CE was lost by the eleventh century and replaced by a compilation of Han Yan 韓延 written in 763–79; see *SJSSa*: 551.

[i] The dates suggested for this treatise vary considerably; I adopt here the viewpoint of Cullen 1993b and 1996, being well aware of other opinions concerning the date of compilation. Martzloff 1997: 124 provides a hardly acceptable period of time: '100 BCE (?) – 600 CE'.

[j] Wang Xiaotong in his 'Preface' to the *Qi gu suan jing* 緝古筭經 mentions Zu Gengzhi 祖暅之 (*b.* before *c.* 480 – *d.* after 525) and not his father Zu Chongzhi as the author of the treatise (*SJSSb*: 415).

[k] Martzloff 1997: 125 suggests for Wang's lifetime the dates '*c.* 650–750' which are impossible given that his treatise was included in the collection of 656 CE.

below. The list could not be chronological either, given that according to the conventional chronology the *Zhou bi* certainly was considered to antedate the treatise *Hai dao* and yet was listed after it. The only suggestion that seems plausible is that the list followed the order in which the treatises were actually studied.[25]

According to the *Tang liu dian* 唐六典 (Six Codes of the Tang [Dynasty]) and to the *Jiu Tang shu* 舊唐書 (Old History of the Tang [Dynasty]), the students of the College were subdivided into two groups each comprising fifteen students. The first group studied treatises [1–8], and the second one treatises [9–10].[26] In Table 15.1 and below I refer to the textbooks of the groups [1–8] and [9–10] as constituting a 'regular programme' and an 'advanced programme', respectively, given that the extant version of the treatise [10] contains more difficult mathematical methods than those found in [1–8] (in particular, solution of cubic equations), and that the now lost treatise [9] was, according to Li Chunfeng, a difficult book (and,

[25] An almost identical list can be found in the *Jiu Tang shu* (Old History of the Tang [dynasty]) (*JTS* 44: 17b), yet the order of the treatises in the 'regular programme' is different: *Jiu zhang, Hai dao, Sun zi, Wu cao, Zhang Qiujian, Xiahou Yang,* and *Zhou bi.* The *San deng shu* is mentioned as *San deng.*

[26] *TLD* 21: 10b, *JTS* 44: 17b. The *Xin Tang shu* only mentions that the number of students amounts to thirty, see *XTS* 44: 1b, des Rotours 1932: 133.

as becomes clear from an inspection of the number of years allotted to the study of the treatises, the most difficult book in either programme).[27] The study in each programme required seven years. Books [11–12] were studied simultaneously with the other treatises in both programmes; the time necessary for their study was not specified.[28]

The conventional identification of the twelve treatises constituting the curriculum is found in a number of modern works and is summarized in Table 15.2.

The conventional identification of the Tang dynasty textbooks with the extant treatises contains a number of points that have never been sufficiently clarified. For instance, there are three treatises listed in the bibliographical section of the dynastic history *Xin Tang shu* which, hypothetically, might be identified as the textbook *Jiu zhang* listed in Table 15.1 and mentioned in the chapter on state examination of the same history: they are the *Jiu zhang suan shu* compiled by Xu Yue, the *Jiu zhang suan jing* compiled by Zhen Luan (*XTS* 59: 13a), and the *Jiu zhang suan shu* commented on (*zhu* 注) by Li Chunfeng (*XTS* 59: 13b), all three treatises in nine chapters (*juan* 卷). If the latter treatise is assumed to be the textbook used for instruction, it remains unclear whether it was identical with the only extant Song dynasty edition of the treatise commented (*zhu* 注) by Liu Hui and accompanied with the explanations of the commentaries (*zhu shi* 注釋) by Li Chunfeng (see below). The *Zhang Qiujian* from the curriculum could be either the *Zhang Qiujian suan jing* 張丘建筭經 in one *juan* commented on by Zhen Luan (*XTS* 59: 13a), or a three-*juan* edition of the treatise commented on by Li Chunfeng (*XTS* 59: 13b); however, the earliest (and only extant) Song dynasty edition in three *juan* mentions Zhen Luan as the commentator while containing only commentaries signed by Li Chunfeng (*SJSSb*: 343). As for the treatise listed in the curriculum as *Xiahou Yang*, the bibliographical chapter of the *Xin Tang shu* mentions two books the titles of which bear reference to this name: one is the *Xiahou Yang suan jing* commented on by Zhen Luan, and

---

[27] Li Chunfeng wrote about Zu Chongzhi and his book as follows: '筭氏之最者也。所著之書名為綴術。學官莫能究其深奧。是故廢而不理。 [He] was the best of mathematicians. The title of the book [he] compiled is *Mending procedures*. No one of the faculty [lit. 'functionaries'] of the [Mathematical?] College was able to comprehend thoroughly the profound [ideas it contained]. This is why [they] abandoned [the book] without [even trying] to understand [it].' (*SS* 16: 4a). Martzloff's translation of the last part of this quotation reads 'He [Zu Chongzhi – A.V.] was excluded (from the textbooks used for teaching) because none of the students of the Imperial College could understand him' (Martzloff 1997: 45, n. 22), and it is somewhat misleading, since Li Chunfeng's statement was clearly pointed against the personnel of the College (and not against its students), while the high esteem he expressed for the book of Zu Chongzhi was apparently related to his decision to introduce the *Zhui shu* into the curriculum as the cornerstone of the advanced programme.

[28] Siu and Volkov 1999.

the other is the *Xiahou Yang suan jing* authored by one Han Yan 韓延 whose lifetime has been a matter of controversy. The hypothesis advanced by Qian Baocong and adopted by other modern authors states that the received book is dated of the eighth century (*SJSSb*: 25–7), yet the extant version contains three *juan* unlike the treatises listed in the *Xin Tang shu*, both containing only one *juan*.

The examination procedure

There were two kinds of examinations held in the Mathematical College: (1) the regular tests conducted every ten days, and (2) the examinations at the end of the year. The regular tests included three questions: two on memorization of a 2000-word excerpt and one on the 'general meaning' (*da yi* 大義) of the excerpt. The examination at the end of each year was held orally; students were asked ten questions on the 'general meaning'. It seems that there was no graduation examination at the end of the entire course.[29]

Those who successfully graduated from the College were allowed to take the examination for the doctoral degree *ming suan* 明筭[30] together with some other categories of candidates.[31] The examination included two parts. The task for the first part was to write an essay answering ten questions related to one of the two programmes, 'regular' or 'advanced'. The second part of the examination in both cases consisted of a test on the memorization of the treatises *San deng shu* and *Shu shu ji yi* held in the form of 'examination by quotation' (literally, 'strip reading' *tie du* 帖讀 or 'strip [reading] of classics' *tie jing* 帖經).[32] The *Xin Tang shu* provides the following description of the examination procedure of the first part:

凡筭學。錄大義〈本〉〔十〕條為問荅。明數造術。詳明術理。然後為
通。試九章三條。海島、孫子、五曹、張丘建、夏侯陽、周髀、五經筭各

---

29 See *XTS* 44: 2a; for translation see des Rotours 1932: 141–2, for a discussion of the procedure see Siu and Volkov 1999.

30 Literally, '[He Who] Understood Computations' (or 'Learned in Mathematics', as Lee 2000: 138 suggests); the 'he' in the translation is imposed by the historical setting in which only men were admissible to the state examinations. The appellation of the degree (and of the related examination) was thus similar to the other titles referring to the degrees and examinations on the Confucian classics (*ming jing* 明經, lit. '[He Who] Understood the Classics'), law (*ming fa* 明法, lit. '[He Who] Understood the [Juridical] Norms'), calligraphy and writing (*ming zi* 明字, lit. '[He Who] Understood the [Chinese] Characters'); see des Rotours 1932: 128.

31 See des Rotours 1932: 128, n. 1 for a detailed description of the candidates.

32 On the procedure of the 'examination by quotation' see des Rotours 1932: 30–31, 141, n. 2; Siu and Volkov 1999: 91, n. 41; see also Lee 2000: 142.

一條。十通六。記遺、三等數。帖讀。十得九。為第。試綴術、緝古。錄
大義為問答者。明數造術。詳明術理。無注者。合數造術。不失義理。然
後為通。綴術七條。緝古三條。十通六。記遺、三等數。帖讀。十得九。
為第。落經者雖通六。不第。 (*XTS* 44: 1b–2a)

All [the candidates examined in] the Mathematical College[33] [have to] produce
records[34] of 'general meaning' for ten[35] tasks [represented with] mathematical
problems (lit. 'problems and answers').[36] [They have to] elucidate the numerical
values [of the problems], [and to] design [computational] procedures [that would
solve them]. [They] elucidate in detail the internal structure of the [computational]
procedures [they designed].[37] [If they do] so, then they pass. [When they are] tested

[33] Des Rotours 1932 : 154 suggests 'For mathematical studies . . .' ('Pour l'étude des
mathématiques . . .'); his suggestion shows that he may have been perplexed by the
heterogeneous headings of the paragraphs describing the examinations: in some cases the
beginning of the description mentions the degree, as in the case of the law examination for
the degrees *jin shi* and *ming fa*: 凡進士 . . . 'All [the candidates for the degree] *jin shi*. . .'; 凡
明法 . . . 'All [the candidates for the degree] *ming fa* . . .' (*XTS* 44: 2b, ll. 11–12), while in the
case of the examinations for the degrees *ming zi* 明字 and *ming suan* 明筭 the names of the
corresponding schools, *shu xue* 書學 and *suan xue* were mentioned instead (*XTS* 44: 2b, ll.
13–14). This specification of the institution can mean that the candidates were examined in
the respective college and/or the only candidates admitted to the examination were those who
graduated from it.

[34] The word used here, *lu* 錄, does not appear in the description of other examinations; des
Rotours 1932: 154, n. 3 writes 'I am not certain of my translation, because I don't understand
well the meaning of the word *lu* 錄' ('Je ne suis pas certain de ma traduction car je ne
comprends pas bien le sens du mot *lu* 錄.'). Indeed, the term *lu* looks somewhat inappropriate
in the context of examination, since one of its principal meanings is 'to copy, to record'. My
interpretation of this term as 'writing a protocol [of computations]' is discussed below.

[35] This emendation of the original text containing the word *ben* 本 ('original') is based on three
premises. Firstly, the descriptions of the other examinations in the *Xin Tang shu* containing
the clause 'V大義X條' with a verb V with the meaning 'to examine', 'to ask', etc., always have
a numeral in the position of X, e.g., 問大義十條 ('ask [to complete] ten tasks on general
meaning'), the examination for the degree *ming jing* 明經 (*XTS* 44: 2b, ln.3); 問大義五十條
('ask [to complete] 50 tasks on general meaning'), the examination on the degree *ming jing*,
option 'Three [Great] commentaries' 三傳科 (*XTS* 44: 2b, lns. 5–6); 問大義百條 ('ask [to
complete] 100 tasks on general meaning'), the examination on the degree *ming jing*, option
'[Dynastic] Histories' 史科 (*XTS* 44: 2b, l. 8); 通大義百條 ('to pass [examination consisting
of] 100 tasks on general meaning'), the examination on the *Rites of the Kai-Yuan era* 開元
禮舉 (*XTS* 44: 2b, l. 4), and 問大義一條 ('ask [to complete] one task on general meaning')
in the description of the oral tests held every ten days in the Mathematical College (*XTS*
44: 2a, l. 5). Secondly, ten is indeed the number of the tasks the candidates were supposed
to complete in this particular case. Thirdly, the word *ben* 本 (as well as its modification 夲)
found in all the extant editions of the history is graphically relatively close to the word 'ten'
十, and the alteration of the text may have happened in an early edition and reproduced in
later editions.

[36] The interpretation of the term *wen da* 問答 as '[mathematical] problem' was argued for in Siu
and Volkov 1999.

[37] A slightly different translation of the two central excerpts of this paragraph was offered in Siu
and Volkov 1999: 92. See also des Rotours 1932: 154–5.

with three tasks on the *Jiu zhang*, and with one task on each [of the treatises] *Hai dao, Sun zi, Wu cao, Zhang Qiujian, Xiahou Yang, Zhou bi, Wu jing suan*, [they] pass [if out of] ten [tasks they complete] six. [For the treatises] *Ji yi* and *San deng shu*, [they do] 'strip reading', and for ten [excerpts they] succeed [if they complete] nine. [When they are] tested with the *Zhui shu* and *Qi gu*, [they] produce records of 'general meaning' taking mathematical problems [as the examination tasks], [they have to] elucidate the numerical values [of the problems], [and to] design [computational] procedures [that would solve them]. [They] elucidate in detail the internal structure of the [computational] procedures [they designed]. As for those [treatises/examination papers] without commentaries,[38] [the candidates have to] make the numerical data coherent, to design [computational] procedures and [should] not make mistakes in the meaning and in the structure [of the procedures]. [If they do] so, then they pass. For the *Zhui shu* [there are] seven tasks; for *Qi gu* [there are] three tasks. [They] pass [if out of] ten [tasks they complete] six. [For the treatises] *Ji yi* and *San deng shu*, [they do] 'strip reading', and for ten [excerpts they] succeed [if they complete] nine. [Under the conditions listed above] they pass the degree examination, [but if they drop] one treatise [of the two], even if [they] completed six [tasks out of ten], [they] will not obtain the degree.[39]

This excerpt leaves several questions unanswered. In particular, it remains unclear whether the examination works of the candidates were written in the same format as tasks on other subjects,[40] or whether they had some specific format relevant to the mathematical contents of the treatises. In Siu and Volkov (1999) the authors suggested the following hypothesis: the candidates were given mathematical problems similar (but not identical) to those contained in the treatises of the chosen 'programme', that is, problems belonging to the categories for which the candidates knew the solutions yet with *modified* numerical parameters. The change of parameters may have implied a modification, sometimes considerable, of the known algorithms

---

[38] The meaning of this phrase remains unclear; see a discussion of it in the concluding section of the present article.

[39] The last remark apparently could refer to the case when the candidate failed all the tasks related to the *Qi gu* 緝古.

[40] A discussion of the expression 'general meaning' is necessary here. This term occurs only in the descriptions of the examinations on the degrees *ming jing* 明經 (in the general description and in the description of two options; see above), *ming suan* 明筭, examination on the *Rites of the Kai-Yuan era* 開元禮舉, as well as the description of the instruction in the Mathematical College (see above). One can suggest that the term 'questions on meaning' refers to a kind of task focusing on the capacity of the examinee to provide a plausible interpretation of a given text or texts. Lee offers two examples of questions and answers on 'general meaning', *da yi* (interestingly, he renders this very term as 'written elucidation') in the context of examination on Confucian classics; he suggests that this kind of questions 'tested mainly familiarity, that is, memory, of the classics' (Lee 2000: 142).

needed for the solution of the problems.[41] In other words, the candidates were asked to design algorithms that were not mere replicas of the algorithms found in the textbooks (otherwise the examination would have been reduced to a simple test of the students' memory) but their generic versions designed according to the modified parameters. This hypothesis, however appealing it might have seemed, could not be provided by Siu and Volkov with any supporting evidence since the examination papers written by the candidates during the mathematics examinations of the Tang and the Song dynasties do not now exist. However, rather unexpectedly, a supporting piece of evidence was found in a Vietnamese mathematical treatise.

Mathematics examinations in traditional Vietnam: the case of a model examination paper

The available information concerning the traditional Vietnamese mathematics and the relevant references to the earlier works can be found elsewhere;[42] it can be very briefly summarized as follows. The number of extant mathematical treatises amounts to twenty-two; the earliest extant treatise is conventionally credited to an author of the fifteenth century while the other treatises were compiled in the eighteenth to early twentieth centuries. Their style and contents are very close to those of Chinese mathematical treatises compiled prior to the introduction of Western mathematics into China.[43]

The Vietnamese system of state education and civil examinations similar to the Chinese one dates back to the eleventh century CE, yet Chinese education and examinations were present in Vietnam well before that time, since the country technically remained a province of China until the mid tenth century.[44] There is no information about institutions specifically focused on mathematics education, yet historical records mention the examinations in 'counting/computations' (Viet. *toán* 算) that took place in 1077, 1179, 1261, 1363, 1404, 1437, 1472, 1505, 1698, 1711, 1725, 1732, 1747, 1762, 1767, and

---

[41] This statement was made in Siu and Volkov 1999 and amply illustrated in Siu 1999 and Siu 2004: 174–7.

[42] Volkov 2002; 2008; 2009.

[43] The reader can find more details on the extant treatises in Volkov 2009: 156–9; the descriptions in Volkov 2002 and Volkov 2008 do not take into account the most recent findings.

[44] The reader can find descriptions of the traditional Vietnamese education in Richomme 1905: 9–28; Tran 1942; Vu 1959: 28–57; Nguyen 1961: 10–40; Woodside 1988: 169–233. The short description of Ennis 1936: 162–4 draws upon the early yet still useful works of Luro (1878) and Schreiner (1900).

1777.[45] The mentions are very short and do not provide any information concerning the contents and the procedure of the examinations. Since the state mathematics examinations were abolished in China by the end of the Song dynasty (960–1279), one can only guess what may have been the procedure and the contents of the Vietnamese state mathematics examinations and their relationship with the Chinese examinations of the Tang and Song dynasties. To my knowledge, no original Vietnamese mathematics examination papers have been found so far. Fortunately, there exists a 'model' mathematics examination paper published in 1820 by Phan Huy Khuông 潘輝框, apparently in order to provide the students with an idea of the best way to answer an examination question. Phan placed the mock examination essay that occupied almost six pages in the last, fourth chapter of his treatise entitled *Chỉ minh lập thành toán pháp* 指明立成籌法 (Guidance for understanding the *Ready-made Computational Methods*) (*CMLT* 4: 30a–32b). This text sheds light on the examination procedure in Vietnam; moreover, it indirectly corroborates the hypothesis concerning the Chinese examination procedure mentioned in the section above.

The original manuscript is preserved in the library of the Institute for Han-Nom Studies (Hanoi).[46] In my work I used a microfilm copy of the manuscript preserved in the library of the Ecole française d'Extrême Orient (Paris). The catalogue Tran and Gros (1993) provides only very sparse information about the author and the contents of the book. The treatise opens with a picture of an abacus (p. 3a) which is an exact reproduction of the picture found in the Chinese mathematical treatise *Suan fa tong zong* 算法統宗 (Summarized fundamentals of computational methods) by Cheng Dawei 程大位 compiled in 1592 (*SFTZ*: 113). The picture is followed by a table of correspondences between powers of 10, monetary units, units of length, weight, and volume (p. 3b). Two following pages present thirty-two diagrams of various plane figures (referred to as 'shapes of fields', Chin. *tian shi* 田勢) (pp. 4a–b) of which the areas are calculated in Chapter 2 of the treatise.

The model examination essay consists of a solution of a mathematical problem written by an imaginary examinee; for the full translation of the examination paper see Appendix 1. The problem reads as follows: three categories of officials, A, B and C, are to be remunerated with 1000 *cân* 斤 of silver, yet out of this amount only the sum $S = 5292$ *lượng* 兩 was supposed to be distributed among the functionaries.[47] It is claimed in the

[45] Volkov 2002.

[46] It is listed under number 433 in Tran and Gros 1993: I 258.

[47] *Cân* 斤 and *lượng* 兩, technically, are measures of weight (1 *cân* = 16 *lượng*), but were also used as monetary units in China and Vietnam, being applied to silver.

problem that the flat-rate distribution method cannot be used to distribute this amount, and the method of weighted distribution is proposed instead. The ratio of the amounts to be given to the functionaries of the three ranks is $7:5:2$, and the numbers of functionaries of each rank are $N_A = 8$, $N_B = 20$ and $N_C = 300$, respectively. There are two questions: (1) to find the amount of silver to award each functionary of the categories A, B and C, and (2) to find the total amount of money allotted to each group of the functionaries.

In modern terms, this is a problem on weighted distribution: one has to find the values $x_1, x_2, \ldots, x_n$ given that $x_1 + x_2 + \ldots + x_n = S$ and $x_1 : x_2 : \ldots : x_n :: k_1 : k_2 : \ldots : k_n$ for given weighting coefficients $k_1, k_2, \ldots, k_n$. Problems of this type as well as the standard procedure for their solution equivalent to the formula

$$x_j = \frac{S k_j}{\sum_{i=1}^{n} k_i}$$

are found in a number of Chinese and Vietnamese mathematical treatises beginning with the Chinese mathematical treatises *Suan shu shu* 筭數書 (Writing on computations with counting rods)[48] and *Jiu zhang suan shu*.[49] However, the problem found in the Vietnamese treatise contains a particularity: it is known that there are three different ranks of functionaries, and for all functionaries of the same rank the weighting coefficients are the same; in our notation, $k_1 = k_2 = \cdots = k_8 = k_A = 7$, $k_9 = k_{10} = \cdots = k_{28} = k_B = 5$, $k_{29} = k_{30} = \cdots = k_{328} = k_C = 2$, and one is asked to find the values x_A, x_B, x_C $(x_A = x_1 = \cdots = x_8, x_B = x_9 = \cdots = x_{28}$, and $x_C = x_{29} = \cdots = x_{328})$ such that $x_A : x_B : x_C :: k_A : k_B : k_C$, and $N_A \cdot x_A + N_B \cdot x_B + N_C \cdot x_C = S$. The examinee is also asked to find the total amount of money allotted to each group of functionaries, that is, to calculate the values $X_A = x_1 + \cdots + x_8$, $X_B = x_9 + \cdots + x_{28}$ and $X_C = x_{29} + \cdots + x_{328}$.

In this chapter I use the term 'aggregated weighted distribution' to identify the category of problems on weighted distribution in which the 'sharers' can be subdivided into groups A, B, C, . . . containing N_A, N_B, N_C, . . . sharers, respectively, such that in each group the weighting coefficients are the same and equal to k_A, k_B, k_C, ... Any problem on aggregated weighted distribution apparently can be solved with the classical algorithm cited above, yet in several sources a modified version of the method was used: the

---

[48] The earliest extant Chinese mathematical treatise *Suan shu shu* was completed no later than the early second century BCE; for English translations, see Cullen 2004 and Dauben 2008.

[49] Cullen 2004: 43–51, 54–6; Dauben 2008: 114–21, 126–7; CG2004: 282–99.

addition of the weighting coefficients is done in two steps: first, the weighting coefficients are multiplied by the numbers of 'sharers' in the respective groups, second, the results of the multiplications are summed up: $K = N_A \cdot k_A + N_B \cdot k_B + N_C \cdot k_C + \cdots$.

The earliest problem on aggregated distribution in China is also found in the *Jiu zhang suan shu* (problem 7 of chapter 3):[50] there are two groups containing three and two persons, respectively, $k_1 = k_2 = k_3 = 3$, $k_4 = k_5 = 2$, $S = 5$ (*SJSSb*: 112). However, the solution offered in the Chinese treatise does not treat specifically this particularity of the condition; the procedure simply suggests to set the weighting coefficients as 3, 3, 3, 2, 2 and to proceed according to the 'classical' method. Chronologically, the earliest extant Chinese treatise featuring the multiplication of the numbers of sharers in each category by the respective weights $N_A \cdot k_A$, $N_B \cdot k_B$, $N_C \cdot k_C$ is the *Sun zi suan jing*; problem 24 of the second chapter (*juan*) of the treatise belongs to this type and contains a detailed description of the computational procedure (*SJSSb*: 274). Problems of this type are also found in the *Zhang Qiujian suan jing* (problem 17 of chapter 1 and problem 13 of chapter 2, *SJSSb*: 303–4, 315–16), *Suan xue qi meng* 筭學啟蒙 (Introduction to the learning of computations, 1299) by Zhu Shijie 朱世傑 (dates unknown) (problem 50 of chapter 2, *SXQM*: 1161), *Jiu zhang suan fa bi lei da quan* 九章算法 比類大全 (Great compendium of the computational methods of nine categories [and their] generics, 1450) by Wu Jing 吳敬 (dates unknown)[51] and *Suan fa tong zong* 算法統宗 (Summarized fundamentals of computational methods, 1592) by Cheng Dawei 程大位 (1533–1606) (Problems 8, 15 and 31 of chapter 5, *SFTZ*: 377, 383, 294, respectively).[52]

The problems on weighted distribution can be found in a number of Vietnamese mathematical treatises. The most interesting case is the systematic introduction of the method found in the *Ý Trai toán pháp nhất đắc lục* 意齋算法一得錄 (*A Record of What Ý Trai Got Right in* Computational Methods, preface 1829) compiled by Nguyễn Hữu Thận 阮有慎.[53] As for the treatise under investigation *Chỉ minh lập thành toán pháp*, chapter 4 contains thirty-eight problems of which twelve are devoted to weighted

---

[50] The *Suan shu shu* does not contain problems on aggregated sharing: in all six problems related to the weighted distribution (problems 11–16, 21 in Cullen 2004) the weights of the sharers are all different.

[51] Problems 5, 33, 36 and 44 of chapter 3 (*DQ* 3: 3a, 14b, 17b, 21b) belong to the category of 'aggregated weighted distribution', but only problem 5 (analogous to problem 7 of the *Jiu zhang suan shu*) is solved with the 'classical' algorithm used in the *Jiu zhang suan shu*.

[52] To numerate the problems, I count the problems *per se* as well as generalized rules given without numerical data.

[53] Volkov forthcoming.

distribution (Problems 5–7, 10–11, 14–19, 38).[54] Among them, only two problems deal with the 'aggregated sharers', namely, problem 6 and problem 38 (which is the problem solved in the 'model examination paper'). Problem 6 represents a case of a 'mixed' weighted distribution combining 'solitary' and 'aggregated' sharers. In this problem one deals with the funds raised by a temple.[55] The setting is as follows (*CMLT* 4: 6a–7b):

The total amount of 240 *cân* 斤 of gold was collected; 3 parts of the total amount were obtained from selling incense, 6 parts from a 'senior donator', 24 ordinary male donators contributed 4 parts each and 5 ordinary female donators contributed 3 parts each. In modern notation one has to find the values $x_1, x_2, \ldots, x_n$, $n = 31$, given that $x_1 + x_2 + \ldots + x_n = S$ and $x_1 : x_2 : \ldots : x_n$ $:: k_1 : k_2 : \ldots : k_n$ for the given weighting coefficients $k_1 = 3$, $k_2 = 6$, $k_i = 4$ for $i = 3, \ldots, 26$ and $k_j = 3$ for $j = 27, \ldots, 31$. The procedure provided in the treatise can be written in modern terms as follows:

- one has to calculate the sum of the coefficients $k_1 + k_2 = 9$;
- find the value $k_3 + k_4 + \cdots + k_{26}$ as $24 \cdot k_3 = 96$;
- find the value $k_{27} + k_{28} + \cdots + k_{31}$ as $5 \cdot k_{27} = 15$;
- find the sum $K = k_1 + k_2 + \cdots + k_n = (k_1 + k_2) + (k_3 + k_4 + \cdots + x_{26})$ $+ (k_{27} + k_{28} + \cdots + x_{31}) = 9 + 96 + 15 = 120$;
- use the obtained total value K to divide the total amount of money and to obtain the 'constant norm' 常法 S/K;
- now one obtains the amounts of money x_i corresponding to the weights k_i: the money for incense $x_1 = k_1 \cdot (S/K)$, the money of the senior donator $x_2 = k_2 \cdot (S/K)$, the money of each ordinary male donator $x_i = k_i \cdot (S/K)$, $i = 3, \ldots, 26$, and the money of each ordinary female donator $x_i = k_i \cdot (S/K)$, $i = 27, \ldots, 31$;
- to obtain the money donated by each group, the reader is given the cases of the incense and the senior donator as examples: here the obtained value S/K is to be used again, and one is told to multiply this value by the 'parts' corresponding to the group. In the case of the incense and the senior donator it will correspond to $x_1 = k_1 \cdot$ (S/K) and $x_2 = k_2 \cdot (S/K)$, respectively. The reader then is told that the

---

[54] It still remains unclear how many problems there were in the original version. In the microfilm of the manuscript preserved in the Ecole française d'Extrême Orient (Paris) the text of problem 14 beginning on page 16a is incomplete. Moreover, Problem 17 (p. 18a) on '8:2 distribution' is misplaced in the section on '6:4 distribution'. These two details suggest that at least one page of the original treatise was not copied by the copyist and other pages may have been copied in a wrong order.

[55] The wording of the problem makes it unclear whether the money is supposed to be *obtained*, or *given* by, the temple; I provided my translation in assuming that historically Vietnamese temples usually obtained rather than distributed money.

remaining operations would be similar. Instead of computing the impact of the ordinary male and female donators as $N_M \cdot x_M$ and $N_F \cdot x_F$, where $N_M = 24$, $x_M = x_3$, $N_F = 5$, $x_F = x_{27}$, the reader is told to compute these values as $(24 \cdot k_3) \cdot (S/K)$ and $(5 \cdot k_{27}) \cdot (S/K)$, respectively. It appears plausible to suggest that the author of the Vietnamese treatise at this point reinterpreted the data, and considered each entire *group* of male and female donators as 'collective donators' of the donated money, possessing $K_M = N_M \cdot k_3$ and $K_F = N_F \cdot k_{27}$ 'shares';

– the problem is concluded with a check-up of the obtained answer; one has to check whether the sum of the amounts obtained from each source is equal to the total amount of the raised money. It is not verified whether the portions of money coming from the four sources indeed constitute the given ratio.

Now we can return to the model examination paper. The solution of the imaginary examinee contains six parts: (1) a formal introduction (p. 30b, ll. 8–11); (2) an explanation why only a part of the awarded silver was actually given to the functionaries (p. 31a, lls. 1–6); (3) an explanation of the fact that the flat-rate distribution could not work (p. 31a, l. 6 – p. 31b, l. 4); (4) a rewording and a solution of the weighted distribution problem (p. 31b, l. 4 – p. 32b, l. 5); (5) a verification of the answer (p. 32b, lls. 5–7); (6) a formal ending of the examination paper (p. 32b, lls. 7–9).

The reader will notice that the examination paper contains more than a solution of just one problem. The imaginary examinee is supposed to check the proposed data, find an explanation for the seeming discrepancy found in the condition (it is stated that 1000 *cân* = 16000 *lượng* is to be given to the functionaries, yet the amount of money distributed among them was only 5292 *lượng*), and solve two problems, one on flat-rate and the other on weighted distribution.

The suggested solution of the weighted distribution problem runs as follows: in order to find x_A, x_B and x_C, at the first step the sum $K = k_1 + k_2 + \cdots + k_{328}$ is calculated; to do so, the imaginary examinee calculates $N_A \cdot k_A = 56$, $N_B \cdot k_B = 100$, $N_C \cdot k_C = 600$ and adds them up to obtain $K = 756$. The term used to refer to these products is rather particular: while talking about the weights k_A, k_B, k_C the examinee uses the word 'shares/parts' (Chinese *fen* 分), but when passing to the 'aggregated shares/parts' $N_A \cdot k_A$, $N_B \cdot k_B$, $N_C \cdot k_C$ he employs a combination of two characters 分率 (Chinese *fenlü*) 'parts–coefficients' or 'multiples of shares/parts'; I shall return to this term later. At the second step, the total amount of money, $S = 5292$ *lượng*, is divided by K yielding 7 *lượng*, called the 'constant norm' 常法, as in problem 6. The amounts of money x_A, x_B and x_C to be obtained by each functionary of the group A, B, C are calculated as the 'constant norm' multiplied by k_A, k_B, k_C, respectively.[56]

In the second part of the solution the imaginary examinee looks for X_A, X_B and X_C which obviously could be found as $N_A \cdot x_A$, $N_B \cdot x_B$, $N_C \cdot x_C$ once x_A, x_B and x_C have been calculated. However, the suggested solution is different: for example, for group A, the author suggests the calculation of $(N_A \cdot k_A) \cdot (S/K)$ instead of calculating $N_A \cdot [(S \cdot k_A)/K]$; for groups B and C similar operations are performed. Once again, it can be understood as if the author considered each entire *group* A, B and C as one 'collective recipient' of the awarded money, possessing $K_A = N_A \cdot k_A$, $K_B = N_B \cdot k_B$ and $K_C = N_C \cdot k_C$ 'shares', respectively, while the sum of the 'shares' $K_A + K_A + K_C$ remained equal to K.

Examinations and commentaries

The solution of the model problem provided in the treatise was based on the algorithm for the 'aggregated sharers' found in a number of Chinese and Vietnamese mathematical treatises, yet it would be reasonable to suggest that the imaginary examinee was supposed to design his solution on the basis of the information found in the same treatise. Indeed, the treatise provides two sources of such information: (1) a general description of the algorithm of weighted distribution (*CMLT* 4: 4b–5a), and (2) the aforementioned problem 6 of chapter 4 on distribution of donations. A cursory inspection of these two sources suggests that the solution in the model paper was designed by analogy with the solution of problem 6; in particular, the term 'parts–multiples' 分率 (or 'multiples of parts') found in the solution of the model problem does appear in the solution of problem 6 but not in the algorithm introduced on p. 5a. It is especially interesting that in this case the Vietnamese author used the term *lü* 率, since the concept of *lü* was one of the key elements in the conceptual system presented in Liu Hui's commentary on the *Jiu zhang suan shu*. In modern notation, a number A is a *lü* 率 (a 'proportional', or 'multiple') of another number, A', if one can establish a proportion in which both numbers occupy the same positions in the ratios involved: A : B : .... :: A' : B' : ....[57] However, the term

---

[56] In Volkov 2008 I suggested a mathematically correct yet 'modernizing' reconstruction of the first part of the Vietnamese procedure.

[57] For a detailed discussion of the term, see CG2004: 135–6, 956–9. Martzloff 1997: 196–7 employs the term 'model' (i.e. one number can be used as a 'model', a representative, of another number).

'parts–multiples' (or 'multiples of parts'?) *fenlü* 分率 introduced by the Vietnamese author appears to be unparalleled in the Chinese mathematical texts of the first millennium CE.

The solution of the imaginary examinee was supposed to be designed as a modification of the solution of a problem from the treatise he, presumably, was supposed to be familiar with. In other words, the examination paper was based on a problem already solved and discussed earlier, but with a modified structure (three groups of functionaries instead of the combination of two individual and two collective donators) and altered numerical data. The entire format of the examination paper was larger than just one problem: it was rather that of a 'research project' in which a given situation was approached with two mathematical 'models', one of flat-rate distribution (rejected as neither fitting into the numerical data nor corresponding to the hierarchical structure of the group of functionaries) and one of weighted distribution.

The mathematical contents of the particular problem solved in the Vietnamese model examination paper are not as important for the present discussion as the very format of the essay suggested by the author of the treatise who apparently was well acquainted with the actual examination procedure. Most importantly for the present discussion, the Vietnamese model examination paper fits, to a large extent, into the format described in the Tang dynasty Chinese source mentioned above, namely: (1) the core of the examination task consists of a mathematical problem; (2) the examinee 'elucidates' the 'numerical values' provided in the given problem (that is, checks the consistency of the given numerical data), and (3) he 'designs a computational procedure' of which (4) the 'structure/rationale' he discusses in detail, that is, he provides a detailed solution in which every step is commented upon. The imaginary Vietnamese examinee styles his text as if he operates with a counting instrument to obtain his result while writing down the results of the operations he is performing. It would be reasonable to assume that the Chinese candidates of the Tang dynasty also employed their counting rods during the examination to solve the problems given to them. If this assumption is correct, their solutions must have contained the protocols of performed computations that would have looked rather similar to that found in the Vietnamese model examination paper. This observation makes it tempting to interpret the term *lu* 錄 ('records, protocols') employed in the description of the mathematics examinations in the *Xin Tang shu* quoted above as referring to this particular feature of the mathematics examination papers.

Back to China

When constructing his solution, the imaginary Vietnamese examinee produced a text the structure of which to a large extent resembles the solution already provided in the treatise, namely, in problem 6 of the same chapter. One can conjecture that the Chinese examinees of the Tang dynasty were also supposed to base their solutions on those provided in the respective mathematical textbooks. Here we come to the focal point of the present chapter, namely, the role the commentaries found in Chinese mathematical treatises played in mathematical instruction and examinations. Table 15.3 provides the names of the commentators of the extant ten mathematical treatises used in the Mathematical College of the Tang dynasty.

Table 15.3 shows that the treatises used for instruction all incorporated commentaries, unlike the extant treatises listed under numbers 1 and 2. The history of transmission of the treatises is so obscure that even if the names of the commentators in the extant treatises coincide with those mentioned in the bibliographies listed in Table 15.3, it remains unknown whether the extant commentaries are indeed identical with those used in the Mathematical College of the Tang dynasty. An inspection of the extant commentaries listed in Table 15.3 shows that they differ considerably as far as their style and contents are considered. The commentaries are mainly focused on the computational procedures designed for solution of the problems, yet the formats adopted by their authors were not the same.

Liu Hui's commentary on the *Jiu zhang suan shu* contains parts written in different styles: the commentator interpreted the operations with fractions exemplified in the treatise using especially coined mathematical terms; used diagrams of plane figures and descriptions of (probably imaginary) three-dimensional models for solution of geometrical and algebraic problems; provided detailed computations in case of the calculation of the value of π close in style to Liu Xiaosun's *cao* or left only obscure indications which, however, may have been referring to some specific mathematical contents.[58] The commentaries of another enigmatic figure, Zhao Shuang 趙爽 or Zhao Junqing 趙君卿 (conventionally these two names are believed to be the aliases of the commentator Zhao Ying mentioned in

[58] For the original text, translation and discussion see CG2004, as well as the works of other authors quoted by Chemla and Guo; on the geometrical diagrams see Volkov 2007. This variety of styles can make one ponder over the authenticity of the received commentary conventionally credited to the authorship of the person known as Liu Hui whose biographical data remain unknown, yet the latter problem, certainly important, is not pertinent in the context of the present inquiry.

Table 15.3. The extant Tang dynasty mathematical textbooks and their commentators[a]

Number	The extant treatises used in the Mathematical College	Commentators as specified in official histories	Commentator(s) of the extant treatises
1	*Sun zi suan jing* 孫子籌經 (Computational treatise of Master Sun)	Zhen Luan (*Jiu Tang shu*);[b] Li Chunfeng (*Xin Tang shu*); Li Chunfeng (*Song shi*)	None.
2	*Wu cao suan jing* 五曹籌經 (Computational treatise of five departments)	Li Chunfeng *et al.* (*Song shi*)	None
3	*Jiu zhang suan shu* (Computational procedures of nine categories)	Li Chunfeng (*Xin Tang shu*); Liu Hui; Li Chunfeng et al. (*Song shi*)[c]	Liu Hui; Li Chunfeng *et al.*
4	*Hai dao suan jing* 海島籌經 (Computational treatise [beginning with a problem] about a sea island)	Li Chunfeng (*Xin Tang shu*)	Li Chunfeng *et al.*
5	*Zhang Qiujian suan jing* 張丘建籌經 (Computational treatise of Zhang Qiujian)	Zhen Luan; Li Chunfeng (*Xin Tang shu*)	Liu Xiaosun 劉孝孫; Li Chunfeng et al.[d]
6	*Xiahou Yang suan jing* 夏侯陽籌經 (Computational treatise of Xiahou Yang)	Zhen Luan (*Jiu Tang shu* and *Xin Tang shu*)	The author (Han Yan 韓延, Tang dynasty)
7	*Zhou bi suan jing* 周髀籌經 (Computational treatise on the gnomon of Zhou [dynasty])	Zhao Ying 趙嬰;[e] Zhen Luan (*Jiu Tang shu*);[f] Zhao Ying; Zhen Luan; Li Chunfeng (*Xin Tang shu*)[g]	Zhao Junqing 趙君卿; Zhen Luan; Li Chunfeng *et al.*
8	*Wu jing suan shu* 五經籌術 (Computational procedures [found] in the five classical books)	Li Chunfeng (*Xin Tang shu*); Li Chunfeng (*Song shi*)[h]	Li Chunfeng *et al.*

Continued

Table 15.3 *Continued*

Number	The extant treatises used in the Mathematical College	Commentators as specified in official histories	Commentator(s) of the extant treatises
9	*Qi gu suan jing* 緝古筭經 (Computational treatise on the continuation of [traditions] of ancient [mathematicians])	Li Chunfeng (?) (*Jiu Tang shu*);[i] Li Chunfeng (*Xin Tang shu*)	The author (Wang Xiaotong 王孝通)
10	*Shu shu ji yi* 數術記遺 (Records of the procedures of numbering left behind for posterity)	Zhen Luan (*Jiu Tang shu* and *Xin Tang shu*)	Zhen Luan

[a] Li 1977: 269–271 quotes these and other sources mentioning the names of commentators.

[b] Zhen Luan is mentioned as the commentator and the author (*JTS* 47: 6b).

[c] The title is mentioned as *Jiu zhang suan jing* (*SS* 207: 3b).

[d] Liu Xiaosun of the Sui dynasty (581–618) authored the 'computations', *cao* 草.

[e] Conventionally identified as Zhao Junqing 趙君卿 also known as Zhao Shuang 趙爽, the author of the commentary found in the extant edition of the treatise.

[f] The *Jiu Tang shu* mentions three different editions of the treatise, two commented upon by Zhao Ying and Zhen Luan, and one *compiled* by Li Chunfeng (*JTS* 47: 5b).

[g] The *Xin Tang shu* mentions four different editions commented upon by the three commentators separately (Li Chunfeng is credited with the authorship of two commentaries) (*XTS* 59: 12b, 13b).

[h] In the *Song shi* the treatise is mentioned as authored by Wang Xiaotong (*SS* 207: 3a).

[i] In the *Jiu Tang shu* both Wang Xiaotong and Li Chunfeng are mentioned as the authors (*JTS* 47: 6b); probably, the text of the history is corrupted and Li Chunfeng was originally mentioned as a commentator.

bibliographical chapters of dynastic histories, as Table 15.3 shows), whose lifetime presumably was not too distant from that of Liu Hui, offer a slightly narrower range of styles. The best-known contribution of Zhao is his justification of a series of quadratic identities with the help of geometrical diagrams, to a certain extent similar to those used by Liu Hui in his commentaries on the ninth chapter of the *Jiu zhang suan shu*.[59]

The actual intentions that Liu Hui and Zhao Shuang had when writing their commentaries on the *Jiu zhang suan shu* and *Zhou bi suan jing*, respectively, do not seem related to any kind of educational activity. However,

[59] Gillon 1977; Cullen 1996: 206–17; CG2004: 695–701.

their commentaries on the oldest and presumably highly respected texts in the collection of the textbooks were edited in the seventh century CE to be used for instruction. The commentaries arguably compiled by Li Chunfeng and his team for educational purposes thus may have corresponded most closely to the style of work with ancient texts practised by the instructors of the Mathematical College.[60] Yet the commentary on the *Hai dao suan jing* by Li Chunfeng *et al.* did not discuss the rationale of the methods; instead, the commentators explained the terms occurring in the conditions of the problems and reproduced the procedures provided by Liu Hui with plugged numerical parameters. That is, for Li Chunfeng the relevant interpretation of a procedure consisted of a correct identification of the parameters involved and the operations with them. The parts of Li Chunfeng's commentary devoted to calculations look similar to the 'computations' (*cao* 草) added by Liu Xiaosun to the *Zhang Qiujian suan jing*, and both texts resemble closely the computations in the Vietnamese model examination paper.

These observations suggest the following conjecture. Even though the format of the Tang dynasty examination papers remains unknown, the format adopted by the author of the model examination work in the Vietnamese treatise fits surprisingly well into the short description of the Tang dynasty mathematics examinations quoted above. The imaginary Vietnamese examinee used as his model the solution of a generic problem found elsewhere in the same treatise and, in particular, provided detailed calculations close enough to those found in the model problem. Now, what kind of explanations of the 'meaning' of the given problems were the actual Chinese examinees of the Tang dynasty expected to provide? It is perhaps not too daring to conjecture that their writings were supposed to resemble those provided by the commentators of the treatises used as textbooks. In other words, it appears plausible to suggest that the commentaries of Liu Hui, Zhao Shuang, Li Chunfeng and others found in the treatises used for instruction in the Mathematical College were used as *the* models for the examination papers; not only did they provide the students with methods used to investigate the validity of the computational procedures presented in the treatises, but they also established the particular format to be imitated by the candidates when writing their examination essays.

The phrase *wu zhu zhe* 無注者 found in the description of the mathematics examinations in the 'advanced programme' and rendered above

---

[60] It appears quite probable that the commentarial activity of Zhen Luan who produced a set of commented mathematical treatises in the second half of the sixth century CE was directly related to a system of state mathematics education established, as some authors have suggested, at the Court of the Northern Zhou dynasty (see above).

as 'As for those [texts/papers] without commentaries' can be understood
in at least three different ways: (1) it refers to a commentary expected to
be written by the examinee in his examination paper but omitted for some
reason; (2) it refers to a commentary missing in one of the two treatises of
the 'advanced programme' which constituted the topic of the examination,
and (3) the word 'commentary' *zhu* had here the technical meaning 'to
preappoint a candidate to a position'.[61] The third option hardly seems to
be relevant in this particular context. Siu and Volkov (1999) have argued
for the first option mainly on the basis of the inspection of the only extant
treatise of the 'advanced programme', the *Qi gu suan jing* 緝古筭經 by
Wang Xiaotong in which almost all the problems are provided with commentaries. However, a large part of the original treatise is lost: according to
the bibliographical sections of the *Jiu Tang shu* and *Xin Tang shu*, the book
originally contained four *juan* (*JTS* 47: 6b; *XTS* 59: 14a) while the *Song
shi* mentions only one *juan* (*SS* 207: 1a). The extant version contains only
twenty problems; the texts of problems 17–20 and of the respective commentaries are partly lost (*SJSSb*: 434–5). It is therefore impossible to know
whether every single problem of the Tang dynasty version of the treatise
was commented upon by Li Chunfeng, or whether a certain number of
the problems were left without commentaries.[62] Moreover, nothing can
be known about Li Chunfeng's commentaries on the second book of the
'advanced programme', the *Zhui shu* by Zu Chongzhi, since the book had
already been lost by the time of the Song dynasty; it is equally possible
that only some problems contained commentaries. If this was the case,
the phrase *wu zhu zhe*, 'as for those without commentaries', may have
referred to paradigmatic problems from the treatises used as textbooks in
the 'advanced programme' which did not contain commentaries on certain
problems. This option leads to the following hypothesis: in the 'advanced
programme' examination tasks were compiled on the basis of problems
from the *Qi gu suan jing* and *Zhui shu*; if the original problem contained
a commentary, the examination criteria were the same as in the 'regular
programme' examination: the examinee had to 'elucidate numbers' and to
'elucidate in detail the internal structure of the [computational] procedure',
that is, to compile a text similar to the original commentary. If the problem
taken as the model for the examination task did not contain a commentary, the candidate was not asked to provide 'elucidations' but to 'make the
numerical data coherent', and 'not to make mistakes in the meaning and

---

[61] Des Rotours 1934: 43, 49, 217, 244, 266, 268; Hucker 1985: 182, nos. 1407–8.

[62] The interested reader will find the annotated translation by Berezkina 1975 highly useful.

in the structure' of the procedure. Each of the terms employed here most probably had a precise technical meaning difficult or even impossible to restore, yet one can safely conjecture that in the latter case the examinee was supposed to provide a sequence of correct operations leading to the solution without their detailed justification.

If the phrase about the 'lack of the commentaries' referred to the compilations of the examinees, one can suggest that they were supposed to write their explanations in the format similar to that of the officially established commentaries and, most probably, used these commentaries as the best available models. If the second interpretation of the phrase is correct, the description of the examination procedure suggests an even larger role of the commentaries found in the treatises used for instruction. Whichever interpretation of the phrase 'as for those without commentaries' is adopted, the role of the commentaries is apparent: they were not only providing explanations or justifications of the algorithms found in the treatises, but also became *the* models for the examination papers.

Conclusions

Until recently the historians of Chinese mathematics tacitly assumed that the commentaries on mathematical texts, especially those authored by Liu Hui and Zhao Shuang, were 'purely mathematical works' written by professional mathematicians for unidentified target groups, presumably small communities of experts and disciples. This assumption is most probably correct; my hypothesis is that the embedding of Liu Hui's and Zhao Shuang's commentaries into the context of state education radically changed the way in which they were interpreted and used. After having been edited by the team of Li Chunfeng, the commentaries on the treatises constituting the curriculum set the guidelines for the instructors and students of the Mathematical College. More specifically, in order to demonstrate their correct understanding of an algorithm found in a mathematical treatise, the students and examinees had to perform the operations the algorithm prescribed with the correctly inserted numerical values. This reconstruction is corroborated by at least three documents: (1) the commentaries of Li Chunfeng's team on the *Hai dao suan jing* written in the seventh century CE with the purpose of being used as didactical material in the Mathematical College and conspicuously featuring computations performed according to the algorithms devised by Liu Hui; (2) the aforementioned description of Tang examinations, and (3) the Vietnamese model examination paper. The commentaries of Li Chunfeng on the *Hai dao suan jing* may have naturally become paradigmatic texts imitated by the authors of examination essays devoted to this particular text, and one can conjecture that the commentaries of Liu Hui and Zhao Shuang, containing justifications of the algorithms, in turn also may have been employed by the students and examinees as models in their oral presentations and written examinations. The commentaries thus provided the standards of persuasiveness and consistency and shaped the style and structure of the mathematical discourse in the branch of the traditional Chinese mathematics perpetuated within the network of official educational institutions of the first millennium CE.

Acknowledgements

I would like to express my gratitude to two anonymous referees for their valuable suggestions, to Karine Chemla for her personal and professional support throughout the preparation of the chapter, and to the Institute for Advanced Study, Princeton where the first draft of the paper was completed in 2007. The financial support for my work in France and Vietnam in 2006–7 was provided by the National Science Council, Taiwan (grant no. 95–2411-H-007–037), by the Leading Edge Research Foundation of the National Tsing Hua University, Taiwan (grant no. 95N2521E21) and by the Institut National de Recherche Pédagogique, France; I would like to express my gratitude to all these institutions.

Appendix 1

The first part of the Appendix contains the original text of the 'model examination paper' from the *Chỉ minh lập thành toán pháp* 指明立成籌法 (Guidance for understanding of the *Ready-Made Computational Methods*) by Phan Huy Khuông's 潘輝框 (*CMLT* 4: 30a–32b). When reproducing the text, I preserved the original layout, that is, one line of the original corresponds to one line of the transcription below. The original text does not contain punctuation, and I introduce my own. The emendations of the text are indicated with the brackets ⟨⟩ and 〔〕 : '⟨A⟩〔B〕' means that the sequence of characters A is suggested to be replaced by the sequence B (either A or B can be an empty sequence, that is, ⟨A⟩ alone means that the sequence A is to be suppressed and 〔B〕stands for the sequence B which is to be added). The second part of the Appendix contains its English translation with the references to the page and line numbers of the original.

/p. 30a/

倣撰籌題試文格式[63]

問。今有奉頒金銀。共一千斤。其這金銀本官奉頒

⟨仍⟩〔乃〕量照銀數五千二百九十二兩。惠許本營屬三

百二十八人。將為平均與人數。頗餘四分八釐。

第高下平等理有未孚。是平分之法不可均用。已

顯。茲欲用這銀均依本屬有差衰。另為三等。甲等

/p. 30b/

八人。每人受七分。乙等二十人。每人〔受〕五分。丙等三

百人。每人受二分。則諸人受分與各該若干。試諸

籌士者。學習精通稱鈞辨別宜悉排陳以觀素蘊。

答曰。

甲等每人獲銀四十九兩。該三百九十二兩。

乙等每人獲銀三十五兩。該七百兩。

丙等每人獲銀十四兩。該四千二百兩。

對。愚謂籌法中來因除不越衰分。上有多少。有差。

此執事籌⟨河⟩〔問〕而愚所以復之也。茲見題中所⟨河⟩〔問〕

惟照奉銀惠及本屬。略說平分而主用差分

之法。諒知籌法無窮之妙用矣。愚請籌而排陳之。

/p. 31a/

於惟奉頒本官金銀一千斤。⟨仍⟩〔乃〕以斤法十六通

之。總得一萬六千兩。且恩霈於上必惠乎下。此金

銀也。本官念其利。不可獨肯以私藏。爰就中奉

頒金銀數所奉領者內取一萬〇七百〇八兩

之貯存銀數。五千二百九十二兩。量照這銀惠許

本屬三百二十八人。則這銀與本營而同其惠者。

若用平分之法。上置人數。下置這銀。以法商除歸。

立成每人受銀十六兩一錢三四釐。然這銀不

盡。頗餘四分八釐。誠可用通分納子之法。第人品

/p. 31b/

有高下而分之。平為一等。此事不稱情其理。有所

未孚。是則平分之法不可均用。故不必排列。信如

題問。蓋已顯然矣。且以人有優劣不齊分之多少

---

[63] This is the title of the section separated from the main body of the text with an indent.

有敘。是優者當受其多。劣者當受其少。分之而有
差等。理固如是。〈仍〉〔乃〕茲款用這銀五千二百九十二
兩均依本屬三百二十八人有差分而人數另為
三等。甲等八人。每人受七分。乙等二十人。每人受
五分。丙等三百人。每人受二分。此是問差分之法。
其法當用。先置甲等八人。以七分因之。得積五十

/p. 32a/

六分率。再置乙等二十人。以五分因之。得積一百
分率。又置丙等三百人。以二分因之。得積六百分
率。〈仍〉〔乃〕以三等分率〈付〉〔副〕併為一。共得七百五
十六分
率。為法。方置這銀五千二百九十二兩。為寔。〈仍〉〔乃〕以
法歸除立之。得每一分率七兩。畱為常法。以因與
各等分率。却先將甲等每七分因之。成甲等每人
獲銀四十九兩。再次將乙等每五分亦因之。成乙
等每人獲銀三十五兩。又將丙等每二分又因之。
成丙等每人獲銀十四兩。〈比〉〔此〕各等每人受分銀已

/p. 32b/

畢。至如各該〔數〕則以各差等分積。亦將乘與常法。即
知該數。〈仍〉〔乃〕以甲等積五十六分率乘之。成甲該銀
三百九十二兩。再以乙等積一百分率乘之。成乙
該銀七百兩。又以丙等積六百分率乘之。成丙該
銀四千二百兩。是各等該銀已成之矣。至若還原。
共併甲、乙、丙三等該銀數者。合而為一。成原銀五
千二百九十二兩。愚也鈍其為學。粗知法式之排
陳。拙於所行。未識多少之辨別。茲因問及淺略答
之。是否如何願執事擇而采之。幸甚。

Translation

/p. 30a/

[1] Imitation of a composition of a mathematical problem [written according to] the format of an examination paper.

[2] Question: [Let us suppose that] now there is money to award [functionaries], the total amount is 1000 *cân* (斤). As for this amount of money, the award assigned to a given [group of] functionaries

[3] had the value of 5292 *lượng* (兩). The award was promised to 328 people affiliated with the given establishment.

[4] [If one] intends to distribute equally according to the number of the people, [then] [it will be] uneven and there will be a remainder of 4 *phan* 8 *li*.

[5] [If for those] ranging from the high to the low [positions] the pattern of 'equal rank [distribution]' (平分) [is applied], [then] there is [something] incorrect. So, the method of 'flat-rate distribution' cannot be universally applied, [it is] already

[6] clear. Now, [one] wishes to use this money to be applied equally [within one rank] according to unequal ranks of the aforementioned corpus [of functionaries] in separating them into three ranks [as follows]. Rank A:

/p. 30b/

[1] 8 persons, each person obtains 7 parts; rank B: 20 persons, each person obtains 5 parts; rank C, 300

[2] persons, each person obtains 2 parts. [If we proceed in this way], then what will be the [amounts of money corresponding to] the parts obtained by all the people and the due amount [of money] for each [of the three groups of functionaries]? [We] examine all

[3] the experts in computations [who] 'study and exercise',[64] [those who] penetrate into the subtleness of weights and measures, [who can] distinguish and differentiate, analyse adequately, [those who know how to] arrange and dispose [the counting rods], in order to inspect the simple as well as the profound [matters].[65]

[4] Answer:[66]

[5] each person of rank A obtains 49 *lượng* of silver; the due amount is 392 *lượng*;

[6] each person of rank B obtains 35 *lượng* of silver; the due amount is 700 *lượng*;

[7] each person of rank C obtains 14 *lượng* of silver; the due amount is 4200 *lượng*.

[8] Response [of the examinee]: [I,] so-and-so,[67] say: [this] computational method involves [the operations of] multiplication and division and does not go beyond the [method of] 'distribution according to grades'

---

[64] A quotation from the first chapter of the Confucian classic *Lun yu* 論語 (*The Analects*).

[65] Probably, this paragraph is a formal ending appended to every problem proposed to candidates at the examination.

[66] The answer is written in smaller characters; it is possible that the answer was supposed to be written by the examinee in the blank space left after the word 'answer'.

[67] A self-depreciatory 愚 (Chinese reading *yu*) indicates the position in which the actual name is to be inserted.

(衰分).[68] Firstly,[69] there is an amount [to be distributed]; [secondly],[70] there are grades.

[9] Here is the computational problem [proposed] by those in charge,[71] and [what is below is] how I answered it. Now it is clear that what is asked in the problem

[10] is solely concerned with the awarded money kindly dispatched to the given groups [of functionaries]. [One] briefly discussed the 'flat-rate distribution', [and after that] used the 'distribution according to grades' as the principal

[11] method. I know that [this] computational method has unlimited miraculous applications! I, so-and-so, ask for counting rods[72] to 'arrange and dispose' them.[73]

/p. 31a/

[1] As for the very [phrase] '[Let us suppose that] now there is money to award [functionaries], the total is 1000 *cân* 斤 [of silver]', [I] make it [= this amount] uniform [with other units] using [the factor] 16, [which is] the 'norm' of *cân*.[74]

[2] The total amount [thus] obtained is 16000 *lượng*. '[If] benevolence is manifested by the superiors, [then] necessarily the subjects are kindly awarded.'[75] As far as this money

[3] is concerned, the said functionaries cared about their benefit and could not themselves accept to keep [the money] privately. Therefore

[4] what the granting authorities kept out of the amount of awarded money was a deposited amount of 10708 *lượng*.[76]

---

[68] This is the term for weighted distribution found in chapter 3 of the *Jiu zhang suan shu*; see *SJSSb*: 109ff.

[69] Or: 'in the upper [position]'.

[70] Or: 'in the lower [position]'.

[71] Here the term 執事 may be a formal title of an official; see Hucker 1985: 162.

[72] It is worth noting that counting rods and not the abacus are mentioned here. According to the report of Giovanni Filippo de Marini (1608–82), counting rods were still in use in Vietnam as late as the mid seventeenth century; see Volkov 2009: 160–4. However, one cannot rule out the possibility that the term *toán* 筭 may have been used here as a metaphorical reference to a counting instrument in general.

[73] Probably, a quotation from the ending of the problem '. . . [those who] arrange and dispose [the counting rods], in order to inspect . . .'

[74] That is, 1 *cân* 斤 = 16 *lượng* 兩, therefore to convert an amount of money from *cân* to *lượng* one has to multiply it by 16.

[75] This phrase does not have any particular mathematical meaning and appears to be a quotation from a text that I have been unable to identify.

[76] That is, the authorities retained some amount of money for the good of the functionaries. This is but a tentative rendering of a rather obscure paragraph explaining why not the entire

[5] As for the [remaining] 5292 *lượng*, [one] measures this amount of money for the awarded

[6] aforesaid corpus of 328 functionaries. Then [if] this money is given to this establishment [= functionaries] and [they are] awarded in the same way,

[7] [it is as] if [one] uses the method of 'flat-rate distribution'. [One] sets above[77] the number of the persons, [one] sets below[78] this [amount of] money.[79] Using the divisor [one] divides [the amount of money] by the 'evaluation division' and by 'returning [division]';[80]

[8] [one] immediately establishes that every person obtains 16 *lượng* 1 *tien* 3 *phan* 4 *li*.[81] Thus this money [could] not

[9] be entirely [paid and] there would be a remainder of 4 *phan* 8 *li*.[82] To get the actual [value], one can use the methods of reduction of fractions to common denominator and of injection [of integer parts of mixed fractions] into numerators.[83] [If] these men's categories

/p. 31b/

[1] are classified as high and low, being at the same level [only within] one rank, [then] this action is not to be called 'analysing [correctly] the inner structure [of it]'[84] and there is [something]

[2] unreliable. [If] this is so, then the 'method of flat-rate distribution'

---

amount of 16000 *lượng* was distributed among the functionaries and why the 10708 *lượng* should have been deducted from the original amount of 1000 *cân*.

[77] Or: 'firstly'.

[78] Or: 'secondly'.

[79] If the counting instrument supposed to be used is the counting rods, then the positions of the operands (divisor in the upper position and the dividend in the lower position) differs from the classical Chinese disposition of the operands represented with the counting rods (divisor below and the dividend above) described in the *Sun zi suan jing* (see *SJSSb*: 262). The standard methods of division performed with the abacus I am aware of all assume that the dividend is to be set in the left (= upper) part of the abacus, and the divisor in its right part. I am thankful to K. Chemla who drew my attention to this particularity of the Vietnamese method (private communication, 2008).

[80] For a very short discussion of the methods of division *shang chu* 商除 and *gui* 歸 (in Mandarin transcription of the characters) mentioned here see LD1987: 181–3.

[81] Indeed, $5292 \div 328 = 16.134(14634)$.

[82] That is, $5292 - 328 \cdot 16.134 = 5292 - 5291.952 = 0.048$.

[83] This phrase can be understood as saying that one can obtain an exact value if a common fraction is used instead of decimal one.

[84] This rather rough translation of the expression 情其理 (*qing qi li* in Mandarin transcription) would require a long discussion of the term *qing* 情 which cannot be offered here; the interested reader is referred to CG2004: 970 for an interpretation of the term as employed by Liu Hui.

cannot be applied to all [the functionaries]. This is why [one] does not need to 'dispose and arrange' [the counting rods in order to solve the problem in this way] and [can]

[3] trust [what was stated] in the problem [viz., that the flat-rate distribution method cannot be used]. It is already clear that this is so! Also, ranging the people according to their unequal capacities, [one has to give them] larger or smaller

[4] awards. So, those who are superior will obtain more, those who are inferior will obtain less. One distributes it [according to]

[5] unequal ranks. The [distribution] pattern certainly [should be] like this. Therefore [one will] use this amount of 5292

[6] *lượng* to distribute this [money] among the aforementioned corpus of 328 persons [while applying] the 'weighted distribution' [method] and having the number of the people subdivided into

[7] three ranks. Rank A: 8 persons, each person obtains 7 parts. Rank B: 20 persons, each person obtains

[8] 5 parts. Rank C: 300 persons, each person obtains 2 parts. This is the method of 'weighted distribution' for [this] problem.

[9] This method should be applied [as follows]: first of all, [I]⁸⁵ set [on the counting device] 8 persons of rank A, multiply them by 7 parts, obtain the product, 56

/p. 32a/

[1] parts–multiples.⁸⁶ Again [I] set 20 persons of rank B, multiply them by five parts, obtain the product, 100

[2] parts–multiples. Also [I] set 300 persons of rank C, multiply them by two parts, obtain the product, 600 parts–multiples.

[3] Then in an auxiliary [position of the counting instrument I] add the three [amounts] of parts–multiples, and obtain in total 756 parts–multiples.

[4] [I] take it as the 'norm' [= divisor]. And at this moment [I] set 5292 *lượng* of this money to be the dividend. Then

[5] [I] divide [this dividend] by the norm, set it [= the result, on the counting instrument], and [thus] obtain [that] one part–multiple equals seven *lượng*. [I] keep it [on the counting instrument] as the 'constant norm' and multiply by it

---

⁸⁵ I translate this part of the examination paper in first person, since its imaginary author is assumed to perform operations with a counting device (hence 'set') and to comment on them.

⁸⁶ On the term 'part–multiple' (Chinese *fenlü* 分率) see the discussion above, pp. 529–30.

[6] the parts-multiples of each rank. That is, first of all, I shall take the seven parts of each [functionary] of rank A, multiply it [by seven *lượng*], and establish that each man of rank A

[7] obtains 49 *lượng* of silver. Then again, [I] take five parts of each [functionary] of rank B, also multiply it [by seven *lượng*], establish that each person of rank B

[8] obtains 35 *lượng* of silver. Again, [I] take two parts of each [functionary] of rank C, also multiply it [by seven *lượng*],

[9] establish that each person of rank C obtains 14 *lượng* of silver. Here [the computation] of the [amount of] silver allotted to each person of each rank is already

/p. 32b/

[1] completed. As for the due [amount of money] for each [rank], [I take] the aggregated parts of each rank, and [I] shall similarly multiply [it] by the 'constant norm', and thus

[2] will know the due amounts. That is, [I] multiply the aggregated 56 parts–multiples for the rank A [by the 'constant norm'] and establish the [amount of] silver due to [all the functionaries of] the rank A,

[3] 392 *lượng*. Again, [I] multiply the aggregated 100 parts–multiples for the rank B [by the 'constant norm'] and establish the [amount of] silver due to [all the functionaries of] the rank B,

[4] 700 *lượng*. Also, [I] multiply the aggregated 600 parts–multiples for the rank C [by the 'constant norm'] and establish the [amount of] silver due to [all the functionaries of]

[5] the rank C, 4200 *lượng*. The silver due to each rank is thereby already established! As for the 'return to the origin',[87]

[6] [I] add together the amounts of silver due to the three ranks A, B and C, uniting them together, and establish the original [amount of] silver,

[7] 5292 *lượng*. [I,] so-and-so, am not clever as far as the 'learning' [is concerned]; [I only] roughly know the 'arrangement and disposition' [of the counting rods] for the [computational] methods and schemes (式);[88]

[8] [I] am bad at what [I] do, and still do not know how to 'distinguish and differentiate'[89] between 'excessive and insufficient'. Now, in answering the question [I] came up with a shallow and approximate answer

---

[87] That is, the check-up conducted in order to verify whether the answer obtained corresponds to the conditions of the problem.

[88] The imaginary examinee apparently makes an allusion to the final part of the problem mentioning '... [those who] arrange and dispose [the counting rods] ...'

[89] Once again, this is a quote from the final part of the problem '... [those who] ... distinguish and differentiate'.

[9] to it. Was it correct or wrong? Hope that those in charge will make [a right] decision. With best regards.[90]

Appendix II

This Appendix contains a list of the titles of Chinese mathematical treatises mentioned in the paper in Chinese characters, *pinyin* transliteration, Wade-Giles transliteration used in Anglo-Saxon countries and in Taiwan, my translation of the title, and the translation adopted in Martzloff 1997.[91] The treatises are listed alphabetically according to the *pinyin* transliteration of their titles.

---

[90] A formal ending.
[91] Martzloff 1997: 17, 20, 56, 124–5, 129.

Title in Chinese	Pinyin transliteration	Wade-Giles transliteration	Translation adopted in this paper	Translation adopted in Martzloff 1997
海島算經	*Hai dao suan jing*	*Hai tao suan ching*	Computational treatise [beginning with a problem] about a sea island	Sea Island Computational Canon
九章算法比類大全	*Jiu zhang suan fa bi lei da quan*	*Chiu chang suan fa pi lei ta chuan*	Great compendium of the computational methods of nine categories [and their] generics	Fully Comprehensive [Collection of] Computational Methods in Nine Chapters with [New Problems and Rules] Devised by Analogy with [Ancient Problems and Rules]
九章算術	*Jiu zhang suan shu*	*Chiu chang suan shu*	Computational procedures of nine categories	Computational Prescriptions in Nine Chapters
緝古算經	*Qi gu suan jing*	*Ch'i ku suan ching*	Computational treatise on the continuation of [traditions] of ancient [mathematicians]	Computational Canon of the Continuation of Ancient
三等數	*San deng shu*	*San teng shu*	Numbers of three ranks	The Art of the Three Degrees
數術記遺	*Shu shu ji yi*	*Shu shu chi i*	Records of the procedures of numbering left behind for posterity	Notes on the Traditions of Arithmo-Numerological Processes
算法統宗	*Suan fa tong zong*	*Suan fa t'ung tsung*	Summarized fundamentals of computational methods	General Source of Computation Methods

筭數書	*Suan shu shu*	*Suan shu shu*	Writing on computations with counting rods	[No translation suggested]
筭學啟蒙	*Suan xue qi meng*	*Suan hsüeh ch'i meng*	Introduction to the learning of computations	Introduction to the Computational Science
孫子筭經	*Sun zi suan jing*	*Sun tzu suan ching*	Computational treatise of Master Sun	Sunzi's Computational Canon
五曹筭經	*Wu cao suan jing*	*Wu tsao suan ching*	Computational treatise of five departments	Computational Canon of the Five Administrative Sections
五經筭術	*Wu jing suan shu*	*Wu ching suan shu*	Computational procedures [found] in the five classical books	Computational Prescriptions of the Five Classics
夏侯陽筭經	*Xiahou Yang suan jing*	*Hsia-hou Yang suan ching*	Computational treatise of Xiahou Yang	Xiahou Yang's Computational Canon
張丘建筭經	*Zhang Qiujian suan jing*	*Chang Ch'iu-chien suan ching*	Computational treatise of Zhang Qiujian	Zhang Qiujian's Computational Canon
周髀筭經	*Zhou bi suan jing*	*Chou pi (pei) suan ching*	Computational treatise on the gnomon of Zhou [dynasty]	Zhou Dynasty Canon of Gnomonic Computations
綴術	*Zhui shu*	*Chui shu*	Mending procedures	[No translation suggested]

Bibliography

Primary sources

CMLT – Phan Huy Khuông 潘輝框. *Chi minh lập thành toán pháp* 指明立成籌法 (Guidance for understanding of the *Ready-made Computational Methods*). Manuscript A1240 preserved in the library of the Institute for Han-Nom Studies, Hanoi, Vietnam.

DQ – Wu Jing 吳敬 (1450) *Jiu zhang suan fa bi lei da quan* 九章算法比類大全 (Great compendium of the computational methods of nine categories [and their] generics). In *Zhongguo kexue jishu dianji tonghui* 中國科學技術典籍通彙 (Comprehensive collection of written sources on Chinese science and technology), (gen. ed.) Ren Jiyu 任繼愈, *Shuxue juan* 數學卷 (Mathematical section), (section ed.) Guo Shuchun 郭書春 vol. II: 5–333. Zhengzhou (1993).

JTS – Liu Xu 劉昫 (gen. ed). *Jiu Tangshu* 舊唐書 (Old history of the Tang [Dynasty]). Taibei (1956).

SFTZ – Mei Rongzhao 梅荣照 and Li Zhaohua李兆华 (eds.). Cheng Dawei程大位. *Suanfa tongzong jiaoshi* 算法統宗校釋 (An annotated edition of the *Summarized Fundamentals of Computational Methods*). Hefei (1990).

SJSSa – Qian Baocong 錢寶琮 (ed.). *Suanjing shishu* 算經十書 (Ten canonical books on computation). Beijing (1963).

SJSSb – Guo Shuchun 郭書春, Liu Dun 劉鈍 (eds.). *Suanjing shishu* 算經十書 (Ten Canonical Books on Computation). Taibei (2001).

SS – Tuo Tuo 脫脫 *et al.* (eds.). *Song shi* 宋史 (History of the Song [dynasty]). Taibei (1956).

SXQM – Zhu Shijie 朱世傑 (1299) *Suan xue qi meng* 籌學啟蒙 (Introduction to the learning of computations). In *Zhongguo kexue jishu dianji tonghui* 中國科學技術典籍通彙 (Comprehensive collection of written sources on Chinese science and technology), (gen. ed.) Ren Jiyu 任繼愈, *Shuxue juan* 數學卷 (Mathematical section), (section ed.) Guo Shuchun 郭書春, vol. I: 1123–200. Zhengzhou (1993).

TLD – Zhang Jiuling 張九齡 *et al. Tang liu dian* 唐六典 (The six codes of the Tang [dynasty]). In *Wenyuange Siku quanshu*, vol. 595: 3–293. Taibei (1983).

XTS – Ouyang Xiu 歐陽脩 and Song Qi 宋祁. *Xin Tang shu* 新唐書 (New history of the Tang [Dynasty]). Taibei (1956).

Secondary works

An Pingqiu 安平秋, Zhang Peiheng 章培恆 (eds.) (1992) *Zhongguo lidai jinshu mulu* 中國歷代禁書目錄 (Catalogues of the Forbidden Books in China Through Generations). *Zhongguo jinshu daguan* 中國禁書大觀 (General History of Forbidden Books in China), vol. v. Taibei.

Bailly, C. (1857) *Réforme de la géométrie*. Paris.

Berezkina, E. (1975) 'Matematicheskii traktat o prodolzhenii drevnikh [metodov]. Vang Syao-tun' (Mathematical treatise on the continuation of ancient [methods], [by] Wang Xiaotong), *Istoriko-matematicheskie issledovaniya* **20**: 329–71.

Biot, É. C. (1847) *Essai sur l'histoire de l'instruction publique en Chine, et de la corporation des lettrés, depuis les anciens temps jusqu'à nos jours: ouvrage entièrement rédigé d'après les documents chinois*. Paris.

Cullen, C. (1993a) '*Chiu chang suan shu* [= *Jiu zhang suan shu*]', in *Early Chinese Texts*, ed. M. Loewe. Berkeley, CA: 16–23.

(1993b) '*Chou pi suan ching* [= *Zhou bi suan jing*]', in *Early Chinese Texts*, ed. M. Loewe. Berkeley, CA: 33–8.

(1996) *Astronomy and Mathematics in Ancient China: The Zhou bi suan jing*. Cambridge.

(2004) The *Suan shu shu 'Writing on reckoning': A Translation of a Chinese Mathematical Collection of the Second Century* BC, *With Explanatory Commentary*. Needham Research Institute Working Papers vol. I. Cambridge.

Dauben, J. W. (2008) '算數書 *Suan shu shu*: a book on numbers and computations', *Archive for the History of Exact Sciences* **62**: 91–178.

Des Rotours, R. (1932) *Le traité des examens, traduit de la Nouvelle histoire des T'ang (chap. 44–45)*. Paris.

Ennis, T. E. (1936) *French Policy and Developments in Indochina*. Chicago, IL.

Gillon, B. S. (1977) 'Introduction, translation, and discussion of Chao Chun-Ch'ing's "Notes to the Diagrams of Short Legs and Long Legs and of Squares and Circles"', *Historia Mathematica* **4**: 253–93.

Guo Shuchun (2001). 'Guanyu "Suan jing shi shu" 關於《算經十書》' (On the *Suan jing shi shu* [Ten classical mathematical treatises]). In *SJSSb*: 1–28.

Hucker, C. O. (1985) *A Dictionary of Official Titles in Imperial China*. Stanford, CA.

Lee, T. H. C. (2000). *Education in Traditional China: A History*. Leiden.

Li Di 李迪 (1982) 'Jiu zhang suan shu' zhengming wenti de gaishu "九章算術"爭鳴問題的概述 (An overview of the controversial questions [related to] the *Jiu zhang suan shu*). In Jiu zhang suan shu *yu Liu Hui* 九章算術與劉徽 (*The* Jiu zhang suan shu *and Liu Hui*), ed. Wu Wenjun 吳文俊. Beijing: 28–50.

Li Yan 李儼 (1977). 'Tang Song Yuan Ming shuxue jiaoyu zhidu' 唐宋元明數學教育制度 (The system of [Chinese] mathematics education of the Tang, Song, Yuan and Ming dynasties). In Li Yan 李儼, *Zhong suan shi luncong* 中算史論叢 (Collected Papers on the History of Chinese Mathematics). Taibei: vol. IV.1: 253–85.

Libbrecht, U. (1973) *Chinese Mathematics in the Thirteenth Century: The Shu-shu chiu-chang of Ch'in Chiu-shao*. Cambridge, MA.

Luro, J.-B.-E. (1878) *Le pays d'Annam: Étude sur l'organisation politique et sociale des annamites*. Paris.

Martzloff, J.-C. (1997) *A History of Chinese Mathematics*. Berlin.

Mikami Yoshio (1913) *The Development of Mathematics in China and Japan*. Leipzig. (Reprinted New York 1961.)

Needham, J. (with the collaboration of Wang Ling) (1959). *Science and Civilisation in China*, vol. III. Cambridge.

Nguyễn Danh Sành (1961) 'Contribution à l'étude des concours littéraires et militaires au Viet-Nam', PhD thesis, University of Rennes.

Richomme, M. (1905) 'De l'instruction publique en Indo-Chine', PhD thesis, Faculté de droit et des sciences économiques de l'Université de Paris.

Robson, E. (2001) 'Neither Sherlock Holmes nor Babylon: a reassessment of Plimpton 322', *Historia Mathematica* **28**: 167–206.

Schreiner, A. (1900) *Les institutions annamites en Basse Cochinchine*. Saigon.

Siu Man-Keung (1995) 'Mathematics education in ancient China: what lessons do we learn from it?' *Historia Scientiarum* **4**: 223–32.

(1999) 'How did candidates pass the state examinations in mathematics in the Tang dynasty (618–917)? – Myth of the "Confucian-Heritage-Culture" classroom', in *Actes du Colloque 'Histoire et épistemologie dans l'éducation mathématique'*. Louvain: 321–34.

(2004) 'Official curriculum in mathematics in ancient China: how did candidates study for the examination?' In *How Chinese Learn Mathematics: Perspectives from Insiders*, ed. Fan Lianghuo, Wong Ngai-Ying, Cai Jinfa and Li Shiqi. Singapore: 157–85.

Siu Man-Keung and Volkov A., (1999) 'Official curriculum in traditional Chinese mathematics: How did candidates pass the examinations?', *Historia Scientiarum* **9**: 87–99.

Sun Peiqing 孫培青 (ed.) (2000) *Zhongguo jiaoyu shi* 中國教育史 (History of education in China). Shanghai.

Tran Van Trai (1942) 'L'enseignement traditionnel en An-Nam', PhD theis, University of Paris.

Volkov, A. (2002) 'On the origins of the *Toan phap dai thanh* (Great Compendium of Mathematical Methods)', in *From China to Paris: 2000 Years' Transmission of Mathematical Ideas*, ed. Y. Dold-Samplonius, J. W. Dauben, M. Folkerts and B. van Dalen. Stuttgart: 369–410.

(2007) 'Geometrical diagrams in Liu Hui's commentary on the *Jiuzhang suanshu*', in *Graphics and Text in the Production of Technical Knowledge in China*, ed. F. Bray, V. Dorofeeva-Lichtmann and G. Métailié. Leiden: 425–59.

(2008) 'Mathematics in Vietnam', in *Encyclopaedia of the History of Non-Western Science: Natural Science, Technology and Medicine*, ed. H. Selin. Heidelberg: 1425–32.

(2009) 'Mathematics and mathematics education in traditional Vietnam', in *Oxford Handbook of the History of Mathematics*, ed. E. Robson and J. Stedall. Oxford: 153–76.

(forthcoming). 'Didactical dimensions of mathematical problems: "weighted distribution" in a Vietnamese mathematical treatise'.

Vu Tam Ich (1959) A *Historical Survey of Educational Developments in Vietnam.* A special issue of the *Bulletin of the Bureau of School Service,* by College of Education, University of Kentucky, Lexington, **32**(2) (December).

Wong Ngai-Ying (2004) 'The CHC learner's phenomenon: its implications on mathematics education', in *How Chinese Learn Mathematics: Perspectives from Insiders,* ed. Fan Lianghuo, Wong Ngai-Ying, Cai Jinfa and Li Shiqi. Singapore: 503–34.

Woodside, A. B. (1988) *Vietnam and the Chinese Model: A Comparative Study of Vietnamese and Chinese Government in the First Half of the Nineteenth Century.* Cambridge, MA.

Yan Dunjie 嚴敦傑 (2000) *Zu Chongzhi kexue zhuzuo jiaoshi* 祖沖之科學著作校釋 (An annotated edition of the Scientific Works of Zu Chongzhi). Shenyang.

Yushkevich, A. P. (1955) 'O dostizheniyakh kitaiskikh uchenykh v oblasti matematiki' (On the achievements of Chinese scholars in the field of mathematics). *Istoriko-matematicheskie issledovaniya (Studies in the history of mathematics)* **8**: 539–72. (In Russian.)

16 | A formal system of the *Gougu* method: a study on Li Rui's *Detailed Outline of Mathematical Procedures for the Right-Angled Triangle*

TIAN MIAO

In contrast to the deductive structure developed in Euclid's *Elements*, which is always taken as the model for ancient Greek mathematical reasoning, the structure of most ancient Chinese mathematical books could be described as that of a collection of problems and procedures. Moreover, these procedures were mostly described within the context of numerical problems. As historians have argued, in some ancient Chinese mathematical texts there are proofs establishing the correctness of the algorithms included. However, these proofs were mostly written by subsequent mathematicians, and were contained in commentaries attached to related procedures.[1] Therefore, as these proofs were specifically brought to bear on procedures that were taken from texts that already existed, they could seldom form a system by themselves, and hence the reasoning model in them looks flexible. This raises two related questions: when did Chinese mathematicians think of developing a formal system of mathematics in their books? Moreover, could the mathematical results developed in ancient China be presented systematically and formally?

In this chapter, I shall rely on a Chinese mathematical book, the *Gougu Suanshu Xicao* (hereafter abbreviated as *GGSX*, *Detailed Outline of Mathematical Procedures for the Right-Angled Triangle*, 1806), to investigate these questions. Furthermore, I hope that the discussion will shed some light upon questions such as why and in which context a formal system of mathematics emerged in China.

---

[1] The best-known examples of proofs in ancient Chinese mathematical texts are those Liu Hui provided in his commentary to *Jiuzhang suanshu*. For greater detail, see Guo Shuchun 1987; Chemla 1992; CG2004: 3–70; Wu Wenjun 1978.

1. *Detailed Outline of Mathematical Procedures for the Right-Angled Triangle*: a formal system for the 'Procedure of the right-angled triangle (*Gougu*)'

The table of contents of *Detailed Outline of Mathematical Procedures for the Right-Angled Triangle (GGSX)*

In the mathematics developed in ancient China, the study of the numerical relations between the sides of a right-angled triangle (the '*gougu*' shape) and the side or diameter of its inscribed and circumscribed square or circle formed a self-contained system, which was entitled the '*gougu* Procedure' (句股術, *Gougu shu*). In contrast to the mathematics developed in Europe, in which the sides of a right-angled triangle were generally named as sides around the right angle and hypotenuse, in ancient China, the two sides of the right angle had different names, the longer one being named *gu*, and the shorter one *gou* (Figure 16.1).[2]

The *GGSX* was completed in 1806 by the Chinese mathematician Li Rui (1769–1817).[3] The whole book was devoted to methods for solving a right-angled triangle when two of the following thirteen items attached to it are known:[4]

> The *gou*, the shortest one of the two sides around the right angle
> The *gu*, the longest one of the two sides around the right angle
> The hypotenuse
> The sum of *gou* and *gu*
> The difference between *gou* and *gu*
> The sum of *gou* and the hypotenuse

---

[2] In his commentary on *The Nine Chapters of Mathematical Procedures*, Liu Hui gave the following definition: 'The shorter side is named *gou*, (and) the longer side is named *gu*' (Liu Hui, Commentary, in *Jiuzhang suanshu*, chapter 9, 1a). When different names are used, it is easy to describe the calculation between them and to name the quantities they yield. In what follows, we will come back to these quantities. During the sixteenth and seventeenth centuries, some Chinese mathematicians named *gu* the vertical side of the right-angled triangle, and *gou* the horizontal side (see Gu Yingxiang, *Discussion on Gougu*, in Gu Yingxiang, 2a). In *GGSX*, the author Li Rui named the sides in the ancient way, which he described in his text.

[3] Liu Dun 1993.

[4] In Yang Hui's *Xiangjie Jiuzhang Suanfa* (*A Detailed Explanation of* The Nine Chapters of Mathematical Procedures, completed in 1261), there is a table containing all of these thirteen items. Guo Shuchun 1988 argues that the main part of this book was written by Jia Xian, and that Yang Hui only provided commentaries on it. If this is so, these thirteen terms were already sorted out in the eleventh century. Note that the names of the last four terms included in *Yang Hui Suanfa* (*Mathematical Methods by Yang Hui*) are not the same as those Li Rui uses in his book. For example, Yang Hui (45a) expressed the sum of *gou* and the sum of *gu* and hypotenuse as 'sum of hypotenuse and the sum (of *gou* and *gu*)'.

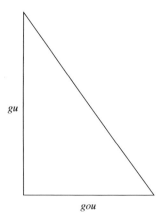

gu

gou

Figure 16.1 The *gougu* shape (right-angled triangle).

The difference between *gou* and the hypotenuse
The sum of *gu* and the hypotenuse
The difference between *gu* and the hypotenuse.
The sum of *gou* and the sum (of *gu* and the hypotenuse)
The sum of *gou* and the difference (between the hypotenuse and *gu*)
The difference between *gou* and the sum (of *gu* and the hypotenuse)
The difference between *gou* and the difference (between the hypotenuse and *gu*).[5]

If we denote *gou*, *gu* and the hypotenuse by *a*, *b* and *c* respectively, Table 16.1 below contains the following items:

Li Rui's text is composed of two parts – the table of contents and the main text. Both are presented in the form of a formal system. First, let us have a look at the table of contents.

The table of contents of the *GGSX* is a list of seventy-eight problems. We know from a basic theorem in combinatorics that if we choose two items out of thirteen, we can have seventy-eight combinations. Therefore, the table of contents of the *GGSX* in fact includes all the problems that can be raised in relation to the topic of the book. This means that Li Rui's solutions to the whole set of problems concerning the right-angled triangle are included in the book. In the table of contents, the problems are laid out according to two different models. We shall come back to them below.

---

[5] One may think that there could be other terms, such as the sum of hypotenuse and the difference between *gou* and *gu*. That could be denoted as hypotenuse + (*gu* – *gou*). However, it is equal to (hypotenuse + *gu*)–*gou*. In fact, this table includes the three sides of a right-angled triangle and the positive differences and sums that can be derived from them.

Table 16.1 The thirteen items of the '*Gougu* Procedure'

a (gou)
b (gu)
c (xian)
b + a (gougu he)
b − a (gougu jiao)
c + a (gouxian he)
c − a (gouxian jiao)
b + c (guxian he)
c − b (guxian jiao)
a + b + c (gouhe he)
b + c − a (gouhe jiao)
a + c − b (goujiao he)
a − c + b (goujiao jiao)

Here is a translation of the first part of the table of contents,[6] in which *gou* is rendered as *a*, *gu* as *b* and the hypotenuse as *c*. I designate the difference in layout by two marks that I place at the beginning of each item.

- *a, b* (being given), find *c*
- *a, c* (being given), find *b*
- *b, c* (being given), find *a*
- ə *a, a + b* (being given), subtract *a* from the sum, the remainder is *b*, enter into this problem by the procedure of *a* and *b*
- ə *a, b − a* (being given), add *a* to the difference, the sum is *b*, enter into this by the procedure of *a* and *b*
- ə *a, a + c* (being given), subtract *a* from the sum, the remainder is *c*, enter into this by the procedure of *a* and *c*
- ə *a, c − a* (being given), add *a* to the difference, enter into this by the procedure of *a* and *c*
- *a, b + c* (being given), find *b* and *c*
- *a, c − b* (being given), find *b* and *c*
- ə *b, a + b* (being given), subtract the difference from *b*, the remainder is *a*, enter into this by the procedure of *a* and *b*
- *b, a + c* (being given), find *a* and *c*
- *b, c − a* (being given), find *a* and *c*
- *b, c + b* (being given), subtract *b* from the sum, the remainder is *c*, enter into this by the procedure of *b* and *c*

---

[6] For the complete table of contents, see Appendix 1. In the original text, there is no mark at the beginning of each problem in the table of contents. In order to clarify the structure of the table and the book, I attach a mark, a circle or a square, to each problem (see below, p. 570).

ə $b, c-b$ (being given), add b to the difference, the sum is c, enter into this by the procedure of b and c

ə $c, a+b$ (being given), find a and b

• $c, b-a$ (being given), find a and b

ə $c, a+c$ (being given), subtract c from the sum, the remainder is a, enter into this by the method of a and c

ə $c, c-a$ (being given), subtract the difference from c, the remainder is a, enter into this by the procedure of a and c.

ə $c, b+c$ (being given), subtract c from the sum, the remainder is b, enter into this by the procedure of b and c.

• ...

• $a+b, (b+c)-a$ (being given), find a, b, and c (two problems).

• ...

• $b-a, a-(c-b)$ (being given), find a, b, and c (four problems).

• $a+c, (b+c)-a$ (being given), find a, b, and c (two problems).

• ...

• $a+c, a-(c-b)$ (being given), find a, b, and c (two problems).

• ...

• $c-a, a+(c-b)$ (being given), find a, b, and c (four problems).

• ...[7]

The table of contents maintains this formal order. For every problem in it, two items are given. The first item is chosen following the order of Table 16.1, while the second item is the one coming after the first item given in Table 16.1 and is also chosen according to the order of Table 16.1. For example, in the first forty-two problems, the following pairs of items are given:

$a, b; a, c; a, b+a; a, b-a; a, c+a; a, c-a; a, b+c; a, c-b; a, a+b+c; a, b+c-a; a, a+c-b; a, a-c+b;$

$b, c; b, b+a; b, b-a; b, c+a; b, c-a; b, b+c; b, c-b; b, a+b+c; b, b+c-a; b, a+c-b; b, a-c+b;$

$c, b+a; c, b-a; c, c+a; c, c-a; c, b+c; c, c-b; c, a+b+c; c, b+c-a; c, a+c-b; c, a-c+b;$

$b+a, b-a; b+a, c+a; b+a, c-a; b+a, b+c; b+a, c-b; b+a, a+b+c; b+a, b+c-a; b+a, a+c-b; b+a, a-c+b;$

...

Through this arrangement, the author of the *GGSX*, Li Rui, gave every problem in the book a definite position in the table of contents and if we

---

[7] Li Rui 1806, Table of contents (Mu, 目), 1a–6b.

want, we can figure out the position of a problem by the items given in the problem.[8]

From the above discussion, we see that the list in the table of contents displays a formal system. Let us analyse the structure of the outlines of problems included in the table of contents. I have translated the beginning of the list of problems into English, and I attached a symbol to each problem at the beginning of the translation of its outline.

The layout of all the problems marked with a black circle is generally the same. All contain two sentences. The first sentence is composed of the names of two items, without any conjunction between them. The second begins with a verb, *qiu* (求, 'find'), and ends with the names of the sides of a right-angled triangle which are sought for in that particular problem.

The problems marked with a square are composed of three parts. The first sentence also consists of the names of two items, without any conjunction. The second part contains one or two procedures. Through the procedure, the items given in the first sentence are transformed into items mentioned in a previous problem. The third sentence is a statement, which begins with *yi* (依, 'according to, relying on'). A procedure named by the two items that are the result of the transformation in the second sentence is then mentioned, and the sentence ends with *ruzhi* (入之, 'enter into it').[9]

Consequently, it is clear that both the order in which the list of problems is given in the table of contents and the way in which the outlines of the procedures are given are all arranged in a systematic way. However, this is

---

[8] Through this arrangement, Li Rui also ensured that he would not leave any problem out. Another Chinese mathematician, Wang Lai, one of Li Rui's friends, gave the general solution to the problem of computing the number of combinations of *n* things taken two or more at a time. See Wang Lai (1799?). Wang Lai does not provide the exact date of the completion of this book; however, he mentions that he attained the results contained in it in 1799. For details of the compilation of Wang Lai's book, see Li Zhaohua 1993.

[9] The whole item means that one solves the problem according to the procedure of the problem in which the resultant items are given. Only the problems marked with a black circle are contained in the main text of the book, the ones marked with a square appearing only in the table of contents. In fact, through the sentences just described, these problems are transformed into one of the other problems. These sentences not only give the way of transforming one problem into another, but also give the reasons why this problem could be solved by the procedure mentioned in the third sentence. For example, the fourth problem reads '*a, a + b* (being given), subtract *a* from the sum, the remainder is *b*, enter into this by the procedure of *a, b*.' The first sentence makes precise the data given in the problem, and the last one indicates that the procedure for the first problem solves this new problem, while the middle one yields the reason for this, that is, $(b + a) - a = a$. In other words, *a* is given, and it is shown how *b* can be found. The problem can hence be solved with the procedure of the problem, the data of which are *a* and *b*. In this way, even though only the problems marked with black circles are solved in the main part of the book, the book indicates how to solve the entire set of seventy-eight problems. We will come back to this point later.

not the only argument on which we rely to reach the conclusion that the *GGSX* has a formal structure. An examination of the main text of the *GGSX* also proves revealing and is particularly significant for our argument.

The main text of the *GGSX*

The main text contains the twenty-five category I items (those marked with black circles above and in the complete list of problems in the *GGSX* as given in the Appendix below). All the seventy-eight problems in the *GGSX* are solved in terms of these twenty-five problems.[10] Now, let us analyse how Li Rui presents and solves these problems in the *GGSX*. The translation of the fourth problem in the *GGSX* is given here as an example, and reads as follows.

Suppose *gou* is (equal to) 12, (and) the sum of *gu* and the hypotenuse is (equal to) 72. One asks how much *gu* and the hypotenuse are.

Answer: *gu*, 35; the hypotenuse, 37.

Procedure: subtract the two squares one from the other, halve the remainder and take it as the dividend, take the sum of *gu* and hypotenuse as the divisor, divide the dividend by the divisor, (one) gets the *gu*; subtract the *gu* from the sum, the remainder is the hypotenuse.

Outline: set up *gu* as the celestial unknown; multiplying it by itself, one gets $\begin{smallmatrix} 0 \\ 0 \\ 1 \end{smallmatrix}$,[11] which makes the square of *gu*. Further, one places (on the computing surface) *gou*, 12; multiplying it by itself, one gets 144, which makes the square of *gou*.

---

[10] See n. 10. In fact, the main text of *GGSX* contains thirty-three problems. For some problems, a note is attached to the outline, which says 'two problems' or 'four problems' (see the table of contents). This is not simply because Li Rui wants to give more examples to special problems. He has better reasons for this. The first kind of problem that is represented by two examples is the one for which '$a+b$ and $(b+c)-a$ (being given), [it is asked to] find a, b, and c.' For this problem Li Rui gives two examples. One relates to the condition $(b+c)-a > a+b$, whereas the other illustrates the condition $(b+c)-a < a+b$. For these two examples, even though the procedure used is the same, in relation to the difference in the conditions, Li Rui has to provide two cases. He gives two different demonstrations and constructs different diagrams for each of them. In the thirteenth century, Li Ye had already encountered this kind of difficulty. Li Rui edited Li Ye's *Ceyuan Haijing* in 1797, so it is likely that he may have been influenced by his research on Li Ye. In one problem, Li Rui provided two different groups of answers for a second-degree equation. This is due to his study on the theory of equations. For Li Rui's study on equations, see Liu Dun 1989.

[11] In ancient China, the degree of the unknown was indicated by the position of its coefficient. In the *GGSX*, the degree of an unknown attached to a given coefficient increases from top to bottom. This polynomial is equivalent to $0 + 0x + 1x^2$. For an explanation of the *tianyuan* method, see LD1987.

Adding the two squares yields $\dfrac{144}{0}$, which makes the square of the hypotenuse.

(Put it aside on the left.) Further, one places the sum of *gu* and the hypotenuse, 72;

subtracting from this the celestial unknown, the *gu*, one gets $\dfrac{72}{-1}$, which makes the

hypotenuse. Multiplying it by itself, one gets $\dfrac{5184}{-144}$, which makes a quantity equal

to (the number put aside on the left). Eliminating with the left (number), one gets

$\dfrac{5040}{-144}$; halving both of them, one gets $\dfrac{2520}{-72}$, the upper one is the dividend, the

lower one is the divisor, (dividing), one gets 35, hence the *gu*. Subtracting the *gu*
from the sum of *gu* and the hypotenuse, 72, there remains 37, hence the hypotenuse. This conforms to what was asked (see Figure 16.2).

Explanation: in the square of the sum, there is one piece of the square of *gu*, one
piece of the square of hypotenuse, and twice the product of *gu* and the hypotenuse.
[Subtracting the square of *gou* from within it, the remainder is twice the square of
gu, subtracting the square of *gou* from the square of the hypotenuse, the remainder
is the square of *gu*][12] and twice the product of *gu* and hypotenuse. Halving them
makes the square of *gu* and the product of *gu* and hypotenuse. Join the two areas
together, hence this is the multiplication by one another of *gu* and the sum of *gu* and
hypotenuse, so, dividing it by the sum, one gets the *gu*.[13]

Except for the first three problems, the layout of every problem is exactly
the same as in the above example. In other words, the text for each problem
is composed of the same components: a numerical problem, an answer
to the problem, a general procedure without specific numbers, an outline
that sets out the computations using the *tianyuan* algebraic method, and
an explanation, which may be regarded as a general and rigorous proof
with a diagram.[14] Furthermore, the order of the different parts remains the
same throughout the whole book.[15] Consequently, not only do most of the

---

[12] In the original text, characters contained in square brackets were printed in smaller size than
the main text. This arrangement indicates that Li Rui did not think that this part belonged
to the main text. In fact, this part provides the reasoning of the previous statement. Li Rui
generally provides reasons for his argument and statements in this way throughout the whole
work.

[13] Li Rui 1806: 8b–9a.

[14] The explanation does not discuss the meaning of the problem or the procedure, but it
highlights the reasons why the procedure given is correct. This is why it can essentially be
considered as a proof of the procedure following the problem.

[15] In the first problem, Li Rui tries to reconstruct the demonstration of the 'Pythagoras
theorem' (which in present-day Chinese is called the '*Gougu* theorem', whereas in the past

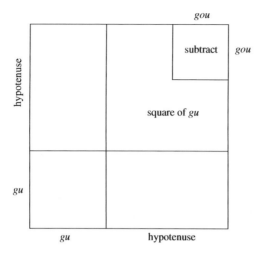

Figure 16.2 Li Rui's diagram for his explanation for the fourth problem in *Detailed Outline of Mathematical Procedures for the Right-Angled Triangle.*

problems in the *GGSX* have the same layout in general, but also the parts of every problem are similarly arranged in a formal way.

Concerning the five parts of each problem in the main text of *GGSX*, there is not much that can be said about the first three. The structure of the presentation of each problem and its solution remains the same for the whole book. The only changes concern the numerical values in the problem and the answers as well as the concrete procedures. We shall focus our analysis on the last two parts of the presentation of each problem: the outline and the explanation.

Let us begin our analysis of the structure of these parts of the problems in the *GGSX* with an inspection of the outline of the calculations. For each of the thirty-three problems contained in the book, Li Rui gives an outline of the calculations. And except for the first three problems, they all bring into play the *tianyuan* method.[16] The first step is to set up the celestial unknown. In addition, Li Rui follows a strict rule in choosing the unknown. The rule

it was called '*Gougu* procedure'), as given by Liu Hui around the year 263. Strictly speaking, the demonstration is not a rigorous one, and it is unknown whether it reflects Liu Hui's original proof or not. For Li Rui's demonstration of the Pythagorean theorem, see Tian Miao, forthcoming. For Liu Hui and his proof of the Pythagoras theorem, see Wu Wenjun 1978; Guo Shuchun 1992; Chemla 1992; CG2004.

[16]   *Tianyuan* algebra is a method for solving problems. It makes use of polynomials with one indeterminate, expressed according to a place-value system, in order to find out an algebraic equation that solves the problem. The equation was also written down according to a place-

is: if *a*, *gou*, is not known in the problem, he sets *a* as the unknown. If *a* is known, and *b* is not known, he sets *b* as the unknown.[17]

The second step of the outline consists of establishing the *tianyuan* equation. To analyse this step, we shall give two examples to show the formal way in which Li Rui does this. Problem 9 reads as follows:

Suppose there is the *gou* (which is equal to) 33, the difference between the hypotenuse and *gu* (which is equal to) 11. Ask for the same items as the previous problem (*gu* and hypotenuse).

Outline: set up *gu* as the celestial unknown, multiplying it by itself, [one] gets $\genfrac{}{}{0pt}{}{0}{1}$, which makes the square of *gu*. Further, one places *gou* 33; multiplying it by itself, one gets 1088, which makes the square of *gou*. Adding the two squares together yields $\genfrac{}{}{0pt}{}{1088}{0}{1}$, which is the square of the hypotenuse. (Put it aside on the left.) Further, one places the difference between the hypotenuse and *gu*, 11, adding it to the celestial unknown, *gu*, one gets $\genfrac{}{}{0pt}{}{11}{1}$, multiplying it by itself, one gets $\genfrac{}{}{0pt}{}{121}{22}{1}$, which makes a quantity equal to (the number put aside on the left). Eliminating with the left (number), one gets $\genfrac{}{}{0pt}{}{-868}{22}$, halving both the upper and the lower, one gets $\genfrac{}{}{0pt}{}{-484}{11}$, the upper one is the dividend, the lower one is the divisor, (dividing), one gets 44, which is the *gu*.[18]

All the thirty problems follow the same pattern. First, Li Rui tries to find the expression of *gou* and *gu* on the basis of the items that are known. He then multiplies each by itself respectively, adds the squares to each other, and puts the result on the left. In a second part, he looks for an expression

value notation. The expression of polynomials and equations makes use of the representation of numbers with counting rods in a place-value number system. Moreover, the notation uses the *tianyuan*, which is supposed to be the unknown and which is represented by a position. This method flourished in thirteenth- to fourteenth-century China. However, it seems that Chinese scholars and mathematicians could no longer understand this algebraic method by the sixteenth century. In the eighteenth century, Chinese mathematicians rediscovered this ancient method, and Li Rui, author of *GGSX*, made the most outstanding contribution to restoring it. For *tianyuan* algebra, see Qian Baocong 1982. On the revival of the *tianyuan* method in eighteenth-century China, see Tian Miao 1999.

[17] Only in the third problem, in which *a* and *b* are known, is *c* chosen as unknown. This problem is solved by a direct application of the Pythagorean theorem, and thus the *tianyuan* method is not used.

[18] Li Rui 1806: 9b.

for the hypotenuse, and squares it. Finally, by eliminating the square of the hypotenuse and the expression put on the left side, he gets the equation. The second example (problem 58) shows that Li Rui deliberately followed the same pattern in the whole book.

Suppose there is the sum of *gou* and the hypotenuse (equal to) 676, the difference between the sum (of *gu* and the hypotenuse) and *gou* is 560. One asks how much the same items as in the previous problem (*gou*, *gu* and the hypotenuse) are.

Draft: set up *gou* as the celestial unknown, multiplying it by itself, one gets $\genfrac{}{}{0pt}{}{0}{1}$, which makes the square of *gou*. Further one places the sum of the hypotenuse and *gou*, 676, and subtracting *gou* from it, one gets the following: $\genfrac{}{}{0pt}{}{676}{-1}$, which is the hypotenuse. Further, one places the difference between the sum and *gou*, 560; adding the celestial unknown *gou* to it, one gets the following formula, $\genfrac{}{}{0pt}{}{560}{1}{676}$, which makes the sum of *gu* and the hypotenuse. Subtracting the hypotenuse, −1 from it, one gets $\genfrac{}{}{0pt}{}{-116}{2}$, which makes *gu*; multiplying it by itself, one gets the following formula, $\genfrac{}{}{0pt}{}{13456}{-464}{4}$, which is the square of *gu*. Adding the two squares together, one gets the following formula: $\genfrac{}{}{0pt}{}{13456}{-464}{5}$, which makes the square of the hypotenuse. (Put it on the left.) Further, multiplying the $\genfrac{}{}{0pt}{}{676}{-1}$ hypotenuse, −1, by itself, one gets $\genfrac{}{}{0pt}{}{456976}{-1352}{1}$, which makes a quantity equal to (the number put aside on the left). Eliminating the left (number), one gets $\genfrac{}{}{0pt}{}{-443520}{888}{4}$; dividing all the numbers from top to bottom by 4, one gets $\genfrac{}{}{0pt}{}{110880}{222}{1}$. Solve the equation of the second degree.

One gets 240, which is the *gou*. Get the *gu* and hypotenuse according to procedure. This answers the problem.[19]

In modern algebra, the above outline could be reformulated into the following procedure:

Take *a*, the *gou*, as *x*,

then, $a^2 = x^2$

as $c + a = 676$

[19] Li Rui 1806: 28b–29a.

so $c = c + a - a = 676 - x$

as $c + b - a = 560$

so, $c + b = 560 + x$

and, $b = c + b - c = 560 + x - (676 - x) = -116 + 2x$

then, $b^2 = 13456 - x + 4x^2$

and, $c^2 = a^2 + b^2 = 13456 - 464x + 5x^2$

while, $c = 676 - x$

so, $c^2 = 456976 - 1352x + x^2$

thus, $13456 - 464x + 5x^2 = 456976 - 1352x + x^2$

so, $-443520 + 888x^2 = 0$

$x = 240$.

In this problem, relying on the items given in the outline, Li Rui first finds the hypotenuse. However, he does not multiply the hypotenuse by itself, to put the result on the left side. Instead, he seeks to find the *gu*, and, only then, he adds the square of *gou* and *gu* and puts the result to the left. It is only in the second step that he computes the square of the hypotenuse and eliminates the result with the number placed on the left side. It is clear that the final equation could not be affected by which number was first put on the left side, and there are reasons to believe that Liu Rui certainly understood this point. Only one reason can account for why Li Rui insisted on determining the *gu* first, namely, that he wanted to follow the same format in presenting each of the outlines.

From the evidence analysed above, we can conclude that throughout the whole book Li Rui follows a formal pattern for the outline of calculation.

Let us now consider how Li Rui presents his explanations in his book. What kinds of rules does Li Rui follow to formulate his proofs?

The eighth problem of the book reads:

Suppose the hypotenuse is (equal to) 75, and the sum of *gou* and *gu* (equal to) 93. One asks how much the *gou* and *gu* are.

The procedure given is as follows:

Subtract the two squares one from the other, halve the remainder and take it as the negative constant. Take the sum (of *gou* and *gu*) as the positive coefficient of the first degree of the unknown, and the negative one as the coefficient of the highest degree of the unknown. Extracting the second degree equation, one gets the *gou*. Subtracting *gou* from the sum, the remainder is *gu*.[20]

---

[20] Li Rui 1806: 11b.

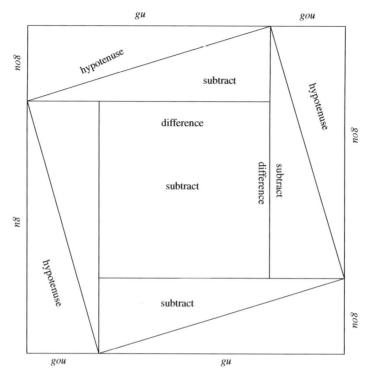

Figure 16.3 Li Rui's diagram for his explanation for the eighth problem in *Detailed Outline of Mathematical Procedures for the Right-Angled Triangle*.

This procedure may be represented in modern algebraic terms by the following equation:

$$x^2 + (a+b)x - [(a+b)^2 - c^2]/2 = 0$$

whose solution is $x = a$.

Li Rui's explanation may be translated as follows:

Explanation: in the square of the sum, there are four pieces of the product of *gou* (*a*) and *gu* (*b*), one piece of the square of the difference between *gou* and *gu*. In the square of the hypotenuse, there are twice the product of *gou* and *gu*, and one piece of the square of the difference (between *gou* and *gu*). Subtracting one from the other, the remainder is twice the product of *gou* and *gu*. Halving it, one gets one piece of the product, which is also the product of *gou* and the sum of *gou* and *gu* minus the square of *gou*. Therefore, take the sum as the negative coefficient of the first degree of the unknown.[21]

Now, let us inquire into the process of explanation (see Figure 16.3). In the first step, Li Rui decomposes the two 'squares' mentioned at the beginning of

---

[21] Li Rui 1806: 12a.

the procedure and gets the geometrical expression of the difference between them, then he transforms half of the difference between the two squares, which is the negative constant term of the equation described in the procedure, into an expression involving the unknown, *gou*, and *gu*. Then, he further changes the product of *gou* and *gu* into an expression depending on the unknown, *gou*, and the given item, *gou+gu*. This yields the same expression as the equation of the procedure. Therefore, the explanation corresponds exactly to the procedure. With the diagram, the explanation is in fact a geometrical proof to account for the correctness of the general procedure.

Except for the first three, all the proofs in the book are obtained by exactly the same process. Therefore, we may conclude that the proofs are also produced in a uniformly formal way.

To recapitulate, in the whole work Li Rui follows a formal way for the outline of the calculation, through which a *tianyuan* algebraic equation – the procedure – is found, as well as for his proofs. With this formal structure of the book, he produces a formal system for the *gougu* procedure strictly based on traditional methods developed in ancient China. From this, we see that the ancient Chinese methods could be used to present mathematical knowledge in the shape of a formal system.

2. Li Rui's intention in developing a formal system of the *Gougu* methods

From the above discussion, we see that the *GGSX* is shaped as a formal and complete system for solving right-angled triangles (*gougu* shape in Chinese). In this section of the chapter, I will tackle two problems. First, did Li Rui deliberately plan his *GGSX* as a formal work? If the answer is yes, we shall then seek to understand why he was interested in creating such a formal system of *gougu* procedures, and what he wanted to show to his readers through such a system.

First, we must establish that Li Rui consciously developed his system. Let us start by summing up the characteristics of the formal expression of the system in the *GGSX*.

(1) The organization of the table of contents of the *GGSX* follows a consistent pattern.
(2) The layout of the problems in the main text follows a consistent pattern too.
(3) *Tianyuan* algebra is used for all the outlines of calculation in the text except the first three.

(4) Li Rui follows a formal and systematic way of choosing the unknown, and seeking the equation in the outline.

(5) The proofs are derived from the corresponding procedure strictly using the same process and methods.

Now, let us see whether it was necessary for Li Rui to follow all the steps listed above.

It is clear that there should be no need for the layout of the table of contents and all problems in the main text to follow a consistent pattern. Moreover, most ancient Chinese mathematical books do not share this feature. We may thus safely assume that if Li Rui took the trouble to design his book in this formal way, he did so intentionally.

Let us now come to the third and fourth features. In ancient China, the study of *gougu* procedures has a history that precedes the invention of *tianyuan* algebra. In the *Nine Chapters of Mathematical Procedures*, an entire chapter is devoted to *gougu* problems, for the solution of which procedures are given.[22] And we have evidence showing that up to the third century, Liu Hui and Zhao Shuang gave proofs to some formulas.[23] Although their diagrams are lost, other books survive that include proofs of some of the formulas, and Li Rui was familiar with most of them.[24] Therefore, he could easily have studied these results and proofs. In fact, in some cases, the proofs could have been more easily and clearly presented without using the *tianyuan* methods. Therefore, it was not necessary for Li Rui to use *tianyuan* algebra for all the problems and proofs in which he used it.

So, it is not far-fetched to conclude that Li Rui chose to use *tianyuan* algebra deliberately. Furthermore, there was no need for him to follow exactly the same order to obtain his equations. As we have already showed above, it was not necessary to obtain systematically first the *gou* and *gu*, and only then the *xian* or hypotenuse. Nor was it necessary to systematically look for the equation on the basis of the Pythagorean theorem, as Li Rui did. A number of formulas existed in ancient Chinese mathematical books, such as *The Nine Chapters*, Yang Hui's *Xiangjie jiuzhang suanfa* and Li Ye's *Ceyuan haijing*. Xu Guangqi and Mei Wending also provide several

---

[22] According to Guo Shuchun, the main part of the *Nine Chapters of Mathematical Procedures*, including the '*Gougu*' chapter, was already formed before the first century BCE. See Guo Shuchun 1992. On the '*Gougu* procedure' in the *Nine Chapters*, see Guo Shuchun 1992: 83.

[23] On Liu Hui's proof of *Gougu* procedures, see CG2004: 704–7.

[24] In 1797, the year he compiled the *Chouren zhuan*, a collection of biographies of mathematicians and astronomers, Li Rui made a serious study of all the mathematical texts that existed in his time, including Yang Hui's *Xiangjie Jiuzhang Suanfa*, Xu Guangqi's *Gougu yi* and Mei Wending's *Gougu juyu*. On Xu Guangqi's *Gougu yi* and Mei Wending's *Gougu juyu*, see Tian Miao, forthcoming.

formulas in their books. Li Rui studied all of these books before he compiled the *GGSX*. Had he wanted to do so, he could have used these formulas to find his equations more easily. Clearly, he insisted on following a uniform pattern throughout his book.

The same remark applies to the proofs. It was also not necessary to follow exactly the same approach throughout. But again, clearly Li Rui obstinately chooses to stick to a rule he has set for himself.

From the above analysis, one can reasonably conclude that Li Rui deliberately shaped a formal system of *gougu* problems in his book.

This conclusion leads us to our last problem: what did he intend to show his readers in forming such a system? Li Rui's preface to the *GGSX* gives us some hints. He writes:

[As for] the Dao of mathematics, the important thing is that one must thoroughly understand the great principles (Yi 義). [If one] seeks [methods] by minor parts, even if his [method] is in accordance (with the problem) in number, it can not be looked upon as a method. In the year of Bingyin, Xu Yunan (Naifan) and Wan Xiaolian (Qiyun) studied with me, [the knowledge they learned] also came down to *gougu* mathematics. In the free time between our discussions, [I] compiled this book and showed it to them. In order to (let them) know that even if procedures are produced according to [specific] problems, they still have a consistent [reason behind] them.[25]

This passage from the preface shows clearly that Li Rui did not aim at achieving new discoveries when he composed the *GGSX*. His aim was to show that there was a consistent reason or theory in mathematics. His essential motivation for writing the book was without doubt didactic.[26]

However, there may have been another reason why Li Rui wrote such a book. Possibly he hoped to show that the mathematical results developed in ancient China had consistent reasons and had their own system. His intention in doing so might have been to reject the opinion that Chinese mathematical books only provided procedures for concrete problems. I do not have hard evidence to support my argument, but considering the context within which the *GGSX* was compiled sheds some light on Li Rui's intention and provides additional support to my argument.

In 1607, the first Chinese translation of Euclid's *Elements* (the first six books) was published under the title *Jihe yuanben*.[27] The two translators, Matteo Ricci and Xu Guangqi, claimed that giving reasons for mathematical

---

[25] Li Rui 1806: preface.
[26] See Liu Dun 1993.
[27] On the transmission of the *Elements* in China, see Engelfriet 1998, Engelfriet 1993.

methods and leaving the reader with no doubt about mathematical knowledge were the essence of Western mathematics. Two years after the publication of the *Jihe yuanben*, in 1609, Xu Guangqi composed *Gougu yi* (*The Principle of Gougu*).[28] To interpret the word *yi*, we have to briefly mention what Xu Guangqi said in the preface of another book, *Celiang fayi* (1607). Peter Engelfriet offers the following analysis:

He [Xu Guangqi] makes a distinction that proves very important in his conception of Western mathematics: a distinction between methods and *yi*. The word *yi* can take on a wide range of meanings, but it is obvious that in this context it must refer to the proofs and explanations given in Western mathematics. For Xu Guangqi states explicitly that only after the *Jihe yuanben* had been translated was it possible to transmit the *yi* of the methods. Moreover, the Western methods of surveying are not essentially different from the methods transmitted in the *Zhoubi suanjing* and the *Jiuzhang suanshu*. What makes Western mathematics more valuable is that it supplies explanations which show why the methods are correct.[29]

In his *Gougu yi*, Xu Guangqi sums up the main topics Chinese mathematicians addressed with respect to *gougu* problems. He stresses that these problems could only be solved on the basis of the Pythagorean theorem,[30] to be found as Proposition 47 of Book I in the *Elements*. He argues:

In the old *Nine Chapters*, there are also [methods] of finding the *gou* and *gu* from each other, [finding] the inscribed square and circle, and [finding] the sums and the differences from each other.[31] But it is only capable of stating the methods, and it is not capable of discussing its principles (*yi*). The methods established [in it] are in disorder and shallow, and do not bear reading.[32]

What is significant for us here is that both Xu Guangqi and Li Rui use the word *yi*. While Xu argues that *The Nine Chapters* did not talk about

---

[28] See Engelfriet 1998: 297–8.

[29] Engelfriet 1998: 297. Engelfriet discusses the meaning of *yi* and the origin of this term in Xu Guangqi's book in more detail in Engelfriet 1993.

[30] The example Xu Guangqi quotes earlier in his text is from the *Zhoubi suanjing* (The *Mathematical Canon of the Zhoubi*, dating from the beginning of the first century BCE). This text contains a general statement of the Pythagorean theorem, including a paragraph which could be regarded as a general proof of it (see Ch'en Liang-ts'so 1982, Li Jimin 1993). In the third century, Zhao Shuang and Liu Hui present clearer proofs in their commentaries to the *Zhoubi Suanjing* and *The Nine Chapters*, respectively. See Qian Baocong 1982; Guo Shuchun 1985; CG2004: 704–45.

[31] *The Nine Chapters of Mathematical Procedures* (dated from the first century BCE to the first century CE). This is one of the most important mathematical classics of ancient China. The ninth chapter of this book is devoted to *gougu* methods. See Guo Shuchun 1985.

[32] Xu Guangqi, preface.

yi, Li Rui argues that one has to understand the *yi*.[33] However, although Xu believed that traditional mathematical learning could not provide any 'principle' for the *gougu* procedure, Li Rui developed a formal system based on traditional methods and mathematical terms.[34] It therefore seems reasonable to assume that one of the reasons why Li Rui wrote the *GGSX* was that he wanted to demonstrate that the traditional methods could be developed into systems and, in doing so, one could also form a system of consistent reasoning.[35]

Let me sum up briefly my conclusions. In 1806, the Chinese mathematician Li Rui shaped a formal system based on the *gougu* procedure. In his work, in seeking procedures and the proof of their correctness, Li Rui strictly follows traditional methods and terms. This provides evidence for whether there could have been a formal system in mathematical research in ancient China. Further analysis shows that Li Rui deliberately constructed such a formal system. Even if he may have had only a didactical aim in mind, it appears that the context of tension between Western mathematical methods and Chinese traditional methods may well lie at the bottom of Li Rui's motivation for compiling the *GGSX*.

Acknowledgements

This paper was primarily finished during the academic year October 2001 – September 2002, when I worked in the University of Paris 7, cooperating with Professor Karine Chemla and being financially supported by the Ministry of Research, France. It was presented at the seminar (March 2002 – June 2002) organized by Karine Chemla, Geoffrey Lloyd, Ian Mueller and Reviel Netz. I benefited a great deal from the attentive discussion and valuable suggestions of all the participants, including Karine Chemla, Catherine Jami, Geoffrey Lloyd, Ian Mueller, Reviel Netz and Alexei Volkov. Joseph W. Dauben and John Moffett read the outline of this chapter, and provided

---

[33] In Liu Hui's commentary (263 of *The Nine Chapters of Mathematical Procedures*), he uses the character *yi* to indicate the reason behind the procedures provided in the *Nine Chapters*. On the meaning of *yi* in ancient Chinese mathematical texts, see Chemla 'Yi' (義)', in CG2004: 1022–3.

[34] From 1797 onwards, Li Rui began helping Ruan Yuan to compile the *Chouren zhuan* (Biographies of mathematicians and astronomers). The main sources for this book were from the *Siku quanshu*. Xu Guangqi's *Gougu yi* was included in this encyclopaedia. Therefore, one can safely assume that Li Rui studied Xu Guangqi's book and knew Xu's opinions concerning traditional *gougu* procedures.

[35] For a detailed analysis of Li Rui's attitude towards Western and traditional mathematics and detailed arguments concerning the compilation of the *GGSX*, see Tian Miao 1999, Tian Miao 2005.

valuable suggestions. I am especially in debt to Karine Chemla and Catherine Jami. As we were discussing and working together frequently during the year, it is not easy to identify all the inspirations I have gained from them. Therefore, here, I would like to take this chance to express my gratitude to them.

Appendix

The content of the *Detailed Outline of Mathematical Procedures for the Right-Angled Triangle*

Problem[a]	Given	Find	Other
•1	a, b	c	
•2	a, c	b	
•3	b, c	a	
□4	$a, b+a$	b, c	Problem 1[b]
□5	$a, b-a$	b, c	Problem 1
□6	$a, c+a$	b, c	Problem 2
□7	$a, c-a$	b, c	Problem 2
•8	$a, c+b$	b, c	
•9	$a, c-b$	b, c	
□10	$b, b+a$	a, c	Problem 1
□11	$b, b-a$	a, c	Problem 1
•12	$b, c+a$	a, c	
•13	$b, c-a$	a, c	
□14	$b, c+b$	a, c	Problem 3
□15	$b, c-b$	a, c	Problem 3
•16	$c, a+b$	a, b	
•17	$c, b-a$	a, b	
□18	$c, c+a$	a, b	Problem 2
□19	$c, c-a$	a, b	Problem 2
□20	$c, b+c$	a, b	Problem 3
□21	$c, c-b$	a, b	Problem 3
□22	$a+b, b-a$	a, b, c	Problem 1
•23	$a+b, a+c$	a, b, c	
•24	$a+b, c-a$	a, b, c	
□25	$a+b, c+b$	a, b, c	Problem 24
□26	$a+b, c-b$	a, b, c	Problem 23
•27	$b-a, a+c$	a, b, c	
•28	$b-a, c-a$	a, b, c	
□29	$b-a, b+c$	a, b, c	Problem 27
□30	$b-a, c-b$	a, b, c	Problem 28

Continued

Appendix *Continued*

Problem[a]	Given	Find	Other
□31	$a+c, c-a$	a, b, c	Problem 2
•32	$a+c, c+b$	a, b, c	Problem 27
□33	$a+c, c-b$	a, b, c	Problem 23
□34	$c-a, b+c$	a, b, c	Problem 24
•35	$c-a, c-b$	a, b, c	Problem 28
□36	$c+b, c-b$	a, b, c	Problem 3
□37	$a, a+b+c$	b, c	Problem 8
□38	$a, c+b-a$	b, c	Problem 8
□39	$a, a+c-b$	b, c	Problem 9
□40	$a, a-c+b$	b, c	Problem 9
□41	$b, a+b+c$	a, c	Problem 12
□42	$b, c+b-a$	a, c	Problem 13
□43	$b, a+c-b$	a, c	Problem 12
□44	$b, a-c+b$	a, c	Problem 13
□45	$c, a+b+c$	a, b	Problem 16
□46	$c, b+c-a$	a, b	Problem 17
□47	$c, a+c-b$	a, b	Problem 17
□48	$c, a-c+b$	a, b	Problem 16
□49	$a+b, a+b+c$	a, b, c	Problem 16
•50a	$a+b, c+b-a$	a, b, c	$a+b>c+b-a$
•50b	$a+b, c+b-a$	a, b, c	$a+b<c+b-a$
•51	$a+b, a+c-b$	a, b, c	
□52	$a+b, a-c+b$	a, b, c	Problem 16
•53	$b-a, a+b+c$	a, b, c	
54□	$b-a, b+c-a$	a, b, c	Problem 17
55□	$b-a, a+c-b$	a, b, c	Problem 17
•56a	$b-a, a-c+b$	a, b, c	$b-a>a-c+b$; $(b-a)-(a-c+b)>a-c+b$
•56b	$b-a, a-c+b$	a, b, c	$b-a>a-c+b$; $(b-a)-(a-c+b)<a-c+b$
•56c	$b-a, a-c+b$	a, b, c	$b-a<a-c+b$; $(a-c+b)-(b-a)>b-a$
•56d	$b-a, a-c+b$	a, b, c	$b-a<a-c+b; (a-c+b)-(b-a)<b-a$
□57	$a+c, a+b+c$	a, b, c	Problem 12
•58a	$a+c, b+c-a$	a, b, c	$a+c>b+c-a$
•58b	$a+cb+c-a$	a, b, c	$a+c<b+c-a$
□59	$a+c, a+c-b$	a, b, c	Problem 12
•60a	$a+c, a-c+b$	a, b, c	
•60b	$a+c, a-c+b$	a, b, c	In this Problem, two answers are given. This means there are two different right-angled triangles with the same data $a+c$ and $a-c+b$

Continued

Appendix *Continued*

Problem[a]	Given	Find	Other
•61	$c-a, a+b+c$	a, b, c	
□62	$c-a, c+b-a$	a, b, c	Problem 13
•63a	$c-a, a+c-b$	a, b, c	$c-a>a+c-b,$
			$(c-a)-(a+c-b)>a+c-b$
•63b	$c-a, a+c-b$	a, b, c	$c-a>a+c-b,$
			$(c-a)-(a+c-b)<a+c-b$
•63c	$c-a, a+c-b$	a, b, c	$c-a<a+c-b, (a+c-b)-(c-a)>c-a$
•63d	$c-a, a+c-b$	a, b, c	$c-a<a+c-b, (a+c-b)-(c-a)<c-a$
□64	$c-a, a-c+b$	a, b, c	Problem 13
□65	$c+b, a+b+c$	a, b, c	Problem 8
□66	$c+b, b+c-a$	a, b, c	Problem 8
•67	$c+b, a+c-b$	a, b, c	
•68	$c+b, a-c+b$	a, b, c	
•69	$c-b, a+b+c$	a, b, c	
•70	$c-b, b+c-a$	a, b, c	
□71	$cv-b, a+c-b$	a, b, c	Problem 9
□72	$c-b, a-c+b$	a, b, c	Problem 9
□73	$a+b+c, b+c-a$	a, b, c	Problem 8
□74	$a+b+c, a+c-b$	a, b, c	Problem 12
□75	$a+b+c, a-c+b$	a, b, c	Problem 16
□76	$b+c-a, a+c-b$	a, b, c	Problem 17
□77	$b+c-a, a-c+b$	a, b, c	Problem 13
□78	$a+c-b, a-c+b$	a, b, c	Problem 9

Notes:

[a] The sign '•' indicates problems that were also discussed by Xu Guangqi in the *Meaning of Gougu.*

[b] This means 'Solve this problem using the method of problem 1'. Similarly hereafter.

Bibliography

Chemla, K. (1992) 'Résonances entre démonstration et procédure: remarques sur le commentaire de Liu Hui aux *Neuf Chapitres sur les Procédures Mathématiques*', in *Regards Obliques sur l'Argumentation en Chine*, ed. K. Chemla. *Extrême-Orient, Extrême-Occident* 14: 91–129.

Ch'en Liang-ts'so (Chen Liangzuo) 陳良佐 (1982) 'Zhao Shuang Gougu yuanfang tuzhu zhi yanjiu 趙爽句股圓方圖注之研究'(Research on the commentary by Zhao Shuang on the figures of the base and the height, the square and the circle). *Dalu zazhi* 大陸雜志 **64**: 33–52.

Engelfrict, P. (1993) 'The Chinese Euclid and its European context', in *L'Europe en Chine*, ed. C. Jami and H. Delahaye. Paris: 111–35.

(1998) *Euclid in China: The Genesis of the First Translation of Euclid's Elements in 1607 and its Reception up to 1723.* Leiden.

Gu Yingxiang 顧應詳 (1553) *Gougu Suanshu* 句股算術 *(Mathematical Procedures on Gougu)*, 1553 edn.

Guo Shuchun 郭書春 (1985) '*Jiuzhang suanshu* "Gougu" zhang de jiaokan he Liu Hui gougu lilun xitong chutan 九章算術句股章的校勘和劉徽句股理論系統初探' (Editorial research on the *Gougu* chapter in the *Nine Chapters* and the system of Liu Hui's *gougu* theory). *Ziran kexue shi yanjiu* 4: 295–304.

(1987) 'Shilun Liu Hui de shuxue lilun tixi 試論劉徽的數學理論體系' (A study on Liu Hui's System of Mathematical Theory). *Ziran bianzheng fa tongxu* 9: 42–48.

(1988) 'Jia Xian *Huangdi Jiuzhang Suanjing Xicao* chutan 賈憲黃帝九章算經細草初探', *Ziran kexue shi yanjiu* 7: 328–334.

(1992) *Gudai shijie shuxue taidou Liu Hui* 古代世界數學泰斗劉徽 *(Liu Hui: A Leading Figure of Ancient World Mathematics)*. Jinan.

Li Jimin 李繼閔 (1993) '"Shang Gao dingli" bianzheng "商高定理"辯證' (Textual research on "Shang Gao" theorem). *Ziran kexueshi yanjiu* 12: 29 41.

Li Rui 李銳 (1806) *Gougu Suanshu Xicao* 句股筭術細草 *(Detailed Outline of Mathematical Procedures of Gougu)*, in *Li shi Yishu* 李氏遺書 *(Posthumous writings of Mr. Li)*, ed. Ding Quzhong 丁取忠 (1875).

Li Zhaohua 李兆华 (1993) 'Wang Lai *Dijian Shuli Sanliang Suanjing* Lüelun 汪萊遞兼數理論略論' (A short discussion on Wang Lai's *Dijian Shuli* and *Sanliang Suanjing*), in *Tantian Sanyou* 談天三友, ed. Horng WannSheng. Taibei: 227–37.

Liu Dun 劉鈍 (1993) '*Gougu suanshu xicao* tiyao 勾股算術細草提要' (Introduction to the *Detailed Outline of Mathematical Procedures for the Right-Angled Triangle*), in *Zhongguo kexue jishu dianji tonghui, shuxue juan*, ed. Guo Shuchun 郭書春, vol. v. Zhengzhou: 67–9.

Qian Baocong 錢寶琮 (1982) *Zhongguo shuxue shi* 中國數學史 *(History of Mathematics in China)*. Beijing.

Tian Miao 田淼 (1999) '*Jiegenfang, Tianyuan,* and *Daishu*: algebra in Qing China', *Historia Scientiarum* 9 (1): 101–119.

(2005) *Zhongguo Shuxue de Xihua Licheng* 中國數學的西化歷程 *(The Westernization of Mathematics in China)*. Jinan.

(forthcoming) 'Rejection and adoption of Western mathematics: Chinese mathematician's study on the *Gougu* Procedure from the beginning of 17th to the beginning of 18th century'.

Wang Lai 汪萊 (1799?) *Dijian Shuli* 遞兼數理 *(The Mathematical Theory of Dijian)*, in *Hengzhai Suanxue* 衡齋算學, book 4, Jiashu tang edn.

Wu Wenjun 吳文俊 (1978) 'Churu xiangbu yuanli 出入相補原理' *(The Out-in Principle)*, in *Zhongguo gudai keji chengjiu* 中國古代科技成就 *(Scientific and Technological Achievements in Ancient China)*. Beijing: 80–100.

Xu Guangqi 徐光啓 (1609) *Gougu Yi* 句股義 *(The Principle of Gougu)*, Tianxue chuhan edn.

Yang Hui (1261) 楊輝 *Xiangjie Jiuzhang Suanfa* 詳解九章筭法 *(A Detailed Explanation of the Nine Chapters of Mathematical Procedures)*, Yijia tang edn.

Index